Structural Mechanics Software Series

Volume I

Structural Mechanics Software Series

Volume I

Edited by

N. Perrone

W. Pilkey

Technical Editor

B. Pilkey

University Press of Virginia
Charlottesville

PREFACE

The primary objective of the Structural Mechanics Software Series is
to provide the technical community with information on structural analysis and design computer programs on a continuing basis. In this manner, computer information will achieve a formalized and archival status.

As evidenced by this first volume, a balance is achieved between
presenting detailed information on a few programs (which are readily
available and can be directly accessed by the reader with a remote
computer terminal from many parts of the United States) and reviews
of many other programs. The first part of this volume contains information on directly callable programs, and the second part deals
with program surveys.

The following computer network vendors have made blocks of computer time available for potential series programs being considered for
publication:

1.   United Computing Systems
2.   TYMSHARE Corporation
3.   University Computing Corporation

To be selected as a participating vendor, it is necessary that
a fairly wide geographical area be covered. The purpose of computer
time being provided by the vendor is to allow candidate programs to
be placed on the system and to be reviewed and assessed. While all
programs placed on the system are publicly available, prospective
users are encouraged to utilize the programs on the vendor system
before considering acquiring them. It may be advisable for users
to continue utilizing the network copy of a given program published
in the series, because updata and mainteinance will then be immediately available to all users. Also, in this way, all the pains of
making the program woik will be short-circuited in a very quick
trial process.

Participating network vendors will provide a computer service
arrangement for anyone who desires to utilize one of the programs
described in this volume (Part I). The editors of the series and the
University Press of Virginia are not involved in effecting arrange-
ments for readers to access any of the series programs. It is necessary to contact individuals described in the availability information
section in the first chapter with regard to questions concerning the
programs. Charges made by network vendors are levied directly to
prospective users; it is emphasized that neither the editors nor the
publishers are involved in this process.

Should a reader opt to obtain a copy of the program (and all
programs, by policy, are publicly available in some form), he should
contact the availability sources listed in the first chapter.

Computer program information presented in the Software Series
should be of interest to a broad segment of the engineering community,
including mechanical, civil, aerospace, nuclear, automotive, and bio-
engineers. In addition, interactions have been effected between the
editors and engineering society committees concerned with computer

software (e.g. Research Committee on Computer Software for ASCE and ASME, Computer Technology, Computing and Applied Mechanics, ASME, AIAA Structures).

Constructive feedback on working programs or surveys are welcome by the editors as well as the authors. Written comments are preferred with copies to the editors.

Potential contributors of computer programs or survey articles for subsequent volumes are urged to communicate their interests in outline form to the editors. In addition, articles related to micro-programs for new computer systems such as the Tektronix 4051, IBM 5500, HP 65, etc., are also welcome.

The programs of the Software Series Library and the documentation presented in this volume are being made available without any repre-sentation or warranty of any kind. The editors and publishers, there-fore, assume no liability of any kind arising from the use of these items.

The editors wish to thank the Department of Engineering Science and Systems of the University of Virginia for their funding, which has made the publication of this volume possible.

We also appreciate the assistance of E. Campbell, D. Wilson, J. Adams, and J. and P. Hamm. Finally, we wish to acknowledge the major editorial effort of B. Pilkey.

February 1977

Walter D. Pilkey
Applied Mechanic Divison
University of Virginia
Charlottesville, Virginia 22901

Nicholas Perrone
Structural Mechanics Program
Office of Naval Research,
* Code 474*
800 N. Quincy St.
Arlington, Virginia 22217

CONTRIBUTORS

Laurent A. Beaubien
Ocean Technology Division
Mechanics of Materials Branch
Naval Research Lab
Washington, D.C. 20375

Charles F. Beck
Computer Services Division
Sargent and Lundy Engineers
55 E. Monroe St
Chicago, Illinois 60603

David Bushnell
Lockheed Missiles and Space Co.
Palo Alto Research Lab
3251 Hanover St
Palo Alto, California 94304

Pin Yu Chang
Hydronautics, Inc.
7210 Pindell School Rd
Laurel, Maryland 20810

Surenda K. Goel
Structural Analytical Division
Sargent and Lundy Engineers
55 E. Monroe St
Chicago, Illinois 60603

Conrad P. Heins
Dept. of Civil Engineering
University of Maryland
College Park, Maryland 20742

Ronald L. Huston
Engineering Science Dept.
College of Engineering
University of Cincinnati
Cincinnati, Ohio 45221

Jarl Jensen
Dept. of Solid Mechanics
The Technical University of Denmark
Building 404
2800 Lyngby
Denmark

Movses J. Kaldjian
Depts. of Civil Engineering and
   Naval Architecture and Marine
   Engineering
The University of Michigan
Ann Arbor, Michigan 48109

Hussein A. Kamel
AME Department
University of Arizona
Tucson, Arizona 85121

Michael W. McCabe
AME Department
University of Arizona
Tucson, Arizona 85721

Frithiof Niordson
Dept. of Solid Mechanics
The Technical University of Denmark
Building 404
2800 Lyngby
Denmark

Walter D. Pilkey
Applied Mechanics Division
School of Engineering and
   Applied Science
University of Virginia
Charlottesville, Virginia 22903

David R. Schelling
Dept. of Civil Engineering
University of Maryland
College Park, Maryland 20742

Glen H. Sikes
Office of Systems Development
Georgia Dept. of Transportation
Atlanta, Georgia 30334

Chirasak Thasanatorn
Dept. of Civil Engineering
University of Virginia
Charlottesville, Virginia 22903

M. Daniel Vanderbilt
Dept. of Civil Engineering
Colorado State University
Ft. Collins, Colorado 80523

Robert K. Waddick
Computer Services Division
Sargent and Lundy Engineers
55 E. Monroe St.
Chicago, Illinois 60603

CONTENTS

PART I

SOFTWARE SERIES LIBRARY
OF COMPUTER PROGRAMS

LIBRARY OF AVAILABLE SOFTWARE SERIES PROGRAMS

INTRODUCTION

The following programs are being made available in this volume as part of the library of Software Series computer programs.

SAP
BOSOR
GIFTS
TOTAL
BEAM
BEAMSTRESS
SHAFT

Each program can be accessed on one or more of the participating computer networks: United Computing Systems (UCS), TYMSHARE, and University Computing Company (UCC). One of the programs is available using the University of Michigan computer network MERIT/TELENET. Usually, connection to the computer requires only a local telephone call. The computer network companies should be contacted directly for information on using the programs on their systems. Appropriate addresses are listed in this chapter.

PROGRAM AND DOCUMENTATION AVAILABILITY

BOSOR

Network Availability
  UCS, TYMSHARE, UCC
Technical Manual
  Use the one in this volume. No other technical manual is adequate.
User Documentation
  Found in this volume.
Program Availability
  Available from
  Lockheed Missiles and Space Co.
  P.O. Box 504
  Sunnyvale, California 94088

Attn. L. W. Besack
     Dept. 40-06, Building 101

An IBM version of the program can be purchased from
V. Weingarten
Dept. of Civil Engineering
University of Southern California
University Park
Los Angeles, California 90007

The price is: $300.

Assistance in Using the Program on the Networks
   Please contact the local representatives of the network.
Technical Problems in Using the Program Contact
   D. Bushnell
   Lockheed Missiles and Space Co.
   Palo Alto Research Lab.
   3251 Hanover St
   Palo Alto, California 94304
   Phone: (415) 493-4411 Ext. 45491

BOSOR – Preprocessor

Network Availability
   UCS
Technical Manual
   None
User Documentation
   See this volume.
Program Availability
   A card deck of the program can be purchased from
   S.K.D. Enterprise
   19 Holt Rd
   Amherst, N.H.   03031

   The price is: $150 on cards.

Assistance in Using the Program on the Network
   Please contact the local representatives of the network or
   S.K.D. Enterprise
Technical Problems in Using the Program Contact
   S.K.D. Enterprise

SAP

Network Availability
   UCS,UCC, MERIT/TELENET
Technical Manual
   Available from
   National Information Service Earthquake Engineering
   College of Engineering
   729 Davis Hall
   University of California, Berkeley
   Berkeley, California 94720

The price for the manual is $5.00.

User Documentation
    Included as part of the technical manual
Program Availability
    An IBM version of the program can be purchased from
    V. Weingarten
    Dept. of Civil Engineering
    University Southern California
    University Park
    Los Angeles, California 90007
    A Control Data version can be purchased from the
    National Information Service Earthquake Engineering
    (address is above)

    The price is $250 for either version.

Assistance in Using the Program on the Network
    Please contact the local representatives of the network.
Technical Problems in Using the Program Contact
    M. Kaldjian
    Dept. of Civil Engineering
    University of Michigan
    Ann Arbor, Michigan 48109
    Phone: (313) 764-8419

PREMSAP - A Preprocessor for SAP

Network Availability for PREMSAP coupled to SAP
    MERIT/TELENET
Technical Manual
    Available from M. Kaldjian with the purchase of the card deck
User Documentation
    Available from M. Kaldjian with the purchase of the card deck
Program Availability
    Card deck of the program can be purchased from
    M. Kaldjian
    Dept. of Civil Engineering
    The University of Michigan
    Ann Arbor, Michigan 48109

    The price is $250, including manuals.

Assistance in Using the Program on the Network
    M. Kaldjian
Technical Problems in Using the Program Contact
    M. Kaldjian
    Phone: (313) 764-8419

TOTAL

Network Availability
  TYMSHARE
Technical Manual
  Available from
  L. Beaubien
  Ocean Technology Division
  Mechanics of Materials Branch
  Naval Research Lab
  Washington, D.C.   20375
User Documentation
  Additional information available from on-line documentation in
  the program
Program Availability
  Contact: L. Beaubien
Assistance in Using the Program on the Network
  Please contact the local representatives of the network.
Technical Problems in Using the Program Contact
  L. Beaubien

BEAM, BEAMSTRESS, SHAFT

Network Availability
  UCS, TYMSHARE, UCC
Technical Manual
  Available from The Structural Members Users Group
  These programs belong to a collection of a dozen programs. The
  technical manual for all of the programs costs $100.
User Documentation
  Contained in this volume
Program Availability
  A tape or deck of the program can be purchased from
  The Structural Members Users Group
  P.O. Box 3958, University Station
  Charlottesville, Virginia 22903

  The price is $500 for all twelve programs, although programs may
  be purchased individually.

Assistance in Using the Program
  Please contact the local representatives of the network.
Technical Problems in Using the Program Contact
  The Structural Members Users Group
  Phone: (804) 296-4906

GIFTS

Network Availability
  UCS
Technical Manual
  Included with the purchase of the program tape

User Documentation
    Included with the purchase of the program tape.
Program Availability
    A tape of the program can be purchased from
    H. Kamel
    Dept. of Aerospace and Mechanical Engineering
    University of Arizona
    Tucson, Arizona 85721

    The price is $150 for recent version and periodic newsletters;
                $500 recent version with newsletter and updates
                    for one year;
              $1500 for recent version with newsletter, updates,
                    and additions for one year.
Assistance in Using the Program on the Network.
    Contact the local representatives of the network.
Technical Problems in Using the Program Contact
    H. A. Kamel

PARTICIPATING NETWORKS

United Computing Systems (UCS)

Local Offices:

Bldg. 1, Suite 106
5825 Glenridge Drive N.E.
Atlanta, Georgia 30328
(404) 256-3610

Fourth Floor
1050 Massachusetts Avenue
Cambridge, Massachusetts 02138
(617) 661-1720

Suite 1910
Bow Valley Square 2
P.O. Box 9235
Calgary, Alberta, Canada T2P2W5
(403) 265-4926

Suite 1016
150 North Wacker Drive
Chicago, Illinois 60606
(312) 782-0865

Two Commerce Park Square
23200 Chagrin Blvd.
Beachwood, Ohio 44122
(216) 464-9205

P.O. Box 781
Delaware, Ohio 43015
(614) 548-6371

Suite 1112, Twin Towers South
8585 Stemmons Freeway
Dallas, Texas 75247
(214) 638-8260

Suite 20C
2460 West 26th Avenue
Denver, Colorado 80211
(303) 458-8001

33 Evergreen Place
East Orange, New Jersey 07018
(201) 677-2400

Suite 101
3702 Rupp Drive
Fort Wayne, Indiana 46805
(219) 484-8522

Ft. Worth, Texas
(214) 263-0584 (Dallas Office)

4544 Post Oak Place
Suite 346
Houston, Texas 77027
(713) 622-5351

500 W. 26th Street
Kansas City, Missouri   64108
(816) 221-9700

Suite 410
101 Continental Boulevard
El Segundo, California   90245
(213) 640-0891

Suite 107
10701 West North Avenue
Wauwatosa, Wisconsin   53226
(414) 475-9392

35 Worth Avenue
Hamden, Connecticut   06518
(203) 288-6287

Suite 1847
Two Pennsylvania Plaza
New York, New York   10001
(212) 868-7785

Suite 252
Northwest Office Center
4334 N.W. Expressway
Oklahoma City, Oklahoma   73116
(405) 843-9784

4120 Birch
Suite 101
Newport Beach, California   92660

Suite 149
7200 Lake Elenor Drive
Orlando, Florida   32809
(305) 855-1810

Suite 217
1032 Elwell Court
Palo Alto, California   94303
(415) 964-6990

Suite 210
500 Office Center
Ft. Washington, Pennsylvania   19034
(215) 542-8600

Suite 104
5350 N. 16th St.
Phoenix, Arizona   85016
(602) 248-9176

Suite 212
1651 East Fourth
Santa Ana, California   92701
(714) 835-3801

Suite 222
681 Market Street
San Francisco, California   94105
(415) 777-1885

Suite B
Koll Commerce Center
699 Strander Blvd.
Tukwila, Washington   98188
(206) 243-8041

Suite 100
7750 Clayton Road
Clayton, Missouri   63117
(314) 781-0123

Suite 518
1000 Ashley Drive
Tampa, Florida   33602
(813) 223-3921

Suite 404
16 East 16 Street
Tulsa, Oklahoma   74119
(918) 582-7291

Suite 319
7115 Leesburg Pike
Falls Church, Virginia   22043
(703) 532-1551

2525 Washington
Kansas City, Missouri   64108
(816) 221-9700

University Computing Company (UCC)

Local Offices:

3 New England Executive Park
Burlington, Massachusetts   01803
(617) 272-6350

747 Third Avenue, 32nd Floor
New York, New York   10017
(212) 421-8850

850 U.S. Rt. 1 Fourth Floor
North Brunswick, New Jersey 08902
(201) 828-3900

9500 Gandy Blvd., Suite 206
St. Petersburg, Fla.   33702
(813) 576-7373

5600 Crooks Road
One Northfield Plaza
Troy, Michigan   48084
(313) 879-9300

120 S. Riverside Plaza,
10th Floor
Chicago, Illinois 60606
(312) 368-0995

823 S. Detroit
Tulsa, Oklahoma   74120
(918) 582-0975

400 Fannin Bank Building
Houston, Texas   77025
(713) 790-1200

888 N. Sepulveda Blvd.
El Segundo, California 90245
(213) 322-3093

1901 S. Bascom, Suite 347
Campbell, California 95008
(408) 377-1775

TYMSHARE

All accounts will be handled by and through:

TYMSHARE
1911 N. Fort Myer Drive
Suite 907
Arlington, Virginia   22209
Attn: Mr. Jack Thomas
(703) 527-1333

MERIT/TELENET

All accounts will be handled by and through:

Chairman
Dept. of Naval Architecture & Marine Engineering
The University of Michigan
445 West Engineering Building
Ann Arbor, Michigan   48109
(313) 764-6470

BOSOR4:   PROGRAM FOR STRESS, BUCKLING, AND VIBRATION OF COMPLEX
SHELLS OF REVOLUTION

David Bushnell

Lockheed Missiles & Space Co., Inc.

INTRODUCTION

A comprehensive computer program, designated BOSOR4, for analysis
of the stress, stability and vibration of segmented, ring-stiffened,
branched shells of revolution and prismatic shells and panels is
described. The program performs large-deflection axisymmetric
stress analysis, small-deflection nonsymmetric stress analysis,
modal vibration analysis with axisymmetric nonlinear prestress included, and buckling analysis with axisymmetric or nonsymmetric
prestress. One of the main advantages of the code is the provision
for realistic engineering details such as eccentric load paths,
internal supports, arbitrary branching conditions, and a 'library'
of wall constructions. The program is based on the finite
difference energy method which is very rapidly convergent with
increasing numbers of mesh points. Overlay charts and core storage
requirements are given for the CDC 6600, IBM 370/165, and UNIVAC
1108/1110 versions of BOSOR4. Several examples are included to
demonstrate the scope and practicality of the program. Some hints
are given to help the user generate appropriate analytical models.
An appendix contains the user's manual for BOSOR4.

Table 1 shows the characteristics and status of BOSOR4. The
program is currently in widespread use and is maintained by the
developer. Notices of any bugs found are promptly circulated to
all known users and data centers that have acquired BOSOR4.

The BOSOR4 program was developed in response to the need for a
tool which would help the engineer to design practical shell
structures. An important class of such shell structures includes
segmented, ring-stiffened branched shells of revolution. These
shells may have various meridional geometries, wall constructions,
boundary conditions, ring reinforcements, and types of loading,
including thermal loading. An example is shown in Fig. 1. The
meridian of the shell of revolution consists of six segments with
various geometries and wall constructions. The first segment
(nearest the bottom, end "A") is a monocoque ogive with variable
thickness; the second is a conical shell with three layers of

Table 1 BOSOR4 at a Glance

Keywords: shells, stress, buckling, vibration, nonlinear, elastic,
    shells of revolution, ring-stiffened, branched, composites,
    discrete model

Purpose: To perform stress, buckling, and modal vibration analyses
    of ring-stiffened, branched shells of revolution loaded either
    axisymmetrically or nonsymmetrically. Complex wall construc-
    tion permitted.

Date: 1972; most recent update 1975

Developer: David Bushnell, 52-33/205
            Lockheed Missiles & Space Co., Inc.
            3251 Hanover Street
            Palo Alto, Ca. 94304
            Tel: (415) 493-4411, X45491 or 43851

Method: Finite difference energy minimization; Fourier superposi-
    tion in circumferential variable; Newton method for solution
    of nonlinear axisymmetric problem; inverse power iteration
    with spectral shifts for eigenvalue extraction; Lagrange
    multipliers for constraint conditions; thin shell theory.

Restrictions: 1500 degrees of freedom (d.o.f.) in nonaxisymmetric
    problems; 1000 d.o.f. in axisymmetric prebuckling stress
    analysis; Maximum of 20 Fourier harmonics per case; Knockdown
    factors for imperfections not included; Radius/thickness
    should be greater than about 10.

Language: FORTRAN IV

Documentation: BOSOR4 User's Manual [1] and about 10 journal
    articles with numerous examples.

Input: Preprocessor written by SKD Enterprise, 9138 Barberry Lane,
    Hickory Hills, Illinois 60457 for free-field input. Required
    for input are shell segment geometries, ring geometries, num-
    ber of mesh points, ranges and increments of circumferential
    wave numbers, load and temperature distributions, shell wall
    construction details, and constraint conditions.

Output: Stress resultants or extreme fiber stresses, buckling
    loads, vibration frequencies; list and plots.

Hardware: UNIVAC 1108/110, CDC 6600/7600, IBM 360/370; SC4020 and
    CALCOMP plotters

Usage: About 100 institutions have obtained BOSOR4. It is cur-
    rently being used on a daily basis by many of them.

Run Time: Typically a job will require 1-10 minutes of computer
    time.

Availability: CDC and UNIVAC versions from developer (see above);
    IBM version from Prof. Victor Weingarten, Dept. of Civil Eng.,
    Univ. of Southern Calif., University Park, Los Angeles, Calif.
    90007; Price: $300. In addition to the Software Series partici-
    pating networks mentioned in this volume, BOSOR4 may be run
    through the following data centers:

            McDonnell-Douglas Automation, Huntington Beach, Calif.
            Control Data Corp., Rockville, Md.
            Westinghouse Telecomputer, Pittsburgh, Penna.
            Information System Design, Oakland, Calif.
            Boeing Computer Service, Seattle, Wash.

temperature-dependent, orthotropic material; the third is a layered, fiber-wound cylinder; the fourth is a toroidal segment with eccentric rings and stringers; the fifth is a spherical segment with eccentric rings and stringers; and the sixth is a flat plate with sandwich construction and eccentric meridional stiffeners. The reference surface is indicated by the dark dash-dot line. It is seen that the meridian of the composite shell structure is discontinuous between the first and second segments, the second and third segments, and the third and fourth segments. In the analysis these discontinuities are accounted for. The shell is supported at the end "A" by a ring which is restrained as shown: axial and radial displacements u* and w* are not permitted at the point "A", which is located a specified distance from the beginning of the reference surface. In the analysis of actual shell structures it is important that support points, junctures, and ring reinforcements be accurately modeled. Seemingly insignificant parameters sometimes have a large effect on the stress, buckling loads, and vibration frequencies. The shell is reinforced by 6 rings of rectangular cross section, the centroids of which are shown in the figure. These rings are treated as discrete elastic structures in the analysis. The shell is submitted to uniform external pressure (not shown), line loads applied at the first and second rings, and the thermal environment depicted on the second segment.

Figures 2 and 3 show computer-generated plots from a linear buckling analysis and free vibration analysis. Normal displacement components w of the modes are shown for the lowest three eigenvalues corresponding to circumferential harmonics n = 4, 6, 8, 10, 12 and 14. The regions of the six shell segments are indicated in Fig. 2. In the buckling analysis the uniform pressure is the eigenvalue parameter, all other mechanical and thermal loads being held fixed. In the vibration analysis the external pressure is 40 psi and all loads are held fixed. Calculation of the 18 eigenvalues requires 8 min for the buckling analysis and 6 min for the vibration analysis. Computations were performed on the UNIVAC 1108, in double precision. There are 460 degrees of freedom in the discrete model.

BOSOR4 has been in use at Lockheed and elsewhere since 1972. During that time it has been used in several projects, some of them involving rather complex shells of revolution. An example is shown in Fig. 4, which depicts a somewhat idealized model of a cryogenic cooler. The axisymmetric structure consists of a series of fiberglas tubes from which are suspended two axisymmetric cryogenic tanks. The object of this study was to determine the natural frequencies of the cooler corresponding to beam-type modes (n=1 circumferential wave). The discretized model is shown in Fig. 5 and the first four vibration modes in Fig. 6.

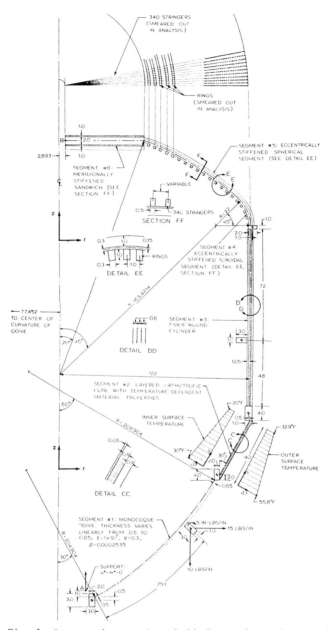

Fig. 1 Segmented composite shell for analysis by BOSOR4

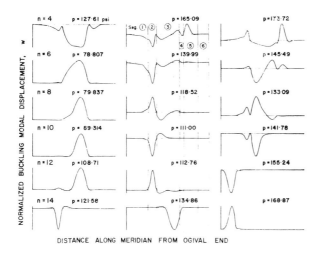

Fig. 2 w-components of eigenvectors for linear buckling analysis
of externally pressurized six-segment shell shown in Fig. 1

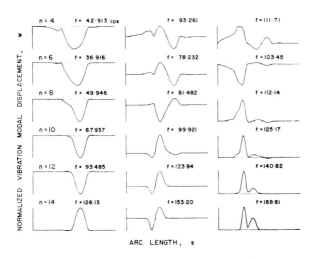

Fig. 3 w-components of eigenvectors for free vibration analysis of
six-segment shell shown in Fig. 1

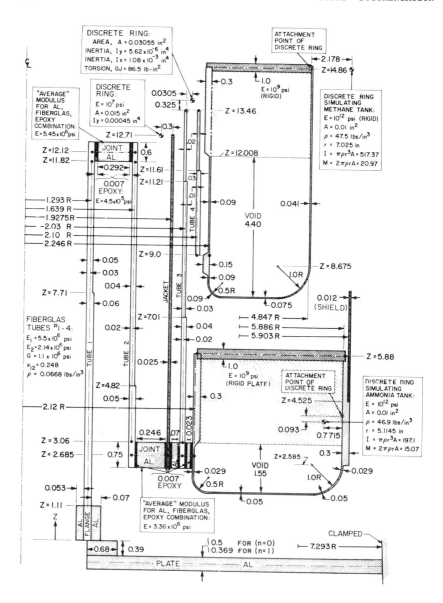

Fig. 4 Cryogenic cooler model for BOSOR4

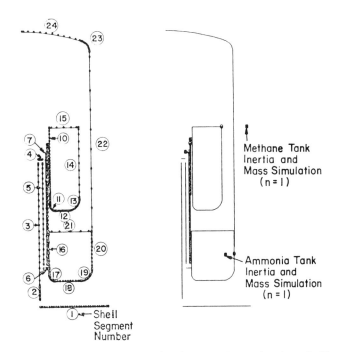

Fig. 5 BOSOR4 model for lateral (n=1) vibration, showing shell
segments, mesh points, and locations of centroids of discrete rings
which simulate mass and moment of inertia of methane and ammonia
tanks

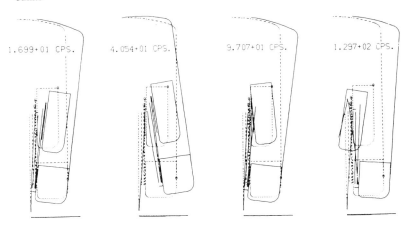

Fig. 6 First four lateral (n=1) vibration modes with BOSOR4 model

SCOPE OF THE BOSOR4 COMPUTER PROGRAM

The BOSOR4 code performs stress, stability, and vibration analyses
of segmented, branched, ring-stiffened, elastic shells of revolution with various wall constructions. Figure 7 shows some examples
of branched structures which can be handled by BOSOR4. Figure 7a
represents part of a multiple-stage rocket treated as a shell of
seven segments; Fig. 7b represents part of a ring-stiffened cylinder in which the ring is treated as two shell segments branching
from the cylinder; Fig. 7c shows the same ring-stiffened cylinder,
but with the ring treated as 'discrete', that is the ring cross
section can rotate and translate but not deform, as it can in the
model shown in Fig. 7b. Figures 7d-f represent branched prismatic
shell structures, which can be treated as shells of revolution
with very large mean circumferential radii of curvature, as described in [2] and later in this paper.

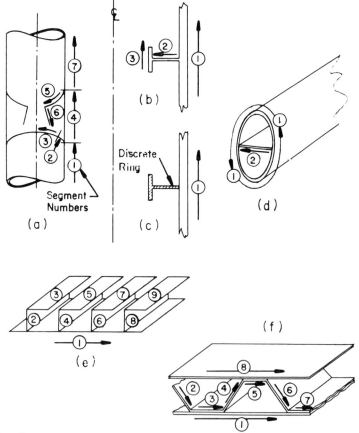

Fig. 7 Examples of branched structures which can be analyzed with
BOSOR4

The program is very general with respect to geometry of meridian, shell-wall design, edge conditions, and loading. It has been thoroughly checked out by comparisons with other known solutions and tests and by extensive use at a number of different institutions over the past three years. The BOSOR4 capability is summarized in Table 2. The code represents three distinct analyses:

1. A nonlinear stress analysis for axisymmetric behavior of axisymmetric shell systems (large deflections, elastic)
2. A linear stress analysis for axisymmetric and nonsymmetric behavior of axisymmetric shell systems submitted to axisymmetric and nonsymmetric loads
3. An eigenvalue analysis in which the eigenvalues represent buckling loads or vibration frequencies of axisymmetric shell systems submitted to axisymmetric loads. (Eigenvectors may correspond to axisymmetric or nonsymmetric modes.)

BOSOR4 has an additional branch corresponding to buckling of non-symmetrically loaded shells of revolution. However, this branch is really a combination of the second and third analyses just listed.

Table 2 BOSOR4 Capability Summary

Type of analysis	Shell geometry	Wall construction	Loading
Nonlinear axisymmetric stress Linear symmetric or nonsymmetric stress Stability with linear symmetric or nonsymmetric prestress or with nonlinear symmetric prestress Vibration with nonlinear prestress analysis Variable mesh point spacing within each segment	Multiple-segment shells, each segment with its own wall construction, geometry, and loading Cylinder, cone, spherical, ogival, toroidal, ellipsoidal, etc. General meridional shape; point-by-point input Axial and radial discontinuities in shell meridian Arbitrary choice of reference surface General edge conditions Branched shells Prismatic shells and composite built-up panels	Monocoque, variable or constant thickness Skew-stiffened shells Fiber-wound shells Layered orthotropic shells Corrugated, with or without skin Layered orthotropic with temperature-dependent material properties Any of above wall types reinforced by stringers and/or rings treated as "smeared out" Any of above wall types further reinforced by rings treated as discrete Wall properties variable along meridian	Axisymmetric or nonsymmetric thermal and/or mechanical line loads and moments Axisymmetric or nonsymmetric thermal and/or mechanical distributed loads Proportional loading Non-proportional loading

In the BOSOR4 code, the user chooses the type of analysis to be performed by means of a control integer INDIC:

INDIC = -2   Stability determinant calculated for given circumferential wave number N for increasing loads until it changes sign. Nonlinear prebuckling effects included. INDIC then changed automatically to -1 and calculations proceed as if INDIC has always been -1.

INDIC = -1   Buckling load and corresponding wave number N determined, including nonlinear prebuckling effects. N corresponding to local minimum critical load $L_{cr}(N)$ is automatically sought.

INDIC = 0   Axisymmetric stresses and displacements calculated for a sequence of stepwise increasing loads from some starting value to some maximum value, including nonlinear effects. Axisymmetric collapse loads can be calculated.

INDIC = 1   Buckling loads calculated with nonlinear bending theory for a fixed load. Buckling loads calculated for a range of circumferential wave numbers. Several buckling loads for each wave number can be calculated.

INDIC = 2   Vibration frequencies and mode shapes calculated, including the effects of prestress obtained from axisymmetric nonlinear analysis. Several frequencies and modes can be calculated for each circumferential wave number.

INDIC = 3   Nonsymmetric or symmetric stresses and displacements calculated for a range of circumferential wave numbers. Linear theory used. Results for each harmonic are automatically superposed. Fourier series for nonsymmetric loads are automatically computed or may be provided by user.

INDIC = 4   Buckling loads calculated for nonsymmetrically loaded shells. Prebuckled state obtained from linear theory (INDIC = 3) or read in from cards. 'Worst' meridional prestress distribution (such as distribution involving maximum negative meridional or hoop prestress resultant) chosen by user, and this particular distribution is assumed to be axisymmetric in the stability analysis, which is the same as that for the branch INDIC = 1.

The variety of buckling analyses (INDIC = -2, -1, 1, and 4) is to permit the user to approach a given problem in a number of different ways. There are cases for which an INDIC = -1 analysis, for example, will not work. The user can then resort to an INDIC = -2 analysis, which requires more computer time, but which is generally more reliable. Buckling of a shallow spherical cap under external pressure is an example. In an INDIC = -1 analysis of the cap, the program generates a sequence of loads that ordinarily should converge to the lowest buckling load, with nonlinear pre-buckling effects included. Depending on the cap geometry and the user-provided initial pressure, however, one of the loads in the sequence may exceed the axisymmetric collapse pressure of the cap. This phenomenon can occur if the bifurcation buckling loads are just slightly smaller than the axisymmetric collapse loads. The user can obtain a solution with use of INDIC = -2, in which the bifurcation load is approached from below in a 'gradual' manner.

The branch INDIC = 1 is provided because it is sometimes desirable to know several buckling eigenvalues for each circum-ferential wave number, N, and because there may exist more than one minimum in the critical load vs N-space. This is especially true for composite shell structures with many segments and load types. Such a structure can buckle in many different ways. The designer may have to eliminate several possible failure modes, not just the one corresponding to the lowest pressure, for example. The INDIC = 4 branch is provided for two reasons: The user can calculate buckling under nonsymmetric loads without having to make two separate runs, an INDIC = 3 run and an INDIC = 1 run. In addition, this branch permits the user to bypass the prebuckling analysis and read prebuckling stress distributions and rotations directly from cards. This second feature is very useful for the treatment of composite branched panels under uniaxial or biaxial compression.

The BOSOR4 program, although applicable to shells of revolu-tion, can be used for the buckling analysis of composite, branched panels by means of a 'trick' described in detail in Ref [2]. This 'trick' permits the analysis of any prismatic shell structure that is simply-supported at particular stations along the length. Any boundary conditions can be used along generators. In [2] many examples are given, including nonuniformly loaded cylinders, non-circular cylinders, corrugated panels, and cylinders with stringers treated as discrete. This paper gives other examples.

ANALYSIS METHOD

The assumptions upon which the BOSOR4 code is based are:

1. The wall material is elastic.
2. Thin shell theory holds; i.e. normals to the undeformed surface remain normal and undeformed.

3. The structure is axisymmetric, and in vibration analysis and nonlinear stress analysis the loads and prebuckling or pre-stress deformations are axisymmetric.

4. The axisymmetric prebuckling deflections in the nonlinear theory (INDIC = 0, -1, 2), while considered finite, are moderate; i.e. the square of the meridional rotation can be neglected com-pared with unity.

5. In the calculation of displacement and stresses in non-symmetrically loaded shells (INDIC = 3), linear theory is used. This branch of the program is based on standard small-deflection analysis.

6. A typical cross sectional dimension of a discrete ring stiffener is small compared with the radius of the ring.

7. The cross sections of the discrete rings remain undeformed as the structure deforms, and the rotation about the ring centroid is equal to the rotation of the shell meridian at the attachment point of the ring (except, of course, if the ring is treated as a flexible shell branch).

8. The discrete ring centroids coincide with their shear centers.

9. If meridional stiffeners are present, they are numerous enough to include in the analysis by an averaging or 'smearing' of their properties over any parallel circle of the shell structure. Meridional stiffeners can be treated as discrete through the 'trick' described in Ref. [2].

The analysis is based on energy minimization with constraint conditions. The total energy of the system includes strain energy of the shell segments and discrete rings, potential energy of the applied line loads and pressures, and kinetic energy of the shell segments and discrete rings. The constraint conditions arise from displacement conditions at the boundaries of the structure, dis-placement conditions that may be prescribed anywhere within the structure, and at junctures between segments. The constraint con-ditions are introduced into the energy function by means of Lagrange multipliers.

These components of energy and constraint conditions are initially integro — differential forms. The circumferential de-pendence is eliminated by separation of variables. Displacements and meridional derivatives of displacements are then written in terms of the shell reference surface components u_i, v_i and w_i at the finite-difference mesh points and Lagrange multipliers λ_i. integration is performed simply by multiplication of the energy per unit length of meridian by the length of the 'finite difference element', to be described below.

In the nonlinear axisymmetric stress analysis the energy ex-pression has terms linear, quadratic, cubic, and quartic in the dependent variables u_i and w_i. The cubic and quartic energy terms arise from the rotation-squared terms that appear in the expres-sion for reference surface meridional strain and in the constraint conditions. Energy minimization leads to a set of nonlinear algebraic equations that are solved by the Newton-Raphson method. Stress and moment resultants are calculated in a straightforward

manner from the mesh-point displacement components through the
constitutive equations and the kinematic relations.

The results from the nonlinear axisymmetric or linear nonsymmetric stress analysis are used in the eigenvalue analyses for
buckling and vibration. The 'prebuckling' or 'prestress' meridional and circumferential stress resultants N_{10} and N_{20} and the
meridional rotation X_o appear as known variable coefficients in
the energy expressions that govern buckling and vibration. These
expressions are homogeneous quadratic forms. The values of a
parameter (load or frequency) that render the quadratic forms
stationary with respect to infinitesimal variations of the dependent variables represent buckling loads or natural frequencies.
These eigenvalues are calculated from a set of linear homogeneous
equations. More will be written about the bifurcation buckling
eigenvalue problems in the following paragraphs.

Details of the analysis are given in [1, 3 and 4]. Only two
aspects will be described here: the finite difference element
and the stability eigenvalue problem.

The 'Finite Difference' Element

BOSOR4 is based on the finite difference energy method. This
method is described in detail and compared with the finite element
method in [5]. Figure 8 shows a typical shell segment meridian
with finite difference mesh points. The 'u' and 'v' points are
located halfway between adjacent 'w' points. The energy contains
up to first derivatives in u and v and up to second derivatives in
w. Hence, the shell energy density evaluated at the point labeled
E (center of the length ℓ) involves the seven points w_{i-1} through
w_{i+1}. The energy per unit circumferential length is simply the
energy per unit area multiplied by the length of the finite
difference element ℓ, which is the arc length of the reference surface between two adjacent u or v points. In Ref. [5] it is shown
that this formulation yields a 7 x 7 stiffness matrix corresponding to a constant strain, constant curvature change finite element
that is incompatible in normal displacement and rotation at its
boundaries but that in general gives very rapidly convergent
results with increasing density of nodal points. Note that two of
the w points lie outside of the element. If the mesh spacing is

Fig. 8 Finite difference discretization:
the 'finite difference element'

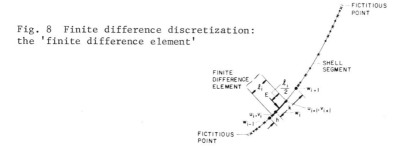

constant, the algebraic equations obtained by minimization of the
energy with respect to nodal degrees of freedom can be shown to be
equivalent to the Euler equations of the variational problem in
finite form. Further description and proofs are given in Ref. [5].

Figures 9 and 10 show rates of convergence with increasing
nodal point density for a poorly conditioned problem — a stress
analysis of a thin, nonsymmetrically loaded hemisphere with a free
edge. The finite element results were obtained by programming
various kinds of finite elements into BOSOR4. The computer time
for computation of the stiffness matrix K_1 is shown in Fig. 10. A
much smaller time for computation of the finite difference K_1 is
required because there are fewer calculations for each Gaussian
integration point and because there is only one Gaussian point
per finite difference element. Other comparisons of rate of convergence with the two methods used in BOSOR4 are shown for buckling
and vibration problems in Ref. [5].

Formulation of the Stability Problem

The bifurcation buckling problem represents perhaps the most difficult of the three types of analyses performed by BOSOR4. It is
practical to consider bifurcation buckling of complex, ring
stiffened shell structures under various systems of loads, some of
which are considered to be known and constant, or 'fixed' and some
of which are considered to be unknown eigenvalue parameters, or
'variable'.

The notion of 'fixed' and 'variable' systems of loads not only
permits the analysis of structures submitted to nonproportionally
varying loads, but also helps in the formulation of a sequence of
simple or 'classical' eigenvalue problems for the solution of problems governed by 'nonclassical' eigenvalue problems. An example
is a shallow spherical cap under external pressure. Very shallow
caps fail by nonlinear collapse, or snap-through buckling, not by
bifurcation buckling. Deep spherical caps fail by bifurcation
buckling in which nonlinearities in prebuckling behavior are not
particularly important. There is a range of cap geometries for
which bifurcation buckling is the mode of failure and for which the
critical pressures are much affected by nonlinearities in prebuckling behavior. The analysis of this intermediate class of
spherical caps is simplified by the concept of 'fixed' and 'variable' pressure.

Figure 11 shows the load deflection curve of a shallow cap in
this intermediate range. Nonlinear axisymmetric collapse (p_{nl}),
linear bifurcation (p_{lb}), and nonlinear bifurcation (p_{nb}) loads are
shown. The purpose of the analysis referred to in this section is
to determine the pressure p_{nb}. It is useful to consider the pressure p_{nb} as composed of two parts

$$p_{nb} = p^f + p^v$$

in which p^f denotes a known or 'fixed' quantity, and p^v denotes an
undetermined or 'variable' quantity. The fixed portion p^f is an

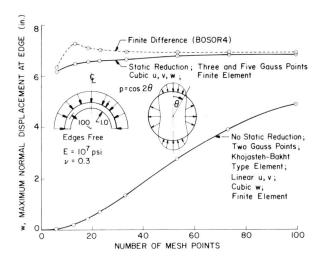

Fig. 9 Normal displacement at free edge of hemisphere with nonuniform pressure $p(s,\theta) = p_o \cos 2\theta$

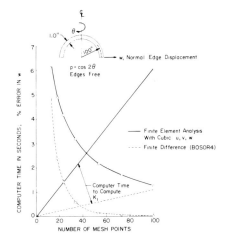

Fig. 10 Computer times to form stiffness matrix K_1 and rates of
convergence of normal edge displacement for free hemisphere with
nonuniform pressure $p(s,\theta) = p_o \cos 2\theta$

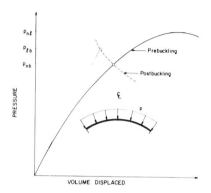

Fig. 11 Load deflection curves for shallow spherical cap, showing bifurcation points from linear prebuckling curve ($p_{\ell b}$) and nonlinear
prebuckling curve (p_{nb})

initial guess or represents the results of a previous iteration.
The variable portion p^V is the remainder, which can be determined
from an eigenvalue problem, as will be described. It is clear from
Fig. 11 that if p^f is fairly close to p_{nb} the behavior in the range
$p = p^f \pm p^V$ is reasonably linear. Thus, the eigenvalue p_{nb} can be
calculated by means of a sequence of eigenvalue problems through
which ever and ever smaller values p^V are determined and added to
the known results p^f from the previous iterations. As the BOSOR4
computer program is written the initial guess p^f need not be close
to the solution p_{nb}.

In the bifurcation stability analysis it is necessary to develop two matrices corresponding to the eigenvalue problem

$$K_1(n)x_n + \lambda_n K_2(n)x_n = 0. \qquad (1)$$

In Eq. (1) $K_1(n)$ is the stiffness matrix of the shell as loaded by
the fixed load system p^f; $K_2(n)$ is the load-geometric matrix
corresponding to the prestress increment caused by the loading increment p^V; λ_n is the eigenvalue; x_n is the eigenvector; and n is
the number of full circumferential waves. Eigenvalues are extracted by inverse power iterations with spectral shifts. Further
details of the theory are given in [6], including the treatment of
the discrete ring stiffeners and constraint conditions.

IMPERFECTION SENSITIVITY IN BUCKLING ANALYSES

It is well known that the load-carrying capability of thin shells is in many cases sensitive to initial imperfections of the geometry of the shell wall. The question so often asked by the analyst is: given the idealized structure and loading, and given the means by which to determine the collapse or bifurcation buckling loads, what "knockdown" factor should be applied to assure a reasonable factor of safety for the actual imperfect structure?

In Fig. 15 is an example of a shell-load system which exhibits load carrying capability considerably greater than that corresponding to the lowest bifurcation eigenvalue. Postbuckling stability is also exhibited by columns and flat plates. On the other hand, it is well known that the critical loads of axially compressed cylindrical shells and externally pressurized spherical shells are extremely sensitive to imperfections less than one wall thick in magnitude. These highly symmetrical systems are very sensitive to imperfections because many different buckling modes are associated with the same eigenvalue, the structure is uniformly compressed in a membrane state, and the buckling modes have many small waves. Very small local imperfections will tend to trigger premature failure. The buckling loads of most practical shell structures are somewhat sensitive to imperfections, but not this sensitive. How much so is a very important question. BOSOR4 does not calculate "knock down" factors to account for imperfections. With BOSOR4 the analyst can calculate buckling loads of shells with arbitrary axisymmetric imperfections. The BOSOR4 user is urged to read the brief survey of imperfection sensitivity theory given in [7] and to consult the references given there.

BOSOR4 PROGRAM ORGANIZATION

The BOSOR4 program consists of a main program MAIN and six overlays called READIT, PRE, ARRAYS, BUCKLE, MODE1, AND PLOT1. Figure 12 gives the core storage in decimal words required for the Univac 1108, IBM 370, and CDC 6600 versions of BOSOR4. The Univac 1108 and IBM 370 versions are written in double precision FORTRAN IV; the CDC version is written in single precision FORTRAN IV.

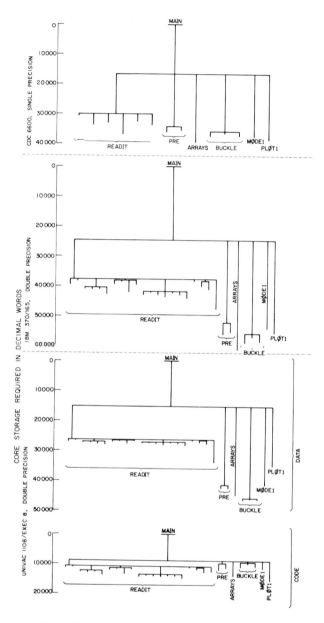

Fig. 12   BOSOR4 core storage requirements

SAMPLE DESIGN PROBLEMS FOR WHICH
BOSOR4 HAS BEEN USED
AND COMPARISON WITH TESTS

A complex design that BOSOR4 was used on is shown in Fig. 4. Other
examples corresponding to various analysis branches (INDIC) are
given in this section.

Nonlinear Stress Analysis (INDIC = 0)

Figure 13 shows part of an internally pressurized elliptical tank
which has been thickened locally near the equator for welding. The
engineering drawings called for an elliptically shaped inner surface with the thickness varying as shown. The maximum stress occurs
at the outer fiber at point C because there is considerable local
bending there due to the rather sudden change in direction, or
eccentricity, of the load path in the short segment ACB. The nonlinear theory gives lower stresses than the linear theory because
the meridional tension causes the tank to change shape in such a
way as to decrease the local excursion of the load path, thereby
decreasing the effective bending moment acting at point C. The
tank had been built and a linear analysis performed. The user of
the tank wanted to know if it would withstand a somewhat higher internal pressure than that for which it had originally been designed.
The lower stress predicted with nonlinear theory gave him enough
margin of safety to avoid the necessity of redesign.

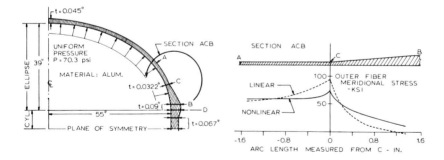

Fig. 13 Linear and nonlinear analysis of internally pressurized
elliptical tank

T-ring Modeled as Branched Shell (INDIC = 0)

Figure 14 shows the discretized model and buckling loads predicted
for a range of circumferential waves N. BOSOR4 gives two minima in
the range $2 \geq N \geq 16$. The minimum at N = 2 is a mode in which the
cross section does not deform, i.e. the ring ovalization mode.
Buckling pressures calculated for this mode are very close to those
computed from the well known formula $q_{cr} = EI(N^2 - 1)/r_c^3$, in which
q_{cr} is the critical line load in lb/in. (pressure integrated in the
direction of segment 1), EI is the bending rigidity of the ring,
and r_c is the radius to the ring centroidal axis. The minimum at
about N = 11 corresponds to buckling of the web. In a test the web
crippled at about 1500 psi. The N = 2 mode was not observed because the ring was held in a mandrel that prevented the unlimited
growth of this mode. Approximately 20 sec of UNIVAC 1108 CPU time
were required for this case.

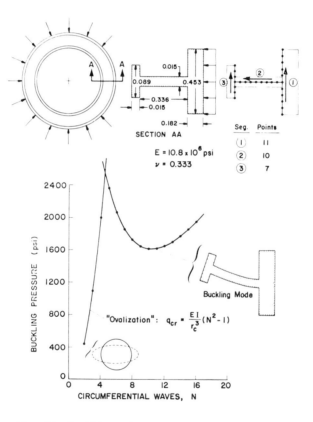

Fig. 14 Buckling of ring treated as branched shell

Nonlinear Bifurcation Buckling (INDIC = -2 and -1)

Point-loaded spherical caps were tested by Penning and Thurston in 1965 [8]. A configuration and predicted and experimental load-deflection curves with bifurcation points are shown in Fig. 15. This system is stable at and beyond the bifurcation points shown.

Figure 16 depicts a short section of the generator of a cylinder stiffened by external corrugations. The corrugations are cut away in the neighborhood of a field joint ring to allow for bolting of the two mating flanges of the ring. The cylinder is axially compressed. Far away from the field joint the axial resultant acts through the centroid of the corrugation-skin combination. In the neighborhood of the field joint the load path moves radially inward, effectively causing an axisymmetric dimple. As the axial compression is increased, hoop compressive stresses build up in the regions reinforced by doublers. Slight asymmetry of the assembly causes the ring to roll over axisymmetrically, which generates higher compressive hoop stresses above the ring and eventually leads to buckling there with many small waves around the circumference of the cylinder. Figure 17 shows the actual failure, which agrees with the BOSOR4 prediction.

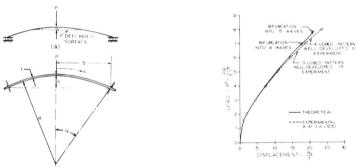

Fig. 15 Point-loaded spherical cap and load-deflection curves obtained from test and from BOSOR4

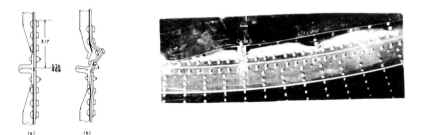

Fig. 16 Field joint geometry and buckle under axial load

Fig. 17 Failure as seen from inside the corrugated cylinder

Nonsymmetric Linear Stress Analysis (INDIC = 3)

Figure 18 gives thermal stresses in a cylinder configured and heated
nonsymmetrically as shown. The test results are from [9]. Twenty
Fourier harmonics were used for representation of the circumferential temperature distribution and calculation of the stress.

Buckling Under Nonsymmetric Loading (INDIC = 4)

Figures 19 and 20 show the model and results. Figure 19 gives the
observed temperature rise distribution at buckling as reported in
[10]. Figure 20 shows the predicted prebuckling stress and displacement distributions and the lowest three eigenvalues and eigenvectors corresponding to 20 circumferential waves. The eigenvalues
denote a factor to be multiplied by the prebuckling temperature
rise distribution at buckling in the test. Twenty Fourier harmonics were used for the prebuckling analysis. The model consists
of 309 degrees of freedom. A total of 74 sec of CPU time on the
UNIVAC 1108 were required for execution of the case.

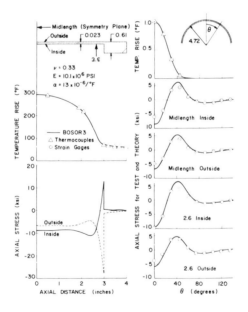

Fig. 18 Comparison of test and theory for thermal stress in non-
symmetrically heated cylinder

Fig. 19
Conical shell
heated along
axial strip

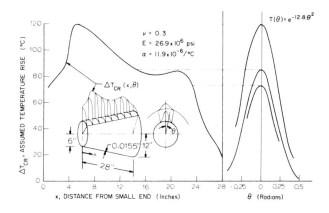

Fig. 20
Prebuckling
state of non-
axisymmetri-
cally heated
cone and
buckling modes

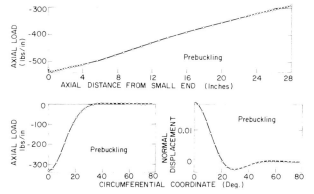

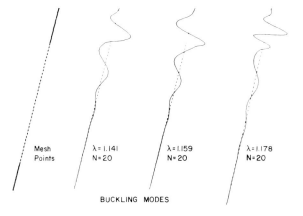

Modal Vibration (INDIC = 2)

Figures 21 and 22 show the geometry and some natural vibration
modes of an aluminum ring stiffened cylinder supported by steel end
plates. The cylinder was tested by Hayek and Pallett [11] and a
previous analysis was performed by Harari and Baron [12]. The experimental results, analytical results from BOSOR4 with eight
different models, and analytical results from [12] are given in
Table 3.

One of the most important points to be made in regard to
Table 3 is that an approximate analysis can by fortuitous coinci-
dence yield very good results because of counteracting errors.
Take the bottom row of Table 3, for example. The relatively crude
model in which the rings are treated as discrete and the end plates
are omitted (modeled as simple supports--v and w restrained, u and
rotation free) leads by chance to a very good prediction (2800 cps)
of the experimental result (2802 cps). However, the stiffness of
each discrete ring is overestimated because its cross section is
not permitted to deform. If each ring is treated as a shell segment with no other changes made in the model, a new frequency of
2663 cps is obtained. This branched model is labeled (1) in
Fig. 21b. If an additional refinement is made by the addition of
the end plates, frequencies of 2682 or 2724 cps are obtained, depending on the degree of constraint assumed to exist between the
end plates and the cylinder. These models are too flexible, however, because axial bending of the cylinder wall is permitted along
the 0.375 in. lengths corresponding to the regions of intersection
of cylinder and rings. If the cylinder is treated as consisting of
six segments with 0.375 in. gaps at the areas where the rings and
cylinder intersect, and if the material in each gap is treated as
a discrete ring with undeformable cross section, the frequencies of
2750 or 2782 or 2833 cps are calculated, depending on whether the
end plates are included and, if they are, on the degree of constraint assumed to exist between them and the cylinder. This
segmented cylinder model is labeled (2) in Fig. 21b. The predicted
vibration mode shapes with n = 6, m = 3 for all of the models are
given in Fig. 22. The test frequency of 2802 cps is bracketed by
the results from the various models. Notice that for other modes
the test frequencies are less well predicted by the cruder discrete
ring model but that they are still bracketed (with the exception of
n = 5, m = 1) by use of the full range of models as just described.
The case n = 6, m = 1 is an example. In the n = 1 case it is important to include the end plates in order to obtain an accurate
prediction of the fundamental beam bending mode of the entire free-
free cylinder end plate system. This mode is depicted in Fig. 22.

During the study of a particular structure the analyst should
set up various models in order to obtain upper and lower bounds on
the behavior if possible. Because of imperfections, it is difficult
to obtain a lower bound for buckling loads. However, since vibration frequencies and modes are not sensitive to imperfections,
vibration test results can usually be regarded as reliable and can
therefore be used to determine which models best simulate the
actual behavior.

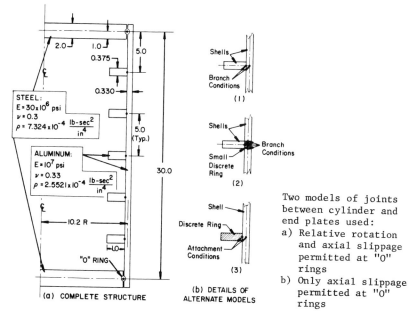

Two models of joints between cylinder and end plates used:
a) Relative rotation and axial slippage permitted at "0" rings
b) Only axial slippage permitted at "0" rings

Fig. 21   (a)   Geometry of ring stiffened cylinder tested by Hayek and Pallet.   (b)   Various models of the rings

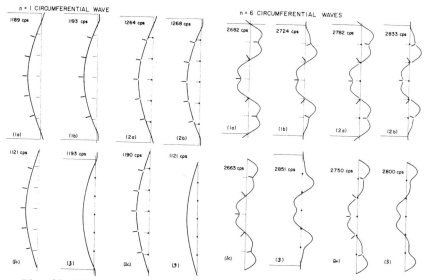

Fig. 22   Vibration modes corresponding to one and six circumferential waves

Table 3   Natural Frequencies for Various Models of Ring-Stiffened Cylinder

Circ. Waves n	Axial Waves m	Test[a] Results	End Plates Included					End Plates Omitted			Harari & Baron	
			Rings Are Shell Branches:				Discrete Rings	Rings Treated As Shell Branches		Discrete Rings	Discrete Rings	Smeared Rings
			Cylinder Is One Segment		Cylinder Is Six Segments[b]			Cylinder Segments:				
			A[c]	B[d]	A	B	B	One	Six		Cylinder is Simply Supported	
1	r.b.[e]	-	0	0	0	0	0	0	0			
1	r.b.[f]	-	0	0	0	0	0	0	0			
1	p.a.[g]	?	0	67	0	69	67	--	--			
1	p.s.	?	0	70	0	73	70	--	--			
1	1	1232	1189	1193	1264	1268	1193	1121	1190	1121	1124	1133
1	u[h]	?	1714	1714	1819	1819	1716	1738	1848	1740	1743	
1	2	?	2189	2198	2301	2313	2199	2175	2282	2177	2183	
1	3	?	2653	2669	2763	2783	2672	2654	2759	2656	2663	
1	4	2870	2863	2887	2962	2991	2890		2960	2868	2875	2893
2	1	627	607	618	648	660	618	609	647	609	611	640
2	p.a.	?	1040	1047	1040	1047	1047	--	--	--	--	
2	p.s.	?	1041	1048	1041	1048	1048	--	--	--	--	
2	2	?	1378	1395	1469	1489	1396	1385	1468	1386	1389	
2	3	?	1960	1983	2075	2103	1985	1967	2073	1969	1974	
2	4	?	2339	2366	2467	2502	2371					
3	1	787	773	783	803	815	796	773	802	786	786	832
3	2	1190	1137	1160	1203	1230	1166	1136	1197	1143	1145	1194
3	3	1602	1588	1619	1690	1726	1622	1587	1679	1589	1594	1650
4	1	1310	1307	1313	1348	1355	1371	1306	1346	1304	1359	1431
4	2	1503	1453	1475	1509	1535	1525	1450	1503	1501	1497	1575
4	3	1806	1714	1752	1797	1842	1788	1708	1784	1745	1744	1826
5	1	1938	1943	1949	2008	2014	2080	1941	2006	2073	2062	2253
5	2	2059	2020	2041	2088	2113	2163	2015	2080	2137	2126	2331
5	3	2276	2170	2214	2251	2304	2317	2159	2232	2262	2252	2474
6	1	2594	2567	2572	2673	2678	2770	2564	2668	2762	2750	3276
6	2	?	2606	2625	2707	2729	2798	2597	2691	2772	2762	
6	3	2802	2682	2724	2782	2833	2851	2663	2750	2800	2790	3424

[a] Tests performed by Hayek and Pallett.

[b] Gaps between segments of cylinder are "filled" by discrete rings with cross-section dimensions .33 x .375.

[c] Model A: Rotation and axial slippage permitted between end plates and cylinder.

[d] Model B: Axial slippage only permitted between end plates and cylinder.

[e] r.b. = "rigid body mode"

[f] p.a. = "plate antisymmetric" = end plates vibrating in phase.

[g] p.s. = "plate symmetric" = end plates vibrating out-of-plane.

[h] u = axial motion predominates.

SOME ASPECTS OF MODELING SHELLS

Some ideas about modeling have just been given. The purpose of this section is to give the user further hints about modeling for stress, buckling, and vibration analyses of practical shell of revolution.

Mesh Point Allocation

The analyst may wish to know what the stresses are in a shell at the bifurcation buckling load. If he sets up a single discretized model for both the stress and the buckling analyses, he must allo-cate nodal points such that stress concentrations as well as buckling modes can be predicted with reasonable accuracy. It is usually fairly easy to guess where the stress concentrations are, but more difficult to predict where the shell will buckle and the shape of the mode. Peak stresses can generally be predicted with enough accuracy if nodal points are spaced a few wall thicknesses apart. If a higher nodal point density is required for adequate convergence, thin shell theory may not represent a good enough model. Good estimates of buckling loads can usually be obtained with more than four nodal points per half wavelength of the buckling mode. Figure 23 depicts a ring stiffened cylinder which is sub-mitted to external pressure. The prebuckling normal displacement and meridional moment and the buckling modal displacement distri-butions are also shown. Notice that mesh points are concentrated near the T-shaped rings and at the boundary where stress concen-trations exist. Half the cylinder is modeled with symmetry conditions applied at the symmetry plane.

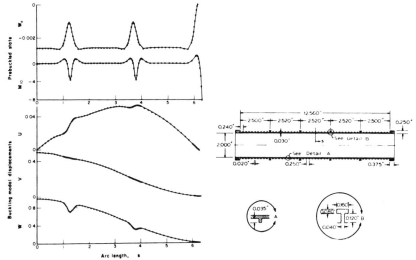

Fig. 23 Prebuckling state and buckling mode of an externally pressurized ring stiffened cylinder

Modeling Discrete Rings When Local Buckling
Between Rings is Possible

Some BOSOR4 users have been concerned that occasionally buckling
loads predicted for externally pressurized ring stiffened cylinders
are unexpectedly high. In these cases the predicted buckling modes
are usually local (deflections between rings with rings at nodes in
the buckling pattern). Aside from the question of initial imperfections, there is another reason that too high buckling loads may be
calculated: in the actual structure the webs of ring stiffeners
probably deform considerably in the local buckling mode. This deformation can be accounted for if the webs of the rings are treated
as flexible shell branches as shown in Fig. 24. The user should
include in his parameter studies such a model, at least for a section of ring stiffened shell spanning two adjacent rings. It is
rarely necessary to include the outstanding flanges as shells, since
they can remain discrete rings.

Figure 25 shows a comparison of predicted buckling pressures of
a cylinder with two models of a ring, one in which its cross section
cannot deform (labeled "Ring") and the other in which it can (labeled "Branched Shell"). Reference [13] has more discussion on this
and other points about modeling discrete rings.

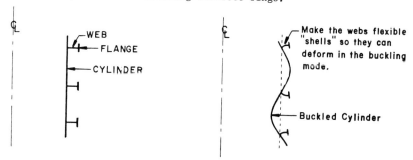

Fig. 24   Cylinder with ring webs modeled as flexible shell branches

When Stiffeners Can Be "Smeared"

If there exists a regular pattern of reasonably closely spaced
stiffeners, their contribution to the wall stiffness of the shell
or plate might be modeled by an averaging of their extensional and
bending rigidities over arc lengths equal to the local spacings between them. Thus, the actual wall is treated as if it were orthotropic. In BOSOR4 this "smearing" process accounts for the fact
that the neutral axes of the stiffeners do not in general lie in
the plane of the reference surface of the shell wall. Predictions
of buckling loads and vibration frequencies of stiffened cylinders
have been found to be very sensitive to this eccentricity effect.
A general rule of thumb for deciding to smear out the stiffeners or

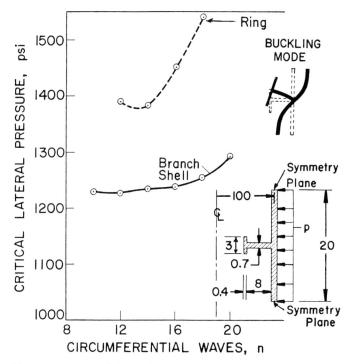

Fig. 25 Comparison of local buckling pressures of a ring stiffened
cylinder for two models of the ring

to treat them as discrete is that for smearing there should be
about 2 to 3 stiffeners per half wavelength of the deformation
pattern. It may be appropriate to smear out stiffeners in a
buckling or vibration analysis but, because of local stress concentrations caused by the stiffeners, not in a stress analyses. The
stiffeners can be smeared as an analytical device to suppress local
buckling and vibration modes. In order to handle problems involving smeared stiffeners, a computerized analysis must include
coupling between bending and extensional energy.

Modeling Prismatic Shell Structures

An interesting and not immediately obvious use of BOSOR4 is for
buckling and vibration analysis of prismatic shell structures, in
particular composite branched panels. This technique of using a
shell of revolution program for the treatment of structures that

are not axisymmetric is discussed in detail in Ref [2]. Figure 26
shows various types of prismatic shell structures that can be
handled by BOSOR4. Examples involving stress and buckling of oval
cylinders, cylinders with nonuniform loads, and corrugated and
beaded panels are given in Ref. [2], as well as a study of vibration
of a stringer stiffened shell in which the stringers are treated as
discrete. In the analysis of buckling of nonuniformly loaded cylinders, the nonsymmetry of the prestress can be accounted for in
the stability analysis. In BOSOR4 the capability described in Ref.
[2] is extended to branched prismatic shell structures.

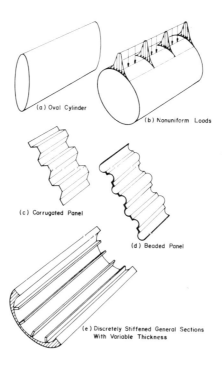

Fig. 26 Some prismatic shell structures that can be analyzed with
use of BOSOR4

Example of Analysis of Prismatic "Shell" Structure

Figure 27 shows two types of semisandwich corrugated construction, bonded and riveted. The panels are treated as giant annuli with mean radius of 2,750 in. and outer radius minus inner radius equal to about 7.4 in. Both panels are assumed to carry an axial compressive stress (panels loaded normal to plane of figure) that is constant along the axis of the panel and over all of the little segments shown at the top of Fig. 27. In the model on the left-hand side of the figure the troughs of the corrugated sheet and the flat skin are assumed to be united by a perfect bond of zero thickness. The thickness of the panel in these areas is equal to the sum of the thickness of the flat sheet and the corrugated sheet. In the riveted panel the displacements and rotations of the corrugated sheet are constrained to be equal to those of the flat skin only at the midlengths of the troughs, thus simulating a rivet of zero diameter in the plane of the paper and continuous in the direction normal to the plane of the paper. The computer generated plots show the undeformed and deformed panels for buckling modes with various wave lengths L in the direction normal to the plane of the paper. The riveted panel is weaker in axial compression because the rivets permit more local distortion of the cross section than does the continuous bonding. The modes shown are more or less general instability modes. One can calculate buckling loads for much shorter L, such as L = 1.0 in., in order to determine the effect of fastening on crippling loads.

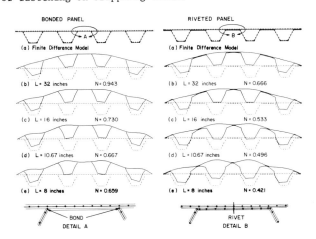

L = Axial Half-Wavelength of Buckling Mode.

$$N = \frac{\text{(Critical Axial Load)}}{\text{(Critical Axial Load With Local Distortion of Wall Cross-Section Not Allowed)}}$$

Fig. 27   Buckling modes and loads for axially compressed bonded and riveted corrugated panels

Modeling Concentrated Loads on Shells

The analyst may be interested in several types of concentrated loads which arise in various ways. If the shell structure is to be subjected to concentrated loads in the ordinary course of its service, such as a tank supported on struts or a rocket stage with discrete payload attach points, it is usually provided that the concentrated loads be applied to reinforced areas such as circumferential rings or longitudinal stringers through which these loads are smoothly diffused into the shell. Therefore, deflections are small, and a linear analysis is generally suitable. If, however, the analyst wants to find out what happens if the shell is accidentally poked somewhere, the concentrated load may be applied to an unreinforced area, and the shell may experience large deflections. Prediction of the effect of these accidental loads may therefore require non-linear analysis. The point-loaded spherical cap, for which a load-deflection curve is shown in Fig. 15, is an example. In BOSOR4 a concentrated load applied such that nonsymmetric displacements occur is modeled as a line load with a triangular distribution around the circumference. Figure 28 shows an example. Each load is simulated by the area within the triangular "pulse" multiplied by some factor provided by the user as an input datum.

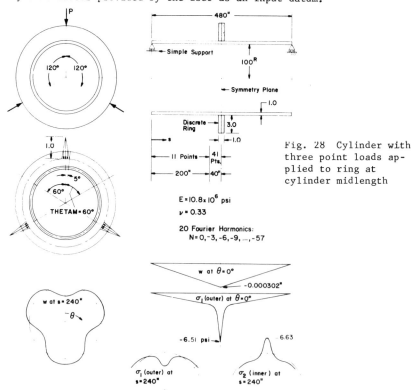

Fig. 28 Cylinder with three point loads applied to ring at cylinder midlength

Constraint Condition Problems to Be Wary Of

There are certain commonly occuring situations in which the program user should take great care with regard to constraint conditions. These involve rigid body behavior, symmetric vs. antisymmetric behavior at planes of symmetry in the structure, singularity conditions at poles of shells of revolution, discontinuities between various branches and segments of a complex shell structure, and unexpected sensitivity of predicted behavior to changes in boundary conditions.

Rigid body displacement. Rigid body displacement of an analytical model of a structure should not be permitted in static stress and buckling problems. In such problems the shell must be held in such a way that no constraints are introduced which are not actually present in the real structure. The proper application of rigid body constraint conditions requires special care in the case of non-symmetrically loaded shells of revolution. These conditions apply only if the displacements are axisymmetric, or if the displacements vary with one circumferential wave around the circumference and must be released for higher displacement harmonics.

Symmetry planes. Many problems are best analyzed by a modeling of a small portion of the actual structure bounded by symmetry planes. In bifurcation buckling and modal vibration problems important modes may be antisymmetrical at one or more of the symmetry planes. This occurrence implies that symmetry boundary conditions should be applied in the prestress analysis and antisymmetry conditions at one or more of the symmetry planes in the eigenvalue analysis for bifurcation buckling or modal vibration. Unless the program user is certain about the behavior at a symmetry plane, he must make multiple runs on the computer, testing for both symmetrical and antisymmetrical behavior at each symmetry plane.

Singularity conditions at a pole. The problem of singularity conditions arises only in the case of shells of revolution or flat circular plates. As with rigid body modes, special conditions must be applied for axisymmetric ($n = 0$) displacements or for displacement modes with one circumferential wave ($n = 1$). If $n \geq 2$ the pole condition acts as a clamped boundary.

Constraint conditions for discontinuous domains. Practical shell structures are very frequently assembled so that the combined reference surfaces of the various branches and segments of the analytical model form a discontinuous domain. The BOSOR4 user should be aware that the constraint conditions governing the compatibility relations between adjacent surfaces imply that a rigid connection exists across the discontinuity. Thus the analytical model is stiffer than the actual structure. Buckling loads and vibration frequencies will be overestimated. It is likely that local discontinuity stresses will also be overestimated.

Unexpected sensitivity of predicted behavior to changes in boundary conditions. Frequently, complicated shell structures are designed and manufactured by more than one company or by more than one organization within a company. Each company or organization is responsible for only one particular segment of the entire structure, and often the properties of the adjoining segments are known only approximately if at all. Therefore some conditions must be assumed at the boundaries of each segment during the design phase of that segment. The purpose of this section is to warn the analyst that predictions of stress, buckling, and vibration of shells may be very sensitive to boundary conditions even though intuition dictates otherwise. Engineers interested in designing a particular segment of a larger structure should make every effort to determine as accurately as possible the actual boundary conditions at the ends of "their" segment. Portions of the adjoining segments should be included in the model, possibly with a cruder mesh. If little is known about the adjoining structures, sensitivity studies should be performed in which both upper and lower bounds on the degree of boundary constraint are assumed.

INPUT DATA

A preprocessor has been written for BOSOR4 by means of which the input data can be prepared in free format [14]. Figure 29 shows a sample BOSOR4 data deck.

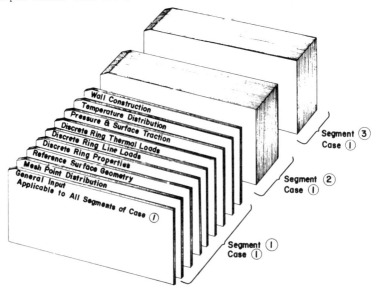

Fig. 29 Sample BOSOR4 data deck

ACKNOWLEDGEMENTS

The author is indebted to Frank Brogan, Tom Peterson, Chet Dyche, Bo Almroth, Bill Loden, and Rod Kure, who wrote some of the subroutines used in the BOSOR4 program. Particular appreciation is expressed for the many fruitful discussions with Frank Brogan and Bo Almroth concerning the numerical aspects of the analysis, and with Jörgen Skogh about ways in which to make the BOSOR4 program easy to use. The author is thankful also for Frank Brogan's assistance in the conversion of BOSOR4 for operation on the CDC 6600 and Tom Peterson's, Pete Smolenski's, and Bob Mitchell's assistance in the conversion for operation on the IBM 370/165.

The development of BOSOR4 was sponsored by the Department of Structural Mechanics of the Naval Ship Research and Development Center under Naval Ship Systems Command, Operation and Maintenance Navy Fund, Contract N00014-71-C-0002. Rembert Jones and Joan Roderick were technical monitors. The work involved in converting BOSOR4 for operation on the CDC 6600 was sponsored by the NASA Langley Research Center, Contract NASI-10929, with Paul Cooper as technical monitor

Some of the numerical studies were performed under the Lockheed Missiles & Space Company's Independent Research Program. The support of ONR under Contract N00014-76-C-0692, with Nicholas Perrone and Kenneth Saczalski as technical monitors, is gratefully acknowledged.

The following figures have been reprinted by permission:

Figs. 1 - 3 from D. Bushnell, B. O. Almroth, and F. Brogan, "Finite-Diference Energy Method for Nonlinear Shell Analysis," Computers & Structures, Vol. 1, 1971, pp. 361-387, © 1971.

Figs. 7, 8, 11, 12, 14, 19, 20, 28, 29 and Table 2 from D. Bushnell, "Stress, Stability and Vibration of Complex, Branched Shells of Revolution," Computers & Structures, Vol. 4, 1974, pp. 399-435, © 1974.

Figs. 9, 10 from D. Bushnell, "Finite-Difference Energy Models versus Finite-Element Models: Two Variational Approaches in One Computer Program," Numerical and Computer Methods in Structural Mechanics, pp. 291-336, © 1973, Academic Press, New York.

Fig. 13 from D. Bushnell, "Nonlinear Analysis for Axisymmetric Elastic Stresses in Ring-Stiffened, Segmented Shells of Revolution," AIAA/ASME 10th Structures, Structural Dynamics and Materials Conference, pp. 104-113, © 1969, ASME.

Fig. 16, 17 from D. Bushnell, "Crippling and Buckling of Corrugated Ring-Stiffened Cylinders," AIAA Journal of Spacecraft and Rockets, Vol. 9, No. 5, 1972, pp. 357-363, © 1972, AIAA.

Fig. 18 from D. Bushnell and S. Smith, "Stress and Buckling of Nonuniformly Heated Cylindrical and Conical Shells, "AIAA Journal, Vol. 9, No. 12, Dec. 1971, pp. 2314-2321, © 1971, AIAA.

Figs. 21 through 23 and Table 3 from D. Bushnell, "Thin Shells," Structural Mechanics Computer Programs, University Press of Virginia, pp. 277-358 © 1972.

Fig. 26 from D. Bushnell, "Stress, Buckling, and Vibration of Prismatic Shells," AIAA Journal, Vol 9, No. 10, Oct. 1971, pp. 2003-2013, © 1971, AIAA.

Fig. 27 from D. Bushnell, "Evaluation of Various Analytical Models for Buckling and Vibration of Stiffened Shells," AIAA Journal, Vol. 11, No. 9, 1973, pp. 1283-1291 © 1973, AIAA.

REFERENCES

1 Bushnell, D., "Stress, Stability, and Vibration of Complex Branched Shells of Revolution, Analysis and User's Manual for BOSOR4," LMSC-D243605, Lockheed Missiles & Space Co., Inc., Sunnyvale, Ca., March 1972.
Also NASA CR-2116, Oct. 1972.
2 Bushnell, D., "Stress, Buckling, and Vibration of Prismatic Shells," AIAA Journal, Vol. 9, No. 10, Oct. 1971, pp. 2004-13.
3 Bushnell, D., Almroth, B. O., and Brogan, F. A., "Finite-Difference Energy Method for Nonlinear Shell Analysis," Journal for Computers & Structures, Vol. 1, 1971, pp. 361-87.
4 Bushnell, D., "Analysis of Ring-Stiffened Shells of Revolution under Combined Thermal and Mechanical Loading," AIAA Journal, Vol. 9, No. 3, March 1971, pp. 401-10.
5 Bushnell, D., "Finite-Difference Energy Models Versus Finite Element Models: Two Variational Approaches in One Computer Program," Numerical and Computer Methods in Structural Mechanics, edited by Fenves, S. J., Perrone, N., Robinson, A. R., and Schnobrich, W. C., Academic Press, Inc., New York and London, 1973, pp. 291-336.
6 Bushnell, D., "Analysis of Buckling and Vibration of Ring-Stiffened, Segmented Shells of Revolution," International Journal of Solids Structures, Vol. 6, 1970, pp. 157-181.
7 Bushnell, D., "Thin Shells," Structural Mechanics Computer Programs, edited by Pilkey, W., Saczalski, K. and Schaeffer, H., University Press of Virginia, Charlottesville, 1974, pp. 277-358.
8 Penning, F. A. and Thurston, G. A., "The Stability of Shallow Spherical Shells Under Concentrated Load," NASA CR-265, July 1965.
9 Holmes, A., "Measurement of Thermal Stresses in Ring-Stiffened Cylinders," LMSC-Y1-69-66-1, Lockheed Missiles & Space Co., Palo Alto, Ca., Dec. 1966.
10 Bushnell, D. and Smith, S., "Stress and Buckling of Nonuniformly Heated Cylindrical and Conical Shells," AIAA Journal, Vol. 9, No. 12, 1971, pp. 2314-2321.
11 Hayek, S. and Pallett, D. S., "Theoretical and Experimental Studies of the Vibration of Fluid Loaded Cylindrical Shells," Symposium on Application of Experimental and Theoretical Structural Dynamics, Southampton University, England, April 1972.
12 Harari, A. and Baron, M. L., "Analysis for the Dynamic Response of Stiffened Shells," ASME Paper No. 73-APM-FFF, to appear J. Appl. Mech.
13 Bushnell, D., "Evaluation of Various Analytical Models for Buckling and Vibration of Stiffened Shells," AIAA Journal, Vol. 11, No. 9, 1973, pp. 1283-1291.
14 BOSOR4 PREPROCESSOR written by and available from SKD Enterprise, 9138 Barberry Lane, Hickory Hills, Illinois 60457.

APPENDIX A

BOSOR4 INPUT DATA

This appendix is organized in the following way: First there is a
page which gives some useful hints on how to set up a case; then
there are two pages which define certain input data that depend on
what type of analysis is to be performed; these two pages are followed by seven pages describing constraint and juncture conditions;
then come three pages on load and temperature multipliers and ranges.
All of these pages just described correspond to the initial cards in
the input deck labeled "General Input--Applicable to All Segments of
Case 1" in Fig. 29.

The remaining input data for a case are defined on pages 61 - 98.
These data are required for each segment of the structure. The data
input section is subdivided into the following subsections:

1. Mesh Point Distribution
2. Reference Surface Geometry
3. Discrete Ring Properties
4. Discrete Ring Line Loads
5. Discrete Ring Thermal Loads
6. Pressure and Surface Traction
7. Temperature Distribution
8. Prestress Input Data for the Option INDI = 4, IPRE = 0
9. Wall Construction

The input data specifications are written in a style very similar to
FORTRAN. It is therefore assumed that the user is familiar with
this language.

Following the input data definition are sample input decks corresponding to each type of analysis. (INDIC = 1, -1, 0, 2, 3, 4, -2).
The user is urged to consult these cases since they will clarify
many of the input specifications which may at first seem rather ar-
cane.

A section entitled "Possible Pitfalls and Recommended Solutions"
then follows. The user should read this section even if he has not
yet encountered a problem. There are some suggestions given there
that may help the user decide how to set up an appropriate model.

Finally, there is a brief description of BOSOR4 output, including sample list and plot output corresponding to the first sample
case.

Some Useful Hints on How to Set Up a Case

1. Decide how many segments the shell should be divided into. Should ring stiffeners be treated as shell segments or discrete rings? It is often advisable to handle ring webs as flexible shell segments rather than as discrete ring segments

2. Decide how to number the segments. Think of the axis of revolution as being vertical and the shell meridian that you are working with as being to the right-hand side of this axis. Try to "travel" along the structure in a generally "northeasterly" direction whenever possible

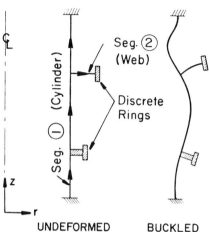

UNDEFORMED   BUCKLED

3. Lay out the entire structure on graph paper

4. Use the middle surface as a reference surface whenever it is reasonably easy to do so. Convergence with increasing mesh point density is fastest that way

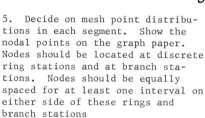

DETAIL A

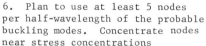

5. Decide on mesh point distributions in each segment. Show the nodal points on the graph paper. Nodes should be located at discrete ring stations and at branch stations. Nodes should be equally spaced for at least one interval on either side of these rings and branch stations

6. Plan to use at least 5 nodes per half-wavelength of the probable buckling modes. Concentrate nodes near stress concentrations

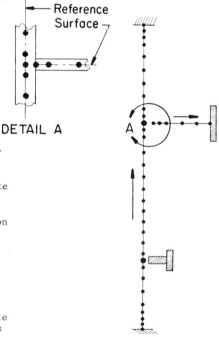

INPUT DATA FOR THE BOSOR4 USER'S MANUAL

Initial Input For Various Types of Analysis (INDIC = 0,-2,-1,1,2)

INDIC = 0 (nonlinear Axisymmetric stress analysis)	INDIC = -2,-1,1,2 (Bifurcation buckling, modal vibration)
● TITLE	● TITLE
● 0, NPRT, NLAST, ISTRES, 0	● INDIC, NPRT, NLAST, ISTRES, 0
● NSEG, NCOND, 0, IRIGID	● NSEG, NCOND, IBOUND, IRIGID
● 0, 0, 0	● 0, 0, 0
● 0, 0, 0, 0, 0	● NOB, NMINB, NMAXB, INCRB, NVEC
● 0, 0, 0	● 0, 0, 0
● 0	● 0
● 0.	● 0.
● 0., 0., 0.	● 0., 0., 0.

Definitions of Input Variables*

TITLE = title of case (72 characters or less).
INDIC = analysis type parameter:
    0 = nonlinear elastic axisymmetric stress analysis,
    -2 = stability determinant calculated for increasing load,
    -1 = bifurcation buckling with nonlinear prebuckling analysis,
    1 = bifurcation buckling with "linear" prebuckling analysis
      (see section on stability)
    2 = modal vibration with axisymmetric nonlinear prestress.
  See the section on scope of BOSOR4 for more details on INDIC.
NPRT = printout options: 1 = minimum, 2 = medium, 3 = max. Use 2.
NLAST = plot option: 0 = yes plots, -1 = no plots.
ISTRES = control for output: 0 = resultants; 1 = stresses. (use 1 with monocoque shells only.)
NSEG = number of shell segments. Must be less than 25.
NCOND = number of points at which constraint conditions are to be imposed, including junctures between segments. Must be less than 50.
IBOUND = control integer for constraint conditions:
    0 means bifurcation buckling and modal vibration constraint conditions are the same as those for axisymmetric prestress analysis,
    1 means that buckling and vibration constraint conditions are different from those for axisymmetric prestress analysis.
IRIGID = control integer for rigid body displacements:
    0 means no extra rigid body constraints are necessary,
    1 means that extra rigid body constraints are necessary.
  By "extra" is meant in addition to regular constraint conditions (still to be specified).

NOB, NMINB, NMAXB, INCRB, NVEC = initial, minimum, maximum circumferential wave numbers to be used in the buckling or vibration analysis; increment in the wave number; number of eigenvalues to calculate for each wave number.

---
* Variables beginning with I, J, K, L, M, N are fixed point. The rest are floating point. The symbol ● means "read".

Initial Input For Various Types of Analysis (Contd) (INDIC = 3,4)

INDIC = 3 (Linear nonsymmetric stress analysis)

- TITLE
- 3, NPRT, NLAST, ISTRES, 0
- NSEG, NCOND, 0, IRIGID
- NSTART, NFIN, INCR
- 0, 0, 0, 0, 0
- NDIST, NCIRC, NTHETA
- ITHETA(I), I = 1, NCIRC
- THETA(I), I = 1, NDIST
- THETAM, 0., 0.

INDIC = 4 (Bifurcation buckling with linear nonsymmetric stress)

- TITLE
- 4, NPRT, NLAST, ISTRES, IPRE
- NSEG, NCOND, IBOUND, IRIGID
- NSTART, NFIN, INCR
- NOB, NMINB, NMAXB, INCRB, NVEC
- NDIST, NCIRC, NTHETA
- ITHETA(I), I = 1, NCIRC
- THETA(I), I = 1, NDIST
- THETAM, THETAS, 0.

Definitions of Input Variables*

TITLE = title of case (72 characters or less).
INDIC = analysis type indicator: 3 = stress, 4 = stress and buckling.
NPRT = printout options: 1 = minimum, 2 = medium, 3 = max; use 2.
NLAST = plot option: 0 = yes plots, -1 = no plots.
ISTRES= 0 = stress resultants; 1 = stresses (1 with monocoque only).
IPRE = 0 = prestress from input data; 1 = prestress calculated.
NSEG = number of shell segments; must be less than 25.
NCOND = number of points at which constraints are applied, including junctions between segments.
IBOUND= control for constraint conditions; see previous page.
IRIGID= control for rigid body displacements; see previous page.
NSTART, NFIN, INCR = starting, ending, and increment in the number of circumferential waves to be used in the nonlinear nonsymmetric stress analysis. May be negative. These are the Fourier harmonics of the linear stress analysis.
NOB, NMINB, NMAXB, INCRB, NVEC = initial, minimum, maximum circumferential wave numbers to be used in the buckling analysis; increment in the wave number; number of eigenvalues to calculate for each wave, n.
NDIST = number of circumferential stations for which meridional distributions will be printed and/or plotted (less than 20). Note: NDIST*IALL*9 < 2700, where IALL = total no. of nodes.
NCIRC = number of meridional stations for which circumferential distributions will be printed and/or plotted (less than 20).
NTHETA= number of points in the output for circumferential distributions; must be less than 100. Note: NCIRC*NTHETA*9 < 2700.
ITHETA= meridional stations for circumferential distributions: e.g., 1011 means segment 1, mesh point 11.
THETA = circumferential stations in degrees for which meridional distributions will be printed and plotted. Must be less than or equal to THETAM.
THETAM= circumferential distributions printed and plotted for $0 \leq \theta \leq$ THETAM (deg.); Loads expanded in Fourier series in the interval $-$THETAM$\leq \theta \leq +$THETAM. THETAM is usually equal to 180.0.
THETAS= meridional distribution of prebuckling stress at $\theta =$ THETAS degrees is used in the stability analysis with options INDIC = 4 and IPRE = 1.

* Variables beginning with I, J, K, L, M, N are fixed point. The rest are floating point. The symbol ● means "read".

Constraint Conditions

Do 3   I = 1, NCOND

● IS1, IP1, IS2, IP2, IU*, IV, IW*, IX, D1, D2

3 Continue

Definitions of Input Variables

NCOND = number of points at which constraints are imposed, including junctures between segments. NCOND = 4 in the example below.   Four
kinds of constraint conditions exist in BOSOR4:
    1. constraints to ground (e.g., boundary conditions)
    2. juncture compatibility conditions,
    3. regularity conditions at poles (where the radius $r = 0$).
    4. constraints to prevent rigid body displacements.

IS1, IP1, IS2, IP2 = segment and node point numbers involved in a constraint condition. For example, a juncture compatibility condition might contain
    IS1, IP1, IS2, IP2 = 1, 25, 2, 5
meaning, "segment 1, point 25 is connected to segment 2,
point 5". A constraint to ground might contain
    IS1, IP1, IS2, IP2 = 1, 25, 1, 25
meaning that segment 1, point 25 is in some way (yet to be
specified) connected to ground. Regularity conditions and
constraints to prevent rigid body displacements are expressed
in the same way as constraints to ground. See the following
examples for further clarification.

IU*, IV, IW*, IX = indicators for no or yes constraint of global displacement components u*, v, w*, X, respectively. 0 means no constraint;
1 means yes there is a constraint of the corresponding displacement component. For example, a juncture compatibility
condition usually contains
    IS1, IP1, IS2, IP2, IU*, IV, IW*, IX = 1, 25, 2, 5, 1, 1, 1, 1
which means that all the displacement components and the
meridional rotation of segment 2, point 5 are "slaved" to
those of segment 1, point 25. A constraint to ground reads:
IS1, IP1, IS2, IP2, IU*, IV, IW*, IX = 1,25, 1,25, 1,1,1,0 which
means that u*, v, w* are zero at segment 1, point 25 and the
meridional rotation is free there (hinge).

D1, D2 = radial, axial components of discontinuity between segments,
or offset of support point from nodal point involved in a
constraint to ground. See Fig. A1 for positive sense of D1, D2.

For the figure here, we might have:
1,1,1,1,1,1,1,1,0.,0.,
1,7,2,1,1,1,1,1,0.,.2
2,5,3,1,1,1,1,1,.1,.4
3,9,3,9,0,0,0,0,0.,0.
(A pole is treated just as
done in the fourth line.
BOSOR4 automatically applies
the correct IU*, IV, IW*, IX,
which depend on circ. n.)

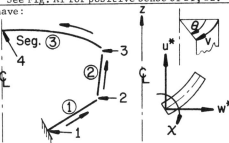

Constraint Conditions (Continued) More on D1 and D2

The figure below shows a meridional discontinuity (a) and boundary
support eccentricity (b). In the figure (a):

D1 and D2 are _positive_ as shown if $J > 0$

D1 and D2 are _negative_ as shown if $J < 0$

This sign convention thus depends only on the relative numbering of
the segments involved in the junction. It does _not_ depend on the
direction of increasing arc length, nor on whether the user specifies
"Segment ISEG is connected to segment ISEG + J" or "Segment ISEG + J is
connected to ISEG." In Fig. Al(b) the "discontinuties" D1 and D2 are
positive as shown, independent of the direction of increasing arc length.

In general, it is recommended that users construct models such
that there are no axial discontinuities (D2 = 0.) between segments.
Axial discontinuities tend to lead to gross overestimates of the
stiffness of a structure, and hence to overestimates of buckling
loads. See the article "Evaluation of various analytical models for
buckling and vibration of stiffened shells" AIAA Journal, Vol. 11,
No. 9, 1973, pp. 1283-1291, for examples.

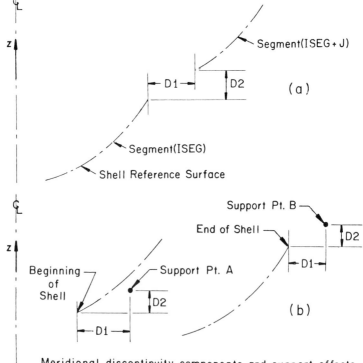

Meridional discontinuity components and support offsets
are positive in the above illustrations.

Fig. Al   Sign convention for discontinuities

Restriction on Frequency of Constraint Points

Constraint conditions can be applied at points in the interior of segments as well as at the boundaries. However, points within a given segment at which constraint conditions are applied must be spaced at intervals of at least three nodes, as shown below:

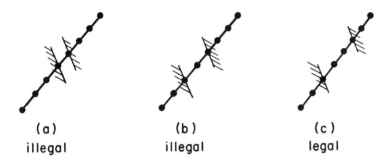

(a)	(b)	(c)
illegal	illegal	legal

Restriction on Branching Conditions

If several segments are joined together, as shown below, the correct way to express the constraint condition input is to connect all higher numbered segments to the lowest numbered segment involved in the juncture. Sample input for IS1, IP1, IS2, IP2, etc. is given below:

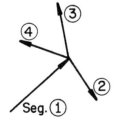

Sample input (IS1, IP1, IS2, IP2, etc.) corresponding to the figure at left:

    1, 25, 2, 1, 1, 1, 1, 1, 0., 0.
    1, 25, 3, 1, 1, 1, 1, 1, 0., 0.
    1, 25, 4, 1, 1, 1, 1, 1, 0., 0.

If the end of Segment J is connected to any previous point, or to ground (b.c.), then the beginning of Segment J+1 cannot be connected to the end of Segment J.

An Example of Constraint Conditions

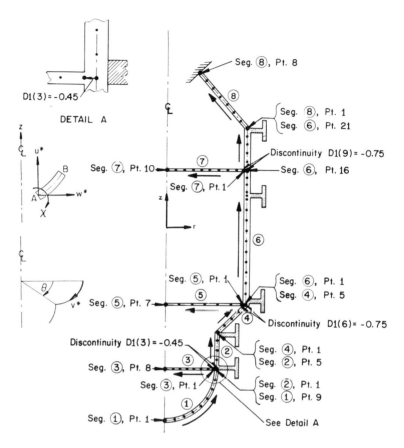

Constraint Condition Input Corresponding to the Figure (NCOND = 12)

```
1, 1, 1, 1, 0,0,0,0, 0., 0.    IS1,IP1,IS2,IP2,IU*,IV,IW*,Iχ,D1( 1),D2( 1)
1, 9, 2, 1, 1,1,1,1, 0., 0.         "                    ,D1( 2),D2( 2)
1, 9, 3, 1, 1,1,1,1,-.45,0.         "                    ,D1( 3),D2( 3)
3, 8, 3, 8, 0,0,0,0, 0., 0.         "                    ,D1( 4),D2( 4)
2, 5, 4, 1, 1,1,1,1, 0., 0.         "                    ,D1( 5),D2( 5)
4, 5, 5, 1, 1,1,1,1,-.75,0.         "                    ,D1( 6),D2( 6)
4, 5, 6, 1, 1,1,1,1, 0., 0.         "                    ,D1( 7),D2( 7)
5, 7, 5, 7, 0,0,0,0, 0., 0.         "                    ,D1( 8),D2( 8)
6,16, 7, 1, 1,1,1,1,-.75,0.         "                    ,D1( 9),D2( 9)
7,10, 7,10, 0,0,0,0, 0., 0.         "                    ,D1(10),D2(10)
6,21, 8, 1, 1,1,1,1, 0., 0.         "                    ,D1(11),D2(11)
8, 8, 8, 8, 1,1,1,1, 0., 0.         "                    ,D1(12),D2(12)
```

Constraint Conditions (Continued)

```
if IBOUND = 0  go to 5

    Do 4  I = 1, NCOND
    ● IUB*, IVB, IWB*, IχB
    4 Continue

5 Continue

if IRIGID = 0  go to 6

    ● IS1,IP1,IS1,IP1, 1,1, 0, 0
    ● IS1,IP1,IS1,IP1, 1,1, 0, 0

6 Continue
```

Definitions of Variables and Explanation

IBOUND = 0 means that prestress and buckling or vibration constraint
conditions are the same. IBOUND = 1 means they are different.
Usually IBOUND = 0. If, however, you have a structure with a
plane of symmetry, and if you want to check buckling or vibration
modes antisymmetric at this plane, then you must set IBOUND = 1
and respecify all the NCOND constraint indicators, even though
most of them are the same as before. Among these will be the
antisymmetry condition at the symmetry plane which will, of
course, differ from the previously specified symmetry condition
that governs the prestress analysis.

IUB^*, IVB, IWB^*, $I_\chi B$ = indicators for no or yes constraint of global
buckling or vibration modal displacement components, u_b^*, v_b, w_b^*
and χ_b, respectively. 0 means no constraint; 1 means yes constraint of the corresponding displacement component. Note that
this input must be specified in the same order as the input for
IU^*, IV, IW^*, I_χ.

IRIGID = control integer for rigid body constraint conditions: 0 means
none needed; 1 means needed. You need specify IRIGID = 1 only if
the previously specified constraint indicators are inadequate to
prevent rigid body displacement in stress and buckling problems.
(Rigid body motion is okay in vibration). Note that rigid body
displacements correspond to n = 0 or n = 1 circumferential waves.
The next page illustrates these modes.

IS1, IP1 = segment and point number at which the rigid body constraint
is applied. Must be the same as in one of the previously specified constraints to ground. It may be necessary to introduce an
extra constraint point, as in the example following, in order to
be able to apply a rigid body constraint.

1,1, 0, 0 = constraint indicators for the rigid body constraint.
Note that u^* and v are constrained to be zero at IS1, IP1.

The two cards read in if IRIGID = 1 should always be identical. The effect of the rigid body constraint is as follows:
At the location specified by IS1 and IP1 the axial displacement
u* and the circumferential displacement v are set equal to zero
for n = 0 and n = 1 circumferential waves only. For higher n
these constraints are automatically replaced by the previously
specified IU* and IV at the location IS1, IP1.

Rigid Body Constraints

There are six rigid body modes, three translational and three rotational. These modes are illustrated below.

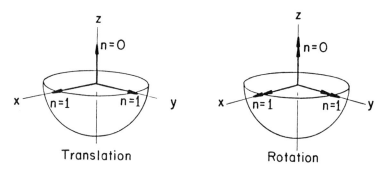

Translation   Rotation

All of these rigid body motions can be prevented by choosing a meridional station at which to restrain the axial displacement u^* and the circumferential displacement v. The figures below show why:

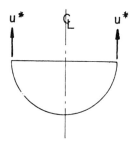 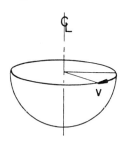

The constraint $u^* = 0$ prevents: The constraint $v = 0$ prevents:

(1) Translation along z axis (n = 0)   (1) Rotation about z axis (n = 0)
(2) Rotation about x axis (n = 1)   (2) Translation along x axis (n = 1)
(3) Rotation about y axis (n = 1)   (3) Translation along y axis (n = 1)

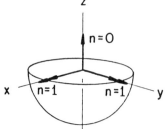 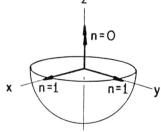

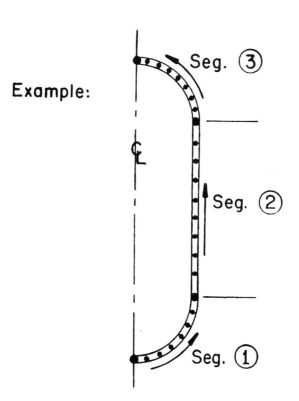

Example:

Seg. ③

₵ L

Seg. ②

Seg. ①

Example of constraint conditions corresponding to the figure above.
Note that an extra constraint point has been provided (NCOND = 5
rather than 4) in order to have a station at which to apply the
rigid body mode constraints for $n = 0$ and $n = 1$ circumferential
waves.

Constraint condition input (NCOND = 5):
```
1, 1, 1, 1, 0, 0, 0, 0, 0., 0.      (pole condition)
1, 8, 2, 1, 1, 1, 1, 1, 0., 0.      (juncture condition)
2, 1, 2, 1, 0, 0, 0, 0, 0., 0.      (extra condition)
2,10, 3, 1, 1, 1, 1, 1, 0., 0.      (juncture condition)
3, 9, 3, 9, 0, 0, 0, 0, 0., 0.      (pole condition)

2, 1, 2, 1, 1, 1, 0, 0            (rigid body condition)
2, 1, 2, 1, 1, 1, 0, 0            (rigid body condition)
```

NOTE: If a constraint to ground is applied at a juncture between two
segments, it must be applied at the first point of the higher-numbered
segment.

Continuation of Initial Input for Various Types of Analysis
INDIC = -2, -1, 0, 1, 2, 3, and 4

INDIC = -2 and 0 (bifurcation buckling   INDIC = -1 and 1 (nonlinear and
    and nonlinear axisymmetric   linear bifurcation buckling)
    stress analysis)

● P, DP, TEMP, DTEMP   ● P, DP, TEMP, DTEMP
● FSTART, FMAX, DF   ● 0., 0., 0.

INDIC = 2 (vibration analysis)   INDIC = 3 and 4 (linear nonaxisym-
                                                metric stress analysis and bi-
                                                furcation buckling with non-
                                                axisymmetric prestress)

● P, 0., TEMP, 0.   ● 0., 0., 0., 0.
● 0., 0., 0.   ● 0., 0., 0.

Definitions of Input Variables and Explanation

P   = pressure or surface traction multiplier. Actual pressure $p(s)$
      is given by $p(s) = P*f(s)$, where $f(s)$ is a meridional distribution
      read in later for each shell segment. P is associated with fixed
      or initial loads. See below for more explanation and examples.

DP   = pressure or surface traction increment multiplier. Actual
      pressure increment is given by $dp(s) = DP*f(s)$. With INDIC = 0 or -2
      the first pressure treated is $P*f(s)$, the second is $(P + DP)*f(s)$ and
      so on up to $FMAX*f(s)$. With INDIC = -1 or 1, DP is an eigenvalue
      parameter. See below for more explanation and examples.

TEMP = temperature rise multiplier. The actual temperature rise
      $T(s,z)$ is given by $T(s,z) = TEMP*g(s)*h(z)$, where $g(s)$ is a meri-
      dional distribution and $h(z)$ is a thickness distribution read in
      later for each shell segment. TEMP is associated with fixed or
      initial loads. See below for more explanation.

DTEMP = temperature rise increment multiplier. Actual temperature
      rise increment is given by $dT(s,z) = DTEMP*g(s)*h(z)$. See defini-
      tion of DP for more details.

FSTART, FMAX, DF = load range delimiters, increment. These may repre-
      sent pressure, temperature, or discrete ring thermal or mechanical
      line loads. These quantities serve only to establish the range of
      loading, and are not used as actual loads in BOSOR4. They simply
      tell the computer when to terminate the case. That is their only
      function in BOSOR4.

More Detailed Explanation of Fixed or Initial (P, TEMP, V) Loads and
Incremental or Eigenvalue (DP, DTEMP, DV) Loads: An Example

The user can introduce into BOSOR4 pressure, surface tractions,
temperature distributions over the shell, and line mechanical and thermal
loads on the discrete rings. Each of these types of loads have two
categories: 1. fixed or initial, and 2. incremental or eigenvalue.
The appropriate use of these two categories of loads for various kinds
of analysis (INDIC) is best communicated by an example. Figure A2a

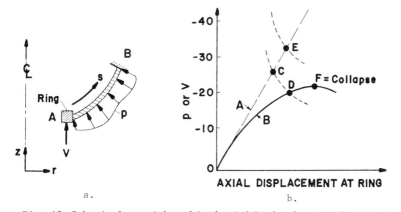

a.   b.

Fig. A2 Spherical cap with combined axial load and external pressure

shows a clamped spherical segment, subjected to a combination of
axial compression V and normal pressure, p. Figure A2b shows typical
load-deflection curves from linear (A) and nonlinear (B) theory. We
wish to:

    1. Calculate the nonlinear axisymmetric behavior (B) (INDIC = 0)
    2. Calculate the bifurcation buckling load (D) (INDIC = -1)
    3. Calculate the bifurcation buckling loads (C,E) (INDIC = 1)
    4. Calculate vibration frequencies for given V_o and p_o (INDIC = 2)
    5. Calculate the stability determinant as a function of load
(INDIC = -2)

Let us suppose for the moment that p is known and fixed at $p_o = -10.0$
(uniform) and that we wish to investigate the above behavior with V
unknown. All loads are assumed to be axisymmetric in this example.
The scale 0 to 40 in the above sketch refers then to V, and the
characteristics of the curves A and B and location of the points C and D
depend on the specified pressure p_o as well as on the geometry,
boundary conditions, and material properties. The table below shows appropriate example values of the load input data for the five types of
analysis just listed. Analyses with INDIC = -2, -1, and 1 involve the
calculation of bifurcation buckling eigenvalues. With INDIC = -2 and
-1 both V and DV are changed during the case, and the buckling load
V_{crit} is printed with the mode shape at the end of the run. With
INDIC = 1 the eigenvalues and eigenvectors are printed, but the user
must obtain the corresponding buckling load V_{crit} from the equation:

$$V_{crit} = V + \text{(eigenvalue)} * DV$$

Table A1 Appropriate Sample Values of P, DP, V, DV, FSTART,
              FMAX, and DF for various values of INDIC

INDIC	P	DP	V	DV	FSTART	FMAX	DF
-2	-10.0	0.	0.	-5.0	0.	-40.0	-5.0
-1	-10.0	0.	-15.0	-1.0	not applicable		
0	-10.0	0.	0.	-5.0	0.	-40.0	-5.0
1	-10.0	0.	0.	-1.0	not applicable		
2	-10.0	0.	$V_o < F$	0.	not applicable		

More Information on the Load Range Delimiters, FSTART, FMAX, DF

The load range delimiters FSTART and FMAX and the increment DF serve only to establish the range of loading and these quantities are not used as actual loads in BOSOR4. They simply "tell" the computer when to terminate the case. That is their only function in BOSOR4. Some examples follow:

Example 1: shell loaded by "fixed" pressure, "variable-in-time" axial
         load:

         $P = 10$ psi $DP = 0.0$ $V(1) = -1000$ lb/in $DV(1) = -200$ lb/in

         FSTART $= -1000$ FMAX $= -5000$ DF $= -200$

Example 2: shell loaded by "variable-in-time" pressure, "fixed" axial
         load:

         $P = 20$ psi $DP = 5$ psi $V(1) = -3000$ lb/in $DV(1) = 0.0$ lb/in

         FSTART $= 20$ FMAX $= 100$ DF $= 5$

Example 3: shell loaded by "variable-in-time" pressure and "variable-in-
         time" axial load:

         $P = 20$ $DP = 5$ psi $V(1) = -1000$ lb/in $DV(1) = -200$ lb/in

         FSTART $= 20$, FMAX $= 100$, DF $= 5$ <u>or</u> FSTART $= -1000$, FMAX $= -5000$,

         DF $= -200$

From the above three examples it is seen that:

    1. The load range delimiters represent the range of one of the "variable-in-time" loads.

    2. The load range delimiters have the same algebraic signs as the corresponding "variable-in-time" load.

    3. In cases involving more than one "variable-in-time" load, the load range delimiters may represent the range of any <u>one</u> of the "variable-in-time" loads.

Input Data for Each Shell Segment   (All Types of Analysis)

The remaining input is read in for each shell segment. The input
manual is constructed as a sort of program, with labeled transfer
points which help tell the user what data to provide next. A summary
of the entire input for each segment is given on this page, and details for each kind of input are given on the following pages.

Summary of Input for Each Segment

     Do 5000 ISEG = 1, NSEG

   12 Read in number and distribution of nodal points.

   15 Read in shell geometry parameters and imperfection shape.

   20 Read in location of reference surface relative to left-
      most surface of the shell wall material.

   25 Read in discrete ring parameters: number of rings, loca-
      tions of the rings, cross-sectional properties, material
      properties.

  100 Read in mechanical line loads: axial, circumferential,
      radial and moment; fixed or initial and eigenvalue or
      incremental.

  300 Read in thermal line loads (thermal hoop resultant and
      thermal moment resultants about two orthogonal axes
      through the centroid of each discrete ring).

  500 Read in pressure and surface traction meridional and cir-
      cumferential distributions.

  900 Read in temperature rise meridional and circumferential
      distributions, and variation through the thickness of the
      shell wall.

 2000 Read in prescribed prestress distribution if INDIC = 4, IPRE = 0.

 3000 Read in shell wall construction parameters: monocoque, layered,
      with or without rings and/or stringers that are "smeared out"
      in the analysis.

 5000 End of input for each segment. Go back to the beginning of the
      loop for the input for the next segment.   If this is the
      last segment, start a new case or type "END".

Number and Distribution of Nodal Points in Segment "ISEG"

12 Continue

● NMESH, NTYPEH, 0   (5 ≤ NMESH ≤ 98)
  if NTYPEH = 1:   (NTYPEH = 1 or 2 or 3)
      ● NHVALU   (2 ≤ NHVALU ≤ 50)
      ● (IHVALU(I), I = 1, NHVALU)
      ● (HVALU(I), I = 1, NHVALU)
  go to 15
  if NTYPEH = 2:
      ● (HVALU(I), I = 1, NMESH - 1)
  go to 15

  if NTYPEH = 3 (uniform nodal point spacing)   go to 15

Definitions of Input Variables and Explanation

NMESH = number of "w" nodal points in the segment, ISEG. NMESH is
    one of the most important variables in the analysis, since it
    governs to a large extent the accuracy of the solution. A feel-
    ing for proper values for NMESH comes with experience. Few
    points are needed for cases in which the solution is expected to
    vary slowly along the shell meridian. Points should be concen-
    trated in areas where the solution is expected to vary rapidly.
    Note that buckling modal displacements may not necessarily vary
    rapidly in the same areas as prebuckling quantities. A jagged
    solution for stress or buckling indicates the need for more mesh
    points.

Limitations on the Total Number of Degrees of Freedom

In the nonlinear prebuckling axisymmetric analysis up to 1000 degrees
of freedom (d.o.f.) are permitted. In the linear nonsymmetric stress
analysis and nonsymmetric bifurcation buckling and vibration analyses
up to 1500 d.o.f. are permitted.
    For the axisymmetric analysis the total d.o.f. are given by:

$$d.o.f. = \sum_{ISEG=1}^{NSEG} (NMESH(ISEG) + 2)*2 + 3*NSEG + 3*NCOND$$

For the nonaxisymmetric analysis, in which there is an additional
displacement variable v, the total number of degrees of freedom is:

$$d.o.f. = \sum_{ISEG=1}^{NSEG} (NMESH(ISEG) + 2)*3 + 4*NSEG + 4*NCOND$$

Location of Finite Difference Nodal Points and Output Points "E"

Figure A3 shows the locations of nodal points in the finite difference
energy method. All BOSOR4 output corresponds to the point labeled "E"

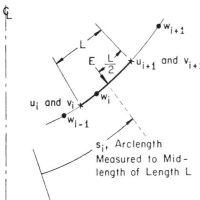

L = elemental integration length, or length of the finite difference element.

E = point where geometry, stresses, strains, displacements are evaluated and where discrete rings and branches are attached.

u and v nodal points are located half-way between w nodal points.

Fig. A3 Location of finite difference nodes and output point "E"

which is the location at which the energy is minimized for each finite difference element. Each "energy point" is located half-way between adjacent u points. As seen from Fig. A3, if the mesh spacing varies, the "energy points" do not coincide with the w points.

Additional w Nodes Automatically Inserted by BOSOR4

Two additional "w" nodes are inserted by BOSOR4 between the first and second and the second-to-last and last points in each segment. This is done in order to reduce the truncation errors associated with boundaries and to prevent spurious modes associated with the fictitious points which lie outside the segment boundaries. If b is the original mesh spacing provided by the user, BOSOR4 inserts the extra w points at a distance a = b/20 from each segment end. It is emphasized that the user does not need to consider these extra nodes in making up a case. All input quantities provided by the user are automatically corrected to account for these extra nodes. The figure below shows an example. Note that the addition of the extra w nodes causes the spacing of the output points E to vary near each end of each segment.

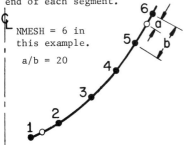

NMESH = 6 in this example.

a/b = 20

● User specified w nodal points.

○ Additional nodal points added by BOSOR4 to reduce truncation error at boundaries of shell segments and to prevent spurious buckling or vibration modes.

Definitions of Input Variables and Explanation

NTYPEH= control integer for nodal point spacing: 1,2 = variable;
                                                    3   = constant.
NHVALU= number of values of mesh spacing (distance between adjacent
   w nodes) which will be read in. Minimum of 2, maximum of 50.
IHVALU= nodal point callouts for which spacing is to be given. Spac-
   will vary linearly between these callouts. See Fig. A4.
 HVALU= spacing between adjacent w nodes at callout points.
   HVALU(I) is the meridional arc length between w(IHVALU(I)) and
   w(IHVALU(I)+1). See Fig. A4 for an example. Only relative
   sizes of spacing are required, not absolute values.

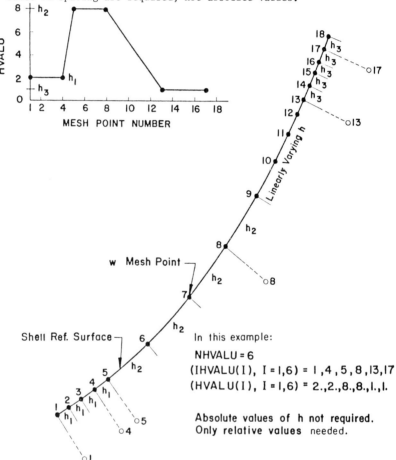

Fig. A4 Input for variable nodal point spacing

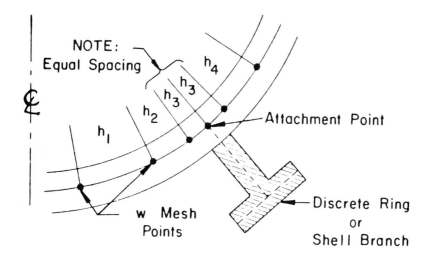

NOTE: w Nodes should be equally spaced for at least one interval (h_3 in example immediately above) on either side of any discrete ring attachment point or shell branch point.

Fig. A5 Appropriate spacing of nodes at discrete ring attachment point or shell branch point

Geometry of the Reference Surface of Shell Segment "ISEG"

15 Continue

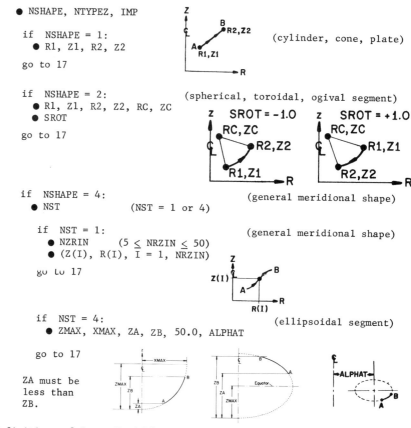

- NSHAPE, NTYPEZ, IMP

  if NSHAPE = 1:   (cylinder, cone, plate)
  - R1, Z1, R2, Z2
  go to 17

  if NSHAPE = 2:   (spherical, toroidal, ogival segment)
  - R1, Z1, R2, Z2, RC, ZC
  - SROT
  go to 17

  if NSHAPE = 4:   (general meridional shape)
  - NST   (NST = 1 or 4)

    if NST = 1:   (general meridional shape)
    - NZRIN   (5 ≤ NRZIN ≤ 50)
    - (Z(I), R(I), I = 1, NRZIN)
    go to 17

    if NST = 4:   (ellipsoidal segment)
    - ZMAX, XMAX, ZA, ZB, 50.0, ALPHAT

    go to 17

    ZA must be
    less than
    ZB.

Definitions of Input Variables

NTYPEZ = control integer for location of reference surface relative
         to the shell wall material:

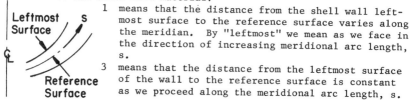

         1 means that the distance from the shell wall left-
            most surface to the reference surface varies along
            the meridian. By "leftmost" we mean as we face in
            the direction of increasing meridional arc length,
            s.
         3 means that the distance from the leftmost surface
            of the wall to the reference surface is constant
            as we proceed along the meridional arc length, s.

IMP   = control integer for imperfection: 0 means none; 1 means some

Imperfection of the Meridional Shape of Segment "ISEG"

17 Continue

   if IMP = 0   (no imperfection)   go to 20

   ● ITYPE   (ITYPE = 1 or 2)

   if ITYPE = 1:

      ● FM, C, FLMIN, FLMAX

   go to 20

   if ITYPE = 2:

      ● WO, WLNGTH

Definitions of Input Variables

ITYPE = control integer for type of axisymmetric imperfection:
       1 means sinusoidal series with random amplitudes and wave-
         lengths,
       2 means pure sinusoidal.

FM   = number of wavelengths to be included in the representation of
       the imperfection.
C   = maximum amplitude of the imperfection.
FLMIN = minimum half-wavelength to be included in the representation
       of the imperfection.
FLMAX = maximum half-wavelength to be included in the representation
       of the imperfection.

WO   = amplitude of sinusoidal imperfection.
WLNGTH= half-wavelength of sinusoidal imperfection.

NOTE: All imperfections must be axisymmetric. Other imperfection
      shapes can be investigated by use of the geometry option for
      general meridional shapes (NSHAPE = 4, NST =1 on previous
      page.)

Location of Reference Surface Relative to Shell Wall Material

20 Continue

    if NTYPEZ = 1:

    ● NZVALU   (2 ≤ NZVALU ≤ 50)
    ● NTYPE   (NTYPE = 2 or 3)

        if NTYPE = 2:
        ● (Z(I), I = 1, NZVALU)
        go to 21

        if NTYPE = 3:
        ● (R(I), I = 1, NZVALU)

21 Continue

    ● (ZVAL(I), I = 1, NZVALU)

    go to 25

    if NTYPEZ = 3:

    ● ZVAL

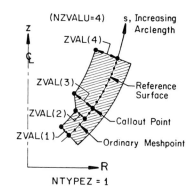

NTYPEZ = 1

Definitions of Input Variables and Explanation

NTYPEZ = control integer for location of reference surface:
         1 means that distance from leftmost surface to reference
            surface varies along the meridional arc length s. The
            meaning of "leftmost" is illustrated in the figure below.
         3 means that the distance from the leftmost surface to the
            reference surface is constant along the meridian.

NZVALU = number of callout points to be used for specification of the
         location of the reference surface relative to the leftmost
         surface. This distance at points intermediate to the call-
         out points is determined automatically by linear interpola-
         tion.

Z   = axial coordinates of callout points. Points must be specified
         from the beginning of the segment to the end, include the end
         points of the segment, and be single valued over the segment.

R   = radial coordinates of callout points. Same restrictions
         apply here as for Z.

ZVAL   = distance from leftmost surface to reference surface at the
         callout points identified by Z or R.

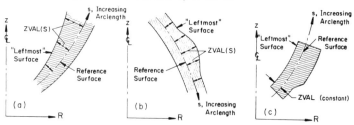

General Comments on Input for Meridionally Varying Quantities

The pattern of input data pertaining to nonconstant reference
surface location, ZVAL(I), I = 1, NZVALU, shown on the previous page,
is typical for any input quantity that varies along the shell meridian, such as temperature, pressure, and thickness. The number,
NZVALU, of stations ("callout points") at which the input quantity
is to be specified is first read in; then a control integer, NTYPE,
is read in. This integer specifies whether the callout points are
to be interpreted as axial distances Z(I) (NTYPE = 2) or radial distances R(I) (NTYPE = 3); then the callout points R(I) or Z(I) are
read in; finally the values, ZVAL(I) themselves, are read in.   In
BOSOR4 the variation of these values along the meridian between
callout points is assumed to be linear.
     When using the input option corresponding to meridionally vary-
ing quantities, the user must always provide input corresponding to
the end points of the segment. Values must be provided in order,
starting from the beginning of the segment and proceeding to the end.
     Corresponding to the figure at the top of the previous page,
the input might be:

4   NZVALU

2   NTYPE

1.0,   1.5,   1.85,   3.0   (Z(I),   I = 1, 4)

0.5,   0.5,   0.80,   0.8   (ZVAL(I), I = 1, 4)

Discrete Rings in Segment "ISEG"

25 Continue

● NRINGS   (0 ≤ NRINGS ≤ 20)

if (NRINGS = 0) (no discrete rings) go to 100

● NTYPE   (NTYPE = 2 or 3)

if (NTYPE = 2): ● (Z(I), I = 1, NRINGS)

if (NTYPE = 3): ● (R(I), I = 1, NRINGS)

● (NTYPER(I), I = 1, NRINGS)   (NTYPER = 0 or 1 or 2 or 4 or 5)

Do 50 I = 1, NRINGS

if (NTYPER(I) = 0): no data read. This is a fake ring. Go to 50

if (NTYPER(I) = 1): ● E, A, RIY, RIX, RIXY, E1, E2, GJ, RM

if (NTYPER(I) = 2): ● E, A, RIS, RIN, RISN, ZC, SC, GJ, RM

if (NTYPER(I) = 3): do not use this option.

if (NTYPER(I) = 4): ● L(1), T(1), L(2), T(2), L(3), T(3)

                     ● E, U, X1P, Y(1), Y(2), Y(3)

                     ● RM

if (NTYPER(I) = 5): ● same input as for NTYPER(I) = 4, except that
                       X,Y axes (Fig. A6) are considered to be
                       normal and tangential, respectively, to the
                       shell reference surface at the ring attach-
                       ment point.

50 Continue   (end of do-loop over the number of discrete rings)

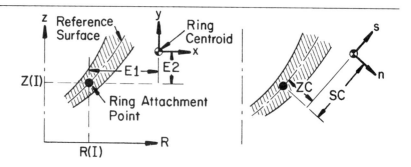

Definitions of Input Variables

NRINGS = number of discrete rings in this segment. Up to 20 rings are
         permitted in one segment; up to 50 rings in the entire struc-
         ture. If line loads are applied at some station, the user
         must supply a fake ring even if no ring is present in the
         actual structure at that point. This is because all line
         loads are considered to act at discrete ring centroids.

Z   = axial coordinates to ring attachment points, which are con-
         sidered to be on the shell reference surface. Must be speci-
         fied from the beginning of the segment to the end and must
         be single-valued.

R   = radial coordinates to ring attachment points. Same restric-
         tions apply here as for Z.

NTYPER = indicator for type of discrete ring. Use 0 if this is a fake
         ring needed only for a place on which to "hang" a line load.

E, A, RIY, RIX, RIXY = Young's modulus, cross-sectional area, moments of
         inertia about y axis, x axis, product of inertia. y and x
         axes are shown in the figure.

E1, E2 = radial, axial distances from ring attachment point to ring
         centroid. Positive as shown in the figure.

GJ; RM = torsional rigidity; mass density (e.g., aluminum = .0002535).

RIS, RIN, RISN = moments of inertia about s axis, n axis, product of
         inertia. s and n axes are shown in the figure.

ZC, SC = normal, tangential distances from ring attachment point to
         ring centroid. Positive as shown on the figure.

L(1), T(1), L(2), T(2), L(3), T(3) = lengths and thicknesses of dis-
         crete ring segments shown in Fig. A6.

E, U   = Young's modulus, Poisson ratio of ring material.

X1P   = radial distance from ring attachment point to first segment
         of discrete ring, shown in Fig. A6.

Y(1), Y(2), Y(3) = axial distances from ring attachment point to cen-
         troids of each of the three segments of the discrete ring.
         These distances are shown in Fig. A6.

NOTE: Users may occasionally want to simulate a massive structure by
a massive discrete ring attached to some point on the meridian. It
has been found that such a massive ring should not be attached to the
end point of a segment, but must be attached at least three points
from either of the segment end points. The reason is that the large
mass located at the end of a segment might give rise to a fictitious
vibration mode associated with exaggerated motion of the fictitious
points located there.

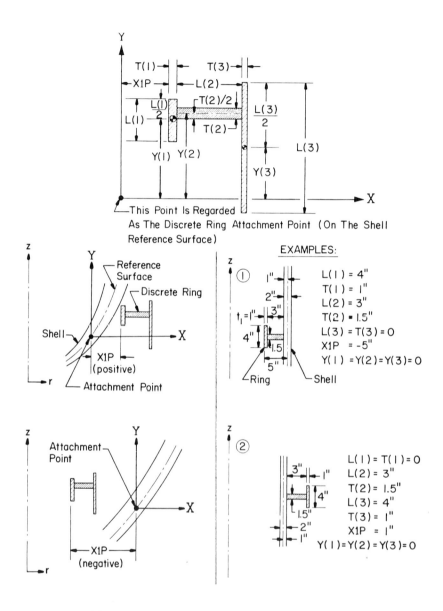

Fig. A6 Input data for discrete ring with use of options
NTYPER(I) = 4 or 5.

Loading on Shell Segment "ISEG"

Four classes of loads are possible:

1. mechanical line loads applied at centroids of discrete rings
2. thermal line loads at discrete rings
3. pressure and surface tractions distributed over shell surface
4. temperature distribution through thickness and over surface

These loads may be axisymmetric or may vary around the circumference. The pressures and temperatures may vary along the meridian as well as around the circumference, and the temperature may vary through the thickness. In cases involving nonsymmetric loading a linear analysis is used; the program finds the Fourier series for the loads, calculates the shell response in each harmonic to the load components with that harmonic, and superposes the results for all harmonics. The superposed displacements and stress resultants are printed and plotted for selected meridional and circumferential stations. Line loads and moments are assumed to be applied at discrete ring centroids. Thermal line loads arise from the presence of discrete rings which may be heated above their zero-stress states. Distributed thermal loads arise from temperature distributions over the shell surface and through the shell wall thickness. Here the input temperature is actually "delta T," the rise in temperature above the zero-stress state, not the ambient temperature.

In many cases a load is represented in the BOSOR4 program as a product of quantities. For example, the initial normal pressure in a nonlinear axisymmetric stress analysis (INDIC = 0) is represented as a product of a multiplier P and a meridional distribution f(s):

$$p(s) = P*f(s) = P*PN(s) \quad or \quad P*(P11 + P12*s^{P13} + P14*s^{P15})$$

The normal pressure for each harmonic in a linear nonsymmetric stress analysis (INDIC = 3 or 4) is represented as a product of a meridional distribution PN(s) and a circumferential harmonic amplitude, PDIST1:

$$p(s,\theta) = PN(s)*PDIST1(L, ISEG)$$

A negative normal pressure can be provided by making either of the factors less than zero.

For each class of load there are two types:

1. initial or fixed loads
2. incremental or eigenvalue parameter loads

The appropriate use of these two types of loads has been illustrated by an example of a spherical cap loaded by a combination of axial compression V and external pressure p (Fig. A2). Other examples are given in Tables A3 and A4.

The various load classes and types and the sign convention are given in Table A2. Notice that for completeness, negative as well as zero and positive circumferential wave numbers n must be used for the Fourier expansions of nonsymmetric loads.

			Table A2 Classes, Types, and Sign Convention for Loads	
FOUR LOAD CLASSES	LOAD TYPES	LOAD NAME	SIGN CONVENTION (axis of revolution is vertical, shell meridian to right of axis)	CIRCUMFERENTIAL VARIATION FOR NONSYMMETRIC LOADS
				zero or positive n	zero or negative n
1 Mechanical line loads	Axial	V, DV	positive downward.	$\sin n\theta$	$\cos n\theta$
	Shear	S	positive out of paper.	$\cos n\theta$	$\sin \lvert n\rvert \theta$
	Radial	H, DH	positive away from axis.	$\sin n\theta$	$\cos n\theta$
	Moment	FM, DM	positive clockwise.	$\sin n\theta$	$\cos n\theta$
2 Thermal line loads	Hoop	TNR	$-\int E_r \alpha_r T dA$	$\sin n\theta$	$\cos n\theta$
	x Moment	TMX	$-\int E_r \alpha_r T y dA$	$\sin n\theta$	$\cos n\theta$
	y Moment	TMY	$-\int E_r \alpha_r T x dA$	$\sin n\theta$	$\cos n\theta$
3 Surface traction and pressure	Meridional traction	P_1	positive parallel to increasing arc length.	$\sin n\theta$	$\cos n\theta$
	Circumfer. traction	P_2	positive out of paper.	$\cos n\theta$	$\sin \lvert n\rvert \theta$
	Normal pressure	P_3	positive to right of increasing arc, s.	$\sin n\theta$	$\cos n\theta$
4 Temperature distribution	Temperature rise	T	positive for temperature rise above ambient.	$\sin n\theta$	$\cos n\theta$

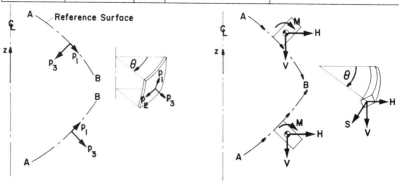

Table A3 BOSOR4 Loads Nomenclature, Axisymmetric Loads				
LOAD CLASSES AND TYPES			**LOAD MAGNITUDES FOR VARIOUS ANALYSES**	
			INDIC = -2,-1,0, and 1	INDIC = 2
CLASS 1	Initial or fixed	Axial	V(I)	V(I)
		Shear	not applicable	not applicable
		Radial	H(I)	H(I)
		Moment	M(I)	M(I)
	Increment or eigenv. parameter	Axial	DV(I)	not applicable
		Shear	not applicable	not applicable
		Radial	DH(I)	not applicable
		Moment	DM(I)	not applicable
CLASS 2	Initial or fixed	Hoop	TNR(I)*TEMP	TNR(I)*TEMP
		x Moment	TMX(I)*TEMP	TMX(I)*TEMP
		y Moment	TMY(I)*TEMP	TMY(I)*TEMP
	Increment or eigenv. parameter	Hoop	TNR(I)*DTEMP	not applicable
		x Moment	TMX(I)*DTEMP	not applicable
		y Moment	TMY(I)*DTEMP	not applicable
CLASS 3	Initial or fixed	Merid.	P*PT(J) or P*(P21+...)	same as INDIC=1
		Circum.	not applicable	same as INDIC=1
		Normal	P*PN(J) or P*(P11+...)	same as INDIC=1
	Increment or eigenv. parameter	Merid.	DP*PT(J) or DP*(P21+..)	not applicable
		Circum.	not applicable	not applicable
		Normal	DP*PN(J) or DP*(P11+..)	not applicable
CLASS 4	Initial or fixed	Temp. rise at points as function of dist. z from reference surface	FUNCT(T1(J),T2(J),T3(J),z)*TEMP or FUNCT(T11+..,T21+..,T31+..,z)*TEMP	
	Increment or eigenv. parameter		FUNCT(T1,T2,T3,z)*DTEMP or FUNCT(T11+,T21+,T31+,z)*DTEMP	not applicable

I = Ith discrete ring in the current segment, ISEG.
J = Jth point in the current segment for which load or temperature is called out (not the Jth nodal point, but the Jth callout).

FUNCT(T1,T2,T3,z) is given for three values of NTGRAD on p. 83.
Sign convention for the loads is given in Table A2.

Table A4 BOSOR4 Loads Nomenclature, Nonsymmetric Loads				
LOAD CLASSES AND TYPES			LOAD MAGNITUDES FOR INDIC = 3 AND 4	
			INDIC = 3	INDIC = 4
CLASS 1	Initial or fixed	Axial Shear Radial Moment	V(I)*PLIN1(L,ISEG) S(I)*PLIN2(L,ISEG) H(I)*PLIN1(L,ISEG) M(I(*PLIN1(L,ISEG)	not applicable not applicable not applicable not applicable
	Increment or eigenv. parameter	Axial Shear Radial Moment	not applicable not applicable not applicable not applicable	V(I)*PLIN1(L,ISEG) S(I)*PLIN2(L,ISEG) H(I)*PLIN1(L,ISEG) M(I)*PLIN1(L,ISEG)
CLASS 2	Initial or fixed	Hoop x Moment y Moment	TNR(I)*TLIN(L,ISEG) TMX(I)*TLIN(L,ISEG) TMY(I)*TLIN(L,ISEG)	not applicable not applicable not applicable
	Increment or eigenv. parameter	Hoop x Moment y Moment	not applicable not applicable not applicable	TNR(I)*TLIN(L,ISEG) TMX(I)*TLIN(L,ISEG) TMY(I)*TLIN(L,ISEG)
CLASS 3	Initial or fixed	Merid. Circum. Normal	PT(J)*PDIST1(L,ISEG) PC(J)*PDIST2(L,ISEG) PN(J)*PDIST1(L,ISEG)	not applicable not applicable not applicable
	Increment or eigenv. parameter	Merid. Circum. Normal	not applicable not applicable not applicable	PT(J)*PDIST1(L,ISEG) PC(J)*PDIST2(L,ISEG) PN(J)*PDIST1(L,ISEG)
CLASS 4	Initial or fixed	Temp. rise at points as function of dist. z from reference surface	FUNCT(T1,T2,T3,z)* TDIST(L,ISEG)	not applicable
	Increment or eigenv. parameter		not applicable	FUNCT(T1,T2,T3,z)* TDIST(L,ISEG)

I = Ith discrete ring in the current segment, ISEG.
J = Jth point in the current segment for which load or temperature
   is called out (not the Jth nodal point, but the Jth <u>callout</u>).
L = Lth harmonic to be processed. Note that the circumferential
   wave number, n, is not necessarily equal to L:
        e.g., L = 1, 2, 3, 4, 5; n = 5, 7, 9, 11, 13
FUNCT(T1,T2,T3,z) is given for three values of NTGRAD on p. 83.
Sign convention for the loads is given in Table A2.

Table A5 Definitions for Nonsymmetric Load Input Data

For Cases in Which NTYPEL = 4

NTHETA = number of circumferential points for specification of the load variation g(θ) in the circumferential direction in the range 0 ≤ θ ≤ THETAM. (THETAM has already been read in. It is usually equal to 180 degrees.) NTHETA must be in the range 2 ≤ NTHETA ≤ 100.

NOPT = control integer for how g(θ) is going to be provided:
1 means that YPLUS(J) and YMINUS(J), J = 1,NTHETA are going to be read in. (required for functions that are neither odd nor even about θ = 0 degrees) YPLUS and YMINUS are the values of g(θ) at the circumferential callout points.

2 means that YPLUS(J) only is going to be read in and that YMINUS(J) can be calculated from YPLUS(J) because the function g(θ) is either odd or even.

3 means that YPLUS(J) and YMINUS(J) are to be calculated from a user-written subroutine, GETY, an example of which is listed below.

NODD = control integer for oddness or evenness or otherwise of g(θ):
1 means g(θ) is even in the range -THETAM ≤0≤+THETAM.
2 means g(θ) is odd.
3 means g(θ) is general (neither even nor odd).

THETA = values of circumferential coordinates of callout points for g(θ) in degrees. The first value must be 0.0 and the last must be THETAM. All values must be positive and less than or equal to 180 degrees. The values need not be evenly spaced in θ and need not cover the entire range θ = 0 to 180. The range covered, however, must be equal to an integer fraction of pi radians (expressed in degrees).

YPLUS = values of g(θ) at the callout points, THETA.
YMINUS = values of g(-θ) at the callout points, THETA.

NOTE: The load factors PLIN1(L,ISEG), PLIN2(L,ISEG), TLIN(L,ISEG), PDIST1(L,ISEG), PDIST2(L,ISEG), and TDIST(L,ISEG) in Table A4 are calculated from the input data just described.

Example of User-Written Subroutine GETY

```
      SUBROUTINE GETY(NTHETA, THETA, YMINUS, YPLUS)
      DIMENSION THETA(NTHETA), YMINUS(NTHETA), YPLUS(NTHETA)
      DO 10 I = 1, NTHETA
      YPLUS(I) = EXP(-12.8*THETA(I)**2)
   10 YMINUS(I) = YPLUS(I)
      RETURN
      END
```

(NOTE: In Sub. GETY THETA(I) is in radians!)

Mechanical Line Loads on Shell Segment "ISEG"
100 Continue

if (INDIC = 4) and (IPRE = 0) go to 2000   (prebuckling stress
                                            resultants to be read
● LINTYP (LINTYP = 0 or 1 or 2 or 3)   in directly as input)

if (LINTYP = 0 or 2) or if (NRINGS = 0) go to 300 (no line loads)

if (INDIC = 3 or 4): ● NTYPEL   (NTYPEL = 3 or 4)

● NLOAD(1), NLOAD(2), NLOAD(3), NLOAD(4)   (NLOAD(j) = 0 or 1)

if (NLOAD(1) = 1) : ● (V(I), I = 1, NRINGS)
if (NLOAD(2) = 1) : ● (S(I), I = 1, NRINGS)
if (NLOAD(3) = 1) : ● (H(I), I = 1, NRINGS)
if (NLOAD(4) = 1) : ● (FM(I), I = 1, NRINGS)
if (INDIC = 3 or 4) go to 105

● NLOAD(1), 0, NLOAD(3), NLOAD(4)   (NLOAD(j) = 0 or 1)

if (NLOAD(1) = 1 : ● (DV(I), I = 1, NRINGS)
if (NLOAD(3) = 1 : ● (DH(I), I = 1, NRINGS)
if (NLOAD(4) = 1 : ● (DM(I), I = 1, NRINGS)

Axisymmetric mechanical line loads have now been read in for seg. "ISEG"
go to 300

---

105 if (NTYPEL = 4) go to 120

● (PLIN1(L,ISEG), L = 1, number of Fourier harmonics)
● (PLIN2(L,ISEG), L = 1, number of Fourier harmonics)

Nonsymmetric mechanical line loads have now been read in for seg. "ISEG"
go to 300

---

120 if (NLOAD(1) = 0 and NLOAD(3) = 0 and NLOAD(4) = 0) go to 140

● NTHETA, NOPT, NODD
● (THETA(J), J = 1, NTHETA)
if NOPT = 1: ● (YPLUS(J), J = 1, NTHETA)
             ● (YMINUS(J), J = 1, NTHETA)

if NOPT = 2: ● (YPLUS(J), J = 1, NTHETA)

if NOPT = 3: ● CALL GETY(NTHETA, THETA, YMINUS, YPLUS)

140 if (NLOAD(2) = 0) go to 300
● NTHETA, NOPT, NODD
● (THETA(J), J = 1, NTHETA)
if NOPT = 1: ● (YPLUS(J), J = 1, NTHETA)
             ● (YMINUS(J), J = 1, NTHETA)

if NOPT = 2: ● (YPLUS(J), J = 1, NTHETA)

if NOPT = 3: ● CALL GETY(NTHETA, THETA, YMINUS, YPLUS)

NOTE: The definitions for NTHETA, NOPT, NODD, etc. are given in
      Table A5.

Definitions of Input Variables and Explanation

INDIC = analysis type. INDIC = 3 means linear nonsymmetric stress
       analysis; INDIC = 4 means nonsymmetric stress with buckling.

IPRE = 1 if prestress is calculated by BOSOR4; 0 if prestress is
       to be read in as input data.

LINTYP= 0 for no line loads; 1 for mechanical line loads only;
       2 for thermal line loads only; 3 for both mech. and thermal.

NRINGS= number of discrete rings in this segment, including fake
       rings required for ringless stations with line loads.

NTYPEL= 3 if Fourier amplitudes for circumferential distribution of
       line loads to be read in for n = NSTART to NFIN in steps of
       INCR.
       4 if line load amplitudes at various circumferential stations
       are to be read in or computed by user-written subroutine GETY.

NOTE: Line loads in each segment must be expressible as a product
$\overline{f(I)}$*g(θ), where I represents the Ith discrete ring. g(θ) can differ
from segment to segment, but must involve the same circumferential
wave numbers, n = NSTART to NFIN in increments or decrements of INCR,
for all segments. The Fourier series for V, H, and FM must be identical in a given segment. The Fourier series for S may be different.

V, S, H, FM = fixed or initial axial, shear, radial, and moment line
             load factors. See Table A4 and the equations below.
DV, DH, DM = incremental or eigenvalue axial, radial, and moment
             line load factors. See Table A3.

NOTE: 1. Line loads are assumed to act at the centroids of discrete
rings. They are positive as shown in the figure under Table A2.
      2. With n = 0 or n = $\pm$1 circumferential waves, the user must
make sure either that these harmonics of the loads are in static
equilibrium or that the constraint conditions prevent rigid body displacements. The user need not provide input for line load reactions,
which do no work during deformations.

PLIN1(L,ISEG) = amplitude factors for axial, radial, moment loads.
PLIN2(L,ISEG) = amplitude factors for shear load. See Table A4.

NOTE: 1. Maximum number of circumferential harmonics is 20
      2. Circumferential wave numbers associated with these harmonics
         are n = NSTART to NFIN in steps of INCR. They may be posi-
         tive or negative or both.
      3. The various line loads at the Ith discrete ring and at a
         circumferential station θ are given by:

N,L=NFIN, no. of harmonics

$$\left\{\begin{matrix} V(I) \\ S(I) \\ H(I) \\ FM(I) \end{matrix}\right\} * \left\{ \sum_{\substack{N,L=NSTART,1 \\ \Delta N=INCR}}^{} \left(\underbrace{\begin{matrix} PLIN1(L,ISEG)*\sin n\theta + PLIN1(L,ISEG)*\cos n\theta \\ PLIN2(L,ISEG)*\cos n\theta + PLIN2(L,ISEG)*\sin|n|\theta \\ PLIN1(L,ISEG)*\sin n\theta + PLIN1(L,ISEG)*\cos n\theta \\ PLIN1(L,ISEG)*\sin n\theta + PLIN1(L,ISEG)*\cos n\theta \end{matrix}}_{\text{positive n} \quad \text{negative n}} \right) \right\}$$

Thermal Line Loads on Shell Segment, "ISEG"

300 Continue

    if (LINTYP = 0 or 1) or if (NRINGS = 0) go to 500 (no line loads)

    if (INDIC = 3 or 4): ● NTYPEL   (NTYPEL = 3 or 4)

    ● NLOAD (1), NLOAD(2), NLOAD(3)   (NLOAD(j) = 0 or 1)

    if (NLOAD(1) = 1) ● (TNR(I), I = 1, NRINGS)
    if (NLOAD(2) = 1) ● (TMX(I), I = 1, NRINGS)
    if (NLOAD(3) = 1) ● (TMY(I), I = 1, NRINGS)

    if (INDIC = 3 or 4) go to 305

    ● 0, 0, 0

Axisymmetric thermal line loads have now been read in for segment
"ISEG." go to 500

---

305 if (NTYPEL = 4) go to 320

    ● (TLIN(L,ISEG), L = 1, number of Fourier harmonics)

Nonsymmetric thermal line loads have now been read in for segment
"ISEG." go to 500

---

320 if (NLOAD (1) = 0 and NLOAD(2) = 0 and NLOAD(3) = 0) go to 500

    ● NTHETA, NOPT, NODD
    ● (THETA(J), J = 1, NTHETA)

    if NOPT = 1: ● (YPLUS(J), J = 1, NTHETA)
               ● (YMINUS(J), J = 1, NTHETA)

    if NOPT = 2: ● (YPLUS(J), J = 1, NTHETA)

    if NOPT = 3: ● CALL GETY(NTHETA, THETA, YMINUS, YPLUS)

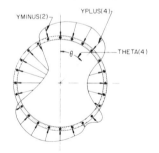

NOTE: The definitions for
          NTHETA, NOPT, NODD, etc.
          are given in Table A5.

Definitions of Input Variables and Explanations

LINTYP = 0 for no line loads; 1 for mechanical line loads only;
2 for thermal line loads only; 3 for both mech. and thermal

NRINGS = number of discrete rings in this segment, including fake
rings required for ringless stations with line loads.

NTYPEL = 3 if Fourier amplitudes for circumferential distribution of
line loads are to be read in for n = NSTART to NFIN in steps
of INCR.
4 if line load amplitudes at various circumferential stations are to be read in or computed by user-written subroutine GETY.

NOTE: With INDIC = 3 or 4 the line loads in each segment must be
expressible as a product $f(I)*g(\theta)$, where I represents the Ith discrete ring. $g(\theta)$ can differ from segment to segment, but must
involve the same circumferential wave numbers, n = NSTART to NFIN in
increments or decrements of INCR, for all segments. The Fourier
series for TNR, TMX, and TMY must be identical in a given segment.

TNR, TMX, TMY = thermal hoop load, moment about x axis, moment about
y axis. These quantities are obtained from the formulas in Table A2 for load class #2. The "T" in those
formulas is a temperature rise distribution. The actual temperature in the ring is the distribution T
times the multiplier, TEMP or DTEMP, or times the
circumferential harmonic, TLIN, depending on the type
of analysis. See Tables A3 and A4 for details.

TLIN(L,ISEG) = circumferential harmonic amplitude factors for TNR,
TMX, TMY. See Table A4.

NOTE: 1. Maximum number of circumferential harmonics is 20
2. Circumferential wave numbers associated with these harmonics
are n = NSTART to NFIN in steps of INCR. They may be positive or negative or both.
3. The various thermal line loads at the Ith discrete ring and
at a circumferential station θ are given by:

N,L=NFIN,no. of harmonics

$$\begin{Bmatrix} TNR(I) \\ TMX(I) \\ TMY(I) \end{Bmatrix} * \sum_{\substack{N,L=NSTART,1 \\ \Delta N=INCR}} \begin{Bmatrix} \underbrace{TLIN(L,ISEG)*\sin n\theta}_{positive\ n} + \underbrace{TLIN(L,ISEG)*\cos n\theta}_{negative\ n} \\ TLIN(L,ISEG)*\sin n\theta + TLIN(L,ISEG)*\cos n\theta \\ TLIN(L,ISEG)*\sin n\theta + TLIN(L,ISEG)*\cos n\theta \end{Bmatrix}$$

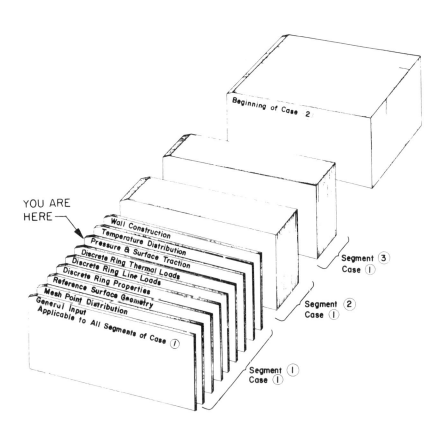

BOSOR4 Data Deck

Loads and Temperatures Distributed over the Surface of Segment "ISEG"

500 Continue

● NLTYPE, NPSTAT, NTSTAT, NTGRAD

Definitions of Input Variables

NLTYPE = control integer for type of loading:

> 0 = no pressure, surface traction of temperature distribu-
> tion on this shell segment.
> 1 = pressure and/or surface traction, but no temperature
> distribution on this shell segment.
> 2 = temperature distribution, but no pressure or surface
> traction on this shell segment.
> 3 = pressure and/or surface traction and temperature distri-
> bution on this shell segment.

NPSTAT = number of meridional stations in this segment for which pressure and surface traction components will be read in. If
INDIC = 3 or 4 and NLTYPE = 1 or 3 NPSTAT must be greater
than or equal to 2, and less than or equal to 20. The NPSTAT
= 0 option can be used only for INDIC = -2, -1, 0, 1, and 2.

NTSTAT = number of meridional stations in this segment for which
temperature rise coefficients T1, T2, and T3 will be read in.
Same discussion applies here as for NPSTAT.

NTGRAD = control integer for type of thermal gradient through the
shell wall thickness:

> 1 means $T(s,z) = T1(s) + T2(s)*z + T3(s)*z^2$
>
> 2 means $T(s,z) = T1(s) + T2(s)*z^{T3(s)}$
>
> 3 means $T(s,z) = T1(s) + T2(s)*exp(z*T3(s))$

> where z is measured from the reference surface positive to
> the right of increasing meridional arc length, s. In
> Tables A3 and A4 the function T(s,z) is called "FUNCT." The
> actual temperature magnitude is given by T(s,z)*TEMP or
> T(s,z)*DTEMP for INDIC = -2, -1, 0, 1, or 2, and for each
> circumferential harmonic by T(s,z)*TDIST(L,ISEG) for INDIC
> equal to 3 or 4.

Pressure and Surface Tractions on Shell Segment "ISEG"

if (NLTYPE = 0) or (NLTYPE = 2) go to 900 (no pressure or
                                                surface traction)

if (NPSTAT greater than 0) go to 510

● P11, P12, P13, P14, P15
● P21, P22, P23, P24, P25

go to 900

510 if (INDIC = 3 or 4): ● NTYPEL   (NTYPEL = 3 or 4)

● NLOAD(1), NLOAD(2), NLOAD(3)   (NLOAD(j) = 0 or 1)

if (NLOAD(1) = 1): ● (PT(I), I = 1, NPSTAT)
if (NLOAD(2) = 1): ● (PC(I), I = 1, NPSTAT)
if (NLOAD(3) = 1): ● (PN(I), I = 1, NPSTAT)

if (INDIC ≠ 3) and (INDIC ≠ 4) go to 700

if (NTYPEL = 4) go to 520

● (PDIST1(L,ISEG), L = 1, number of harmonics)
● (PDIST2(L,ISEG), L = 1, number of harmonics)

go to 700

---

520 if (NLOAD(1) = 0 and NLOAD(3) = 0) go to 530

● NTHETA, NOPT, NODD
● (THETA(J), J = 1, NTHETA)
if NOPT = 1: ● (YPLUS(J), J = 1, NTHETA)
              ● (YMINUS(J), J = 1, NTHETA)
if NOPT = 2: ● (YPLUS(J), J = 1, NTHETA)
if NOPT = 3: ● CALL GETY(NTHETA, THETA, YMINUS, YPLUS)

530 if (NLOAD(2) = 0) go to 700

● NTHETA, NOPT, NODD
● (THETA(J), J = 1, NTHETA)
if NOPT = 1: ● (YPLUS(J), J = 1, NTHETA)
               ● (YMINUS(J), J = 1, NTHETA)
if NOPT = 2: ● (YPLUS(J), J = 1, NTHETA)
if NOPT = 3: ● CALL GETY(NTHETA, THETA, YMINUS, YPLUS)

---

700 Continue

● NTYPE   (NTYPE = 2 or 3)

if (NTYPE = 2): ● (Z(I), I = 1, NPSTAT)
if (NTYPE = 3): ● (R(I), I = 1, NPSTAT)

NOTE: The definitions for NTHETA, NOPT, NODD, etc. are given in
        Table A5.

Definitions of Input Variables and Explanation

NLTYPE = 0 for no loading; 1 for pressure and surface tractions only;
2 for temperature only; 3 for both pressure and temperature.

NPSTAT = number of meridional callout points for pressure.

P11, P12, P13, P14, P15 = coefficients for $f(s) = P11 + P12 * s^{P13} + P14 * s^{P15}$
in which s is the meridional arc length from the beginning
of the segment. This function corresponds to the meridional
distribution of the normal pressure. As seen in Table A3,
the actual pressure is a product $P*f(s)$ or $DP*f(s)$.

P21, P22, P23, P24, P25 = coefficients for $g(s)$ of same form as $f(s)$;
$g(s)$ refers to meridional traction.

NTYPEL = 3 if Fourier amplitudes for circumferential distribution of
loads are to be read in for n = NSTART to NFIN in steps of
INCR.
4 if load amplitudes at various circumferential stations are
to be read in or computed by user-written subroutine GETY.

NOTE: With INDIC = 3 or 4 the pressure and surface tractions in each
segment must be expressible as a product $f(s)*g(\theta)$. $g(\theta)$ can differ
from segment to segment, but must involve the same circumferential
wave numbers, n = NSTART to NFIN in increments or decrements of INCR,
for all segments. The Fourier series for normal and meridional components must be identical; that for the circumferential component can
be different.

PT(I), PC(I), PN(I) = meridional, circumferential, normal components
at the Ith meridional callout point. Sign convention is
shown in the figure beneath Table A2. See Table A4 and below.

PDIST1(L,ISEG) = amplitude factors for meridional traction and normal
pressure.
PDIST2(L,ISEG) = amplitude factors for circumferential traction.

NOTE: 1. Maximum number of circumferential harmonics is 20.
2. Circumferential wave numbers associated with these harmonics
are n = NSTART to NFIN in steps of INCR. They may be positive or negative or both.
3. The various surface loads at the Ith meridional callout and
at a circumferential station θ are given by:

$$\begin{Bmatrix} PT(I) \\ PC(I) \\ PN(I) \end{Bmatrix} * \sum_{\substack{N,L=NSTART,1 \\ \Delta N=INCR}}^{N,L=NFIN,\text{ no. of harmonics}} \begin{Bmatrix} \underbrace{PDIST1(L,ISEG)*\sin n\theta}_{\text{positive } n} + \underbrace{PDIST1(L,ISEG)*\cos n\theta}_{\text{negative } n} \\ PDIST2(L,ISEG)*\cos n\theta + PDIST2(L,ISEG)*\sin n\theta \\ PDIST1(L,ISEG)*\sin n\theta + PDIST1(L,ISEG)*\cos n\theta \end{Bmatrix}$$

Z(I) = axial coordinate of Ith meridional callout point where surface
load components are specified.

R(I) = radial coordinate of Ith meridional callout point where surface
load components are specified.

Temperature Distribution in Shell Segment "ISEG"

900 Continue

    if (NLTYPE = 0) or (NLTYPE = 1) go to 3000 (no temperature)

    if (NTSTAT greater than 0) go to 910
- T11, T12, T13, T14, T15
- T21, T22, T23, T24, T25
- T31, T32, T33, T34, T35

    go to 3000

910 if (INDIC = 3 or INDIC = 4): ● NTYPEL   (NTYPEL = 3 or 4)

    ● NLOAD(1), NLOAD(2), NLOAD(3)   (NLOAD(j) = 0 or 1)
    if (NLOAD(1) = 1): ● (T1(I), I = 1, NTSTAT)
    if (NLOAD(2) = 1): ● (T2(I), I = 1, NTSTAT)
    if (NLOAD(3) = 1): ● (T3(I), I = 1, NTSTAT)
    if (INDIC ≠ 3) and (INDIC ≠ 4) go to 970
    if (NTYPEL = 4) go to 920
    ● (TDIST(L,ISEG), L = 1, number of harmonics)
    go to 970

---

920 if (NLOAD(1) = 0 and NLOAD(2) = 0 and NLOAD(3) = 0) go to 3000
    ● NTHETA, NOPT, NODD
    ● (THETA(J), J = 1, NTHETA)
    if NOPT = 1: ● (YPLUS(J), J = 1, NTHETA)
                ● (YMINUS(J), J = 1, NTHETA)
    if NOPT = 2: ● (YPLUS(J), J = 1, NTHETA)
    if NOPT = 3: ● CALL GETY(NTHETA, THETA, YMINUS, YPLUS)

---

970 Continue
    ● NTYPE   (NTYPE = 2 or 3)
    if (NTYPE = 2): ● (Z(I), I = 1, NTSTAT)
    if (NTYPE = 3): ● (R(I), I = 1, NTSTAT)

NOTE: The definitions for NTHETA, NOPT, NODD, etc. are given in
       Table A5.

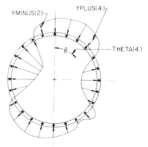

Definitions of Input Variables and Explanation

NLTYPE = 0 for no loading; 1 for pressure and surface tractions only;
         2 for temperature only; 3 for both pressure and temperature.

NTSTAT = number of meridional callout points for temperature.

T11, T12, T13, T14, T15   Coefficients for T1(s), T2(s), and T3(s)
T21, T22, T23, T24, T25   which appear in the functions of tempera-
T31, T32, T33, T34, T35   ture with thickness coordinate, z, given
                                 previously in connection with NTGRAD.

For example, the function $T1(s) = T11 + T12*s^{T13} + T14*s^{T15}$. The
other functions T2(s) and T3(s) have the same form. Note that the
actual temperature rise distribution is the function T(s,z) =
FUNCT(T1(s), T2(s), T3(s), z) multiplied by TEMP or DTEMP if
INDIC = -2, -1, 0, 1, or 2 and by TDIST(L,ISEG) if INDIC = 3 or 4.
See Tables A3 and A4 and the equations below.

NTYPEL = 3 if Fourier amplitudes for circumferential distribution of
           temperature are to be read in for n = NSTART to NFIN in steps
           of INCR.
         4 if temperature amplitudes at various circumferential sta-
           tions are to be read in or computed by user-written
           subroutine GETY.

NOTE: With INDIC = 3 or 4 the temperature in each segment must be
expressible as a product $f(s)*g(\theta)$. $g(\theta)$ can differ from segment to
segment, but must involve the same circumferential wave numbers, n =
NSTART to NFIN in increments or decrements of INCR, for all segments.

T1(I), T2(I), T3(I) = temperature rise coefficients at Ith meridional
           callout point. These are the coefficients that appear in the
           functions of temperature with thickness coordinate z given
           in connection with the description associated with NTGRAD.

TDIST(L,ISEG) = amplitude factors for circumferential distribution of
           temperature.
NOTE: 1. Maximum number of circumferential harmonics is 20.
       2. Circumferential wave numbers associated with these harmonics
          are n = NSTART to NFIN in steps of INCR. They may be posi-
          tive or negative or both.
       3. The temperature rise coefficients T1, T2, T3 at the Ith
          meridional callout and at a circumferential station θ are:

$$\left\{\begin{matrix} T1(I) \\ T2(I) \\ T3(I) \end{matrix}\right\} \ * \ \sum_{\substack{N,L=NSTART,1 \\ N=INCR}}^{N,L=NFIN, \text{ no. of harmonics}} \left(\begin{matrix} \underbrace{TDIST(L,ISEG)*\sin n\theta}_{} + \underbrace{TDIST(L,ISEG)*\cos n\theta}_{} \\ TDIST(L,ISEG)*\sin n\theta + TDIST(L,ISEG)*\cos n\theta \\ TDIST(L,ISEG)*\sin n\theta + TDIST(L,ISEG)*\cos n\theta \end{matrix}\right)$$

positive n   negative n

Z(I) = axial coordinate of the Ith meridional callout point where
           temperature rise coefficients are specified.

R(I) = radial coordinate of the Ith meridional callout point where
           temperature rise coefficients are specified.

Prestress Input Data for Option INDIC = 4, IPRE = 0, Segment "ISEG"

2000 Continue

    if (INDIC ≠ 4) or (IPRE ≠ 0)   go to 3000

    ● NSTRES, NRLOAD

    if (NSTRES = 0) go to 2100

    ● NTYPE

    if (NTYPE = 2): ● (Z(I), I = 1, NSTRES)

    if (NTYPE = 3): ● (R(I), I = 1, NSTRES)

    ● (FN10(I), I = 1, NSTRES)
    ● (FN20(I), I = 1, NSTRES)
    ● (CHIO(I), I = 1, NSTRES)

2100 if (NRLOAD = 0) go to 3000

    ● (IRING(I), I = 1, NRLOAD)
    ● (RLOAD(I), I = 1, NRLOAD)

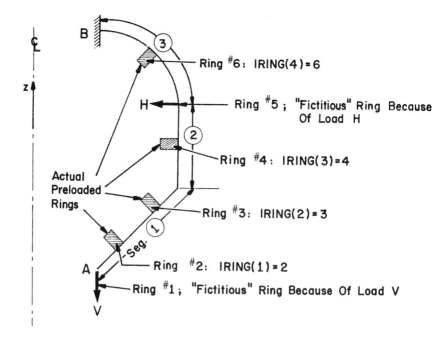

Fig. A7 Actual and fictitious rings

Definitions of Input Variables

INDIC .... analysis type; INDIC = 4 means buckling with nonsymmetric prestress

IPRE ..... used only with INDIC = 4; 0 = prestress meridional distribution read in, 1 = prestress meridional distribution calculated

NSTRES ... number of stations along the meridian in segment ISEG for which prestress resultants FN10 and FN20 and meridional rotation CHIO will be read in (less than 50)

NRLOAD ... number of discrete rings in entire shell for which prebuckling hoop loads will be read in; note that NRLOAD applies to all of the preloaded rings in the entire shell, an exception to the segment-by-segment handling of the input data in BOSOR4. This quantity is read in only with data associated segment #1 (less than 50).

Z(I) ..... axial coordinate of the Ith mesh point callout where prestresses FN10(I), FN20(I), and meridional rotation CHIO(I) are to be specified

R(I) ..... radial coordinate of the Ith mesh point callout

FN10(I) .. meridional prestress resultant at Ith mesh point callout (positive for tension)

FN20(I) .. circumferential prestress resultant at Ith mesh point callout (tension positive)

CHIO(I) .. meridional prestress rotation at Ith mesh point callout (positive for clockwise rotation, as with M in the figure beneath Table A2)

IRING(I) . index number of discrete ring with hoop prestress RLOAD(I). Indices for all preloaded discrete rings are read in when ISEG = 1.

RLOAD(I) . hoop preload in discrete rings; tension is positive. Read in data for all preloaded discrete rings in shell when ISEG, the current segment number, equals one.

Never include input for IRING or RLOAD if ISEG is greater than 1.

NOTE: Prestresses and meridional rotation vary linearly between stations where they are called out. Be sure to include the first and last points in the segment as callout points.

The following special branches calling for simple input data are provided:

    1.   general wall; the $C(i,j)$ are read in, see the equation below
    2.   monocoque wall
    3.   shells with skew stiffeners
    4.   fiber-reinforced shells laid up in layers (e.g., fiberglass)
    5.   layered shells with orthotropic layers
    6.   corrugated shells
    7.   corrugated semisandwich shells
    8.   layered shells with orthotropic layers, each layer of which
has temperature-dependent material properties

Any of these types of shells can be reinforced by two types of stiffeners: 1. rings and stringers which are "smeared out" in the analysis and 2. rings which are treated as discrete elastic structures.
    The discrete ring input data has already been described.
    The shell wall properties are permitted to vary along the meridian. The smeared ring and stringer properties are also permitted to vary along the meridian. The wall properties of each segment are specified independently of those of the other segments.
    In BOSOR4 the wall properties of each segment are determined in one of the subroutines CFB1, CFB2, etc. Each of these subroutines calculates the coefficients $C(i,j)$ of the constitutive equations which relate stress and moment resultants to reference surface strains and changes in curvature:

$$\left\{ \begin{array}{c} N_1 \\ N_2 \\ N_{12} \\ M_1 \\ M_2 \\ M_{12} \end{array} \right\} = [C]\{\epsilon\} = \left[\begin{array}{cccccc} C_{11} & C_{12} & 0 & C_{14} & C_{15} & 0 \\ C_{12} & C_{22} & 0 & C_{24} & C_{25} & 0 \\ 0 & 0 & C_{33} & 0 & 0 & C_{36} \\ C_{14} & C_{24} & 0 & C_{44} & C_{45} & 0 \\ C_{15} & C_{25} & 0 & C_{45} & C_{55} & 0 \\ 0 & 0 & C_{36} & 0 & 0 & C_{66} \end{array} \right] \left\{ \begin{array}{c} \epsilon_1 \\ \epsilon_2 \\ \epsilon_{12} \\ \kappa_1 \\ \kappa_2 \\ 2\kappa_{12} \end{array} \right\}$$

    In the BOSOR4 analysis it is always assumed that the meridional and circumferential independent variables s and θ can be separated. Thus, certain of the $C(i,j)$ are assumed to be zero. This is a limitation of the BOSOR4 analysis, although in most cases not a serious one.
    In the following pages input data for all of the wall construction options except 3, 6, and 7 are identified. For input data for options 3, 6, and 7 the reader is referred to the BOSOR4 User's Manual [1].

Wall Construction (continued), NWALL and GENERAL C(i,j)

3000 Continue

● NWALL   (NWALL = 1, 2, 3, 4, 5, 6, 7, 8)

go to (3100, 3200, 3300, 3400, 3500, 3600, 3700, 3800), NWALL

3100 Continue   (NWALL = 1, general C(i,j))

● SMPA
● C11, C12, C14, C15, C22, C24
● C25, C33, C44, C45, C55, C66
● C36, ANRS   (ANRS = 0.0 or 1.0)

if (ANRS=1.0) ● read data as directed in Table A6.

go to 5000   (end of input for segment ISEG)

Definitions of Input Variables

NWALL = control integer for choice of wall construction:

    1 = general C(i,j)
    2 = monocoque
    3 = skew-stiffened, constant properties along meridional arc
    4 = fiberwound, layered, constant thickness; smeared stif-
        feners possible
    5 = layered orthotropic; variable thickness; smeared stif-
        feners possible
    6 = corrugated; properties constant along meridian; smeared
        stiffeners possible
    7 = corrugated with one smooth skin (semi-sandwich); Smooth
        skin can have variable thickness; smeared stiffeners
    8 = layered orthotropic with temperature-dependent material
        properties; variable thickness; smeared stiffeners o.k.

NWALL = 1 input data description:

SMPA = shell wall mass/area

C11, C12, etc. = coefficients in the constitutive law given on the
                 previous page.

ANRS = control variable for addition of smeared stiffeners:
       0.0 means no smeared stiffeners to be added to wall
       1.0 means yes smeared stiffeners to be added. (Note that add-
       ing the smeared stiffeners will change the C(i,j).)

Wall Construction (continued): MONOCOQUE (NWALL = 2)

3200 Continue   (NWALL = 2, monocoque wall)

● E, U, SM, ALPHA, ANRS, SUR

if (SUR = -1.0): ● NTYPET   (NTYPET = 1 or 2 or 3)

    if (NTYPET = 1): ● NTVALU
                ● NTYPE   (NTYPE = 2 or 3)
                if (NTYPE = 2): ● (Z(I), I = 1, NTVALU)
                if (NTYPE = 3): ● (R(I), I = 1, NTVALU)
                ● (TVAL(I), I = 1, NTVALU)

    if (NTYPET = 2): ● TH1, TH2, TH3, TH4, TH5

    if (NTYPET = 3): ● TVAL

if (ANRS = 1.0): ● read data as directed in Table A6.

go to 5000   (end of input for segment ISEG)

Description of Input Variables

E, U = Young's modulus, Poisson ratio.
SM   = mass density (e.g., aluminum = 0.0002535 lb-sec^2/in.^{4}).
ALPHA = coefficient of thermal expansion.
ANRS = 0.0 for no smeared stiffeners to be added,
        1.0 for yes smeared stiffeners to be added.

SUR   = control variable for thickness input:
        0.0 means reference surface is the middle surface. Since we al-
        ready know the distance from the leftmost surface to the reference
        surface, we do not need any more data to determine the wall thick-
        ness.

        1.0 means the reference surface is the outer or rightmost surface.
        This is the same as the distance from the leftmost surface to the
        reference surface, which has already been read in. Hence, no ad-
        ditional data are needed for specification of the shell thickness.

        -1.0 means that the reference surface is arbitrarily located with
        respect to the leftmost surface. (It might be the leftmost sur-
        face itself.) Therefore, additional data will be needed for
        specification of the thickness.

NTVALU= number of meridional callout points for which the thickness
        will be read in.

Z(I) = axial coordinate to the Ith meridional callout for thickness
R(I) = radial coordinate to the Ith meridional callout for thickness
TVAL(I) = thickness at the Ith meridional callout; thickness varies
          linearly between meridional stations where it is called out

TH1,TH2,TH3,TH4,TH5 = coefficients in t(s)=TH1 + TH2*s^{TH3} + TH4*s^{TH5}

TVAL = thickness (constant in this segment)

Wall Construction (continued), Fiberwound, Layered (NWALL = 4)

3400 Continued   (NWALL = 4, fiberwound layered)

- EF, EM, UF, UM, AK, ANRS
- (T(I), I = 1, AK)
- (X(I), I = 1, AK)
- (BE(I), I = 1, AK)
- (C(I), I = 1, AK)
- (SM(I), I = 1, AK)

   if (ANRS = 1.0): ● read data as directed in Table A6.

   go to 5000   (end of input for segment ISEG)

Description of Input Variables

EF   = Young's modulus for fibers
EM   = Young's modulus for matrix
UF   = Poisson ratio for fibers
UM   = Poisson ratio for matrix
AK   = number of layers (maximum is 20.0) (floating point input!)

ANRS = 0.0 for no smeared stiffeners to be added
       1.0 for yes smeared stiffeners to be added

T(I) = thickness of layer; leftmost layer is no. 1; rightmost layer
       is no. AK.
X(I) = matrix content by volume of Ith layer
BE(I) = winding angle (degrees) between fiber direction and meridian
C(I) = contiguity factor: 0.2 to 0.3 is the usual range
SM(I) = mass density of Ith layer. (aluminum = .0002535 $lb\text{-}sec^2/in.^4$)

Wall Construction (continued): Layered Orthotropic (NWALL = 5)

3500 Continue   ⟨NWALL = 5, Layered orthotropic)

    ● WRAPS, ANRS, TYPET

    if (TYPET = 0.0): ● (T(I), I = 1, WRAPS)

    ● (G(I), I = 1, WRAPS)
    ● (EX(I), I = 1, WRAPS)
    ● (EY(I), I = 1, WRAPS)
    ● (UXY(I), I = 1, WRAPS)   NOTE: EY*UXY = EX*UYX
    ● (SM(I), I = 1, WRAPS)
    ● (ALPHA1(I), I = 1, WRAPS)
    ● (ALPHA2(I), I = 1, WRAPS)

    if (TYPET = 1.0): ● NTIN   (NTYPE = 2 or 3)
                   ● NTYPE
                   if (NTYPE = 2): ● (Z(I), I = 1, NTIN)
                   if (NTYPE = 3): ● (R(I), I = 1, NTIN)

    if (TYPET = 1.0): Do 3550 I = 1, WRAPS

            3550 ● (TIN(J), J = 1, NTIN)

    if (ANRS = 1.0): ● read data as directed in Table A6.

    go to 5000   (end of input for segment ISEG)

Description of Input Data

WRAPS	= number of layers (maximum is 20.0) (floating point input!)
ANRS	= 0.0 for no smeared stiffeners to be added
	1.0 for yes smeared stiffeners to be added
TYPET	= 0.0 layer thicknesses constant; 1.0 layer thicknesses vary
T(I)	= thickness of Ith layer. I = 1 is leftmost, = WRAPS is rightmost
G(I)	= shear modulus of Ith layer
EX(I)	= modulus in meridional direction
EY(I)	= modulus in circumferential direction
UXY(I)	= Poisson ratio
SM(I)	= mass density (e.g., aluminum = .0002535 $lb\text{-}sec^2/in.^4$)
ALPHA1(I)	= coefficient of thermal expansion in meridional direction
ALPHA2(I)	= coefficient of thermal expansion in circumfer. direction
NTIN	= number of meridional callouts for which thicknesses of all layers will be read in
Z(I)	= axial coordinates of meridional callouts for thicknesses
R(I)	= radial coordinates of meridional callouts for thicknesses
TIN(J)	= thickness of a layer at the Jth meridional callout

NOTE: thicknesses vary linearly between meridional callouts.

Wall Construction (continued):Layered Orthotropic with Temperature-
Dependent Material Properties (NWALL = 8)

```
3800 Continue                          NWALL = 8, temp. dependent props)

     ● WRAPS, ANRS, TYPET                    (TYPET = 0.0 or 1.0)

     if (TYPET = 0.0): ● (T(I), I = 1, WRAPS)
                         go to 3900

     if (TYPET = 1.0): ● NTIN
                       ● NTYPE                (NTYPE = 2 or 3)
                       if (NTYPE = 2): ● (Z(I), I = 1, NTIN)
                       if (NTYPE = 3): ● (R(I), I = 1, NTIN)

     if (TYPET = 1.0): Do 3850 I = 1, WRAPS

               3850 ● (TIN(J), J = 1, NTIN)

3900 ● (    SM(I), I = 1, WRAPS)
     ● (NPOINT(I), I = 1, WRAPS)

     Do 3950  I = 1, WRAPS

     ● (HEAT(I,K), K = 1, NPOINT(I))
     ● (    G(K,I), K = 1, NPOINT(I))
     ● (   EX(K,I), K = 1, NPOINT(I))
     ● (   EY(K,I), K = 1, NPOINT(I))
     ● (  UXY(K,I), K = 1, NPOINT(I))
     ● (   A1(K,I), K = 1, NPOINT(I))
     ● (   A2(K,I), K = 1, NPOINT(I))

3950 Continue

if (ANRS = 1.0): ● read data as directed in Table A6.

go to 5000                          (end of input data for this segment)
```

Description of Input Variables

WRAPS = number of layers (maximum is 5.0) (floating point input!)
ANRS = 0.0 for no smeared stiffeners; 1.0 for yes stiffeners
TYPET = 0.0 for constant thicknesses; 1.0 for variable thicknesses
$T(I)$ = thickness of Ith layer; I = 1 is leftmost,=WRAPS is rightmost
NTIN = number of meridional callouts for layer thicknesses
$Z(I)$ = axial coordinates of meridional callouts for thicknesses
$R(I)$ = radial coordinates of meridional callouts for thicknesses
$TIN(J)$ = thickness of a layer at the Jth meridional callout
        NOTE: thicknesses vary linearly between meridional callouts.
$SM(I)$ = mass density of Ith layer material
$NPOINT(I)$ = number of temperature values for which properties of the
        Ith layer are given; maximum of 20 values/layer
$HEAT(I,K)$ = temperature above zero-stress temperature for which wall
        properties of the Ith layer will be read in
$G(K,I)$ = shear modulus of Ith layer at the Kth temperature, $HEAT(I,K)$
$EX(K,I)$= Young's modulus in meridional direction, Ith layer, Kth temp
$EY(K,I)$= Young's modulus in circumfer. direction, Ith layer, Kth temp
$UXY(K,I)$= Poisson ratio; note that EY*UXY = EX*UYX
$A1(K,I)$ = thermal expansion coefficient in meridional direction
$A2(K,I)$ = thermal expansion coefficient in circumferential direction
NOTE: The temperature multiplier TEMP must be unity for this option!

Table A6 "Smeared" Stringer and Ring Properties in Segment "ISEG"

(The following data are to be read in if ANRS = 1.0 for the NWALL
option, even if no stringers or rings are present.)

● IRECT1, IRECT2, IVAR1, IVAR2   (IRECT, IVAR = 0 or 1)

---

if (IRECT1 = 1) and (IVAR1 = 0)	● N1, K1
	● El, Ul, STIFMD
(constant, rectangular)	● T1, H1
	go to 4000 (stringer input done)

---

if (IRECT1 = 1) and (IVAR1 = 1) ● NSTATN, N1, K1
                                 ● NTYPE   (NTYPE = 2 or 3)
(variable, rectangular)   if (NTYPE=2): ● (Z(I), I = 1, NSTATN)
                                 if (NTYPE=3): ● (R(I), I = 1, NSTATN)
                                 ● El, Ul, STIFMD
                                 Do 3970 I = 1, NSTATN
                            3970 ● T(I), H(I)
                                 go to 4000   (stringer input done)

---

if (IRECT1 = 0) and (IVAR1 = 0) ● N1, K1
                                 ● El, Ul, STIFMD
(constant, nonrectangular)   ● XS, A1, XI1, XJ1
                                 go to 4000   (stringer input done)

---

if (IRECT1 = 0) and (IVAR1 = 1) ● NSTATN, N1, K1
                                 ● NTYPE   (NTYPE = 2 or 3)
(variable, nonrectangular)   if (NTYPE=2): ● (Z(I), I = 1, NSTATN)
                                 if (NTYPE=3): ● (R(I), I = 1, NSTATN)
                                 ● El, Ul, STIFMD
                                 Do 3980 I = 1, NSTATN
                            3980 ● X(I), A(I), XI(I), XJ(I)
                                 go to 4000   (stringer input done)

IRECT1 = 1 for stringers with rectangular cross section
         0 for stringers with arbitrary cross section
IVAR1 = 1 for stringers with properties varying along meridian
         0 for stringers with constant properties along meridian

N1 = number of stringers in 360 degrees
K1 = 0 for stringers attached to leftmost surface; 1 rightmost surf.
El, Ul, STIFMD = stringer modulus, Poisson ratio, mass density
T1; H1 = stringer thickness (dimension parallel to shell wall); height
NSTATN = number of meridional callouts for stringer properties
Z(I) = axial coordinates to meridional callout points
R(I) = radial coordinates to meridional callout points
T(I), H(I) = stringer thickness, height at meridional callout point
XS = distance from neutral axis of stringer to closest shell surface
A1 = cross-sectional area of stringer
XI1= centroidal moment of inertia about axis parallel to circumference
XJ1= torsional constant J
X(I)= distance from neutral axis to closest shell surf. at Ith callout
A(I)= cross-sectional area of stringer at Ith meridional callout
XI(I)=centroidal moment of inertia about axis parallel to circumference
XJ(I)=torsional constant J of stringer at Ith meridional callout

Table A6 (continued)   "Smeared" Ring Properties in Segment "ISEG"

(The following data are to be read in if ANRS = 1.0 for the NWALL
option, even if no smeared rings are present.)

4000 Continue

if (IRECT2 = 1) and (IVAR2 = 0) ● K2
                                 ● E2, U2, RGMD
  (constant, rectangular)   ● D2, T2, H2
                                 go to 5000   (ring input done)

---

if (IRECT2 = 1) and (IVAR2 = 1) ● NRINGS, K2
                                 ● NTYPE   (NTYPE = 2 or 3)
  (variable, rectangular)   if (NTYPE=2): ● (Z(I), I = 1, NRINGS)
                                 if (NTYPE=3): ● (R(I), I = 1, NRINGS)
                                 ● E2, U2, RGMD
                                 Do 4100 I = 1, NRINGS
                            4100 ● D(I), T(I), H(I)
                                 go to 5000   (ring input done)

---

if (IRECT2 = 0) and (IVAR2 = 0) ● K2
                                 ● E2, U2, RGMD
  (constant, nonrectangular)   ● XR, D2, A2, XI2, XJ2
                                 go to 5000   (ring input done)

---

if (IRECT2 = 0) and (IVAR2 = 1) ● NRINGS, K2
                                 ● NTYPE   (NTYPE = 2 or 3)
  (variable, nonrectangular)   if (NTYPE=2): ● Z(I), I = 1, NRINGS)
                                 if (NTYPE=3): ● R(I), I = 1, NRINGS)
                                 ● E2, U2, RGMD
                                 Do 4200 I = 1, NRINGS
                            4200 ● K(I), D(I), A(I), XI(I), XJ(I)
5000 Continue   (end of input for this segment)

IRECT2 = 1 for rings with rectangular cross sections
         0 for rings with arbitrary cross sections
IVAR2 = 1 for rings with properties which vary along the meridian
         0 for rings with constant properties along the meridian

K2 = 0 for rings attached to the leftmost surface; 1 rightmost surf.
E2, U2, RGMD = ring modulus, Poisson ratio, mass density
D2 = arc length between adjacent rings (constant over segment)
T2; H2 = ring thickness (dimension parallel to shell wall), height

NRINGS = number of meridional callouts for ring properties
Z(I)   = axial coordinates to meridional callout points
R(I)   = radial coordinates to meridional callout points
T(I), H(I) = ring thickness, height at Ith meridional callout
D(I)   = average ring spacing at the Ith meridional callout

XR = distance from neutral axis of ring to closest shell surface
A2 = cross-sectional area of ring
X12= centroidal moment of inertia about axis parallel to meridian
XJ2= ring torsional constant, J

X(I)= distance from neutral axis to closest shell surf. at Ith callout
A(I)= average ring cross-sectional area at Ith meridional callout
XI(J)= average ring centroidal moment of inertia at Ith callout
XJ(I)= average ring torsional constant J at Ith meridional callout

How to Run a Case with Smeared Stiffeners Including Thermal Effects

It is not possible to use the smeared stiffener option (Table 9)
if the smeared stiffeners experience a temperature rise above or drop
below their zero-stress (reference) temperature. However, such a
problem can be solved by treatment of the stiffeners as a shell
layer or layers as shown below. The NWALL = 5 option (orthotropic
layered shell) is used.

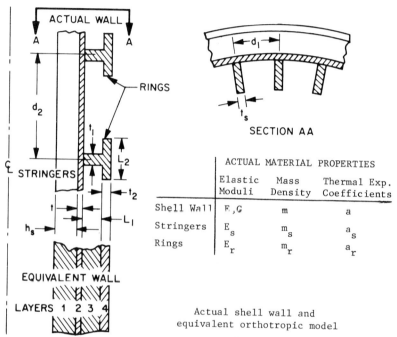

ACTUAL MATERIAL PROPERTIES

	Elastic Moduli	Mass Density	Thermal Exp. Coefficients
Shell Wall	E, G	m	a
Stringers	E_s	m_s	a_s
Rings	E_r	m_r	a_r

Actual shell wall and
equivalent orthotropic model

Equivalent Layered Orthotropic Shell Wall

Shell Wall Layer	Thickness	G	EX	EY	UXY	SM	A1	A2
1	h_s	0	$E_s t_s/d_1$	0	0	$m_s t_s/d_1$	a_s	0
2	t	G	E	E	ν	m	a	a
3	L_1	0	0	$E_r t_1/d_2$	0	$m_r t_1/d_2$	0	a_r
4	t_2	0	0	$E_r L_2/d_2$	0	$m_r L_2/d_2$	0	a_r

SAMPLE CASES

This section contains input data for 7 cases which test all of the
analysis branches, INDIC = -2, -1, 0, 1, 2, 3, and 4. Table A 7 sum-
arizes the cases and gives reasons why each case was chosen as a
demonstration. The BOSOR4 user is urged to consult this table and the
sample input on the following pages whenever he encounters difficulties in solving problems similar to these.

Table A 7   Sample Cases for BOSOR4

INDIC	CASE NAME	THE PURPOSE OF THE CASE IS TO DEMONSTRATE:
1	Aluminum Frame Buckling	1. linear bifurcation buckling 2. branched shells 3. various locations of reference surface 4. two different failure modes, local and general, leading to two minimum critical loads $p(n)$
-1	Cylinder Buckling	1. nonlinear bifurcation buckling 2. "smeared" stiffeners 3. variable node point spacing 4. discrete rings 5. fake ring for line load 6. hydrostatic pressure: $V = pr/2$ 7. change of boundary conditions from prebuckling to buckling analysis 8. local and general instability
0	Uniformly Loaded Plate	1. nonlinear axisymmetric stress analysis 2. two load steps for linear and nonlinear action
2	Hemisphere Vibration	1. modal vibration analysis 2. rigid body displacement constraint conditions
3	Cylinder with Three Point Loads	1. linear nonsymmetric stress analysis 2. modeling of concentrated loads 3. modeling discrete ring at symmetry plane 4. variable node point spacing 5. point loads repeating at regular intervals around the circumference
4	Buckling of Cone Heated on Axial Strip	1. bifurcation buckling of nonaxisymmetrically loaded shell 2. load which varies along the meridian 3. variable node point spacing
-2	Spherical Cap Buckling	1. nonlinear bifurcation buckling by successive calculation of the stability determinant 2. sign convention of pressure depending on the direction of travel along a meridian 3. problem in which axisymmetric collapse load and bifurcation buckling load are fairly close

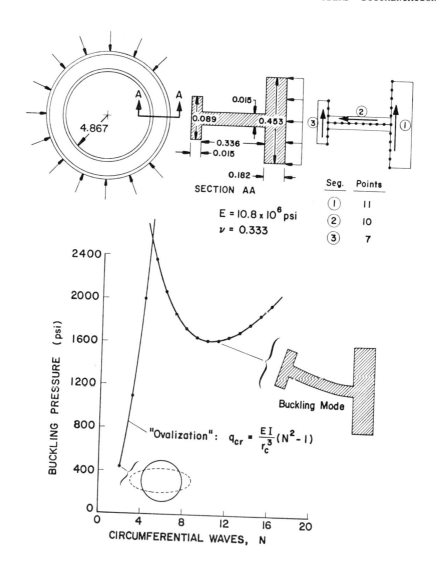

Fig. A8 Aluminum frame buckling (INDIC = 1)

Example of Aluminum Frame Buckling

```
ALUMINUM FRAME BUCKLING (INDIC=1) TITLE
1, 2, 0, 0, 0                     INDIC, NPRT, NLAST, ISTRES, IPRE
3, 3, 0, 0                        NSEG, NCOND, IBOUND, IRIGID
0, 0, 0                           NSTART, NFIN, INCR
2, 2,14, 4, 1                     NOB, NMINB, NMAXB, INCRB, NVEC
0, 0, 0                           NDIST, NCIRC, NTHETA
0                                 (ITHETA(I), I = 1, NCIRC)
0.                                ( THETA(I), I = 1, NDIST)
0., 0., 0.                        THETAM, THETAS, 0.
1, 1, 1, 1, 1, 0, 0, 0, 0., 0.    IS1,IP1,IS2,IP2,IU*,IV,IW*,IX,D1,D2
1, 6, 2, 1, 1, 1, 1, 1, 0., 0.    IS1,IP1,IS2,IP2,IU*,IV,IW*,IX,D1,D2
2,10, 3, 4, 1, 1, 1, 1, 0., 0.    IS1,IP1,IS2,IP2,IU*,IV,IW*,IX,D1,D2
0., -1., 0., 0.                   P, DP, TEMP, DTEMP
0., 0., 0.                        FSTART, FMAX, DF
11, 3, 0                          NMESH, NTYPEH, 0 ......Segment #1
 1, 3, 0                          NSHAPE, NTYPEZ, IMP
5.218, 0., 5.218, .453            R1, Z1, R2, Z2
0.                                ZVAL
0                                 NRINGS
0                                 LINTYP
1, 0, 0, 0                        NLTYPE, NPSTAT, NTSTAT, NTGRAD
1., 0., 0., 0., 0.                P11, P12, P13, P14, P15
0., 0., 0., 0., 0.                P21, P22, P23, P24, P25
2                                 NWALL
10800000., .333, 0., 0., 0., -1.  E, U, SM, ALPHA, ANRS, SUR
3                                 NTYPET
.182                              TVAL
10, 3, 0                          NMESH, NTYPEH, 0 ......Segment #2
 1, 3, 0                          NSHAPE, NTYPEZ, IMP
5.218, .2265, 4.882, .2265        R1, Z1, R2, Z2
.0075                             ZVAL
0                                 NRINGS
0                                 LINTYP
0, 0, 0, 0                        NLTYPE, NPSTAT, NTSTAT, NTGRAD
2                                 NWALL
10800000., 0.333, 0., 0., 0., 0.  E, U, SM, ALPHA, ANRS, SUR
 7, 3, 0                          NMESH, NTYPEH, 0 ......Segment #3
 1, 3, 0                          NSHAPE, NTYPEZ, IMP
4.882, .182, 4.882, .271          R1, Z1, R2, Z2
.015                              ZVAL
0                                 NRINGS
0                                 LINTYP
0, 0, 0, 0                        NLTYPE, NPSTAT, NTSTAT, NTGRAD
2                                 NWALL
10800000., 0.333, 0., 0., 0., 1.  E, U, SM, ALPHA, ANRS, SUR
```

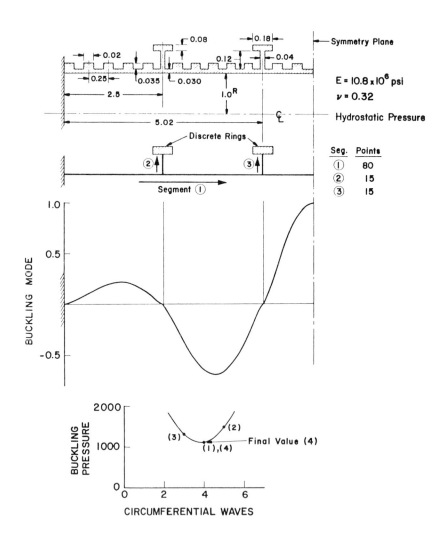

Fig. A9 Cylinder buckling (INDIC = -1)

Example of Cylinder Buckling

CYLINDER BUCKLING (INDIC = -1)	TITLE
-1, 2, 0, 0, 0	INDIC, NPRT, NLAST, ISTRES, IPRE
3, 4, 1, 0	NSEG, NCOND, IBOUND, IRIGID
0, 0, 0	NSTART, NFIN, INCR
4, 1, 6, 1, 1	NOB, NMINB, NMAXB, INCRB, NVEC
0, 0, 0	NDIST, NCIRC, NTHETA
0	(ITHETA(I), I = 1, NCIRC)
0.	(THETA(I), I = 1, NDIST)
0., 0., 0.	THETAM, THETAS, O.
1, 1, 1, 1, 0, 1, 1, 1, 0., 0.	IS1,IP1,IS2,IP2,IU*,IV,IW*,IX,D1,D2
1,30, 2, 1, 1, 1, 1, 1, 0., 0.	IS1,IP1,IS2,IP2,IU*,IV,IW*,IX,D1,D2
1,63, 3, 1, 1, 1, 1, 1, 0., 0.	IS1,IP1,IS2,IP2,IU*,IV,IW*,IX,D1,D2
1,80, 1,80, 1, 0, 0, 1, 0., 0.	IS1,IP1,IS2,IP2,IU*,IV,IW*,IX,D1,D2
1, 1, 1, 1	IUB*, IVB, IWB*, IXB
1, 1, 1, 1	IUB*, IVB, IWB*, IXB
1, 1, 1, 1	IUB*, IVB, IWB*, IXB
1, 0, 0, 1	IUB*, IVB, IWB*, IXB
0., -1., 0., 0.	P, DP, TEMP, DTEMP
0., 0., 0.	FSTART, FMAX, DF
80, 1, 0	NMESH, NTYPEH, 0 ......Segment #1
11	NHVALU
1, 21, 22, 37, 38, 54, 55, 70, 71, 78, 79	(IHVALU(I), I = 1, NHVALU)
1., 1., .5, .5, 1., 1., .5, .5, 1., 1., .8	(HVALU(I), I = 1, NHVALU)
1, 3, 0	NSHAPE, NTYPEZ, IMP
1.015, 0., 1.015, 6.28	R1, Z1, R2, Z2
.015	ZVAL
1	NRINGS
2	NTYPE
0.	Z(1)
0	NTYPER(1) (fake ring)
1	LINTYP
0, 0, 0, 0	(NLOAD(M), M = 1,4)
1, 0, 0, 0	(NLOAD(M), M = 1,4)
-.5075	DV(1) (DV = DP*R1/2.)
1, 0, 0, 0	NLTYPE, NPSTAT, NTSTAT, NTGRAD
1., 0., 0., 0., 0.	P11, P12, P13, P14, P15
0., 0., 0., 0., 0.	P21, P22, P23, P24, P25
2	NWALL
10800000., 0.32, 0., 0., 1., 0.	E, U, SM, ALPHA, ANRS, SUR
1, 1, 0, 0	IRECT1, IRECT2, IVAR1, IVAR2
0, 0	N1, K1
0., 0., 0.	E1, U1, STIFMD
0., 0.	T1, H1
1	K2
10800000., 0.32, 0.	E2, U2, RGMD
.25, .02, .035	D2, T2, H2

```
15, 1, 0                              NMESH, NTYPEH, 0 ......Segment #2
3                                     NHVALU
1, 13, 14                             (IHVALU(I), I = 1, NHVALU)
1., 1., .5                            ( HVALU(I), I = 1, NHVALU)
1, 3, 0                               NSHAPE, NTYPEZ, IMP
1.015, 2.5, 1.150, 2.5                R1, Z1, R2, Z2
.02                                   ZVAL
1                                     NRINGS
3                                     NTYPE
1.150                                 R(1)
1                                     NTYPER(1)
10800000., .0144, .00000768,          E, A, RIY,
.00003888, 0., .04, 0., 90.4, 0.      RIX, RIXY, E1, E2, GJ, RM
0                                     LINTYP
0, 0, 0, 0                            NLTYPE, NPSTAT, NTSTAT, NTGRAD
2                                     NWALL
10800000., .32, 0., 0., 0., 0.        E, SM, ALPHA, ANRS, SUR
15, 1, 0                              NMESH, NTYPEH, 0 ......Segment #3
3                                     NHVALU
1, 13, 14                             (IHVALU(I), I = 1, NHVALU)
1., 1., .5                            ( HVALU(I), I = 1, NHVALU)
1, 3, 0                               NSHAPE, NTYPEZ, IMP
1.015, 5.02, 1.150, 5.02              R1, Z1, R2, Z2
.02                                   ZVAL
1                                     NRINGS
3                                     NTYPE
1.150                                 R(1)
1                                     NTYPER(1)
10800000., .0144, .00000768,          E, A, RIY,
.00003888, 0., .04, 0., 90.4, 0.      RIX, RIXY, E1, E2, GJ, RM
0                                     LINTYP
0, 0, 0, 0                            NLTYPE, NPSTAT, NTSTAT, NTGRAD
2                                     NWALL
10800000., 0.32, 0., 0., 0., 0.       E, U, SM, ALPHA, ANRS, SUR
```

Note: In this case, the boundary conditions for the prebuckling analysis are different from those of the bifurcation buckling analysis. In
the prebuckling analysis u* is free at segment 1, point 1, as indicated on the first IS1, IP1, IS2, IP2, etc. card, and the rest of the
displacement components, v, w*, and X are set equal to zero. In the
bifurcation buckling analysis this boundary is clamped; all displacement components are set equal to zero, as seen from the first card
for IUB*, IVB, IWB*, and IXB. This change from prebuckling to buckling analysis is necessary because the axial load DV=DP*R1/2 arising
from the hydrostatic pressure must be permitted to do work in the
axisymmetric prebuckling phase of the problem. Axial motions are
restrained in the nonsymmetric buckling phase by a large end ring
which was present in the test of this specimen, but which is not
included in the analytical model.

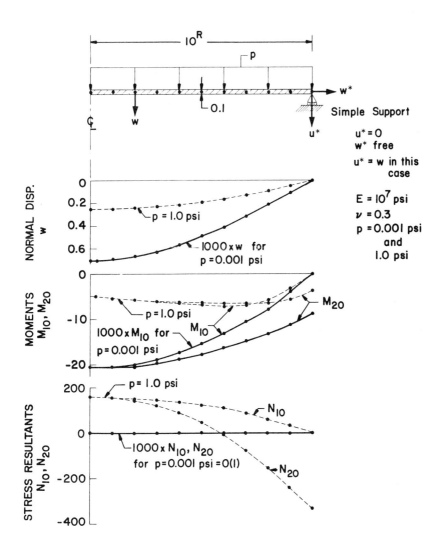

Fig. A10 Uniformly loaded plate (INDIC = 0)

Example of Uniformly Loaded Plate

UNIFORMLY LOADED PLATE (INDIC= 0)	TITLE
0, 2, 0, 1, 0	INDIC, NPRT, NLAST, ISTRES, IPRE
1, 2, 0, 0	NSEG, NCOND, IBOUND, IRIGID
0, 0, 0	NSTART, NFIN, INCR
0, 0, 0, 0, 0	NOB, NMINB, NMAXB, INCRB, NVEC
0, 0, 0	NDIST, NCIRC, NTHETA
0	(ITHETA(I), I = 1, NCIRC)
0.	(THETA(I), I = 1, NDIST)
0., 0., 0.	THETAM, THETAS, 0.
1, 1, 1, 1, 0, 0, 0, 0, 0., 0.	IS1,IP1,IS2,IP2,IU*,IV,IW*,IX,D1,D2
1,11, 1,11, 1, 1, 0, 0, 0., 0.	IS1,IP1,IS2,IP2,IU*,IV,IW*,IX,D1,D2
.001, .999, 0., 0.	P, DP, TEMP, DTEMP
.001, 1.0, .999	FSTART, FMAX, DF
11, 3, 0	NMESH, NTYPEH, 0 ......Segment #1
1, 3, 0	NSHAPE, NTYPEZ, IMP
0., 0., 10., 0.	R1, Z1, R2, Z2
.05	ZVAL
0	NRINGS
0	LINTYP
1, 0, 0, 0	NLTYPE, NPSTAT, NTSTAT, NTGRAD
1., 0., 0., 0., 0.	P11, P12, P13, P14, P15
0., 0., 0., 0., 0.	P21, P22, P23, P24, P25
2	NWALL
10000000., 0.3, 0., 0., 0., 0.	E, U, SM, ALPHA, ANRS, SUR
HEMISPHERE VIBRATION (INDIC = 2)	TITLE
2, 2, 0, 0, 0	INDIC, NPRT, NLAST, ISTRES, IPRE
1, 2, 0, 1	NSEG, NCOND, IBOUND, IRIGID
0, 0, 0	NSTART, NFIN, INCR
0, 0, 3, 1, 3	NOB, NMINB, NMAXB, INCRB, NVEC
0, 0, 0	NDIST, NCIRC, NTHETA
0	(ITHETA(I), I = 1, NCIRC)
0.	(THETA(I), I = 1, NDIST)
0., 0., 0.	THETAM, THETAS, 0.
1, 1, 1, 1, 0, 0, 0, 0, 0., 0.	IS1,IP1,IS2,IP2,IU*,IV,IW*IX,D1,D2
1,31, 1,31, 0, 0, 0, 0, 0., 0.	IS1,IP1,IS2,IP2,IU*,IV,IW*IX,D1,D2
1,31, 1,31, 1, 1, 0, 0	IS1,IP1,IS1,IP1,IUR*,IVR,IW*,IX
1,31, 1,31, 1, 1, 0, 0	IS1,IP1,IS1,IP1,IUR*,IVR,IW*,IX
0., 0., 0., 0.	P, DP, TEMP, DTEMP
0., 0., 0.	FSTART, FMAX, DF
31, 3, 0	NMESH, NTYPEH, 0 .....Segment #1
2, 3, 0	NSHAPE, NTYPEZ, IMP
0., 0., 100., 100., 0., 100.	R1, Z1, R2, Z2, RC, ZC
-1.0	SROT
.5	ZVAL
0	NRINGS
0	LINTYP
0, 0, 0, 0	NLTYPE, NPSTAT, NTSTAT, NTGRAD
2	NWALL
10000000., 0.3, .0002535,0.,0.,0.	E, U, SM, ALPHA, ANRS, SUR

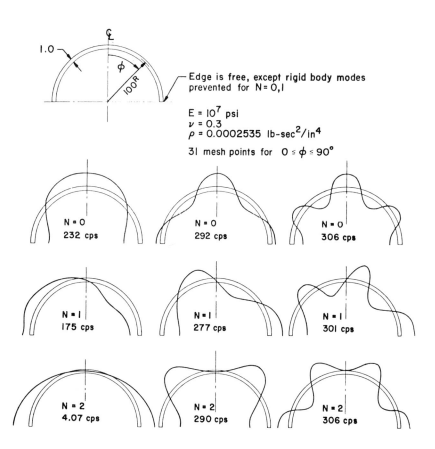

Fig. A11   Hemisphere vibration (INDIC = 2)

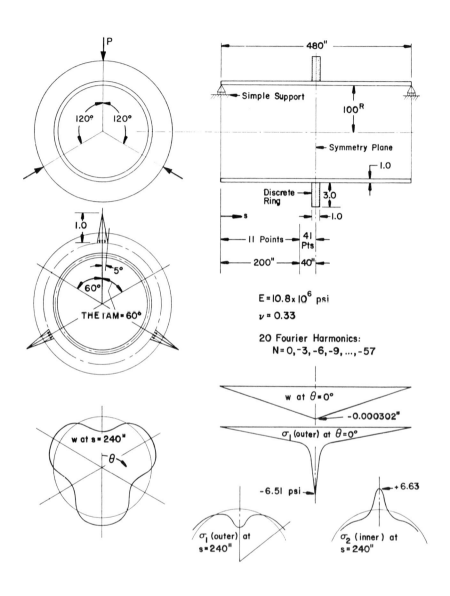

Fig. A12 Cylinder with three point loads (INDIC = 3)

Example of Cylinder with Three Point Loads

CYL. WITH THREE POINT LOADS (INDIC=3) TITLE	
3, 2, 0, 1, 0	INDIC, NPRT, NLAST, ISTRES, IPRE
1, 2, 0, 0	NSEG, NCOND, IBOUND, IRIGID
0, -57, -3	NSTART, NFIN, INCR
0, 0, 0, 0, 0	NOB, NMINB, NMAXB, INCRB, NVEC
5, 5, 31	NDIST, NCIRC, NTHETA
1011, 1026, 1043, 1049, 1052	(ITHETA(I), I = 1, NCIRC)
0., 10., 20., 35., 60.	(THETA(I), I = 1, NDIST)
60., 0., 0.	THETAM, THETAS, 0.
1, 1, 1, 1, 0, 1, 1, 0, 0., 0.	IS1,IP1,IS2,IP2,IU*,IV,IW*,IX,D1,D2
1,52, 1,52, 1, 0, 0, 1, 0., 0.	IS1,IP1,IS2,IP2,IU*,IV,IW*,IX,D1,D2
0., 0., 0., 0.	P, DP, TEMP, DTEMP
0., 0., 0.	FSTART, FMAX, DF
52, 1, 0	NMESH, NTYPEH, 0 ......Segment #1
4	NHVALU
1,10,11,51	(IHVALU(I), I = 1, NHVALU)
1., 1., .05, .05	(HVALU(I), I = 1, NHVALU)
1, 3, 0	NSHAPE, NTYPEZ, IMP
100.5, 0., 100.5, 240.	R1, Z1, R2, Z2
.5	ZVAL
1	NRINGS
2	NTYPE
240.0	Z(1)
1	NTYPER(1)
5400000., 3., 2.25, .25, 0., 2.,	E, A, RIY, RIX, RIXY, E1,
0., 1639000., 0.	E2, GJ, RM
1	LINTYP
4	NTYPEL
0, 0, 1, 0	(NLOAD(M), M = 1, 4)
1.0	H(1)
3, 2, 1	NTHETA, NOPT, NODD
0., 5., 60.	(THETA(J), J = 1, NTHETA)
-1., 0., 0.	(YPLUS(J), J = 1, NTHETA)
0, 0, 0, 0	NLTYPE, NPSTAT, NTSTAT, NTGRAD
2	NWALL
10800000., .33, 0., 0., 0., 0.	E, U, SM, ALPHA, ANRS, SUR

Note: Since there are three point loads applied at 120 degree intervals around the circumference, it is necessary only to expand the
circumferential variation in the interval
$$-\text{THETAM} \le \theta \le + \text{THETAM} = -60. \le \theta \le + 60.$$
and to set INCR = -3, since only every third harmonic contributes to
the load function. If there are m equally spaced loads around the
circumference one can expand in the interval
$$-(180/m) \le \theta \le + (180/m)$$
and set INCR = - m or + m, depending on whether the function is even
(-m) or odd (+m) about $\theta = 0$.

Another note: For discrete rings at symmetry planes: cut the modulus
E and the torsional rigidity GJ and the density RM in half and leave
all other variables alone.

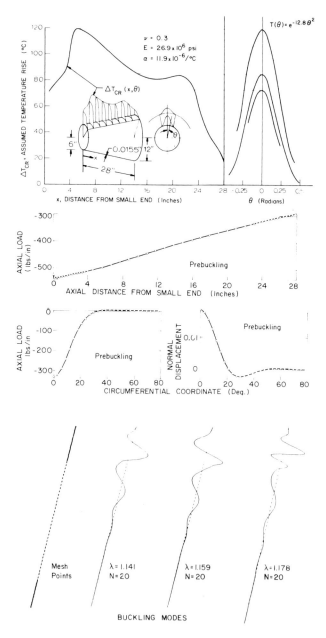

Fig. A13   Buckling of cone heated on an axial strip (INDIC = 4)

Example of the Buckling of a Cone Heated on an Axial Strip

BUCKLING OF CONE HEATED ON AXIAL STRIP (INDIC=4)	TITLE
4, 2, 0, 0, 1	INDIC, NPRT, NLAST, ISTRES, IPRE
1, 2, 0, 0	NSEG, NCOND, IBOUND, IRIGID
0, -19, -1	NSTART, NFIN, INCR
20, 20, 20, 1, 3	NOB, NMINB, NMAXB, INCRB, NVEC
1, 1, 61	NDIST, NCIRC, NTHETA
1066	(ITHETA(I), I = 1, NCIRC)
0.	(THETA(I), I = 1, NDIST)
180., 0., 0.	THETAM, THETAS, 0.
1, 1, 1, 1, 1, 1, 1, 1, 0., 0.	IS1,IP1,IS2,IP2,IU*,IV,IW*,IX,D1,D2
1,97, 1,97, 1, 1, 1, 1, 0., 0.	IS1,IP1,IS2,IP2,IU*,IV,IW*,IX,D1,D2
0., 0., 0., 0.	P, DP, TEMP, DTEMP
0., 0., 0.	FSTART, FMAX, DF
97, 1, 0	NMESH, NTYPEH, INTVAL
6	NHVALU
1, 28, 29, 64, 65, 96	(IHVALU(I) I = 1, NHVALU)
.143, .143, .5, .5, .167, .167	(HVALU(I) I = 1, NHVALU)
1, 3, 0	NSHAPE, NTYPEZ, IMP
6., 0., 12., 27.35	R1, Z1, R2, Z2
.00775	ZVAL
0	NRINGS
0	LINTYP
2, 0, 18, 1	NLTYPE, NPSTAT, NTSTAT, NTGRAD
4	NTYPEL
1, 0, 0	NLOAD(1), NLOAD(2), NLOAD(3)
68., 80., 85., 90., 105, 119.5,	(T(I), I = 1, NTSTAT)
118., 112., 93.5, 82., 81.4, 83.5,	
84.2, 82., 75.5, 50., 35., 20.	
20, 3, 1	NTHETA, NOPT, NODD
0., 1.72, 3.44, 5.16, 6.88, 8.59,	(THETA(J), J = 1, NTHETA)
10.3, 12.0, 13.8, 15.5, 17.2,	
20.6, 24.1, 27.5, 30.9, 34.4,	
37.8, 41.3, 51.6, 180.	
2	NTYPE
0., 1.95, 2.93, 3.42, 3.91, 4.88,	(Z(I), I = 1, NTSTAT)
5.86, 7.81, 11.7, 15.6, 17.6,	
19.5, 20.5, 21.5, 22.5, 23.9,	
25.4, 27.35	
2	NWALL
26900000., .3, 0.,.0000119,0.,0.	E, U, SM, ALPHA, ANRS, SUR

Note: NOPT = 3, which means that the circumferential variation of the temperature is determined by a user-written subroutine. In this case the user-written routine is:

```
      SUBROUTINE GETY(NTHETA, THETA, YMINUS, YPLUS)
      DIMENSION THETA(100), YMINUS(100), YPLUS(100)
      DO 10 I = 1, NTHETA
      YPLUS(I) = EXP(-12.8*THETA(I)**2)
   10 YMINUS(I) = YPLUS(I)
      RETURN
      END
```

Note: The variable THETA ( ) is in radians in this subroutine!

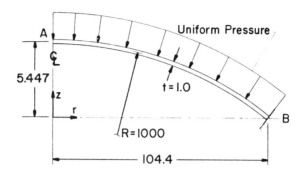

$$E = 30 \times 10^6 \text{ psi}$$
$$\nu = 0.3$$

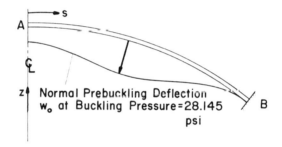

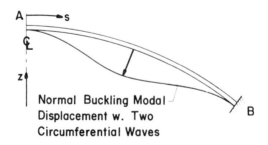

Fig. A14   Spherical cap buckling (INDIC = -2)

Example of Spherical Cap Buckling

```
SPHERICAL CAP BUCKLING (INDIC=-2) TITLE
-2, 2, 0, 0, 0                    INDIC, NPRT, NLAST, ISTRES, IPRE
 1, 2, 0, 0                       NSEG, NCOND, IBOUND, IRIGID
 0, 0, 0                          NSTART, NFIN, INCR
 2, 0,10, 1, 1                    NOB, NMINB, NMAXB, INCRB, NVEC
 0, 0, 0                          NDIST, NCIRC, NTHETA
 0                                (ITHETA(I), I = 1, NCIRC)
 0.                               ( THETA(I), I = 1, NDIST)
 0., 0., 0.                       THETAM, THETAS, 0.
 1, 1, 1, 1, 0, 0, 0, 0, 0., 0.   IS1,IP1,IS2,IP2,IU*,IV,IW*,IX,D1,D2
 1,20, 1,20, 1, 1, 1, 1, 0., 0.   IS1,IP1,IS2,IP2,IU*,IV,IW*,IX,D1,D2
18., 4., 0., 0.                   P, DP, TEMP, DTEMP
18., 50., 4.                      FSTART, FMAX, DF
20, 3, 0                          NMESH, NTYPEH, 0 ......Segment #1
 2, 3, 0                          NSHAPE, NTYPEZ, IMP
 0., 5.447, 104.4, 0., 0., -994.6 R1, Z1, R2, Z2, RC, ZC
1.0                               SROT
.5                                ZVAL
0                                 NRINGS
0                                 LINTYP
1, 0, 0, 0                        NLTYPE, NPSTAT, NTSTAT, NTGRAD
1., 0., 0., 0., 0.                P11, P12, P13, P14, P15
0., 0., 0., 0., 0.                P21, P22, P23, P24, P25
2                                 NWALL
30000000., .3, 0., 0., 0., 0.     E, U, SM, ALPHA, ANRS, SUR
```

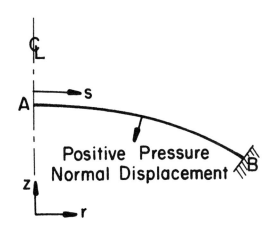

POSSIBLE PITFALLS AND RECOMMENDED SOLUTIONS

The following is a compilation of items which may cause the user
of the BOSOR4 program some difficulty. Suggestions are given for
overcoming the difficulties.

Provision of Consistent Input Data

In the initial use of a complex program such as BOSOR4 it is possible that the input data may not be consistent. The user is
urged to check carefully the list and plot output for errors in the
input data. In particular, boundary conditions, position of discrete ring stiffeners, meridian shape, line loads, and surface loads
should be checked. Often the best way the user can familiarize
himself with the input procedures is to run cases for which he
knows the answers beforehand. A check of the mode shapes and
stress distributions often reveals possible errors in input. It is
emphasized that the user should check the sample cases in the
BOSOR4 manual to see if they might help him to set up a new case.

Finding the Minimum Minimum Buckling Load:
Appropriate Choices for NOB, NMINB, NMAXB, INCRB

The theory on which BOSOR4 is based does not exclude the possibility that several values of circumferential wave number N may be
associated with minimum buckling loads. One must always find the
minimum minimum. This problem frequently arises in the calculation of buckling loads for complex shells or ring stiffened shells.
A ring stiffened conical shell under external pressure is such a
case (Fig. A15). Here there could be a minimum buckling load
corresponding to general instability and additional minima (at
higher values of N) corresponding to the local failure of each
conical frustrum (the bays between the rings). Physical intuition
is invaluable as a guide for finding the absolute minimum load.
One may idealize each bay of a ring stiffened shell by assuming
that the bay is simply supported, calculate corresponding "panel"
buckling loads with certain appropriate ranges of N, and then use
the critical loads and values of N as starting points in an investigation of the assembled structure.
    It is not necessary always to increase the circumferential
wave number N by one. In the search for the minimum buckling load,
for example, one may only be certain that the N corresponding
to the minimum buckling load, N (critical), lies in the range
$2 \le N \le 100$. One might, therefore, choose INCRB = 10 and "zero in"
on a more accurate value in a subsequent run. The user should
ordinarily set INCRB = 0.05*(NMINB + NMAXB).
    Experimental evidence is of course very useful in determining
a good choice of NOB, NMINB, and NMAXB. If none is available the
user is advised to try the following formulas:

(1) "Square" buckles for short shells or panel buckling

N = $\pi r/L$, where L is the shell meridional arc length
between nodes of the buckling mode.

(2) For monocoque deep shells, axial compression:

$$N = [\text{(Nominal circumferential rad. of curve)}/t]^{1/2}(1 - \upsilon^2)$$

(3) For shallow spherical caps supported rigidly at their
edges; external pressure:

$$N = 1.8 * \alpha_2 * (R/t)^{1/2} - 5$$

(4) For axially compressed conical shells and frustrums:

Use formula 2 where the circumferential radius of
curvature, R, is the average of the radii at the ends.

(5) Spherical segments of any depth under axial tension

$$N = 1.8 * (R/t)^{1/2} \sin [\alpha_1 + 4.2 (t/R)^{1/2}]$$

where α_1 and α_2 are the meridional angles at the
segment beginning and end, respectively.

The above list of formulas is by no means complete. However, notice
that $(R/t)^{1/2}$ is a significant parameter. If N is known for a shell
of a given geometry loaded in a certain way, a new value can be predicted for a new R/t through the knowledge that N often seems to vary
as $(R/t)^{1/2}$. (R is the circumferential radius of curvature.)

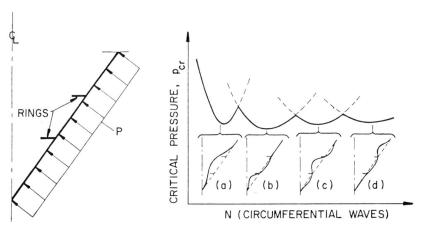

Fig. A15 Several buckling modes for ring stiffened conical shell
(a) General instability (b) 1st bay buckling (c) 2nd bay buckling
(d) 3rd bay buckling

Experience in the use of the program will lead to further competence
in the selection of appropriate values for NOB, the initial guess at
N. Again, the user must be sure that the input range NMINB$\leq$ N$\leq$ NMAXB
includes the <u>minimum</u> minimum buckling load.

Stress Resultant or Stress Discontinuities at
Junctures and Boundaries

Stress resultants and stresses need not be continuous at segment
junctures in all cases, of course. However, the user of BOSOR4 will
notice that for some cases in which these quantities should be continuous there exist small discontinuities right at junctures. These
discontinuities arise from the fact that the finite-difference energy
method leads to larger truncation errors at boundaries than inside
domains. If the user is particularly interested in stress at a
juncture or boundary, it is urged that he concentrate mesh points in
these areas to minimize truncation error. In any case, the BOSOR4
program is written so as to minimize the effect of boundary truncation error. The stress resultants are "corrected" as described on
pages of 172 and 173 of [6]. In addition, "extra" mesh points are
automatically inserted near the points on junctures and boundaries
in order to make the truncation error as small as is feasible without
encountering difficulties associated with precision round-off error.
This feature is more completely described in the input data section.

Correct Modeling of Discrete Rings

It has been common in past analyses to neglect out-of-plane bending
stiffness (terms involving I_x) which is called "RIX" in the
manual and torsional stiffness (terms involving GJ) in the analysis
of shells with discrete rings. The user is cautioned not to neglect
these terms, in particular not to neglect the out-of-plane bending
stiffness of the discrete rings (I_x). Such neglect may lead to very
low estimates of the buckling loads, particularly in cases in which
the ring is prestressed in compression and in which its centroid is
located at several shell thicknesses away from the reference surface.
Note also, that if the web of the ring is very thin in comparison
with its length (height), the composite shell-ring structure may fail
by crippling or "sidesway" of the web. These failure modes can be
predicted by treatment of the webs as shell branches rather than as
parts of the discrete rings, as described in previous sections. If
a discrete ring occurs at a plane of symmetry, and this plane is used
as a boundary in the analytical model, the user should set the ring
modulus E, torsional rigidity GJ, and density RM, equal to 1/2 their
actual values. All other quantities remain unchanged.
    Also see the note given on the page where the discrete ring input
is defined. This note has to do with the use of discrete rings to
simulate a large mass.

Rigid Body Displacement

For n = 0 and n = 1 circumferential waves, rigid body motion is
possible if the shell is not sufficiently constrained by the boundary
conditions. The six possible rigid body modes, three translational
and three rotational, can be prevented by choosing a meridional
station at which to restrain the axial displacement u^* and the circumferential displacement v. The BOSOR4 manual describes an input
variable, IRIGID, through which rigid body constraints are introduced in order to prevent n = 0 and n = 1 rigid body displacements.
For n > 1 these constraints are automatically released and replaced
by whatever the user has specified for IU^*, IV, IW^*, I_χ at the segment number and mesh point number corresponding to the meridional
location at which the rigid body constraints have been applied. In
this way rigid body displacements are prevented without introduction
of spurious stresses.

Behavior at Apex of Shell

Certain regularity conditions exist at the apex of shells the
meridians of which intersect the axis of revolution. These conditions have been satisfied to the extent which the finite difference
model permits. Because of the "half-station" spacing of u and v,
however, all of the regularity conditions are not satisfied exactly
at the apex. This truncation error leads to errors in the local
values of the stress resultants in the immediate neighborhood of the
apex. The actual stress resultants at the apex can be obtained
simply by extrapolating the solution from a region slightly away from
the apex in which it is regular.

Buckling and Vibration of Structures with Planes of Symmetry

A fairly common oversight on the part of a program user is the
failure to run a case in which buckling and vibration modes are
sought which are antisymmetric with respect to a plane of symmetry.
If half a shell or a part of a shell is being analyzed because of
the existence of planes of symmetry, then the analyst should check
for buckling and vibration both symmetrical and antisymmetrical with
respect to the planes of symmetry. See the paragraph on "Correct Modeling of Discrete Rings" for how to model a discrete ring at a plane
of symmetry.

Calculation of Same Eigenvalue Twice, Eigenvalues Out of Order

In problems for which the user requires more than about 5 eigenvalues
for a given circumferential wave number N, the eigenvalue extraction
routine occasionally computes the same eigenvalue and eigenvector more
than once. It is also possible on occasion that eigenvalues will be
calculated out of order or that an eigenvalue will be missed. Un-
fortunately, there is no way to make an eigenvalue finder based on

equations of the type used in the BOSOR4 program 100% reliable. The
calculated eigenvalues are always eigenvalues of the system, but
occasionally some eigenvalues may be repeated or missed. If it is
suspected that an eigenvalue has been missed, it may help to run the
case with a different number of mesh points, or to run the same case
with a higher value of NVEC.

Multiple or Closely-Space Eigenvalues

In the case of ring stiffened shells it may turn out that eigenvalues
corresponding to vibration frequencies or buckling loads are close
together. This is particularly true of ring stiffened cylinders
where the rings are equally spaced and rather stiff in bending compared to the shell bending stiffness. With such a configuration
there are many modes in which the motion of the rings is of small
amplitude compared to that of the shell. The bays between the rings
vibrate at frequencies or buckle at loads which may approximate
those corresponding to a simply-supported cylinder of the same
geometry as the bay. Multiple or close-spaced eigenvalues correspond to modes in which one or more of the bays is vibrating or
buckling while others are unaffected. True multiple eigenvalues are
generally eliminated by use of symmetry and antisymmetry conditions
at planes of symmetry in the shell. In eigenvalue problems the user
should always analyze as small a segment of shell as possible in
order to avoid numerical difficulties associated with multiple
eigenvalues.

Block Sizes Too Large

On occasion the user will encounter the diagnostic "Block size of
Segment No. ..... exceeds maximum allowable ..... .
    What is a block? In BOSOR4 the stiffness, mass, and load-
geometric matrices are stored on disk or drum in blocks. The logic
in the program is set up such that a given block must contain the information relevant to assembly of complete shell segments. The
lowest possible number of segments per block is one, of course.
Figure A16 shows a stiffness matrix configuration. Only the elements
inside the "skyline" — the heavy line enclosing all non-zero elements
below and including the main diagonal — are stored. The block size
is equal to the number of little squares. In prebuckling problems
the maximum block size is 2850; in stability, vibration, and nonsymmetric stress problems the maximum block size is 3333. The program
checks at the end of each segment to see if the elements corresponding to the next segment will cause the block to overflow. If they do,
a new block is started.

It occasionally happens that the number of elements within the "skyline" corresponding to a single segment exceeds one or both of the allowable limits of 2850 or 3333. For example, referring to Figure A16, one can imagine that if the horizontal "skyscrapers" corresponding to the juncture conditions in segment ② were very long, or if there were very many of them, the number of little squares within the skyline from Equation 30 to Equation 64 (Segment ②) might exceed the allowable limits. It is this situation that causes the message "Block size ... exceeds maximum allowable...." to be printed and the run to be aborted. The user can almost always find a way around this problem by reordering the segments or dividing up the segment with many branch conditions into more than one segment.

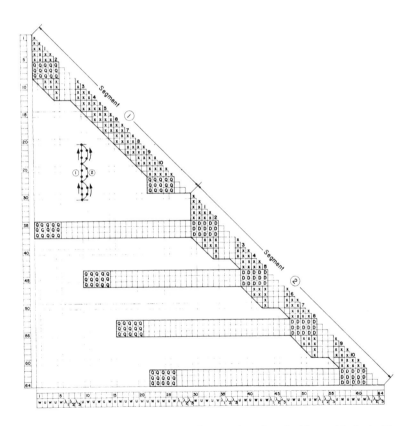

Fig. A16 Stiffness matrix configuration for double-walled shell fastened intermittently.

Moment Resultants and Reference Surface Location

More than one BOSOR4 user has indicated concern about the values
obtained for the moment resultants M10, M20 or M1, M2. In this paragraph it is emphasized that these moment resultants are the values
with respect to the reference surface, which may not necessarily be
the middle surface. The magnitude of the moment resultants depends,
therefore, on the location of the reference surface relative to the
shell wall material. For example, in a uniformly loaded monocoque
cylinder, if the inner or outer surface is used as the reference
surface, the moments M1, M2 will approach the values

$$\left| M1 \right| = \left| N1 \right| t/2; \quad \left| M2 \right| = \left| N2 \right| t/2$$

far away from the edges. (t = thickness; N1, N2 = stress resultants)
Note, however, that the extreme fiber stresses are of course not
dependent on the location of the reference surface. In this connection please recall that the commonly used formula for extreme fiber
stress

$$\sigma = \frac{N}{t} \pm \frac{6M}{t^2}$$

only applies if the shell is monocoque and if the middle surface is
used as the reference surface.

Remarks on the Hemisphere Vibration

In this sample case the control integer IRIGID is set equal to unity.
While this case does illustrate the proper mechanical use of the
IRIGID ≠ 0 option to prevent rigid body motion associated with n = 0
and n = 1 circumferential waves, the choice of a vibration analysis for
the demonstration is a poor one, since the frequencies corresponding to
n = 0 and n = 1 will depend upon the location of the constraints. The
frequencies and modes will correspond to the actual free-free hemisphere vibrations only if the constraints are imposed such that the
center of mass of the structures does not move during vibration in the
n = 0 or n = 1 modes. Actually, in vibration analyses it is never
necessary to set IRIGID ≠ 0. To put it more clearly, IRIGID should be
zero in vibration analyses. Note, however, that this case does
illustrate the proper way to handle the problem of rigid body motion,
which must be handled in stress and stability analyses.

Modeling Global Moments and Shear Forces

The user may wish to determine local stresses in a shell structure
caused by certain known global moments and shear forces. Figure A17
shows one way in which the global forces might be converted into
equivalent line loads. A cylinder with an end ring is loaded by a net
shear force and moment (a). The shear force is assumed to act uniformly around the circumference as shown in (b). At every circumferential station θ , the shear force in (b) is resolved into components

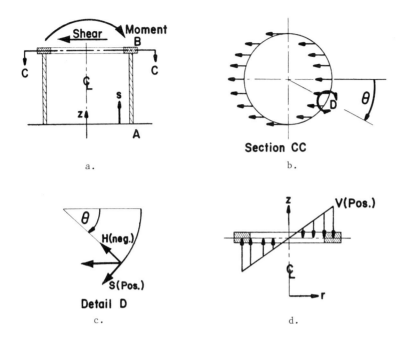

Fig. A17 Modeling global moments and shear forces

normal (H) and tangential (S) to the ring centroidal axis (c). The
"global" moment M is modeled as an axial load which varies around the
circumference as shown in (d). With the coordinate system shown it is
clear that

$$V = V_o \cos\theta, \; S = S_o \sin\theta, \; H = H_o \cos\theta$$

with V_o and S_o positive and H_o negative. Referring to Table A2 we
see that for this circumferential distribution of line loads we must
use n = -1 as input to BOSOR4. (NSTART = NFIN = -1, INCR = 1 or -1)

Shear Line Loads, Concentrated or Otherwise

BOSOR4 users have had difficulty providing the correct input for shear
line loads. This paragraph should help to clear up the trouble.
Figure A18 shows an example of a ring with equal concentrated loads S
applied at $\theta = 90^\circ$ and $\theta = 270^\circ$. In BOSOR4 concentrated

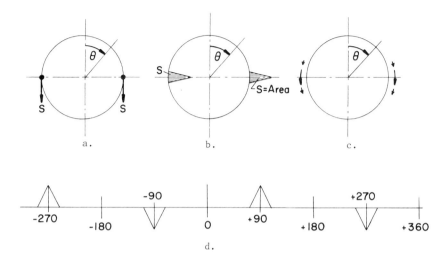

Fig. A18 Concentrated shear loads

loads are handled by spreading them out over a finite angle, say 5°
or 10°, as shown in Fig. A18. The sign convention for shear loads
is such that positive S is in the direction of increasing circumferential coordinate θ. Thus, if we plotted the triangular peaks
shown in Fig. A18b on a rectilinear scale, we would obtain the odd
function shown in Fig. A18d. It is emphasized that even though the
shear loading is symmetrical about $\theta=0$, as seen from Fig. A18a, it
is described by an odd function in the interval $-180°<\theta<180°$. In
this example, therefore, THETAM would be $180°$, NODD would be 2, and
the Fourier Harmonics −1 through −39 in steps of −2 would be used,
since negative harmonics imply that the shear force varies as $\sin|N|\theta$.
Also note that the entire range $-180°< \theta <180°$ must be used, since
the function repeats every 360°. If in Fig. A18a the S at 270° pointed
upward, then the function would be even, THETAM would be 90°, and the
Fourier harmonics would be +0, +2, +4, ..., +38.

Best Way to Run Cases with the INDIC = 1 Option

The BOSOR4 User's Manual says that with INDIC = 1 a linear buckling
analysis is performed. Actually, this is not strictly so. With
INDIC = 1 BOSOR4 performs a nonlinear prebuckling analysis for the
"fixed" or "initial" loads, P, V ( ), etc., and then another nonlinear prebuckling analysis for P + DP, V( ) + DV( ), etc. The
prestresses and shape change (meridional rotation distribution χ_o)
corresponding to the initial loads P, V( ), etc., modify the stability

stiffness matrix. The changes in meridional and hoop stress resultants N_{10} and N_{20} due to the load increments DP, DV( ), etc., contribute terms to the so-called "load-geometric" matrix or "Lambda-matrix." The critical loads are then

$$P_{cr} = (P + (Eigenvalue)*DP)*PDIST$$

$$V( )_{cr} = V( ) + (eigenvalue)*DV( ); \text{ etc.},$$

where PDIST represents the meridional distribution of pressure. It is best, when doing an INDIC = 1 type of buckling analysis, to observe the following two rules:

1. Never have both non-zero initial load and non-zero increment for the same type of load.

EXAMPLE: P = 0.0, DP = 1.0 is O.K.

P = 50.0, DP = 1.0 is inadvisable, mainly because the user could easily err in interpreting the eigenvalue.

ANOTHER EXAMPLE: P = 0.0, DP = -1.0

V(1) = 75.0, DV(1) = 0.0 is O.K. because P and V(1) are different kinds of loads.

2. Always choose loads that are small compared to the design load of the structure. In other words, choose magnitudes of the loads for which the prebuckling behavior really is linear. It is generally advisable to set DP = -1.0, for example, since the eigenvalue then represents the critical pressure directly. Remember that the actual pressure is DP*f(s), where f(s) is the meridional distribution. (In the examples it is tacitly assumed that f(s) = 1.0.)

Miscellaneous Suggestions

It is often advisable in buckling analyses to use INDIC = 1 with a rather wide range for N for the first run through the computer (linear buckling analysis). With this choice NVEC buckling loads are obtained for circumferential wavenumbers from N = NOB to N = NMAXB in steps of INCRB. The user can obtain multiple buckling loads at a given N only with INDIC = 1 and 4. Computer time is often saved in this manner, since the wavenumber corresponding to the minimum load is often not known a priori, even approximately. Also, there are cases for which two minima exist, and the user must find the absolute minimum. With

INDIC = -1, only the relative minimum will be found unless more than one case is run, each case with its own range of N.

The capability of finding more than one buckling load at a given N is particularly useful to the designer who wishes to find the allowable buckling of a complex shell such as that shown in Fig. 1. The lowest buckling pressure might correspond to buckling of the cylinder, but at a few psi higher the ogive might buckle. Thus, the designer would not greatly improve the overall structure by strengthening just the cylinder. He must know the loads for which each of the segments buckles when these segments are analyzed as part of a larger structure.

In cases for which two eigenvalues are close together or for which bifurcation buckling loads are close to axisymmetric collapse loads, it is occasionally advisable to use INDIC = -2. In this way the first vanishing point of the stability determinant is approached gradually, and if axisymmetric collapse occurs at higher loads than nonsymmetric buckling, the stability determinant will change sign and the bifurcation buckling load will be determined.

With INDIC = 4 there are two possible flows of calculations: If IPRE = 0 the prebuckling stress resultants N_{10} and N_{20} and the prebuckling meridional rotation χ_o are read in directly for a certain number, NSTRES, of meridional stations. Linear interpolation is performed internally for calculation of these prebuckling quantities at all of the mesh stations of each segment. Buckling loads (NVEC eigenvalues for each circumferential wave number N) are then calculated for the range NOB to NMAXB in steps of INCRB. If IPRE ≠ 0 the prebuckling quantities are calculated from the linear theory for nonsymmetrically loaded shells, just as if INDIC were equal to 3. The user preselects the meridian (value of θ, called THETAS, which he feels represents the "worst" prestress from the point of view of stability. For example, a cylinder submitted to external pressure which varies around the circumference will generally buckle where the pressure has the highest amplitude. The BOSOR4 program will use the meridional stress distribution at θ = THETAS in the stability calculations. In the stability analysis the flow of calculations for both cases IPRE = 0 and IPRE ≠ 0 is the same as that for INDIC = 1.

BOSOR4 OUTPUT

Nomenclature of the BOSOR4 Output (Sample Units)

(Units do not have to be in in. and lb)

ALPHA1	angle from axis to beginning of spherical segment (degrees)
ALPHA2	angle from axis to end of spherical segment
ALPHAT	distance from axis to center of curvature of spherical segment
AREA	discrete ring cross-sectional area $(in.^2)$
BETA	meridional rotation, denoted χ in analysis (radians)
CHIO	prebuckling rotation χ_o (radians)
CUR1	meridional curvature, $1/R_1$ $(in.^{-1})$
CUR2	normal circumferential curvature, $1/R_2$ $(in.^{-1})$
CUR1D	s derivative of meridional curvature, $(1/R_1)$ $(in.^{-2})$
DET	stability determinant "mantissa": Determinant = $DET*10^{NEX}$
DH	eigenvalue radial line load or radial line load increment (lb/in.)
DM	eigenvalue meridional moment, or meridional moment increment (in.-lb/in.)
DP	eigenvalue pressure multiplier, or pressure increment multiplier (psi)
DTEMP	eigenvalue temperature rise multiplier, or temperature rise increment multiplier
DV	eigenvalue axial line load or axial line load increment (lbs/in.)
EIGENVALUE	Meaning depends upon case. (See following section)
ER	discrete ring modulus of elasticity (psi)
E1	discrete ring radial eccentricity (in.)
E2	discrete ring axial eccentricity (in.)
GJ	discrete ring torsional rigidity $(lb\text{-}in.^2)$
H	"fixed" or initial radial line load (lb/in.)
ITER	number of Newton-Raphson iterations for convergence of nonlinear axisymmetric stress analysis to within 0.1%
IX	discrete ring moment of inertia about x axis $(in.^4)$
IY	discrete ring moment of inertia about y axis $(in.^4)$
IXY	discrete ring product of inertia $(in.^4)$

M	"fixed" or initial meridional line moment (in.-lb/in.)
M10, M20	prestress or prebuckling meridional, circumferential moment resultants, (in.-lb/in.)
M1, M2, MT	linear stress analysis meridional, circumferential, twisting moment resultants, (in.-lb/in.)
N10, N20	prestress or prebuckling meridional, circumferential, resultants (lb/in.)
N	circumferential wave number
NEX	exponent for stability determinant (see DET)
P	pressure multiplier (psi)
PU, PV, PW	p_1, p_2, p_3: meridional, circumferential, normal pressure components (psi) for given wave number N
PND	derivative of normal pressure with respect to arc length s
RAD	radius of parallel circle, r, (in.)
RADD	derivative of r with respect to arc length s (r')
RC	radius of discrete ring measured to centroid (in.)
RM	ring material mass density (lb-sec^2/in.^{4})
S(K)	arc length to kth discrete ring (in.)
SHEAR	applied shear line load, (lb/in.)

SIGMA1(IN), S1(IN)	inner fiber meridional stress (psi)	"inner" fiber on left side of increasing arc length. Outer fiber on right side.
SIGMA1(OUT), S1(OUT)	outer fiber meridional stress (psi)	
SIGMA2(IN), S1(IN)	inner fiber circumferential stress (psi)	
SIGMA2(OUT), S2(OUT)	outer fiber circumferential stress (psi)	
SIGMAE(IN), SVON(IN)	inner fiber von Mises "effective" stress (psi)	
SIGMAE(OUT), SVON(OUT)	outer fiber von Mises "effective" stress (psi)	

TEMP	"fixed" or initial temperature rise multiplier
TMR	thermal line moment about x axis M_x^T

TMRX   thermal line moment about y axis M_y^T

TNR   thermal hoop force N_r^T

TN1, TN2   meridional, circumferential thermal stress resultants
            N_1^T, N_2^T.

TM1, TM2   meridional, circumferential thermal moment resultants
            M_1^T, M_2^T

U, UO   meridional displacement component (modal or linear stress
            analysis, prestress analysis) (in.)

UV, USTAR   axial displacement (u^*) for prestress analysis (in.)

V, VSTAR   circumferential displacement component v, v^* in
            nonsymmetric analysis (in.)

V   "fixed" or initial axial line load (lb/in.)

W, WO   normal outward displacement component (modal or linear
            stress analysis, prestress analysis) (in.)

WSTAR   radial displacement w^*

Z   distance from shell leftmost surface to reference
            surface (in.)

Description of Output From Case 1:
Aluminum Frame Buckling (INDIC = 1)

Figure A8 shows the problem. The input data are listed on page 101. This case represents a general buckling and crippling analysis of a "T" shaped frame, and illustrates the phenomenon of more than one minimum in the "plot" of buckling load vs. circumferential wave number.

The frame is treated as a branched "shell" of three segments, the geometry of which is given (with constraint conditions) on the first three pages of output. The user will notice that each segment has two mesh points more than the number provided as input.

Two additional w points are "inserted" automatically between the first and second and last and second-to-last points in each segment. This measure is taken in order to reduce the truncation errors associated with boundaries and to prevent spurious modes associated with the fictitious points. If h is the original mesh spacing at the edges, the "extra" w points are located at h/20 in from the edges. It is emphasized that the user does not need to consider these extra points in making up a case. All quantities are automatically "shifted" to account for the internal change.

It is important to point out that the "stations" and "arc lengths" printed out on page 2 of the output refer to the points at which the energy density E is evaluated and not in general to the w mesh points. Each "energy point" is located half way between adjacent u points. As seen from the sketch below, if the mesh

spacing varies, as it does at the ends of each segment, the "energy
points" do not coincide with the "w points" in regions of varying
spacing.

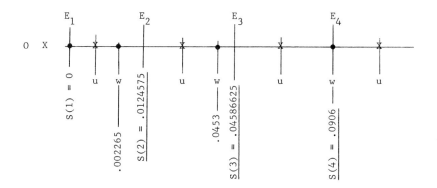

The positions of the first four stations, S(1) - S(4) in this case
are shown in the above sketch. All of the output quantities correspond to the "energy stations" E_1. In addition, discrete rings
are assumed to be attached at the "energy stations," and not at the
"w points." Branch locations also correspond to "energy points,"
and not to "w points."
      Page 4 of the output gives data related to the constraint con-
ditions. Two sets of data appear: those corresponding to the axis-
symmetric prestress problem, and those corresponding to the nonsymmetric bifurcation buckling problem.
      Pages 5 and 6 show the prestress distribution corresponding to
the "fixed" or "initial" components of the loads, that is, corresponding to P and TEMP (and line loads V, H, and M, if such were
present). Pages 6 and 7 show the "total" prestress state, that is
the prestress quantities N_{10}, N_{20}, and χ_o which correspond to loads
P+DP and TEMP+DTEMP (also V+DV, H+DF, M+DM, if such were present).
The prestress distributions corresponding to the predicted buckling
loads λ are given by:

$$N_{10_{cr}} = \left(N_{10_{tot}} - N_{10_{fixed}} \right) \lambda + N_{10_{fixed}}$$

$$N_{20_{cr}} = \left(N_{20_{tot}} - N_{20_{fixed}} \right) \lambda + N_{20_{fixed}}$$

$$\chi_{o_{cr}} = \left(\chi_{o_{tot}} - \chi_{o_{fixed}} \right) \lambda + \chi_{o_{fixed}}$$

in which subscript "fixed" denotes the quantities listed on pages 5 and 6 and "tot" denotes the quantities listed on output pages 6 and 7.

The output on page 7 has to do with calculation of the matrices K_1 and K_2 which is done in the overlay ARRAYS and calculation of the lowest eigenvalue, which is done in the overlay BUCKLE. All of these calculations correspond to two circumferential waves. The line "9 NEGATIVE ROOTS FOR SHIFT, AXT = 0.00" may help the user to determine if any eigenvalues (roots) have been missed. In this case there are nine negative roots for zero shift because there are nine Lagrange multipliers associated with the nine "non-zero" constraint conditions (see integers listed under USTAR VSTAR WSTAR BETA on page 1). The quantity of negative roots for zero shift should always be equal to the quantity of "ones" listed under USTAR VSTAR WSTAR BETA for the stability and vibration and nonsymmetric stress constraint conditions. If several eigenvalues are to be calculated for each wavenumber N, and if the user discovers that a root has been skipped, the lines "9 negative roots ..." can be used with the shifts, AXT to bracket the missing roots, if any. The statement "THERE ARE 1 EIGENVALUES BETWEEN .000 AND .4255236+03" will tell the user if all of the roots in a given load range have been found. This number of roots should equal the input value, NVEC.

The buckling eigenvalues λ and mode shapes for N = 2, 6, 10 and 14 waves are given on pages 8 to 14. The user can see that N = 2 corresponds to overall "ovalization" of the ring with virtually no distortion of the ring cross section. The buckling load q for this type of deformation is approximately

$$L_1 \lambda = q = EI(N^2 - 1)/r_c^3$$

in which L_1 is the length of the first segment (L_1 = .453 in Fig. All) over which the uniform pressure is applied. The buckling loads for higher values of N correspond to crippling of the web (Segment 2).

(1)

START READING DATA FOR THIS CASE
ELAPSED TIME = 0: 0: 0. 75

*ADD,P DB*B4TESTDATA.

BEGINNING OF NEXT CASE

ALUMINUM FRAME BUCKLING (INDIC = 1)

STABILITY ANALYSIS WITH LINEAR BENDING PREBUCKLING
ANALYSIS. BUCKLING LOADS CALCULATED FOR N(.LT.,.LT.,NM
AX.

ANALYSIS TYPE = 1, PRINT OPTION = 1, PLOT OPTION = 0, STRESS OPTION = 0, PRESTRESS CALCULATION OPTION = 1

NUMBER OF SHELL SEGMENTS = 3

STRESS CALCULATED FOR CIRCUMFERENTIAL WAVES FROM 0 TO 0 IN INCREMENTS OF 1

INITIAL BUCKLING OR VIBRATION WAVE NO.= 2, MINIMUM WAVE NO.= 2, MAXIMUM WAVE NO.= 16, INCREMENT= 4

1 EIGENVALUES SOUGHT FOR EACH CIRCUMFERENTIAL WAVE NUMBER.

CONSTRAINT CONDITION DATA FOLLOW

SEG. POINT	CONNECTED TO SEG. POINT	USTAR	VSTAR	WSTAR	BETA	RADIAL DISC. D1(I)	AXIAL DISC. D2(I)
1	6	1	1	1	0	0.00000000	0.00000000
1	10	1	1	1	1	0.00000000	0.00000000
2	3	1	1	1	1	0.00000000	0.00000000

PRESSURE MULTIPLIER P = 0.0000 , INCREMENT DP= -1.0000+00, TEMPERATURE MULT,TEMP= 0.0000 , INCREMENT DTEMP= 0.0000

INITIAL LOAD, FSTART = 0.0000 , MAXIMUM LOAD, FMAX = -1.0000+00, STEP SIZE, DP= -1.0000+00

SEGMENT NO, 1 IS A CYLINDER OR CONE,
END POINT COORDINATES (.5218+01, .0000) AND (.5218+01, .4530+00)
REFERENCE SURFACE GEOMETRY FOR SEGMENT NO, 1

STATION	ARC LENGTH	RAD	RADD	CUR1	CUR2	CURID	Z
1	.0000000	.5218000+01	.0000000	.0000000	.1916431+00	.00000000	.00000000
2	.1245750-01	.5218000+01	.0000000	.0000000	.1916431+00	.00000000	.00000000
3	.4586624-01	.5218000+01	.0000000	.0000000	.1916431+00	.00000000	.00000000
4	.9059999-01	.5218000+01	.0000000	.0000000	.1916431+00	.00000000	.00000000
5	.1359000+00	.5218000+01	.0000000	.0000000	.1916431+00	.00000000	.00000000
6	.1812000+00	.5218000+01	.0000000	.0000000	.1916431+00	.00000000	.00000000
7	.2265000+00	.5218000+01	.0000000	.0000000	.1916431+00	.00000000	.00000000
8	.2718000+00	.5218000+01	.0000000	.0000000	.1916431+00	.00000000	.00000000
9	.3171000+00	.5218000+01	.0000000	.0000000	.1916431+00	.00000000	.00000000
10	.3624000+00	.5218000+01	.0000000	.0000000	.1916431+00	.00000000	.00000000
11	.4071337+00	.5218000+01	.0000000	.0000000	.1916431+00	.00000000	.00000000
12	.4405424+00	.5218000+01	.0000000	.0000000	.1916431+00	.00000000	.00000000
13	.4529999+00	.5218000+01	.0000000	.0000000	.1916431+00	.00000000	.00000000

PHYSICAL PROPERTIES OF SEGMENT NO, 1

ANALYSIS IS FOR A MONOCOQUE SHELL

MODULUS OF ELASTICITY= .10400+08   POISSON RATIO= .33300+00   SHELL DENSITY = .00000   THERMAL EXP COEF, = .00000

MESH POINT	STATION	REF, SURFACE	THICKNESS
1	0.00000	0.00000	1.82000-01
2	1.24575-02	0.00000	1.82000-01
3	4.58662-02	0.00000	1.82000-01
4	9.05900-02	0.00000	1.82000-01
5	1.35900-01	0.00000	1.82000-01
6	1.81200-01	0.00000	1.82000-01
7	2.26500-01	0.00000	1.82000-01
8	2.71800-01	0.00000	1.82000-01
9	3.17100-01	0.00000	1.82000-01
10	3.62400-01	0.00000	1.82000-01
11	4.07134-01	0.00000	1.82000-01
12	4.40542-01	0.00000	1.82000-01
13	4.53000-01	0.00000	1.82000-01

SEGMENT NO, 2 IS A CYLINDER OR CONE,

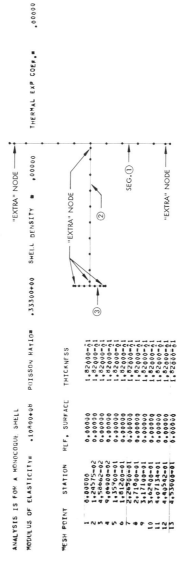

"EXTRA" NODE

"EXTRA" NODE

②

③

SEG. ①

"EXTRA" NODE

③

END POINT COORDINATES (.5218+01, .0000) AND (.4882+01, .0000)
REFERENCE SURFACE GEOMETRY FOR SEGMENT NO. 2

STATION	ARC LENGTH	RAD	RADD	CUR1	CUR2	CURID	Z
1	.4529999+00	.5218000+01	-.1000000+01	.0000000	.0000000	.0000000	.7500000-02
2	.4632005+00	.5247333+01	-.1000000+01	.0000000	.0000000	.0000000	.7500000-02
3	.4979998+00	.5180200+01	-.1000000+01	.0000000	.0000000	.0000000	.7500000-02
4	.5270006+00	.5143333+01	-.1000000+01	.0000000	.0000000	.0000000	.7500000-02
5	.5693397+00	.5106001+01	-.1000000+01	.0000000	.0000000	.0000000	.7500000-02
6	.6023330+00	.5068067+01	-.1000000+01	.0000000	.0000000	.0000000	.7500000-02
7	.6399962+00	.5031334+01	-.1000000+01	.0000000	.0000000	.0000000	.7500000-02
8	.6799996+00	.4994001+01	-.1000000+01	.0000000	.0000000	.0000000	.7500000-02
9	.7143333+00	.4956667+01	-.1000000+01	.0000000	.0000000	.0000000	.7500000-02
10	.7433326+00	.4919335+01	-.1000000+01	.0000000	.0000000	.0000000	.7500000-02
11	.7813328+00	.4882000+01	-.1000000+01	.0000000	.0000000	.0000000	.7500000-02
12	.7899994+00	.4882001+01	-.1000000+01	.0000000	.0000000	.0000000	.7500000-02

PHYSICAL PROPERTIES OF SEGMENT NO. 2

ANALYSIS IS FOR A MONOCOQUE SHELL

MODULUS OF ELASTICITY= .1080000+08   POISSON RATIO= .3330+00   SHELL DENSITY = .00000   THERMAL EXP COEF.= .00000

MESH POINT	STATION	REF. SURFACE	THICKNESS
1	4.53000-01	7.50000-03	1.50000-02
2	4.63267-01	7.50000-03	1.50000-02
3	4.90800-01	7.50000-03	1.50000-02
4	5.27007-01	7.50000-03	1.50000-02
5	5.65000-01	7.50000-03	1.50000-02
6	6.02333-01	7.50000-03	1.50000-02
7	6.39067-01	7.50000-03	1.50000-02
8	6.77000-01	7.50000-03	1.50000-02
9	7.14333-01	7.50000-03	1.50000-02
10	7.41200-01	7.50000-03	1.50000-02
11	7.78733-01	7.50000-03	1.50000-02
12	7.89000-01	7.50000-03	1.50000-02

SEGMENT NO. 3 IS A CYLINDER OR CONE.
END POINT COORDINATES (.4882+01, .0000) AND (.4882+01, .8900-01)
REFERENCE SURFACE GEOMETRY FOR SEGMENT NO. 3

STATION	ARC LENGTH	RAD	RADD	CUR1	CUR2	CURID	Z
1	.7899994+00	.4882020+01	.0000000	.0000000	.2443408+00	.0000000	.1500000-01
2	.7937791+00	.4882020+01	.0000000	.0000000	.2443408+00	.0000000	.1500000-01
3	.8040168+00	.4882000+01	.0000000	.0000000	.2443408+00	.0000000	.1500000-01
4	.8186660+00	.4882000+01	.0000000	.0000000	.2443408+00	.0000000	.1500000-01
5	.8339990+00	.4882000+01	.0000000	.0000000	.2443408+00	.0000000	.1500000-01
6	.8483427+00	.4882000+01	.0000000	.0000000	.2443408+00	.0000000	.1500000-01
7	.8629811+00	.4882000+01	.0000000	.0000000	.2443408+00	.0000000	.1500000-01

```
8   .87392077+00   .4882000+01   .00000000   .00000000   .00000000   .24253408+00   .00000000   .1500000-01
9   .8779999+00    .4882000+01   .00000000   .00000000   .24253408+00   .00000000   .1500000-01   .00000
```

PHYSICAL PROPERTIES OF SEGMENT NO. 3

ANALYSIS IS FOR A MONOCOQUE SHELL

MODULUS OF ELASTICITY= .10600+08   POISSON RATIO= .33300+00   SHELL DENSITY = .00000   THERMAL EXP COEF.= .00000

AXISYMMETRIC PRESTRESS INPUT CONSTRAINT CONDITIONS FOLLOW

```
CONSTRAINT NO. 1  SEGMENT NO. 1  POINT  1  CONNECTED TO SEGMENT NO. 1  POINT  1...TYPE OF CONSTRAINT = 1
CONSTRAINT NO. 2  SEGMENT NO. 2  POINT  7  CONNECTED TO SEGMENT NO. 2  POINT  2...TYPE OF CONSTRAINT = 4
CONSTRAINT NO. 3  SEGMENT NO. 3  POINT 12  CONNECTED TO SEGMENT NO. 3  POINT  5...TYPE OF CONSTRAINT = 4
```

LOCAL MATRIX DIMENSION= 5 OVERLAP= 3 NO. CONSTRAINT CONDS, PER CONSTRAINT POINT= 3 SYSTEM RANK= 86 NUMBER OF BLOCKS= 1

```
NUMBER OF EQUATIONS ASSOCIATED WITH SEGMENT NO. 1 EQUALS 32.   NO. OF CONSTRAINT PTS. EQUALS 1
NUMBER OF EQUATIONS ASSOCIATED WITH SEGMENT NO. 2 EQUALS 30.   NO. OF CONSTRAINT PTS. EQUALS 1
NUMBER OF EQUATIONS ASSOCIATED WITH SEGMENT NO. 3 EQUALS 24.   NO. OF CONSTRAINT PTS. EQUALS 1
BLOCK NUMBER= 1 LAST EQ. IN BLOCK= 86 LOWEST UNK IN BLOCK= 1, MAX. OFF-DIAGONAL WIDTH= 24
```

STABILITY,VIBRATION OR NON-SYMMETRIC STRESS INPUT CONSTRAINT CONDITIONS FOLLOW

```
CONSTRAINT NO. 1  SEGMENT NO. 1  POINT  1  CONNECTED TO SEGMENT NO. 1  POINT  1...TYPE OF CONSTRAINT = 1
CONSTRAINT NO. 2  SEGMENT NO. 2  POINT  7  CONNECTED TO SEGMENT NO. 2  POINT  2...TYPE OF CONSTRAINT = 4
CONSTRAINT NO. 3  SEGMENT NO. 3  POINT 12  CONNECTED TO SEGMENT NO. 3  POINT  5...TYPE OF CONSTRAINT = 4
```

LOCAL MATRIX DIMENSION= 7 OVERLAP= 4 NO. CONSTRAINT CONDS, PER CONSTRAINT POINT= 4 SYSTEM RANK= 126 NUMBER OF BLOCKS= 1

```
NUMBER OF EQUATIONS ASSOCIATED WITH SEGMENT NO. 1 EQUALS 47.   NO. OF CONSTRAINT PTS. EQUALS 1
NUMBER OF EQUATIONS ASSOCIATED WITH SEGMENT NO. 2 EQUALS 44.   NO. OF CONSTRAINT PTS. EQUALS 1
NUMBER OF EQUATIONS ASSOCIATED WITH SEGMENT NO. 3 EQUALS 35.   NO. OF CONSTRAINT PTS. EQUALS 1
BLOCK NUMBER= 1 LAST EQ. IN BLOCK= 126 LOWEST UNK IN BLOCK= 1, MAX. OFF-DIAGONAL WIDTH= 35
```

DATA READ IN AND PROCESSED FOR THIS CASE, LEAVING SUBROUTINE READIT
ELAPSED TIME = 0: 0: 0.715

ENTERING SUBROUTINE PRE, AXISYMMETRIC PRESTRESS CALCULATOR

⑤

****

PRESSURE MULTIPLIER,P = 0.000000   TEMPERATURE MULTIPLIER TEMP = 0.000000

FIXED PART OF AXISYMMETRIC PRESTRESS STATE, THESE QUANTITIES ARE NOT MULTIPLIED BY EIGENVALUE,

PRESTRESS-- MERIDIONAL RESULTANT, N10   CIRCUMFERENTIAL RESULTANT, N20   MERIDIONAL ROTATION, CHIO   FOR SEGMENT 1

	N10	N20	CHIO
1	0.00000000	0.00000000	0.00000000
2	0.00000000	0.00000000	0.00000000
3	0.00000000	0.00000000	0.00000000
4	0.00000000	0.00000000	0.00000000
5	0.00000000	0.00000000	0.00000000
6	0.00000000	0.00000000	0.00000000
7	0.00000000	0.00000000	0.00000000
8	0.00000000	0.00000000	0.00000000
9	0.00000000	0.00000000	0.00000000
10	0.00000000	0.00000000	0.00000000
11	0.00000000	0.00000000	0.00000000
12	0.00000000	0.00000000	0.00000000
13	0.00000000		

FIXED PART OF AXISYMMETRIC PRESTRESS STATE, THESE QUANTITIES ARE NOT MULTIPLIED BY EIGENVALUE,

PRESTRESS-- MERIDIONAL RESULTANT, N10   CIRCUMFERENTIAL RESULTANT, N20   MERIDIONAL ROTATION, CHIO   FOR SEGMENT 2

	N10	N20	CHIO
1	0.00000000	0.00000000	0.00000000
2	0.00000000	0.00000000	0.00000000
3	0.00000000	0.00000000	0.00000000
4	0.00000000	0.00000000	0.00000000
5	0.00000000	0.00000000	0.00000000
6	0.00000000	0.00000000	0.00000000
7	0.00000000	0.00000000	0.00000000
8	0.00000000	0.00000000	0.00000000
9	0.00000000	0.00000000	0.00000000
10	0.00000000	0.00000000	0.00000000
11	0.00000000	0.00000000	0.00000000
12	0.00000000	0.00000000	0.00000000

FIXED PART OF AXISYMMETRIC PRESTRESS STATE, THESE QUANTITIES ARE NOT MULTIPLIED BY EIGENVALUE,

PRESTRESS-- MERIDIONAL RESULTANT, N10   CIRCUMFERENTIAL RESULTANT, N20   MERIDIONAL ROTATION, CHIO   FOR SEGMENT 3

```
1    0.00000000    0.00000000
2    0.00000000    0.00000000
3    0.00000000    0.00000000
4    0.00000000    0.00000000
5    0.00000000    0.00000000
6    0.00000000    0.00000000
7    0.00000000    0.00000000
8    0.00000000    0.00000000
```

ENTERING SUBROUTINE PRE, AXISYMMETRIC PRESTRESS CALCULATOR

****

PRESSURE MULTIPLIER,P = -1.000000+00   TEMPERATURE MULTIPLIER,TEMP =   0.000000

TOTAL PRESTRESS STATE. THESE QUANTITIES MINUS CORRESPONDING FIXED QUANTITIES ARE MULTIPLIED BY EIGENVALUE.

PRESTRESS-- MERIDIONAL RESULTANT, N10   CIRCUMFERENTIAL RESULTANT,N20   MERIDIONAL ROTATION, CHIO   FOR SEGMENT   1

```
 1   -1.3969838-09   -4.7449073+00    2.3155299-08
 2    9.3132575-10   -4.7449777+00    2.3177901+00
 3    6.5288667-09   -4.7451177+00    2.2992009-08
 4   -1.6873628-08   -4.7441405+00    2.1732724-08
 5   -4.8944552-09   -4.7438125+00    1.8287556-08
 6   -4.9581209-09   -4.7435757+00    1.1591312-08
 7    1.3271367-08   -4.7434994+00    1.4651080-15
 8   -5.4924596-09   -4.7435757+00   -1.1591280-08
 9    4.4237822-09   -4.7438125+00   -1.8287527-08
10   -1.6415322-08   -4.7441405+00   -2.1732721-08
11    6.5192586-09   -4.7451017+00   -2.2992005-08
12    9.3132575-10   -4.7449777+00   -2.3177932-08
13   -1.3969838-09   -4.7449073+00   -2.3155298-08
```

TOTAL PRESTRESS STATE. THESE QUANTITIES MINUS CORRESPONDING FIXED QUANTITIES ARE MULTIPLIED BY EIGENVALUE.

PRESTRESS-- MERIDIONAL RESULTANT, N10   CIRCUMFERENTIAL RESULTANT,N20   MERIDIONAL ROTATION, CHIO   FOR SEGMENT   2

```
1   -3.3967737-02   -4.0224989-01    1.4581309-15
2   -3.3240409-02   -4.0297085-01    8.0600857-16
3   -5.1268280-02   -4.0494965-01   -9.4712225-16
```

⑦

```
 4   -2.8500360-02   -4.0763720-01   -3.3013845-15
 5   -2.5798330I-02  -4.1010913-01   -5.7103803-15
 6   -2.2954927P-02  -4.1326231-01   -8.1254413-15
 7   -2.0479981-02   -4.1616924-01   -1.0587013-14
 8   -1.7075829-02   -4.1911617-01   -1.3501900-14
 9   -1.4935852-02   -4.2181405-01   -1.5532494-14
10   -6.0300333-02   -4.2525120-01   -1.9002844-14
11   -6.636759-03    -4.2735230-07   -1.9850003-14
12   -7.7487822-03   -4.2846436-01   -2.0537047-14
```

TOTAL PRESTRESS STATE, THESE QUANTITIES MINUS CORRESPONDING FIXED QUANTITIES ARE MULTIPLIED BY EIGENVALUE.

PRESTRESS-- MERIDIONAL RESULTANT, N10   CIRCUMFERENTIAL RESULTANT, N20   MERIDIONAL ROTATION, CHIO   FOR SEGMENT   3

```
1   -2.2919265-09    -4.2544842I-01   -3.6590458-07
2   -6.9121597J-11   -4.2549816I-01   -3.6796217-07
3   -4.6202309-10    -4.2563181-01    -3.5385556-07
4    9.2496617-10    -4.2579425-01    -3.4629209-07
5   -1.0259102-09    -4.258A637-01    -2.6529209-07
6    9.2406617-10    -4.2579425-01    -2.0537051-14
7   -4.3291947-10    -4.2563181-01     3.5385011-07
8   -6.9121597J-11   -4.2549816-01     3.6786217-07
9   -2.2919265-09    -4.2548421-01     3.6990395-07
```

ENTER SUBROUTINE ARRAYS TO CALCULATE STIFFNESS MATRIX, LOAD*GEOMETRIC MATRIX*L**2 MATRIX, OR MASS MATRIX,   2 WAVES

ENTER FAND2 TO CALCULATE LOWEST   1   EIGENVALUES.   *AVENUMBER*N=   2 WAVES

Q   NEGATIVE ROOTS FOR SHIFT, AXT =   0.00000

ITERATIONS HAVE CONVERGED FOR EIGENVALUE NO.   1   BUCKLING LOAD FACTOR=   4.25596+02,   2 CIRCUMFERENTIAL WAVES
ELAPSED TIME = 01 01 2.936

10   NEGATIVE ROOTS   FOR SHIFT, AXT =   -4.2552+02

THERE ARE   1 EIGENVALUES BETWEEN   .000000   AND   .4255236+03

BUCKLING LOADS AND MODES FOLLOW

CIRCUMFERENTIAL WAVE NUMBER, N =   2

⑧

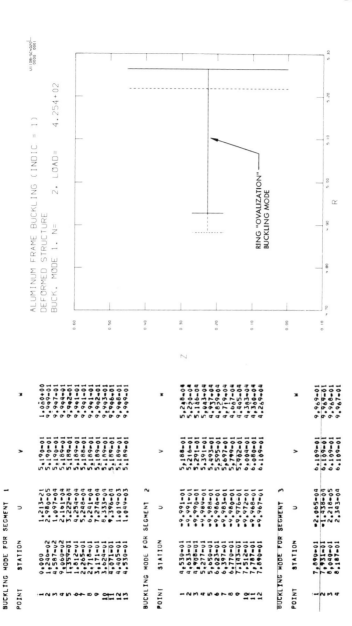

ALUMINUM FRAME BUCKLING (INDIC = 1)
DEFORMED STRUCTURE
BUCK. MODE 1. N=   2. LOAD=   4.254+02

RING "OVALIZATION"
BUCKLING MODE

EIGENVALUE9 =   4.25396+02

MODE SHAPE FOR EIGENVALUE NO. 1 FOLLOWS

BUCKLING MODE FOR SEGMENT 1

POINT	STATION	U	V	W
1	0.000	1.213−21	5.190−01	1.000+00
2	1.240−02	2.980−05	5.190−01	9.999−01
3	4.587−02	1.697−04	5.189−01	9.997−01
4	9.060−02	2.181−04	5.188−01	9.994−01
5	1.359−01	3.222−04	5.189−01	9.992−01
6	1.812−01	4.254−04	5.189−01	9.991−01
7	2.265−01	5.248−04	5.188−01	9.991−01
8	2.718−01	7.201−04	5.189−01	9.991−01
9	3.171−01	7.274−04	5.189−01	9.992−01
10	3.624−01	8.333−04	5.189−01	9.993−01
11	4.071−01	9.396−04	5.189−01	9.996−01
12	4.405−01	1.019−03	5.189−01	9.998−01
13	4.530−01	1.049−03	5.189−01	9.999−01

BUCKLING MODE FOR SEGMENT 2

POINT	STATION	U	V	W
1	4.530−01	−9.991−01	5.188−01	5.248−04
2	4.633−01	−9.991−01	5.216−01	5.220−04
3	4.905−01	−9.990−01	5.291−01	5.186−04
4	5.277−01	−9.989−01	5.492−01	5.043−04
5	5.650−01	−9.988−01	5.595−01	4.937−04
6	6.023−01	−9.986−01	5.697−01	4.852−04
7	6.397−01	−9.983−01	5.799−01	4.719−04
8	6.770−01	−9.980−01	5.902−01	4.607−04
9	7.143−01	−9.976−01	6.004−01	4.495−04
10	7.512−01	−9.972−01	6.004−01	4.383−04
11	7.788−01	−9.968−01	6.080−01	4.300−04
12	7.890−01	−9.967−01	6.109−01	4.269−04

BUCKLING MODE FOR SEGMENT 3

POINT	STATION	U	V	W
1	7.890−01	−2.005−04	6.109−01	9.969−01
2	7.931−01	−1.438−04	6.109−01	9.969−01
3	8.040−01	2.218−05	6.109−01	9.968−01
4	8.187−01	2.343−04	6.109−01	9.967−01

(9)

```
5    8.335-01    4.269-04    6.109-01    9.967-01
6    8.483-01    6.194-04    6.109-01    9.967-01
7    8.630-01    8.315-04    6.109-01    9.968-01
8    8.739-01    9.975-04    6.109-01    9.969-01
9    8.780-01    1.060-03    6.109-01    9.969-01
                 ELAPSED TIME = 01 01 3.329
```

ENTERING SUBROUTINE PLOT

WE ARE ENTERING S-H GEOPLT TO PLOT THE UNDEFORMED STRUCTURE

WE ARE ENTERING S-R GEOPLT TO PLOT THE DEFORMED STRUCTURE

ENTER SUBROUTINE ARRAYS TO CALCULATE STIFFNESS MATRIX, LOAD-GEOMETRIC MATRIX(L**2 MATRIX), OR MASS MATRIX,   6 WAVES

ENTER FBAND2 TO CALCULATE LOWEST 1 EIGENVALUES.   WAVENUMBER,N=   6 WAVES

9 NEGATIVE ROOTS FOR SHIFT, AXT = 0.00000

9 NEGATIVE ROOTS FOR SHIFT, AXT = -2.11715+03

THERE ARE   0 EIGENVALUES BETWEEN   .0000000 AND .2117150+04

ITERATIONS HAVE CONVERGED FOR EIGENVALUE NO. 1, BUCKLING LOAD FACTOR= 2.13839+03,   6 CIRCUMFERENTIAL WAVES
          ELAPSED TIME = 01 01 5.287

10 NEGATIVE ROOTS FOR SHIFT, AXT = -2.13904+03

THERE ARE 1 EIGENVALUES BETWEEN   .0000000 AND .2139035+04

BUCKLING LOADS AND MODES FOLLOW

CIRCUMFERENTIAL WAVE NUMBER, N =   6

⑩

ALUMINUM FRAME BUCKLING (INDIC = 1)
DEFORMED STRUCTURE
BUCK. MODE 1. N=   6. LOAD=   2.138+03

WEB CRIPPLING
BUCKLING MODE

EIGENVALUES =   2.1383+03

MODE SHAPE FOR EIGENVALUE NO. 1 FOLLOWS

BUCKLING MODE FOR SEGMENT 1

POINT	STATION	U	V	W
1	0.000	2.504-23	-8.058-04	-4.495-03
2	1.286-02	4.121-06	-8.347-04	-4.186-03
3	4.587-02	1.779-05	-6.969-04	-3.517-03
4	9.060-02	4.133-05	-5.112-04	-2.016-03
5	1.335-01	7.231-05	-3.213-04	-1.694-03
6	1.842-01	1.197-04	-1.297-04	-1.657-04
7	2.265-01	1.270-04	2.160-05	1.670-04
8	2.718-01	9.218-05	2.546-05	2.154-03
9	3.171-01	1.050-04	4.494-04	2.149-03
10	3.624-01	9.038-05	6.405-04	3.107-03
11	4.071-01	8.312-05	8.278-04	3.959-03
12	4.405-01	8.107-05	9.669-04	4.667-03
13	4.530-01	8.213-05	1.019-03	4.984-03

BUCKLING MODE FOR SEGMENT 2

POINT	STATION	U	V	W
1	4.530-01	-1.970-04	6.340-04	1.359-04
2	4.653-01	-1.969-04	6.475-05	1.665-03
3	4.908-01	-1.965-04	6.825-05	2.052-02
4	5.277-01	-1.959-04	7.305-05	7.717-02
5	5.650-01	-1.952-04	7.800-05	1.582-01
6	6.023-01	-1.945-04	8.325-05	2.064-01
7	6.397-01	-1.937-04	8.860-05	3.975-01
8	6.779-01	-1.929-04	9.431-05	5.343-01
9	7.143-01	-1.920-04	1.002-04	6.817-01
10	7.512-01	-1.910-04	1.064-04	8.356-01
11	7.787-01	-1.902-04	1.112-04	9.499-01
12	7.890-01	-1.899-04	1.131-04	9.973-01

BUCKLING MODE FOR SEGMENT 3

POINT	STATION	U	V	W
1	7.890-01	9.916-01	5.812-02	-1.833-01
2	7.931-01	9.917-01	5.279-02	-1.665-01
3	8.049-01	9.920-01	3.851-02	-1.214-01
4	8.335-01	9.923-01	1.942-02	-6.165-02
5	8.483-01	9.923-01	1.131-04	1.869-04
6	8.483-01	9.922-01	-1.920-02	6.281-02
7	8.630-01	9.920-01	-3.029-02	1.218-01
8	8.739-01	9.917-01	-5.257-02	1.048-01
9	8.780-01	9.916-01	-5.779-02	1.386-01

ELAPSED TIME = 01 01 5.690

```
ENTERING SUBROUTINE PLOT
WE ARE ENTERING S-R GEOPLT TO PLOT THE DEFORMED STRUCTURE


ENTER SUBROUTINE ARRAYS TO CALCULATE STIFFNESS MATRIX, LOAD-GEOMETRIC MATRIX,L**2 MATRIX, OR MASS MATRIX,    10 WAVES

ENTER ERAND2 TO CALCULATE LOWEST   1 EIGENVALUES.          WAVENUMBER,N=    10 WAVES

9 NEGATIVE ROOTS FOR SHIFT, AXT =   0.0000^

9 NEGATIVE ROOTS FOR SHIFT, AXT =  -1.65636+03

THERE ARE    0 EIGENVALUES BETWEEN    .000000^   AND   .165630+04

ITERATIONS HAVE CONVERGED FOR EIGENVALUE NO, 1  BUCKLING LOAD FACTOR=   1.67303+03,    10 CIRCUMFERENTIAL WAVES
                ELAPSED TIME =   0: 0: 7.367

10 NEGATIVE ROOTS FOR SHIFT, AXT =  -1.67353+03

THERE ARE    1 EIGENVALUES BETWEEN    .000000^   AND   .167353+04

BUCKLING LOADS AND MODES FOLLOW

CIRCUMFERENTIAL WAVE NUMBER, N =    10

EIGENVALUES =    1.67303+03  ───── CRITICAL (MINIMUM) LOAD

MODE SHAPE FOR EIGENVALUE NO. 1 FOLLOWS
```

(12)

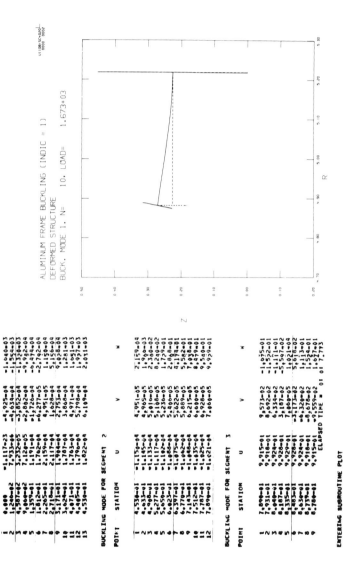

ALUMINUM FRAME BUCKLING (INDIC = 1)
DEFORMED STRUCTURE
BUCK. MODE 1. N= 10. LOAD= 1.673+03

BUCKLING MODE FOR SEGMENT 1

POINT	STATION	U	V	W
1	0.000	-1.117-23	-4.925-04	-1.040-03
2	1.240-02	7.933-06	-4.634-04	-1.554-03
3	4.587-02	3.232-05	-3.852-04	-1.326-03
4	9.066-02	7.120-05	-2.802-04	-9.992-04
5	1.355-01	1.191-04	-1.726-04	-6.474-04
6	1.812-01	1.762-04	-6.277-05	-2.792-04
7	2.265-01	2.159-04	4.951-05	-1.150-04
8	2.719-01	2.117-04	1.928-04	5.156-04
9	3.171-01	1.944-04	2.755-04	4.098-04
10	3.624-01	1.783-04	3.896-04	1.281-03
11	4.077-01	1.783-04	4.971-04	1.651-03
12	4.485-01	1.779-04	5.798-04	1.937-03
13	4.538-01	1.622-04	6.108-04	2.031-03

BUCKLING MODE FOR SEGMENT 2

POINT	STATION	U	V	W
1	4.538-01	-1.159-04	4.951-05	2.159-04
2	4.633-01	-1.145-04	4.965-05	1.906-03
3	4.790-01	-1.133-04	5.010-05	2.300-02
4	5.257-01	-1.117-04	5.106-05	8.290-02
5	6.023-01	-1.122-04	5.236-05	1.729-01
6	6.397-01	-1.075-04	5.400-05	4.176-01
7	6.770-01	-1.062-04	5.589-05	5.582-01
8	7.143-01	-1.046-04	6.215-05	7.059-01
9	7.512-01	-1.035-04	6.600-05	8.497-01
10	7.787-01	-1.025-04	6.928-05	9.540-01
11	7.899-01	-1.021-04	7.060-05	9.929-01

BUCKLING MODE FOR SEGMENT 3

POINT	STATION	U	V	W
1	7.899-01	9.915-01	9.573-02	-1.675-01
2	7.931-01	9.931-01	6.692-02	-1.152-01
3	8.082-01	9.928-01	6.134-02	-5.111-02
4	8.187-01	9.928-01	3.187-02	-5.697-02
5	8.335-01	9.929-01	7.060-05	-3.173-04
6	8.485-01	9.929-01	-3.173-02	5.062-02
7	8.636-01	9.924-01	-6.320-02	1.113-01
8	8.735-01	9.918-01	-8.678-02	1.534-01
9	8.780-01	9.915-01	-9.559-02	1.677-01

ELAPSED TIME = 01 01 7.773

ENTERING SUBROUTINE PLOT

WE ARE ENTERING S-R GEOPLT TO PLOT THE DEFORMED STRUCTURE

(13)

```
ENTER SUBROUTINE ARRAYS TO CALCULATE STIFFNESS MATRIX, LOAD-GEOMETRIC MATRIX,L**2 MATRIX, OR MASS MATRIX,    14 WAVES

ENTER ERAND2 TO CALCULATE LOWEST  1 EIGENVALUES.        WAVENUMBER,N=    14 WAVES

  9 NEGATIVE ROOTS FOR SHIFT, AXT =    0.00000

ITERATIONS HAVE CONVERGED FOR EIGENVALUE NO.  1  BUCKLING LOAD FACTOR=   1.83719+03,    14 CIRCUMFERENTIAL WAVES
                                     ELAPSED TIME = 01 01 9- 90

 10 NEGATIVE ROOTS FOR SHIFT, AXT =  -1.83769+03

THERE ARE  1 EIGENVALUES BETWEEN    .0000000   AND   .183769+04

BUCKLING LOADS AND MODES FOLLOW

CIRCUMFERENTIAL WAVE NUMBER, N =    14

EIGENVALUES =   1.83719+03

MODE SHAPE FOR EIGENVALUE NO.  1 FOLLOWS

BUCKLING MODE FOR SEGMENT  1
POINT  STATION       U          V          W
  1    0.000      1.15R-23   -2.67B-04   -8.150-04
  2    1.246-02   1.50-05    -2.51-04    -7.781-04
  3    4.587-02   5.799-05   -2.084-04   -6.871-04
  4    9.060-02   1.21-04    -1.148-04   -5.36-04
  5    1.359-01   1.944-04   -8.483-05   -3.503-04
  6    1.812-01   2.77-04    -1.643-05   -1.41-04
  7    2.266-01   3.365-04    5.687-05    1.098-04
  8    2.718-01   3.343-04    1.322-04    3.06-04
```

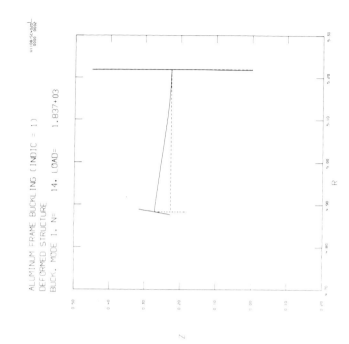

ALUMINUM FRAME BUCKLING (INDIC = 1)
DEFORMED STRUCTURE
BUCK. MODE 1. N=   14. LOAD=   1.837+03

```
 9   3.171-01   3.079-04   2.062-04   5.999-04
10   3.624-01   2.934-04   2.783-04   8.287-04
11   4.071-01   2.792-04   3.491-04   1.050-03
12   4.405-01   2.938-04   4.024-04   1.215-03
13   4.530-01   2.967-04   4.225-04   1.277-03

BUCKLING MODE FOR SEGMENT  2

POINT   STATION      U          V          W

 1   4.530-01  -1.044-04   5.687-05   5.365-04
 2   4.633-01  -1.337-04   5.602-05   2.432-03
 3   4.908-01  -1.210-04   5.394-05   2.795-02
 4   5.277-01  -9.766-05   5.164-05   9.784-02
 5   5.650-01  -9.471-05   4.990-05   2.068-01
 6   6.023-01  -9.211-05   4.900-05   3.257-01
 7   6.397-01  -8.981-05   4.882-05   4.639-01
 8   6.770-01  -8.776-05   4.995-05   6.038-01
 9   7.143-01  -8.588-05   5.110-05   7.418-01
10   7.516-01  -8.412-05   5.384-05   8.719-01
11   7.787-01  -8.283-05   5.650-05   9.615-01
12   7.890-01  -8.235-05   5.766-05   9.941-01

BUCKLING MODE FOR SEGMENT  3

POINT   STATION      U          V          W

 1   7.890-01   9.916-01   1.321-01  -1.391-01
 2   7.931-01   9.921-01   1.199-01  -1.284-01
 3   8.049-01   9.931-01   8.725-02  -9.294-02
 4   8.187-01   9.939-01   4.384-02  -4.665-02
 5   8.335-01   9.941-01   5.766-05   6.215-05
 6   8.484-01   9.939-01  -4.372-02   4.682-02
 7   8.630-01   9.931-01  -8.714-02   9.258-02
 8   8.739-01   9.921-01  -1.197-01   1.265-01
 9   8.780-01   9.916-01  -1.320-01   1.392-01
              ELAPSED TIME =  0: 0: 9.504
```

ENTERING SUBROUTINE PLOT

WE ARE ENTERING S-R GEOPLT TO PLOT THE DEFORMED STRUCTURE

            ELAPSED TIME = 01 01 9.762

START READING DATA FOR THIS CASE
            ELAPSED TIME = 01 01 0.   4

BEGINNING OF NEXT CASE

GIFTS: GRAPHICS ORIENTED INTERACTIVE FINITE ELEMENT TIME-SHARING SYSTEM

Hussein A. Kamel and Michael W. McCabe

University of Arizona

INTRODUCTION

In solving problems using the finite element method, complex models
are generated which need large amounts of data to describe. The process of generating these models is time-consuming. The effort is error
prone and needs extensive checking.

The term model generation is used to denote the total process
of generating nodal coordinates and freedoms, element connectivities
and properties, as well as loads and boundary conditions. GIFTS
represents an attempt to provide the user with a unified and coherent
approach to model generation, model display, analysis, and result
display.

Apart from the lack of a unified approach, finite element program
users have been exposed to other inconveniences. Accessibility of
computers and programs has been inadequate. The turnaround time is
often slow. Analysis programs have different input schemes. Most
available codes can only operate in a large core area, leading to
delays in job execution. Many small engineering outfits may not have
access to a large computer, but are in possession of an in-house
minicomputer which may be utilized to generate and display models, and
indeed to solve them. In larger companies, a specialized group may opt
for installing a minicomputer linked, via a high-speed transmission
line, to the outfit's large batch facility. Thus the mini is utilized
for pre- and postprocessing of models, and the large computer is used
for the solution process, in a batch mode.

The GIFTS 4 system is a collection of program modules operating
on a unified data base (UDB) designed to facilitate the process of
finite element analysis, using modern computer systems. Each program
module has a unique name, such as BULKM, STIFF, and so on. The
following demonstrates how GIFTS can be used to provide a more user-
oriented environment in finite element analysis:

1. One of the primary design goals for the GIFTS package has been
low core requirements. Therefore, it is operational on a number of
large time-sharing systems based on a multitude of main-frames, as
well as on a number of minicomputers. The amount of core required

depends on the program module being executed as well as the particular
computer being utilized. To give examples, 24K to 32K are sufficient
on a minicomputer with overlayed program modules. On a time-sharing
system, 16K to 24K are usually required. The low core requirement
does not restrict program capacity.
   2. GIFTS may be used as a pre- and postprocessor for other
packages. All data generated by the system are stored in a number of
files, called the Unified Data Base (UDB). The format of this UDB
is fixed for a particular GIFTS version, and is well documented. In
order to interface the system to a particular analysis program, it is
only necessary to write two simple linking programs to pass data back
and forth between two sets of program files.
   3. GIFTS is designed to retrieve, for the user, data contained
in a data file, and to present it in numerical or graphic form.
   4. The standard GIFTS terminal is an inexpensive storage tube
device such as a Tektronix 4010 or equivalent. A hard-copy device
is available for such terminals so that report-ready plots can be obtained at the press of a button.
   5. If the computer center stores a number of finite element programs, the user may use GIFTS as the standard pre- and postprocessor
for all of them. Care has been taken that the UDB accepts and stores
data for a wide variety of finite element applications, even though
GIFTS may not be capable of performing the associated computation.

   GIFTS 4 is not a single program but a collection of modules
present in a program library. Individual modules run independently
of each other and communicate only via the UDB. To perform a complete
analysis using GIFTS, the user executes a GIFTS procedure using a number
of modules in a specified order. An overview of the various procedures available is given in the section SYSTEM CAPABILITIES.
   The GIFTS 4 system supports an element library. For details of
the elements and the extent of support offered, the user is referred
to the section THE ELEMENT LIBRARY.
   The section THE UNIFIED DATA BASE explains the concept of the UDB.
The section INSTRUCTION FORMAT AND SOME INSTRUCTIONS OF GENERAL INTEREST
discusses the standard GIFTS 4 instruction format. The HELP COMMAND
describes the HELP command, which may be used to obtain information
regarding the system at execution time. Since this manual is condensed
in order to conserve space, the HELP command is indispensable to the
reader in obtaining additional information regarding the system. It
will always produce up-to-date information on the GIFTS package.
Another source of information is the unabbreviated users' manual, obtainable from the University of Arizona.
   Many GIFTS 4 modules are used in a number of procedures. Therefore, they are described in separate chapters and reference is made
to them in the sections of the manual devoted to the individual procedures. The section MODEL GENERATION AND EDITING deals with modules
used in generating and displaying the model. The section LOAD AND
BOUNDARY CONDITIONS GENERATION, DISPLAY, AND EDITING describes load
and boundary conditions generation and display. The section GENERAL
PURPOSE COMPUTATIONAL AND RESULT DISPLAY MODULES lists computational
modules of general use.
   The section THE GIFTS 4 STATIC SOLUTION PACKAGE describes the basic
static analysis procedure. The section THE GIFTS 4 NATURAL VIBRATION
PACKAGE contains the natural vibration capabilities, whereas the section

THE GIFTS 4 TRANSIENT RESPONSE PACKAGE (DIRECT INTEGRATION) deals with transient response analysis using direct integration. The section THE GIFTS CONSTRAINED SUBSTRUCTURING PACKAGE describes analysis by substructures.

The full GIFTS 4 documentation contains a more detailed users' manual, a theoretical, and a system's manual. The program listing is well commented, which serves as additional documentation.

This document serves as an introduction to the GIFTS system. The user may expect that many additional facilities are available, which are not described here. He may obtain up-to-date information regarding these capabilities by using the HELP command or may obtain documentation by writing to the first author.

How to Use This Manual

Start by reading the introductory sections through THE 'HELP" COMMAND. Now suppose that you want to run a static analysis. Read the section THE GIFTS 4 STATIC SOLUTION PACKAGE, which describes the correct module-running sequence. Try to follow the example given, referring wherever necessary to sections describing the various modules in detail.

SYSTEM CAPABILITIES

The GIFTS system has the following capabilities:

1. Model generation, display, editing, and verification.
2. Display of displacement and stress results.
3. Static analysis using a complete basic library of elements suitable for two-dimensional trusses, frames, and elasticity problems as well as three-dimensional trusses, frames, and shells.
4. Analysis by (constrained) substructures (COSUBs). A major structure may be subdivided into smaller parts, called substructures. These substructures are generated as separate finite element models. Kinematic constraints may be applied to the substructure boundaries in order to reduce the number of external freedoms and, therefore, the number of unknowns and half bandwidth in the main analysis. After the stiffness matrix for such a substructure has been assembled, it is partially decomposed, condensed, and later assembled, together with other substructures and ordinary finite elements, to form the complete structure. Substructures may be attached to the major structure any number of times and intermingled with ordinary finite elements. At the time of assembly, certain transformations of the stiffness and load matrices are possible.

After the main analysis of the complete model has been performed, it is possible to conduct local analyses of each substructure in order to obtain detailed deflections and stresses within it.

5. Free vibration analysis. Any model generated using standard GIFTS elements may be analyzed for a number of the lowest vibrational frequencies and corresponding modes of vibration. The Subspace Iteration method, as developed by Bathe and Wilson, is utilized with im-

proved, automatically generated starting vectors. The vibrational
frequencies are obtained numerically, and the modes may be superimposed
on the model geometry and plotted as a deflected shape. It is also
possible to compute the stresses associated with the mode shape and
plot them using any of the standard stress plotting options. Structures have to be adequately supported.

6. Transient response analysis. The user may define a time-
varying load, to which the structure is subjected. GIFTS will proceed
to obtain the structural response (displacements) using specified time
steps. The user specifies a number of displacement components, for which
a histogram is produced upon request at any time during the analysis.
The full deflected shape may be obtained at any time and the associated
stresses may be computed and plotted. In the analysis both inertia
and damping forces are considered. The Houbolt method (third order
backward difference scheme) is utilized in the time integration process.

THE ELEMENT LIBRARY

The GIFTS system is capable of handling a wide variety of finite
elements. However, the extent of the GIFTS support depends on the
element type. Elements are classified into several categories:

1. Full support. Elements classified under this heading may be
generated and displayed in unstressed and in stressed form. GIFTS is
capable of computing their mass distribution, stiffness matrix, equivalent nodal loads, and stresses. All data pertaining to them may be
accommodated within the UDB according to the GIFTS standard storage
conventions.

Elements within this category include the ROD2, BEAM2, TM3, QM4,
TB3,QB4, and COSUB. (See later for an explanation of mnemonics.)

2. Generation and display only. In this category are elements
that may be generated and displayed using standard GIFTS modules.
The display capability includes both the undeformed and deformed states.
Although it is assumed that element properties will be evaluated in
the analysis program, GIFTS will provide some capability in the area
of mass and load computation. Elements within this category include
ROD3, ROD4, TM6, TM10, QM9, QM16, TB6, TB10, QB9, and QM16.

3. Storage only. In this category elements are included that may
be stored in the UDB according to standard storage conventions. This
category includes practically all other finite element families. In
particular, the following solid elements may be mentioned: TET4,
TET10, SLD8, and SLD27.

NOTE: Should GIFTS continue to be upgraded, it is expected
that elements previously listed under C may be upgraded to B, and
those under B to A.

Elements Enjoying Full Support

ROD2 Element

The constant strain rod element (Fig. 1) joins two nodes. It is
suitable for the modeling of two- and three-dimensional trusses, and
as a stiffener element in conjunction with simple membrane and plate
elements (TM3, QM4, TB3, QB4).

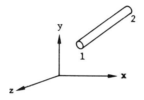

Fig. 1   The constant strain rod (ROD2) element

BEAM2 Element

GIFTS has an extensive BEAM analysis capability. Several common
beam cross section types can be defined using a minimum amount of user-
oriented geometric data. The program then computes all cross-sectional
properties and displays them upon request. All cross sections include
the effect of nonsymmetric bending, shear strains, torsional rigidity,
and position of the shear center and allow for an arbitrary point of
attachment.

A BEAM2 element is defined in terms of three points. The first
two are points of attachment (structural nodes) while the third is
used to define a geometric reference plane. The local horizontal
(reference) axis of the beam cross section (z') lies by default in the
1,2,3 plane and points to the side on which point 3 lies. It may,
however, be tilted at an arbitrary angle, THETA, defined by the user.
Figure 2 shows the most general form of the beam definition.

A cross section is defined in a local geometric reference axis
system, z', y', which corresponds with the "natural" orientation of
the cross section. Figure 3 gives examples of such cross sections. In
beam cross section plots, the beam cross section's principal axes are
plotted on the side and are denoted by p and q. For the purpose of
plots, p and q are chosen such that Ipp .GE. Iqq. The position of the
centroid and shear center of the cross section are also computed and
given as ZG,YG and ZO,YO, respectively, in the offset area of the
screen.

The point of attachment of the beam is, by default, the beam

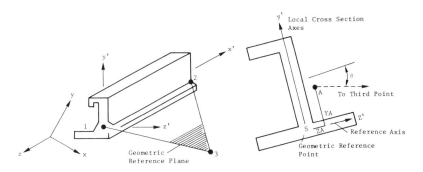

Fig. 2 Definition of the general beam cross section

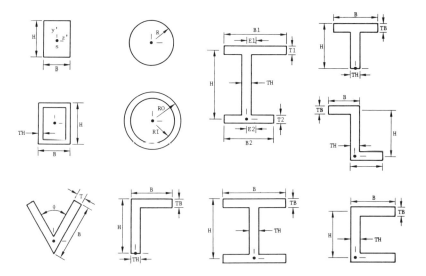

Fig. 3 Standard beam cross sections

centroid. The user may change this, however, by using a special mode
parameter at the time of cross section definition. In this case, the
coordinates of the user-defined point of attachment must be supplied
relative to a standard point of reference whose position depends on
the type of cross section used. In all cross section definitions
(see Figs. 3 to 13) this standard reference point is denoted 'S', and
the direction of the cross section geometric reference axes are clearly
marked.

Once a cross section has been defined, it is considered as a thickness group and may be used to define any number of beam elements. The following standard cross section types are included:

1. Solid circular cross section (CIRCS). The solid circular cross section is defined by its radius R.
2. Hollow circular cross section (CIRCH). The hollow circular cross section is defined by its outside and inside radii, RO and RI.
3. Solid rectangular cross section (RECTS). The solid rectangular cross section is defined by its outside dimensions H and B.
4. Hollow rectangular cross section (RECTH). The hollow rectangular cross section is defined by its outside dimensions H and B, as well as its wall thicknesses TH and TB.
5. Oblique angle (OBANG). The oblique angle cross section is defined with two equal sides of length B, inclined to one another at an angle of PHI. The thickness of the two sides is TH.
6. Generalized I beam (GIBEAM). The general purpose I beam is the basis for a large number of simpler cross sections, which will be described below. It also provides the user with a fairly powerful configuration that may be used to model unusual shapes. The cross section is defined in terms of its height H, width of upper and lower flanges B1 and B2, the thicknesses of web, upper, and lower flanges TH, T1, and T2, as well as flange eccentricities E1 and E2.
7. I beam (IBEAM)--a doubly symmetric I beam whose properties are given by its height H, flange width B, web and flange thicknesses TH and TB.
8. T-section (TBEAM). The T-section, a special case of the general I beam, is defined in terms of its height H, width B, and web and flange thicknesses TH and TB.
9. Z-section (ZBEAM). The Z-section is described in terms of the height and width H and B, as well as the web and flange thicknesses TH and TB.
10. Standard channel (CHANNEL)--a symmetric channel section described in terms of height and width H and B, as well as the web and flange thicknesses TH and TB.
11. Standard angle (ANGLE)--a right angle with unequal lengths, described by the height and width H and B and the thicknesses of its vertical and horizontal walls TH and TB.

TM3 Element

The constant strain membrane triangle TM3 (Fig. 4) is the simplest membrane element for the analysis of two-dimensional elasticity and stiffened membrane problems. It may, however, be oriented in three-dimensional space. The TM3 element is based on the standard assumptions of linearly varying displacements and, therefore, constant strains and stresses.

QM4 Element

A first order isoparametric quadrilateral membrane element is shown in Fig. 5.

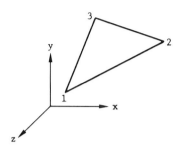

Fig. 4   The triangular membrane element

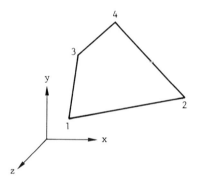

Fig. 5   The quadrilateral membrane element

CAUTION: Quadrilateral membrane elements, whether generated by
the user directly or by an automatic mesh generator, should not be so
highly distorted as to produce poor numerical results. We define
unacceptable distortion as that which produces a ratio of two of the
sides that is greater than four, or a vertex angle smaller than fifteen
degrees or greater than 150 degrees.

TB3 Element

The triangular bending element (Fig. 6) is the primary bending plate
element used to model plates and curved shell elements, as well as
stiffened complex structures. It includes both bending and membrane
effects. The membrane properties are identical to those of the TM3
element. The bending part assumes a linear variation of internal

plate moments, including the twist. The TB3 element has in-plane
bending capabilities controlled by a factor BETA, which may be altered
by the user.

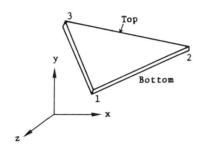

Fig. 6   The triangular bending element

QB4 Element

The quadrilateral bending element (Fig. 7) is made out of a combination
of two TB3 elements. Stress values are averaged, and a separate set
of values is given for each face.

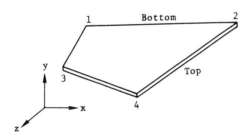

Fig. 7   The quadrilateral bending element

COSUB Element

Definition. The COSUB element (Fig. 8) is a substructure made out of
several elements and nodes. A COSUB is generated during a separate
run, in which its stiffness, mass, and other properties are generated and stored in a separate set of UDB files.
    The COSUB nodes are divided into boundary nodes and internal
nodes. The boundary nodes are, in turn, divided into master nodes and
dependent nodes. Boundary nodes are those along the COSUB/structure
interface. The number of dependent and/or internal nodes may be zero.

The maximum number of external nodes depends on the current GIFTS configuration. At the moment it is set to be 27.

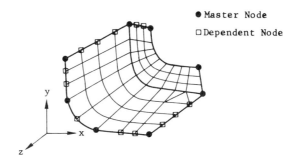

Fig. 8   The constrained substructure element (COSUB)

Generation and assembly of COSUBs.   At the time of assembly of the COSUB to the main structure, only the master nodes are assembled. The displacements of the dependent nodes are kinematically constrained to those of the master nodes. This means that once the displacements of the master nodes are fixed, those of the dependent nodes are found by interpolation and, therefore, are not regarded as free displacements. The internal nodes of the substructure are statically condensed. This means that their displacements are related to those of the master nodes such that equilibrium is satisfied at all internal nodes. COSUBs are handled as ordinary elements by the GIFTS solution and display routines.

If a COSUB is subjected to internal loading, its loads are formed in the usual manner during COSUB generation. At the time of condensation, a condensed stiffness matrix and a condensed load matrix are formed and stored in special files. In effect, the COSUB stiffness matrix is computed in terms of the freedoms of the master nodes alone. The stiffness routine assembles this matrix as an ordinary element stiffness during the main analysis. Similarly, the master node loads, kinematically equivalent to the COSUB loads, are applied to the main structure during the process of loading.

The above explains how the COSUB elements contribute to the main structure stiffness and load matrices. The structure, which may be made out of both ordinary elements and COSUBS, can now be analyzed for displacements and stresses. Since the internal details of the COSUBs are not available within the main structure files, a special local analysis procedure has to be followed to obtain the detailed deflections and stresses within a COSUB.

Boundary constraints.   The following kinematic constraints may be applied to COSUB boundaries:

1.   Rigid constraints, in which dependent nodes are rigidly

attached to a master node.

  2. Linear constraints, in which the translational displacements of dependent nodes are interpolated linearly from those of two master nodes.

  3. Cubic interpolation--the displacements of dependent nodes, except the translation along the line connecting the two master nodes and the rotation about this line, are interpolated from the appropriate translational and rotational displacements of the master nodes using a cubic scheme similar to the displacement functions of beam bending. The two remaining displacements associated with the line connecting the master nodes are interpolated linearly.

  NOTE: In all the above interpolation schemes the dependent points need not lie directly on the straight line joining the master nodes.

Equilibrium checks. One of the advantages of using the COSUB method is the possibility of checking the accuracy of the COSUB solution by examining the equilibrium of the COSUB stiffness matrix. The basis for such an examination is automatically provided by program REDCS.

Order of assembly of COSUB external (master) nodes. In defining the COSUB nodes during COSUB generation and in describing the COSUB within the main structure, it is important to ensure that the nodes are listed in one-to-one correspondence so that the assembly is performed correctly.

Elements for Generation and Storage

The following elements may be generated and displayed using standard GIFTS modules. The GIFTS 4 computational procedures, however, do not support them. These elements are intended primarily as input for other finite element programs. GIFTS is capable of processing the results produced by such programs, provided they are entered in the UDB in the correct format.

  For the elements listed under this section it is possible to:

  1. Generate the elements using BULKM and EDITM.
  2. Display the elements using BULKM and EDITM.
  3. Optimize band width using OPTIM.
  4. Generate loads using BULKLB and EDITLB. This includes diagonal mass matrices, inertia loads, and pressure loads.
  5. Display loads using EDITLB.
  6. Display deflections and stresses using RESULT.

  The following items are elements currently classified under this category.

ROD3 Element

The ROD3 element (Fig. 9) is a higher order linear strain stiffener
element designed for use with TM6, QM9, TB6, and QB9 elements.

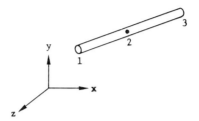

Fig. 9   The linear strain stiffener element ROD3

TM6 and TM10 Elements

The TM6 and TM10 elements (Fig. 10) are quadratic and cubic displacement elements used for accurate determination of displacements and
stresses in two-dimensional elasticity problems.

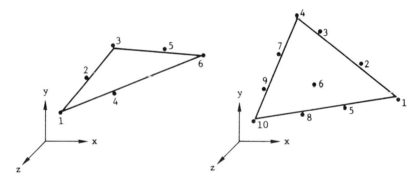

Fig. 10   The higher order membrane triangles TM6 and TM10

QM9 and QM16 Elements

The QM9 and QM16 elements (Fig. 11) are biquadratic and bicubic displacement quadrilateral membrane elements.   They are used to obtain
more accurate solutions to two-dimensional membrane problems, but may
be arbitrarily oriented in space.

Higher Order Bending Triangles TB6 and TB10

The exact derivation of these elements depends on the program being

utilized for displacement and stress computation. They are essentially higher order bending triangles with six or ten corner nodes,
as shown in Fig. 12.

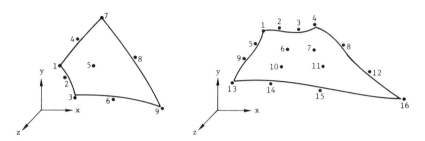

Fig. 11   The higher order membrane quadrilaterals QM9 and QM16

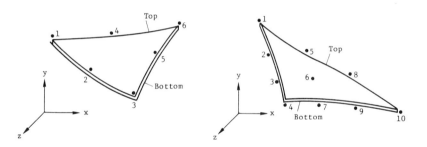

Fig. 12   The TB6 and TB10 bending elements

Second Order Bending Quadrilaterals QB9 and QB16

The detailed derivation of these elements depends on the program being
utilized for displacement and stress computation. They are higher
order bending quadrilateral elements with nine or sixteen nodes, as
shown in Fig. 13.

Elements for Storage Only

Several additional element types have been considered in the design
of the UDB, so that they may be included in the package at a later
date. There are no display, generation, or computational capabilities provided, but conventions have been chosen for their accommoda-

tion in the UDB. Additional modules to handle them may be provided
by the University of Arizona or by some of the GIFTS users at a later
date. Examples of such elements are: solid tetrahedron elements,
solid brick elements, and axisymmetric shell elements.

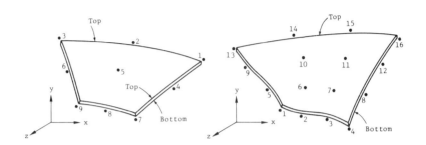

Fig. 13   The QB9 and QB16 bending elements

THE UNIFIED DATA BASE

The GIFTS system stores data relevant to a problem on a number of
files. Typically, a file name is made of two parts. The first part
is identical to the job name, and the second (called the extension)
describes the data. In all time-sharing systems it is possible to
identify the individual files in the disk directory. It is usually
not necessary for the user to manipulate the UDB files directly.
However, it would perhaps be necessary in order to list the extensions of some of the most common files. A detailed description of
the UDB is included in the GIFTS 4 systems manual. Table 1 summa-
rizes basic UDB files.

INSTRUCTION FORMAT AND SOME INSTRUCTIONS OF GENERAL INTEREST

General Instruction Format and On-Line Operation

After the initial loading of a GIFTS interactive module, the program
responds with an asterisk, denoting its readiness to accept commands.
Commands have the general form:

    FUNCTION,MODES
    DATA

    The data may be input on several lines following the function
line. The input of the data is requested by the program through a
prompting character (>). Some systems add a prompting character of
their own. For example, a question mark may be used. After the
data input is complete, a bell is heard from the terminal. Upon

Table 1   Summary of the basic UDB files

File Extension	File Contents
PAR	System and problem control parameters, status list
FIL	File sizes and data management parameters
LIN	BULKM line generation logic
SUR	BULKM Grid (Surface) generation logic
PTS	Nodal point parameters
ELT	Structural element parameters
MAT	Material definition
THS	Thickness definition
SCS	Beam cross section definition
LDS	Nodal point loads
SDY	Stiffness submatrix pointers (Directory)
STF	Stiffness matrix submatrices
DNS	Nodal point deflections
STR	Element stress file

completion of the computation associated with the instruction, a
second bell is heard. In an actual run, the terminal display will
appear as follows:

```
*                       Program instruction prompting
?BOX                    Instruction by user
>                       Program data prompting
?0,50.                  User data
?-5,150.2               Additional data
?-100.5,0               Additional data
                        BELL (Input done)
                        BELL (Computing done)
*                       Program ready for next instruction
?
```

GIFTS instructions are entered in free format. If several variables are entered on the same line, separators are used in between.
A valid separator may be a blank, a series of blanks, a comma, or a
combination of one comma and several blanks in any order. Two successive commas separated by nothing or by one or more blanks denote

the presence of a zero (or blank) variable at the given position.

Each instruction may need no data, or a combination of alphanumeric, integer, and floating point data. The first set of data
is the mode variables, required for some instructions if the execution
is to follow a non-default option. One or two mode variables may
be present. They are always entered as a single integer variable,
following the instruction.

After the line containing the function and modes is entered,
the rest of the data are organized in the following order:

FUNCTION,MODES	MODES is a 2-digit integer (e.g., 21).
ALPHANUMERIC VARIABLES	(1 or more lines)
INTEGER VARIABLES	(1 or more lines)
FLOATING POINT VARIABLES	(1 or more lines)

On-Line Batch Mode of Operation (OLB)

Instructions for interactive GIFTS modules may be created in advance,
using the system text editor, and preserved on a disk file. In this
manner it is possible to repeat an interactive computation with few
changes without having to retype all the necessary commands. The
interactive capabilities are not compromised but enhanced by this
OLB feature.

OLB FILE	Initiates execution from disk file "FILESRC". It continues execution until it encounters another OLB, END, JOB, or QUIT instruction. Terminating the file with the command OLB will result in the continuation of OLB operation, but from a new disk file.
END	Transfers control back to the user, who may continue to input instructions via the terminal.
QUIT	Causes the termination of execution of the program.
JOB	Terminates input from file, finalizes and closes job files, and reinitiates the program for a new job.

Repetitive and Nonrepetitive Instructions

From experience, many functions are executed several times over
once they are called. To avoid retyping the function mnemonic every
time, such functions will automatically ask for one set of data
after another until they encounter a blank or zero data item, which
provides an exit to the next command. It is possible to treat a
nonrepetitive instruction as a repetitive one, since GIFTS ignores
blank instructions. The opposite, however, is not true and will
create errors. As a general rule, all GIFTS 4 commands that require
data, apart from commands which set and reset switches, are repetitive.

Common Plotting Instructions

There are several plotting instructions that are general enough to be included in almost all of the GIFTS plotting programs. These include:

PLOT	Produces a model plot using the current plot switches. The plot is properly labeled.
PLOTNL	Similar to PLOT, but no labeling is produced. Executes faster.
VDIR K, L, M	Sets viewing direction for subsequent plotting parallel to the line through point (K,L,M) and the origin. Default values are (0,0,1) (view down the z-axis). K, L, and M may be either positive or negative. The y-axis is always vertical.
ROTV(,K) AL1(,AL2,AL3)	Specifies that the viewed model is to be rotated about one (or all) of the three screen axes. K specifies the axis about which to rotate the figure: K = 0 All axes (all three ALPHAs read)--In this case, rotation is about the x-axis by AL1, followed by a y-axis rotation of AL2, and then a rotation about the z-axis by AL3. K = 1 Screen x-axis (horizontal axis), by AL1. K = 2 Screen y-axis (vertical axis), by AL1. K = 3 Screen z-axis (perpendicular to screen), by AL1.
VDIS H	Specifies the viewing distance (for perspective) as H units away from the center of the boxed area.
PN	Causes user point numbers to appear and disappear.
SN	Causes system point numbers to appear and disappear.
EN	Causes element numbers to appear and disappear.
ETY	Causes element types to appear and disappear.
MN	Causes material numbers to appear and disappear.
THN	Causes thickness group numbers to appear and disappear.
BOX XMIN,XMAX YMIN,YMAX ZMIN,ZMAX	Restricts viewed area to the region bounded by the given x, y, and z limits. If any pair (e.g., XMIN,XMAX) is given zero or identical values, the model limits along that axis are used.
ELEMENTS	Indicates that elements are to be plotted subsequently. To deactivate, use LINES command.

TYON TYPE	Indicates that elements of type TYPE are to be subsequently plotted. Type may be any of the standard element mnemonics (e.g., TM3, QM4).
TYOFF TYPE	Indicates that elements of type TYPE are not to be subsequently plotted.
LINES	Indicates that only model grid boundaries are to be displayed (not elements).
RESET	Resets all plot parameters to their default values.
WINDOW	Causes a cursor to appear twice on the screen. Each time the user may select a point by moving the cursor to the desired position and pressing any of the keys. The two points chosen by the user are interpreted as the upper left-hand and lower right corners of a window to be used in subsequent plots.

Common Information Commands

As is the case with the plot commands listed above, there are some information commands that are common to most of the interactive program modules in GIFTS. They are:

INFMOD	Produces general information concerning the model being analyzed.
INFP NF(,NL,NT)	Produces a listing of the coordinates and freedom pattern of NT regularly numbered user nodes NF through NL. Default: NL = NF, NT = NL + 1 - NF.
INFE NF(,NL,NT)	Produces a printout of the composition and connectivity of NT regularly numbered elements NF to NL. Default: NL = NF, NT = NL + 1 - NF.

Additional commands which produce listings of other information, such as line and surface definitions, nodal point loads, stresses, and deflections, are available under the appropriate modules. They may be obtained by using the HELP command or by referring to the full users' manual.

THE "HELP" COMMAND

If, during the run, the user needs to refresh his (or her) memory, he (or she) may do this via the HELP command. It is possible, during the execution of any of the GIFTS interactive commands, to request information about the GIFTS 4 procedures, any of the GIFTS modules, or any individual instruction used in any of the modules. This is achieved by typing as data the item on which information is required.
    The HELP command is a repetitive instruction. (See the section above, Repetitive and Nonrepetitive Instructions.) Typical command formats are:

```
    *
    HELP
    >
    GIFTS              Prints out information about all GIFTS proce-
                       dures.
    >
    STATIC             Gives information regarding static analysis
                       procedure.
    >
    EDITM              Describes the module EDITM.
    >
    PLOTNL             Explains the command  PLOTNL .
    >
    >                  New data requested.
    .
    .
```

MODEL GENERATION AND EDITING

Three programs are available in GIFTS 4 for the generation of two-
and three-dimensional trusses and frames as well as plate and shell
problems. The package can be extended to other areas, e.g., 3-D
solids.

A finite element model may be generated using either module
BULKM or EDITM or both. Constrained substructure models are generated in the same manner. In addition, program DEFCS defines the
constrained substructure boundaries.

BULKM is an automated three-dimensional plate and shell model
generator. It is suitable for structures that can be modeled by
generation of interconnected point and element patterns.

EDITM is designed to update and correct BULKM models, although
it can be used to generate simple models and ones too complex for
BULKM.

DEFCS accepts information regarding external and dependent
boundary nodes in a constrained substructure (COSUB).

The Bulk Model Generator (BULKM)

BULKM is an automatic three-dimensional plate and shell model generator. When loaded, it responds with:

```
    BULKM Vxx
    TYPE JOB NAME
```

and waits for the user to type a 4-character job name. The program
checks for the presence of the job on disk. If it does not find it,
it initializes the job and types out a message to that effect. It
then awaits commands from the user.

There are four steps involved in generating a model in BULKM:

    1. Specification of material properties and element thickness
definitions.
    2. Generation of key nodes by number and coordinates.
    3. Generation of lines by alphanumeric identifier (8 charac-
ters), based on previously defined key nodes. Lines may be straight
(SLINE), circular (CARC), or parametric (PARAM2, PARAM3).
    4. Generation of surfaces (grids), defined by line edges and
identified by an 8-character alphanumeric identifier.

    Each element thickness group defines an element dimension and
is assigned a thickness group number. In the case of a rod, the
thickness refers to the cross-sectional area, whereas in a plate or
membrane, it refers to the plate thickness. For beam elements, the
cross section to be used is regarded as a thickness group, and
assigned a number. The appropriate thickness record will contain
the properties of the section as computed by BULKM, from user-provided dimensions. A special file contains the cross section dimensions as originally specified by the user. The command ETH is used
to specify thickness values. For beams, special commands for cross
section definition (CIRCS, TBEAM, ...) are used.
    The command ELMAT is used to specify material properties.
MSTEEL, SSTEEL, and AALLOY define standard materials whose properties are present in the GIFTS 4 library.
    Key nodes can be specified one at a time or in a string using
the KPOINT command. The generation of straight lines, arcs, and
parametric curves uses the key nodes to describe their geometry.
The commands are SLINE, CARC, PARAM2, and PARAM3. The user may
generate rod or beam elements along the lines by setting the appropriate mode parameter. To specify the line element type, the line
element command LETY should be used before a line is generated.
    To generate grids (3-D surfaces) covered with plane elements,
previously defined lines are used in one of the commands: GRID3,
GRID4, GRID3S, GRID4S, ... The elements to be used are specified
via the GETY command before the grid is generated. This sets
the surface element type, thickness, and material number. All subsequent surface element generation will be of that type, thickness,
and material until it is changed. It is also possible to generate
line element stiffeners within the grids by using the LETY command,
while activating the appropriate mode parameters in the grid generation instruction.
    Following is a list of some of the most widely used instruc-
tions and the parameters they require. For a more complete list,
the user should obtain the expanded GIFTS users' manual or use the
HELP instruction described above.

Thickness and Material Specification

ETH,M	Defines an element thickness group, made out of
NTH	variables describing element dimensions. It
T1(,T2,T3,...)	may also be used to redefine an already defined
	set. NTH is the property group number. T1,
	T2, etc., are the thickness parameters. M

determines how many thickness parameters are to
be read and stored on the file. Valid values
for M are 1 or more. For the TM3 element, M
would be 1, and the thickness would be read as
T1. Property set number one defaults to a set
with T1 = 1., T2, ... = 0..

RECTS(,MN)
NTH
H,B
(XA,YA)
(THETA)

Solid rectangular beam cross section definition. H and B are the cross section height and
width, respectively. If M > 0, XA and YA give
the coordinates of the attachment point relative to the center of the beam. (They are
assumed zero otherwise.) If N > 0, THETA specifies the orientation angle of the cross section (relative to the third point). NTH is
the element property group number.

RECTH(,MN)
NTH
H,B
TH,TB
(XA,YA)
(THETA)

Hollow rectangular beam cross section definition. H and B are the cross section height
and width (outside), while TH and TB are the
corresponding wall thicknesses. The attachment
point (XA,YA) relative to the beam center is
read if M > 0. The orientation angle THETA is
read if N > 0.

Additional beam cross section definitions which are similar
to RECTS and RECTH are CIRCS and CIRCH.

GIBEAM(,MN)
NTH
H,B1,B2
TH,T1,T2
E1,E2
(XA,YA)
(THETA)

Generalized I beam cross section definition. H
is the web height. B1 and B2 are the widths
of the upper and lower flanges, respectively.
TH is the thickness of the web, while T1 and
T2 are the thicknesses of the upper and lower
flanges. E1 and E2 are the upper and lower
flange offsets, measured from the web end to
the center of the respective flange. (XA,YA)
is measured from the bottom of the web.

Additional cross section definition instructions similar in
construction to GIBEAM are IBEAM, ANGLE, CHANNEL, TBEAM, and ZBEAM.

OBANG(,MN)
NTH
B
T
PHI
(XA,YA)
(THETA)

Oblique angle cross section definition. B is
the width of both legs of the angle, and T is
their thickness. PHI is the angle (in degrees)
between the legs of the angle. (XA,YA) (read
for M > 0) gives the attachment point coordinates relative to the apex of the angle (where
the y-axis bisects the angle). The orientation
angle THETA is read if N is nonzero.

ELMAT(,M)
NMAT
SY(,E,V,P,A)

Defines isotropic material number NMAT. Its
properties are Young's modulus E, Poisson's
ratio V, yield stress SY, density P, and thermal expansion coefficient A. M gives the number of properties to be defined. Nonprescribed

properties assume default (aluminum) values.
G is not specified, but is calculated from E
and V.

MSTEEL(,M) NMAT (SY,E,V,P,A)	Defines material number NMAT as mild steel. M gives number of properties to be redefined. Default values are: SY = 34000., E = 29.5E6, V = .29, P = 7.339E-4, A = 6.5E-6. (Cf. 1976 ABS rules.)

Other standard materials are stainless steel (SSTEEL) and aluminum alloy (AALLOY).

Element Type Specification

LETY TYPE NMAT,NTH	Specifies that all line elements generated along lines, or as surface stiffeners, will be of type TYPE, with material type NMAT and thick- ness group NTH, until a new line element type instruction is given. TYPE = ROD2, NMAT = NTH = 1 is the default line element specification.
GETY TYPE NMAT,NTH	Specifies that all surface elements generated subsequently by any of the surface grid commands will be of type TYPE, with material type NMAT and thickness group NTH, until a new surface element type instruction is given. TYPE = TM3, NMAT = NTH = 1 is the default surface element specification.

Point and Line Generation

KPOINT NF(,NL,NT) XF,YF,ZF (XL,YL,ZL)	Defines NT regularly numbered key nodes, NF,..., NL. The coordinates of the first node are given by XF,YF,ZF, and those of the last node by XL,YL,ZL. The nodes are assumed to lie on a straight line and to be equally spaced. Default values are NL = NF and NT = NL + 1 - NF.

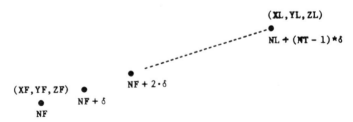

Fig. 14 Generation of key node strings

SLINE (,MN)	Creates a series of NLN straight lines with
NAM	alphanumeric identifiers NAM, NAM+NDM, etc.
M1,M2,MP(,IB,NLN)	The first line connects nodes M1 and M2 with
(N1,N2,NP,JB,NDM)	MP nodes in all, and a bias parameter of IB.
(MG,NG)	The last line joins N1 to N2 with NP nodes

in all, and a bias parameter of JB. It is
assumed that the line sequence is regularly
numbered. (Cf. Fig. 15.)

M = 0   No line element generation along
          NAM.

M = 1   Line element generation--If beam
          elements are being generated, MG(,NG)
          are expected. They provide the beam
          third point for the first (and last)
          lines.

N = 0   No bias--points equally spaced

N = 1   End bias--points biased toward N2
          for positive and toward N1 for nega-
          tive. Magnitude of IB determines
          biasing.

N = 2   Center bias--points denser in center
          for positive, denser toward ends for
          negative.

IB is related to the ratio between the lengths
of the last and first line segments. In more
precise terms:

R = (length of 1st segment/length of last
    segment)

  = $(1 + ABS(IB/100)$**s

where s is the sign of IB.

Examples: If IB = 50, R = 3/2

              If IB = -250, R = 2/7

Other curve generation commands are CARC, PARAM2, PARAM3, and
COMPLINE. Details of these may be obtained from the full manual or
through the HELP command.

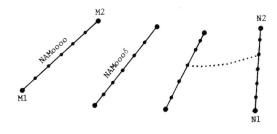

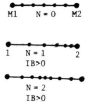

Effect of Bias
Parameter

Fig. 15 Straight-line generation

Grid Generation

BULKM can generate a variety of grid types, as can be verified through the HELP command. The following is only an example of the most widely used grid types.

GRID4(,M)   Generates four-sided grid GNAME bounded
GNAME   by edges NAME1 to NAME4, using a scheme
NAME1,NAME2,NAME3,NAME4   which transforms the shape of line
                           NAME1 to that of NAME3 as the gener-
                           ation proceeds from one end of the
                           grid to the other. The number of
                           intermediate points in the lines on
                           opposite sides of the grid must be
                           equal, or an error will result. The
                           appropriate choice of M results in
                           automatic generation of line stiff-
                           eners:
                           M = 0   No stiffeners
                           M = 1   Stiffeners parallel to side
                                   NAME1
                           M = 2   Stiffeners parallel to side
                                   NAME2
                           M = 3   Stiffeners parallel to both
                                   side NAME1 and NAME2

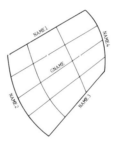

Fig. 16   Scheme for generation of four sides and grid (GRID4)

Other grid generation commands are GRID4S, GRID3, GRID3S, GRIDT, GRIDC, PGRID, and COMPGRID.

Plotting Commands

For common plotting commands, refer to the appropriate section. In addition the following commands are allowed:

KN   Causes key node numbers to appear and disappear.
LNAM   Causes line names to appear and disappear.
GNAM   Causes grid names to appear and disappear.

Information Commands

Apart from the usual information commands, the following special
instructions are available:

INFK	Prints the coordinates of NT regularly numbered
NF(,NL,NT)	key nodes NF,...,NL. Default: NL = NF, NT = NL + 1 - NF.
INFL	Prints the definition of NT regularly numbered
NF(,NL,NT)	lines NF,...,NL. Default: NL = NF, NT = NL + 1 - NF.
INFG	Prints the definition of NT regularly numbered
NF(,NL,NT)	grids NF,...,NL. Default: NL = NF, NT = NL + 1 - NF.

On-Line Batch (OLB) Commands

All standard commands, described previously, are allowed.

Model Editor and Display Program (EDITM)

EDITM is a model editor designed primarily to correct and update
models generated by BULKM. Additionally, it may be used to generate
simple models or ones that are too complex to automate. The initialization procedure is similar to that of BULKM. EDITM has more plotting capabilities than BULKM, particularly detailed node and element
plots. EDITM also has the capability to produce information on a
model in tabular form.

Model Generation with EDITM

To generate a model with EDITM, the points must be generated first
using the POINT command. This command may generate points singly
or in strings.
    The material and thickness of elements generated in EDITM are
defined by ELMAT, ORMAT, MSTEEL, SSTEEL, AALLOY, and ETH, CIRCS, etc.
They are activated by material and thickness pointers. These pointers
are set by the PTRM and PTRTH commands or by any of the beam
cross section definition commands. The pointer will continue to
specify a given material or thickness until it is changed. Elements
are generated directly with user points as the corners.

Editing a Model with EDITM

The POINT command can be used to reposition nodes, as well as to
create them. Connectivity, thickness, type, and material can all
be redefined for an element or elements using the REDEC, REDETH,
REDETY, and REDEM commands, respectively. A point or points can be
deleted using the DELP command. An element or elements can be deleted with DELE.
    Following is a listing of the most widely used instructions

and their parameters. For a complete list see the full GIFTS manual
or use the HELP command.

Plotting Commands

All common plotting commands are allowed. In addition:

PLOTBC NTH	Plots the cross section associated with element property group number NTH. An error will result if NTH has no cross section definition associated with it.

Information Commands

All common information commands are permitted. In addition:

INFM NF(,NL,NT)	Lists material properties for NT regularly numbered materials NF to NL.
INFTH NF(,NL,NT)	Lists element thicknesses for NT regularly numbered thickness groups NF,...,NL.

Material and Thickness Specifications

All the BULKM thickness, material, and cross section definition
commands are permitted, such as ETH, RECTS, RECTH, CIRCS, GIBEAM,
IBEAM, ANGLE, CHANNEL, TBEAM, ZBEAM, OBANG, ELMAT, MSTEEL, SSTEEL,
and AALLOY. In addition:

PTRTH N	Changes thickness pointer to N, so that all elements subsequently generated will be assigned thickness N.
PTRM N	Sets material pointer to N so that all subsequent elements generated will be assigned material N.

Point Editing Commands

POINT NF(,NL,NT) XF,YF,ZF (XL,YL,ZL)	Creates or repositions NT regularly numbered nodes NF,...,NL. Coordinates of the first node, NF, are given by XF,YF,ZF, and those of the last node, by XL,YL,ZL. The nodes are assumed equally spaced. Default NL = NF, NT = NI + 1 - NF.
MERGEP NF1,NL1,NT NF2,NL2	Merges NT regularly numbered points NF1,...,NL1 to another set of NT regularly numbered points NF2,...,NL2. Points NF1 are deleted and are made "dependent" on the points into which they are merged.
SPHERE X,Y,Z R	Defines a sphere with center X,Y,Z and radius R. Nodes may be forced to lie on this surface with the command PROJECT.

CONE X1,Y1,Z1 R1 X2,Y2,Z2 R2	Defines a right circular conic surface whose axis passes through (X1,Y1,Z1) and (X2,Y2,Z2) with cross-sectional radii R1 at (X1,Y1,Z1) and R2 at (X2,Y2,Z2). Nodes may be forced to lie on this surface with the command PROJECT.
PROJECT NF(,NL,NT)	Forces NT regularly numbered nodes NF through NL to lie on the surface defined by a preceding SPHERE or CONE command. The nodes will be moved to the point on the surface nearest to the original location of the node.
DELP NF(,NL,NT)	Deletes NT regularly defined points NF to NL. Any element connected to any of these points will be automatically deleted.
ACTIVP NF(,NL,NT)	Reactivates NT regularly numbered, previously de-leted user nodes NF,...,NL. The instruction, how-ever, does **not** reactivate deactivated elements connected to them.

Element Editing Commands

REDEC NF(,NL,NT) M1,M2,M3,... (N1,N2,N3)	Redefines connectivity of NT regularly numbered elements NF through NL, without changing their type, material, or thickness. Program expects same number of nodes as before. The new connec-tivities are M1, M2,... for the first element, and N1, N2,... for the last.
REDETH NF(,NL,NT) NTH	Redefines thickness group of NT regularly numbered elements NF through NL to NTH, without changing their type, material, or connectivity.
REDETY NF(,NL,NT) TYPE	Redefines type of NT regularly numbered elements NF through NL, without changing their material, thickness, or connectivity. New type is given by TYPE, which may be any of the standard element mnemonics ROD2, TM3, QM9,....
REDEM NF(,NL,NT) NMAT	Redefines material of NT regularly numbered ele-ments NF through NL, without changing their type, thickness, or connectivity.
DELE NF(,NL,NT)	Deactivates NT regularly numbered elements NF to NL.
ACTIVE NF(,NL,NT)	Reactivates NT regularly numbered elements NF, ...,NL.
ROD2 M1,M2(,NT) (N1,N2)	Generates a rod or series of NT regularly numbered rods. The first connects M1, M2 and the last, N1, N2. Default NT = 1.
BEAM2 M1,M2,M3(,NT) (N1,N2,N3)	Similar to ROD2 in construction. Third point defines reference plane (not necessarily a struc-tural point). Before BEAM2 element is created,

the cross section has to be defined and thickness pointer set.

```
TM3 [TB3]        **
M1,M2,M3(,NT)     * Similar to ROD2 in construction.  These in-
(N1,N2,N3)        * structions generate membrane (bending) tri-
                  * angles and membrane (bending) quadrilaterals.
QM4 [QB4]         *
M1,M2,M3,M4(,NT)  *
(N1,N2,N3,N4)    **
```

Other elements which may be generated in a similar fashion include TM6, TM10, TB6, TB10,.... For a full listing, use the HELP command.

```
COSUB(,MN)        Defines one or more COSUB modules by the
RNAME             name of RNAME.  NCP is the number of master
NCP(,NT)          nodes, and M1,M2,... are the nodes to which
M1,M2,M3,...      the first COSUB nodes are attached.  These
(N1,N2,N3,...)    nodes must be in one-to-one correspondence
(ALS,ALL)         with the external nodes defined for the
                  COSUB module in DEFCS.  EDITM does not check
                  to see if the COSUB exists or if the correct
                  number of master points have been specified.
                  The process is repeated NT times, the node
                  numbers being incremented by constant amounts
                  until the last COSUB is assembled to N1,
                  N2, N3,....  M is a mode parameter.  If
                  M = 0 or M is omitted, the COSUB is assembled
                  unchanged.  If M = 1, the COSUB stiffness
                  matrix is multiplied by ALS.  The mode para-
                  meter N has a similar effect on the COSUB
                  internal load assembly.  The load multipli-
                  cation factor is ALL.
```

On-Line Batch (OLB) Commands

Commands OLB, JOB, END, and QUIT are also available. For a more complete description, see the appropriate section.

Constrained Substructure Definition Routine (DEFCS)

Program DEFCS is used to define a model as a constrained substructure (COSUB module) prior to reduction. In addition to that, DEFCS is used to define the external (master) nodes of the COSUB, by which the decomposed COSUB will be attached to the master analysis model. It also requests the dependent nodes, whose displacements are inter-polated from specified external nodes (see Fig. 17) according to the appropriate kinematic constraint (rigid, linear, or cubic--Fig. 18).

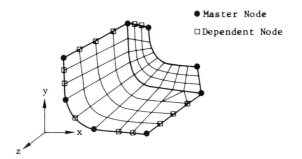

Fig. 17   Constrained substructure (COSUB)

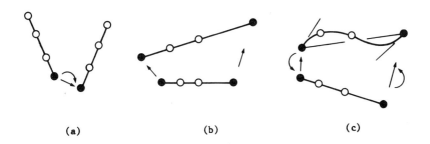

(a)   (b)   (c)

Fig. 18   Boundary interpolation schemes

DEFCS may be run on any model, whether or not it was generated by BULKM, although it has commands that reference line data generated by BULKM. DEFCS requests the number of external nodes (maximum of 27) and a list of the user numbers of these nodes. The program will await a command from the list below.

Boundary Definition Commands

RIGIDL,N   Specifies that line LNAME is to be a rigid boun-
LNAME   dary. N (= 1 or 2) specifies which endpoint of
                  the line is to be the master node. All internal
                  nodes of the line, as well as the other endpoint,
                  will be dependent nodes.

LINEARL   Specifies that line LNAME is to be a linear boun-
LNAME   dary. Both endpoints will be external nodes, and
                  all internal line nodes will be dependent nodes.

CUBICL LNAME	Specifies that line LNAME is to be a cubic boundary. Both endpoints will be external nodes, and all internal line nodes will be dependent nodes.
RIGIDBY NEP ND1,ND2,...	Defines a rigid boundary with external node NEP and a list of dependent nodes ND1, ND2,.... If more dependent nodes than can fit on a line are desired, they must be broken up into two or more boundaries with the same external node.
LINEARBY NE1,NE2 ND1,ND2,...	Defines a linear boundary with external nodes NE1 and NE2, and dependent nodes ND1, ND2,.... As with RIGIDBY, if more dependent nodes than will fit on one line are needed, they must be divided into more than one boundary.
CUBICBY NE1,NE2 ND1,ND2,...	Defines a cubic boundary. Parameters are the same as in command LINEARBY.

On-Line Batch and Program Termination

Instructions OLB, QUIT, END, or JOB may be used.

Mesh Generation Example

The following simple example serves to illustrate some of the GIFTS mesh generation capabilities.

A cylinder of radius 5 in. and length 7 in. is capped by a sphere of the same radius. Only a quarter of the structure is generated.

The cylindrical part is divided into two grids named CYLT and CYLB. CYLT is generated as a parametric grid, and CYLB is generated as a flat grid to be forced later into a conical shape in EDITM using the PROJECT command.

The spherical part is generated from three four-sided grids SPHT, SPHL, and SPHR. All are generated using straight line edges with a view to projecting them on the sphere later in EDITM.

In order to illustrate the use of multiple materials and thicknesses, the following thickness and material properties are used for the various grids:

Grid	Thickness (in.)	Young's modulus (lb/in.^{2})	Poisson's ratio	Element type
CYLT	0.1	1.0×10^7	0.33	TB3
CYLB	0.1	1.2×10^7	0.33	TB3
SPHT	0.11	1.0×10^7	0.33	TB3
SPHL	0.11	1.0×10^7	0.33	TB3
SPHR	0.11	1.0×10^7	0.33	TB3

```
E BULK                           Command to start execution
BULKM VP4A                       ( machine dependent )
TYPE JOB NAME
CYL                              Underlined text is
JOB CYL BEING CREATED            produced by program,
*                                and not user.
KPOINT                           Key point generation
>
1
7,5,0.
>          Prompting character, computer generated.
2
7,,5.
>
3
12,,
>
4
0,5
>
5
,3.535534,3.535534
>
6
,,5
>
11
0,4.619398,1.913417
>
12
7,4.619398,1.913417
>
7
7,3.535534,3.535534
>
8
12,,3
>
9
10,3,0
>
10
12,3,3
>
0000                             Zero point number
*                                to terminate key point
SLINE                            input.
>
L39
3,9,5
>                                Straight line generation.
L910
9,10,5
>
L910
7,10,5
>
L39
3,9,5
>
C27
2,7,5
>
C56
5,6,5
>
                                 Blank name to terminate.
*
```

```
SLINE,B1
>
L14                              Generation of biased
1,4,10,-300                      straight lines.
>
L57
7,5,10,-300
>
L26
2,6,10,-300
>
L19
1,9,5,-300
>
L710
7,10,5,-300
>
L28
2,8,5,-300
>

*
CARC
>                                Circular arc generation.
C45
4,11,5,5
>
C17
1,12,7,5
>

*
ELMAT 2                          Definition of material
>                                properties.
1                                ( 2 materials)
10700.,1.E7,.33
>
2
13000,1.2E7,.35
>
0000
*
ETH ,1
>                                Definition of element
1                                thicknesses
0.1
>                                ( 2 in all)
2
0.11
>
0000
*
GETY                             Define grid (surface) element
>                                type as triangular bending
TB3                              mat=1, thickness=0.1
1,1
*
GRID4
>                                Generate grid CYLT.
CYLT
C17,L14,C45,L57
>

*
GETY
>                                Change element material to #2
TB3
2,1
*
```

```
GRID4
>                        Generate grid CYLB, t=0.I,
CYLB                     material=#2
L57,C27,L26,C56
>

*
CBTY                     Change back to material #I,
>                        but t=0.II
T=3
1,2
*
GRID4
>                        Generate grids.
SPHT
L19,C17,L710,L910
>
SPHL
L910,L29,C27,L710
>
SPHR
L39,L38,L910,L910
>

*
QUIT
                         User requests termination of
LINES BEING GENERATED:            execution.
L39
L910
L910
L38
C27
C56
L14
L57
L26
L19
L710
L29
C45
C17

GRIDS BEING GENERATED:
CYLT
CYLB
SPHT
SPHL
SPHR

ASSIGNING USER NUMBERS
STOP  000000
                         Program stops
```

```
E EDITM
>                        Commence execution of
EDITM VP4A                EDITM, in order to finalize
                          model shape.
TYPE JOB NAME
CYL
*
SPHERE                   Define sphere.
>
7,0,0
5
*
PROJECT                  Move nodes to lie on sphere.
>
1,3
>
7,10
>
13,24
>
55,63
>
118,144
>

*
CONE                     Define cylinder.
>
!,
5
7,0,0
5
*
PROJECT                  Move nodes to lie on cylinder.
>
25,30
>
94,117
>

*
QUIT
STOP  000000             Terminate.
```

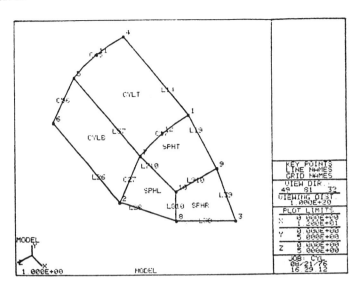

Fig. 19   Arrangement of lines and grids, plotted by program BULKM

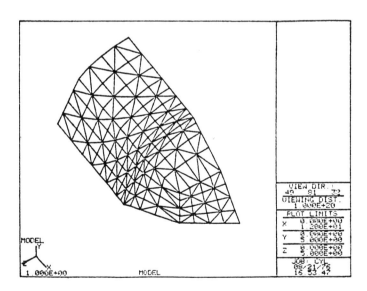

Fig. 20   Grid before node projection, plotted via EDITM

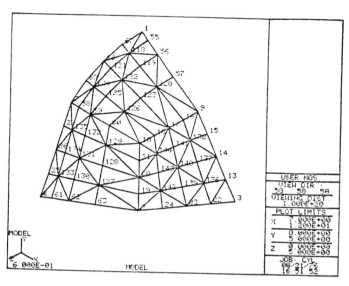

Fig. 21 Numbering of nodes in spherical part before projection, produced by EDITM

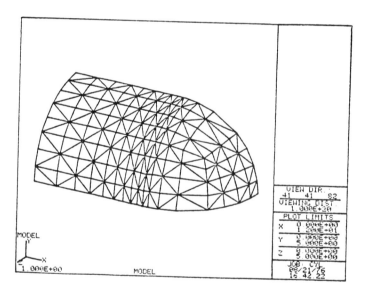

Fig. 22 Final model, plotted via EDITM

LOAD AND BOUNDARY CONDITION GENERATION, DISPLAY, AND EDITING

Three basic programs are provided in GIFTS 4 for the generation of
model loads and boundary conditions. They are:

BULKF   intended to allow only those freedoms which a
model can support, thereby relieving the user of
the necessity of suppressing all superfluous
freedoms by hand.

BULKLB   a bulk load and boundary condition generator
designed to apply loads to models generated with
BULKM. It may be used to apply distributed line
and surface loads and masses, prescribed
displacements along lines and surfaces, and
inertial loads.

EDITLB   is a display and edit routine intended to provide
local modification capability to loads and
boundary conditions applied by BULKLB. It may also
be used to generate simple loading on models, or
loading on models not generated with BULKM.

Automatic Freedom Generator (BULKF)

BULKF is intended to allow only those freedoms which a model can
support, thereby relieving the user of the necessity to suppress all
superfluous freedoms by hand. When BULKF is loaded, it requests and
reads a four-character job name. The program then checks the computation status list to ensure that all prerequisites have been satisfied, and then proceeds to compute and store the freedoms that the
model can support, and terminates when finished.

BULKF is not set up to allow the correct freedom patterns for
COSUB modules. At present, it assumes that they can support all six
degrees of freedom. If this contradicts the nature of the problem,
the freedom pattern must be corrected by the user, using BULKB or
EDITLB.

Bulk Load and Boundary Condition Generator (BULKLB)

BULKLB is a bulk load and boundary condition generator designed to
apply loads to models generated with BULKM. Upon loading, the user is
asked to define the number of loading cases:

NUMBER OF LOADING CASES?

Valid response is any positive integer. After that BULKLB is
ready for user commands.

There are three types of operations that can be performed with
BULKLB. Loads can be applied to key nodes, lines, or grids. Masses
and damping coefficients can be applied and inertia loading produced.

Node freedoms can be suppressed and released. Freedom suppression
of key nodes, lines, and grids is done with the commands SUPK, SUPL,
and SUPG. Freedom release of key nodes, lines, and grids is done
with the commands RELK, RELL, and RELG.

At the beginning of the execution, a pointer is set to load case
1. If other load cases are to be generated, the pointer has to be
reset before the associated loads are applied. This is accomplished
with the LDCASE command.

Loads can be applied to key nodes, lines, and grids with the
commands LOADK, LOADL, and LOADG, respectively. The command HEADG
applies a liquid pressure head to a given grid.

Masses can be added to key nodes, lines, and grids by the use of
commands MASSK, MASSL, and MASSG, respectively. The command MASS
computes the diagonalized mass matrix of the model. Once mass has
been introduced, inertial loading can be generated with the commands
ANGVEL and TRANACC.

Following is a listing of commands and their parameters.

Model Loading Commands

LDCASE N	Sets the loading case pointer to N. All loads subsequently applied become part of the load case N.
UNLOAD	Zeroizes all loads for the current loading case.
UNLOADK NF(,NL,NT)	Zeroizes all loads on NT regularly numbered key nodes NF, ..., NL for current load case.
UNLOADL LNAME	Zeroizes all loads on line LNAME for current load case.
UNLOADG GNAME	Zeroizes all loads on grid GNAME for current load case.
LOADK ,M NF(,NL,NT) VF(,VL)	Applies a load with freedom M to NT regularly numbered key nodes NF, ..., NL. The load value is linearly interpolated from the end values VF and VL. Valid values for M are: 　　M = 1 -- force along x 　　　= 2 -- force along y 　　　= 3 -- force along z 　　　= 4 -- moment around x 　　　= 5 -- moment around y 　　　= 6 -- moment around z
LOADL,M LNAME (K) V1,V2	Applies a distributed line load in direction M to line LNAME. V1 is the value of the load at end 1 and V2 at end 2. The load is distributed linearly along the length of the line. If M = 0, the load is along the line from end 1 toward end 2. If M = 7, the integer K is read (1, 2, or 3 for x-, y-, z-axes), and the loads are applied in the direction of the cross product of e(K) X R(1,2), where e(K) is a unit vector in the direction of the appropriate

axis, and R(1,2) is a vector in the direction of
each line segment.

LOADG,M   Applies a distributed surface pressure on grid
GNAME   GNAME. V1 through V4 are the pressure values at
V1,V2,V3,V4   the corners, as in Figure 23. The load distribu-
                    tion is linear across the surface. If M = 0, the
                    load is perpendicular to the surface in the direc-
                    tion of R(1,3) x R(2,4) (see Fig. 24). If M is
                    not zero, it gives the direction of load applica-
                    tion (1 = x, 2 = y, 3 = z).

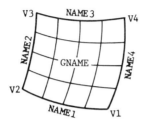

Fig. 23 Scheme for the application of load values to the corners
of a surface

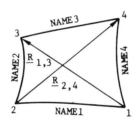

Fig. 24 Definition of vectors used in the application of loads
perpendicular to a surface

HEADG,M   Applies a pressure head to grid GNAME. M specifies
GNAME   the axis of the pressure gradient, and C1 and C2
C1,V1   give the coordinates on that axis that have pres-
C2,V2   sure values V1 and V2. The head loads are applied
                    only up to the zero head line. The loads are ap-
                    plied in the direction of R(1,3) x R(2,4) (see
                    Fig. 24).

Introducing Mass and Damping Coefficients

MASS   Calculates and stores the mass matrix of the entire
                        model using the lumped mass approach.

MASSK,M   Adds a lumped mass at freedom M to NT regularly
NF(,NL,NT)   numbered key nodes NF, ..., NL. VF is the value
VF(,VL)   at node NF, and VL at NL. M may take on any of
                        the values 0-3. M > 0 specifies that the mass is to
                        be applied in the specified direction. If M = 0, it
                        is applied in all three coordinate directions.

MASSL,M   Adds a linearly distributed line mass to line
LNAME   LNAME. V1 and V2 are the values at ends 1 and 2,
V1,V2   respectively. M has same meaning as in MASSK.

MASSG,M   Adds a distributed surface mass to grid GNAME. V1
V1,V2,V3,V4   through V4 are the values at the corners, as in
                        LOADG. M may take values as in MASSK.

PROPDAM   Computes a diagonal damping matrix that is ALPHA
ALPHA,BETA   times the mass, plus BETA times the diagonal of the
                        stiffness matrix.

DAMK,M   **
                         * Identical to MASSK, MASSL, AND MASSG, except
DAML,M   * these commands apply damping coefficients instead
DAMC,M   * of masses.
                        **

TRANACC(,K)   Used to define translational inertia loading on
V   the structure. V is the acceleration, and P, Q,
(P,Q,R)   and R give the direction cosines of the acceleration
                        vector. If K is specified (1,2,3), the accelera-
                        tion is along one of the coordinate axes and P, Q,
                        and R are omitted.

ANGVEL(,K)   Applies centripetal inertia loads due to model
V   rotation about an axis with angular velocity V. If
(P,Q,R)   K is specified (1,2,3), the axis of rotation is the
(X,Y,Z)   specified coordinate axis. If K = 0, the axis of
                        rotation is the axis passing through X,Y,Z, with
                        direction cosines P,Q,R.

SUM   Causes the program to compute the load resultants
                        on the model about the coordinate origin, and to
                        print them out.

BALANCE   Computes a set of inertial loads and applies them
                        to all nodes, so that the total structure is under
                        equilibrium. (Use only for unsupported structures.)

Freedom Pattern Modification

SUPK(,M)   Suppresses freedom M of key nodes NF through NL.
NF(,NL,NT)   If M = 0, all freedoms are suppressed.

SUPL(,M)   Suppresses freedom M in all nodes of line LNAME.
LNAME   If M = 0, all freedoms are suppressed.

SUPG(,M) Suppresses freedom M in all nodes of grid GNAME.
GNAME   If M ≠ 0, all freedoms are suppressed.

RELK, RELL, and RELG are used to release freedoms of key points, lines,and grids. The formats are similar to SUPK, SUPL,and SUPG.

Setting Time Values (Used for Transient Response)

TIME   Specifies that the current loading case represents
V   the load vector at time V.

On-Line Batch (OLB) and Termination Commands

Commands OLB, JOB, QUIT, and END may be used as usual.

EDITOR FOR LOADS AND BOUNDARY CONDITIONS (EDITLB)

EDITLB is intended to provide local modifications to loads and boundary conditions applied by BULKLB. It may also be used to generate simple loading on models or loading on models not generated with BULKM. Once loaded, it requests the desired number of loading cases if it has not been set previously.

NUMBER OF LOADING CASES?

Valid response is any positive integer. It is used by the program to create the load file.
The LDCASE command defines the loading case to be considered. Default value is 1. Commands LOADP, SUPP, RELP, MASSP, and DAMP may be used to load, suppress,and release point freedoms, as well as add masses and define damping coefficients.
Standard plotting commands are applicable with a few additions, such as command SCALELD, which scales the displayed loads.
EDITLB has two information commands in addition to the standard commands. INFLD produces the loads on the model. INFPMD produces point masses and damping coefficients.
Following is a list of the commands and their parameters.

Load Modification Commands

Commands LDCASE, UNLOAD, SUM, and BALANCE may be used in a similar manner to module BULKLB.

UNLOADP Zeroizes all loads NF for NT regularly numbered
NF(,NL,NT) nodes NF,.. NL for the current loading case.
      Default: NL = NF, NT = NL + 1 - NF.

LOADP(,M) Adds loads at freedom M to NT regularly numbered
NF(,NL,NT) nodes NF,..., NL. Legal values for M are 1 through
V1(,V2)   6.

LOADCS NAME	Applies the condensed load matrix (all loading cases) of all COSUBs with identifier NAME, whose loads have not yet been applied, to the model. It tags them accordingly.
UNLOADCS NAME	Subtacts the condensed load matrix (all loading cases) of all COSUBs with identifier NAME, whose loads have been applied, from the model, and resets them accordingly.

NOTE: If UNLOAD is to be used at any time after a LOADCS command, UNLOADCS must be given for all those COSUBs for which a LOADCS was issued. Then UNLOAD may be issued, followed by another LOADCS for each of the COSUBs. This is necessary since, while LOADCS and UNLOADCS apply to all loading cases, UNLOAD only applies to the current loading case, and hence may not update their loading status correctly.

Mass and Damping Coefficient Application Commands

MASSP(,M) NF(,NL,NT) VMF(,VML)	Adds a mass of value VM in the specified direction to NT regularly numbered nodes NF,..., NL. If M = 0, the mass will be applied in all three directions. Default: Nl = NF, NT = NL + 1 - NF.
DAMP(,M) NF(,NL,NT) VDCF(,VDCL)	Sets the damping coefficient in the specified direction of NT regularly numbered nodes NF through NL. If M = 0, the damping coefficients will be applied in all directions.

Node Suppression and Release

SUPP(,M) NF(,NL,NT)	Suppresses freedoms for NT regularly numbered nodes NF, ..., NL. If M = 0, all freedoms are suppressed. If M > 0, it specifies the particular freedom that is to be suppressed: 1 = x, 2 = y, 3 = z, 4 = rx, 5 = ry, 6 = rz. Default: NL = NF, NT = NL + 1 - NF.
RELP(,M) NF(,NL,NT)	Releases freedoms for NT regularly numbered nodes NF, ..., NL. If M = 0, all freedoms are suppressed. If M > 0, it specifies the particular freedom that is to be released: 1 = x, 2 = y, 3 = z, 4 = rx, 5 = ry, 6 = rz. Default: NL = NF, NT = NL + 1 - NF.

Setting Time Values (Used for Transient Response)

TIME V	Specifies that the current loading case describes the load vector at time V.

Plotting Commands

Commands such as BOX, VDIR, VDIS, TYON, TYOFF, LINES, PN, and EN may be used. (See appropriate section.) In addition:

SCALELD   Scales load display (vector length) to V times the
V   default length.

FORCOM(,M)   Specifies that force components are to be displayed
            M = 0 --- Force resultants (translational)
            M = 1, 2, or 3 --- Force x, y, or z components.

MOMCOM(,M)   Specifies that moment components, M, are to be displayed. M is interpreted as in FORCOM.

TRANFR   Indicates translational freedoms are to be displayed as lines in the direction of each freedom to the lower right of each point.

ROTFR   Indicates rotational freedoms are to displayed.

Information Commands

In addition to the usual commands, the following commands may be used:

INFLD   Produces a numerical printout of the loads at NT
NF(,NL,NT)   regularly numbered nodes NF,..., NL. Nodes with zero loads will not be printed.

INFPMD   Lists the directional masses and damping coeffi-
NF(,NL,NT)   cients for NT regularly numbered user nodes NF, ..., NL.

On-Line Batch(OLB) and Termination Commands

The commands OLB, JOB, END, and QUIT may be used.

GENERAL PURPOSE COMPUTATIONAL AND RESULT DISPLAY MODULES

The following are computational modules of general applicability that may be used, at least once, during each of the standard GIFTS procedures. These modules are listed here for convenient reference.

OPTIM   Bandwidth optimization program. Although GIFTS is designed to handle problems without size or bandwidth restriction, it is very important that the problem be optimized before the solution proceeds. Experience has shown that run times can be reduced by a factor of two to ten if the procedure is used. OPTIM may be called several times until the best node numbering scheme has been achieved.

STIFF   Computes and assembles element stiffness matrices
             to produce the master stiffness matrix.

DECOM   Introduces kinematic boundary conditions and
             decomposes the stiffness matrix using the Cholesky
             method.

DEFL   Computes the deflections from the current loading
             conditions and the decomposed stiffness matrix.

STRESS   Computes element stresses based on current deflec-
             tions.

RESULT   Displays deflections and stresses. It has many
             options that may be used to process and plot the
             results for optimum comprehension.

The following gives detailed descriptions of these modules.

Bandwidth Optimizer (OPTIM)

OPTIM is used to reduce the spread (half bandwidth) of the model
stiffness matrix in order to increase the solution efficiency. Once
the user responds with a valid job name, OPTIM requests the user number of the node at which it should begin the renumbering:

STARTING NODE

The response should be the user number of the desired starting node.
    After node renumbering, the user may still address the original
node numbers throughout the rest of the computations. The internal
numbering scheme may be obtained on a plot in EDITM, EDITLB, or
RESULT by using the SN command as explained under plotting instructions.
    OPTIM must be run before stiffness matrix assembly, as it results
in the destruction of both the stiffness matrix and the stiffness
directory, if present.
    It is not necessary to run OPTIM before loads and boundary
conditions are applied, as it reorganizes them, if present.

Stiffness Assembler (STIFF)

STIFF is a program designed to compute and assemble element stiffness
matrices to form a global stiffness matrix. The program reads the
job name. It then checks for the status of the stiffness matrix. If
it has already been computed, no subsequent model changes have been
made, and the matrix has not been decomposed, the program will terminate. Otherwise it will compute the stiffness matrix and update the
status list accordingly.

Stiffness Matrix Decomposition (DECOM)

The program reads the job name. Next, it checks if the stiffness
matrix has been computed and the boundary conditions applied. If so,
it proceeds with the generalized Cholesky decomposition procedure,
using partitioned matrix representation, and updates the status list
accordingly. DECOM terminates if the stiffness matrix has already
been decomposed.

The program, furthermore, prints current status messages at the
end of each partition. A partition contains 18 degrees of freedom or
less. For shell problems, for example, each 3 nodes constitute a
partition. For a two-dimensional elasticity problem each group
contains 9 nodes. For substructures, only a partial decomposition is
performed, involving only the internal nodes as pivots. In addition,
DECOM tests for the presence of singularities and prints a list of
any encountered during the computation.

Deflection Computation (DEFL)

The program reads the job name, after which it checks if the stiffness
matrix has been decomposed and loads have been applied to the model.
Then it solves for the deflections and updates the status list
accordingly.

Stress Computation (STRESS)

The STRESS program checks for the completion of the deflection computation and then calculates the stress values for each element and
stores them on disk. Upon completion it sets the appropriate status
switch and terminates.

Result Display (RESULT)

The RESULT program is designed to display the deflections and stresses
of one loading case or a linear combination of the computed loading
cases. After the user specifies the job name, RESULT checks for the
presence of the job and the completion of deflection calculation.
Stress computation need not have been performed, in which case all
stresses will be zero.

The use of RESULT consists typically of specifying a loading
case, plotting the model, using user-set switches, or using the
information commands for alphanumeric information.

Following is a list of the commands and their parameters.

Loading Case Specification

LDCASE   Sets a pointer to loading case N.
N

COMP   Defines, for display, a composite loading case
N1,N2,...   combining loading cases N1, N2, ... using weight-
W1,W2,...   ing factors W1, W2, etc.

Plotting Commands

Apart from the usual commands, the following special instructions are
available:

PRINST   Specifies that the positive principal stresses are
                to be plotted in vector form. Compressive stresses
                are plotted separately, via use of command
                SCALEST (see below).

TOP   Specifies that subsequent principal stress plots
                will be of stresses at the top of bending plate
                elements. The top is defined in the element des-
                cription section.

MIDDLE,BOTTOM   Similar to TOP, but specify that the stresses
                will be those in the middle or bottom of the
                bending plate elements.

FC   Failure criterion is to be displayed using a
                character plot. If no ranges were specified,
                default values are computed (evenly spaced between
                min. and max. values (see RANGE command) of the
                model).

RANGE(,N)   Defines N equally spaced ranges between failure
C   criterion values FC1 and FC2, to be used in
FC1,FC2   failure criterion character plots. FC1 and FC2
                are expressed as percentages of the yield stress.
                The first range defined will be given the label C,
                and subsequent ranges will be denoted by the next
                series of letters from the alphabet.

CONTOUR   Specifies that failure criterion contours are to be
                plotted. If the contour value list is empty,
                RESULT will compute default values in percentage of
                the yield stress, covering the entire range of
                failure criteria.

CONTV   Specifies V as a failure criterion value to be
V   traced in a contour plot. V is interpreted as a
                percentage of the yield stress (current maximum
                of 20 values).

CONTS   Directs the program to compute its own contour
FC1,FC2   values covering the range FC1 to FC2. The values
                will be evenly spaced and expressed in rounded
                percentages of the yield stress.

NOST   No stresses (contours, vectors, or labels) are to
                be displayed.

RESETFC   Zeroizes the failure criterion range list so that

	it may be recreated.
RESETCR	Zeroizes the contour value list so that it may be recreated.
SCALEDN V	Displacements are to be scaled by V times the default (computed) scale factor.
SCALEST V	Specifies that principal stress vectors are to be scaled by V times the default scale factor. If V is positive, tensile stresses will be displayed. If V is negative, compressive stresses will be plotted. Default is +1.
NSEG N	Specifies that beams are to be plotted in N longitudinal segments. Default value is 3.
PLOTBST NEL	Plots the normal and shear stress distribution over the cross section of the standard beam element NEL.

Information Commands

Apart from the common information commands, the following special instructions are available:

EXTFC	Gives maximum and minimum failure criterion values of all elements included within the current plot limits.
INFDN NF(,NL,NT)	Produces numerical values of deflections of NT regularly numbered user nodes NF,..., NL. Default: NL = NF, NT = NL + 1 - NF.
INFST NF(,NL,NT)	Produces numerical stress information for NT regularly numbered elements NF,...,NL. The interpretation of the values depends on the type of element in question. For membrane elements, the values are those of the local Cartesian stresses sx, sy,txy. For a bending plate element, two sets of values are provided: one for the top and one for the bottom fibers. The x-axis is defined as parallel to the first edge of the element. If the elements were generated using BULKM, the first edge will be always parallel to the first edge of the grid. The definition of top and bottom is given under element description. For rod elements, only the axial stress is printed. For beam elements, the axial force N, shear forces Sp and Sq, the torque T, and the two bending moments Mp and Mq measured relative to the cross section principal axes, p and q, are given.
INFFC NF(,NL,NT)	Produces the failure criterion for NT regularly numbered elements NF,...,NL. The values are given as percentages of the yield stress.

INFSTR   Lists detailed stress data for all elements whose
FC1,FC2   failure criterion lies within the range FC1 to
                    FC2. FC1 and FC2 are expected as percentages of
                    the yield stress. The interpretation of the stress
                    values is supplied under command INFST.

On-Line Batch (OLB) and Termination Commands

As usual, commands OLB, JOB, QUIT, and END may be used.

THE GIFTS STATIC SOLUTION PACKAGE

Program Running Sequence

Although the model and loads are usually generated interactively,
the computer analysis is best performed in a batch mode. The process consists of forming the stiffness matrix, decomposing it, computing deflections, and calculating the stress values for each element.
Each one of these operations is done by a separate program. The procedure then is to run the modules in the following order:

BULKM	Model generation.
EDITM	

BULKF	
BULKLB	Load and boundary condition definition.
EDITLB	

OPTIM	Band width optimization.
STIFF	Stiffness matrix formation.
DECOM	Stiffness matrix decomposition.
DEFL	Computation of model deflections.
STRESS	Stress computation.

RESULT	Result display.

Static Analysis Example

The problem chosen is that of stress concentration around a hole
4 in. in diameter at the center of a square (20 in. x 20 in.) plate
loaded by a uniform edge load. The thickness of the plate is assumed
to be 0.1 in., and the edge load has the value of 1 lb/in.
    Only a quarter of the plate is analyzed. It is divided into
two unequal grids. Bias parameters are set to produce a fine mesh
at the stress concentration area.
    Two loading cases are considered, one in which the loading is
on a vertical edge, and the other when the loading is on the horizontal edge.
    Only Young's modulus and Poisson's ratio are defined using

ELMAT. The shear modulus is automatically computed. The rest of the material properties are left at the default values. In particular, the yield stress is equal to 6×10^4 lb/in.^{2}

The results show the stress contour closest to the stress concentration areas assigned a value of 4.2×10^{-2} (% of the yield stress). This is equivalent to a stress concentration factor given by:

$$n = 4.2 \times 10^{-2} \times 6 \times 10^4/100/10 = 2.52$$

The same value is obtained in both loading cases, in spite of the nonsymmetry of the grid.

The following gives a summary of the commands used to generate the model and a display of all relevant data. Some numerical values, from RESULT, are also included. The user is advised to attempt this problem first before modeling any complex structures. A number of selected plots have been added. They should be self-explanatory.

```
E BULKM
                        Execute module BULKM
BULKM VP4A              ( PDP-15. format)

TYPE JOB NAME
HOLE
JOB HOLE BEING CREATED
*
KPOINT
>                       Key points.
1
1,1.7321,0
>
2
2,0,0
>
3
10,0,0
>
4
10,10,0
>
5
2,10,0
>
6
0,2,0
>
7
0.5176,1.9319,0
>
8
1.7321,1,0
>
0000
*
SLINE,01
>                       Line boundaries
L56                     ( Straight lines)
5,6,8,400
>
L14
1,4,7,-400
>
L23
2,3,8,-400
>
L45
4,5,6
>
L34
3,4,6
>
*
CARC,01
>                       Circular arcs.
C16
1,7,6,6,100
>
C12
1,8,2,6,-50
>
*
ETH 1
>
1                       Thickness and material
0.1                                        definition
>
2000
*
```

```
ELMAT 3
>
1
32200,1.E7,.3333333
>
0000
*
GETY
>                       Define element, material and
OM4                     thickness to be used in grid
1,1                     generation.
*
GRID4
>                       Grid generation.
TOP
L14,L45,L56,C16
>
BOT
L23,L34,L14,C12
>

*
QUIT
                                    Terminate.
LINES BEING GENERATED:
L56
L14
L23
L45
L34
C16
C12

GRIDS BEING GENERATED:
TOP
BOT

ASSIGNING USER NUMBERS
STOP 000000
 E OPTIM
                        Bandwidth optimization.
OPTIM VP4A

TYPE JOB NAME
HOLE

STARTING NODE
2

   90 NODES
   70 ELEMENTS

H.B.W. BEFORE AND AFTER
  HBW   NEL
  270    70
   51    44
OPTIMIZATION TIME     0:22.5
STOP 000000

E BULKF                 Automatic selection of overall
BULKF VP4A              freedom pattern.

TYPE JOB NAME
HOLE

BULKF TIME -- 0:19.8
STOP 000000
```

```
E BULKLB              Definition of loads and boundary
BULKLB VP4A           conditions.

TYPE JOB NAME
HOLE

NUMBER OF LOADING CASES?
2
*
LOADL 1
>                     Load perpendicular to line
L34                   L34
1,1
>

*
LDCASE
>                     Define second load case.
2
*
LOADL 2
>
L45
1,1                   Vertical line load on L45.
>

*
SUPL 1                Introduce symmetry boundary
>                     conditions. Suppress x freedom
L56                   of boundary L56.
>

*
SUPL 2
>                     Suppress y freedom of boundary
L23                   L23.
>

*
QUIT                  Exit.
STOP   000000
E STIFF
                      Compute stiffness matrix.
STIFF VP4A

TYPE JOB NAME
HOLE
STIFFNESS ASSEMBLY TIME   3:55.0
STOP   000000
                      All times are for PDP-15
                      without floating point hardware.
                      They are in minutes & seconds.
E DECOM               Stiffness matrix decomposition.

DECOM VP4A

TYPE JOB NAME
HOLE
CONDENSING ROW    1      Program produces
CONDENSING ROW    2      intermediate printouts.
CONDENSING ROW    3
CONDENSIN' ROW    4
CONDENSING ROW    5
CONDENSING ROW    6
CONDENSING ROW    7
CONDENSING ROW    8
CONDENSING ROW    9
CONDENSING ROW   10

DECOMPOSITION TIME   2:45.3  (minutes:seconds)
STOP   000000
                      PDP-15 w/o floating
                      point hardware.
```

```
E DEFL                Solution of equations for
DEFL VP4A             deflections.

TYPE JOB NAME
HOLE

DEFLECTION TIME   1:30.9 (minutes:seconds)
STOP   000000
                      PDP-15 times.

E STRESS
                      Stress computation.
STRESS VP4A

TYPE JOB NAME
HOLE
STRESS TIME --    0:39.2
STOP   000000

E RESULT              Display results and obtain
                      information regarding deflections
RESULT VP4A           and stresses

TYPE JOB NAME
HOLE
* *
INFDN
>
71,86
          JOB:HOLE      08/20/76     LOADING CASE
NP          U            V            W           TH
71  -2.727E-06   1.240E-06   0.000E-01
72  -2.601E-06   1.196E-06   0.000E-01
73  -3.495E-06   3.196E-06   0.000E-01
74  -3.034E-06   2.724E-06   0.000E-01
75  -2.678E-06   2.344E-06   0.000E-01
76  -2.431E-06   2.108E-06   0.000E-01
77  -2.273E-06   2.065E-06   0.000E-01
78  -2.184E-06   2.307E-06   0.000E-01
79  -3.054E-06   4.813E-06   0.000E-01
80  -2.628E-06   4.100E-06   0.000E-01
81  -2.248E-06   3.530E-06   0.000E-01
82  -1.947E-06   3.164E-06   0.000E-01
83  -1.745E-06   3.063E-06   0.000E-01
84  -1.676E-06   3.326E-06   0.000E-01
85  -2.620E-06   6.413E-06   0.000E-01
86  -2.250E-06   5.440E-06   0.000E-01
>

*
EXTFC
EXTREMUM FOR PLOT:

FCMIN =  1.1454E-02 AT ELEMENT    34
FCMAX =  8.2471E-02 AT ELEMEN4    42
*
INFST
>
40,42
          JOB:HOLE      08/20/76      LOADING CASE
NE                                     STRESSES
40  3.605E+00   1.405E+01  -2.468E+00
41  4.027E+00   1.793E+01  -2.570E+00
42  2.466E+00   2.577E+01  -2.368E+00
>

*
QUIT
STOP   000000
```

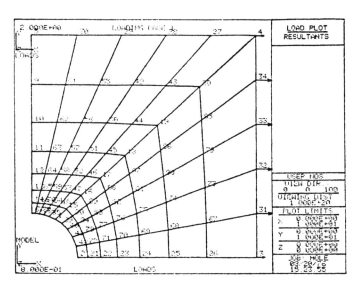

Fig. 25   Display of model and loads for load case 1, produced by EDITLB

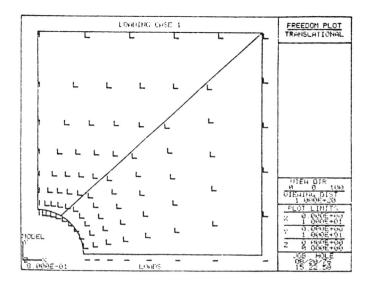

Fig. 26   Display of boundary conditions, produced by EDITLB

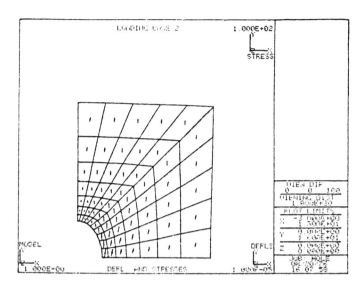

Fig. 27 Positive principal stress vector plot for load case 2, produced by RESULT

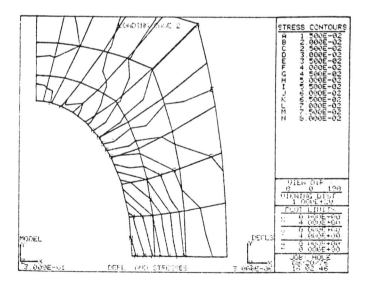

Fig. 28 Contours of Von Mises yield criterion near hole, produced by RESULT

THE GIFTS NATURAL VIBRATION PACKAGE

Program Running Sequence

The GIFTS free vibration package is a package designed to compute
the lowest frequencies of vibration and the associated modes. The
frequencies are printed out on the terminal, while the deflections
are stored in the displacement file, thereby allowing the user to
display the modes using RESULT.
     The method utilized is the subspace iteration method. The
starting vectors are either harmonic or power functions of x, y,
and z. The user may override the automatic initial vector generation
scheme and substitute his own loads, using BULKLB and/or EDITLB.
The program sequence is as follows:

BULKM	Generate model.
EDITM	Edit and display model.
BULKF	Determine basic freedom pattern.
OPTIM	Optimize bandwidth.
BULKLB	Define number of modes desired and kinematic boundary conditions.
EDITLB	Define number of modes desired and kinematic boundary conditions.
AUTOL	Automatic load generation. User chooses between harmonic and power vectors.
STIFF	Compute stiffness matrix.
DECOM	Matrix decomposition.
SUBS	Subspace iteration routine. Performs one iteration or more until user wishes to interrupt or convergence occurs.
STRESS	Computes stresses connected with vibration modes. (Optional.)
RESULT	Displays current shapes of vibrational modes. May be used to display stresses, if computed.

Eigenmode Computation of a Tailplane Model

The following is an illustration of the use of GIFTS to compute
eigenmodes and frequencies of a structure. A simplified model of a
tailplane is generated and used for the purpose.
     The power series option is chosen in the automatic generation
of the initial load vectors (AUTOL). Convergence is rapid, as shown
in the following pages.
     After the modes are obtained, deflections and stresses may be
displayed.
     We note that although the subspace iteration method only claims
accurate convergence for the first 5 or 6 modes, it has been our
experience that all but the last mode are satisfactory. This example strengthens this belief.

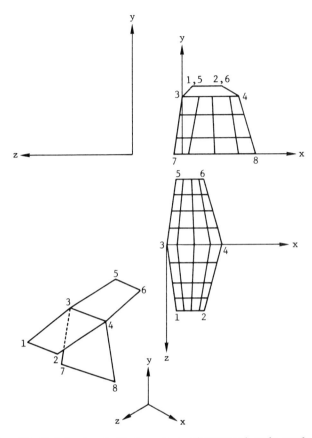

Fig. 29 Model of a tailplane for vibrational mode analysis

```
 E  PULYM

 PULYM  VP4A

 TYPE JOB NAME
 TAIL
 JOB TAIL BEING CREATED
 *
 ETY  1
 >                              Generate tailplane model
 1                              as simple plates.
 1,2
 >
 2                              Thicknesses.
 2.
 >
 2002
 *
 ELMAT 3
 >
 1                              Material properties.
 10000.,1.E7,.33
 >
 0000
 *
 GETY
 >
 TP3                            Select element, material,
 1,1                            and  thickness, for horizontal
 *                              surface.
 XPOINT
 >
 1
 10,70,70
 >                              Keypoints.
 2
 40,70,70
 >
 3
 0,60,0
 >
 4
 60,60,0
 >
 5
 10,70,-70
 >
 6
 40,70,-70
 >
 7
 -10,0,0
 >
 8
 90,0,0
 >
 0000
 *
 SLINE
 >                              Straight line edges.
 L12
 1 2 5
 >
 L34
 3 4 5
 >
 L56
 5 6 5
 >
 L13
 1 3 5
 >
 L24
 2 4 5
```

```
 >
 L35
 3 5 5
 >
 L46
 4 6 5
 >
 L37
 3 7 4
 >
 L48
 4 8 4
 >
 L78
 7 8 5
 >

 *
 GRID4
 >                              Generate horizontal surface.
 TOPL
 L12,L24,L34,L13
 >
 TOPR
 L34,L46,L56,L35
 >

 *
 GETY
 >                              Select element, material and
 TP3                            thickness for vertical surface.
 1,2
 *
 GRID4
 >                              Generate vertical surface.
 VERT
 L37,L78,L48,L34
 >

 *
 QUIT                           Terminate BULKM

 LINES BEING GENERATED:
 L12
 L34
 L56
 L13
 L24
 L35
 L46
 L37
 L48
 L78

 GRIDS BEING GENERATED:
 TOPL
 TOPR
 VERT

 ASSIGNING USER NUMBERS
 STOP  000000

  E BULKF               Select model overall freedom
                               pattern.
 BULKF  VP4A

 TYPE JOB NAME
 TAIL

 BULKF TIME -- 0:14.7
 STOP  000000
```

E OPTIM   Bandwidth optimization.

OPTIM VP4A

TYPE JOB NAME
TAIL

STARTING NODE
35

   62 NODES
   88 ELEMENTS

H.B.W. BEFORE AND AFTER
  HBW   NEL
  342   87
   72   39
OPTIMIZATION TIME   0:21.3
STOP 000000

E BULKLB   Introduce boundary conditions,
                    compute masses, and define no. of
BULKLB VP4A   modes required.

TYPE JOB NAME
TAIL

NUMBER OF LOADING CASES?
6
*   No. of loading cases=no. of modes
SUPL   to be computed.
>
L78   Boundary conditions.
>

*
MASS
*   Compute mass.
QUIT
STOP 000000

DOS-15 UV3A000
$$JOB
E STIFF
                    Compute & assemble stiffness matrix.
STIFF VP4A

TYPE JOB NAME
TAIL
STIFFNESS ASSEMBLY TIME 18:29.5
STOP 000000

E AUTOL
                    Automatic generation of starting
AUTOLD VP4A   load vectors.

TYPE JOB NAME
TAIL
NUMBER OF LOADING CASES?
6
HARMONIC(H) OR POWER(P)   =no. of required modes.
P   power series selected.
DO YOU WANT LOADS APPLIED IN THE X DIRECTION
Y
DO YOU WANT LOADS APPLIED IN THE Y DIRECTION
Y
DO YOU WANT LOADS APPLIED IN THE Z DIRECTION
Y
STOP 000000   Loads to be applied in all
                      three directions.

E DECOM   Decompose stiffness matrix.

DECOM VP4A

TYPE JOB NAME
TAIL
CONDENSING ROW   1
CONDENSINGSROW   2
CONDENSING ROW   3
CONDENSING ROW   4
CONDENSING ROW   5
CONDENSING ROW   6
CONDENSING ROW   7
CONDENSING ROW   8
CONDENSING ROW   9
CONDENSING ROW   10
CONDENSING ROW   11
CONDENSING ROW   12
CONDENSING ROW   13
CONDENSING ROW   14
CONDENSING ROW   15
CONDENSIN' ROW   16
CONDENSING ROW   17
CONDENSING ROW   18
CONDENSING ROW   19

DECOMPOSITION TIME 17:20.3
STOP 000000

E SUBS
               Perform one iteration for S.S.I.method
SUBS VP4A

TYPE JOB NAME
TAIL
MODE   E.VALUES   FREQ. C.P.S.
 1   1.7557E-06   3.2159E+00
 2   1.3435E-05   5.6537E+00
 3   3.8881E-04   7.2181E+00
 4   4.8617E-04   8.0714E+00
 5   7.9245E-04   4.3422E+01
 6   2.4493E-03   1.2012E+02

SUBSPACE ITERATION TIME --   7:22.6
STOP 000000

```
DOS-15 UV3ACC2
SOJOB
E SUBS      Second iteration.

SUBS VP 4A

TYPE JOB NAME
TAIL
MODE     E.VALUES      FREQ. C.P.S.
  1    9.3897E-06    3.2155E+00   O.K.
  2    3.2051E-05    5.6315E+00   Almost
  3    3.9223E-04    7.2107E+00   Close
  4    4.3713E-04    8.0362E+00   Close
  5    7.9871E-04    2.8113E+01
  6    2.4499E-03    5.2162E+01

SUBSPACE ITERATION TIME --   7: 9.9
STOP  000000
```

```
E SUBS          Third iteration.

SUBS VP 4A

TYPE JOB NAME
TAIL
MODE     E.VALUES      FREQ. C.P.S.
  1    3.1907E-05    3.2155E+00   O.K.
  2    5.6813E-05    5.6315E+00   O.K.
  3    3.9226E-04    7.2106E+00   O.K.
  4    4.3719E-04    8.0358E+00   v.close
  5    7.9871E-04    2.1115E+01
  6    2.4499E-03    2.8540E+01

SUBSPACE ITERATION TIME --   7: 9.8
STOP  000000
```

```
E SUBS          Fourth iteration.

SUBS VP 4A

TYPE JOB NAME
TAIL
MODE     E.VALUES      FREQ. C.P.S.
  1    3.1121E-05    3.2155E+00   O.K.
  2    5.7184E-05    5.6315E+00   O.K.
  3    3.9226E-04    7.2106E+00   O.K.
  4    4.3719E-04    8.0359E+00   O.K.
  5    7.9871E-04    2.1047E+01   GETTING THERE
  6    2.4499E-03    2.8529E+01   Close

SUBSPACE ITERATION TIME --   7: 8.8
STOP  000000
```

```
E SUBS          Fifth iteration

SUBS VP 4A

TYPE JOB NAME
TAIL
MODE     E.VALUES      FREQ. C.P.S.
  1    3.1122E-05    3.2155E+00   O.K.
  2    5.7136E-05    5.6315E+00   O.K.
  3    3.9226E-04    7.2106E+00   O.K.
  4    4.3719E-04    8.0358E+00   O.K.
  5    7.9871E-04    2.1046E+01   v.close
  6    2.4499E-03    2.8529E+01   O.K.

SUBSPACE ITERATION TIME --   7: 8.4
STOP  000000
```

```
E SUBS          Sixth iteration.

SUBS VP 4A          Not really necessary !!!!

TYPE JOB NAME
TAIL
MODE     E.VALUES      FREQ. C.P.S.
  1    3.1124E-05    3.2155E+00   O.K.
  2    5.7136E-05    5.6315E+00   O.K.
  3    3.9226E-04    7.2106E+00   O.K.
  4    4.3719E-04    8.0358E+00   O.K.
  5    7.9871E-04    2.1046E+01   O.K.
  6    2.4499E-03    2.8528E+01   O.K.

SUBSPACE ITERATION TIME --   7: 8.1
STOP  000000
```

```
E SUBS

SUBS VP 4A

TYPE JOB NAME
TAIL
MODE     E.VALUES      FREQ. C.P.S.
  1    3.1126E-05    3.2155E+00
  2    5.7136E-05    5.6315E+00
  3    3.9226E-04    7.2106E+00
  4    4.3719E-04    8.0358E+00
  5    7.9871E-04    2.1046E+01
  6    2.4499E-03    2.8527E+01

SUBSPACE ITERATION TIME --   7: 8.4
STOP  000000
```

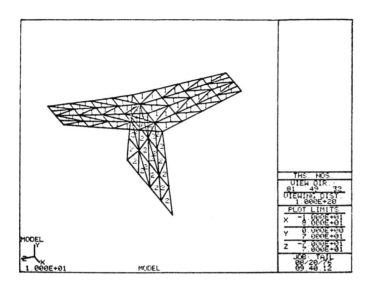

Fig. 30   Model with thickness code display, plotted by program EDITM

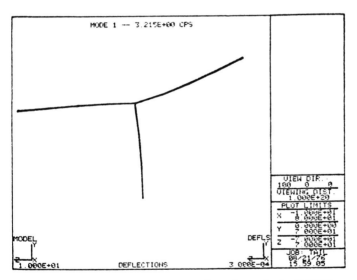

Fig. 31   First vibrational mode, plotted via RESULT

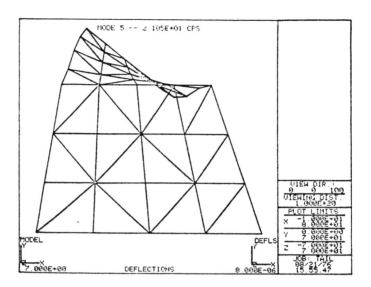

Fig. 32   Fifth vibrational mode, plotted by RESULT

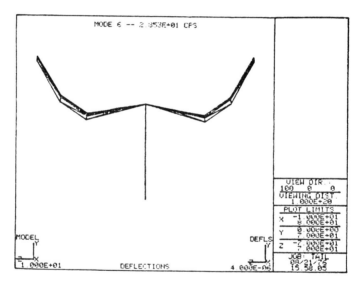

Fig. 33   Sixth mode of vibration, plotted by RESULT

THE GIFTS TRANSIENT RESPONSE PACKAGE (DIRECT INTEGRATION)

Program Execution Sequence

A typical transient response solution will follow the procedure
shown below.

BULKM EDITM	Generation of model.
BULKF BULKLB EDITLB	Generation of load function as a series of loading cases at different time values. Also mass and damping coefficient generation.
OPTIM STIFF	
TRAN1 DECOM TRAN2 DECOM	Definition of time step size and initiation of integration procedure.
TRANS	User-controlled time integration. Will provide histogram plots of up to four point/freedom combinations specified by the user as an aid to determining when the integration has been carried far enough.
STRESS RESULT	Computes stresses of time steps set up by TRANS. Displays result at time steps set up by TRANS.

Transient Response Initiation, First Phase (TRAN1)

TRAN1 is to be run on a transient response model immediately after
stiffness assembly. It is used to specify the time step to be used
in the time integration process. When loaded, TRAN1 checks for
completion of stiffness assembly and of mass matrix generation.
    TRAN1 will then ask for the time step size. It will check to
ensure that all loading cases defined have a set time value (command
TIME in BULKLB and EDITLB) and will sort the loading cases according
to time values. If no loading case with a time value of T = 0 is
found, the initial loads are assumed to be zero.
    TRAN1 then computes the initial acceleration. Next, it saves
the stiffness file on sequential file JOB,SAV for use in the next
step of transient analysis, and replaces it with an auxiliary matrix
used in the initialization process.

Transient Response Initiation, Second Phase (TRAN2)

TRAN2 is to be run after TRAN1 and DECOM have been executed. When called, TRAN2 checks for satisfactory fulfillment of the required prerequisites to execution.

TRAN2 then computes the displacement matrix for time t = DEL, where DEL is the time step to be used in the integration process, using the auxiliary matrix created by TRAN1.

Next TRAN2 computes the displacement matrix for t = -DEL. Finally, it replaces the auxiliary stiffness matrix with another one to be used in the recurrence formula of the Houbolt method. When it is finished, TRAN2 will destroy the saved stiffness file.

Transient Response Computation (TRANS)

After the second step of transient response initiation (TRAN2) has been run and the auxiliary matrix created and decomposed with DECOM, all time steps (after t = DEL) are computed by program TRANS. It is interactive to give the user better control over the number of steps to be performed. TRANS maintains and plots histograms of the displacements of up to four different freedoms to aid the user in determining when to terminate the computation. TRANS may be executed any number of times on the same model.

When loaded, TRANS checks the job status for completion of TRAN2 and DECOM. During the first time TRANS is run, the program requests four point/freedom combinations for the histogram plot. They are entered as (point number, freedom number), one combination to a line. If less than four are desired, entry or blank point number will terminate input. TRANS then saves the deflection vectors for t = 0 and t = DEL in file JOB,DNH and initiates the histograms for the time steps. It then enters its command loop.

The following is a list of the valid commands for TRANS.

Transient response commands.

STEP	Computes one time step.
SAVE	Saves last step computed on file JOB,DNH.
STEPS NST,ND	Computes next NST steps in model response and saves every NDth deflection vector on file JOB, DNH, starting with the NDth step.
RUN	Computes response throughout duration of applied load vectors and saves all deflection vectors.

Saved vector information command.

INFSTEPS	Produces a list of all saved deflection vectors giving their position in file JOB,DNH and the time at which the deflection occurred.

Histogram plotting command.

PLOTHST	Produces histogram plots of point/freedom pairs specified by the user at beginning of program.

Stress and result preparation command.

SETUP   Copies NT regularly numbered time steps, NF to NL,
NF(,NL,NT)   from the deflection save file JOB,DNH to the
                 regular deflection file JOB,DNS for stress compu-
                 tation by STRESS and plotting of the deflected
                 model by RESULT.

On-line batch and termination commands. Commands OLB, JOB, END,
and QUIT may be used as usual.

Transient Response of an Aircraft Tail

As an example for the use of the direct integration scheme for the
determination of deflection and stress histories, the tailplane used
before in the vibration mode analysis example is employed. The
example takes into consideration all degrees of freedom of the structure. Knowledge of the frequencies of vibration helps in the choice
of the time step.
     The time-dependent load consists of two parts. A rudder load
(oversimplified) applied gradually from $t = 0$ to $t = 0.2$ sec, then
kept constant, and an elevator load (again oversimplified) applied
gradually between $t = 0$ and $t = 0.2$ sec, kept constant until $t = 0.4$
sec, and then reduced until zero at $t = 0.6$ sec and kept zero after-
wards.
     The time step was chosen as 0.025 sec. For comparison, the
cycle time for the lowest natural frequency is 0.3 sec. It appears,
nevertheless, that the time step is still too large, as exhibited
by the noticeable numerical damping in the results--a characteristic
of the Houbolt method.

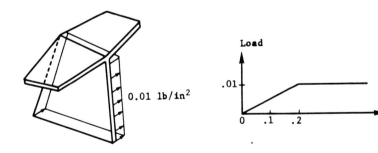

Fig. 34   Rudder load

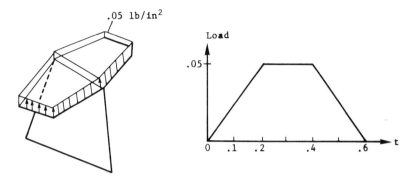

Fig. 35   Elevator load

```
SE BULKM

BULKM VP4A

TYPE JOB NAME
TAIL
JOB TAIL BEING CREATED
*
ETH 2                Generate tailplane model
>                    as simple plates.
1
1.2,.025
>                    Thicknesses.
2
2.0,.025
>
0000
*
ELMAT 3
>
1
40000.,1.E7,.33      Material properties.
>
0000
*
GETY
>
TB3                  Select element type, material,
1,1                  and thickness for horizontal
*                    surface.
KPOINT
>
1
10,70,70
>
2
40,70,70             Keypoints.
>
3
0,60,0
>
4
60,60,0
>
5
10,70,-70
>
6
40,70,-70
>
7
-10,0,0
>
8
80,0,0
>
0000
*
SLINE
>
L12
1,2,3
>                    Straight line edges.
L34
3,4,3
>
L56
5,6,3
>
L13
1,3,4
>
```

```
L24
2,4,4
>
L35
3,5,4
>
L46
4,6,4
>
L37
3,7,4
>
L48
4,8,4
>
L78
7,8,3
>

*
GRID4
>
TOPL
L12,L24,L34,L13
TOPR                          Generate horizontal surface.
L34,L46,L56,L35
>

*
GETY
>                             Select element type, material,
TB3                           and thickness for vertical
1,2                           surface.
*
GRID4
>
VERT
L37,L78,L48,L34    Generate vertical surface.
>

*
QUIT                          Terminate BULKM.

LINES BEING GENERATED:
L12
L34
L56
L13
L24
L35
L46
L37
L48
L78

GRIDS BEING GENERATED:
TOPL
TOPR
VERT

ASSIGNING USER NUMBERS
STOP  000000

E BULKF
                              Generate model's overall
BULKF VP4A                    freedom pattern.

TYPE JOB NAME
TAIL

BULKF TIME --  0: 7.2
STOP  000000
```

```
E OPTIM

OPTIM VP4A           Bandwidth optimization.

TYPE JOB NAME
TAIL

STARTING NODE
3

   30 NODES
   36 ELEMENTS

H.B.W. BEFORE AND AFTER
  HBW   NEL
  162   35
   78   28
OPTIMIZATION TIME    0:16.0
STOP  000000


E BULKLB
                     Introduce boundary conditions,
BULKLB VP4A          compute masses, and define
                     time-varying loads as a series
TYPE JOB NAME        of load vectors at specified
TAIL                 time values.

NUMBER OF LOADING CASES?
3
*
MASS                 Compute mass.
*
SUPL
>
L78                  Boundary conditions.
>


*
LOADG 3
>
VERT
-.01,-.01,-.01,-.01  Rudder load, T=.2
>

*
LOADG 2
>
TOPL
.05,.05,.05,.05      Elevator load, T=.2
>
TOPR
.05,.05,.05,.05
>


*
TIME
>                    Time value (.2)
.2
*
LDCASE
>
2
*
LOADG 3
>
VERT                 Rudder load, T=.4
-.01,-.01,-.01,-.01
>
```

```
*
LOADG 2
>
TOPL
.05,.05,.05,.05
>                    Elevator load, T=.4
TOPR
.05,.05,.05,.05
>

*
TIME
>                    Time value (.4)
.4
*
LDCASE
>
3
*
LOADG 3
>
VERT                 Rudder load, T=.6
-.01,-.01,-.01,-.01
>

*
TIME
>                    Time value (.6)
.6
*
QUIT
STOP  000000


E STIFF

STIFF VP4A
                     Compute & assemble
TYPE JOB NAME        stiffness matrix.
TAIL
STIFFNESS ASSEMBLY TIME   7:50.8
STOP  000000

E TRAN1

TRAN1 VP4A
                     Transient response
TYPE JOB NAME        initiation (first
TAIL                 phase).

TIME STEP SIZE? (SEC.)   Set time step size.
.025

TRAN1 TIME --    0:39.1
STOP  000000

E DECOM

DECOM VP4A           Decompose K* (used to
                     compute first time step).
TYPE JOB NAME
TAIL
CONDENSING ROW    1
CONDENSING ROW    2
CONDENSING ROW    3
CONDENSING ROW    4
CONDENSING ROW    5
CONDENSING ROW    6
CONDENSING ROW    7
CONDENSING ROW    8
CONDENSING ROW    9

DECOMPOSITION TIME    7:16.1
STOP  000000
```

```
E TRAN2

TRAN2 VP4A

TYPE JOB NAME        Transient response initiation
TAIL                 (second phase).

TRAN2 TIME --   1:31.5
STOP  000000

E DECOM

DECOM VP4A           Decompose K** (used for all
                     subsequent time steps).
TYPE JOB NAME
TAIL
CONDENSING ROW   1
CONDENSING ROW   2
CONDENSING ROW   3
CONDENSING ROW   4
CONDENSING ROW   5
CONDENSING ROW   6
CONDENSING ROW   7
CONDENSING ROW   8
CONDENSING ROW   9

DECOMPOSITION TIME   7:16.9
STOP  000000


E TRANS

TRANS VP4A

TYPE JOB NAME        Transient response integration
TAIL                 routine.

LIST 4 PT./FRDM. COMBINATIONS FOR HISTOGRAM
4,2
4,3                  Specify 4 freedom values for
6,2                  which a histogram will be retained
6,3                  (to help in determining when
*                    integration has been carried far
STEP                 enough).
*
SAVE                 Compute and save one time step.
*
STEPS
>                    Compute 10 time steps, and save
10,2                 every second one.
>

*
PAGEOFF              Turn information paging off.
*
INFSTEPS
                     List time values of all saved
                     steps in the integration.

 JOB: TAIL           09/07/76          16
STEP    TIME
  1     0.0000
  2     0.0250
  3     0.0500
  4     0.1000
  5     0.1500
  6     0.2000
  7     0.2500
  8     0.3000
*
PLOTHST              Plot current histogram.
*
```

```
STEPS
>                    Compute 20 time steps, and save
20,2                 every other one.
>>> LOAD MATRIX EXCEEDED.  LAST LOAD VECTOR E
>

*
INFSTEPS
                     List time values of all saved
                     steps.

 JOB: TAIL                09/07/76          17
STEP    TIME
  1     0.0000
  2     0.0250
  3     0.0500
  4     0.1000
  5     0.1500
  6     0.2000
  7     0.2500
  8     0.3000
  9     0.3500
 10     0.4000
 11     0.4500
 12     0.5000
 13     0.5500
 14     0.6000
 15     0.6500
 16     0.7000
 17     0.7500
 18     0.8000
*
PLOTHST              Plot current histogram.
*
SETUP                Set up deflection file with
>                    steps at 0.1, 0.2, ..., 0.8
4,18,8               sec.
>

*
QUIT                 Terminate integration run.

STOP  000000


$E STRESS


STRESS VP4A          Compute stresses for the time
                     steps in the deflection file.
TYPE JOB NAME
TAIL
STRESS TIME --   2: 4.0
STOP  000000


              RESULT run.
```

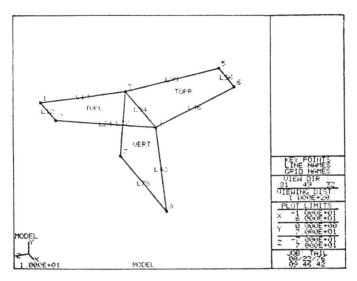

Fig. 36   Key points, lines, and grids (plotted by BULKM)

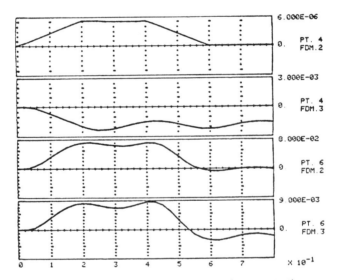

Fig. 37   Final histogram plot (from TRANS)

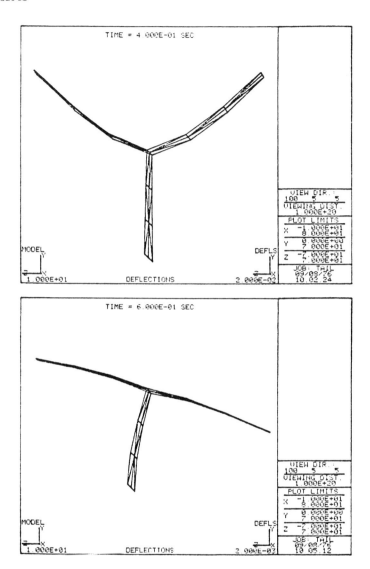

Fig. 38 Tailplane deflected shapes at t = 0.4 and t = 0.6 sec

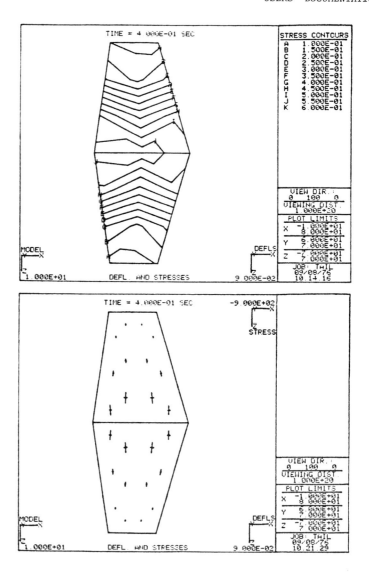

Fig. 39   Failure criterion contour plot (top) and compressive stress
principal stress plot for the top side of the elevator at t = 0.4 sec

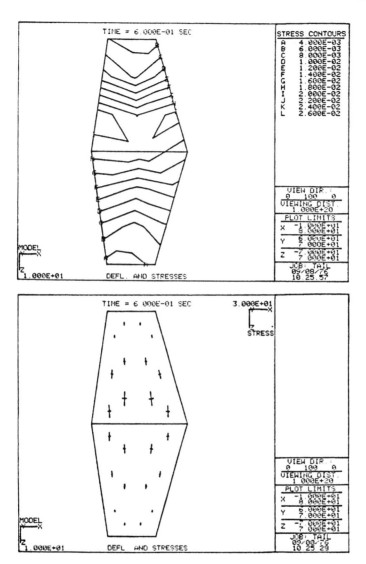

Fig. 40 Failure criterion contour plot (top) and tensile stress
principal stress plot for the top side of the elevator at t = 0.6 sec

THE GIFTS CONSTRAINED SUBSTRUCTURING PACKAGE

Program Running Sequence

A typical run involving COSUBs follows the shown procedure:

Generation of Typical COSUB model

BULKM	
EDITM	Generation of model, including loads and freedom
BULKF	pattern. No constraints should be applied.
BULKLB	
EDITLB	
OPTIM	
DEFCS	Definition of external and dependent nodes.
STIFF	
DECOM	
REDCS	Condenses stiffness and load matrices. Prints
	residual forces as check on accuracy of COSUB
	generation.

Generation of Main Analysis Model

BULKM	
EDITM	Apart from usual functions, used to attach
	COSUBs to the model.
BULKF	Ignores COSUBs in determining freedom pattern.
BULKLB	
EDITLB	
OPTIM	
STIFF	Assembles COSUBs as well as ordinary finite
	elements.
DECOM	
DEFL	
STRESS	Computes stresses only in ordinary finite elements.

Local Analysis of Typical COSUB

LOCAL	Computes local COSUB deflections.
STRESS	Computes COSUB stresses.

Constrained Substructure Reduction Routine (REDCS)

Before a COSUB module may be used in a master analysis run, it must
be processed by program REDCS to form the COSUB stiffness matrix and
its reduced load matrix (if internal loads are present). After initialization, REDCS checks the correctness and completion of the previous related steps. If all prerequisites are satisfied, REDCS
proceeds to compute the condensed stiffness and load matrices, as
well as the internal node deflection matrix, due to internal loads
on the COSUB (if any). This partial deflection matrix will be used
after the master analysis run for local analyses.
    Just before termination, REDCS checks the equilibrium of the
condensed stiffness matrix and provides a printout of the residual
force and moment resultants associated with each degree of freedom.
    The residual forces are to be compared with the diagonal ele-
ments of the reduced stiffness matrix. The diagonal elements represent the largest terms occurring during the summation. Care must
be taken, however, to scale the moment residuals by a typical COSUB
dimension before comparing it to a diagonal force value, and vice
versa. If the residual forces are too large, the COSUB generation
is unsuccessful. Previous steps should be checked, and the computation repeated.

Local Analysis of a Constrained Substructure (LOCAL)

After a solution run has been performed on the master analysis model
in a problem involving COSUB modules, a local analysis of any of the
COSUBs comprising the model may be performed. This local analysis
will give the details of the displacements within each of the COSUB
building blocks of the model.
    The purpose of program LOCAL is to extract the deflections of
each of the external nodes of the desired COSUB from the master
analysis model and to use them to compute the displacements of all
of the dependent boundary points and, together with the partial
displacement matrix due to internal loading (computed by REDCS),
all of the internal nodes of the COSUB model. After termination of
LOCAL, stresses within the COSUB may be computed by STRESS.
    As it is usually desired to do local analyses on more than one
of the COSUBs in a model, LOCAL is run using the job name of the master analysis model, and the COSUBs on which a local analysis is
desired are specified, one at a time. Since the data base of each
COSUB can only support one deflection file, only the most recent local analysis involving that COSUB is maintained. Hence, it is not
possible to perform local analyses of all substructures in a master
analysis model during the same run of LOCAL if two or more of them
are duplicates of the same COSUB.
    When loaded, LOCAL checks for completion of the master deflection
calculation. LOCAL then enters its command loop. The instructions
to which LOCAL will respond are listed below.

Plotting Commands

All common plotting commands may be used.

Information Commands

Commands INFP and INFE may be used to help identify COSUBs.

Local Analysis Command

    LOCALAN   Initiates local analysis of the COSUB whose number
    NEL   is NEL, if element number NEL is not a COSUB.

On-Line Batch and Termination Commands

As usual, commands OLB, JOB, QUIT, and END may be used.

Substructuring Example

A uniform sheet of metal (16 in. x 4 in.) is perforated at equal
intervals by a series of holes of diameter 0.8 in. each. A constrained substructure, UNIT, is formed and assembled sixteen times
to form the main model, which is then analyzed and followed by a local
analysis of some interesting COSUBs.

    In order to help determine critical COSUBs for local analysis,
quadrilateral membrane elements in 'stress only' mode were generated
in the main analysis model. Based on the stress values in these
quadrilaterals, the COSUBs at the bottom corners were picked out for
analysis.

    Two loading cases were chosen: an inertia loading in the hori-
zontal direction and one in the vertical direction. The loads were
applied on the substructures. The loads are automatically condensed
by REDCS, but have to be assembled by the LCSUB command in EDITLB.

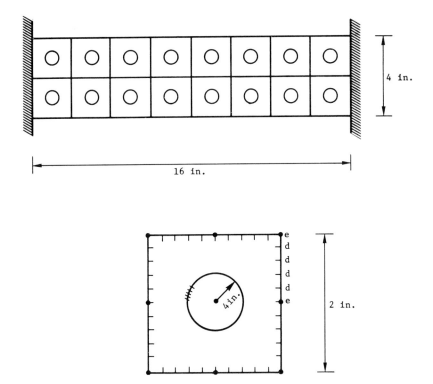

Fig. 41   Solution of perforated beam using constrained substructures

Table 2   COSUB key points

1	−1.0	1.0	0.
2	0.	1.0	0.
3	1.0	1.0	0.
4	1.0	0.	0.
5	1.0	−1.0	0.
6	0.	−1.0	0.
7	−1.0	−1.0	0.
8	−1.0	0.	0.
9	−0.282843	0.282843	0.
10	0.	0.4	0.
11	0.282843	0.282843	0.
12	0.4	0.	0.
13	0.282843	−0.282843	0.
14	0.	−0.4	0.
15	−0.282843	−0.282843	0.
16	−0.4	0.	0.
17	−0.153073	0.369552	0.
18	0.153073	0.369552	0.
19	0.369552	0.153073	0.
20	0.369552	−0.153073	0.
21	0.153073	−0.369552	0.
22	−0.153073	−0.369552	0.
23	−0.369552	−0.153073	0.
24	−0.369552	0.153073	0.

```
 Ξ BULKM

BULKM VP4A

TYPE JOB NAME
UNIT
JOB UNIT BEIN' CREATED
*
ETH 1
>                    Generate substructure model.
1
0.1
>
0000
*
ELMAT 3
>
1
1.E4,1.E7,.3333333
>
0000
*
GETY
>
QM4
1,1                  Choose isoparametric quadrilateral
*                         membrane elements.
KPOINT
>
1
-1,1,0
>
2
0,1,0
>
3
1,1,0
>
4
1,0,0
>
5
1,-1,0
>
6
0,-1,0
>
7
-1,-1,0
>
8
-1,0,0
>
9
-.282843,.282843,0
>
10
0,.4,0
>
11
.282843,.282843,0
>
12
.4,0,0
>
13
.282843,-.282843,0
>
14
0,-.4,0
>
15
-.282843,-.282843,0
```

```
>
16
-.4,0,0
>
17
-.153073,.369552,0
>
18
.153073,.369552,0
>
19
.369552,.153073,0
>
20
.369552,-.153073,0
>
21
.153073,-.369552,0
>
22
-.153073,-.369552,0
>
23
-.369552,-.153073,0
>
24
-.369552,.153073,0
>
0000
*
SLINE,01             Biased lines result in finer
>                    grid near hole.
L12
1,2,6
>
L23
2,3,6
>
L34
3,4,6
>
L45
4,5,6
>
L56
5,6,6
>
L67
6,7,6
>
L78
7,8,6
>
L18
1,8,6
>
L19
1,9,6,100
>
L210
2,10,6,100
>
L311
3,11,6,100
>
L412
4,12,6,100
>
L513
5,13,6,100
>
L614
6,14,6,100
```

```
>
L715
7,15,6,100
>
L816
8,16,6,100
>

*
CARC
>
C910
9,17,10,6
>
C1011
10,18,11,6
>
C1112
11,19,12,6
>
C1213
12,20,13,6
>
C1314
13,21,14,6
>
C1415
14,22,15,6
>
C1516
15,23,16,6
>
C916
9,24,16,6
>

*
GRID4                        Generate eight interconnected
>                            grids.
G1
L210,L12,L19,C910
>
G2
L311,L23,L210,C1011
>
G3
L412,L34,L311,C1112
>
G4
L513,L45,L412,C1213
>
G5
L614,L56,L513,C1314
>
G6
L614,L67,L715,C1415
>
G7
L816,L78,L715,C1516
>
G8
L19,L18,L816,C916
>

*
QUIT

LINES BEING GENERATED:
L12
L23
L34
  :
  :
C1516
C916

GRIDS BEING GENERATED:
G1
G2
G3
G4
G5
```

```
G6
G7
G8

ASSIGNING USER NUMBERS
STOP  000000

E BULKF              Automatic allocation of basic
                     freedom pattern.
BULKF VP4A

TYPE JOB NAME
UNIT

BULKF TIME --  1: 7.5
STOP  000000


E OPTIM              Bandwidth optimization

OPTIM VP4A

TYPE JOB NAME
UNIT

STARTING NODE
8

 248 NODES
 200 ELEMENTS

H.B.W. BEFORE AND AFTER
 HBW   NZL
 714   196
  66    46
OPTIMIZATION TIME      0:55.7
STOP  000000

E EDITM

EDITM VP4A       Generate main analysis model.

TYPE JOB NAME
BEAMH

JOB BEAM BEING CREATED
*
ELMAT,3          Material definition only necessary
>               for stress element, to insure
1               results compatible with
1.E4,1.E7,.3333333  constrained substructure.
>
0
*
POINT           Generate point grid directly as
>               user nodes, regularly numbered.
1,81,17
0.,0.,0.
16.,0.,0.
>
2,82,17
0.0,1.0,0.0
16.,1.0,0.0
>
3,83,17
0.0,2.0,0.0
16.,2.0,0.0
>
4,84,17
0.0,3.0,0.0
16.,3.0,0.0
>
5,85,17
0.0,4.0,0.0
16.,4.0,0.0
>
0
```

```
*
COSUB              Define COSUBs. Observe one to one
>                  correspondence of attachment nodes
UNIT               to definition of master nodes in
8,8                   program DEFCS. (see later).
3,8,13,12,11,6,1,2
73,78,83,82,81,76,71,72
>
UNIT
8,8                Each command generates 8 COSUBs.
5,10,15,14,13,8,3,4
75,80,85,84,83,78,73,74
>

*
EMODE              Prepare for generation of stress
>                  elements. These elements do not
STRESS             influence results in any way. They
*                  serve only to give overall stress
QM4                patterns before COSUBs are selected
>                  for local analysis.
2,6,8,12,8
72,76,78,82
>                  First set of stress elements are
4,8,10,14,8        QM4s.
74,78,80,84
>
0
*
TM3
>                  Next set of stress elements are
1,6,2,8            TM3 elements.
71,76,72
>
6,11,12,8
76,81,82
>
12,13,8,8
82,83,78
>
2,8,3,8
72,78,73
>
3,8,4,8
73,78,74
>
8,13,14,8
78,83,84
>
14,15,10,8
84,85,80
>
4,10,5,8
74,80,75
0
*
QUIT               Main analysis model is complete.
STOP   000000

E BULKF            Assign overall freedom pattern to
                   main analysis model.
BULKF VP4A

TYPE JOB NAME
BEAMH

BULKF TIME --  0: 9.2
STOP   000000

E OPTIM            Optimize half bandwidth for main
                   analysis model.
OPTIM VP4A

TYPE JOB NAME      Observe that since nodes were
BEAMH              already in optimum order, and
                   since program does not produce
STARTING NODE      absolute optimum, things got a bit
78                 worse.

   85  NODES
   96  ELEMENTS
```

```
H.B.W. BEFORE AND AFTER
  HBW   NEL
   78    1
   84   15
OPTIMIZATION TIME      0:22.8
STOP   000000

E BULKLB           Apply loads to COSUB. It is
                   important to note that COSUB
BULKLB VP4A        should be left as free body and
                   NOT constrained in any way.
TYPE JOB NAME
UNIT

NUMBER OF LOADING CASES?
2
*
MASS

TRANACC 1          First loading case :
>                  Own weight applied horizontally.
-1.
*
LDCASE
>
2
*
TRANACC 2          Second load case :
>                  Own weight applied vertically.
1.
*
QUIT               Internal COSUB loads applied.
STOP   000000

E EDITLB           Apply boundary conditions to
                   main analysis model. Also remove
EDITLB VP4A        superfluous freedoms. Allow
                   z rotations at COSUB nodes, since
TYPE JOB NAME      cubic boundary constraints are
BEAMH              used( see DEFCS later) .

NUMBER OF LOADING CASES?
2
*
SUPP               Introduce supports at both ends
>                  of beam.
1,5,5
>
81,85,5
>
0000
*
SUPP,3             Remove w freedom at all nodes.
>
1,85
*
0000
ILLEGAL COMMAND -- 0000
*
SUPP,4             Remove x rotation at all nodes.
>
1,85
*
0000
ILLEGAL COMMAND -- 0000
*
SUPP,5             Remove y rotation at all nodes.
>
1,85
*
0000
ILLEGAL COMMAND -- 0000
*
QUIT
STOP   000000
```

E DEFCS   Define UNIT as COSUB, and introduce
                 boundary constraints.
DEFCS VP4A

TYPE JOB NAME
UNIT

NO. OF EXTERNAL PTS.?
8

LIST OF EXTERNAL PTS.?
1,2,3,4,5,6,7,8   List key points on outside
*   boundary as master points.
CUBICL
>
L12
>   Introduce cubic constraints along
L23   boundary lines generated by BULKM.
>
L34   End points of each line become
>   master points, and aquire a
L45   rotational freedom, in addition
>   to the two translational ones.
L56
>
L67
>
L78
>
L18
"

*
QUIT   Definition of COSUB and boundary
STOP   000000   constraints is complete.

E STIFF   Compute stiffness matrix for COSUB.

STIFF VP4A

TYPE JOB NAME
UNIT
STIFFNESS ASSEM"LY TIME   12:45.6
STOP   000000

E DECOM   (Partial) decomposition of COSUB
                 stiffness matrix. Only internal
DECOM VP4A   nodes are statically condensed.

TYPE JOB NAME
UNIT
CONDENSING ROW   8
CONDENSING ROW   9
CONDENSING ROW   10
CONDENSING ROW   11
CONDENSING ROW   12
CONDENSING ROW   13
CONDENSING ROW   14
CONDENSING ROW   15
CONDENSING ROW   16
CONDENSING ROW   17
CONDENSING ROW   18
CONSENSING ROW   19
CONDENSING ROW   20
CONDENSING ROW   21
CONDENSING ROW   22
CONDENSING ROW   23
CONSENSING ROW   24
CONDENSING ROW   25
CONDENSING ROW   26
CONDENSING ROW   27
CONDENSING ROW   28
CONDENSING ROW   29
CONDENSI.G ROW   30

DECOMPOSITION TIME   8: 4.9
STOP   000000

E REDCS   Generation of condensed stiffness
                 and load matrices for COSUB. Also
REDCS VP4A   produces check on solution of COSUB.'

TYPE JOB NAME
UNIT

NP	NF	SUM X	SUM Y	SUM Z	SUM MX	SUM MY	SUM MZ	COMP TO
1	1	7.1E-01	1.2E-01	0.0E-01	0.0E-01	0.0E-01	2.7E-01	3.6E+05
1	2	-2.3E-01	1.7E-01	0.0E-01	0.0E-01	0.0E-01	-1.2E-01	3.6E+05
1	3	0.0E-01	0.0E-01	0.0E-01	0.0E-01	0.0E-01	0.0E-01	0.0E-01
1	4	0.0E-01	0.0E-01	0.0E-01	0.0E-01	0.0E-01	0.0E-01	0.0E-01
1	5	0.0E-01	0.0E-01	0.0E-01	0.0E-01	0.0E-01	0.0E-01	0.0E-01
1	6	5.1E-02	9.8E-04	0.0E-01	0.0E-01	0.0E-01	3.1E-02	3.2E+04
2	1	9.2E-01	-3.5E-02	0.0E-01	0.0E-01	0.0E-01	2.3E-01	6.6E+05
7	2	-2.3E-02	3.4E-01	0.0E-01	0.0E-01	0.0E-01	8.2E-02	3.6E+05
7	3	0.0E-01	0.0E-01	0.0E-01	0.0E-01	0.0E-01	0.0E-01	0.0E-01
7	4	0.0E-01	0.0E-01	0.0E-01	0.0E-01	0.0E-01	0.0E-01	0.0E-01
7	5	0.0E-01	0.0E-01	0.0E-01	0.0E-01	0.0E-01	0.0E-01	0.0E-01
7	6	-5.6E-02	6.1E-02	0.0E-01	0.0E-01	0.0E-01	5.9E-02	3.2E+04
8	1	5.9E-01	2.0E-03	0.0E-01	0.0E-01	0.0E-01	-1.4E-01	6.1E+05
8	2	7.5E-02	1.7E-01	0.0E-01	0.0E-01	0.0E-01	-1.7E-01	6.6E+05
8	3	0.0E-01	0.0E-01	0.0E-01	0.0E-01	0.0E-01	0.0E-01	0.0E-01
8	4	0.0E-01	0.0E-01	0.0E-01	0.0E-01	0.0E-01	0.0E-01	0.0E-01
8	5	0.0E-01	0.0E-01	0.0E-01	0.0E-01	0.0E-01	0.0E-01	0.0E-01
8	6	-3.3E-02	-3.4E-03	0.0E-01	0.0E-01	0.0E-01	7.3E-02	3.3E+04

COSUB DECOMPOSITION TIME   26:49.1
STOP   000000

Above check shows equilibrium
satisfied to approximately 6 figures.

E STIFF   Compute stiffness matrix for main
                 analysis. It seeks and assembles
STIFF VP4A   COSUB condensed stiffness matrices
                 and ignores all stress elements.
TYPE JOB NAME
BEAMH
STIFFNESS ASSEMBLY TIME   2:24.8
STOP 000000

E DECOM   Decompose stiffness matrix of main
                 analysis.
DECOM VP4A

TYPE JOB NAME
BEAMH
CONDENSING ROW   1
CONDENSING ROW   2
CONDENSING ROW   3
CONDENSING ROW   4
CONDENSING ROW   5
CONSENSYNG ROW   6
CONDENSING ROW   7
CONSENSING ROW   8
CONDENSING ROW   9
CONDE.SING ROW   10

DECOMPOSITION TIME   4:26.1
STOP 000000

E EDITLB   EDITLB is used here only to apply
                 COSUB condensed loads (including
EDITLB VP4A   'fixed end' moments).

TYPE JOB NAME
BEAMH
*
LOADCS   Apply all loads of COSUB 'UNIT',
>   for all load cases, wherever the
UNIT   COSUB occurs.
>

*
QUIT
STOP 000000

E DEFL   Compute deflections for main
                 analysis.
DEFL VP4A

TYPE JOB NAME
BEAMH

DEFLECTION TIME   1:50.8
STOP 000000

E STRESS   Compute stresses in main analysis
                 stress elements. COSUBs will be
                 ignored.
STRESS VP4A

TYPE JOB NAM%
BEAMH
STRESS TIME --   0:42.6
STOP 000000

E LOCAL   Perform local analysis on chosen
                 COSUB.

LOCAL VP4A

TYPE JOB NAM%
BEAMH
*

LOCALAN   Local analysis of COSUB at bottom
>   right hand corner.
8
*
QUIT

STOP 000000

E STRESS

STRESS VP4A   Stress computation for COSUB
                  undergoing local analysis.
TYPE JOB NIME
UNIT
STRESS TIME --   1:41.3
STOP 000000

DOS-15 UV3A000

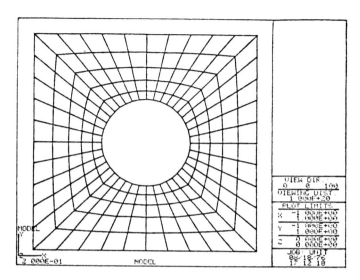

Fig. 42 COSUB model showing element pattern, displayed via EDITM

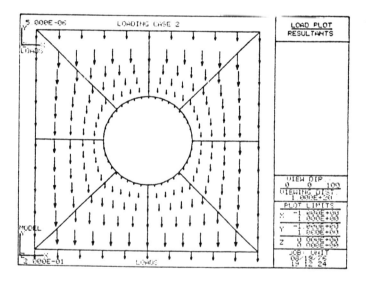

Fig. 43 COSUB under its own weight, plotted using EDITLB

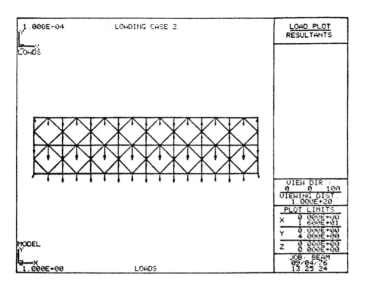

Fig. 44   Main analysis showing assembled COSUB loads, plotted using
EDITLB.   (Plot does not show "fixed end moments"; use instruction
MOMCOM.)

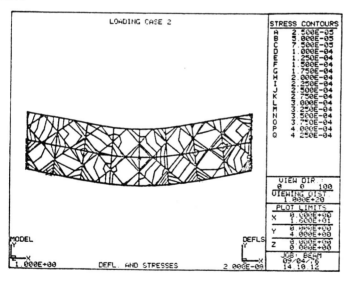

Fig. 45   Stress contours in deflected structure, plotted via RESULT

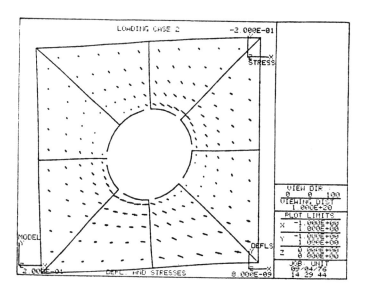

Fig. 46 Negative principle stress vector plot in selected COSUB,
plotted using RESULT

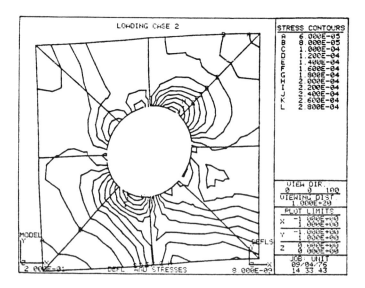

Fig. 47 Von Mises yield stress contours, plotted using RESULT

INTERACTIVE AND DATA MODE PREPROCESSOR FOR SAP

Movses J. Kaldjian

The University of Michigan

INTRODUCTION

An interactive and data mode input preprocessor program called PREMSAP is described briefly in this chapter. PREMSAP prepares the input data for the Michigan Structural Analysis Program (MSAP) and MSAPLOT [1], its graphic partner.

MSAP, which is a modified version of SOLID SAP [2] or SAP IV, is a linear general purpose two- or three-dimensional finite element program. Its input format is rather involved for ordinary use, especially since there are many options available. Insufficient experience with computers and complicated description of input format statements often discourage the uninitiated student and engineer alike from using it to full advantage.

The purpose of PREMSAP, therefore, is to provide the student and the engineer with an easy guide and an efficient way of communicating his mathematical problem to the computer and to allow him to obtain results by avoiding unnecessary and time-consuming mistakes, i.e., to bypass the tedious work of learning and preparing formatted input data statements for MSAP and MSAPLOT.

PREMSAP is a format-free interactive data preprocessor program and can be run from any terminal on a time-sharing computer system or in batch when using the data mode. It is written in FORTRAN IV and is operational on IBM 370/168.

It is the successor of an earlier version [3], and is intended for all structural problems both large and small. PREMSAP does away almost completely with formatted card preparation. It has nodal point and element mesh generation features as well as a data mode option.

In the data mode, prompting is essentially suppressed so that the data can be typed line after line without prompting interruptions in between. The data mode can only be used if a similar problem is first run on the interactive mode, otherwise there is no way of knowing for certain what information is being requested at a given instant.

The nodal point coordinates, x, y, z, may be given also in polar form (as defined by SAP IV) [4] if desired. The latter, however, is limited at present to shells and 3-D solids and when nodal mesh generation option is not required.

Input data formats of MSAP and MSAPLOT are identical with those of SOLID SAP [2] and SAP IV [4] (in static mode with element type 9 excluded). Thus PREMSAP can be used equally well with SOLID SAP or SAP IV.

INPUT/OUTPUT

PREMSAP is an interactive and data mode input program developed to lead the user each step of the way in communicating all the details of his problem to the computer.

After the user has defined his problem with proper sketches and dimensions, he calls on PREMSAP from the terminal. The computer responds by printing a statement requesting some specific piece of information from the user regarding his problem. The user answers back by typing the required information and then returns the carriage. Multiple items on a line must be separated by commas. Either integer or floating point numbers can be used throughout.

The process of requesting information and the user responding to it continues until the last bit of information necessary to complete the input data for MSAP is accomplished.

All the information received above is stored internally by the computer on two separate tapes with different formats. The first tape is printed on file -CDATA when requested. Its main purpose is to be able to detect errors. The second tape is stored either on a temporary or a permanent file and is to be named by the user as he chooses. It contains the information supplied by -CDATA, edited and arranged according to MSAP input format ready to be run in MSAP or MSAPLOT.

It is of course recommended, though not essential for simple problems, to read the MSAP (SOLID SAP or SAP IV) manual and get acquainted with finite element techniques before running PREMSAP on the terminal.

In an indirect fashion, PREMSAP may be used in complicated structural problems also. Since the overall skeleton of the MSAP input data format is the same for simple as well as complicated problems, the user can first obtain his MSAP input data from PREMSAP for a small simplified model of his problem. Then he edits it by adding and modifying directly as required by the actual problem, thereby reducing heavy dependence on formatted statements and general purpose program complications. Note that a similar approach to the above may also be followed when a dynamic response analysis is called for.

PROGRAM DESCRIPTION

MSAP contains the following eight element types (see SOLID SAP or SAP IV [4] manual and Appendix for details).

1. Three-dimensional truss
2. Three-dimensional beam
3. Plane stress membrane
4. Plane stress, plane strain, and axisymmetric elements
5. Three-dimensional solid

    6.   Plate and shell
    7.   Boundary
    8.   Thick-shell element

The above element types are grouped by PREMSAP into four categories, namely:

Two-dimensional problems
    1.   Truss, plane stress, plane strain, axisymmetric, and boundary elements
    2.   beam, plate and shell, and boundary elements
Three-dimensional problems
    3.   truss, three-dimensional solid, thick shell, and boundary elements
    4.   beam, plate and shell, and boundary elements

The first information to be supplied is the input mode type, 0 for interactive and 1 for data mode. Note that with a data mode there is essentially no more prompting; the user is on his own the rest of the way. The next bit of information to be supplied is the title of the problem on one line. This is followed by the number of joints (nodal points), the number of element types, and the number of load cases. Then through three yes or no type questions PREMSAP identifies the category and the nodal mesh generation option of the problem being studied. These are:

. . . IS THE PROBLEM 2-DIMENSIONAL?
. . . ENTER Y FOR YES OR N FOR NO

. . . ARE THERE BEAM, THIN SHELL OR PLATE ELEMENTS INVOLVED
. . . IN THE PROBLEM? (ENTER Y OR N)

and

. . . IS NODAL POINT MESH GENERATION
. . . TO BE PERFORMED? (ENTER Y OR N)

After these questions are answered, the program prompts the user for specific information according to the category of the element and the mesh generation option being used. They include:

    1.   Nodal Point Mesh Generation
        Number of times mesh generation to be used
        First and last nodal points in the series and the
           mesh generation increment KN for each set
    2.   Nodal Point Data
        The coordinates
        The boundary condition codes (0 for free, 1 for constrained)
    3.   Element Mesh Generation
        Number of times mesh generation to be used
        First and last element in the series and the mesh generation increment K
        Element type number

Number of elements
Number of different materials
   a. Material properties
   b. Geometric properties
Element nodal points
(Repeat item 3 for each different element type)
4. Load Data
Number of joints with concentrated loads and moments

As mentioned earlier, all the data the user enters in the computer is stored in the temporary file −CDATA created by the program. The user may ask for the listing of −CDATA and check his figures. If there are mistakes −CDATA must be edited and revised.

If no listing is desired or after the corrections are made, the program reads the data from −CDATA into a second file (FILE2) which is to be named by the user himself. FILE2 is the required input for MSAP.

The user is now ready to obtain his results by typing

        $RUN MSAP 5=FILE2   (for Structural Analysis)
        $RUN MSAPLOT   (for Graphic Display)

COMPUTER EXAMPLES AND PLOTS

For detailed description of the preceding the reader is encouraged to study the five numerical examples given in this chapter, namely:

Example	Title	Element Types Used
1	Five-Story Frame Building	(2)
2	Beam on Elastic Foundation	(1) and (4)
3	Folded Roof	(2) and (6)
4	Cantilever Plate	(5), (7), and (8)
5	Bordered Membrane Shed	(2) and (3)

These are direct computer outputs and are obtained by running PREMSAP. Eight different element types are incorporated into these examples.

The Calcomp plots shown at the end of each example attest to the validity of PREMSAP results. They were obtained by running the MSAPLOT program.

Example 1- Five Story Frame Building

<u>ELEMENT TYPES</u>

Beam   (2)

SECTION PROPERTIES

	I	II	III
A_{ax}	16.20 in^2	17.70	13.20
A_{sh}	7.80 in^2	4.25	3.54
I	1140 in^4	354	249

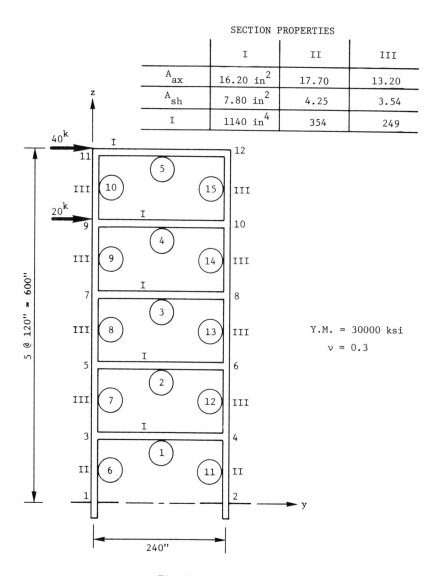

Y.M. = 30000 ksi

$\nu = 0.3$

Fig. 1   Five story frame building

```
#RUN CENA:PREMSAP

...ENTER INPUT MODE TYPE NUMBER
...(0 FOR INTERACTIVE, 1 FOR DATA MODE)
   0

...ENTER PROBLEM TITLE (ONE LINE ONLY)
   FIVE-STORY FRAME BUILDING

...ENTER NUMBER OF JOINTS, NUMBER OF ELEMENT TYPES, AND
...NUMBER OF LOAD CASES (ON ONE LINE SEPARATED BY COMMA)
   12,1,1

...IS THE PROBLEM 2-DIMENSIONAL?
...ENTER Y FOR YES OR N FOR NO
   Y

...NOTE: FOR 2-D PROBLEMS, ALL DATA MUST BE PREPARED IN Y-Z PLANE

...ARE THERE BEAM, THIN SHELL OR PLATE ELEMENTS
...INVOLVED IN THE PROBLEM? (ENTER Y OR N)
   Y

...IS NODAL POINT MESH GENERATION
...TO BE PERFORMED? (ENTER Y OR N)
   Y

...ENTER THE NUMBER OF TIMES THE NODAL POINT
...MESH GENERATION WILL BE USED IN THIS PROBLEM
   2

...FOR EACH MESH GENERATION SET STATED ABOVE,
...ENTER FOLLOWING PER LINE (IN INCREASING SEQ.)
...THE FIRST NODAL POINT NUMBER,THE LAST N. P. NUMBER,
...AND THE MESH GENERATION INCREMENT KN
   3,11,2
   4,12,2

   *** JOINT DATA

...FOR EACH JOINT ENTER FOLLOWING PER LINE
...THE Y-, Z-COORDINATES, AND BOUNDARY COND. CODES (0 FOR
...FREE, 1 FOR CONSTRAINED) IN Y-, Z-DIR., AND X-ROT.
    1:-   0,0,1,1,1
    2:-   240,0,1,1,1
    3:-   0,120
   11:-   0,600
    4:-   240,120
   12:-   240,600
```

```
    *** ELEMENT DATA

...ENTER ELEMENT TYPE NUMBER
...   (1=TRUSS, 2=BEAM, 3=PLANE STRESS MEMBRANE,
...    4=PLANE STRESS, PLANE STRAIN, AND AXISYMMETRIC,
...    5= 3D SOLID 8-NODE-BRICK, 6=PLATE AND THIN SHELL,
...    7=BOUNDARY ELEMENT, 8= 3D THICK SHELL 16-NODE-BRICK)
    2

...IS ELEMENT MESH GENERATION
...TO BE PERFORMED? (ENTER Y OR N)
    Y

...ENTER THE NUMBER OF TIMES THE MESH GENERATION
...WILL BE USED FOR THIS ELEMENT TYPE
    3

...FOR EVERY MESH GENERATION STATED ABOVE
...ENTER FOLLOWING PER LINE (IN INCREASING SEQ.)
...THE FIRST ELEMENT NUMBER,THE LAST ELEM. NUMBER,
...AND THE MESH GENERATION INCREMENT K
    1,5,2
    7,10,2
    12,15,2

    *** BEAM ELEMENTS

...ENTER NUMBER OF ELEMENTS,NUMBER OF DIFF. GEOMETRY,
...AND NUMBER OF DIFF. MATERIALS
    15,3,1

...FOR EACH DIFF. MATERIAL ENTER FOLLOWING PER LINE
...MODULUS OF ELASTICITY AND POISSONS RATIO
    1:-  30000, 0.3

...FOR EACH DIFF. GEOMETRY ENTER FOLLOWING PER LINE
...AXIAL AREA, SHEAR AREA, MOMENT OF INERTIA
...(TO NEGLECT SHEAR DEFORMATIONS SET SHEAR AREAS = 0.)
    1:-  16.20, 7.80, 1140
    2:-  17.70, 4.25, 354
    3:-  13.20, 3.54, 249

...FOR EACH ELEMENT ENTER FOLLOWING PER LINE
...JOINT NOS., I-(BEGINNING), J-(ENDING), K-
...(K IS ANY POINT A DISTANCE AWAY FROM LINE I-J),
...AND I.D. NOS., OF MATERIAL AND GEOMETRY
    1:-   3,4,2,1,1
    5:-   11,12,10,1,1
    6:-   1,3,4,1,2
    7:-   3,5,6,1,3
    10:-  9,11,12,1,3
```

```
          11:-  2,4,3,1,2
          12:-  4,6,5,1,3
          15:-  10,12,11,1,3

       ***CONCENTRATED LOAD DATA

     ...ENTER NUMBER OF JOINTS WITH CONCENTRATED LOADS
          2

     ...FOR EACH LOADED JOINT ENTER FOLLOWING PER LINE
     ...JOINT NO.(IN INCREASING SEQ.), LOADS IN Y-, Z-DIR.,
     ...AND MOMENT X-X
          9, 20
          11, 40

     ...IS LISTING OF ABOVE DATA DESIRED?
     ...ENTER Y FOR YES OR N FOR NO
          Y
  #$LIST -CDATA
  >      1        FIVE-STORY FRAME BUILDING
  >      2           12    1    1
  >      3            1    1    1    1     0.0          0.0        0      0.0
  >      4            2    1    1    1   240.000        0.0        0      0.0
  >      5            3    0    0    0     0.0        120.000      0      0.0
  >      6           11    0    0    0     0.0        600.000      2      0.0
  >      7            4    0    0    0   240.000      120.000      0      0.0
  >      8           12    0    0    0   240.000      600.000      2      0.0
  >      9            2
  >     10           15    3    1
  >     11            1   30000.    0.300000
  >     12            1  1.62E+01  7.80E+00   1.14E+03
  >     13            2  1.77E+01  4.25E+00   3.54E+02
  >     14            3  1.32E+01  3.54E+00   2.49E+02
  >     15            1    3    4    2    1    1    2
  >     16            5   11   12   10    1    1    2
  >     17            6    1    3    4    1    2    0
  >     18            7    3    5    6    1    3    2
  >     19           10    9   11   12    1    3    2
  >     20           11    2    4    3    1    2    0
  >     21           12    4    6    5    1    3    2
  >     22           15   10   12   11    1    3    2
  >     23            2
  >     24            9   20.000      0.0         0.0
  >     25           11   40.000      0.0         0.0
  #

     ...IS ABOVE DATA CORRECT? (ENTER Y OR N)
          Y
```

```
...THE PROGRAM IS READY TO STORE ABOVE DATA IN YOUR OWN FILE
...ACCORDING TO THE INPUT FORMAT OF MSAP
...ENTER YOUR OWN FILE NAME (8 OR LESS CHARACTERS)
   FRAME5

...YOU ARE NOW READY TO OBTAIN YOUR RESULTS BY TYPING
...$RUN CENA:MSAP 5=FRAME5     - FOR STRUCTURAL ANALYSIS
...$RUN CENA:MSAPLOT   FRAME5  - FOR GRAPHIC DISPLAY

#COPY FRAME5
>FIVE-STORY FRAME BUILDING
>  12
^   1  -1   1   1  -1  -1    0.0      0.0      0.0    0   0.0
^   2  -1   1   1  -1  -1    0.0    240.000    0.0    0   0.0
^   3  -1   1   0  -1  -1    0.0      0.0    120.000  2   0.0
^  11  -1   0   0  -1  -1    0.0      0.0    600.000  2
^   4  -1   0   0  -1  -1    0.0    240.000  120.000  2
^  12  -1   0   1  -1  -1    0.0    240.000  600.000  2
^   2  15   3   3.00E+01
^   1  3.00E+04  3.00E-01   0.0   1.14E-01  1.14E-01  1.14E+03
^   2  1.62E+01  7.80E+00   0.0   3.54E-02  3.54E-02  3.54E+02
^   3  1.77E+01  4.25E+00   0.0   2.49E-02  2.49E-02  2.49E+02
^      1.32E+01  3.54E+00
^
^   1   3   4   2   1   1   1   0   0   0   0   2
^   5  11  12  10   1   1   1   0   0   0   0   2
^   6   1   3   4   1   1   2   0   0   0   0   0
^   7   3   5   6   1   1   3   0   0   0   0   2
^  10   9  11  12   1   1   1   0   0   0   0   2
^  11   2   4   1   1   1   2   0   0   0   0   0
^  12   4   6   5   1   1   2   0   0   0   0   2
^  15  10  12  11   1   1   3   0   0   0   0   2
^   9   1   1   1  20.000   0.0   0.0   0.0   0.0   0.0
^  11   1   0   0  40.000   0.0   0.0   0.0   0.0   0.0
>
#
```

```
#RUN CENA:PREMSAP

...ENTER INPUT MODE TYPE NUMBER
...(0 FOR INTERACTIVE, 1 FOR DATA MODE)
   1
    FIVE-STORY FRAME BUILDING
   12,1,1
   Y
   Y
   Y
   2
   3,11,2
   4,12,2

   *** JOINT DATA
    1:-   0,0,1,1,1
    2:-   240,0,1,1,1
    3:-   0,120
   11:-   0,600
    4:-   240,120
   12:-   240,600

   *** ELEMENT DATA
    2
    Y
    3
   1,5,2
   7,10,2
   12,15,2
   15,3,1
    1:-   30000, 0.3
    1:-   16.20, 7.80, 1140
    2:-   17.70, 4.25, 354
    3:-   13.20, 3.54, 249
    1:-   3,4,2,1,1
    5:-   11,12,10,1,1
    6:-   1,3,4,1,2
    7:-   3,5,6,1,3
   10:-   9,11,12,1,3
   11:-   2,4,3,1,2
   12:-   4,6,5,1,3
   15:-   10,12,11,1,3

   ***CONCENTRATED LOAD DATA
    2
     9, 20
    11, 40
    Y
```

```
#$LIST -CDATA
>    1       FIVE-STORY FRAME BUILDING
>    2       12   1   1
>    3        1   1   1   1      0.0        0.0       0     0.0
>    4        2   1   1   1    240.000      0.0       0     0.0
>    5        3   0   0   0      0.0      120.000     0     0.0
>    6       11   0   0   0      0.0      600.000     2     0.0
>    7        4   0   0   0    240.000    120.000     0     0.0
>    8       12   0   0   0    240.000    600.000     2     0.0
>    9        2
>   10       15   3   1
>   11        1     30000.   0.300000
>   12        1  1.62E+01  7.80E+00   1.14E+03
>   13        2  1.77E+01  4.25E+00   3.54E+02
>   14        3  1.32E+01  3.54E+00   2.49E+02
>   15        1   3   4   2   1   1   2
>   16        5  11  12  10   1   1   2
>   17        6   1   3   4   1   2   0
>   18        7   3   5   6   1   3   2
>   19       10   9  11  12   1   3   2
>   20       11   2   4   3   1   2   0
>   21       12   4   6   5   1   3   2
>   22       15  10  12  11   1   3   2
>   23        2
>   24        9   20.000     0.0        0.0
>   25       11   40.000     0.0        0.0
#
    ...IS ABOVE DATA CORRECT? (ENTER Y OR N)
       Y
       -FRAME5

    ...YOU ARE NOW READY TO OBTAIN YOUR RESULTS BY TYPING
    ...$RUN CENA:MSAP 5=-FRAME5        - FOR STRUCTURAL ANALYSIS
    ...$RUN CENA:MSAPLOT               - FOR GRAPHIC DISPLAY
```

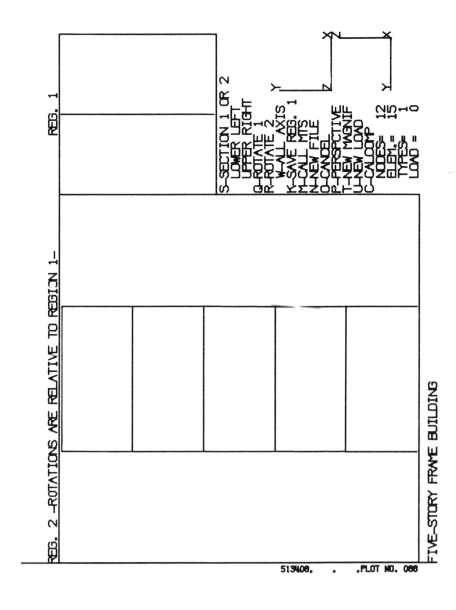

Example 2– Beam On Elastic Foundation

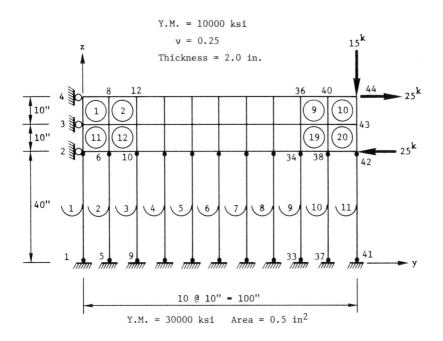

ELEMENT TYPES

Truss   (1)
Plane stress (4)

Y.M. = 10000 ksi
 ν = 0.25
Thickness = 2.0 in.

Fig. 3 Beam on elastic foundation

```
#RUN CENA:PREMSAP

...ENTER INPUT MODE TYPE NUMBER
...(0 FOR INTERACTIVE, 1 FOR DATA MODE)
   0

...ENTER PROBLEM TITLE (ONE LINE ONLY)
   BEAM ON ELASTIC FOUNDATION

...ENTER NUMBER OF JOINTS, NUMBER OF ELEMENT TYPES, AND
...NUMBER OF LOAD CASES (ON ONE LINE SEPARATED BY COMMA)
   44,2,1

...IS THE PROBLEM 2-DIMENSIONAL?
...ENTER Y FOR YES OR N FOR NO
   Y

...NOTE: FOR 2-D PROBLEMS, ALL DATA MUST BE PREPARED IN Y-Z PLANE

...ARE THERE BEAM, THIN SHELL OR PLATE ELEMENTS
...INVOLVED IN THE PROBLEM? (ENTER Y OR N)
   N

...IS NODAL POINT MESH GENERATION
...TO BE PERFORMED? (ENTER Y OR N)
   Y

...ENTER THE NUMBER OF TIMES THE NODAL POINT
...MESH GENERATION WILL BE USED IN THIS PROBLEM
   4

...FOR EACH MESH GENERATION SET STATED ABOVE,
...ENTER FOLLOWING PER LINE (IN INCREASING SEQ.)
...THE FIRST NODAL POINT NUMBER,THE LAST N. P. NUMBER,
...AND THE MESH GENERATION INCREMENT KN
   1,41,4
   6,42,4
   7,43,4
   8,44,4

   *** JOINT DATA

...FOR EACH JOINT ENTER FOLLOWING PER LINE
...THE Y-, Z-COORDINATES ,AND BOUNDARY COND. CODES
...(0 FOR FREE, 1 FOR CONSTRAINED) IN Y-DIR., IN Z-DIR.
    1:-   0,0,1,1
   41:- 100,0,1,1
    2:-   0,40,1,0
    3:-   0,50,1,0
    4:-   0,60,1,0
    6:-  10,40
   42:- 100,40
    7:-  10,50
   43:- 100,50
    8:-  10,60
   44:- 100,60
```

```
     *** ELEMENT DATA

...ENTER ELEMENT TYPE NUMBER
...   (1=TRUSS, 2=BEAM, 3=PLANE STRESS MEMBRANE,
...    4=PLANE STRESS, PLANE STRAIN, AND AXISYMMETRIC,
...    5= 3D SOLID 8-NODE-BRICK, 6=PLATE AND THIN SHELL,
...    7=BOUNDARY ELEMENT, 8= 3D THICK SHELL 16-NODE-BRICK)
     1

...IS ELEMENT MESH GENERATION
...TO BE PERFORMED? (ENTER Y OR N)
     Y

...ENTER THE NUMBER OF TIMES THE MESH GENERATION
...WILL BE USED FOR THIS ELEMENT TYPE
     1

...FOR EVERY MESH GENERATION STATED ABOVE
..ENTER FOLLOWING PER LINE (IN INCREASING SEQ.)
...THE FIRST ELEMENT NUMBER,THE LAST ELEM. NUMBER,
..AND THE MESH GENERATION INCREMENT K
     1,11,4

     *** TRUSS ELEMENTS

...ENTER NUMBER OF ELEMENTS AND NUMBER OF DIFF. MATERIALS
...(INCLUDE DIFF. AREAS IN THE LATTER)
     11,1

...FOR EACH DIFF. MATERIAL (OR AREA) ENTER FOLLOWING PER LINE
...MODULUS OF ELASTICITY AND CROSS-SECTIONAL AREA
     1:-  30000, 0.3

...FOR EACH ELEMENT ENTER FOLLOWING PER LINE
...JOINT NOS. I-(BEGINNING), J-(ENDING), AND MATERIAL I.D. NO.
     1:-  1,2,1
     11:-  41,42,1

...ENTER ELEMENT TYPE NUMBER
...   (1=TRUSS, 2=BEAM, 3=PLANE STRESS MEMBRANE,
...    4=PLANE STRESS, PLANE STRAIN, AND AXISYMMETRIC,
...    5= 3D SOLID 8-NODE-BRICK, 6=PLATE AND THIN SHELL,
...    7=BOUNDARY ELEMENT, 8= 3D THICK SHELL 16-NODE-BRICK)
     4

...IS ELEMENT MESH GENERATION
...TO BE PERFORMED? (ENTER Y OR N)
     Y

...ENTER THE NUMBER OF TIMES THE MESH GENERATION
...WILL BE USED FOR THIS ELEMENT TYPE
     2

...FOR EVERY MESH GENERATION STATED ABOVE
...ENTER FOLLOWING PER LINE (IN INCREASING SEQ.)
...THE FIRST ELEMENT NUMBER,THE LAST ELEM. NUMBER,
..AND THE MESH GENERATION INCREMENT K
     1,10,4
     11,20,4
```

```
     *** 2-DIMENSIONAL FINITE ELEMENTS

...ENTER NUMBER OF ELEMENTS, AND NUMBER OF DIFF. MATERIALS
     20,1

...ENTER ANALYSIS TYPE NUMBER
...( 0 = AXISYMMETRIC, 1 = PLANE STRAIN, 2 = PLANE STRESS)
     2

...FOR EACH DIFF. MATERIAL ENTER FOLLOWING PER LINE
...MODULUS OF ELASTICITY AND POISSONS RATIO
     1:-  10000, .25

...FOR EACH ELEMENT ENTER FOLLOWING PER LINE
...NODES I, J, K, L(FOR TRIANGULAR ELEM. L=K), MATERIAL I.D. NO.,
...NSPRT (SEE NOTE), ELEMENT THICKNESS (FOR PLANE STRESS ONLY)
...  (NSPRT= 0  FOR STRESS OUTPUT AT ELEMENT CENTER
...          1  FOR NO STRESS OUTPUT
...          8  FOR STRESS AT CENTER & MIDPOINT OF SIDE I-L
...         20  FOR STRESS AT CENTER & MIDPOINT OF ALL SIDES)
     1:-   3,7,8,4,1,20,2
    10:-  39,43,44,40,1,20,2
    11:-   2,6,7,3,1,20,2
    20:-  38,42,43,39,1,20,2

     ***CONCENTRATED LOAD DATA

...ENTER NUMBER OF JOINTS WITH CONCENTRATED LOADS
     2

...FOR EACH LOADED JOINT ENTER FOLLOWING PER LINE
...JOINT NO.(IN INCREASING SEQ.), AND LOADS IN Y-, Z-DIR.
     42,  -25, 0
     44,   20, -15

...IS LISTING OF ABOVE DATA DESIRED?
...ENTER Y FOR YES OR N FOR NO
     N

...THE PROGRAM IS READY TO STORE ABOVE DATA IN YOUR OWN FILE
...ACCORDING TO THE INPUT FORMAT OF MSAP
...ENTER YOUR OWN FILE NAME(8 OR LESS CHARACTERS)
     ELASTIC

...YOU ARE NOW READY TO OBTAIN YOUR RESULTS BY TYPING
...$RUN CENA:MSAP 5=ELASTIC    - FOR STRUCTURAL ANALYSIS
...$RUN CENA:MSAPLOT           - FOR GRAPHIC DISPLAY
```

```
#COPY ELASTIC
>BEAM ON ELASTIC FOUNDATION
^ 44  2  1  1  1 -1 -1  0.0    0.0      0.0    0  0.0
^ 41  1  1  1  1 -1 -1  0.0  100.000    0.0    0  0.0
^  2 -1  1  0  1 -1 -1  0.0    0.0     40.000  4  0.0
^  3 -1  1  0  0 -1 -1  0.0    0.0     50.000  0  0.0
^  4 -1  1  0  0 -1 -1  0.0    0.0     60.000  0  0.0
^  6 -1  1  0  0 -1 -1  0.0   10.000   40.000  0  0.0
^ 42 -1  1  0  0 -1 -1  0.0  100.000   50.000  4  0.0
^  7 -1  0  0  0 -1 -1  0.0   10.000   50.000  0  0.0
^ 43 -1  0  0  0 -1 -1  0.0  100.000   50.000  4  0.0
^  8 -1  0  0  0 -1 -1  0.0   10.000   60.000  0  0.0
^ 44 -1  0  0  1 -1 -1  0.0  100.000   60.000  4  0.0
^  1 11  1  1  1 -1
^  1  3.00E+04  0.0  0.0  0.0  3.00E-01  0.0
^
^ 11  1  1  2  1  1  0.0
^ 11 41 42  1  4  4
^  4 20  1  2
^  1 10000. 10000. 10000. 10000. 0.250000 0.250000 0.250000 4000.
^
^  1  3  7  8  4  1  0.0  0.0  20 20  2.00000
^ 10 39 43 44 40  1  0.0  0.0  20 20  2.00000
^ 11  2  6  7  3  1  0.0  0.0  20 20  2.00000
^ 20 38 42 43 39  1  0.0  0.0  20 20  2.00000
^ 42  1  1  0.0 -25.000  -0.0  0.0  0.0  0.0  0.0
^ 44  1  1  0.0  20.000 -15.000 0.0  0.0  0.0  0.0
#
```

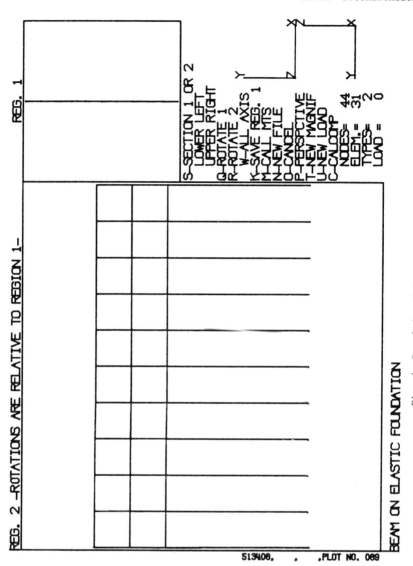

Fig. 4 Resulting Calcomp plot for Example 2

Example 3- Folded Roof

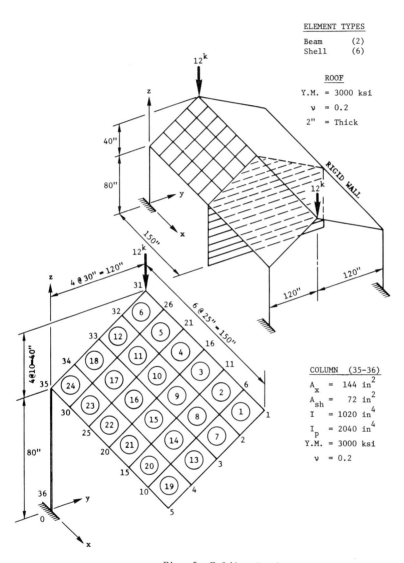

ELEMENT TYPES

| Beam | (2) |
| Shell | (6) |

ROOF

Y.M. = 3000 ksi

ν = 0.2

2" = Thick

COLUMN (35-36)

A_x = 144 in^2

A_{sh} = 72 in^2

I = 1020 in^4

I_p = 2040 in^4

Y.M. = 3000 ksi

ν = 0.2

Fig. 5 Folding Roof

‡RUN CENA:PRE MSAP

...ENTER INPUT MODE TYPE NUMBER
...(0 FOR INTERACTIVE, 1 FOR DATA MODE)
    0

...ENTER PROBLEM TITLE (ONE LINE ONLY)
    FOLDED ROOF

...ENTER NUMBER OF JOINTS, NUMBER OF ELEMENT TYPES, AND
...NUMBER OF LOAD CASES (ON ONE LINE SEPARATED BY COMMA)
    36,2,1

...IS THE PROBLEM 2-DIMENSIONAL?
...ENTER Y FOR YES OR N FOR NO
    N

...ARE THERE BEAM, THIN SHELL OR PLATE ELEMENTS
...INVOLVED IN THE PROBLEM? (ENTER Y OR N)
    Y

...IS NODAL POINT MESH GENERATION
...TO BE PERFORMED? (ENTER Y OR N)
    Y

...ENTER THE NUMBER OF TIMES THE NODAL POINT
...MESH GENERATION WILL BE USED IN THIS PROBLEM
    6

...FOR EACH MESH GENERATION SET STATED ABOVE,
...ENTER FOLLOWING PER LINE (IN INCREASING SEQ.)
...THE FIRST NODAL POINT NUMBER,THE LAST N. P. NUMBER,
...AND THE MESH GENERATION INCREMENT KN
    1,5,1
    6,31,5
    7,32,5
    8,33,5
    9,34,5
    10,35,5

    *** JOINT DATA

...FOR EACH JOINT ENTER FOLLOWING PER LINE
...THE X-, Y-, Z-COORD., BOUNDARY COND. CODES (0 FOR
...FREE, 1 FOR CONSTRND) IN X-, Y-, Z-DIR., X-, Y-, Z-ROT.,
...AND COORD. TYPE (0 FOR RECTANGULAR, 1 FOR CYLINDRICAL)
    1:-   150,120,120,1,1,1,1,1,1
    5:-   150,0,80,1,1,1,1,1,1
    6:-   125,120,120,1,1,0,1,0,1
   31:-   0,120,120,1,1,0,1,0,1
    7:-   125,90,110
   32:-   0,90,110
    8:-   125,60,100

```
33:-   0,60,100
 9:-   125,30,90
34:-   0,30,90
10:-   125,0,80
35:-   0,0,80
36:-   0,0,0,1,1,1,1,1,1
```

*** ELEMENT DATA

...ENTER ELEMENT TYPE NUMBER
...   (1=TRUSS, 2=BEAM, 3=PLANE STRESS MEMBRANE,
...   4=PLANE STRESS, PLANE STRAIN, AND AXISYMMETRIC,
...   5= 3D SOLID 8-NODE-BRICK, 6=PLATE AND THIN SHELL,
...   7=BOUNDARY ELEMENT, 8= 3D THICK SHELL 16-NODE-BRICK)
    6

...IS ELEMENT MESH GENERATION
...TO BE PERFORMED? (ENTER Y OR N)
    Y

...ENTER THE NUMBER OF TIMES THE MESH GENERATION
...WILL BE USED FOR THIS ELEMENT TYPE
    4

...FOR EVERY MESH GENERATION STATED ABOVE
...ENTER FOLLOWING PER LINE (IN INCREASING SEQ.)
...THE FIRST ELEMENT NUMBER,THE LAST ELEM. NUMBER,
...AND THE MESH GENERATION INCREMENT K
    1,6,5
    7,12,5
    13,18,5
    19,24,5
```

*** PLATE OR THIN SHELL ELEMENTS

...ENTER NUMBER OF ELEMENTS, AND NUMBER OF DIFF. MATERIALS
    24,1

...FOR EACH DIFF. MATERIAL ENTER FOLLOWING PER LINE
...MODULUS OF ELASTICITY AND POISSONS RATIO
    1:-   3000, .2

...FOR EACH ELEMENT ENTER FOLLOWING PER LINE
...NODES I, J, K, L(FOR TRIANGULAR ELEM. L=0), MATERIAL I.D. NO.,
...AND ELEMENT THICKNESS
```
    1:-   1,6,7,2,1,2
    6:-   26,31,32,27,1,2
    7:-   2,7,8,3,1,2
   12:-   27,32,33,28,1,2
   13:-   3,8,9,4,1,2
   18:-   28,33,34,29,1,2
   19:-   4,9,10,5,1,2
   24:-   29,34,35,30,1,2
```
```

```
...ENTER ELEMENT TYPE NUMBER
...   (1=TRUSS, 2=BEAM, 3=PLANE STRESS MEMBRANE,
...    4=PLANE STRESS, PLANE STRAIN, AND AXISYMMETRIC,
...    5= 3D SOLID 8-NODE-BRICK, 6=PLATE AND THIN SHELL,
...    7=BOUNDARY ELEMENT, 8= 3D THICK SHELL 16-NODE-BRICK)
     2

...IS ELEMENT MESH GENERATION
...TO BE PERFORMED? (ENTER Y OR N)
     N

   *** BEAM ELEMENTS

...ENTER NUMBER OF ELEMENTS,NUMBER OF DIFF. GEOMETRY,
...AND NUMBER OF DIFF. MATERIALS
     1,1,1

...FOR EACH DIFF. MATERIAL ENTER FOLLOWING PER LINE
...MODULUS OF ELASTICITY AND POISSONS RATIO
     1:-  3000, .2

...FOR EACH DIFF. GEOMETRY ENTER FOLLOWING PER LINE
...AXIAL AREA, SHEAR AREAS IN LOCAL 2-, 3-DIR., AND
...MOMENT OF INERTIAS ABOUT LOCAL 1-1(TORSION), 2-2, 3-3 AXES
     1:-  144,72,72,2040,1020,1020

...FOR EACH ELEMENT ENTER FOLLOWING PER LINE
...JOINT NOS., I-(BEGINNING), J-(ENDING), K-
...(K IS ANY POINT A DISTANCE AWAY FROM LINE I-J),
...AND I.D. NOS., OF MATERIAL AND GEOMETRY
     1:-  36,35,5,1,1

   ***CONCENTRATED LOAD DATA

...ENTER NUMBER OF JOINTS WITH CONCENTRATED LOADS
     1

...FOR EACH LOADED JOINT ENTER FOLLOWING PER LINE
...JOINT NO.(IN INCREASING SEQ.), LOADS IN X-, Y-, Z-DIR.,
...AND MOMENTS ABOUT X-X, Y-Y, Z-Z
     31,0,0,-12

...IS LISTING OF ABOVE DATA DESIRED?
...ENTER Y FOR YES OR N FOR NO
     N

...THE PROGRAM IS READY TO STORE ABOVE DATA IN YOUR OWN FILE
...ACCORDING TO THE INPUT FORMAT OF MSAP
...ENTER YOUR OWN FILE NAME(8 OR LESS CHARACTERS)
     ROOF

...YOU ARE NOW READY TO OBTAIN YOUR RESULTS BY TYPING
...$RUN CENA:MSAP 5=ROOF       - FOR STRUCTURAL ANALYSIS
...$RUN CENA:MSAPLOT           - FOR GRAPHIC DISPLAY
```

```
#COPY ROOF
>FOLDED ROOF
> 36   1  1  1  1  1  1   150.000   120.000   120.000   0   0.0
> 1    1  1  1  1  1  1   150.000     0.0      80.000    1   0.0
> 5    1  1  0  1  1  1   125.000   120.000   120.000    5   0.0
> 6    1  1  0  0  1  1     0.0     120.000   120.000    5   0.0
> 31   1  0  0  0  0  0   125.000    90.000   110.000    5   0.0
> 7    0  0  0  0  0  0     0.0      90.000   110.000    5   0.0
> 32   0  0  0  0  0  0   125.000    60.000   100.000    5   0.0
> 8    0  0  0  0  0  0     0.0      60.000   100.000    5   0.0
> 33   0  0  0  0  0  0   125.000    30.000    90.000    5   0.0
> 9    0  0  0  0  0  0     0.0      30.000    90.000    5   0.0
> 34   0  0  1  0  0  0   125.000     0.0      80.000    5   0.0
> 10   0  1  1  0  0  0     0.0       0.0      80.000    5   0.0
> 35   1  1  0  1  1  0     0.0       0.0       0.0      0   0.0
> 36   1  1  1  1  1  1
> 6   24  1  1              625.0   3125.0    0.0     1250.0   0.0
> 3125.0   0.0   0.0   0.0   0.0   0.0
```

```
> 1    6   7   2   5   5   2.00000   0.0   0.0   0   0.0
> 26  31  32  27   5   5   2.00000   0.0   0.0   0   0.0
> 2    7   8   3   5   5   2.00000   0.0   0.0   0   0.0
> 27  32  33  28   5   5   2.00000   0.0   0.0   0   0.0
> 3    8   9   4   5   5   2.00000   0.0   0.0   0   0.0
> 28  33  34  29   5   5   2.00000   0.0   0.0   0   0.0
> 4    9  10   5   5   5   2.00000   0.0   0.0   0   0.0
> 29  34  35  30   5   5   2.00000   0.0   0.0   0   0.0
> 2    1   0   1
> 1        1
> 1   3.00E+03   2.00E-01   0.0    7.20E+01   1.02E+03   1.02E+03
>    1.44E+02    7.20E+01  -12.000                        0.0
> 1   36  35   5   1   0   0   0   0
> 31   1   0.0   0.0   0.0
#
```

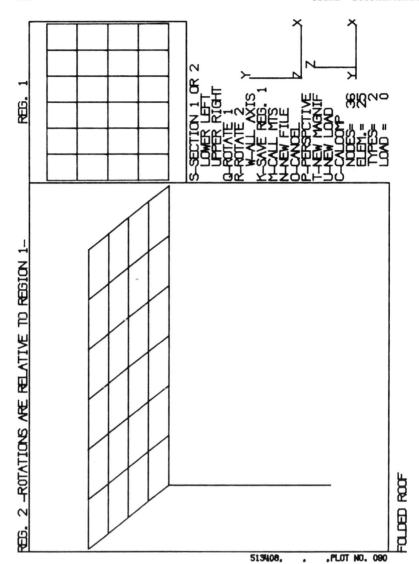

Fig. 6   Calcomp plot for Example 3

Example 4- Cantilever Plate

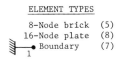

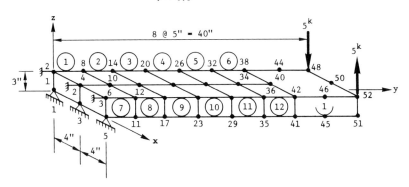

Fig. 7   Cantilever plate showing input for Example 4

```
#RUN CENA:PREMSAP

...ENTER INPUT MODE TYPE NUMBER
...(0 FOR INTERACTIVE, 1 FOR DATA MODE)
   0

...ENTER PROBLEM TITLE (ONE LINE ONLY)
   THREE-D CANTILEVER FLAT BAR

...ENTER NUMBER OF JOINTS, NUMBER OF ELEMENT TYPES, AND
...NUMBER OF LOAD CASES (ON ONE LINE SEPARATED BY COMMA)
   52,3,1

...IS THE PROBLEM 2-DIMENSIONAL?
...ENTER Y FOR YES OR N FOR NO
   N

...ARE THERE BEAM, THIN SHELL OR PLATE ELEMENTS
...INVOLVED IN THE PROBLEM? (ENTER Y OR N)
   N

...IS NODAL POINT MESH GENERATION
...TO BE PERFORMED? (ENTER Y OR N)
   Y

...ENTER THE NUMBER OF TIMES THE NODAL POINT
...MESH GENERATION WILL BE USED IN THIS PROBLEM
   9

...FOR EACH MESH GENERATION SET STATED ABOVE,
...ENTER FOLLOWING PER LINE (IN INCREASING SEQ.)
...THE FIRST NODAL POINT NUMBER,THE LAST N. P. NUMBER,
...AND THE MESH GENERATION INCREMENT KN
   1,5,2
   2,38,6
   4,40,6
   6,42,6
   7,37,6
   9,39,6
   11,41,6
   47,51,2
   48,52,2

   *** JOINT DATA

...FOR EACH JOINT ENTER FOLLOWING PER LINE
...THE X-, Y-, Z-COORDINATES, BOUNDARY COND. CODES
...(0 FOR FREE, 1 FOR CONSTRAINED) IN X- ,Y-, Z-DIR.,
...AND COORD. TYPE (0 FOR RECTANGULAR, 1 FOR CYLINDRICAL)
   1:-  0,0,0,1,1,1
   5:-  8,0,0,1,1,1
```

```
 2:-   0,0,3
38:-   0,30,3
 4:-   4,0,3
40:-   4,30,3
 6:-   8,0,3
42:-   8,30,3
 7:-   0,5,0
37:-   0,30,0
 9:-   4,5,0
39:-   4,30,0
11:-   8,5,0
41:-   8,30,0
43:-   0,35,0
44:-   0,35,3
45:-   8,35,0
46:-   8,35,3
47:-   0,40,0
51:-   8,40,0
48:-   0,40,3
52:-   8,40,3
```

*** ELEMENT DATA

...ENTER ELEMENT TYPE NUMBER
...   (1=TRUSS, 2=BEAM, 3=PLANE STRESS MEMBRANE,
...   4=PLANE STRESS, PLANE STRAIN, AND AXISYMMETRIC,
...   5= 3D SOLID 8-NODE-BRICK, 6=PLATE AND THIN SHELL,
...   7=BOUNDARY ELEMENT, 8= 3D THICK SHELL 16-NODE-BRICK)
    5

...IS ELEMENT MESH GENERATION
...TO BE PERFORMED? (ENTER Y OR N)
    Y

...ENTER THE NUMBER OF TIMES THE MESH GENERATION
...WILL BE USED FOR THIS ELEMENT TYPE
    2

...FOR EVERY MESH GENERATION STATED ABOVE
...ENTER FOLLOWING PER LINE (IN INCREASING SEQ.)
...THE FIRST ELEMENT NUMBER,THE LAST ELEM. NUMBER,
...AND THE MESH GENERATION INCREMENT K
    1,6,6
    7,12,6

*** 3-D SOLID ELEMENTS

...ENTER NUMBER OF ELEMENTS, AND NUMBER OF DIFF. MATERIALS
    12,1

...FOR EACH DIFF. MATERIAL ENTER FOLLOWING PER LINE
...MODULUS OF ELASTICITY, AND POISSONS RATIO
    1:-   10000, .3

```
...FOR EACH ELEMENT ENTER FOLLOWING PER LINE
...NODE NOS.(CORRESPONDING TO ELEM. NODES 1,2,3,4,5,6,7,8),
...INTERGRATION ORDER (2 FOR RECTANGULAR ELEM., OR 3 FOR SKEWED ELEM.),
...MATERIAL I.D. NO., AND TWO FACE NUMBERS
...(FOR STRESS OUTPUT FROM FOLLOWING NOS. 0,1,2,3,4,5, OR 6)
    1:-   3,9,7,1,4,10,8,2,2,1,6,0
    6:-   33,39,37,31,34,40,38,32,2,1,6,0
    7:-   5,11,9,3,6,12,10,4,2,1,6,0
   12:-   35,41,39,33,36,42,40,34,2,1,6,0

...ENTER ELEMENT TYPE NUMBER
...   (1=TRUSS, 2=BEAM, 3=PLANE STRESS MEMBRANE,
...    4=PLANE STRESS, PLANE STRAIN, AND AXISYMMETRIC,
...    5= 3D SOLID 8-NODE-BRICK, 6=PLATE AND THIN SHELL,
...    7=BOUNDARY ELEMENT, 8= 3D THICK SHELL 16-NODE-BRICK)
     8

...IS ELEMENT MESH GENERATION
...TO BE PERFORMED? (ENTER Y OR N)
     N

    *** 3-D THICK SHELL ELEMENTS

...ENTER NUMBER OF ELEMENTS, NUMBER OF DIFF. MATERIALS
     1,1

...FOR EACH DIFF. MATERIAL ENTER FOLLOWING PER LINE
...MODULUS OF ELASTICITY AND POISSONS RATIO
     1:-   10000, .3

...FOR EACH ELEMENT ENTER FOLLOWING PER LINE
...INTEGRATION ORDER (3 FOR REGULAR SHAPE, 4 FOR IRREGULAR SHAPE),
...MATERIAL I.D. NO., AND SIXTEEN NODAL POINT NOS.
...CORRESPONDING TO ELEMENT LOCAL NODES (1 TO 16)
     1:-   3,1,52,48,38,42,51,47,37,41,50,44,40,46,49,43,39,45

...ENTER ELEMENT TYPE NUMBER
...   (1=TRUSS, 2=BEAM, 3=PLANE STRESS MEMBRANE,
...    4=PLANE STRESS, PLANE STRAIN, AND AXISYMMETRIC,
...    5= 3D SOLID 8-NODE-BRICK, 6=PLATE AND THIN SHELL,
...    7=BOUNDARY ELEMENT, 8= 3D THICK SHELL 16-NODE-BRICK)
     7

...IS ELEMENT MESH GENERATION
...TO BE PERFORMED? (ENTER Y OR N)
     Y

...ENTER THE NUMBER OF TIMES THE MESH GENERATION
...WILL BE USED FOR THIS ELEMENT TYPE
     1
```

```
...FOR EVERY MESH GENERATION STATED ABOVE
...ENTER FOLLOWING PER LINE (IN INCREASING SEQ.)
...THE FIRST ELEMENT NUMBER,THE LAST ELEM. NUMBER,
...AND THE MESH GENERATION INCREMENT K
   1,3,2

   *** BOUNDARY ELEMENTS

...ENTER NUMBER OF ELEMENTS
   3

...FOR EACH ELEMENT ENTER FOLLOWING PER LINE
...NODE N (WHERE THE ELEMENT IS PLACED, IN ASCENDING ORDER),
...NODE I (THIS DEFINES THE DIRECTION OF THE ELEMENT),
...DISPLACEMENT CODE(0 OR 1), ROTATION CODE(0 OR 1),
...SPECIFIED DISPLACEMENT, SPECIFIED ROTATION, AND
...SPRING STIFFNESS (SET TO 1.0*E10 IF LEFT BLANK)
   1:-  2,8,1
   3:-  6,12,1

   ***CONCENTRATED LOAD DATA

...ENTER NUMBER OF JOINTS WITH CONCENTRATED LOADS
   2

...FOR EACH LOADED JOINT ENTER FOLLOWING PER LINE
...JOINT NO.(IN INCREASING SEQ.), AND LOADS IN X-, Y-, Z-DIR.
   48, 0, 0, -5
   52, 0, 0,  5

...IS LISTING OF ABOVE DATA DESIRED?
...ENTER Y FOR YES OR N FOR NO
   N

...THE PROGRAM IS READY TO STORE ABOVE DATA IN YOUR OWN FILE
...ACCORDING TO THE INPUT FORMAT OF MSAP
...ENTER YOUR OWN FILE NAME(8 OR LESS CHARACTERS)
   FLATBAR

...YOU ARE NOW READY TO OBTAIN YOUR RESULTS BY TYPING
...$RUN CENA:MSAP 5=FLATBAR     - FOR STRUCTURAL ANALYSIS
...$RUN CENA:MSAPLOT            - FOR GRAPHIC DISPLAY
```

```
#COPY FLATBAR
>THREE-D CANTILEVER FLAT BAR
> 52  3  1  1  1 -1 -1 -1     0.000    0.0       0.0       2   0.0   0.0
>  1  1  1  1  0 -1 -1 -1     8.000    0.0       0.0       0   0.0   0.0
>  5  1  1  0  0 -1 -1 -1     0.000    0.0       6.0       0.0
>  2  0  0  0  0 -1 -1 -1     0.000   30.000     3.000     6   0.0   0.0
> 38  0  0  0  0 -1 -1 -1     4.000    0.0       3.000     6   0.0   0.0
>  4  0  0  0  0 -1 -1 -1     4.000   30.000     3.000     6   0.0   0.0
> 40  0  0  0  0 -1 -1 -1     8.000    0.0       3.000     6   0.0   0.0
>  6  0  0  0  0 -1 -1 -1     8.000   30.000     3.000     6   0.0   0.0
> 42  0  0  0  0 -1 -1 -1     0.000    5.000     0.0       0   0.0   0.0
>  7  0  0  0  0 -1 -1 -1     4.000   30.000     0.0       0   0.0   0.0
> 37  0  0  0  0 -1 -1 -1     0.000    5.000     0.0       0   0.0   0.0
>  9  0  0  0  0 -1 -1 -1     8.000   30.000     0.0       0   0.0   0.0
> 39  0  0  0  0 -1 -1 -1     0.000    5.000     3.000     6   0.0   0.0
> 11  0  0  0  0 -1 -1 -1     8.000   30.000     3.000     6   0.0   0.0
> 41  0  0  0  0 -1 -1 -1     0.000   35.000     0.0       0   0.0   0.0
> 43  0  0  0  0 -1 -1 -1     8.000   35.000     0.0       0   0.0   0.0
> 44  0  0  0  0 -1 -1 -1     0.000   35.000     3.000     6   0.0   0.0
> 45  0  0  0  0 -1 -1 -1     8.000   35.000     0.0       0   0.0   0.0
> 46  0  0  0  0 -1 -1 -1     0.000   40.000     0.0       0   0.0   0.0
> 47  0  0  0  0 -1 -1 -1     8.000   40.000     3.000     6   0.0   0.0
> 51  0  0  0  0 -1 -1 -1     0.000   40.000     0.0       2   0.0   0.0
> 48  0  0  0  0 -1 -1 -1     0.000   40.000     0.0       0   0.0   0.0
> 52  0  0  0  0 -1 -1 -1     8.000   40.000     3.000     2   0.0   0.0
>  5 12  1  1  1 -1             10000.     0.300000
>  1
>  6 33 39 31 34 40 38 32  2  1  6  60  0.0
```

```
7    5   11    9    3    6   12   10    4    2    1    6   60  0.0
12   35   41   39   33   36   42   40   34    2    1    6   60  0.0
 8    1    1
 1        10000. 0.300000

                                    45
                                    39
                                    43
                                    49
                                    46
                                    40
                                    44
                                    50
                                    41
                                    37
                                    47
                                    51
                                    42
                                    38

 1    3    1    0    3    0.0  1    0    2    0    0    0.0  0.0  0.0  0.0
52   48   38   42   51   0.0  1    0    2    0   -5.000 0.0  0.0  0.0  0.0
 7    3                               37   41        5.000
 1.0

 2    8
 6   12
48    1
52    1

 1.00

^^^^^^^^^^^^^^^^^^^^^^^^^^^^#
```

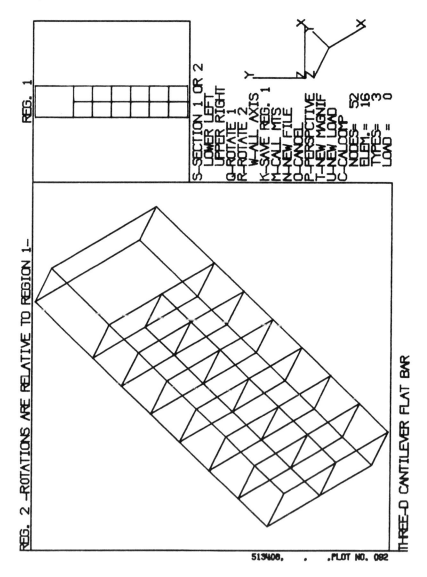

REG. 1

REG. 2 —ROTATIONS ARE RELATIVE TO REGION 1—

S—SECTION 1 OR 2
LOWER LEFT
UPPER RIGHT
Q—ROTATE 1
R—ROTATE 2
W—ALL AXIS
K—SAVE REG. 1
M—CALL MTS
N—NEW FILE
O—CANCEL
P—PERSPCTIVE
T—NEW MAGNIF
U—NEW LOAD
C—CALCOMP

NODES= 52
ELEM.= 16
TYPES= 3
LOAD = 0

THREE-D CANTILEVER FLAT BAR

513408,   .   .PLOT NO. 082

Fig. 8 Calcomp plot for Example 4

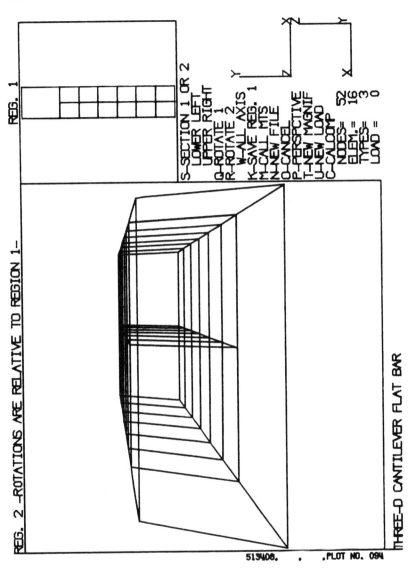

Fig. 9 Calcomp plot for Example 4

Example 5-   Bordered Membrane Shed

ELEMENT TYPES

Beam   (2)
Membrane   (3)

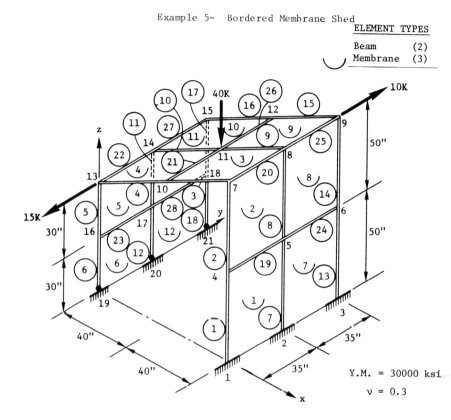

Membrane .125 in. thick

Section Properties

	A_x	A_{s2}	A_{s3}	J	I_2	I_3
Frames	6.20	2.38	1.84	.210	107	10.8
Horiz. Beams	5.01	1.96	1.62	.147	56.6	7.44

Load cases	1	2	3
Loads	10,15	40	10,40,15

Fig. 10 Diagram showing input data for Example 5

```
#RUN CENA:PREMSAP

...ENTER INPUT MODE TYPE NUMBER
...(0 FOR INTERACTIVE, 1 FOR DATA MODE)
     0

...ENTER PROBLEM TITLE (ONE LINE ONLY)
     BORDERED MEMBRANE SHED

...ENTER NUMBER OF JOINTS, NUMBER OF ELEMENT TYPES, AND
...NUMBER OF LOAD CASES (ON ONE LINE SEPARATED BY COMMA)
     21,2,3

...IS THE PROBLEM 2-DIMENSIONAL?
...ENTER Y FOR YES OR N FOR NO
     N

...ARE THERE BEAM, THIN SHELL OR PLATE ELEMENTS
...INVOLVED IN THE PROBLEM? (ENTER Y OR N)
     Y

...IS NODAL POINT MESH GENERATION
...TO BE PERFORMED? (ENTER Y OR N)
     Y

...ENTER THE NUMBER OF TIMES THE NODAL POINT
...MESH GENERATION WILL BE USED IN THIS PROBLEM
     7

...FOR EACH MESH GENERATION SET STATED ABOVE,
...ENTER FOLLOWING PER LINE (IN INCREASING SEQ.)
...THE FIRST NODAL POINT NUMBER,THE LAST N. P. NUMBER,
...AND THE MESH GENERATION INCREMENT KN
     1,3,1
     4,6,1
     7,9,1
     10,12,1
     13,15,1
     16,18,1
     19,21,1

   *** JOINT DATA

...FOR EACH JOINT ENTER FOLLOWING PER LINE
...THE X-, Y-, Z-COORD., BOUNDARY COND. CODES (0 FOR
...FREE, 1 FOR CONSTRND) IN X-, Y-, Z-DIR., X-, Y-, Z-ROT.,
...AND COORD. TYPE (0 FOR RECTANGULAR, 1 FOR CYLINDRICAL)
     1:-   80,0,0,1,1,1,1,1,1
     3:-   80,70,0,1,1,1,1,1,1
     4:-   80,0,50
     6:-   80,70,50
```

```
    7:-   80,0,100
    9:-   80,70,100
   10:-   40,0,80
   12:-   40,70,80
   13:-   0,0,60
   15:-   0,7u,60
   16:-   0,0,30
   18:-   0,70,30
   19:-   0,0,0,1,1,1
   21:-   0,70,0,1,1,1
```

    *** ELEMENT DATA

...ENTER ELEMENT TYPE NUMBER
...   (1=TRUSS, 2=BEAM, 3=PLANE STRESS MEMBRANE,
...   4=PLANE STRESS, PLANE STRAIN, AND AXISYMMETRIC,
...   5= 3D SOLID 8-NODE-BRICK, 6=PLATE AND THIN SHELL,
...   7=BOUNDARY ELEMENT, 8= 3D THICK SHELL 16-NODE-BRICK)
    2

...IS ELEMENT MESH GENERATION
...TO BE PERFORMED? (ENTER Y OR N)
    Y

...ENTER THE NUMBER OF TIMES THE MESH GENERATION
...WILL BE USED FOR THIS ELEMENT TYPE
    3

...FOR EVERY MESH GENERATION STATED ABOVE
...ENTER FOLLOWING PER LINE (IN INCREASING SEQ.)
...THE FIRST ELEMENT NUMBER,THE LAST ELEM. NUMBER,
...AND THE MESH GENERATION INCREMENT K
    1,6,3
    7,12,3
    13,18,3

    *** BEAM ELEMENTS

...ENTER NUMBER OF ELEMENTS,NUMBER OF DIFF. GEOMETRY,
...AND NUMBER OF DIFF. MATERIALS
    28,2,1

...FOR EACH DIFF. MATERIAL ENTER FOLLOWING PER LINE
...MODULUS OF ELASTICITY AND POISSONS RATIO
    1:-   30000., .3

```
...FOR EACH DIFF. GEOMETRY ENTER FOLLOWING PER LINE
...AXIAL AREA, SHEAR AREAS IN LOCAL 2-, 3-DIR., AND
...MOMENT OF INERTIAS ABOUT LOCAL 1-1(TORSION), 2-2, 3-3 AXES
    1:-  6.20,2.38,1.84,.210,107.,10.8
    2:-  5.01,1.96,1.62,.147,56.6,7.44

...FOR EACH ELEMENT ENTER FOLLOWING PER LINE
...JOINT NOS., I-(BEGINNING), J-(ENDING), K-
...(K IS ANY POINT A DISTANCE AWAY FROM LINE I-J),
...AND I.D. NOS., OF MATERIAL AND GEOMETRY
    1:-   1,4,2,1,1
    6:-  16,19,17,1,1
    7:-   2,5,3,1,1
   12:-  17,20,18,1,1
   13:-   3,6,2,1,1
   18:-  18,21,17,1,1
   19:-   4,5,8,1,2
   20:-   7,8,5,1,2
   21:-  10,11,8,1,2
   22:-  13,14,11,1,2
   23:-  16,17,14,1,2
   24:-   5,6,9,1,2
   25:-   8,9,6,1,2
   26:-  11,12,9,1,2
   27:-  14,15,12,1,2
   28:-  17,18,15,1,2

...ENTER ELEMENT TYPE NUMBER
...    (1=TRUSS, 2=BEAM, 3=PLANE STRESS MEMBRANE,
...     4=PLANE STRESS, PLANE STRAIN, AND AXISYMMETRIC,
...     5= 3D SOLID 8-NODE-BRICK, 6=PLATE AND THIN SHELL,
...     7=BOUNDARY ELEMENT, 8= 3D THICK SHELL 16-NODE-BRICK)
      3

...IS ELEMENT MESH GENERATION
...TO BE PERFORMED? (ENTER Y OR N)
      Y

...ENTER THE NUMBER OF TIMES THE MESH GENERATION
...WILL BE USED FOR THIS ELEMENT TYPE
      2

...FOR EVERY MESH GENERATION STATED ABOVE
...ENTER FOLLOWING PER LINE (IN INCREASING SEQ.)
...THE FIRST ELEMENT NUMBER,THE LAST ELEM. NUMBER,
...AND THE MESH GENERATION INCREMENT K
    1,6,3
    7,12,3
```

```
    *** PLANE STRESS MEMBRANE ELEMENTS

...ENTER NUMBER OF ELEMENTS, AND NUMBER OF DIFF. MATERIALS
    12,1

    ...FOR EACH DIFF. MATERIAL ENTER FOLLOWING PER LINE
...MODULUS OF ELASTICITY AND POISSONS RATIO
    1:-  30000., .3

...FOR EACH ELEMENT ENTER FOLLOWING PER LINE
...NODES I, J, K, L(FOR TRIANGULAR ELEM. L=K), MATERIAL I.D. NO.,
...NSPRT (SEE NOTE), ELEMENT THICKNESS (FOR PLANE STRESS ONLY)
... (NSPRT= 0  FOR STRESS OUTPUT AT ELEMENT CENTER
...          1  FOR NO STRESS OUTPUT
...          8  FOR STRESS AT CENTER & MIDPOINT OF SIDE I-L
...         20  FOR STRESS AT CENTER & MIDPOINT OF ALL SIDES)
    1:-  1,2,5,4,1,8,.125
    6:-  2,3,6,5,1,8,.125
    7:-  20,19,16,17,1,8,.125
   12:-  21,20,17,18,1,8,.125

...ENTER NUMBER OF JOINTS WITH CONCENTRATED LOADS
...FOR ALL LOAD CASES
    6

...FOR EACH LOADED JOINT ENTER FOLLOWING PER LINE
...JOINT AND LOAD CASE NOS. (IN INCREASING SEQ.)
...LOADS IN X-, Y-, Z-DIR.,
...AND MOMENTS X-X, Y-Y, Z-Z
    9, 1, 0., 10.
    9, 3, 0., 10.
    11, 2, 0.,0.,-40.
    11, 3, 0.,0.,-40.
    13, 1, 0.,-15.
    13, 3, 0.,-15.

...IS LISTING OF ABOVE DATA DESIRED?
...ENTER Y FOR YES OR N FOR NO
    N

...THE PROGRAM IS READY TO STORE ABOVE DATA IN YOUR OWN FILE
...ACCORDING TO THE INPUT FORMAT OF MSAP
...ENTER YOUR OWN FILE NAME(8 OR LESS CHARACTERS)
    SHEDD

...YOU ARE NOW READY TO OBTAIN YOUR RESULTS BY TYPING
...$RUN CENA:MSAP 5=SHEDD       - FOR STRUCTURAL ANALYSIS
...$RUN CENA:MSAPLOT            - FOR GRAPHIC DISPLAY
```

#LIST SHEDD

BORDERED MEMBRANE SHED

```
                                              11538.

 0  0  0  0        0.300000        0.12500  0
 0  0  0  0                        0.12500  0
                                   0.12500  0
                                   0.12500  0
                                            0.0
                                            0.0
                                            0.0
                                            0.0

 0  0  0  0        0.300000     3  3  3  3
 0  0  0  0                                 0.0
                                            0.0
                                            0.0
                   0.300000     8  8  8  8  0.0
                                            0.0
 0  0  0  0        0.300000                 0.0
 0  0  0  0                                 0.0
                                            0.0
                                            0.0
                                            0.0
                                            0.0

 0  0  0  0        30000.                   0.0    0.000
 0  0  0  0                                 0.0    0.000
                                            0.0  -40.000
                                            0.0  -40.000
                                            0.0    0.0
                                            0.0    0.0

 2  2  2  3        30000.        1  1  1  1  0
 1  1  1  1                      4           10.000   0.0
                                 5           10.000   0.0
                                17           0.0
                                18           0.0
                                             0.0    -15.000
                                                    -15.000

 6  9 -2 15        30000.        5  6 16 17
 9 12 15 18 1                    2           0.0
                                 3 19        0.0
                                   20        0.0
                                             0.0
                                             0.0

 8 11 14 17 12                   1  2 20 21  3  2  3  1  3

25 26 27 28  3  1                1  6  7 12  9  9 11 11 13 13
```

```
   36 >
   37 >
   38 >
   39 >
   40 >
   41 >
   42 >
   43 >
   44 >
   45 >
   46 >
   47 >
   48 >
   49 >
   50 >
   51 >
   52 >
   53 >
   54 >
   55 >
   56 >
   57 >
   58 >
   59 >
   60 >
   61 >
```

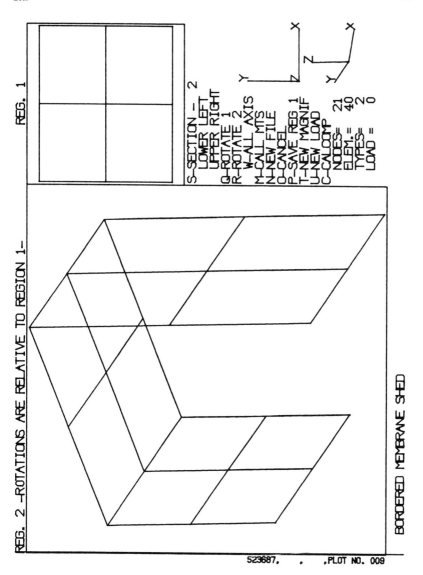

Fig. 11 Calcomp plot for Example 5

SUMMARY AND CONCLUSIONS

The preceding interactive and data mode program PREMSAP is very easy to use. It is intended to facilitate and thereby encourage beginners as well as experienced students and engineers to use MSAP (SOLID SAP, SAP IV) and MSAPLOT in various structural problems encountered in the classroom or in the office. In short, PREMSAP makes preparing tedious formatted input statements for MSAP almost obsolete.

PREMSAP is format free and requires a minimal knowledge of the computer and finite element methods.

Knowledge of MSAP (SOLID SAP or SAP IV) and MSAPLOT manuals is encouraged for a better understanding of the mechanics behind the PREMSAP process.

For the sake of simplicity, a number of options, such as gravity, temperature,and pressure loads are purposely deleted from the program. They can be added with ease by editing the PREMSAP output, namely file FILE2.

REFERENCES

1 Kaldjian, M. J., and Huang, K. N., "Users Guide to MSAPLOT - A 3-D Interactive Graphic Display Program for the Input and Output Data of Michigan Structural Program MSAP," No. 172,Dept. of Naval Arch. and Marine Engineering, Univ. of Mich., Ann Arbor, Mich. 48109, June 1975.

2 Wilson, E. L., "SOLID SAP - A Static Analysis Program for 3-D Solid Structures," UC-SESM 71-19, Dept. ot Civil Eng'g., Univ. of Calif., Berkeley, Dec. 1972.

3 Kaldjian, M. J., "Interactive Data Preprocessor Program for Michigan SAP (MSAP)," Proceedings 2nd National Symposium on Computerized Structural Analysis and Design, George Washington Univ., Washington, D.C., March 1976.

4 Bathe, K. J., Wilson, E. L., and Peterson, F. E., "SAP IV - A Structural Analysis Program for Static and Dynamic Response of Linear Systems," EERC 73-11, Earthquake Eng'g., Research Center, College of Eng'g., Univ. of Calif., Berkeley, June 1973.

NOTE

APPENDIXES A and B are direct reproductions from the SAP IV [4] Manual. This manual, as well as SOLID SAP, can be ordered for $5 each, from NISEE, 729 Davis Hall, University of California, Berkeley, California, 94720, Attn: Ken Wong.

APPENDIX I

THE ELEMENT LIBRARY

The element library of SAP IV consists of eight different element
types. These elements can be used in either a static or dynamic
analysis. They are shown in Fig. A1 and are briefly described below.

Three-Dimensional Truss Element

The derivation of the truss element stiffness is given in Refs. [A1,
A2]. The element can be subjected to a uniform temperature change.

Three-Dimensional Beam Element

The beam element included in the program considers torsion, bending
about two axes, axial, and shearing deformations. The element is
prismatic. The development of its stiffness properties is standard
and is given in Ref. [A2]. Inertia loading in three directions and
specified fixed-end forces form the element load cases. Forces
(axial and shear) and moments (bending and torsion) are calculated in
the beam local coordinate system.
   A typical beam element is shown in Fig. A1. A plane which
defines the principal bending axis of the beam is specified by the
plane i,j,k. Only the geometry of nodal point k is needed; therefore,
no additional degrees of freedom for nodal point k are used in the
computer program. A unique option of the beam member is that the
ends of the beam can be geometrically constrained to a master node.
Slave degrees of freedom at the end of the beam are eliminated from
the formulation and replaced by the transformed degrees of freedom of
the master node [A3,A2]. This technique reduces the total number
of joint equilibrium equations in the system (while possibly increasing the bandwidth) and greatly reduces the possibility of numerical sensitivities in many types of structures. Also, the method can
be used to specify rigid floor diaphragms in building analysis.

Plane Stress, Plane Strain, and Axisymmetric Elements

A plane stress quadrilateral (or triangular) element with orthotropic
material properties is available. Each plane stress element may be
of different thickness and may be located in an arbitrary plane with
respect to the three-dimensional coordinate system. The plane strain
and axisymmetric elements are restricted to the y,z plane. Gravity,
inertia and temperature loadings may be considered. Stresses may be
computed at the center of the element and at the center of each side.
The element is based on an isoparametric formulation [A4,A5].

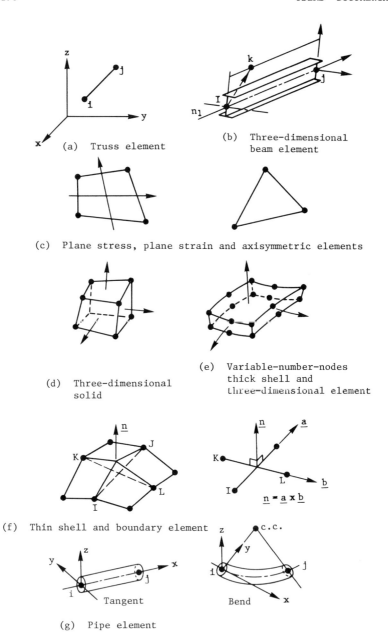

(a) Truss element

(b) Three-dimensional
     beam element

(c) Plane stress, plane strain and axisymmetric elements

(d) Three-dimensional
     solid

(e) Variable-number-nodes
     thick shell and
     three-dimensional element

(f) Thin shell and boundary element

(g) Pipe element

Fig. A1 Element library of SAP IV

Incompatible displacement modes can be included in order to improve
the bending properties of the element [A6,A2,A7].

Three-Dimensional Solid Element

A general eight-nodal point "brick" element, with three translational degrees of freedom per nodal point can be used (see Fig. A1d).
Isotropic material properties are assumed, and element loading consists of temperature, surface pressure, and inertia loads in three
directions. Stresses (six components) may be computed at the center
of the element and at the center of each face. The element employs
incompatible modes, which can be very effective if rectangular elements are used [A6].

Variable-Number-Nodes Thick-Shell and Three-Dimensional Element

A general three-dimensional isoparametric or subparametric element
which may have from 8 to 21 nodes can be used for three-dimensional
or thick-shell analysis (see Fig. A1e) [A8,A9]. General orthotropic
material properties can be assigned to the element. The loading may
consist of applied surface pressure, hydrostatic loads, inertia loads
in three directions, and thermal loads. Six global stresses are output at up to seven locations within an element.

Thin Plate and Shell Element

The thin-shell element available in the program is a quadrilateral of
arbitrary geometry formed from four compatible triangles. The bending and plane stress properties of the element are described in
references [A10,A11]. The shell element uses the constant strain
triangle and the LCCT9 element to represent the membrane and bending
behavior, respectively. The central node is located at the average
of the coordinates of the four corner nodes. The element has six
interior degrees of freedom which are eliminated at the element level
prior to assembly; therefore, the resulting quadrilateral element has
twenty-four degrees of freedom, i.e., six degrees of freedom per node
in the global coordinate system.
     In the analysis of flat plates the stiffness associated with the
rotation normal to the shell surface is not defined; therefore, the
rotation normal degree of freedom must not be included in the analysis.
For curved shells, the normal rotation need be included as an extra
degree of freedom. In case the curvature is very small, the degree
of freedom should be restrained by the addition of a "Boundary
Element" with a small normal rotational stiffness, say of less or
about 10% of the element bending stiffness [A12,A5].

Boundary Element

The boundary element, shown in Fig. A1f can be used for the following:

1. in the idealization of an external elastic support at a
node;
2. in the idealization of an inclined roller support;
3. to specify a displacement, or
4. to eliminate the numerical difficulty associated with the
'sixth' degree of freedom in the analysis of nearly flat shells.

The element is one-dimensional with an axial or torsional stiffness.
The element stiffness coefficients are added directly to the total
stiffness matrix.

Pipe Element

The pipe element (Fig. Alg) can represent a straight element
(tangent) or a circularly curved segment (bend); both elements require
a uniform section and uniform material properties. Elements can be
directed arbitrarily in space. The member stiffness matrices account
for bending, torsional, axial,and shearing deformations. In addition,
the effect of internal pressure on the stiffness of curved pipe elements is considered.
    The types of structure loads contributed by the pipe elements
include gravity loading in the global directions and loads due to
thermal distortions and deformations induced by internal pressure.
Forces and moments acting at the member ends (i,j) and at the center
of each bend are calculated in coordinate systems aligned with the
member's cross section.
    The pipe element stiffness matrix is formed by first evaluating
the flexibility matrix corresponding to the six degrees of freedom at
end j as given by Poley [A13]. With the corresponding stiffness
matrix, the equilibrium transformations outlined by Hall et al.
[A14] are used to form the complete element stiffness matrix. Dis-
torsions due to element loads are premultiplied by the stiffness
matrix to compute restrained nodal forces due to thermal, pressure,or
gravity loads.

APPENDIX II

STATIC ANALYSIS

A static analysis involves the solution of the equilibrium equations

$$Ku = R \qquad (1)$$

followed by the calculation of element stresses.

Solution of Equilibrium Equations

The load vectors R have been assembled at the same time as the structure stiffness matrix and mass matrix were formed. The solution of the equations is obtained using the large capacity linear equation solver SESOL [A15]. This subroutine uses Gauss elimination on the positive-definite symmetrical system of equations. The algorithm performs a minimum number of operations; i.e., there are no operations with zero elements. In the program, the $L^{T}DL$ decomposition of K is used, hence Eq. (1) can be written as

$$L^{T}v = R \qquad (2)$$

and

$$v = DLu \qquad (3)$$

where the solution for v in Eq. (2) is obtained by a reduction of the load vectors; the displacement vectors u are then calculated by a back-substitution.

In the solution, the load vectors are reduced at the same time as K is decomposed. In all operations it is necessary to have at any one time the required matrix elements in high-speed storage. In the reduction, two blocks are in high-speed storage (as was also the case in the formation of the stiffness matrix and mass matrix), i.e., the "leading" block, which finally stores the elements of L and D, and in succession those blocks which are affected by the decomposition of the "leading" block.

Evaluation of Element Stresses

After the nodal point displacements have been evaluated, the element stress-displacement matrices are read sequentually from low-speed storage, and the element stresses are calculated.

REFERENCES FOR APPENDIXES

A1 Przemieniecki, J. S., Theory of Matrix Structural Analysis, McGraw-Hill, New York, 1968.

A2 Wilson, E. L., "SOLID SAP - A Static Analysis Program for Three-Dimensional Solid Structures," SESM Report 71-19, Dept. of Civil Engineering, University of California, Berkeley, 1971.

A3 Irons, B. M., "Structural Eigenvalue Problems: Elimination of Unwanted Variables," Journal A.I.A.A., Vol. 3, 1965.

A4 Irons, B. M., Numerical Integration Applied to Finite Element Methods," Conf. on Use of Digital Computers in Structural Engineering, University of New Castle, England, July 1966.

A5 Zienkiewicz, O. C., The Finite Element Method in Engineering Science, McGraw-Hill, New York, 1971.

A6 Strang, G., and Fix, G. J., "Analysis of the Finite Element Method," Prentice Hall, Englewood Cliffs, N.J., 1973.

A7 Wilson, E. L., Taylor, R. L., Doherty, W. P., and Ghaboussi, J., "Incompatible Displacement Models," ONR Symposium on Matrix Methods in Structural Mechanics, University of Illinois, Urbana, Illinois, Sept. 1971.

A8 Bathe, K. J., and Wilson, E. L., "Thick Shell Structures," in Structural Mechanics Software Programs, University Press of Virginia, 1974.

A9 Bathe, K. J., Wilson, E. L., and Iding, R. H., "NONSAP - A Structural Analysis Program for Static and Dynamic Response of Nonlinear Systems," SESM Report 74-3, Department of Civil Engineering, University of California, Berkeley, 1974.

A10 Clough, R. W., and Felippa, C. A., "A Refined Quadrilateral Element for Analysis of Plate Bending," Proceedings 2nd Conference on Matrix Methods in Structural Mechanics, Wright Patterson AFB, Ohio, 1968.

A11 Felippa, C. A., "Refined Finite Element Analysis of Linear and Nonlinear Two-dimensional Structures," SESM Report 66-2, Dept. of Civil Engineering, University of California, Berkeley, 1966.

A12 Clough, R. W., and Wilson, E. L., "Dynamic Finite Element Analysis of Arbitrary Thin Shells," Computers and Structures, Vol. 1, No. 1, 1971.

A13 Poley, S., "Mesh Analysis of Piping Systems," IBM New York Scientific Center Technical Report No. 320-2939, March 1968.

A14 Hall, A. S., Tezcan, S. S., and Bulent, D., Discussion of paper "Curved Beam Stiffness Coefficients," ASCE Journal of Struct. Div., Feb. 1969.

A15 Wilson, E. L., Bathe, K. J., and Doherty, W. P., "Direct Solution of Large Systems of Linear Equations," Computers and Structures, to appear.

TOTAL: INTERACTIVE GRAPHICS SYSTEM FOR THE TWO-DIMENSIONAL ANALYSIS OF LINEAR ELASTIC SOLIDS

Laurent A. Beaubien

Naval Research Laboratory

INTRODUCTION

The TOTAL (Two dimensional, Orthotropic, Time-sharing structural Analysis Library) system is basically a collection of 28 versatile pre- and postprocessing routines presently linked to an elementary finite element solution scheme (but easily mated to more complex solution methods), and accessible in real time from any alphanumeric or graphic terminal. This system is capable of rapidly handling widely differing classes of linear elastic, two-dimensional continuum mechanics problems. Areas of applicability range from complex boundary problems (such as those formerly solved by photoelastic methods) to simulation of failure mechanisms of layered orthotropic bodies using global fracture mechanics criteria. Material property conditions may range from homogeneous isotropic to nonhomogeneous (particulate) orthotropic. Any compatible set of boundary conditions involving concentrated or distributed forces, displacements, or fixed points either on or inside the boundary may be specified.

Among the preprocessing capabilities are several easily learned schemes for automatic generation of complex geometries as well as several methods of rapid and automatic specifications of boundary conditions and element material assignment. In addition, several routines are provided for large-scale manipulation and modification of existing geometries, including shifting of whole interior sub-regions, and linking together of initially separate geometries. Routines for bandwidth reduction and geometry error checking are also available.

Postprocessing capabilities include selective searching of result files for sequences of extreme values, linear combinations of any compatible result files, and, when a cathode ray tube (CRT) is used, a comprehensive graphics package which can rapidly produce several different representations of results in a single run, including two-dimensional contours and three-dimensional surfaces.

The emphasis in the design of this system has been placed on ease of use, and rapid turn-around of design- and multiple-simulation-type problems for which "engineering accuracy" (e.g., 5-10%) is satisfactory. (The problem illustrated in Fig. 1 was solved from

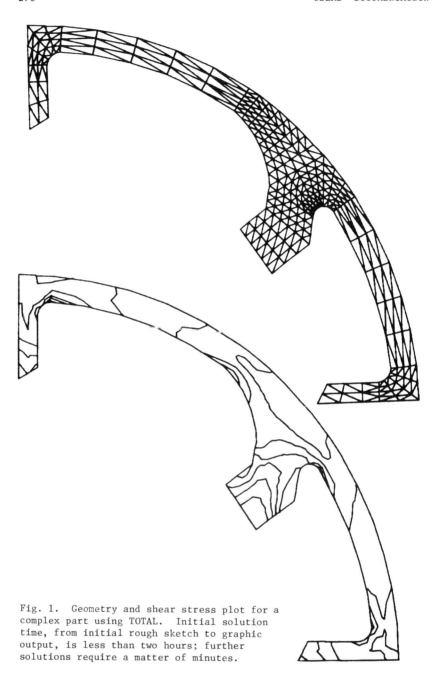

Fig. 1. Geometry and shear stress plot for a
complex part using TOTAL. Initial solution
time, from initial rough sketch to graphic
output, is less than two hours; further
solutions require a matter of minutes.

scratch, including graphics output, in less than two hours, with subsequent solutions taking a matter of minutes.) The finite element solution scheme is based on constant strain triangles and on an in-core solution of a banded matrix. There are several methods of smoothing and extrapolating results to provide an improvement in the accuracy normally achieved with these elements.

A considerable effort has been expended on optimizing user-program interaction. The system is extremely modular, with highly mnemonic names for the routines. For example, a typical problem might be solved by calling, in order, programs POINTS, ELMNTS, MTRIAL, LOADS, STFGEN, SOLVE, STRAIN, STRESS, with each program doing just what its name implies and creating its own type of disk file to be used by other routines when needed. The input to each program is completely unformatted and is specifically requested by the dialog, which has been so structured as to provide an auto-instructional aspect for the novice without getting in the way of the experienced user. In fact, data file modes can be used to by-pass much of the dialog in some routines, such as those for geometry input.

The ultimate goal of this system has been the implementation of a "black box" approach to stress analysis to provide the user with a vehicle for comprehensive numerical simulation without formal training in numerical techniques.

As a final word to the prospective reader and user, in the case of some of the more complex programs (e.g., POINTS, ELMNTS, PLOT) it is not advisable to first carefully read all of the descriptive text and then proceed to the following related dialog. Since the auto-instructional aspects of the prompting dialog make some parts of the basic text almost superfluous, it is best to look at this dialog after only a brief scanning of the text. The reader can then return for further study of the more complex capabilities which might not be obvious from the dialog examples.

SYSTEM DOCUMENTATION

The TOTAL system, in addition to being self-prompting, is also self-documenting. In order to preserve this character of the system, this chapter consists primarily of selected excerpts from the full set of system and program information files which comprise the full user's manual, and which can be printed out in complete form on an alphanumerics terminal. The only additional information for this publication consists of the graphical display output. This procedure has the following advantages. First, it preserves the flavor of the medium being presented, since it is felt that the concept of such a self-documenting, modular, interactive system as TOTAL is as important as its actual availability as a computational tool. Second, as the on-line documentation evolves with the system, new information file printouts can easily be used to replace the equivalent older sections of this chapter.

PRELIMINARY INFORMATION

The on-line documentation of the TOTAL system is structured in such
a way that a prospective user can access and learn the system knowing only its name. After logging on the computer system he need
only call the one-page system information file TOTAL, which will
direct him in accessing other information files, in suitable sequence. Adherence to this access and learning procedure is ob-
viously not necessary when using the manual as presented in this
Software Series. However, the organization and names of the sections (information files) of the manual, and the internal refer-
encing within these sections have been left in the on-line documentation format. Therefore, the following selected subset of the
full manual starts with the brief on-line introduction, to TOTAL, as
it would be printed out at a terminal in response to a TY TOTAL
command.

TOTAL

The TOTAL system is a collection of finite element and related programs which operate on a broadly structured disk file data base to
provide a highly flexible capability for efficiently solving the
simplest and most complex plane elastic boundary value problems.
A more detailed listing of system capabilities and features can be
found in information file INFCAP. Additional brief discussions of
capabilities can be found in the one-line descriptions of individual programs in the program information file INFPRO. TOTAL is extremely user oriented. All input is in unformatted (each individual
number separated by a comma) form, and is always requested specifically by the program. All that the new user need do is read a few
of the brief information files, pick a five-or-less character name
for his problem, and start running the system programs. The more
complex capabilities of the system open to the more experienced user
are always available as options, but never get in the way of the new
user.
      There are only two commands required to use the system. The
RUN command is used to initiate all programs (e.g., RUN "program
name"). The TY (or TYPE) command is used to list all information
files to the terminal (e.g., TY "INF---"). In addition, all YES-NO
questions are answered with "1" for YES and "-1" for NO. The programs available are listed in INFPRO and described in other "INF---"
files as detailed in INFORM.
      The best way of learning the system is to first read the one-
page terminology file INFTER, and then go to the use file INFUSE,
which contains illustrative dialogs for the analysis of a cantilever
beam. These dialogs should then be tried at the terminal before
proceeding to the information files on the individual programs, with
their more extensive discussion and dialog examples. In addition
most program description files have dialog examples related to a
single illustrative problem, that of a circular cylinder under radial
external compression.

CAPABILITY PROFILE (INFCAP)

Following are some of the more important and/or unique capabilities
and features of the TOTAL system, with related programs in parentheses.

o Liberal use of graphics for both input and results

o Self-prompting programs with brief, specific requests for all
  input

o Optional bypassing of dialog in some routines using a data file
  mode (POINTS, ELMNTS, MTRIAL)

o Keyboard-available information files describing all programs, and
  system features and usage (INFORM)

o Rapid automatic generation of complex geometries using only a few
  simple commands (POINTS, ELMNTS)

o Provision for rapid modification of existing geometries, including:
    1. "Zooming," with reapplication of previously computed dis-
       placements as input loads to a refined mesh (ZOOM)
    2. Shifting of whole interior regions without changing con-
       nectivity (SHIFT)
    3. Disassembly of geometries either for renumbering or for
       reassembly of subregions as separate geometries (GEOMET)

o Linking of two or more previously created geometries, independent
  of their initial relative scales or orientation (LINK)

o Application of any point displacement and/or force at any node,
  interior or exterior, and of a uniform or linearly varying distributed normal or shear load along any contour in or on the
  region (LOADS)

o Specification, for each individual element if wanted, of any
  orthotropic or isotropic set of elastic constants with any orientation (MTRIAL)

o Mixing of plane stress and plane strain elements (MTRIAL)

o Bandwidth reduction, with automatic mapping of the reduced node
  numbering system to the original numbering system in later programs (SHRINK)

o Thickness modulation by several methods, including linear X-Y or
  radial variations (THICK); also display of generated surfaces
  (PLOT)

o Multi-level selective search for extreme result values (STRESS,
  PRINC, ENERGY, DSTRIB)

o Linear combination of input or result files (COMBIN)

o Optional plot scaling, including expansion by a constant ratio for piecing together large copies (PLOT)

o Linear plotting of one or more result curves along any path, either in-place within a boundary plot, or in a standard X-Y form (LINPLT)

o Single-run solution looping for combinations of geometry, material, and loading changes (SOLOOP)

o Calculation of fracture criteria quantities such as J-integrals (JNTGRL)

SYSTEM PROGRAMS (INFPRO)

Table 1 lists the available system programs, with brief descriptions of their functions, the type of files they use (IN) and create (OUT), and the page location of the section describing them. Asterisks in the page column denote programs whose descriptions have been either omitted from, or abbreviated for, this chapter. Complete descriptions for these programs can be found in the on-line documentation.

Table 1 System Programs and their Function

PROGRAM NAME	PROGRAM FUNCTION	ASSOCIATED FILES	PAGE
POINTS	Creates mesh points location	IN: KEYBOARD, .PIN, .PTS OUT: .PTS	296*
ELMNTS	Creates and connects elements	IN: KEYBOARD, .EIN, .ELE OUT: .ELE	307*
GEOMET	Combines point and element files into geometry file	IN: .PTS, .ELE, .GEO OUT: .GEO	314*
CHECK	Checks points and elements for gross errors; creates geometry file	IN: .PTS, .ELE OUT: .GEO	336*
MTRIAL	Assigns material properties to elements	IN: KEYBOARD OUT: .MAT	315
LOADS	Applies force, displacement, and constraint boundary conditions	IN: KEYBOARD, .LDF, .LDD, .LDZ OUT: .LDF, .LDD, .LDZ	322

TABLE 1 (cont.)

PROGRAM NAME	PROGRAM FUNCTION	ASSOCIATED FILES	PAGE
STFGEN	Creates local and global stiffness	IN: .GEO, .MAT OUT: .STF	*
SOLVE	Solves for displacements	IN: .STF, .LDF, .LDD, .LDZ OUT: .DIS	*
PLOT	Gives CRT displays of geometry, or of results (stress, energy, etc.) in integer, 3-D surface, or 2-D contour form	IN: .GEO, .STS, .STN, .PRI, .ELE, .THI .END	327
STRAIN	Computes strains from displacements	IN: .DIS, .GEO, .MAT OUT: .STN	*
STRESS	Computes stresses from strains	IN: .STN, .MAT OUT: .STS	326
GDCHNG	Lists and redefines points and elements in problem coordinates	IN: .GEO, KEYBOARD OUT: .GEO	*
ZOOM	Applies solution displacements to a refined interior subregion as displacement loads	IN: .DIS, KEYBOARD OUT: .LDD	*
FORCES	Computes forces at loaded and constrained points	IN: .DIS, .STF OUT: .FOR	*
FILCHK	Checks contents of arbitrary files	IN: .---	*
SHRINK	Reduces bandwidth of geometry file	IN: .GEO OUT: .GEO	337*
DSPLAC	Provides listing and/or plot capabilities for displacements	IN: .DIS, .GEO	335
ENERGY	Calculates strain energy density and total energy	IN: .STS, .STN OUT: .END	

TABLE 1 (cont.)

PROGRAM NAME	PROGRAM FUNCTION	ASSOCIATES FILES	PAGE
SHIFT	Moves interior sub-regions invariantly maintaining overall connectivity	IN: .GEO OUT: .GEO	338*
ELPNT	Decomposes geometry file into point and element files	IN: .GEO OUT: .PTS, .ELE	*
THICK	Modulates element thickness	IN: .GEO, .MAT, .THI OUT: .MAT, .THI	339*
PRINC	Calculates principal stresses	IN: .STS OUT: .PRI	*
COMBIN	Produces linear com-binations of input or result files	IN: .LDF, .LDD, .DIS, .STS, .STN, .END OUT: (SAME)	340*
STFSOL	A combination of STFGEN, SOLVE, FORCE	IN: .GEO, .MAT, .LDF, .LDD, .LDZ OUT: .DIS, OPTIONAL: .STF, .FOR	325
RESULT	A selective combina-tion of STRAIN, STRESS, PRINC, ENERGY	IN: .DIS OUT: .STN, .STS, .PRI, .END	325
DSTRIB	Distributes and extra-polates element results to nodes	IN: .STS, .PRI, .END OUT: (SAME)	340*
LINK	Links previously created geometries	IN: .GEO OUT: .GEO	340*
LINPLT	Produces linear plots of results, either in place or in standard X-Y form	IN: .GEO, .STS, .PRI, .END, .STN	342*
SOLOOP	Loops through solutions for changes in geometry, material, or loading	IN: .GEO, .MAT, .LDF, .LDD, .LDZ OUT: .DIS, .FOR	*
JNTGRL	Calculates family of path-invariant integrals used for predicting fracture	IN: .DIS, .MAT, .GEO	*

TERMINOLOGY (INFTER)

File name. When requested by any program, a file name consists of any five or less alphanumeric characters chosen by the user. See the section on files for a further discussion.

YES-NO answers and the "ZERO" answer. YES-NO questions are answered with: 1 for YES; -1 for NO. There are also many cases when a "ZERO" answer to a YES-NO question (or to a request for a node number or node number pair) can be used to initiate an alternate computation path. The "ZERO" option is usually listed in the question dialog itself, but is always described in the INF--- file for the program in question.

Range. When the program asks for a range (e.g., node range) a pair of integers is to be entered.

Node length. The number of node points lying along any continuous path (e.g., edge) in the mesh is called the node length of that path (edge). For quadrilaterals with equal numbers of nodes along opposite sides, sequential and transverse node lengths are defined as follows. The sequential node length (SNL) is the node length of the sides having consecutive numbering. The transverse node length (TNL) is the node length of the other two sides. These terms are illustrated in Fig. 2. The node length concept also applies to generalized quadrilaterals, figures equivalent to the above but with curved edges and/or lines, and spanning points numbered by SNLxTNL consecutive integers. See illustration in the discussion of PROGRAM POINTS

Dialog input convention. In all illustrative dialogs, all numerical information entered by the user is preceded by an "ENTER" or "?" indication. All other numerical information is output from computer.

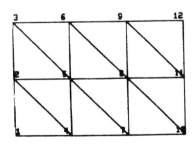
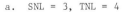
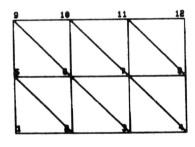

a. SNL = 3, TNL = 4   b. SNL = 4, TNL = 3

Fig. 2   Illustration of node length definition

SYSTEM USE WITH DIALOG TUTORIAL (INFUSE)

Preliminary

The first step in the use of the TOTAL system is to create on graph
paper a point mesh simulating the region to be analyzed. The smallest interval on the graph paper can be conveniently used as the
unit length. This unit can later be converted to a physical dimension with the scale factors available in the mesh point input program POINTS. It is important to have the highest mesh resolution
in regions where the maximum stress gradient is expected, and to
locate node points at all physical points where a force, displacement, or displacement constraint is to be specified. If possible,
node numbers should be assigned so as to minimize the greatest maximum difference between the three node numbers defining any triangular element over the whole region. This is usually equivalent
to having the node numbers increasing approximately monotonically
with distance from the first node point. This results in reduced
bandwidth of the stiffness matrix to be inverted, and reduces computer time significantly. It is also well to arrange the points
such that large regions are equivalent to quadrilaterals as described in INFELM and can therefore be generated automatically by
program ELMNTS. This type of arranging will also usually ensure
that much of the point generation can be done automatically by program POINTS.

Program Calling Sequence

The problem can now be solved by running, in order, the following
programs. For each the procedure is to type: RUN "PROGRAM NAME".

    o POINTS
    o ELMNTS
    o GEOMET (or CHECK)
    o MTRIAL
    o LOADS
    o STFGEN
    o SOLVE
      (or STFSOL in place of STFGEN and SOLVE)

At this point the stiffness matrix has been solved for the displacements, and the problem essentially solved. Other quantities of
interest can be calculated by the following programs.

    o STRAIN
    o STRESS
    o ENERGY
    o PRINC
      (or RESULT in place of the above four)

Dialog Example

In this dialog example, a cantilever beam is analyzed for two different loadings, a linear combination is made of the two resulting
stress files, and a fiberstress (sigma-X) plot is made. The total
time required for the two solutions, including their linear combination and a plot of the 108-element geometry was 11 minutes elapsed
time at the terminal, and 25 actual CPU seconds on a PDP10. The
time for the stress plot was 3 minutes elapsed terminal time and
19 CPU seconds. In general, only the simplest program features,
evident from the dialog, are used in this example. Those few more
complicated entries are briefly described in footnotes.

   In the first sequence below, programs POINTS and ELMNTS are run
to generate and connect the 70 node points of a 6 by 30 cantilever
beam (see Fig. 3a), fixed at the left end (nodes 1-7) and loaded
along the top edge (nodes 7, 14, 21, 28, 35, 42, 49, 56, 63, 70).
Programs MTRIAL and LOADS are then run to assign material properties
and boundary conditions (uniform downward pressure along the top
surface and a fixed left end). Program STFSOL is used to generate
and solve the stiffness matrix for the displacements. Program
RESULT is run to calculate only the stresses from among the several
result calculation options available, and then program STRESS is
run to search for the three most extreme element fiber stresses.

Note. Numerical entries not preceded by "ENTER" or "?" are output
from the computer. All flag options, parenthetically appended to
input requests, should be ignored, except for the three described
in footnotes.

   R UN PØINTS

   GET ØLD FILE?
   - 1
   A UTØ PØINT GENERATØR WANTED?
   1
   ENTER NØDE RANGE (NEG, NØN-LIN; O, DATA FILE) [1]
   -1,70
   ENTER NØDE NØ, X-CØØRD, Y-CØØRD (NEG, QUAD) [1]
   -1,0.,0.
   ENTER (NØDE NØ,X,Y) FØR NEXT 3 QUAD PTS
   7,0.,6.
   64,30.,0.
   70,30.,6.

---

[1]When entering points over any input range (here, 1-70) a negative sign on a node number is a flag to the program that this node
is to be interpreted as the first of four corner nodes of a quadrilateral (a four-sided figure with either straight or curved sides
and with equal numbers of nodes on opposite sides), and the program
then requests the next three corner nodes, as entered on the next
three lines.

```
ENTER 4 SCALE FACTORS: (SFS1,SFS2,SFT1,SFT2)²
1.,1.,5.,5.
FURTHER AUTO GENER? (2, TRANSP)
-1
LISTING WANTED? (2, GENER)
-1
LEAVING AUTO GENERATOR
FURTHER INPUT?
-1
STORE PTS? (0, SCALE; 2, LOCAL EXPANS)
1
ENTER FILE NAME
BEAM
NO OF NODES STORED
70

END OF EXECUTION
CPU TIME 1.22   ELAPSED TIME 1:14.73


RUN ELMNTS

GET OLD FILE?
-1
AUTO ELEMENT GENERATOR WANTED?
1
ENTER NAME OF POINT FILE
BEAM
NO OF NODES AVAILABLE
70
NO OF REGIONS TO BE GENER? (0,DATA FILE; NEG,OPT LIST)
1
ENTER, FOR EACH REGION (NEG DIAG OPT)
FIRST ELEM NO, FIRST NODE NO, LAST NODE NO ³
1,1,70
SEQUEN NODE LENGTH, TRANSV NODE LENGTH? ³
7,10
```

---

[2]In response to the negative flag used in the node range entry (-1,70) seven lines earlier, the program requests the scale factors defining the nonlinear spacing of points along the four sides of the quadrilateral; first the two in the direction of numbering (sequential), and then the two in the other direction (transverse). These scale factors are the ratio of the last generated interval in a given direction to the first generated interval.

[3]Connectivity of any quadrilateral is completely determined by five parameters: the first element number used in the quadrilateral (must be "1" for a geometry consisting of a single quadrilateral), the first and last node numbers, and the number of nodes along the sides in the direction of numbering (sequential node length) and in the direction transverse to numbering (transverse node length).

```
ELEM RANGE GENERATED
1,108
LISTING WANTED? (0 FOR PLOT)
0
NO OF ELEMS AVAILABLE
108
INPUT ELEM RANGE (NEG FOR SCALE)
-1,108
ENTER SCALE FACTOR
.8
WANT ELEM NOS, NODE NOS, 90 DEG ROT?
1,1,-1
```

(Fig. 3a plotted)

```
FURTHER PLOTS?
-1
LISTING WANTED?
-1
FURTHER AUTO GENER WANTED?
-1
CREATE GEOM FILE?
1
ENTER NAME OF GEOM FILE
BEAM
NO OF NODES, NO OF ELEMS, BANDWIDTH
70,108,16
LEAVING AUTO GENERATOR
STORE ELEMS?
1
ENTER FILE NAME
BEAM
NO OF ELEMS STORED
108
BANDWIDTH, ELEM NO
16,1

END OF EXECUTION
CPU TIME 10.51 (3.35 WITHOUT PLOT)
ELAPSED TIME 4:10 (1:08 WITHOUT PLOT)



RUN MTRIAL

TOTAL NO FO ELEMS?
108
ENTER NOD OF ISO MATS, ORTHO MATS (0,0 FOR DATA FILE)
1,0
FOR ISOTROPIC MAT (NEG MOD FOR PL STN)
INPUT YOUNGS MOD, POISSONS RATIO
10000000.,.35
```

```
PRINT ØF CIJ WANTED?
- 1
ENTER NAME ØF MAT FILE
BEAM

END ØF EXECUTIØN
CPU TIME 0.68   ELAPSED TIME 31.42



RUN LØADS

ALL FILES UNDER SAME NAME?
1
ENTER PRØBLEM NAME
BEAM
WANT FØRCE, DISPL, CØNSTR LØADS ( 0 FØR ØLD FILE)
1,-1,1
DISTRIBUTED FØRCES WANTED? (O FØR CØNVEN)
0
INTENSITY CØNVENTIØN: NØRMAL LØAD - PØSITIVE,
                     TANGENT LØAD - NEGATIVE
DIRECTIØN CØNVENTIØN: LIST NØDES DEFINING EDGE IN
CCW ØRDER FØR PRESSURE ØR FØR CCW SHEAR, IN
CW ØRDER FØR NØRMAL TENSIØN ØF CW SHEAR
1
NØ ØF NØDES IN GEØM FILE
70
NØ ØF EDGES TØ BE LØADED?
1
ENTER INTENS, NØ ØF EDGE NØDES (O, TRI; O, RANGE)
100.,10
ENTER NØDE NØS IN PRØPER ØRDER
70,63,56,49,42,35,28,21,14,7
LISTING ØF NØN-ZERØ FØRCES WANTED?
- 1
FURTHER DISTRIBUTED LØADS WANTED?
- 1
CØNCENTRATED FØRCES WANTED?
- 1
STØRE FØRCES?
1
NØ ØF X-CØNSTRAINTS TØ BE SET?
7
ENTER NØDE NØS (NEG TØ FREE)
1,2,3,4,5,6,7
NØ ØF Y-CØNSTRAINTS TØ BE SET?
1
ENTER NØDE NØS (NEG TØ FREE)
1
DISPLAY CØNSTRAINED NØDES?
- 1
```

```
STØRE CØNSTRAINTS?
1

END ØF EXECUTIØN
CPU TIME 1.70  ELAPSED TIME 1:42.78



RUN STFSØL

ALL FILES UNDER SAME NAME?
1
ENTER PRØBLEM NAME
BEAM
NØDES, ELEMENTS, BANDWIDTH
70, 108, 16
STIFFNESS MATRIX BEING GENERATED
STØRE STIFF MATRIX?
-1
FØRCE INPUT?
1
DISPLACEMENT INPUT?
-1
CØNSTRAINT INPUT?
1
DISPLACEMENT LISTING WANTED?
-1
CALCULATED NØDE FØRCES?
-1

END ØF EXECUTIØN
CPU TIME 6.22  ELAPSED TIME 53.65



RUN RESULT

INPUT UNDER SAME NAME? (0, ØUTPUT ALSØ)
0
ENTER INPUT NAME
BEAM
STØRE STRAIN,STRESS,PRIN STRESS,ENERGY?
-1,1,-1,-1
NØDES, ELEMENTS
FULL ELEM RANGE WANTED?
1

END ØF EXECUTIØN
CPU TIME 3.07  ELAPSED TIME 22.57
```

```
RUN STRESS

FILES ALL UNDER SAME NAME?
1
ENTER PROBLEM NAME
BEAM
CREATE NEW STRESS FILE?
-1
LIST STRESSES? (O FOR MAX,MIN)
0
ENTER STRESS CODE (NEG,MULT SEARCH; O,CODE LIST)
0
.1, SIG-X; 2, SIG-Y; 3, SIG-XY; 4, SIG-Z
ENTER STRESS CODE  (NEG,MULT SEARCH; O,CODE LIST)
-1
ENTER SEARCH LEVEL NO
3
SIG-X: MAX,ELEM; MIN,ELEM
   6859. ,12, -7585., 1
   5880. ,24, -5844., 13
   4816. ,36, -4649., 25
LIST STRESSES? O FOR MAX,MIN)
-1

END OF EXECUTION
CPU TIME 1.58 ELAPSED TIME 50.83
```

In this second sequence, program LOADS is rerun to change the upper
surface loading to a trapezoidal one, and then the STFSOL and RESULT
programs are rerun (dialog not included), leaving everything else
unchanged. Program COMBIN is then run to form a linear combination
of the two stress files. Finally, program PLOT is run to generate
contour plots of the fiber stress (sigma-X) distribution of the
combined case.

```
RUN LOADS

ALL FILES UNDER SAME NAME?
-1
WANT FORCE,DISPL,CONSTR LOADS (O FOR OLD FILE)
1,-1,-1
DISTRIBUTED FORCES WANTED?
1
ENTER NAME OF GEOM FILE
BEAM
NO OF NODES IN GEOM FILE
70
NO OF EDGES TO BE LOADED?
1
ENTER INTENS, NO OF EDGE NODES (0.,TRI; 0, RANGE)
0.,10
```

```
ENTER NØDE NØS IN PRØPER ØRDER
70,63,56,49,42,35,28,21,14,7
ENTER BEGIN,END INTENS
50.,10.
LISTING ØF NØN-ZERØ FØRCES WANTED?
-1
FURTHER DISTRIBUTED LØADS WANTED?
CØNCENTRATED FØRCES WANTED?
-1
-1
STØRE FØRCES?
1
ENTER NAME ØF FØRCE FILE
BEAM1

END ØF EXECUTIØN
CPU TIME 1.53  ELAPSED TIME 2:7.27



RUN STFSØL   (Dialog not included)



RUN RESULT   (Dialog not included)



RUN CØMBIN

FILE CØDE: 1-FØRCE LØADS, 2-DISPL LDS, 3-DISPLACEMENTS,
4-STRESSES, 5-STRAINS, 6-ENERGY DENSITY
ENTER CØDE NØ
4
ENTER NØ ØF FILES TØ BE CØMBINED
2
ENTER INPUT FILE NAME
BEAM1
ENTER LINEAR CØEFFICIENT
2.
ENTER INPUT FILE NAME
BEAM
ENTER LINEAR CØEFFICIENT
1.
ENTER NAME ØF CØMBINED FILE
BEAM2
FURTHER CØMBINATIØNS? (O FØR NEW CØDE)
-1

END ØF EXECUTIØN
CPU TIME 4.26  ELAPSED TIME 1:12.93
```

```
R UN PLØT

? NAME ØF GEØM FILE
B EAM
NØ ØF ELEMS AVAILABLE
1 08
? ØPT NØ (O FØR LIST)
O
1, GEØM; 2, INTENS INTEG; 3, INTENS SURF; 4, CØNTØURS
? ØPT NØ (O FØR LIST)
4
NAME ØF RESULT FILE?
B EAM2
? FILE CØDE (O FØR LIST)
O
FILE CØDE: 1-STRESS; 2-PRIN STRESS; 3-ENERGY DENS
? FILE CØDE
1
? PLØT CØDE
O
PLØT CØDE: 1-SIG-X; 2-SIG-Y; 3-SIG-XY; 4-SIG-Z
? PLØT CØDE (O FØR LIST)
1
LIST NØDE VALUES? (O FØR MAX,MIN)
O
MIN VAL, NØDE NØ; MAX VAL, NØDE NØ
-13056. , 1, 9655., 14
LIST NØDE VALUES? (O FØR MAX,MIN)
- 1
? ELEM PLØT RANGE (NEG, SCALE)
-1,108
? EXPANS FACTØR
.8
? CØNTUR INTERVAL (NEG FØR NUMBERED)
1 000.
GET STØRED BØUND?
- 1
STØRE BØUND?
- 1

(Fig. 3b plotted)

CØNTINUE? (O ØPT)
- 1
NEW ØPTIØN?
- 1

END ØF EXECUTIØN

CPU TIME 33.54 ELAPSED TIME 9:53
```

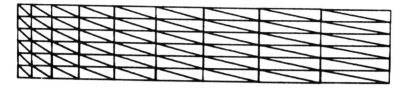

a. Automatically generated mesh

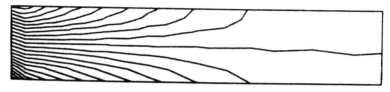

b. Fiber stress contours

Fig. 3. Cantilever beam problem

ON LINE DOCUMENTATION (INFORM)

The on-line documentation of the TOTAL system consists of information files of the name-form "INF---". To print out any of these
files, simply type "TY INF---". Since the information files of
primary interest are larger than can be accommodated on a CRT screen,
it is best to list them on a hard-copy printer such as a teletype.
   The information files fall basically into two categories, system description files and program description files. Program description files are usually of the form "INF---",where these last
three characters are the first three characters of the program name.
For example, the information file on program POINTS is obtained by
typing "TY INFPOI". For completeness, the names of program information files and their corresponding programs are listed below following the system file names.

System Information Files

o INFUSE Describes the general use of the TOTAL system to solve a
          problem, including the preliminary planning of the mesh,
          and what programs to call in what order

o INFPRO Lists programs with one-line descriptions of their
          function

o INFTER   Defines terminology having special meaning in the TOTAL
           system

o INFFIL   Describes system file structure and handling

o INFCAP   Contains a list of important and/or unique system capa-
           bilities

o INFUPD   Provides updates and cautions as needed

o INFMOD   Discusses modifications which may be necessary to imple-
           ment the reference coding (PDP10-FORTRAN 10) of TOTAL on
           other computer system

o INFTEC   Briefly discusses technical features

                        Program Information Files

o INFPOI-POINTS   o INFSTS-STRESS   o INFELP-ELPNT

o INFELM-ELMNTS   o INFENE-ENERGY   o INFTHI-THICK

o INFGEO-GEOMET   o INFGDC-GDCHNG   o INFPRI-PRINC

o INFCHE-CHECK   o INFZOO-ZOOM   o INFCOM-COMBIN

o INFMTR-MTRIAL   o INFJNT-JNTGRL   o INFRES-RESULT

o INFLOA-LOADS   o INFFOR-FORCES   o INFSFS-STFSOL

o INFSTF-STFGEN   o INFFLC FILCHK   o INFDST-DSTRIB

o INFSOL-SOLVE   o INFSHR-SHRINK   o INFLNK-LINK

o INFPLO-PLOT   o INFDSP-DSPLAC   o INFLPL-LINPLT

o INFSTN-STRAIN   o INFSHI-SHIFT   o INFSLP-SOLOOP

                 FILE HANDLING AND STRUCTURE (INFFIL)

                         File Names and Use

At the heart of the TOTAL system is the disk file structure and
handling system. The five character name assigned to a file by the
user is actually only the first part of the file name as used by the
system. The system assigns as a second part of any entered name a
four character extension which indicates the type of information in
the file. This extension is ordinarily not seen by the user; it
consists of a period followed by three characters. For example, the
GEOMET program takes mesh point locations stored in a NAME 1.PTS
file and element connectivity information stored in a NAME 2.ELE file,

and creates a full geometry file "NAME 3.GEO" which is used by the
rest of the TOTAL programs. For a simple problem the entered names
can be kept the same (e.g., NAME 1 = NAME 2 = NAME 3) and this
option can be elected at the start of all programs using files with
several different extensions. However, the flexibility of using
different file names when solving multi-conditioned problems will
become readily apparent to the user. As an aid to the user, gross
mismatches of files (e.g., an element file requiring more points
then a coupled point file) are picked up by the system, which either
issues a warning or terminates the run. Descriptions of individual
programs contain the extensions either created or used.

There are two situations in which the full nine character file
name must be entered by the user. The first is the general purpose
file checking program FILCHK. Use of this program is generally
not required, but it is described in INFFLC. The second situation
occurs when a user inadvertently enters a wrong file name at any
point. In this event (in the PDP10 system) the computer will print
out a message requesting a new file name, and will include in the
message a dummy file name including the proper extension. To re-
sume without interruption the user should type in the proper five
(or less) character name with the extension attached, followed by
an "Escape" rather than a "Carriage Return".

Reading Files

Most programs which create files of a given type also have the capability of reading and listing an old file of the same type. In
fact, each of these programs asks initially if you wish to read and
list an old file, for possible modification in the case of input
generation programs.

Data Files

Basically, all files are created by the individual programs. However, programs POINTS, ELMNTS, and MTRIAL accept as input data files
which are created using a system editor, and the form of these files
is described not only below, but also in more detail in the respective program information files. In addition, using the file formats
described below, a file of any type can be created, either using an
editor or by some other user-built program, as long as the file
name includes the proper extension. As a simple example, a force
loads file (NAME .LDF) could be created with an editor and then
called by program LOADS as an old file.

File Structure

See on-line documentation INFFIL for a description of individual
file structures.

PROGRAM INFORMATION FILES

Information files, including descriptions, use, sample dialogs and
graphical illustrations are given below for the following programs:
POINTS, ELMNTS*, GEOMET*, MTRIAL, LOADS, STFSOL**, RESULT**, STRESS,
PLOT, DSPLAC, CHECK*, SHRINK*, SHIFT, THICK*, COMBIN* DSTRIB*,
LINK*. Asterisks in the above list denote programs for which a
considerable amount of additional documentation is available via
terminal access. Double asterisks denote programs for which illustrative dialogs can be found in the section SYSTEM USE . The
name of the on-line information file is given in parentheses after
the program name. All file types associated with each program are
specified at various points.

PROGRAM POINTS (INFPOI)

POINTS is a program for entering the node number and location of
points defining a mesh, and storing this information in a points
(.PTS) file. Old point files may be read and modified and graphic
display is available while modifying a point file for which an element connectivity (.ELE) file has already been created by program
ELMNTS.

Paper coordinates and problem coordinates. Paper coordinates are
those used to enter the location of points in the POINTS program,
and usually correspond to locations in terms of the arbitrary units
used in a mesh-planning sketch. They are converted to problem coordinates, the actual coordinates to be used for solution, by input
scale factors. All input and listing, with one exception, in program POINTS are in paper coordinates, but storage is in problem coordinates. A single exception to listing in paper coordinates is
provided at the end of the program session, when the question
"STORE?" is asked. (See STORING below)

Data Entry

Mesh point information can be entered either (1) individually, one
at a time, (2) automatically by using the automatic generator, or
(3) by a combination of the two methods. In all methods the information required by each mesh point consists of a triplet of numbers
of the form: (Point number, X coordinate, Y coordinate). The program always asks for the range (N1,N2) of point numbers to be entered. Input (in triplets as above) is then requested until the
point number reaches N2. Another range of points may then be entered.
The final point file must consist of points with numbers starting
at 1, and continuing consecutively. No numbering gaps are permitted.
     The program first asks if an old file is wanted. If so,the name
is requested, and the old file becomes available for listing and/or
modifying (including enlarging). Next the choice of automatic or

individual input is made. For any run using both types of entry,
the automatic mode must be used first. However, the brief discussion of the individual entry mode, which is seldom needed, should
be read first.

Nonautomatic Entry

Manual Entry

In this mode, the program next asks the input range (N1,N2). (A
"0,0" entry for any range request during individual entry will activate the "data file" mode, and then bring another input range request. See below.) The program then requests node information
until the second of the range pair numbers is reached, at which point
listing of further input is available. The entry to define a node
point consists of the node number followed by its X and Y coordinates: (Node No. X,Y). In this mode each triplet entered generates
only one point. In the (N1, N2) range, any point numbers skipped
are assigned X=Y=99999.0 for ease of identification when listing.
Any later specification of a point location replaces the previously
specified location.

Data-File Entry

A node point data file consists of an un-line-numbered file, previously created under the name (NAME.PIN)(the extension must be included), with each line consisting of the node number followed by
the defining coordinate pair (Node No. X,Y). When this entry mode
has been elected by entering "0,0" in response to a range request
the response to the following range request should be the first and
last node numbers in the data file (or some subset). The name of
the data file (without extension) is then requested, the file is
entered, and the program then returns to the manual mode with listing and further entry options. The data-file option is normally
used only when entering large numbers of irregularly located and
arranged nodes.

Automatic Generation

This method also operates on a point input range (N1,N2), and defining triplets are requested until the range is filled. However,
skipping either one or a consecutive sequence of node numbers results in interpolation of the missing points along a straight line
connecting the two node numbers adjacent to the gap. For example,
entering coordinate information for points 1, 2, 8, 9, and 10 over a
range (1,10) results in interpolation of points 3, 4, 5, 6, 7
equally spaced (linear interpolation) along a line joining points
2 and 8.

Generation Options

Circular arc option. A circular arc may be generated to span the gap connecting two non-consecutive nodes by appending a negative sign to the node number following the gap. The program will then request a radius, with the sign convention (+ for curvature to right, – to left) listed. Entry of "ZERO" for this radius will bring a request for a third point on the arc. In the discussion immediately preceding, if the information for node 8 is entered as "-8, X8, Y8" then a circular arc containing points 3-7 will be generated between points 2 and 8.

Non linear interpolation option. Appending a negative sign to the input range (e.g., –N1, N2) at any point in the automatic generator will activate this option. When operating under this nonlinear option, the last generated interval between interpolated points will exceed the first generated interval by a multiplicative scale factor requested when needed by the program. In the above example, for the non-linear option, when the (N, X, Y) triplet is entered for point 8, the program will ask for a scale factor (>0). If 10.0 is entered as the scale factor, the interval between 7 and 8 will be ten times as long as the interval between 2 and 3. The scale factor may be greater or less than one. (See Dialog L.)

Quadrilateral option. A simple quadrilateral array of points with equal numbers of nodes along opposite straight sides is generated using only four input (corner) points as follows. When entering the (N, X, Y) triplet for any point "N" in a (N1, N2) range, a minus sign is assigned to the point number "N". The negative sign is a flag to the system that this point is to be interpreted as the first quadrilateral corner point "NQ1". The program then requests triplets defining the number and location of the other three corner points "NQ2, NQ3, NQ4", which must be in the sequence N1≤NQ1<NQ2<NQ3< NQ4≤N2. Any inconsistent numerical relation between the corner points is detected by the program and the first point is rerequested. Fig. 4a illustrates a 20-point quadrilateral generated by entering only the four corner points 1, 4, 17, 20.

Curved quadrilateral option 1. A generalized quadrilateral, with circular arcs along either or both of the transverse (non-sequentially numbered) edges can be easily generated as follows. In the above input for the simple quadrilateral, use of a negative node number in the triplet defining the third corner point "NQ3" (e.g., –NQ3, X, Y) will later bring a request for the radius (or third point) of a circular arc joining corner points "NQ1" and "NQ3", with intervening points spaced evenly along this arc. (All radius input request dialogs, here and in similar options, are properly labeled to avoid confusing the different arcs) Likewise, corner point "NQ4"

can be entered negative to generate an arc between "NQ2" and "NQ4".
All interior transverse lines will be curved proportionately to fit
the curved edges. Curvature of sequential edges can be accomplished
using Option 2 immediately following, or using the transposition
capability discussed later. Figure 4b illustrates a curved quadrilateral generated by entering corner points 17 and 20 with a negative sign, and then entering proper radii defining arcs between
points 1 and 17 and between points 4 and 20.

Curved quadrilateral option 2. Circular arcs can be generated along
all four sides of a generalized quadrilateral by entering the number of the second quadrilateral point "NQ2" with a negative sign.
Four radii will be requested later, with the already discussed third
point option available for any of the four arcs. Any of the four
sides in this option can be straightened simply by entering a very
large radius (e.g., 10.E6). The quadrilateral illustrated in Fig.
4b can be generated using this option by entering the triplet for
point 4 with a negative sign (-4,X4,Y4), the same transverse radii
(arcs 1-17, 4-20) as for Option 2 above, and "infinite" sequential
radii (arcs 1-4, 17-20). Dialog 4 illustrates use of this option
in generating a circular region.

Nonlinear quadrilateral option. When a negative sign on the input
range has been used to elect nonlinear interpolation prior to the
use of the quadrilateral option, the program will request four scale
factors (1.0 for linear spacing), one for each of the sides (or arcs)
in the following order (with corresponding sides in parentheses):
SFS1 (NQ1-NQ2), SFS2 (NQ3-NQ4), SFT1 (NQ1-NQ3), SFT2 (NQ2-NQ4).
Spacing along all interior lines will be adjusted proportionately.
Fig. 4c illustrates a 20 point quadrilateral with curved edges and
nonlinear spacing along two edges. (See Dialog 1.)

Auto-generation data file option. As in the manual mode, a data
file consists of an un-line-numbered file previously created with an
editor under the name "-----.PIN", and a data file read is activated
by a "0,0" entry as a range for automatic generation. However, the
similarity ends here. The "Auto" data file consists of a node range
(negative if wanted) followed by answers to all questions as they
would be entered at the terminal over this range. For experienced
users this is by far the best way of entering complex geometries.
One node range, consisting of many quadrilateral-defining entries,
complete with curves and nonlinear generation, can be entered from
one data file, with no intervening dialog. See Dialog 5 for a two-
quadrilateral example.

Transpositions

At each "FURTHER AUTO GENERATION?" request, entry of a "2" will initiate the transposition option. A transposition is the switching of

sequential and transverse directions in the numbering of a generalized quadrilateral. The program simply asks the starting node number and the new sequential (SNL) and transverse (TNL) node lengths.
Transposition of the node numbering of Fig. 4b to that of Fig. 4d
can be achieved by entering 1 as the starting node and (5,4) as the
(SNL, TNL) pair. To transpose points in an old file, simply request the old file and enter its name. The program will then ask
if points are to be entered, with a "ZERO" option to go directly to
the transposition mode. (See Dialog 2)

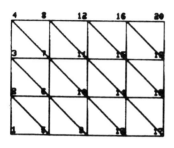

a. Simple quadrilateral

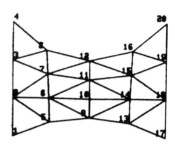

b. Curved quadrilateral

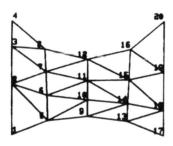

c. Quadrilateral with
   nonlinear spacing

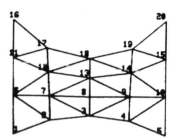

d. Transposed quadrilateral

Fig. 4. Various cases of quadrilateral generation

Storing, Scaling, and Problem Coordinate Listing

At the end of the run, the question "STORE?" is asked. A "YES"
answer brings a request for a file name, and the points are stored
with unit scale factors (equal paper and problem coordinates). A
"ZERO" answer activates the global scale factor option, and a "2"
answer activates a local scaling (expansion) capability.

Scaling. If scaling is elected with a "ZERO" answer, X- and Y-scale factors are requested, all coordinates are multiplied by these factors, and then listing in the new problem coordinates is available before storing. The scale factors may also be changed after listing. The problem coordinates are then stored under a chosen name. Problem coordinate listing is also available using program GDCHNG.

Local expansion. If local scaling (expansion) is chosen with a "2" answer to the "STORE?" question, the following takes place. First a set of nodes to be moved is entered. Then one of three expansion modes is chosen: X-, Y-, or R(radial)-expansion. An expansion factor is then entered, and also a fixed locus (X-, Y-, or R-). Also, for the radial case, a reference central node (or location) is entered. The expansion now takes place, with all points to be expanded being expanded linearly with respect to the fixed locus.

Listing and Plotting

Listing. At several appropriate points, the question "LISTING WANTED?" is asked. A "YES" (1) answer brings a request for a node range pair "N1,N2", and the coordinates of points in this range are then printed.

As an option, listing of coordinates over any nonconsecutive set of node numbers can be elected by entering "N,0" for the listing range, where "N" is the number of nodes to be listed. The program will then request the nodes to be listed. The "LISTING WANTED?" request is repeated until entry of a "NO" (-1) answer.

Plotting. A "ZERO" answer activates the plotting routine, and a request follows for the name of an element connectivity (.ELE) file. This plotting mode is usually used only when modifying (or simply displaying) a previously generated point file for which a corresponding connectivity file has been created. However, for a new point file it is possible for the experienced user to use any compatible (.ELE) file available. The capabilities of the plot mode are similar to those of program PLOT as detailed in INFPLO.

Temporary Back-Up Files

Whenever the program asks if further input is wanted, a "ZERO" answer causes temporary storage of all previously generated data on a file with the name TEMP. If program operation is aborted during succeeding input, due to either user error or system failure, then the program can be rerun and the previously generated data recovered by recalling TEMP as an old file. The availability of this temporary storage capability makes it preferable to enter large numbers of points in several successive node range entries rather than in one entry over the whole range, except for data file use.

Nonaborting Mistakes

If a mistake such as the entry of a wrong node number or coordinate
occurs during input over a range (N1,N2), immediate entry of the
final (N2,XN2,YN2) triplet will usually terminate the input over
this range without aborting the run. The node range input can then
be redone, either completely or starting after the last correctly
generated point.

Dialog Examples for Point File Generation

NOTE. Two more dialogs, illustrating individual entry, linear automatic line and quadrilateral generation, scale factors, problem coordinate listing and manual data file entry are contained in the on-
line documentation (TY INFPOI).

Dialog 1 (Nonlinear Curved Quadrilateral)

The following dialog will generate a 90-point mesh, illustrated in
Fig. 5 a and 6, for analyzing one quadrant (X>0,Y>0) of a thick-
walled cylinder with an outside radius of 10 and an inside radius of
1, complete with nonlinear spacing to produce smaller elements and
greater resolution near the center (Lame problem). The problem
will be followed all the way through the documentation of other programs.

```
RUN POINTS

GET OLD FILE?
-1
AUTO POINT GENERATOR WANTED?
1
ENTER NODE RANGE (NEG,NONLIN; 0,DATA FILE)
-1,90
ENTER NODE NO, X-COORD, Y-COORD (NEG,QUAD)
-1,0.,1.
ENTER (NODE NO,X,Y) FOR NEXT 3 QUAD PTS
10,0.,10.
-81,1.,0.
-90,10.,0.
ENTER 4 SCALE FACTORS: SFS1,SFS2,SFT1,SFT2
5.,5.,1.,1.
ENTER 1-3 RADIUS: + TO RT, - TO LE (0.0 FOR 3RD PT)
1.
ENTER 2-4 RADIUS: + TO RT, - TO LE (0.0 FOR 3RD PT)
10.0
FURTHER AUTO GENER? (2, TRANSP)
-1
LISTING WANTED?
-1
LEAVING AUTO GENERATOR
```

```
     FURTHER INPUT?
     -1
     STØRE PØINTS? (0 ,SCALE; 2,LØCAL EXP)
     1
     ENTER FILE NAME
     CYLDR
     NØ ØF NØDES STØRED
     90,

     END ØF EXECUTIØN
     CPU TIME: 1.26  ELAPSED TIME 1:50.52
     EXIT
```

Dialog 2 (Transpositions)

The 90 points generated above are numbered sequentially along 9
radial lines, with numbers 1-10 along the positive Y axis and 81-90
along the positive X axis. Use of the transposition option as below
will renumber the points so that sequential numbering is along circular arcs, with numbers 1-9 along the inside surface (R = 1.0) and
82-90 along the outside surface (R=10.0). This transposed geometry,
stored under the name "CYLDR" (replacing the old file), is used for
the rest of the cylinder problem.

(Continuing from corresponding point in Dialog 1)

```
     FURTHER AUTØ GENER WANTED? (2, TRANSP)
     2
     ENTER START NØDE NØ, SEQ LENG, TRANS LENG
     1,9,10
     FURTHER TRANSP? (0,LIST; 2,GENER)
     -1
     LEAVING AUTØ GENERATØR
```

(Etc.)

Dialog 3 (Circular Arc, Plotting, Old File Option)

In the following dialog, the previously stored "CYLDR" points file
is recalled as an old file. Points 1-9, which lie along the inner
circular edge (R = 1), are moved inward radially a distance of 0.5
using the quadrilateral generator to create a single circular arc.
The inner elements (1-48) are then plotted, using the previously
generated elements file since connectivity is not affected by moving
these points.

```
RUN POINTS

GET OLD FILE?
1
ENTER OLD FILE NAME
CYLDR
NO OF NODES READ IN
90
ENTER POINTS? (O FOR TRANSPOS ONLY)
1
AUTO POINT GENERATOR WANTED?
1
ENTER NODE RANGE (NEG,NONLIN; O,DATA FILE)
1,9
ENTER NODE NO, X-COORD, Y-COORD (NEG,QUAD)
1,0.,.5
NODE NO, X-COORD, Y-COORD?
-9,.5,0.
ENTER RADIUS: + TO RT, - TO LE (0.0 FOR 3RD PT)
.5
FURTHER AUTO GENER? (2,TRANSP)
-1
LISTING WANTED?
0
ENTER NAME OF ELEM FILE
CYLDR
NO OF ELEMS AVAILABLE
144
ELEMENT PLOT RANGE? (NEG FOR SCALE)
1,48
WANT ELEM NOS, NODE NOS, 90 DEG ROT?
-1,-1,-1
```

(Fig. 5c plotted)

```
FURTHER PLOTS?
-1
LISTING WANTED?
-1
LEAVING AUTO GENERATOR
```

(Etc.)

Dialog 4 (Auto-Generation with Four Circular Sides)

An 11x11 mesh representing a circle passing through points 1,11,111, 121 is generated as one quadrilateral by flagging the second quadri-lateral point (11) with a negative sign. The resulting mesh, after connecting with program ELMNTS is shown in Fig. 5d.

```
    RUN POINTS

    GET OLD FILE?
    -1
    AUTO POINT GENERATOR WANTED?
    1
    ENTER NODE RANGE (NEG, NON LIN; 0, DATA FILE)
    1,121
    ENTER NODE NO, X-COORD, Y-COORD (NEG, QUAD)
    -1,0.,0.
    ENTER (NODE NO,X,Y) FOR NEXT 3 QUAD PTS
    -11,0.,10.
    111,10.,0.
    121,10.,10.
    ENTER 4 RAD IN 1-3,2-4,1-2,3-4 ORDER (0 OPTS)
    -7.07,7.07,7.07,-7.07
    FURTHER AUTO GENER? (2,TRANSP)
    -1
    LISTING WANTED? (2,GENER)
    -1
```

(Etc.)

Dialog 5 (Auto-Generation Data Files)

In this dialog, the points for a 90-point geometry similar to the
"CYLDR" problem are entered using a data file. The difference between this geometry and "CYLDR" is that the outer radial surface of
"CYLDR" is replaced by two straight-line segments intersecting at
point 10,10 . The resulting geometry is one quadrant of a 19x19
square plate with a central hole, and the five edges require the use
of two quadrilaterals to generate it (see Fig. 8d in PROGRAM
ELMNTS). These two quadrilaterals are best joined along a 45 degree
line (points 41-50), and the data file described and used below consists of answers to questions as they would be asked for two quadrilaterals having corner points 1,10,41,50 and 41,50,81,90 spanning
the node range 1-90, including negative flags as needed to signify
nonlinear generation and circular edges. As is generally the case,
it is easiest to regenerate the connecting nodes 41-50 when generating the second quadrilateral. The data file has been previously
created without line numbers, under the name "SQUAR.PIN", in the
following form:

```
    -1,90                         -41,.707,./07
    -1,0.,1.                      50,10.,10.
    10,0.,10.                     -81.1.,0.
    -41,.707,.707                 90,10.,0.
    50,10.,10.                    5.,5.,1.,1.
    5.,5.,1.,1.                   1.
    1.
```

```
RUN POINTS

GET OLD FILE?
- 1
AUTO POINT GENERATOR WANTED?
1
ENTER NODE RANGE (NEG, NON LIN; 0, DATA FILE)
0,0
ENTER NAME OF DATA FILE
SQUAR
LISTING WANTED?
```
(Etc.)

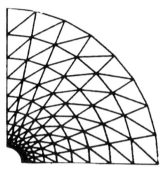

a. Full CYLDR geometry
    (Dialogs 1 and 2) generated
    from four entered points

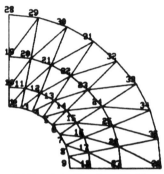

b. Inner detail of radially
    numbered CYLDR geometry
    (Dialog 1)

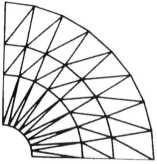

c. Inner detail of CYLDR
    geometry after radial
    shift of inner boundary
    (Dialog 3)

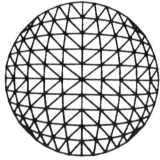

d. Circular region gen-
    erated from four entered
    points (Dialog 4)

Fig. 5. Geometry generated by dialog examples (Note:
Connectivity for plotting requires element generation
using ELMNTS)

PROGRAM ELMNTS (INFELM)

ELMNTS is a program for entering the connectivity of a mesh of triangular elements in terms of triplets (N1,N2,N3) of node numbers defining each individual triangle and for storing the information in an
elements (.ELE) file. Old element files may also be read and modified. The sense of element-defining triplets must be counterclockwise (CCW) to be consistent with the TOTAL system convention of positive tension and negative compression. All automatic generation
options produce CCW sensing when properly used. Defining of element
connectivity usually follows creation of a corresponding points
(.PTS) file, and such a points file is required for use of the automatic element generator. Graphical display of the mesh is provided
when a points file is available. At the end of the program run, the
bandwidth of the mesh is printed out, with its location, and is
stored in the element file.

Data Entry

As in the POINTS program, element connectivity information can be
entered either (1) individually, an element at a time, (2) automatically by using the automatic generator, or (3) by a combination of
the two. Element connectivity is defined by a triplet of node numbers (N1,N2,N3) entered in CCW order. The program asks the range
(ELEM1 ,ELEM2) of element numbers to be entered. Input is then requested until the last element entered (or automatically generated)
equals ELEM2. Another range of elements may then be entered. The
final element file must consist of elements with numbers starting at
1, and continuing consecutively. No numbering gaps are permitted.
    The program first asks if an old file is wanted. If so, the
name is requested, and the old file becomes available for listing
and/or modifying (including enlarging). Next the choice of automatic or individual input is made. For any run using both types of
entry, the automatic mode must be used first. However, individual
entry is briefly discussed first.

NonAutomatic Entry

Manual Entry

In this mode, the program next asks the input range (ELM1,ELM2). (A
"0,0" entry for any range request during individual entry will activate the DATA FILE mode, and then bring another input range request. See below.) The program then requests element information
until the second range number is reached, at which point listing or
further input is available. The entry to define an element consists
of the element number followed by the required triplet of node numbers (ELEM NO,N1,N2,N3), where N1,N2,N3 must be in counterclockwise
(CCW) order. In the ELEM1,ELEM2 input range any elements skipped
are assigned the node number triplet 0,0,0 for ease in identification when listing. These gaps must be filled with real elements

before the mesh can be used, and before any attempt to exercise the
plotting capabilities. Any later specification of the triplet defining an element, either manually or automatically, replaces the
earlier specification.

Data File Entry

An element data file consists of an un-line-numbered file, previously created under the name NAME.EIN (the extension must be included),
with each line consisting of the element number followed by the defining triplet (ELEM NO,N1,N2,N3). When this entry mode has been
elected by entering "0,0" for the first range request, the response
to the second range request should be the first and last element
numbers in the data file (or some subset). The name of the data
file (without extension) is then requested, the file is entered,
and the program then returns to the manual mode with listing and
further entry options. The data file option is normally used only
when entering elements connecting a large number of irregularly arranged nodes.

Automatic Generation

This program option provides automatic generation of elements in any
region which is equivalent in connectivity to a quadrilateral with
equal node lengths on opposite sides, and also of several irregular
(or transition) regions. The simple quadrilateral case is illustrated by the figures in cases 1 and 2 in the "Node Length" discussion
in INFTER, and the case of a more general equivalent region is illustrated by the region spanned by nodes 1-12 in Fig. 6a and b.
The program firsts asks for the number of regions to be generated (NAGR). This is simply a looping parameter for data request,
and is not critical since later the program will ask if more regions
are wanted. (A "ZERO" entry for NAGR activates a data-file mode
discussed below. A negative entry for NAGR activates the non-
standard region options and brings a list of the available options.
See below.) For each region the program asks first the starting element number and the node range of the region entered as a triplet
(ELEM NO,N1,N2). The last requested inputs are the node lengths of
the region in the form (NLSEQ,NLTRANS). The following two cases
indicate two possible node range conditions and the type of results
produced.

Standard Region Option

Case 1.   Standard node range (N1,N2) option: $N1 \le N2$
Entry for (first ELEM NO,N1,N2): (1,1,12)
Entry for (NLSEQ,NLTRANS): (3,4)
Result: Generation of a 12 element mesh connecting points 1-12, with
         element 1 starting at the "POINT 1" corner and element 12
         ending at the "POINT 12" corner.

<u>Note</u>. Connection of almost all quadrilateral regions can be accom-
plished with Case 1 above. Case 2 below, though available, is rarely needed.

<u>Case 2</u>.   Reverse node range (N1,N2) option: N1>N2
Entry for (first ELEM NO,N1,N2):   (1,12,1)
Entry for (NLSEG,NLTRANS):   (3,4)
Result: Generation of a 12 element mesh connecting points 1-12, with
         element 1 starting at the "POINT 12" corner.

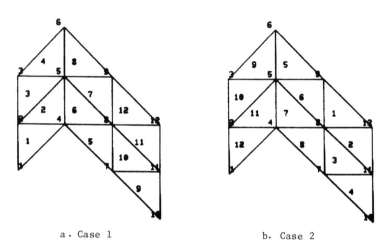

a. Case 1   b. Case 2

Fig. 6.   Two types of connectivity for one-point file

Auto-Generation Data File

Entry of "ZERO" for the number (NAGR) of regions to be generated activates a data file mode. The name of a data file (.EIN) is requested, and the information for any number of regions will then be
read from this file. This type of data file, created without numbers
under the name "-----.EIN", starts with "NAGR" on the first line, and
then contains two one-line answers to the two questions that would be
asked by the program for each region. See Dialogs 2 and 3 for an example of entry of the same data with and without the use of a data
file.

Nonstandard Region Options

A "-1" answer for "NAGR" brings a choice of automatically connecting
any number of the following special regions by entering the proper
code number.

Fan-Shaped Region (Code 1): one in which a central point is connected to N outer points with N-1 triangles, each having the
central point as one of its nodes. The program requests the central
node number, the node range N1,N2 (N1<N2 or N1>N2) of the outer
nodes in CW order, and then the first element number. Entry of
"N,0" for the node range, where N is the number of outer nodes activates the discrete (nonconsecutive) entry mode, and the program
then requests the outer nodes in CW order. Fig. 7a illustrates the
connecting of central node 1 to outer nodes 2-10 .

Transition Region (Code 2): a single bay of elements connecting two
lines of points, with twice as many intervals along one line as along
the other (or, equivalently, with N points on one line and 2 x N-1
on the other). This option is of particular value when increasing
(or decreasing) element density from one subregion to the next. The
user enters two sets of node numbers, in either consecutive or nonconsecutive order (see FAN option above), first for the dense edge
(greater number of points and intervals), and then for the sparse
edge. Figure 7b illustrates a transition region connecting a
five-node side to a three-node side.

Irregular Region (Code 3): a quadrilateral of dimension 2xN (or
Nx2) with the node numbers along one or both of the N-length sides
not being in sequential numerical order. Such a region will usually
be used as a transition between two larger automatically generated
regular regions. It is similar to the transition region described
above (Code 2), but with equal numbers of points (and intervals)
along each of the two longer sides. The input is also similar, with
entry of two sets of points, entered in the same direction for the
two long sides (consecutive or nonconsecutive entry), followed by
the starting element number. Figure 7c illustrates an irregular
region with one consecutive and one nonconsecutive edge-node set.

Standard Input (Code 4): returns user to standard auto-generation.

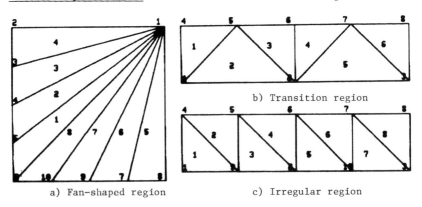

a) Fan-shaped region   c) Irregular region

Fig. 7.   Nonstandard regions connected by auto-generator

Listing and Plotting

Listing and plotting options are the same as for program POINTS with
the plotting option being activated by a "ZERO" answer to the "LIST-
ING WANTED?" question. (See PROGRAM POINTS section)

Shortest Diagonals

Diagonal discussion. In the ELMNTS program, meshes are generated by
successive creation of 4 point quadrilaterals, each of which is then
split into two triangles by a diagonal. The shortest of the two
diagonals is chosen by the program, since this usually results in
triangles with the best aspect ratios and a consequently better solution. However, there are cases when the long diagonal may be preferable over all or part of a geometry. As an example, location of
element centroids as close as possible to a point of stress concentration may require local use of the longest diagonal. When the
mesh being generated is rectangular, both possible diagonals will be
of the same length, and the program chooses one as a default. In
such a region, symmetry of the mesh about some axis of physical
symmetry may be accomplished by electing the longest diagonal on one
side of the axis, which will result in the use of the other equal
diagonal. However, this symmetry can only be realized readily for
meshes in which the symmetry line lies in the direction of sequential
numbering.

Longest diagonal option. The longest diagonal may be elected over
any region by appending a negative sign to the number of the first
element to be used in generating the region, e.g. (-ELEM NO,N1,N2).
Dialog 2 illustrates the use of this switch to produce a symmetric
mesh.

Geometry Files

Since both point and element information is available during automatic generation, the user has the option before leaving the automatic generator of creating a geometry (.GEO) file immediately without later use of the CHECK or GEOMET programs.

                            Dialog Examples

Note. Six more pages of dialog illustrating the different standard
and non-standard connectivity options can be found in the on-line
documentation (INFELM).

Dialog 1 (CYLDR Problem)

The following dialog will generate a 144 element mesh connecting the
90 points in the transposed CYLDR point file as generated in Dialog 2

of INFPOI, with elements 1-16 lying along the inner edge (R=1), and
119-144 along the outer edge (R=10). The resulting mesh (Figs. 8a
and 8b) is used throughout the result of the CYLDR problem solution.
It will result in some lack of symmetry in the solution since it
can be seen that the mesh is not symmetric about a 45-deg line.

```
R UN ELMNTS

GET ØLD FILE
- 1
A UTØ GENERATIØN WANTED?
1
ENTER NAME ØF PØINT FILE
CYLDR
NØ ØF NØDES AVAILABLE
90,
NØ ØF REGIØNS TØ BE GENERATED? (0 FØR ØPTIØNS)
1
FØR EACH REGIØN (NEG DIAG ØPT)
ENTER FIRST ELEM NØ, FIRST NØDE NØ, LAST NØDE NØ
1,1,90
ENTER SEQUEN NØDE LENGTH, TRANSV NØDE LENGTH
9,10
LISTING WANTED?
- 1
FURTHER AUTØ GENER WANTED?
- 1
CREATE GEØM FILE?
1
ENTER NAME ØF GEØM FILE
CYLDR
NØ ØF NØDES, NØ ØF ELEMS, BANDWIDTH
90,144,22
LEAVING AUTØ GENERATØR
STØRE ELEMS?
```

(Etc.)

Note. A dialog identical to the above could be used to generate the
connectivity of a mesh similar to the cylindrical geometry but with
the outer circular surface replaced by two lines intersecting at
10,10, or in other words a square plate with a hole. Even though
the periphery now appears to consist of five edges, Fig. 8d shows
that this region is also equivalent to a single quadrilateral with
node lengths 9,10 .

Dialog 2 (Diagonal Option)

In this dialog, the radially numbered geometry created in Dialog 1 of
INFPOI is connected by using two separate regions, and electing the

longest diagonal option in the second region to produce symmetry
about a 45-deg line. The results are illustrated in Fig. 8c. Data
file entry of the same information follows in Dialog 3.

(Continuing from corresponding point in Dialog 1)

```
NØ ØF REGIØNS TØ BE GENERATED? (O FØR ØPTIØNS)
2
FØR EACH REGIØN (NEG DIAG ØPT)
ENTER FIRST ELEM NØ, FIRST NØDE NØ, LAST NØDE NØ
1,1,50
ENTER SEQUEN NØDE LENGTH, TRANSV NØDE LENGTH
10,5
ELEM RANGE GENERATED
1,72
ENTER FIRST ELEM NØ, FIRST NØDE NØ, LAST NØDE NØ
-73,41,90
ENTER SEQUEN NØDE LENGTH, TRANSV NØDE LENGTH
10,5
ELEM RANGE GENERATED
73,144
```

(Etc.)

Dialog 3 (Auto-Generation Data Files)

In this dialog, the information entered in answer to the questions of
Dialog 2 above is read from a data file previously created under the
name "CYLDR.EIN", and consisting of the following five lines:

```
2
1,1,50
10,5
-73,41,90
10,5
```

(Continuing from corresponding point in Dialog 2)

```
NØ ØF REGIØNS TØ BE GENERATED? (O,DATA FILE; NEG,ØPT LIST)
0
ENTER NAME ØF DATA FILE
CYLDR
ELEM RANGE GENERATED
1,72
ELEM RANGE GENERATED
73,144
```

(Etc.)

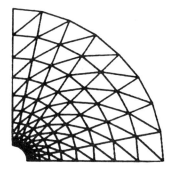

a. CYLDR geometry generated
   as one region (Dialog 1).

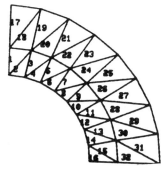

b. Inner detail of CYLDR with
   element numbers.

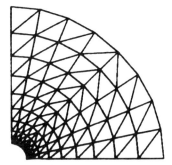

c. Symmetric CYLDR geometry
   generated as two regions
   (Dialog 2).

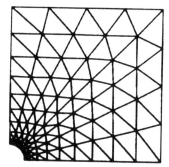

d. Mesh having connectivity
   interchangeable with that of
   symmetric CYLDR mesh.

Fig. 8. Connectivities generated by dialog examples for
node locations created by program POINTS

PROGRAM GEOMET (INFGEO)

GEOMET is a program for combining a points (.PTS) and elements (.ELE)
file into a geometry (.GEO) file which is used for geometric information by all subsequent programs. In its simplest form it combines a
complete points file with a complete file of elements spanning the
full range of the points file. However, there are options whereby
continuous compatible subsets of points and elements files can be
linked together and automatically renumbered to produce a subset of
the full geometry file. This subset option can also be used to renumber the nodes and elements of the original geometry.

Data Entry

Full Geometry

After requesting the names of the points and elements files, the
program asks if the full range of nodes and elements is wanted. For
a "YES" answer, a complete geometry file is created under a requested name.

Subset Geometry

If the answer to the "FULL RANGE" question is "NO", the program requests a node range pair (N1,N2), renumbers all nodes in this range
starting with the number 1 , and then asks if a listing is wanted.
A "YES" answer brings a list of new node numbers and corresponding
old node numbers and their X-Y location. A "ZERO" answer brings a
request for another node range to be appended sequentially to the
previously renumbered nodes. A "NO" answer transfers the user to
element input, with a request for the first range of elements to be
renumbered. Further requests and input of elements are then identical to those described above for nodes. When a fully compatible
geometry subset (or renumbered full geometry) is assembled, a new
bandwidth is calculated and printed, and a geometry (.GEO) file can
be stored under any chosen name.

Dialog Example

```
RUN GEØMET

ALL FILES UNDER SAME NAME?
1
ENTER FILE NAME
CYLDR
FULL ELEM, NØDE RANGES WANTED FØR GEØM FILE?
1
NØ ØF NØDES, NØ ØF ELEMS, BANDWIDTH
90,144,24

END ØF EXECUTIØN
```

PROGRAM MTRIAL (INFMTR)

MTRIAL is a program which takes keyboard- or data-file-input material
property information, including element material axis orientation for
the orthotropic case, assigns the proper information to each element,
and stores all the needed quantities in a material (.MAT) file. The
default mode of this program, and of the TOTAL system, is plane
stress. The plane strain mode may be elected for any set of elements

and their corresponding materials, by appending a negative sign to
the first modulus quantity requested under any of the material
property entry modes discussed below. A mixed mode solution is allowed. All material properties are converted at input to either
plane stress- or plane strain-modified form before storing. In
either case, the elastic properties are consistent with per-unit-
thickness stress and strain variables. (See "PROGRAM THICK" to modify (.MAT) file for variable or constant nonunit thickness.) All
material properties are stored in full orthotropic C(IJ) form, including isotropic materials, and the listing option after material
property entry will produce a full C(IJ) listing for each material
rather than in the format as entered. The negative sign on C11
should be ignored for materials entered in the plane strain mode.
MTRIAL does not presently have the capability for reading and/or
modifying a previously created (.MAT) file; any changes require the
creation of a new file. However, reusable information, for further
use and/or modification by MTRIAL, can be stored in the following
data files: (.MPR), material properties; (.MEL), element material
assignment; (.MRO), element material axis orientation. The order
of input of elastic constants as described below is also listed in
the request dialog of the program.
    Note. For the simplest case of one isotropic material assigned
to all elements, read the first sample dialog before continuing.

                              Data Entry

The program first asks for the total number (NEL) of elements to
which material properties are to be assigned. A general utility
material file for a single homogeneous material (isotropic or orthotropic) may be set up by simply defining NEL to be greater than required for any foreseen application. The programs which use the
material file will accept such over dimensioning, although sometimes
a warning will be issued. The next request is for a number pair
(NMATIS,NMATOR) giving the number of isotropic and orthotropic materials for which elastic constants are to be entered. (A "0,0"
entry here activates the data-file mode and brings a request for the
name of the material property data file (.MPR). The program prints
the number of materials read in, and input then returns to the terminal. See data file discussion below.) The elastic constants, isotropic followed by orthotropic, are then entered as follows.

Isotropic Input (skipped for orthotropic only)

For each isotorpic material, the required input is a real-number pair
(E,PR) giving the elastic modulus and Poisson's ratio. The program
continues to request such pairs for the full range of the parameter
 NMATIS . Entry of the modulus with a negative sign elects a plane
strain mode for all elements to which the material properties are assigned. A mixed plane stress-plane strain situation for a single
material can be elected by entering two materials, with the same
properties except for a negative sign on one modulus, and then

assigning element properties accordingly. See below.

Orthotropic Input (skipped for isotropic only)

For the orthotropic case, there are two modes of input, the C(IJ)
mode and the E(I),PR(I,J) mode. The program asks the number NCIJ of
materials to be read in C(IJ) mode. For NCIJ=0, the program proceeds to the E,PR mode below.

C(IJ) input. For each material, over the full range of NCIJ , the
C(IJ)'s are requested in the order: C11, C12, C13, C22, C23, C33,
C66. The notation used here is (STRESS(I)=C(IJ)xSTRAIN(J);I,J=1,6;
1=XX, 2=YY, 3=ZZ, 4=YZ, 5=XZ, 6=XY). The strain used here, and
throughout the TOTAL system, is the engineering strain (without the
½ factor on the shear components). A negative C11 will elect the
plane strain mode.

E(I),PR(IJ) input. If NCIJ<NMATOR, the properties for the remainder
of the orthotropic materials are requested in the order   E1, PR12,
PR13, E2, PR21, PR23, E3, PR31, PR32, G12 (XY shear modulus). The
notation used here is (-PR(I)) is the strain in the J direction
caused by the application of a stress in the I direction sufficient
to cause a unit strain in the I direction; since only three of the
six Poisson ratios are independent, only three independent real
values need to entered. The other three entries can be zeros,
which serve as a flag to the program to calculate actual values consistent with the other three. (E.g., if PR12 is entered, PR21 may
be set to zero, and will then be calculated by the program.) A
negative "E1" elects plane strain.

Material Property Listing

At this point, a listing can be made of all material properties in
C(IJ) form.

Element Material Assignment (skipped for one material only)

If more than one material has been specified, the program requests
a code number (1-5) specifying the mode of assignment of materials
to elements. (A "ZERO" code entry brings a listing of these options.)
Any combination of modes may be used, and after termination of any
mode there is an option to list results or to enter another mode.
There are also options to list the assignments, and to create an element assignment data file (.MEL).

Consecutive assignment (Code 1). Program requests triplets N1,N2,
NMP, where the first pair defines an element range over which material
number "NMP" is assigned. Input ceases when the second range number
equals the total number of elements. However, when modifying an

element data file which has been read in (Code 3 below), input ceases
when a "0,0,0" triplet is entered.

Discrete entry (Code 2). Program requests a material number and
the number of elements to which it is to be assigned. These element numbers are then entered, in any order. Entry requests in
this mode cease when a "0,0" pair is entered.

Data file entry (Code 3). Program requests the name of an element
assignment data file (.MEL) which has been previously created, either
with an editor or during a previous run of MTRIAL. The form of
this data file is discussed below. The data file read in can be
modified with any of the other entry modes.

Window entry (Code 4). In this option, the name of a geometry file
is requested, and then a material property number and four node numbers are requested. These latter four numbers define the minimum
and maximum X-, and minimum and maximum Y-extent of a rectangular
window within which all elements are assigned the same material
number.

   Radial window. As an added option, the material property number in the window entry can be entered with a negative sign to signify that the entries to follow are to be interpreted as defining a
radial window. In this case, the four nodes (or coordinates) entered with the property number define points at minimum and maximum
radial distances from a central point which is next requested. (Normally, the second pair (NYMIN,NYMAX) duplicates the first pair
(NXMIN,NXMAX).) Entry of "ZERO" for the central node number brings
a request for its X,Y coordinates. The window now consists of all
points which lie radially, with respect to the central point, at
distances equal to those between the minimum and maximum points,
independent of angular location. Successive use of this option will
assume the radial case, with the same central point, until a new
negative material number is entered, at which time the option re-
verts to the rectangular case.

Quit (Code 5). Entry of this code terminates material assignment,
and bypasses listing and element data file (.MEL) store options.

Element Material Axes (skipped for isotropic only)

If orthotropic material properties have been entered, the program
will ask if any material axis rotations are required. If the answer
is "YES", then assignment options similar to those above for material
assignment are available. The material axis angle is defined as the
angle from the material X axis of the element to the global geometric
X axis. Angle input is in degrees.

Data-File Use

All three data files may be created by a computer system editor as un-line-numbered files, following the format described below. The last two listed files can also be created directly by MTRIAL.

Material properties (.MPR). Files containing material constants of up to six different materials, plus required parameters, can be stored as follows. (See above for parameter definitions.)

First line:	NMATIS, NMATOR
Second line:	NCIJ
Following lines:	Elastic constants of materials
	First: All isotropic
	Second: All CIJ orthotropic
	Last: All E,PR orthotropic
	NOTE: Property list for any one material may extend into a second line, but each new material must start on a new line.

If wanted, alphanumeric text labeling the properties may be appended to the end of the (.MPR) file. See second dialog below.

Element material assignment (.MEL). First line: N1,N2 (element range of file); each following line: element number, assigned material number. For editor-entered files, gaps are permitted in element numbers, but list must be numerically increasing, with last element number equal to N2.

Material axis orientation (.MRO). Same form as (.MEL) file, with rotation angle, in degrees, replacing material number.

Dialog Examples

Dialog 1

In the following dialog, a material file is created for the CYLDR problem, with one isotropic material assigned to all 144 elements. Plane strain is elected over the plane stress default by appending a negative sign to the modulus.

```
RUN MTRIAL

TOTAL NO ELEM?
144
ENTER NO OF ISO MATS, NO OF ORTHO MATS
1,0
FOR ISOTROP MAT
INPUT YOUNGS MOD, POISSONS RATIO
-10000000.,.35
```

```
PRINT ØF CIJ WANTED?
-1

ENTER NAME ØF MAT FILE
CYLDR

END ØF EXECUTIØN
CPU TIME 0.70    ELAPSED TIME 42.78
```

Dialog 2

In the following dialog, a three-material data file is read in, an element assignment data file is also read in and modified to assign material 3 to elements 1-48, and a material axis angle of 45 deg is assigned to all elements. The material property data file is listed first, including an appended index (for illustrative purposes, the three materials are identical).

Data file "CYLDR.MPR"

```
1,2
1
10000000.,,.35
16029380.,8641976.,8641976.,16049380.,8641976.
16049380.,3703704.
10000000.,,.35,.35,10000000.,0.0,.35,10000000.,0.0,0.0
3703704.
No of iso mats, no of ortho mats
No of ortho mats in "CIJ" mode
Properties of following materials:  Aluminum
                                    Aluminum
                                    Aluminum
```

```
RUN MTRIAL

TØTAL NØ ELEM?
144
ENTER NØ ØF ISØ MATS, ØRTHØ MATS (0,0 FØR DATA FILE)
0,0
ENTER NAME ØF MAT PRØP DATA FILE
CYLDR
NØ ØF ISØ MATS, ØRTHØ MATS
1,2
PRINT ØF CIJ WANTED?
-1
ASSIGN ELEM MAT? (0 FØR DATA FILE)
0
ENTER NAME ØF ELEM DATA FILE
CYLDR
RANGE READ IN
1,144
```

```
LISTING WANTED?
-1
ASSIGN ELEM MAT? (0 FØR DATA FILE)
1
ENTER ELEM RANGE, MAT PRØP NØ (0,0,0 TØ END)
1,48,3
ENTER ELEM RANGE, MAT PRØP NØ (0,0,0 TØ END)
0,0,0
STØRE ELEM MAT?
-1
ASSIGN ELEM RØT? (0 FØR DATA FILE)
1
ENTER ELEM RANGE, ANGLE IN DEG
1,144,45.
STØRE ELEM RØT?
-1
ENTER NAME ØF MAT FILE
CYLDR

END ØF EXECUTIØN
CPU TIME: 2.29 ELAPSED TIME: 3:34.53
```

Dialog 3

In this dialog example, elements 1-32 of the CYLDR problem are assigned material property 1, and elements 33-144 property 2 by using the radial window option. Note that the negative flag on the material number to signify radial assignment is not mentioned in the input request dialog.

```
RUN MTRIAL

TØTAL NØ ØF ELEM?
ENTER NØ ØF ISØ MATS, ØRTHØ MATS (0,0 FØR DATA FILE)
2,0
FØR ISØ MAT
INPUT YØUNGS MØD, PØISSØNS RAT
10000000.,.35
INPUT YØUNGS MØD, PØISSØNS RAT
10000000.,.35
PRINT ØF CIJ WANTED?
-1
ENTER ELEM ASSIGN CØDE (0 FØR ØPT LIST)
0
CØDE:1,CØNT; 2,DISCR; 3,DATA FILE; 4,WIND; 5,QUIT
ENTER ELEM ASSIGN CØDE
4
ENTER NAME ØF GEØM FILE
CYLDR
NØDES, ELEMS
90,144
```

```
ENTER ASSIGN NØ,NXMIN,NXMAX,NYMIN,NYMAX (0 CØØRD ØPT)
-1,1,19,1,19
ENTER CENTR NØDE NØ (0, X-Y ENTRY)
0
ENTER CENTR X,Y
0.,0.
FURTH ELEM ASSI? (0,LIST; 2,CREATE ELEM FILE)
1
ENTER ELEM ASSIGN CØDE (0 FØR ØPT LIST)
4
ENTER ASSIG NØ,NXMIN,NXMAX,NYMIN,NYMAX (0 CØØRD ØPT)
2,19,82,19,82
FURTH ELEM ASSI? (0,LIST, 2,CREATE ELEM FILE)
0
ENTER ELEM RANGE
32,33
ELEM NØ, MAT PRØP NØ
32,1
33,2
LISTING WANTED? (0,FURTH ASS)
-1
ENTER NAME ØF MAT FILE
CYLDR

END ØF EXECUTIØN
CPU TIME: 3.35 ELAPSED TIME 2:18.37
```

PROGRAM LOADS (INFLOA)

This program provides force, displacement, and displacement constraint boundary conditions. Any consistent combination of forces
and displacements can be applied at any node point (not just on the
boundary). Of course, the force and displacement in one direction
cannot both be specified at a point. Constraints (zero displacements)
on motion of nodes are entered not as displacements, but separately
as constraint inputs. There must be enough properly constrained
points to prevent rigid body translation and rotation, except when
sufficient nonzero displacements have been imposed. Force-only
loading requires at least one fully constrained point and another
point constrained in either the X- or Y-direction. The order of input to the program is forces, displacements, and constraints. Three
individual load files for the three types of loads are stored separately when each has been generated. Previously created load files
may be read for listing and/or modification.

Although each load is created and stored independently, they
must all refer to the same mesh. The number of nodes is automatically assigned by an old file call or by the geometry file used by
distributed forces. Otherwise, the program will request the number
of nodes when first needed.

Data Entry

Creation of each of the three types of load files is essentially independent. Unless the "SAME NAME" option is elected initially,
names of new output files (and of old files, if wanted) are requested
for all three. A geometry (.GEO) file is required for distributed
forces. After the "SAME NAME?" option request, the program asks:
"WANT FORCE, DISPL, CONSTR LOADS? (0,Old File)". Any combination of
the three load types can be elected with 1 or -1; a "ZERO" answer
for any of the three will permit the reading in of an old file.

Force Loads (.LDF)

The user has the choice of distributed and/or point force input,
with distributed input required first. A "ZERO" answer when asked
if distributed forces are wanted will first bring a display of the
proper conventions (see below) before further input request.

Distributed forces. The first request is for the number of edges to
be loaded. An edge here is defined as any continuous contour in
the mesh, starting and ending at a node point, on which the load is
distributed. The next request is for a number pair (FDIS,NNOD)
giving the intensity of a uniform distributed force and the number
of nodes on the loaded edge. The load intensity convention is
positive for all normal forces, and negative for all tangential
(shear) forces. Load direction is specified by the order in which
the edge nodes are entered. An edge is input to the program as a
set of node points progressing continuously from one end to the
other: in CCW sense for pressure and CCW shear; in CW sense for
normal tension and CW shear. Entry of "ZERO" for the intensity
initiates the "linearly varying" load option, and the program then
requests the intensities at either end of the edge, in the order defined by the node entry. Entry of "ZERO" for the number of edge
nodes initiates the consecutive node option, and a node range pair,
in proper order, is requested.

Point forces. The first request is for the number of X forces to be
entered. For each such force the program then requests a number pair
(NNOD,FOR) giving the node number and the value of the force, positive for positive X direction, negative for negative direction. A
similar procedure is then followed for Y forces.

Displacement Loads (.LLD)

The input format for displacements is identical to that described just
above for point forces.

Constraints (.LDZ) files

The program code for point constraint in a given (X or Y) direction

is: 1, free; 0, fixed. For a new constraint file, the program automatically assigns free (1) conditions to all points. The program
first asks for the number of X constraints to be set. After entering this number, the user enters the proper node numbers, in any
order, and these points are constrained in the X direction. Previously constrained nodes may be freed simply by making the corresponding node number entries negative. A similar procedure is
then followed for Y constraints.

Dialog Example

<u>Note</u>. More extensive dialogs can be found in the cantilever beam
example in the section "System Use with Dialog Tutorial."

The following dialog will generate a pressure of 1000 on the outer
surface of the CYLDR geometry and fix the vertical edge in the X
direction and the horizontal edge in the Y direction.

```
RUN LOADS

ALL FILES UNDER SAME NAME?
1
ENTER PROBLEM NAME
CYLDR
FORCE LOADS WANTED? (O FOR OLD FILE)
1
DISTRIBUTED FORCES WANTED? (O FOR CONVEN)
0

INTENSITY CONVENTION: NORMAL LOAD - POSITIVE,  TANGENT
LOAD NEGATIVE

DIRECTION CONVENTION: LIST NODES DEFINING EDGE
IN CCW ORDER FOR PRESSURE OR FOR CCW SHEAR, IN CW
ORDER FOR NORMAL TENSION OR CW SHEAR.

NO OF NODES IN GEOM FILE
90
NO OF EDGES TO BE LOADED?
1
ENTER LOAD INTENSITY, NO OF NODES ON EDGE
1000.,9
ENTER NODE NOS IN PROPER ORDER
90,89,88,87,86,85,84,83,82
LISTING OF NON-ZERO FORCES WANTED?
-1
FURTHER DISTRIBUTED LOADS WANTED?
-1
CONCENTRATED FORCES WANTED?
-1
STORE FORCES?
1
```

```
DISPLACEMENT LOADS WANTED? (O FOR OLD FILE)
-1
DISPL CONSTRAINTS WANTED? (O FOR OLD FILE)
1
NO OF X-CONSTRAINTS TO BE SET?
10
ENTER NODE NOS (NEG TO FREE)
1,10,19,28,37,46,55,64,73,82
NO OF Y-CONSTRAINTS TO BE SET?
10
ENTER NODE NOS (NEG TO FREE)
1,9,18,27,36,45,54,63,72,81,90
DISPLAY CONSTRAINED NODES?
-1
STORE CONSTRAINTS?
1

END OF EXECUTION
CPU TIME: 1.87  ELAPSED TIME: 5:36.03
```

PROGRAM STFSOL (INFSFS)

STFSOL is basically a combination of STFGEN and SOLVE into a solution
sequence which obtains the displacements (.DIS) directly from the
basic input (geometry, material, loads) without requiring the intermediate steps of storing and recovering the stiffness matrix. As
options, the node forces can be calculated and stored, and the stiffness matrix can also be stored.

The only input required is the names of the geometry (.GEO) and
material (.MAT) files, and the combination of boundary condition
files (.LDF,.LDD,.LDZ) wanted and their names; also the names of
the forces (.FOR) and stiffness (.STF) files if they are to be
stored.

PROGRAM RESULT (INFRES)

RESULT is a combination of programs STRAIN, STRESS, PRINC, and ENERGY
which allows selective calculation and storing of strain (.STN),
stress (.STS), principal stress (.PRI) and energy density (.END)
without intermediate storage and retrieval. It is capable only of
creating new files, and listing requires subsequent use of the corresponding result quantity program.

Note. Since seven file name entries are possible in this program, the normal "SAME NAME" option at the start of the program is
broken into two options, one for the three required input files
(.GEO,.MAT,.DIS), and a second for the four optional output files.
In addition, the "SAME NAME" option may be selected for all seven
file types by answering "ZERO" rather than "YES" when electing the
input-name option. These choices are evident from the dialog.

The input required is the choice of the name-entering options,
the entry of names as required by these options, and the choice of

which of the four possible file types are to be stored.

PROGRAM STRESS (INFSTS)

STRESS is a program for calculating stresses over the element range
of a previously created strain file, or for reading and listing an
old stress file. A search for minimum and maximum values of any
stress quantity is provided in the listing procedure, and is described below.

Data Entry

The old/new file option is first requested. For an old file (.STS)
the name is requested, the element range of the file printed, and
selective listing is then available. For a new file, the names of
the strain (.STN) and material (.MAT) files are requested, stresses
are calculated, and listing and store options are then available.

Listing Capabilities

Continuous and discrete listing. If listing is elected, then the
standard option is the entry of an element range, and a printout
then follows of the stresses over this continuous range of elements.
However, if a N,0 pair is entered for the range, the program then
requests N element numbers, and then prints out the stresses for
these N discrete elements.

Extreme value search. A "ZERO" answer to the "LISTING WANTED?"
question activates the extreme value search, and brings a request
for the code (1-4) defining the quantity of interest (SIG-X,SIG-Y,
TAU-XY,SIG-Z). (A "ZERO" entry brings a code listing.) The maximum
and minimum of this quantity are then printed out with their element
locations. A multisearch capability is activated by entering the
code number with a negative sign. A search-level number is then requested, and this number of successively decreasing extreme values
is then printed.

Dialog Example

Dialog for Cylinder Problem

```
RUN STRESS

FILES UNDER SAME NAME?
1
ENTER PRØBLEM NAME
CYLDR
```

```
CREATE NEW STRESS FILE?
1
ELEM RANGE ØF STRAIN FILE
1,144
LIST ØF STRESSES WANTED? (O FØR MAX,MIN)
0
ENTER STRESS CØDE (NEG, MULT SEARCH; 0 FØR CØDE LIST)
-1
ENTER SEARCH LEVEL
2
SIG-X: MAX,ELEM; MIN,ELEM
-208.,15,-2064.,2
-300.,16,-1885.,4
LIST ØF STRESSES WANTED? (O FØR MAX,MIN)
1
ELEM RANGE? (N,O FØR DISCR)
2,0
ENTER ELEM NØS
1,16
ELEM NØ, X-, Y-, XY-, Z-STRESS
1, -1466., -333., 35., 0.
16, -300., -2045., 166., 0.
LIST ØF STRESS WANTED? (O FØR MAX,MIN)
-1
STØRE STRESSES?
1

END ØF EXECUTIØN
CPU TIME: 3.68 ELAPSED TIME: 2:3.08
```

PROGRAM PLOT (INFPLO)

PLOT is a general purpose plotting routine which operates in any or all of the following four modes:

1. Original geometry plot.
2. Plot of the geometry with element numbers replaced by "intensity integers" representing the intensity of such resultant quantities are stress, principal stress, and energy (and also strain by "fooling the program"; see below).
3. Isometric plots of surface representing the distribution of the above resultant quantities, superimposed, if wanted, on a "zero intensity" plane.
4. Contour plots, consisting of lines on which any chosen resultant quantity remains constant.

NOTE. Element thicknesses may also be displayed in modes 2-4. A more specific discussion can be found under "Intensity Surface Mode" below.

Only one basic geometry file name may be used in each run of
PLOT, but the names of result files in modes 2-4 may be changed as
wanted. As many plots as wanted can be made using any combination
of plot mode, result file name, and plot quantity. (See discussion
of "CONTINU?" options below.) In all modes, plotting takes place
over a continuous element range (NE1,NE2) entered by the user.

Plotting Modes

Geometry Mode   (Mode 1)

In this mode, regions consisting of elements of the initial mesh
are plotted, with or without element and node numbers.

Intensity Number Mode   (Mode 2)

In this mode, a result file name is entered, a file-type (e.g.,
stress) is chosen by entering a file code number ("ZERO" brings a
prompting list), and then similarly a plot code number is entered
representing a plot quantity (e.g., sig-X, if the stress file has
been chosen). The maximum and minimum values of the plot quantity
and their element location are printed. The program next requests
the number of intervals (1-99) wanted to span the range from zero
to the largest absolute value to be plotted. A listing of the range
covered by each intensity integer is available. An initial geometry
over a selected range of elements is then plotted, and the intensity
integers (+ or -) are printed in place of element numbers.

Intensity Surface Mode   (Mode 3)

In this mode, a choice is made of result file name, file type, and
plot quantity as in Mode 2. The program then distributes element
values to the nodes, and listing (with max/min-value-only option)
is available for the resulting node quantities. The user then enters
two angles defining the isometric view, the first being the in-plane
rotation from the Y axis, the second being the tilt angle of the X,Y
plane. This program now requests a scale factor for the plot quantity, and a reasonable choice will usually be one that reduces the
greatest absolute plot-quantity value, as listed earlier by the program, to a range of 0-1.0. (Entry of "0.0" for the scale factor
brings the user the option of "zeroing" of node quantities, usually
on a boundary, which are known to be zero physically but which do not
quite reach zero in the element-to-node distribution. Various combinations of angles and scale factor can be tried; a value of 30 degrees for
both angles is a reasonable start. The option is given of overlaying
the surface on a "ZERO" reference plane, which often improves interpretation, particularly if the two surfaces intersect. A dotted line option
for the reference plane further improves the plots but considerably increases the plotting time.

Thickness surface display. As a special case of this mode, entry of
a 4 for file type, and of the name of a thickness file as a result-
file allows the plot of thicknesses as generated by program THICK.
For a plate in which the two surfaces are symmetric about a center
plane, a scale factor of 0.5 will actually produce a 3-D view of
the upper surface, to scale. Thickness numbers (Mode 2) and contours (Mode 4) can also be displayed.

Contour Mode   (Mode 4)

In this mode, a result file name, file code, and plot code are entered and node-distributed quantities are calculated (with listing
available) as in Mode 3. After the element plotting range is entered, the program requests a contour interval. Entry of a negative
value here will result in the printing of a contour number (+ or -)
at the intersection of each contour with the boundary of the region
being plotted. The value along any contour is the product of the
contour interval and the printed contour number. Contours which do
not intersect the boundary are not numbered.

Boundary search. The boundary lines required in the contour option
are not part of the basic geometry file. Therefore, PLOT has the
capability of searching out and storing a boundary file (.BND) for
any continuous set of elements, or of reading in a previously created file. Boundaries created by program DSTRIB can also be used.
Since finding the boundary of a very large number of elements is
one of the longest and most costly processes in the TOTAL system,
large boundaries should be initially stored, and then erased when
no longer needed. A new boundary is required with each new choice of
element range when plotting contours. The various boundary options
are requested, when needed, after entry of the contour interval.

Other Features

Option List

At several points in the program, starting with the initial plot-mode
choice, code numbers (1-4) are requested. A "ZERO" answer to any of
these requests brings a list of available options and code numbers,
followed by another code number request.

Scaling

All plots are automatically scaled to fill the screen. However, if
a negative sign is appended to the element plot range (e.g., -1,10),
a separate scaling factor (SF) is requested, which does the following: for SF=1.0, any region will be plotted to a scale in which the
full geometry would fill the screen and any smaller subregion would
be proportionately smaller; for SF>1.0 the whole plot is expanded

so that the full geometry will no longer fit the screen, with sub-
regions being proportionately smaller. This scaling option is very
useful for creating plots of a given size for reports, etc.

Zooming

When a plotting element range smaller than the full (NEL1=1,NEL2=
Total number of elements) geometry is entered, the plot is expanded to fill the screen, thereby providing a "zoom" capability
for regions consisting of consecutive element numbers. An additional zoom capability is provided (in the dialog) at some points
in the program, whereby entry of "0,0" for the plotting range
brings a request for four node numbers defining the upper and lower
X and Y limits of a plotting window. All elements within this
window are expanded and plotted.

Plot Numbering and Rotation

The last question asked in the simple geometry mode is "WANT NODE
NOS, ELEM NOS, 90 DEG ROTATION?", and a triplet of 1's or -1's must
be entered. Numbers are ordinarily used only when the smallest elements to be plotted are of a reasonable size, and the rotation is
used when the region is larger in the Y direction. Similar questions are asked in other modes, but all three options are not always
available.

The "CONTINUE?" Question and Changing of Plot Modes

After each plot is finished, a "CONTINUE?" question is printed in
the upper left hand corner. A "YES" answer brings a request for a
new element range to be plotted, without changing any of the other
plotting parameters or data. A "NO" answer brings the opportunity
either to quit or to start over in a new plotting mode (same geometry). With the entry of a "ZERO" answer to the "CONTINUE?" questions, the program starts asking for possible changes within the
same plotting mode. These changes can run from a simple change in
the display parameters, to the entry of a new file name with all
the required following input. The actual form and sequence of these
requests depends on which mode is being used, and is best learned by
reading the examples and trying the various options.

Strain plots and "fooling" the program. If a strain (.STN) plot is
wanted, do not enter anything for the intensity file name, and then
proceed as for the corresponding file name. The program will eventually give an error message requesting the full name of the file
and "Name.STN" should be entered, followed by "ESCAPE" instead of
"CARRIAGE RETURN".

Program Use

Basically, all the user need do to use this program is enter the
name of the geometry (.GEO) file, and, if needed, the names of the
element result (.STS,.PRI,.ENE,.THI) file to be plotted, and answer
the other questions as asked. The "ZERO" answer to yes-no questions
can be used as indicated to affect operational changes in the program,
depending on which mode is being used. The sequence of plotting
parameter input is best illustrated by the following dialog.

Dialog Example

In the following dialog, four plots of results for the CYLDR problem
are made as follows:

1. Stress intensity (sig-X) numbers for elements 1-48
2. Numbered stress (sig-X) contours for elements 1-48
3. Principal stress (sig-II) contours for elements 1-48
4. Principal stress (sig-II) surface for elements 1-64 with "ZERO"
   reference surface.

```
RUN PLØT

? NAME ØF GEØM FILE
CYLDR
NØ ØF ELEMENTS AVAILABLE
144
? ØPT NØ (O FØR LIST)
0
1, GEØM; 2, INTENS INTEG; 3, INTENS SURF; 4, CØNTØURS
? ØPT NØ (O FØR LIST)
2
? NAME ØF RESULT FILE
CYLDR
? FILE CØDE (O FØR LIST)
0
FILE CØDE: 1, STRESS; 2, PRIN STRESS; 3, ENERGY DENS
          4, THICKNNESS
? FILE CØDE (O FØR LIST)
1
? PLØT CØDE (O FØR LIST)
0
PLØT CØDE: 1, SIG-X; 2, SIG-Y; 3, SIG-XY; 4, SIG-Z
? PLØT CØDE (O FØR LIST)
1
MIN VALUE, ELEM NØ; MAX VALUE, ELEM NØ
  -2169.9      , 2,  -117.04      , 15,
```

```
? NØ ØF INTERVALS
10
INTERVAL INCREMENT VALUE
216.99
LIST ØF INTERVALS?
-1
? ELEM PLØT RANGE (NEG, SCALE; 0, ZØØM)
1,48
WANT NØDE NØS, 90-DEG RØT?
-1,-1
```

(Fig. 9a plotted)

```
CØNTINUE (0 ØPT)?
-1
NEW ØPTIØN?
1
? ØPT NØ (0 FØR LIST)
4
CHANGE PLØT INFØRM?
-1
LIST NØDE VALUES? (0 FØR MAX, MIN)
0
 -1858.96    , 2,  -368.41    , 9,
LIST NØDE VALUES? (0 FØR MAX, MIN)
-1
? ELEM PLØT RANGE (NEG, SCALE)
1,48
? CØNTØUR INTERVAL (NEG FØR NUMBERED)
-250.
GET STØRED BØUND?
-1
STØRE BØUND?
1
? NAME ØF BØUND FILE
CYL48
```

(Fig. 9b plotted)

```
CØNTINUE (0 ØPT)?
0
CHANGE PLØT INFØRM? (0 FØR PLØT PARAM ØNLY)
1
CHANGE FILE CØDE? (0 FØR NEW FILE NAME)
1
? FILE CØDE (0 FØR LIST)
2
```

```
? PLØT CØDE (0 FØR LIST)
2
LIST NØDE VALUES? (0 FØR MAX, MIN)
-1
? ELEM PLØT RANGE
1,48
? CØNTØUR INTERVAL (NEG FØR NUMBERED)
100.
```

(Fig. 9c plotted)

```
CØNTINUE (0 ØPT)?
-1
NEW ØPTIØN?
1
? ØPT NØ (0 FØR LIST)
3
CHANGE PLØT INFØRM?
-1
LIST NØDE VALUES?
-1
? IN-PLANE RØTATIØN ANGLE FRØM Y-AXIS
30.
? TILT ANGLE FRØM X-Y PLANE
15.
? VERT SCALE FACTØR (0.0 FØR ZERØING)
.001
ZERØ SURFACE ØVERLAY? (0 FØR DASHED)
1
? ELEM PLØT RANGE (NEG, SCALE; 0, ZØØM)
1,64
```

(Fig. 9d plotted)

```
CØNTINUE (0 ØPT)?
-1
NEW ØPTIØN?
-1

END ØF EXECUTIØN
CPU TIME: 1:17.77  ELAPSED TIME: 22:1.63
```

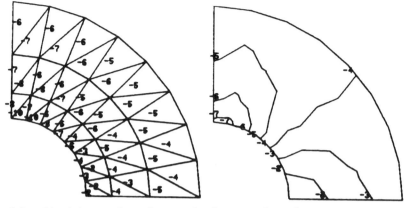

a · Intensity integer plot of   b . Contour plot of sigma-X
    sigma-X

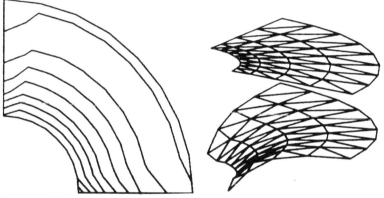

c . Contour plot of largest   d. Isometric surface of largest
    principal stress   principal stress, with "ZERO"
                                         reference surface

Fig. 9. Graphic representation of CYLDR problem results
provided by one run of program PLOT.

PROGRAM DSPLAC (INFDSP)

DSPLAC is a program for listing displacements and for plotting the
distorted mesh, overlaying the original mesh if wanted. Separate
X and Y scale factors can be applied to exaggerate the displacements as needed for plotting.

Program Use

After entering the name of the displacement (.DIS) file, the user is
asked if a listing is wanted. A "YES" answer to this question
brings listings over any node-ranges wanted. A "ZERO" answer here,
or to any "LISTING WANTED?" request later, activates the plot mode
and brings a request for the name of a geometry (.GEO) file. Scale
factors to expand the displacements for plotting are entered, and
the program then asks if any overlay (distorted mesh over original)
is wanted. A "ZERO" answer to this overlay question results in a
dashed original mesh. The user then chooses an element range for
plotting, with the standard element and node number and rotation
options. A "ZERO" answer to the "CONTINUE PLOTTING?" question provides the opportunity to change scale factors and/or elect or re-
fuse the overlay option before further plotting over a new element
range.

Plot scaling. Normally all plots are expanded to fill the screen.
However, attaching a negative sign to any plotting range brings the
capability of either expanding or contracting the plot. This capability is fully described in "PROGRAM PLOT".

Caution. Since the use of dashed lines for the original mesh takes
a considerable amount of time, it is advisable to determine the proper scale factors and element range before electing the overlay option for a final plot.

Dialog Example

In the following dialog, a distorted plot of elements 113-144 at the
outside edge of the "CYLDR" problem is overlayed over the same un-
distorted region. Of course, since the displacements in this problem
are radial, little information is gained from such a plot.

```
RUN DSPLAC

ENTER NAME ØF DISPL FILE
CYLDR
NØ ØF NØDES IN DISPL FILE
90,
LISTING WANTED? TYPE 0 FØR PLØT
0
```

```
ENTER NAME ØF GEØM FILE
CYLDR
ENTER X-, Y-DISPL SCALE FACTØRS: SFXD, SFYD
1000.,1000.
ØVERLAY WANTED? (O FØR DASHED ØRIGINAL)
O
NØ ØF ELEMENTS AVAILABLE
144
ELEMENT PLØT RANGE? (NEG FØR SCALE)
113,144
WANT ELEM NØS, NØDE NØS, 90 DEG RØT?
-1,-1,-1


CØNTINUE PLØT? (O FØR SCALE ØR ØVERLAY ØPT CHANGE)
-1
LISTING WANTED?: TYPE O FØR PLØT
-1
```

(Ftc.)

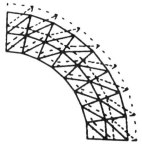
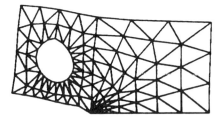

a. Distorted CYLDR geometry   b. Distorted test specimen

Fig. 10.   Illustrations of displacement plotting capabilities

PROGRAM CHECK (INFCHE)

CHECK is a program which searches geometric input for gross mistakes
in either coordinate location or element connectivity. It is of particular value when the graphics capabilities cannot be used for visu-
al checking and when large amounts of non-automatically generated input have been entered. If no mistakes are found, then a geometry
(.GEO) file can be created immediately from the input points (.PTS)
and elements (.ELE) files.

The following checks are made:

1. Calculation and display of maximum and minimum coordinate

values (in true problem coordinates)
    2. Detection of any overlapping elements (optional)
    3. Detection of triangle aspect rations greater than a specified
maximum value
    4. Detection and redefinition of any improperly sense triangles

PROGRAM SHRINK (INFSHR)

SHRINK is a goemetrically founded bandwidth reduction program. It
is based on the principle that in most meshes the lowest bandwidth
can be achieved by having the numbers of the nodes increase with distance from the first node. Since reduction is achieved at the geometry (.GEO) level, rather than at the stiffness matrix level, one
reduction can be used for any solution involving the same geometric
connectivity. Two options are provided.

Reduction Options

One of the following scanning options will always significantly reduce gross bandwidth problems (e.g., higher node numbers assigned as
an afterthought in the neighborhood of low numbered nodes). Its effectiveness decreases somewhat as the mesh becomes very irregular
and/or departs from being rectangular.

Radial scan option. In this case, node numbers are assigned sequentially with increasing radial distance from a reference point entered
by the user. This point should ordinarily be chosen at a considerable
distance from the mesh, and in a direction such that radial lines to
the mesh, are perpendicular to the direction of smallest dimension
of the mesh. A notable exception to choosing a distant reference
point is a radial mesh, in which case the radial center of the mesh
may work best. Different starting nodes may be chosen, and the one
giving the lowest bandwidth used.

Rectangular scan option. In this option, two rectangular scans are
made, and the best of the two results is chosen by the program. Basically, the lower-left-most point is chosen as the first node, and
succeeding nodes are numbered on the basis of their X(Y)-distances
being ordered by their Y(X)-distance from the first node. This option is best for most equi-dimensioned figures, and in fact gives
the lowest bandwidth possible for wholly rectangular meshes (simply
connected regions).

Automatic Mapping

Although the new geometry has a new numbering system, this system
need not be known by the user. All associated files which depend on
node locations and numbering (e.g., load files created by program
LOADS) may be created using the original numbering. All subsequent
programs using the "reduced" geometry file (e.g., STFSOL, STFGEN,

SOLVE, FORCES) automatically accommodate the two numbering systems, and the final displacement file is created in terms of the original numbering.

This automatic point-mapping may be defeated, and the new numbering used for all related files, if a "ZERO" answer is given to the "STORE NEW GEOMETRY?" question at the end of the run. In this case, node numbering of reduces geometry file must then be used in programs LOADS, STFGEN, SLOVE, STRAIN (and also in DSPLAC, FORCES if wanted). Programs following STRAIN in the logical solution sequence operate only on element quantities and can use the original geometry (when required for such purposes as plotting, etc.).

PROGRAM SHIFT (INFSHI)

SHIFT is a program which allows any interior region of a mesh to be shifted in an X and/or Y direction, maintaining the connectivity of the whole mesh. X and Y shifts are accomplished separately and identically and only the X shift will be discussed. First an outer X,Y window, and then an inner X,Y window, is defined. Then a X shift distance is entered and the following takes place. All points outside, or on, the outer window remain unchanged. Inside and on the inner window, all points are shifted by the amount specified; points between the two windows are shifted proportionately to maintain continuity. The eight points defining the two windows can be entered as nodes, or as actual coordinates. The X boundaries of the inner window may coincide, defining a vertical boundary line with X expansion and contraction on either side of this line as it moves. All four points defining the interior window may also coincide. The same procedure is followed for a Y shift.

Data Entry

The name of a geometry file (.GEO) is first entered. If an X shift is elected, four node numbers defining the outside window are requested as follows: NXMIN,NXMAX,NYMIN,NYMAX. The first two nodes define the minimum and maximum extent of the outer window, and the second two define the Y extent. A similar set of four nodes is then requested to define the inner window. Entering of "ZERO" for any of the node numbers will bring a request for an actual coordinate value, and this option is indicated in the prompting. The desired X shift of the interior region is then requested. The same procedure is followed for a Y shift, if wanted. The name of the output geometry (.GEO) file is then requested.

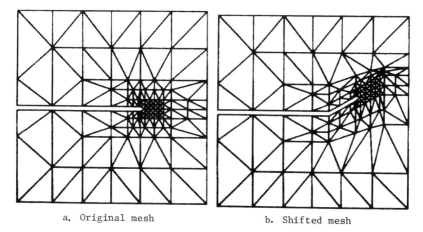

a. Original mesh   b. Shifted mesh

Fig. 11. Modified inner region of test specimen using SHIFT.

PROGRAM THICK (INFTHI)

THICK is a program for modulating the thickness of a model in a plane stress situation. It has the capability of creating either or both of the following files:

    1. A thickness file (.THI) containing a thickness for each element.

    2. A modified material file (.MAT) which consists of a normal material file with the element thicknesses appended, and a switch to indicate this modification to all programs subsequently using the material file.

A previously stored thickness file can be read initially, modified as below if wanted, and appended to any material file, or a new thickness file may be created and appended.

Data Entry

1. Gradient option (X,Y or radial). A reference point is entered, either directly or by specifying a node number, together with the thickness at that point and X and Y (or radial) thickness-gradients. Thicknesses for other elements are then extrapolated linearly on the basis of the X and Y distances of their centers from the reference point, or on the basis of a radial distance from some arbitrary central point. Listing, including maximum and minimum values, is then available. The procedure can be repeated with different gradients, if wanted, until a satisfactory distribution is found.

2. Constant thickness region option. A constant thickness value can be specified over any consecutive range of elements, or within any specified X,Y window.

3. Individual entry option. Thickness can be entered individually for each element, either directly or from a data file.

PROGRAM COMBIN (INFCOM)

COMBIN is a program for producing linear combinations of existing files of the same type (extension) and storing the result under a chosen name with the proper extension. File types which can be combined are: input force (.LDF) and displacement (.LDD) load files; and resultant displacement (.DIS), stress (.STS), strain (.STN), and energy (.END) files.

The program first lists the code integers representing each of the suitable file types, and the user enters the proper code. The number of files of the chosen type to be combined is then entered. The program then requests the required number of file names, together with a linear combination factor (+ or -) for each file. A name for the resulting combined file is then requested, and the file is stored. Listing of the combined file can be obtained by going to the proper program.

PROGRAM DSTRIB (INFDST)

DSTRIB is a program which provides several choices of interpolation and extrapolation of initially computed element results (e.g., strain, stress, principal stress, energy density) to produce node result quantities. The basic interpolation, a weighted distribution of element results to neighboring node locations, is automatic and the resulting node quantities are believed to be the best possible values obtainable from constant strain triangles for all interior points (nodes). Three optional methods of extrapolation of interior values to a boundary are provided, which can be selected based on the experience of the analyst and on his interpretation of the initial distribtuion. All three will give exact results for a linear distribution; for nonlinear variations, their results will differ, depending primarily on whether the gradient of the interior values is increasing or decreasing as the boundary is approached.

A description of the interpolation and extrapolation schemes, with pertinent dialogs, is available in the on-line documentation (INFDST).

PROGRAM LINK (INFLNK)

Program LINK is used to connect two or more previously created geometries, with the only input required being sets of nodes (of equal number) from each geometry which are to be identified. The

initial geometries need not be of the same scale or properly oriented. The program automatically scales and rotates so that the
intersection sets are coincident. Duplicate node numbers are
eliminated, and the second geometry is then renumbered. This renumbering usually produces a very high bandwidth which should be reduced with program SHRINK. More detailed discussion and dialogs
can be found in the on-line documentation (INFLNK).

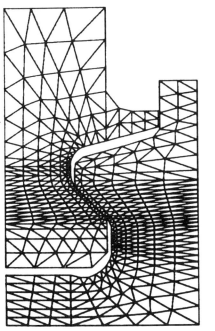 

a. A turbine blade-lug configura-   b. Three steps in the creation of
   tion which has been linked   a ring from a ring quadrant;
   together at seven points   the quadrant is first linked
                                           to itself, and then the half-
                                           ring is linked to itself in
                                           the same run

Fig. 12.   Creation of geometries by linking subregions.

PROGRAM LINPLT (INFLPL)

LINPLT provides a capability for plotting results (stress, principal stress, energy density) along any path, curved or straight, in
the solution region. Two basic plotting modes are available:

X,Y modes. This is simply the usual type of linear plot consisting
of a continuous curve representing result intensity (+ or -) with
respect to a horizontal reference line. In the case of a curved
path, distances in the horizontal direction represent arc length
distances along the curved path.

In-place mode. In this mode, the actual path of interest is plotted
properly oriented with respect to a selected closed boundary. Then
the result curve is plotted using this path (straight or curved)
as the reference (zero) line. At any point along the reference
curve the intensity is plotted with respect to the reference curve,
but in a direction perpendicular to a line joining the first and
last points of the curve, and not along a line normal to the curve.
This parallel-projection type of plot normally precludes choosing
a plotting path with a change in angle of over 90 degrees.
   Within each of these basic modes, there are several options.
Plots of a single result quantity for up to ten differently located
paths may be made at one time, using a common intensity scale but
different numbers of plot points, if wanted. All curves may be
plotted with or without parallel straight lines joining the calculation points on the curve to their respective points on the intensity curve. The plot paths may be entered as discrete points,
using any combination of mode numbers and X,Y locations. Alterna-
tively, for straight lines paths, the beginning and end point locations can be entered, and the desired number of calculation points
will be interpolated.

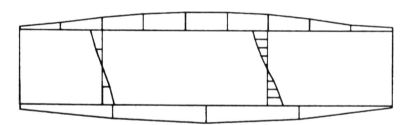

Fig. 13. In-place plot of fiber stresses along four
          paths for a uniformly loaded beam

ACKNOWLEDGMENT

Development of the TOTAL system was supported by the Naval Research Laboratory's in-house program (Project 84F01-04) funded by the Office of Naval Research under the Structural Mechanics Subelement (Task RR023-03-45). Appreciation is also due to: J. Swedlow of Carnegie Mellon University for his stiffness generation and solution coding; H. Kamel and M. McCabe of the University of Arizona for valuable discussions leading to the concept and implementation of the TOTAL system, particularly the file-handling concepts; R. J. Sanford of the Naval Research Laboratory for his comments and suggestions based on his dubious distinction as the primary "trial horse" user; finally, and especially, N. Perrone of the Office of Naval Research (ONR) and the Catholic University of America for his encouragement and suggestions based on use of the system by himself and by many of his students.

APPENDIX 1

MODIFICATIONS FOR OTHER HARDWARE (INFMOD)

With the exception of four commands related to I/O, all coding in
the TOTAL system consists of elementary FORTRAN statements common
to all major time-sharing processors. The reference version of TOTAL
was written for the DEC PDP-10 system, and the I/O coding is standard
DEC FORTRAN 10. The system-dependent I/O statements are used in such
a way that they can be quickly replaced by other equivalent statements using any editor with a global string replacement capability.
Likely modifications and discussion of the functions of related
statements are as follows.

TYPE Statements

All dialog is produced using the TYPE statement, with a related
format statement, as in the following example:

        TYPE 400
    400 FORMAT ('ENTER PROBLFM NAME')

Combinations of this type are contained throughout all TOTAL programs, and string replacement edits for each program can be used to
produce a new equivalent coding. As an example, for a system using
"WRITE" instead of "TYPE", and stars instead of single quotes as
literal delimiters in the format statements, replacement of the
three strings TYPE with new strings WRITE would produce the proper
form:

        WRITE 400
    400 FORMAT (*ENTER PROBLEM NAME*)

READ and WRITE Statements

All reading and writing of data and responses to questions, from
either the keyboard or disk file, is unformatted (list directed)
and of the form:

        READ (5,*) I,A,B,J,.........
        WRITE (6,*) I,A,B,J,.........

The form of the list indicates the first four entries are "integer,
real, real, integer". Unit 5 is always used for reading, and this

unit is assigned (see below) alternately to the terminal keyboard
and disk as required; unit 6 is similarly always used for writing.
These read and write statements are found in the above form in all
programs, and can be easily changed with global string replacement
as above.

Please note that any attempt to implement TOTAL on an operating
system not having list-directed I/O capabilities for both keyboard
and disk will require a major revision effort in individually for-
matting each I/O statement.

OPEN and CLOSE Statements

The assignment of unit numbers to devices, and opening and closing
of disk files of a given name for either reading or writing are accomplished with OPEN and CLOSE statements. As used in the TOTAL
programs, these statements are of the form:

    OPEN (Unit = 5, Device = "DSK", Access - "SEQIN", File = "TITL")
    CLOSE (Unit = 5)

At the beginning of each program there is an assignment of unit 6 to
the terminal, of the form: "OPEN (Unit = 6, Device = "TTY")"; Unit 5
is automatically assigned to the terminal by the DEC 10 system.
There are no further OPEN or CLOSE statements in the programs themselves. All assignments of units to the disk and then back to the
terminal are accomplished in subroutines RDFIL and WRTFIL which are
loaded with all programs as part of the file-handling library
TOTLIB. (See "Loading of Programs" below.) Any equivalent file-
and unit-assignment-handling statements can be easily substituted
at the beginning of each program, and at the four points at which
they occur in the TOTLIB subroutine.

File Names

As described in INFFIL, file names consist of two parts, a five-or-
less character problem name, read under an (A5) format in each program, and a second part consisting of three alphabetic characters,
which is assigned as needed by subroutine NAMFIL (part of TOTLIB),
using a Holerith format. (In the PDP-10 reference version, the
second part includes a preceding "." (period), and is assigned with
a "4H" format.) The only real requirement is that the second part
include at least the three characters defining the type of file
(e.g., "PTS" for the points files). The first part may consist of
any number of characters which can be input with a single "A-Format"
read.

As an example of possible modifications, consider the case of
a computer system allowing only an "A4" (or less) read, and allowing
only alphanumeric characters in a file name. In this situation, the
formats on all terminal reads of problem names (e.g., Read (5,5)
TITL (1) must be changed from "A5" to "A4" (one change per program),
and all assignments of the second part (TITL(2) in subroutine NAMFIL

must be changed from "4H" to "3H", and the period removed from each
assignment;   e.g., "TITL(2) = 4H.PTS" becomes "TITL(2) = 3HPTS".

RUN and TY Commands

In the reference PDP 10 version, the information files are obtained
by using the TY file-name command. If necessary, the TY command
should be replaced by a similar command which lists non-line-
numbered alphanumeric files to the terminal.
    All programs in the reference version are stored in a pre-
loaded and linked form (.SAV files), which require only the RUN
"Program Name" command to initiate running. For operating systems
not supporting this type of "RUN" file, the loading procedures described below must be implemented, using available commands.

Loading of Programs

The RUN form of each TOTAL program consists of a compiled coding
of the program, linked with from one to three sets of library subroutines. For instance, the loaded version of POINTS (e.g.,
POINT.SAV for the PDP 10) is obtained by the command "LOAD POINTS,
TOTLIB, TOTPLT"). The three subroutine libraries, with their
functions, are:

       TOTLIB: File naming and handling
       TOTELC: Elastic coefficient handling
       TOTPLT: Plotting subroutines (from Tektronix Plot 10 package)

All programs require TOTLIB to be loaded with them; all programs
using material (.MAT) files require TOTELC; all programs with plotting capabilities require TOTPLT.

BEAM: A PROGRAM FOR THE STATIC, STABILITY, AND DYNAMIC RESPONSE OF BEAMS

Walter D. Pilkey

University of Virginia

Pin Yu Chang

Hydronautics, Inc.

INTRODUCTION

The program BEAM is for the flexural analysis of simple and complex beams. It calculates the deflection, slope, bending moment, and shear force for static and steady state conditions. The critical axial load and mode shape are found for stability. The natural frequencies and mode shapes are computed for free transverse vibrations. The beam can be formed of segments with any mechanical or thermal loading, in-span supports, foundations, and boundary conditions. The user can include any or all of bending, shear deformation, and rotary inertia effects. BEAM is a part of a family of computer programs for structural members and mechanical elements, e.g., rods, thin-walled beams, plates, gridworks, torsional systems, shafts, and shells, maintained by the Structural Members Users Group.

GENERAL INFORMATION

Sign Convention

The beam is considered to be in a horizontal position. The sign conventions for loading and the state variables are: transverse force, concentrated or distributed, is positive downwards; applied moment is positive if it has a clockwise sense of rotation about a point inside a free body element; and finally an internal moment is positive if it tends to bend the element concave upwards. The sign convention for the deflections, slopes, bending moments, and shear forces that are calculated is shown in Fig. 1.

Solution Method

The transfer matrix method is employed. The analysis starts at the left end of the beam and moves progressively to the right end. Based on the data furnished by the user, the program will determine the needed transfer matrices. However, if the user wishes, he may choose to supply his own matrices for the entire member or any portion of the member.

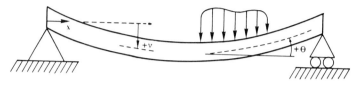

a. Positive displacement v and slope θ

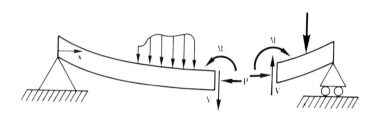

b. Positive internal bending moment M and shear force V

Fig. 1

Technical Background

The underlying theory for the program, including derivations and a tabulation of a wide array of transfer matrices, is provided in Ref. [1].

Calculation of Buckling Loads and Natural Frequencies

Buckling loads and natural frequencies of the beam are found by searching a characteristic equation for its roots. That is, the buckling loads or natural frequencies are those critical values that make the characteristic equation equal to zero. The user inputs an estimated value for a buckling load or the lowest desired natural frequency. This estimated value should be somewhat less than what is thought to be the actual value. The user also inputs a search increment. The program then searches for the buckling load or natural frequencies by computing the value of the characteristic equation using the estimated value, and then the estimated value +nΔ, n = 1,2, 3,. . ., where Δ is the search increment (Fig. 2). When the characteristic equation changes sign, the computer program employs a root-finding scheme to converge to the desired buckling load or frequency.

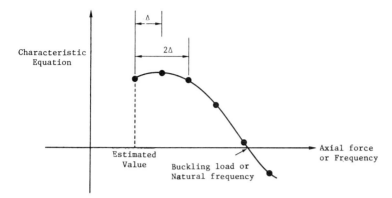

Fig. 2 Search for buckling load or natural frequencies

Since the program is set to search through an upper limit of 50 increments, it is important to choose an estimated value-search increment
combination that will encompass the desired buckling load or natural
frequency within 50 search increments.

The estimates for natural frequencies higher than the first calculated frequency are selected automatically by the computer program.

Ramp Loadings

For force or moment ramp loads, the computer program calls for the input of the gradient (rate of change) of the loading. A positive
gradient is assumed to increase from left to right along the beam.
This means that a loading such as shown in Fig. 3 is very simply

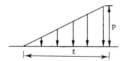

Fig. 3 Ramp loading increasing to the right

included. The gradient in this case is p/ℓ. However, other situations may require special attention. For example, the case of Fig. 4

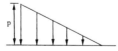

Fig. 4 Ramp loading decreasing to the right

is input as an equivalent uniform load and ramp load with a negative
gradient as shown in Fig. 5.

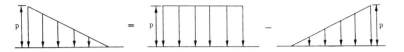

Fig. 5   Loading equivalent to the ramp of Fig. 4

In a similar fashion the case of Fig. 6 is also replaced by an

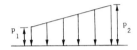

Fig. 6   General linearly varying load

equivalent uniform load and ramp load.

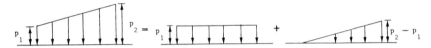

Fig. 7   Loading equivalent to the general load of Fig. 6

Accessing and Executing the Program

Three options of data input are provided for this beam program: the
prompting mode, the nonprompting mode, and the use of input from a
previously created data file.

In the prompting mode of input, the user responds to questions
put forth by the program, thereby furnishing the relevant data for his
problem.   In the nonprompting mode, the supportive questions are suppressed and the user enters his data according to the sequence and
format given in the description of each program.   In both modes of input a file with data in the same sequence as the nonprompting input
is automatically generated.   This file may be saved at the end of each
run.   The third input capability of the program, i.e., input from a
data file, enables the user to call out his previously created data
file, modify his data, and then run the same problem.   And of course
he may simply run the problem using a data file without any modification at all.

The program is FORTRAN coded.   However, to use it, a minimal knowledge of computer language, or even none at all, is assumed on the
user's part.   All that is required is minimal familiarity with the use
of a terminal such as a teletype.   All questions asked by the programs
are self-explanatory.   The program will lead the user through the input.   Numerical data input is free-formatted.   This means that the
user simply treats numbers the way he is accustomed to without concern as to whether the numbers lie in particular columns.   Commas or
blanks are inserted between numbers being input.   Of course, if one

line is not long enough for the data, the user can go to the next lines until his data list is satisfied.

The following pages, in combination with the system manuals for the computer in question, should provide the necessary information to access and begin using the program. The example problems provided later in this documentation should appear similar on all systems as far as content is concerned; system differences may cause output to differ in appearance by including spurious line feeds, question marks, etc.

Outline of Procedure to Access and Use the Program

1. Dial the nearest phone number for the computer system. When the system responds with a high-pitched tone, place the phone in the acoustic coupler and wait for the system to print something.

2. Log in according to the instructions given in the system's reference manual. The system will give some message indicating it is ready to accept your commands.

3. You are now ready to execute the program. A brief outline of the user response and execution sequence for the program follows. It should be noted that after each line of instruction to the computer is completed, the user signifies that he has finished a line of instruction by hitting the carriage return key (CR). To begin the programs, type the name BEAM, followed by a return. In some cases a variation to the name is required. Consult your system manual.

4. The computer will print "WILL INPUT BE FROM THE TERMINAL (ENTER 1) OR FORM A PREVIOUSLY CREATED DATA FILE (ENTER 2)?" These are the two distinct modes in which the BEAM program operates. If input is to come from a data file, skip to step 8.

5. The computer will print "DO YOU WANT TO SAVE A COPY OF YOUR INPUT DATA? (TYPE 'YES' OR 'NO')." This refers to the file which is automatically generated containing a copy of the input data. If you do not wish to save this file, skip to step 7.

6. The computer will reply "UNDER WHAT NAME?" Reply with the name of the file you wish this data to be written on. The created file will be accessible after the current run by this name. Note that if a file already exists with this name it will be destroyed. In some cases more than one name is required; consult your system manual.

7. The computer will print a message indicating the program has begun executing.

8. If the input is to be from a data file already in existence, the computer will print "ENTER FILE NAME." Enter the name of the data file previously created. The format is the same as in step 6.

9. The computer will print "WILL YOU WISH TO MODIFY YOUR DATA FILE? (TYPE 'YES' OR 'NO')." If you desire to modify the data on your file before running the program, type "YES"; otherwise type "NO" and proceed to step 12. Note that the original copy of the data will not be altered.

10. The computer will respond with "WILL YOU WISH TO SAVE THE MODIFIED COPY? (TYPE 'YES' OR 'NO')." If you want the new version of your data to be saved, answer "YES". If not, the program will run once with the modified copy of the data and then discard it. If this is desired, answer "NO" and proceed to step 12.

11. The computer will print "UNDER WHAT NAME?" Respond as in
step 6. The name of the original data file may be given here. In
this case the modified copy will replace the original file, which
will be destroyed.

12. The computer will print a message indicating the program has
begun executing.

Input from a Data File and Modification

To execute a program with input from a data file either previously
created or generated internally by the prompting or nonprompting
mode of input, the user simply indicates this wish in executing the
programs and specifies the file name. The user may also modify the
data file before using it with the system editor. A simple editor is
provided with this program and modifications may be made to data files
after the program begins execution.

Each line in a data file always begins with a 8-digit line number
followed by a blank. This number serves the dual purpose of identifying as well as sequencing a data line. Thus when a line of data is
to be deleted, the user simply retypes its line number with nothing
following. Also, new lines of data can be inserted between any two
lines by using appropriate line numbers. Although the program will automatically attach line numbers (with an increment of 10) for the data
file generated in a prompting or a nonprompting input, the user must
enter them for his data file created otherwise (see the examples in
the following sections).

Modifications can be made by retyping the whole line (including
the line number) which contains the item(s) to be changed, or if
necessary, by adding a new line of data. It is important that the
user makes all necessary associated changes; e.g., if he decides to
change the number of material properties, he must change several input
parameters such as NUME (the number of materials) as well as EO(I),
NUO(I) (moduli of elasticity and Poisson's ratios). The user is allowed to enter as many data as space allows on a line so long as they
are separated by a comma (or at least one blank). Furthermore, the
new entries do not have to be in the same format as the replaced ones,
e.g. the user may want to re-enter a number, say, 120.5, simply as
120.5 instead of 1.205E+02 as it would appear on the data file. The
commands L and Q are available to list the current state of the
data file or quit (exit from editor). For more sophisticated manipulation of his data file, the user should refer to the appropriate system reference manual.

Terminology

Field: The span of length over which a material property, e.g., mass
        density, or a loading, e.g., temperature differential, remains
        unchanged.

Number of changes in . . .: One change is counted whenever a material
        property or a loading changes its magnitude at some point; "0"
        (zero) should be entered if a material property or loading remains
        unchanged over the entire member.

Occurrence: An abrupt change in the magnitude of a geometrical, physical, or material property, e.g., a change in cross-sectional
area or in distributed loading, or the application of a concentrate parameter.

Availability and Assistance

The program is available from and is maintained by The Structural
Members Users Group, P. O. Box 3958, University Station, Charlottesville, Virginia, 22903, phone 804-924-4906. Questions on using
the program should be addressed to this organization.

EXAMPLE PROBLEMS

An array of example problems, illustrating all input options, are presented in this section.

Example 1.   Static Analysis of a Fixed-fixed Beam

Compute the displacements, slope, bending moment, and shear force
along the steel beam of Fig. 8.   This example illustrates the prompting form of input.

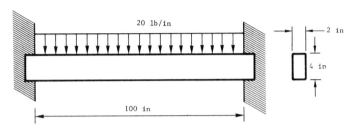

Fig. 8   Example 1

```
WILL INPUT BE FROM THE TERMINAL (ENTER 1)
OR FROM A PREVIOUSLY CREATED DATA FILE (ENTER 2)
 ? 1
DO YOU WANT TO SAVE A COPY OF YOUR INPUT DATA (YES OR NO)
 ? YES
UNDER WHAT NAME?
 ? BEAMEX1


****************** PROGRAM BEAMRESPONSE- DATA INPUT ******************

DO YOU WANT A PROMPTING (ENTER 1) OR A NON-PROMPTING (ENTER 2) INPUT,
OR DO YOU WISH TO ENTER DATA FROM YOUR DATA FILE (ENTER 3)
 ? 1

DO YOU HAVE A SIMPLE BEAM (NO CHANGES IN CROSS SECTION OR MODULUS OF
ELASTICITY, NO INSPAN SUPPORTS, NO ELASTIC FOUNDATIONS, FORCE AND
MOMENT LOADING ONLY, YES OR NO)
 ? YES

INDICATE THE TYPE OF ANALYSIS DESIRED BY ENTERING
        1 FOR STATIC RESPONSE
        2 FOR STEADY STATE
        3 FOR STABILITY
OR      4 FOR FREE DYNAMICS
 ? 1

LENGTH OF BEAM =
 ? 100

        ********** END AND INSPAN SUPPORTS **********
USING 1=FIXED, 2=PINNED, 3=FREE, 4=GUIDED, SPECIFY THE END SUPPORTS:
(NL,NR), WHERE NL=TYPE OF LEFT END SUPPORT
               NR=TYPE OF RIGHT END SUPPORT
(NL,NR)
 ? 1,1

DO YOU WISH TO SUPPLY YOUR OWN TRANSFER MATRICES (YES OR NO)
 ? NO

ENTER THE MODULUS OF ELASTICITY [E]
 ? 30.0E+06
```

```
DO YOU WISH TO HAVE THE MOMENT OF INERTIA CALCULATED FOR YOU
(YES OR NO)
 ? YES

INDICATE THE CROSS SECTION SHAPE BY ENTERING
          1 FOR RECTANGULAR
          2 FOR HOLLOW RECT.
          3 FOR CIRCLE
          4 FOR HOLLOW CIR.
 OR       5 FOR I SECTION
 ? 1

ENTER, CONSECUTIVELY, THE DATA SET (INITIAL POSITION,
WIDTH,HEIGHT)
FOR ALL I FIELDS:
 ? 0,2,4

ENTER THE DATA SET (NDF,NRAF), WHERE
          NDF =NO. OF UNIFORM FORCES
          NRAF=NO. OF RAMPED FORCES

(NDF,NRAF)
 ? 1,0

ENTER, CONSECUTIVELY, (INITIAL POSITION,END POSITION,MAGNITUDE)
FOR ALL UNIFORM FORCES
 ? 0,100,20

ENTER THE DATA SET (NCF,NCMO), WHERE
          NCF =NO. OF CONCENTRATED FORCES
          NCMO=NO. OF CONCENTRATED MOMENTS

(NCF,NCMO)
 ? 0,0

NO. OF POINTS BETWEEN OCCURRENCES FOR PRINTING RESULTS (MAX.200)
 ? 9

DO YOU WISH TO HAVE THE RESULTS PLOTTED (YES OR NO)
 ? NO

DO YOU WANT A SUMMARY OF YOUR INPUT DATA (YES OR NO)
 ? NO


******************** PROGRAM BEAMRESPONSE- OUTPUT ********************
```

LOCATION	DEFLECTION	SLOPE	MOMENT	SHEAR
0.	0.	0.	-1.6667E+04	1.0000E+03
1.0000E+01	2.1094E-03	-3.7500E-04	-7.6667E+03	8.0000E+02
2.0000E+01	6.6667E-03	-5.0000E-04	-6.6667E+02	6.0000E+02
3.0000E+01	1.1484E-02	-4.3750E-04	4.3333E+03	4.0000E+02
4.0000E+01	1.5000E-02	-2.5000E-04	7.3333E+03	2.0000E+02
5.0000E+01	1.6276E-02	0.	8.3333E+03	-3.6380E-12
6.0000E+01	1.5000E-02	2.5000E-04	7.3333E+03	-2.0000E+02
7.0000E+01	1.1484E-02	4.3750E-04	4.3333E+03	-4.0000E+02
8.0000E+01	6.6667E-03	5.0000E-04	-6.6667E+02	-6.0000E+02
9.0000E+01	2.1094E-03	3.7500E-04	-7.6667E+03	-8.0000E+02
1.0000E+02	3.5527E-15	0.	-1.6667E+04	-1.0000E+03

Example 2.   Stability of Analysis of a Column of
Variable Cross Section

Find the critical axial force for the column of Fig. 9.   It is prescribed that P_2 is always one-half the magnitude of P_1.
We estimate that the critical value of P_1 is 10^5 lb.   This estimated value should always be somewhat less than the actual critical
load.   Choose 10^5 lb as the increment for the critical load search.
The prompting input option will be employed.

```
WILL INPUT BE FROM THE TERMINAL (ENTER 1)
OR FROM A PREVIOUSLY CREATED DATA FILE (ENTER 2)
  ? 1
DO YOU WANT TO SAVE A COPY OF YOUR INPUT DATA (YES OR NO)
  ? YES
UNDER WHAT NAME?
  ? BEAMEX2
```

```
****************** PROGRAM BEAMRESPONSE- DATA INPUT ******************

DO YOU WANT A PROMPTING (ENTER 1) OR A NON-PROMPTING (ENTER 2) INPUT,
OR DO YOU WISH TO ENTER DATA FROM YOUR DATA FILE (ENTER 3)
  ? 1
```

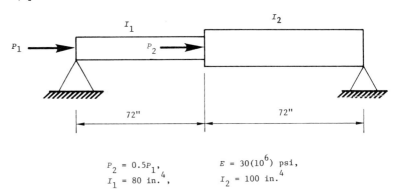

$$P_2 = 0.5P_1,$$
$$I_1 = 80 \text{ in.}^4,$$

$$E = 30(10^6) \text{ psi},$$
$$I_2 = 100 \text{ in.}^4$$

Fig. 9 Example 2

```
DO YOU HAVE A SIMPLE BEAM (NO CHANGES IN CROSS SECTION OR MODULUS OF
ELASTICITY, NO INSPAN SUPPORTS, NO ELASTIC FOUNDATIONS, FORCE AND
MOMENT LOADING ONLY, YES OR NO)
  ? NO

INDICATE THE TYPE OF ANALYSIS DESIRED BY ENTERING
          1 FOR STATIC RESPONSE
          2 FOR STEADY STATE
          3 FOR STABILITY
OR        4 FOR FREE DYNAMICS
  ? 3

YOU HAVE A STABILITY ANALYSIS PROBLEM. ENTER BELOW THE DATA SET
(SP,DEL), WHERE SP=YOUR ESTIMATE OF THE CRITICAL LOAD
               DEL=INCREMENT FOR CRITICAL LOAD SEARCH
```

```
(SP,DEL)
? 1.0E+05,1.0E+05

LENGTH OF BEAM =
? 144

          ********** END AND INSPAN SUPPORTS **********
USING 1=FIXED, 2=PINNED, 3=FREE, 4=GUIDED, SPECIFY THE END SUPPORTS:
(NL,NR), WHERE NL=TYPE OF LEFT END SUPPORT
                NR=TYPE OF RIGHT END SUPPORT
(NL,NR)
? 2,2

NUMBER OF INSPAN SUPPORTS (SHEAR RELEASE, MOMENT RELEASE, GUIDE, AND
RIGID SUPPORTS, O IF NONE)
? O

DO YOU WISH TO SUPPLY YOUR OWN TRANSFER MATRICES (YES OR NO)
? NO

          ********** MATERIAL AND GEOMETRIC PROPERTIES **********
DO YOU WISH TO HAVE THE MOMENT OF INERTIA CALCULATED FOR YOU
(YES OR NO)
? NO

ENTER THE FOLLOWING DATA SET (NEY,NIN)
WHERE    NEY = NO. OF CHANGES IN MODULUS OF ELASTICITY,
         NIN = NO. OF CHANGES IN MOMENT OF INERTIA (O IF UNCHANGED).

(NEY,NIN)
? 0,1

ENTER, CONSECUTIVELY, THE DATA SET (INITIAL POSITION,MAGNITUDE)
FOR ALL E FIELDS:

? 0,30.0E+06

ENTER THE SAME DATA SET FOR ALL I FIELDS:

? 0,80,72,100

IS SHEAR DEFORMATION TO BE CONSIDERED (YES OR NO)
? NO

NO. OF ELASTIC (WINKLER) FOUNDATIONS (O IF NONE)
? O

NO. OF ROTARY FOUNDATIONS (O IF NONE)
? O

NO. OF AXIAL LOADS (INCLUDING REACTION AT LEFT END, O IF NONE)
? 2

ENTER, CONSECUTIVELY, THE DATA SET (APPLIED POSITION,MAGNITUDE RELA-
TIVE TO ONE OF THE LOADS) FOR THE AXIAL LOADS (INCLUDING THE REFERENCE
WHICH IS TAKEN AS 1, POSITIVE IF DIRECTED TO THE RIGHT)
? 0,1,72,.5

NOTE: THE CRITICAL LOAD THUS OBTAINED IS THE CRITICAL VALUE OF THE
REFERENCED LOAD.

          ********** CONCENTRATED PARAMETERS **********
A CONCENTRATED PARAMETER IS ONE OF THE FOLLOWING: CONC. FORCE, CONC.
MOMENT, CONC. MASS, CONC. ROTARY INERTIA, LINEAR AND ROTARY SPRINGS.

DO YOU HAVE ANY CONCENTRATED PARAMETERS (YES OR NO)
? NO

DO YOU WISH TO HAVE THE TRACE OF CRITICAL LOAD SEARCH PRINTED OUT
(YES OR NO)
? YES
```

```
DO YOU WISH TO HAVE THE MODE SHAPES PRINTED OUT (YES OR NO)
? NO

DO YOU WISH TO HAVE THE RESULTS PLOTTED (YES OR NO)
? NO

DO YOU WANT A SUMMARY OF YOUR INPUT DATA (YES OR NO)
? NO


******************** PROGRAM BEAMRESPONSE- OUTPUT ********************


TRACE OF SEARCH:
        TRIAL LOAD      DETERMINANT
        1.00000E+05    -1.75692E+04
        2.00000E+05    -1.46986E+04
        3.00000E+05    -1.21045E+04
        4.00000E+05    -9.76785E+03
        5.00000E+05    -7.67087E+03
        6.00000E+05    -5.79663E+03
        7.00000E+05    -4.12911E+03
        8.00000E+05    -2.65319E+03
        9.00000E+05    -1.35459E+03
        1.00000E+06    -2.19793E+02
        1.10000E+06     7.63918E+02
        1.06117E+06     3.99120E+02
        1.04176E+06     2.08646E+02
        1.02234E+06     1.26713E+01
        1.00293E+06    -1.88892E+02
        1.01203E+06    -9.37444E+01
        1.01657E+06    -4.66353E+01
        1.01885E+06    -2.31964E+01
        1.01999E+06    -1.15058E+01
        1.02112E+06     1.65561E-01


CRITICAL LOAD=  1.0211E+06
```

Example 3.   Static Response of a Uniformly Loaded Beam.

This example illustrates the use of a nonprompting option of input
as well as data modification. Consider the beam of Fig. 10 with a
uniform load of 10 lb/in. For the moment, ignore the 2000-lb concentrated force.

The nonprompting option of input is the same as the prompting
mode except the questions are deleted. Here, the input is entered
according to the instructions of the final section of this chapter.
The nonprompting mode is particularly useful to those who are very
familiar with the prompted input.

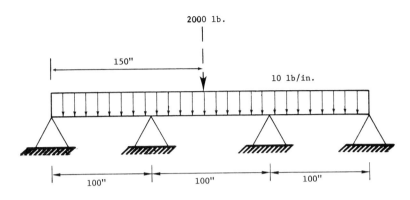

Fig. 10   Example 3

```
WILL INPUT BE FROM THE TERMINAL (ENTER 1)
OR FROM A PREVIOUSLY CREATED DATA FILE (ENTER 2)
 ? 1
DO YOU WANT TO SAVE A COPY OF YOUR INPUT DATA (YES OR NO)
 ? YES
UNDER WHAT NAME?
 ? BEAMEX3


****************** PROGRAM BEAMRESPONSE- DATA INPUT ******************

DO YOU WANT A PROMPTING (ENTER 1) OR A NON-PROMPTING (ENTER 2) INPUT,
OR DO YOU WISH TO ENTER DATA FROM YOUR DATA FILE (ENTER 3)
 ? 2
 ? 0
 ? 1
 ? 300,2,2,2
 ? 100,4,200,4
 ? NO
 ? NO
 ? 0,0
 ? 0,30.0E+06
 ? 0,1000
 ? NO
 ? 0
 ? 0
 ? YES
 ? 1,0,0,0,0,0
 ? 0,300,10
 ? 0
 ? NO
 ? 1

DO YOU WISH TO HAVE THE RESULTS PLOTTED (YES OR NO)
 ? NO

DO YOU WANT A SUMMARY OF YOUR INPUT DATA (YES OR NO)
 ? NO
```

******************** PROGRAM BEAMRESPONSE- OUTPUT ********************

LOCATION	DEFLECTION	SLOPE	MOMENT	SHEAR
0.	0.	-8.3333E-06	0.	4.0000E+02
5.0000E+01	2.2569E-04	1.3889E-06	7.5000E+03	-1.0000E+02
1.0000E+02	-1.3878E-17	2.7778E-06	-1.0000E+04	5.0000E+02
1.5000E+02	1.7361E-05	0.	2.5000E+03	1.4552E-11
2.0000E+02	-5.1387E-17	-2.7778E-06	-1.0000E+04	6.0000E+02
2.5000E+02	2.2569E-04	-1.3889E-06	7.5000E+03	1.0000E+02
3.0000E+02	-9.6402E-17	8.3333E-06	0.	-4.0000E+02

Suppose that after the results are printed, the problem is changed by the addition of a 2000-lb force at 150 in. from the left end. The data file generated during the nonprompting input should be saved under a name of your choice (see the instructions for your computer system). As can be seen in the following printout, the new force is taken into account by changing line number 260 to "YES", then inserting the pertinent data in line numbers 262 and 264. A second run using these new data was executed, with the results printed out below.

```
WILL INPUT BE FROM THE TERMINAL (ENTER 1)
OR FROM A PREVIOUSLY CREATED DATA FILE (ENTER 2)
 ? 2
ENTER FILE NAME
 ? BEAMEX3
WILL YOU WISH TO MODIFY YOUR DATA FILE (YES OR NO)
 ? YES
WILL YOU WISH TO SAVE THE MODIFIED COPY (YES OR NO)
 ? YES
UNDER WHAT NAME?
 ? MODBM3


******************** PROGRAM BEAMRESPONSE- DATA INPUT ********************

DO YOU WANT A PROMPTING (ENTER 1) OR A NON-PROMPTING (ENTER 2) INPUT,
OR DO YOU WISH TO ENTER DATA FROM YOUR DATA FILE (ENTER 3)
 ? 3
DO YOU WISH TO MODIFY YOUR DATA FILE
 ? YES


BEGIN EDITING, ENTER Q TO STOP, L TO LIST.


 ? L
100   0
110   1
120   3.000E+02  2  2  2
130   1.000E+02  4  2.000E+02  4
140  NO
150  NO
160   0   0
170       0.        3.000E+07
180       0.        1.000E+03
190  NO
200   0
210   0
220  YES
230   1  0  0  0  0  0
```

```
240      0.      3.000E+02  1.000E+01
250   0
260 NO
270   1
? 260    YES
? 262    1  0  0  0  0  0
? 264    150  2000
? Q

DO YOU WISH TO HAVE THE RESULTS PLOTTED (YES OR NO)
? NO

DO YOU WANT A SUMMARY OF YOUR INPUT DATA (YES OR NO)
? NO


******************* PROGRAM BEAMRESPONSE- OUTPUT ********************
```

LOCATION	DEFLECTION	SLOPE	MOMENT	SHEAR
0.	0.	9.4739E-20	0.	2.5000E+02
5.0000E+01	-8.6806E-05	3.4722E-06	-1.1642E-10	-2.5000E+02
1.0000E+02	0.	-1.3889E-05	-2.5000E+04	1.5000E+03
1.2500E+02	4.8286E-04	-1.9965E-05	9.3750E+03	1.2500E+03
1.5000E+02	7.8125E-04	-7.5894E-19	3.7500E+04	-1.0000E+03
1.7500E+02	4.8286E-04	1.9965E-05	9.3750E+03	-1.2500E+03
2.0000E+02	6.5055E-17	1.3889E-05	-2.5000E+04	7.5000E+02
2.5000E+02	-8.6806E-05	-3.4722E-06	0.	2.5000E+02
3.0000E+02	3.8511E-17	-3.4694E-18	-3.7253E-09	-2.5000E+02

Example 4.   Natural Frequencies of a Beam of a Variable Cross Section

This example shows how to create a data file and then use it to find
the natural frequencies of the beam of Fig. 11, taking into account
shear deformation effects.   The areas indicated have been adjusted
by the shear shape factor.
     The first natural frequency is estimated to be somewhat greater
than 30 cps and an increment of 2 cps was chosen for the frequency
search.
     Create the data file off-line and save it.   (See the instructions
for your computer system for the proper commands.)

```
100   0
110   4
120   3.000E+01  2.000E+00 1      0.
130 NO
140   3.540E+02  2  2  1
150   2.360E+02 4
160 NO
170 NO
180   0  1
190       0.     3.000E+07
200       0.     2.480E+04  2.360E+02  6.200E+03
210 YES
220   1  0
230       0.     5.455E+02  2.360E+02  2.728E+02
240       0.     3.000E-01
250 NO
260   1
270       0.     4.000E-01  2.360E+02  2.000E-01
280   0
290   0
300 NO
310   1  0  0
```

$$E = 30 \times 10^6 \text{ lb/in}^2, \text{ I}_1 = 24800 \text{ in}^4, \text{ I}_2 = 6200 \text{ in}^4, \; \rho_1 = 0.4 \text{ lb-sec}^2/\text{in}^2,$$

$$\rho_2 = 0.2 \text{ lb-sec}^2/\text{in}^2, \text{ A}_1 = 545.53 \text{ in}^2, \text{ A}_2 = 272.76 \text{ in}^2, \quad \nu = 0.3$$

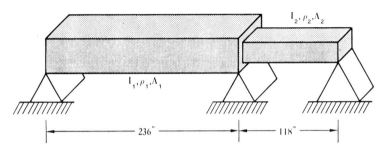

Fig. 11   Example 4

```
WILL INPUT BE FROM THE TERMINAL (ENTER 1)
OR FROM A PREVIOUSLY CREATED DATA FILE (ENTER 2)
? 2
ENTER FILE NAME
? BEAMEX4
WILL YOU WISH TO MODIFY YOUR DATA FILE (YES OR NO)
? NO

***************** PROGRAM BEAMRESPONSE- DATA INPUT ******************

DO YOU WANT A PROMPTING (ENTER 1) OR A NON-PROMPTING (ENTER 2) INPUT,
OR DO YOU WISH TO ENTER DATA FROM YOUR DATA FILE (ENTER 3)
? 3
DO YOU WISH TO MODIFY YOUR DATA FILE
? NO

DO YOU WISH TO HAVE THE RESULTS PLOTTED (YES OR NO)
? NO

DO YOU WANT A SUMMARY OF YOUR INPUT DATA (YES OR NO)
? NO

******************* PROGRAM BEAMRESPONSE- OUTPUT *********************

TRACE OF SEARCH:
        TRIAL FREQ.      DETERMINANT
        3.00000E+01      7.62688E+04
        3.20000E+01      6.44097E+04
        3.40000E+01      5.21665E+04
        3.60000E+01      3.96034E+04
        3.80000E+01      2.67860E+04
        4.00000E+01      1.37816E+04
        4.20000E+01      6.58376E+02
        4.40000E+01     -1.25148E+04
        4.30500E+01     -6.25554E+03
        4.25750E+01     -3.12662E+03
        4.23375E+01     -1.56274E+03
        4.22187E+01     -7.80988E+02
        4.21594E+01     -3.90170E+02
        4.21000E+01      6.09734E-01


FREQUENCY OF MODE   1= 4.2100E+01 CYCLES/SEC.
```

Example 5.   Beam on Elastic Foundation

Find the deflection, slope, bending moment, and shear force along
the statically loaded beam of Fig. 12.   Use the nonprompting input
option.

$$E = 30 \times 10^6 \text{ lb/in.}^2, \ I = 25 \text{ in.}^4$$

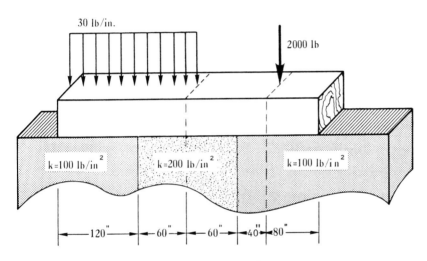

Fig. 12   Example 5

```
WILL INPUT BE FROM THE TERMINAL (ENTER 1)
OR FROM A PREVIOUSLY CREATED DATA FILE (ENTER 2)
 ? 1
DO YOU WANT TO SAVE A COPY OF YOUR INPUT DATA (YES OR NO)
 ? YES
UNDER WHAT NAME?
 ? BEAMEX5


****************** PROGRAM BEAMRESPONSE- DATA INPUT ******************

DO YOU WANT A PROMPTING (ENTER 1) OR A NON-PROMPTING (ENTER 2) INPUT,
OR DO YOU WISH TO ENTER DATA FROM YOUR DATA FILE (ENTER 3)
 ? 2
 ? 0
 ? 1
 ? 360,3,3,0
 ? NO
 ? NO
 ? 0,0
 ? 0,30.0E+06
 ? 0,25
 ? NO
 ? 3
 ? 0,120,100,120,240,200,240,360,100
 ? 0
```

```
? YES
? 1,0,0,0,0,0
? 0,180,30
? 0
? YES
? 1,0,0,0,0,0
? 280,2000
? 3

DO YOU WISH TO HAVE THE RESULTS PLOTTED (YES OR NO)
? NO

DO YOU WANT A SUMMARY OF YOUR INPUT DATA (YES OR NO)
? NO

******************* PROGRAM BEAMRESPONSE- OUTPUT ********************
```

LOCATION	DEFLECTION	SLOPE	MOMENT	SHEAR
0.	3.4725E-01	1.1517E-03	0.	0.
3.0000E+01	3.1251E-01	1.1749E-03	1.6072E+03	8.9799E+01
6.0000E+01	2.7574E-01	1.2952E-03	4.3258E+03	7.3080E+01
9.0000E+01	2.3399E-01	1.4916E-03	4.8225E+03	-6.0832E+01
1.2000E+02	1.8706E-01	1.6015E-03	-6.6306E+02	-3.2840E+02
1.3500E+02	1.6336E-01	1.5436E-03	-4.9345E+03	-2.5299E+02
1.5000E+02	1.4113E-01	1.4081E-03	-8.5993E+03	-2.4676E+02
1.6500E+02	1.2149E-01	1.1970E-03	-1.2653E+04	-3.0362E+02
1.8000E+02	1.0568E-01	8.9350E-04	-1.7976E+04	-4.1400E+02
1.9500E+02	9.5226E-02	4.8727E-04	-2.1898E+04	-1.1417E+02
2.1000E+02	9.1234E-02	4.6239E-05	-2.1511E+04	1.6386E+02
2.2500E+02	9.3593E-02	-3.4569E-04	-1.6993E+04	4.3963E+02
2.4000E+02	1.0094E-01	-6.0534E-04	-8.2454E+03	7.3046E+02
2.5000E+02	1.0738E-01	-6.6430E-04	-4.2563E+02	8.3457E+02
2.6000E+02	1.1386E-01	-6.1192E-04	8.4679E+03	9.4523E+02
2.7000E+02	1.1920E-01	-4.3343E-04	1.8499E+04	1.0619E+03
2.8000E+02	1.2206E-01	-1.1331E-04	2.9720E+04	-8.1720E+02
3.0000E+02	1.1774E-01	4.8298E-04	1.5809E+04	-5.7542E+02
3.2000E+02	1.0479E-01	7.7154E-04	6.5788E+03	-3.5194E+02
3.4000E+02	8.8136E-02	8.7104E-04	1.5281E+03	-1.5869E+02
3.6000E+02	7.0515E-02	8.8436E-04	0.	-4.3656E-11

Example 6. Steady State Response

Compute the response of the harmonically loaded beam of Fig. 13. The
time variation of the responses is found by multiplying the amplitude
listed below by $\cos \Omega t$.

$$W = 3000 \text{ lb}, \quad \Omega = 100 \text{ rad./sec.} = 15.9155 \text{ cps.}$$

$$E = 30 \times 10^6 \text{ lb/in.}^2, \quad I = 108 \text{ in.}^4, \quad \rho = 0.0264 \text{ lb-sec.}^2/\text{in.}^2$$

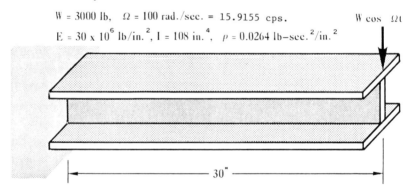

Fig. 13 Example 6

```
WILL INPUT BE FROM THE TERMINAL (ENTER 1)
OR FROM A PREVIOUSLY CREATED DATA FILE (ENTER 2)
 ? 1
DO YOU WANT TO SAVE A COPY OF YOUR INPUT DATA (YES OR NO)
 ? YES
UNDER WHAT NAME?
 ? BEAMEX6


***************** PROGRAM BEAMRESPONSE- DATA INPUT ******************

DO YOU WANT A PROMPTING (ENTER 1) OR A NON-PROMPTING (ENTER 2) INPUT,
OR DO YOU WISH TO ENTER DATA FROM YOUR DATA FILE (ENTER 3)
 ? 2
 ? 1
 ? 2
 ? 15.9155
 ? 30,1,3,0
 ? NO
 ? 30.0E+06
 ? NO
 ? 108
 ? 0.0264
 ? 0,0
 ? 1,0
 ? 30,3000
 ? 9

DO YOU WISH TO HAVE THE RESULTS PLOTTED (YES OR NO)
 ? NO

DO YOU WANT A SUMMARY OF YOUR INPUT DATA (YES OR NO)
 ? NO


******************* PROGRAM BEAMRESPONSE- OUTPUT ********************
```

LOCATION	DEFLECTION	SLOPE	MOMENT	SHEAR
0.	0.	0.	-9.0547E+04	3.0249E+03
3.0000E+00	1.2156E-04	-7.9639E-05	-8.1473E+04	3.0249E+03
6.0000E+00	4.6943E-04	-1.5088E-04	-7.2399E+04	3.0246E+03
9.0000E+00	1.0184E-03	-2.1371E-04	-6.3325E+04	3.0241E+03
1.2000E+01	1.7433E-03	-2.6815E-04	-5.4255E+04	3.0230E+03
1.5000E+01	2.6189E-03	-3.1418E-04	-4.5188E+04	3.0213E+03
1.8000E+01	3.6200E-03	-3.5183E-04	-3.6128E+04	3.0188E+03
2.1000E+01	4.7215E-03	-3.8109E-04	-2.7076E+04	3.0155E+03
2.4000E+01	5.8982E-03	-4.0197E-04	-1.8036E+04	3.0113E+03
2.7000E+01	7.1250E-03	-4.1449E-04	-9.0095E+03	3.0061E+03
3.0000E+01	8.3768E-03	-4.1866E-04	4.6566E-10	3.0000E+03

Example 7.   Buckling of Beam Column of Variable Cross Section

Calculate the value of P_0 that would make the beam of Fig. 14 unstable. P_1, P_2, P_3, and P_4 remain in proportion to the nominal value P_0 throughout the loading process. We estimate the lower bound on P_0 to be 5 MN and choose 0.5 MN as the increment for the critical load search.

Note that P_0 is input as being of magnitude 1, while the magnitudes of P_1, P_2, P_3, and P_4 relative to P_0 are entered. BEAM then finds the critical value of P_0.

Use the nonprompting input option.

$E = 200 \ \mathrm{GN/m}^2 = 200 \times 10^9 \ \mathrm{N/m}^2$, $I_1 = 43500 \ \mathrm{cm}^4 = 4.35 \times 10^{-4} \ \mathrm{m}^4$, $I_2 = 6.5 \times 10^{-4} \ \mathrm{m}^4$

$I_3 = I_4 = 9.3 \times 10^{-4} \ \mathrm{m}^4$, $I_5 = 1.12 \times 10^{-3} \ \mathrm{m}^4$

$P_1/P_0 = 0.967$, $P_2/P_0 = 0.917$, $P_3/P_0 = 1.05$, $P_4/P_0 = 2.15$

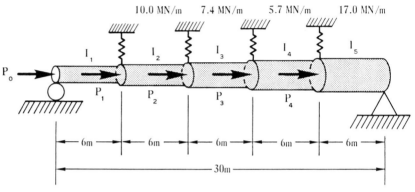

Fig. 14   Example 7

```
WILL INPUT BE FROM THE TERMINAL (ENTER 1)
OR FROM A PREVIOUSLY CREATED DATA FILE (ENTER 2)
 ? 1
DO YOU WANT TO SAVE A COPY OF YOUR INPUT DATA (YES OR NO)
 ? YES
UNDER WHAT NAME?
 ? BEAMEX7


***************** PROGRAM BEAMRESPONSE- DATA INPUT ******************

DO YOU WANT A PROMPTING (ENTER 1) OR A NON-PROMPTING (ENTER 2) INPUT,
OR DO YOU WISH TO ENTER DATA FROM YOUR DATA FILE (ENTER 3)
 ? 2
 ? 0
 ? 3
 ? 5.0E+06,5.0E+05
 ? 30,2,2,0
 ? NO
 ? NO
 ? 0,3
 ? 0,200.0E+09
 ? 0,4.35E-04,6,6.5E-04,12,9.3E-04,24,1.12E-03
 ? NO
 ? 0
 ? 0
 ? 5
 ? 0,1,6,.967,12,.917,18,1.05,24,2.15
 ? YES
 ? 0,0,0,0,4,0
 ? 6,1.0E+07,12,7.4E+06,18,5.7E+06,24,1.7E+07
 ? 1,0,0
```

```
DO YOU WISH TO HAVE THE RESULTS PLOTTED (YES OR NO)
? NO

DO YOU WANT A SUMMARY OF YOUR INPUT DATA (YES OR NO)
? NO


******************** PROGRAM BEAMRESPONSE- OUTPUT ********************


TRACE OF SEARCH:
        TRIAL LOAD        DETERMINANT
        5.00000E+06      -3.54014E+04
        5.50000E+06      -2.21214E+04
        6.00000E+06      -1.33703E+04
        6.50000E+06      -7.74371E+03
        7.00000E+06      -4.23370E+03
        7.50000E+06      -2.12654E+03
        8.00000E+06      -9.24888E+02
        8.50000E+06      -2.88546E+02
        9.00000E+06       1.00203E+01
        8.98322E+06       3.72990E+00
        8.96644E+06      -2.77355E+00
        8.97360E+06       2.63395E-02


CRITICAL LOAD=   8.9736E+06
```

Example 8. Beam on Elastic Supports

Find the deflection, slope, bending moment, and shear force in the axially loaded beam of Fig. 15. The nonprompting input option will be employed.

The 5650 N·m moment is negative as it acts counterclockwise. The springs on the ends of the beam are input the same as springs within the span and not as boundary conditions. The end conditions are hinged-guided.

$$E = 200 \text{ GN/m}^2 = 200 \times 10^9 \text{ N/m}^2, \quad I_1 = 125 \text{ cm}^4 = 1.25 \times 10^{-6} \text{m}^4, \quad I_2 = 2.5 \times 10^{-6} \text{m}^4$$

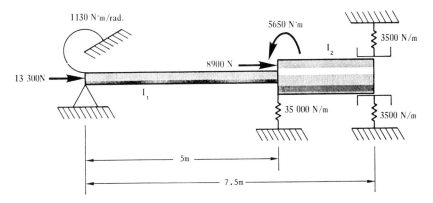

Fig. 15   Example 8

```
WILL INPUT BE FROM THE TERMINAL (ENTER 1)
OR FROM A PREVIOUSLY CREATED DATA FILE (ENTER 2)
 ? 1
DO YOU WANT TO SAVE A COPY OF YOUR INPUT DATA (YES OR NO)
 ? YES
UNDER WHAT NAME?
 ? BEAMEX8


***************** PROGRAM BEAMRESPONSE- DATA INPUT ******************

DO YOU WANT A PROMPTING (ENTER 1) OR A NON-PROMPTING (ENTER 2) INPUT,
OR DO YOU WISH TO ENTER DATA FROM YOUR DATA FILE (ENTER 3)
 ? 2
 ? 0
 ? 1
 ? 7.5,2,4,0
 ? NO
 ? NO
 ? 0,1
 ? 0,200.0E+09
 ? 0,1.25E-06,5,2.5E-06
 ? NO
 ? 0
 ? 0
 ? NO
 ? 2
 ? 0,13300,5,8900
 ? YES
 ? 0,1,0,0,2,1
 ? 5,-5650
 ? 5,35000,7.5,7000
 ? 0,1130
 ? 4

DO YOU WISH TO HAVE THE RESULTS PLOTTED (YES OR NO)
 ? NO

DO YOU WANT A SUMMARY OF YOUR INPUT DATA (YES OR NO)
 ? NO


****************** PROGRAM BEAMRESPONSE- OUTPUT *********************
```

LOCATION	DEFLECTION	SLOPE	MOMENT	SHEAR
0.	0.	-7.1350E-03	-8.0626E+00	4.6120E+02
1.0000E+00	6.7813E-03	-6.0597E-03	5.4333E+02	4.6120E+02
2.0000E+00	1.1399E-02	-2.8268E-03	1.0659E+03	4.6120E+02
3.0000E+00	1.1772E-02	2.3924E-03	1.5321E+03	4.6120E+02
4.0000E+00	6.0431E-03	9.3216E-03	1.9171E+03	4.6120E+02
5.0000E+00	-7.3199E-03	1.7594E-02	-3.4494E+03	2.0500E+02
5.5000E+00	-1.5247E-02	1.4104E-02	-3.5229E+03	2.0500E+02
6.0000E+00	-2.1415E-02	1.0561E-02	-3.5573E+03	2.0500E+02
6.5000E+00	-2.5806E-02	7.0028E-03	-3.5523E+03	2.0500E+02
7.0000E+00	-2.8422E-02	3.4694E-03	-3.5079E+03	2.0500E+02
7.5000E+00	-2.9286E-02	-1.1102E-16	-3.4246E+03	2.0500E+02

Example 9. Thermally Loaded Beam

Find the deflection, slope, bending moment, and shear force in a
thermally loaded uniform beam on an elastic foundation (Fig. 16).
This steel beam with a moment of inertia of 1000 in.^{4} is 100 in. long
and rests on an elastic foundation of modulus 100,000 lb/in.^{2} The
ends are simply supported. A uniform thermal moment of 1000 lb-in.
is applied along the beam. Use the nonprompting input option.

Uniform applied thermal moment

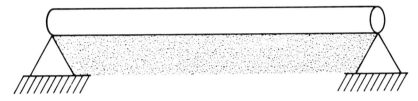

Fig. 16   Example 9

```
WILL INPUT BE FROM THE TERMINAL (ENTER 1)
OR FROM A PREVIOUSLY CREATED DATA FILE (ENTER 2)
 ? 1
DO YOU WANT TO SAVE A COPY OF YOUR INPUT DATA (YES OR NO)
 ? YES
UNDER WHAT NAME?
 ? BEAMEX9


****************** PROGRAM BEAMRESPONSE- DATA INPUT ******************

DO YOU WANT A PROMPTING (ENTER 1) OR A NON-PROMPTING (ENTER 2) INPUT,
OR DO YOU WISH TO ENTER DATA FROM YOUR DATA FILE (ENTER 3)
 ? 2
 ? 0
 ? 1
 ? 100,2,2,0
 ? NO
 ? NO
 ? 0,0
 ? 0,30.0E+06
 ? 0,1000
 ? NO
 ? 1
 ? 0,100,1.0E+05
 ? 0
 ? YES
 ? 0,0,0,0,1,0
 ? 0,100,1000
 ? 0
 ? NO
 ? 3
```

```
DO YOU WISH TO HAVE THE RESULTS PLOTTED (YES OR NO)
? NO

DO YOU WANT A SUMMARY OF YOUR INPUT DATA (YES OR NO)
? NO

******************** PROGRAM BEAMRESPONSE- OUTPUT ********************


          LOCATION    DEFLECTION    SLOPE        MOMENT       SHEAR

             0.          0.       -6.1479E-07      0.       -3.2894E+01
          2.5000E+01  7.6751E-06  -9.8573E-08  -7.0778E+02  -2.0635E+01
          5.0000E+01  8.4520E-06  -2.0329E-20  -9.6929E+02      0.
          7.5000E+01  7.6751E-06   9.8573E-08  -7.0778E+02   2.0635E+01
          1.0000E+02 -1.0842E-19   6.1479E-07  -5.8208E-11   3.2894E+01
```

INPUT DEFINITIONS

The definitions necessary to create an input data file or to use the nonprompting input option are presented in this section.

1. KP   Do you have a simple beam (no changes in cross section or modulus of elasticity, no in span supports, no elastic foundation, force and moment loading only)
             0 = No
             1 = Yes

2. ID   Type of analysis desired
             1 = static response
             2 = steady state
             3 = stability
             4 = natural frequencies

3. Skip to item number 4 if static problem, otherwise choose one:
    SP   for steady state
         value of frequency in cps of applied loading

    SP, DEL   for stability analysis
      SP: Estimate of critical load. Choose a value less than the actual critical load
     DEL: Increment for critical load search

    SP, DEL, NF, WHIRL   for free vibration
      SP: Estimate in cps of first natural frequency. Choose a value less than the actual frequency
     DEL: Increment for frequency search
      NF: Number of natural frequencies desired
   WHIRL: 0 if vibrating beam
            1 if rotating shaft and the whirl is in the same direction as rotation
            -1 if rotating shaft and the whirl is in the same direction as rotation

3a. For free vibration problems of nonsimple beams only

      ANSO   (Yes or No) Is a lumped parameter model to be used?

4. BL, NL, NR, NSUP

         BL: Total beam length

     NL, NR: Left and right end conditions

              1 = fixed

              2 = simply supported

              3 = free

              4 = guided

              Ends with applied loads are treated as free boundaries since the loads are entered as applied loadings and not as boundary conditions. Similarly, ends with concentrated masses or springs are also treated as being free.

      NSUP: Number of inspan supports (rigid supports, moment release, guide, shear release)

              Skip to item number 6 if no inspan supports (NSUP=0)

5. SUP(1), MTYP(1), SUP(2), MTYP(2), ..., SUP(NSUP), MTYP(NSUP)

     SUP(I): Position of the Ith inspan support

    MTYP(I): Type of support

              1 = shear release

              2 = moment release

              3 = guide

              4 = rigid support

6. ANS1   (YES or NO) Do you wish to supply your own transfer matrices?

    Skip to item number 7 if ANS1 = NO.

6a. NTM   Number of transfer matrices to be entered.

6b. TMI(1), TME(1), TM1(2), TME(2), ..., TMI(NTM), TME(NTM)

              Initial and final positions of the transfer matrices

6c. S(1,1,1), S(1,1,3), ..., S(1,1,5), S(1,2,1), S(1,2,2), ..., S(1,2,5), ..., S(1,4,1), S(1,4,2), ..., S(1,4,5)

              Deflection, slope, moment, shear and loading elements of the first transfer matrix

— — — — — — — — — — — — — — — — — —

    S(NTM,1,1,) S(NTM,1,2), ..., S(NTM,1,5), S(NTM,2,1), S(NTM,2,2), ..., S(NTM,2,5), ..., S(NTM,4,1), S(NTM,4,2), ..., S(NTM,4,5)

              Deflection, slope, moment, shear and loading elements of the last transfer matrix

6d. ANS2   (YES or NO) Are these the matrices for the entire beam? If ANS2 = YES; skip to item number 19a for static or steady problem of simple beam. skip to item number 20 for stability or free vibration problem of simple beam. skip to item number 19 for nonsimple beam.

7. Skip to item number 8 for non-simple beam.
    EY1   for simple beam
          EY1: Modulus of elasticity of the beam (force/length^2)

8. ANSR   (YES or NO) Do you wish to have the moment of inertia
             calculated for you?
             If ANSR = YES, skip to item number 10 for simple beam
             option.

8a. Skip to item 9 for non-simple beam.
    XII   for simple beam
          XII: Moment of inertia of the beam (length^4)
             After this entry skip to item number 14 if vibration
             problem, skip to item number 17a if static problem, skip
             to item number 20 if stability problem.

9. NEY, NIN for non-simple beam
          NEY: Number of changes in modulus of elasticity (E)
          NIN: Number of changes in moment of inertia (I)

9a. ELAS(1), EY(1), ELAS(2), EY(2), ..., ELAS(NEY+1), EY(NEY+1)
          Initial positions and magnitudes of all E fields
          Skip to item number 10 if ANSR = YES

9b. XINS(1), XI(1), XINS(2), XI(2), ..., XINS(NIN+1), XI(NIN+1)
          Initial positions and magnitudes of all I fields
          Skip to item number 11 if ANSR = NO

10. ICS   Shape of cross section
             1 = rectangular
             2 = hollow rectangular
             3 = circle
             4 = hollow circle
             5 = I section

10a. (Choose one)
     POS(1), X(1), X(2), ..., POS(NIN+1), X(2*(NIN+1), X(2*(NIN+1))
          for rectangular section
          Initial position, width and height of the section

     POS(1), X(1), X(2), X(3), X(4), ..., POS(NIN+1), X(4*(NON+1)-3),
     X(4*(NIN+1)-2), X(4*(NIN+1)-1), X(4*(NIN+1)))
          for hollow rectangular section
          Initial position, outer width, outer height, inner
          width, inner height of the section

     POS(1), X(1), ..., POS(NIN+1), X(NIN+1)
          for circular section
          Initial position and radius of the section

     POS(1), X(1), X(2), ..., POS(NIN+1), X(2*(NIN+1)-1), X(2*(NIN+1))
          for hollow circular section
          Initial position, inner radius, and outer radius of
          the section

POS(1), X(1), X(2), X(3), X(4), ..., POS(NIN+1), X(4*(NIN+1)-3),
X(4*(NIN+1)-2), X(4*(NIN+1)-1), X(4*(NIN+1)))
> for I section
>
> Initial position, width, height, web thickness, flange
> thickness for the section
>
> For simple beam only, after this entry skip to item
> number 14 if vibration problem, skip to item number 17a
> if static problem, skip to item number 20 if stability
> problem.

11. ANS3   (YES or NO) Shear deformation to be considered? If
> NO skip to item number 13
>
> Skip to item number 12 if ANSR = YES

11a. NARE, NPO
> NARE: Number of changes in cross-sectional area (length^2).
> This area should be adjusted by multiplying by shear
> shape factor.
>
> NPO: Number of changes in Poisson's ratio

11b. AREA(1), A(1), AREA(2), A(2), ..., AREA(NARE+1), A(NARE+1)
> Initial position and cross-sectional areas for all
> area fields

11c. POI(1), PI(1), POI(2), PI(2), ..., POI(NPO+1), PI(NPO+1)
> Initial positions and Poisson's ratios of all Poisson
> ratio fields
>
> Skip to item number 13.

12. PI(1)   Poisson's ratio

13. (skip to item number 15 if static (ID=1) or stability (ID=3)
problem.)
> ANS4   (YES or NO) Rotary inertia to be considered? If NO, go
> to item number 14.

13a. NRG   Number of changes in radius of gyration (length)

13b. GYR(1), RG(1), GYR(2), RG(2), ..., GYR(NRG+1), RG(NRG+1)
> Initial positions and radii of gyration of the rotary
> inertia fields

14. Skip to item number 15 if lumped parameter model is to be used
for free vibration problem of non-simple beam (ANSO = YES)

> (choose one)
> DM   for simple beam, magnitude of mass density fields
> (mass/length). (After this entry skip to item number
> 17a if steady state problem, to item number 20 if free
> vibration problem.)
>
> NDM   for non-simple beam, number of changes in mass density

14a. DENS(1), DM(1), DENS(2), DM(2), ..., DENS(NDM+1), DM(NDM+1)
        Initial positions and magnitudes of the mass density
        fields

15. NEF   Number of elastic (Winkler) foundations
           Skip to item number 16 if NEF=0.

15a. EFI(1), EFE(1), XK(1), EFI(2), EFE(2), XK(2), ..., EFI(NEF),
        EFE(NEF), XK(NEF)
           Initial positions, end positions, and elastic moduli
           of elastic foundations (force/length^2).

16. NRF   number of rotary foundations
           Skip to item number 17 if NRF = 0.

16a. RFI(1), RFE(1), RK(1), RFI(2), RFE(2), RK(2), ..., RFI(NRF),
        RFE(NRF), RK(NRF)
           Initial positions, end positions, and moduli of rotary
           foundations (force-length/length^2).

17. Skip to item number 19 if free vibration problem, to item 18 if
    stability problem.
    ASN7   (YES or NO) Any distributed loading?
           If NO, skip the following entries, go to item 18.

17a. NDF, NRAF for simple beam
     NDF, NDMO, NRAF, NRAM, NUT, NRT for non-simple beam
        NDF: number of uniformly distributed transverse forces
        NDMO: number of uniformly distributed moments
        NRAF: number of linearly varying distributed transverse forces
        NRAM: number of linearly varying distributed moments
        NUT: number of uniform thermal moments
        NRT: number of ramped thermal moments

           Skip any of the following entries if the number of a
           distributed loading associated with that entry is zero.

17b. DFI(1), DFE(1), F(1), DFI(2), DFE(2), F(2), ..., DFI(NDF),
        DFE(NDF), F(NDF)
           Initial positions, end positions, and magnitudes of the
           uniform forces, (force/length), positive downwards

17c. DMI(1), DME(1), BM(1), DMI(2), DME(2), BM(2), ..., DMI(NDMO),
        DME(NDMO), BM(NDMO)
           Initial positions, end positions, and magnitudes of the
           uniform moments (force-length/length), positive clockwise.

17d. RFI(1), RFE(1), FI(1), RFI(2), RFE(2), FI(2), ..., RFI(NRAF),
        RFE(NRAF), FI(NRAF)
           Initial positions, end positions, and gradients (force/
           length^2) of the ramped forces, positive if the downwards
           force increases from left to right end of the beam

17e. RMI(1), RME(1), BMI(1), RMI(2), RME(2), BMI(2), ..., RMI(NRAM)
RME(NRAM), BMI(NRAM)
   Initial positions, end positions, and gradients (force-
   length/length^2) of the ramped moments, positive if the clockwise moments increase from the left to the right end of the
   beam

17f. TMI(1), TME(1), TMI(2), TME(2), TM(2), ..., TMI(NUT), TME(NUT)
TM(NUT)
   Initial positions, end positions, and magnitudes of the
   uniform thermal moments

   If the thermal moment is represented by M_T, then
   $$M_T = \int_A E\alpha \; \Delta T \; z \; dA$$

   E = modulus of elasticity (force/length^2)
   α = coefficient of thermal expansion (length/length-degree)
   ΔT = change in termperature (degrees), i.e., the tempera-
        ture rise with respect to the reference temperature
   A = cross-sectional area
   z = vertical coordinate, positive downwards, measured
        from the neutral axis

17g. TGI(1), TGE(1), TG(1), TGI(2), TGE(2), TG(2), ..., TGI(NRT),
TGE(NRT), TG(NRT)
   Initial positions, end positions, and gradients of the
   ramped thermal moments

18. Skip to item 19a if simple beam.

   NAXF   Number of axial loads, including reaction at left end
           if applicable

   Skip to item number 19 if NAXF = 0

18a. AXF(1), FA(1), AXF(2), FA(2), ..., AXF(NAXF), FA(NAXF)
   Applied positions and magnitudes of axial loads; positive
   if directed to the right. For stability problems, if more
   than one axial load is present (so that the axial force
   varies along the length of the beam), magnitudes relative
   to one of the loads which is taken as 1 should be entered.
   The critical load thus obtained is the critical value of
   the reference load.

19. ANS8 (YES or NO) Any concentrated parameters? If NO, skip
    the following entries to item number 20.

19a. (choose one)
   NCF, NCMO for simple beam
   NCF, NCMO, NCMA, NCR, NSP, NRS for non-simple beam
   NCF: Number of concentrated transverse forces (positive
        downwards)

NCMO: Number of concentrated moments (positive clockwise)
NCMA: Number of concentraded masses
NCR: Number of concentraded rotary inertia
NSP: Number of linear extension springs
NRS: Number of rotary springs

Skip any of the following entries if the number of a concentrated parameter associated with that entry is zero.

19b. CF(1), CP(1), CF(2), CP(2), ..., CF(NCF, CP(NCF)
     Positions and magnitudes of the concentrated forces (force).

19c. CMO(1), CBM(1), CMO(2), CBM(2), ..., CMO(NCMO), CBM(NCMO)
     Positions and magnitudes of the concentrated moments (force-length).

19d. CMA(1), CM(1), CMA(2), CM(2), ..., CMA(NCMA), CM(NCMA)
     Positions and magnitudes of the concentrated masses (mass).

19e. CRI(1), CN(1), CRI(2), CN(2), ..., CRI(NCR), CN(NCR)
     Positions and magnitudes of the concentrated rotary inertia $(mass\text{-}length^2)$.

19f. SPR(1), CK(1), SPR(2), CK(2), ..., SPR(NSP), CK(NSP)
     Positions and spring constants of the extension springs (force/length).

19g. RSP(1), BK(1), RSP(2), BK(2), ..., RSP(NRS), BK(NRS)
     Positions and spring constants of the rotary springs (force-length/length).

20. (choose one)
     NA for static or steady state problems
     NP, NM, NA for stability or free vibration problems
        NM = 1 for modeshape printout
             0 otherwise
        NP = 1 for printing trace of critical load or natural frequency search
             0 otherwise
        NA = Number of points for printing results between occurrences

REFERENCE

    1 Pilkey, W. D., and Chang, P. Y., *Modern Formulas for Statics, Dynamics, and Stability: Shafts, Beams, Plates, and Shells*, McGraw Hill, New York, 1977.

BEAMSTRESS: A PROGRAM FOR DETERMINING THE CROSS-SECTIONAL
PROPERTIES AND STRESSES OF A BAR

Walter D. Pilkey
Chirasak Thasanatorn

University of Virginia

Pin Yu Chang

Hydronautics, Inc.

INTRODUCTION

The program BEAMSTRESS is for determining the section properties and
stresses in an arbitrary homogeneous or composite cross section of a
straight bar. Properties include cross-sectional area, centroid,
moments of inertia about any axes, polar moment of inertia, radii of
gyration, angle of inclination of principal axes, principal moments
of inertia, location of shear center, shear deformation coefficients,
torsional constant and warping constant. For composite cross sections,
these cross-sectional properties are calculated as modulus weighted
properties. The stresses include normal stresses due to bending
moments, axial forces, and constrained warping and shear stresses
due to torsion, tranverse shear forces, and constrained warping.
   BEAMSTRESS is one of a family of computer programs for structural
members and mechanical elements, e.g., rods, beams, shafts, thin-walled
beams, plates, gridworks, torsional systems, shells, maintained by
The Structural Members Users Group.

GENERAL INFORMATION

Modeling of the Cross Section

An arbitrary section can be modeled by the user as an assemblage of
quadrilaterals or elements, as shown in Fig. 1. The four corners of
an element are called <u>nodal points</u> or <u>nodes</u>. For computing normal
(bending and axial) stresses, cross-sectional area, centroid, moments
of inertia, product of inertia, angle of inclination of principal
axes, radii of gyration, polar moment of inertia, and principal
moments of inertia, i.e., non-shear related cross-sectional properties,
the cross section can be modeled by convenient elements of <u>any size</u>
(Fig. 1a). In finding the shear stresses, shear center, shear deformation coefficients, warping function, torsional constant, warping constant, and stresses due to warping, i.e., shear and warping related
properties, the accuracy of the results will depend upon the fineness
of the elements used in the model. The computed shear and warping
related results will converge to the exact solution as the fineness

of the element mesh is increased, e.g., Fig. 1b. Since most of the
stresses are printed out at the centroid of each element, the user
may wish to arrange the elements in such a way that the centroid of
an element is at a point of interest.

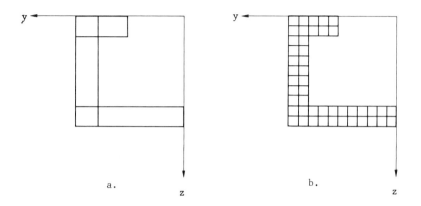

Fig. 1

If the cross section (and material properties for a composite
beam) is symmetrical about one or two axes, the symmetry options of
the program (with the exception of constrained warping problems) can
be utilized by establishing the y,z coordinate system along the
line(s) of symmetry. Then, only one-half or one-quarter of the cross
section (the first quadrant, bounded by the positive y,z axes) needs
to be input.

Solution Method

The shear related properties are calculated using the finite element
method as described in Refs. [1,2,3]. In fact some of the coding was
provided by the authors of Refs. [1,2].

Bandwidth and Numbering

After the user has established the nodes and elements, it is economi-
cal, as far as computer time in computing shear related properties is

concerned, to number the nodal points so as to minimize the bandwidth of a matrix. The bandwidth may be thought of as the greatest difference in magnitude between any two nodal point numbers of the same element plus one. The minimization of the bandwidth is done by numbering the nodal points in such a way that the difference between any two nodal point numbers on each element is a minimum and not greater than 50. For a cross section consisting of long straight segments such as a thin-walled beam section or a cross section which can be modeled by straight lines, the automatic nodal and element generation, which is incorporated in the program and is to be discussed later, may be used to reduce the amount of input efforts. The disadvantage of the automatic nodal and element generation is that it may be difficult to achieve a near minimum bandwidth. Figure 2a,b illustrates the different numbered elements for the same section.

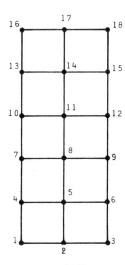
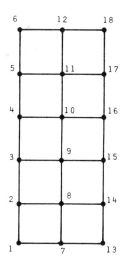

The greatest difference between any two nodal point numbers on any element is 4; i.e., this leads to a bandwidth of 5. The number of input lines is 17, i.e., 12 nodal point and 5 element lines.

The greatest difference between any two nodal point numbers on any element is 7; i.e., this leads to a bandwidth of 8. The number of input lines is 8, i.e., 6 nodal point and 2 element lines. Relative to case (a), this is a poorly numbered configuration.

Fig. 2 Nodal point numbering

The groups of four node numbers which define an element must be entered as input in a counterclockwise sequence as shown in Fig. 3.

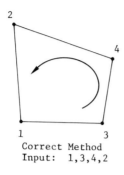

Correct Method
Input: 1,3,4,2

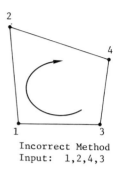

Incorrect Method
Input: 1,2,4,3

Fig. 3

Element Shape

The shapes of quadrilaterals can be arbitrary. They need not be rectangles or squares, but these configurations are often most convenient to use. Very thin rectangles should be avoided while computing shear related properties because the accuracy of the results in that element sometimes depends on the aspect ratio (length/width) of the rectangle. All element interior angles must be 180° or less. See Fig. 4 for illustrations of proper and improper quadrilaterals.

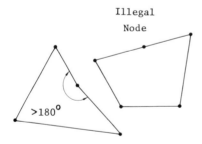

Improper Quadrilaterals

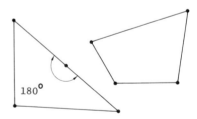

Proper Quadrilaterals

Fig. 4

Node Generation

If a series of nodal points lie in a straight line and are equally spaced, the user may input the two nodal point numbers (in ascending order) and coordinates for the nodes at each end. The program automatically generates the omitted intermediate nodal points by incrementing the preceding nodal point number by one. This automatic generation of nodal information is demonstrated in Fig. 5, where the user inputs only nodes 2 and 5 and their coordinates.

Input Data:

    2, 1.5, 1.5   {node no., y coordinate, z coordinate}

    5, 6.0, 1.5

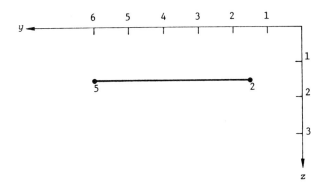

This program automatically generates the additional information:

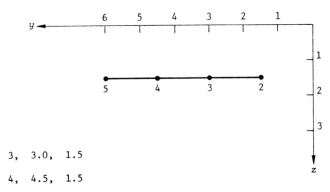

   3, 3.0, 1.5

   4, 4.5, 1.5

Fig. 5

Element Generation

The program assigns an element number to each quadrilateral or element according to the input order of the quadrilateral definition
line (a set of four nodes which defines an element). The quadrilateral on the first line will be assigned element number 1, that on the
second line will be assigned element number 2, and so on. The program can automatically generate a sequence of elements. The first
element in a line must be specified, along with the number of elements
to be created. The node and element numbers of the omitted elements
will be generated by increasing the previous nodal point and element
numbers by 1.

    The automatic generation of four elements is illustrated in Fig.
6. The user must input a set of four nodal point numbers of the
first element in the row (1, 2, 8, 7) and the number of omitted elements (4). If element 1, 2, 8, 7 is the first quadrilateral definition line to be input, the element number 1 will be assigned to
this element as shown in Fig. 6b. The element number on the next
entered quadrilateral definition line will be assigned element number
6, and so on.

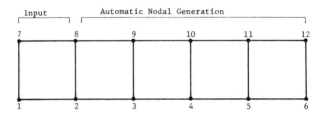

a. Four elements are to be generated automatically

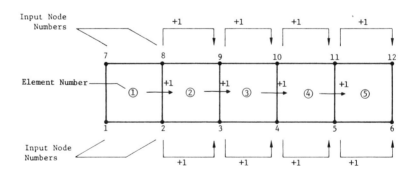

b. Numbers are sequentially increased by one

Fig. 6

Special Modeling of the Thin-walled Section for a Constrained
Warping Stress Analysis

If the constrained torsional warping stresses are to be calculated,
the thin-walled section should be divided into segments which will
be called _thin segments_. It is natural to consider the thin plate
between a free edge and plate junction, e.g., flange of the Zee section, or the thin plate between any two plate junctions, e.g., web of
the Zee section, as a thin segment (see Fig. 7a).

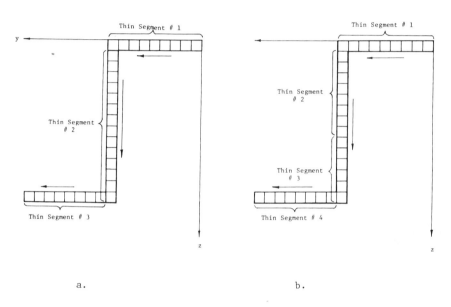

a.   b.

Fig. 7

The user may wish to divide the thin-walled section into the
shorter thin segments as in Fig. 7b in order that the bandwidth
(the greatest difference in magnitude between any two nodal point
numbers in the same element plus one) can be minimized when the
automatic nodal and element generation option is utilized. Figure
8 illustrates the modeling of some thin-walled sections.

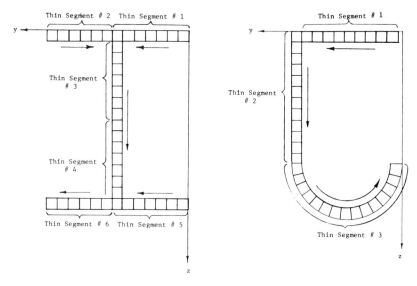

Fig. 8

The element definition lines (a set of four nodes which defines an element) must be entered in such an order that the element numbers are increased successively from any chosen free edge to the other edge of the thin-walled section, e.g., in the direction of arrows in Figs. 7, 8, and 9. An automatic element generation option can also be used to generate the sequence of elements in the directions of the arrows. If the element generation option is used, the numbering of the nodal points must be done in such a way that the nodal point numbers are increased successively in the directions of arrows as in Figs. 7 and 8 (further information on numbering can be found under "Element Generation"). The element generation option enables the user to reduce the amount of input data substantially.

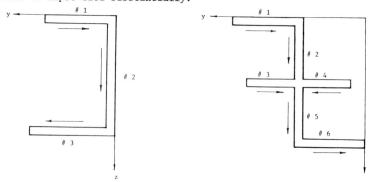

Fig. 9

Figure 10a illustrates in detail how the nodal and element generation option can be used to create the nodal point numbers and element numbers as required for constrained torsional warping stress
analysis of thin-walled sections. The encircled nodal point numbers
must be entered, as must the element number definitions for the
shaded elements. The number shown inside each element is the element
number.

INTERPRETATION OF CONSTRAINED WARPING STRESSES

Constrained Torsional Warping Normal Stresses

The computed constrained warping normal stresses are given at the centroid of each element. Tensile normal stresses are positive, compressive stresses are negative.

Constrained Torsional Warping Shear Flows

The computed shear flows due to constrained warping are given at the
center lines of thin segments, i.e., at the center of a segment of the
thin-walled section. Their locations and directions deserve some
explanation. Typical partial output for the warping shear flows on
the Zee section of Fig. 10a would appear as:

ELEMENT NUMBER	WARPING SHEAR FLOWS
1	0.
1	15.571E+01
2	28.096E+01
3	37.574E+01
4	44.006E+01
5	47.391E+01
6	47.730E+01
7	45.022E+01
8	39.335E+01
9	33.751E+01
10	28.096E+01
11	22.477E+01

The first line gives the shear flow (0.) on the initial edge of
element 1, i.e., at the center of line joining nodes 16 and 31; the
second line gives the shear flow (15.571E+01) on the final edge of
element 1, i.e., at the center of line joining nodes 17 and 32; and the
positive shear flow is in the direction of the arrow. If the shear
flow is in the opposite direction to the arrow, the result will be
negative. The third line gives the shear flow (28.096E+01) on the
final edge of element 2 acting at the center line of the thin segment,
i.e., at the center of line joining nodes 18 and 33, and so on. Figure
10b demonstrates some results of the shear flows on the thin segment

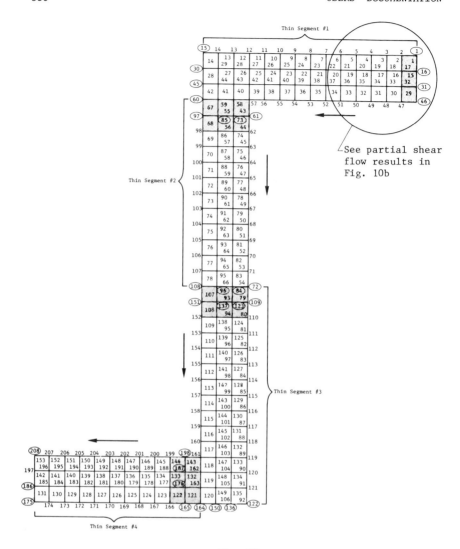

See partial shear
flow results in
Fig. 10b

Fig. 10a

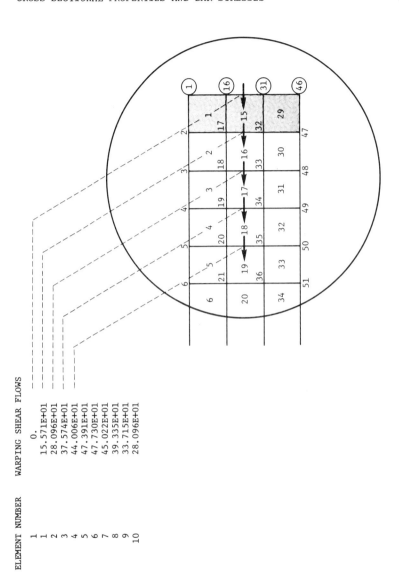

ELEMENT NUMBER	WARPING SHEAR FLOWS
1	0.
1	15.571E+01
2	28.096E+01
3	37.574E+01
4	44.006E+01
5	47.391E+01
6	47.730E+01
7	45.022E+01
8	39.335E+01
9	33.715E+01
10	28.096E+01

Fig. 10b

number 1 of the Zee section in Fig. 10a. <u>One or more than two rows</u>
<u>of elements</u> should be used to avoid numerical errors.

Sign Conventions

Positive internal forces are shown in Fig. 11. Forces in opposite
directions are negative and must be entered in the input data with
negative signs. These forces adhere to the sign conventions of the
technical manual of Ref. [4] and to those of the internal forces
produced by the response programs. It is important to follow these
sign conventions for the bimoment and warping torque which are
required if warping stresses are computed. Shear stresses are positive if they "point" in the direction of positive axes. Tensile normal stresses are positive; compressive stresses are negative. The
sign conventions for shear flows due to constrained warping were discussed in the subsection "Interpretation of Constrained Warping
Shear Flows."

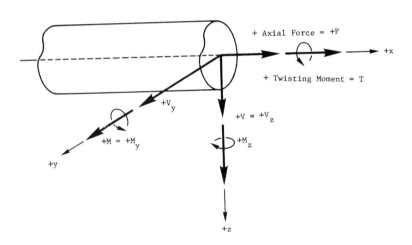

Fig. 11   Positive internal forces

Accessing and Executing the Program

Three options of data input are provided for this program: The prompting mode, the nonprompting mode, and the use of input from a previously created data file.

In the prompting mode of input, the user responds to questions put forth by the program, thereby furnishing the relevant data for his problem. In the nonprompting mode, the supportive questions are suppressed and the user enters his data according to the sequence and format given in the description of this program. In both modes of input a file with data in the same sequence as the nonprompting input is automatically generated. This file may be saved at the end of each run. The third input capability of the program, i.e., input from a data file, enables the user to call out his previously created data file, modify his data, and then run the same problem. And of course, he may simply run the problem using a data file without any modification at all.

The program is FORTRAN coded. However, to use it, a minimal knowledge of computer language, or even none at all, is assumed on the user's part. All that is required is minimal familiarity with the use of a terminal such as a teletype. All questions asked by the program are self-explanatory. The program will lead the user through the input. Numerical data input is free-formatted. This means that the user simply treats numbers the way he is most accustomed to without concern as to whether the numbers lie in particular columns. Commas or blanks are inserted between numbers being input. Of course, if one line is not long enough for the data, the user can go to the next lines until his data list is satisfied.

The following pages, in combination with the system manuals for the computer in question, should provide the necessary information to access and begin using the program. The example problems provided later in this documentation should appear similar on all systems as far as content is concerned; system differences may cause output to differ in appearance by including spurious line feeds, question marks, etc.

Outline of Procedure to Access and Use the Program

1. Dial the nearest phone number for the computer system. When the system responds with a high-pitched tone, place the phone in the acoustic coupler and wait for the system to print something.

2. Log in according to the instructions given the system's reference manual. The system will give some message indicating it is ready to accept your commands.

3.   You are now ready to execute the program. A brief outline of the user response and execution sequence for the program follows. It should be noted that after each line of instruction to the computer is completed, the user signifies that he has finished a line of instruction by hitting the carriage return key (CR). To begin the program, type the name BEAMSTR, followed by a return. In some cases a variation to the name is required. Consult your system manual.

4.   The computer will print "WILL INPUT BE FROM THE TERMINAL (ENTER 1) OR FROM A PREVIOUSLY CREATED DATA FILE (ENTER 2)?" These are the two distinct modes in which the BEAMST program operates. If input is to come from a data file, skip to step 8.

5.   The computer will print "DO YOU WANT TO SAVE A COPY OF YOUR INPUT DATA? (TYPE 'YES' OR 'NO')". This refers to the file which is automatically generated containing a copy of the input data. If you do not wish to save this file, skip to step 7.

6.   The computer will reply "UNDER WHAT NAME?". Reply with the name of the file you wish this data to be written on. The created file will be accessible after the current run by this name. Note that if a file with this name already exists, it will be destroyed. In some cases more than one name is required; consult your system manual.

7.   The computer will print a message indicating the program has begun executing.

8.   If the input is to be from a data file already in existence, the computer will print "ENTER FILE NAME". Enter the name of the data file previously created. The format is the same as in step 6.

9.   The computer will print "WILL YOU WISH TO MODIFY YOUR DATA FILE? (TYPE 'YES' OR 'NO')". If you desire to modify the data on your file before running the program, type "YES"; otherwise type "NO" and proceed to step 12. Note that the original copy of the data will not be altered.

10.   The computer will respond with "WILL YOU WISH TO SAVE THE MODIFIED COPY? (TYPE 'YES' OR 'NO')". If you want the new version of your data to be saved, answer "YES". If not, the program will run once with the modified copy of the data and then discard it. If this is desired, answer "NO" and proceed to step 12.

11.   The computer will print "UNDER WHAT NAME?". Respond as in step 6. The name of the original data file may be given here. In this case the modified copy will replace the original file, which will be destroyed.

12.   The computer will print a message indicating the program has begun executing.

Input from a Data File and Modification

To execute a program with input from a data file either previously created or generated internally by the prompting or non-prompting mode of input, the user simply indicates this wish in executing the programs and specifies the file name. The user may also modify the data file before using it with the system editor. A simple editor is provided with this program and modifications may be made to data files after the program begins execution.

Each line in a data file always begins with a 3-digit line number followed by a blank. This number serves the dual purpose of identifying as well as sequencing a data line. Thus when a line of data is to be deleted, the user simply retypes its line number with nothing following. Also, new lines of data can be inserted between any two lines by using appropriate line numbers. While the program will automatically attach line numbers (with an increment of 10) for the data file generated in a prompting or a non-prompting input, the user must enter them for his data file created otherwise (see the examples in the following sections).

Modifications can be made by retyping the whole line (including the line number) which contains the item(s) to be changed, or if necessary, by adding a new line of data. It is important that the user makes all necessary associated changes, e.g. if he decides to change the number of material properties, he must change several input parameters such as NUME (the number of materials) as well as EO(I), NUO(I) (modulii of elasticity and Poisson's ratios). The user is allowed to enter as many data as space allows on a line so long as they are separated by a comma (or at least one blank). Furthermore, the new entries do not have to be in the same format as the replaced ones, e.g. the user may want to re-enter a number, say, 120.5 simply as 120.5 instead of 1.205E+02 as it would appear on the data file. The commands 'L' and 'Q' are available to list the current state of the data file or quit (exit from editor). For more sophisticated manipulation of his data file, the user should refer to the appropriate system reference manual.

Availability and Assistance

The program is available from and is maintained by The Structural Members Users Group, P.O. Box 3958, University of Virginia Station, Charlottesville, Va. 22903, phone (804)296-4906.

Charlottesville, Virginia 22903, phone 804-296-4906. Questions on
using the program should be addressed to this organization.

EXAMPLE PROBLEMS

An array of example problems, illustrating all input options, are
presented in this section. User responses are underlined.

Example 1: Normal Stress Analysis of Z-Section

This example and the following example illustrate the use of the
prompting mode of input. The problem is to find the normal stresses
(axial and bending stresses) and non-shear-related cross-sectional
properties of the cross section shown in Fig. 12 subjected to the
loadings: bending moment about y' axis = 10,000 in-lb, bending
moment about z' axis = 2,000 in-lb, compressive axial force of 500 lb
applied at y = 3 in. and z = 4 in.
     Note that the total moment about the y' axis is 10,000 - 500
(0.75) = 9,625 in-lb, where the effect of the axial force is taken
into account. The selection of quadrilaterals along with the numbering of the nodal points is illustrated in Fig. 12. Note that large
quadrilaterals will suffice for this problem since only non-shear-
related properties are requested and the results do not depend on the
size of the elements chosen. However, if,for example, the torsional
constant is to be calculated, the number of quadrilaterals must be
increased.

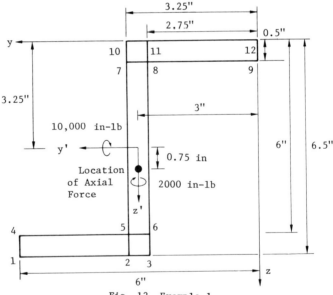

Fig. 12 Example 1

```
WILL INPUT BE FROM THE TERMINAL (ENTER 1)
OR FROM A PREVIOUSLY CREATED DATA FILE (ENTER 2)
? 1

DO YOU WANT TO SAVE A COPY OF YOUR INPUT DATA?
(TYPE 'YES' OR 'NO')
? YES

UNDER WHAT NAME?
? EXAM1

*************** PROGRAM BEAMSTRESS - DATA INPUT ***************

WHAT TYPE OF INPUT FORMAT DO YOU DESIRE
     1-PROMPTED
     2-NON-PROMPTED
     3-INPUT FROM DATA FILE
  ? 1
INPUT PROBLEM TITLE
  ? EXAMPLE 1 NORMAL STRESS ANALYSIS OF ZEE SECTION
ENTER OPT1,WHERE:
     1-ONLY CROSS-SECTIONAL PROPERTIES
     2-ONLY NORMAL STRESSES(WARPING EFFECTS NOT INCLUDED)
       AND CROSS-SECTIONAL PROPERTIES
     3-NORMAL AND SHEAR STRESSES(WARPING EFFECTS NOT INCLUDED)
       AND CROSS-SECTIONAL PROPERTIES
     4-NORMAL AND SHEAR STRESSES,INCLUDED CONSTRAINED WARPING
       EFFECTS,AND CROSS-SECTIONAL PROPERTIES
       WARPING SHEAR STRESSES ARE ACCURATE ONLY FOR THIN-WALLED
       OPEN SECTIONS AND REQUIRE A SUBSTANTIAL INCREASE
       IN THE AMOUNT OF INPUT
  ? 2
ENTER OPT2,WHERE:
     1-HOMOGENEOUS CROSS SECTION
     2-COMPOSITE CROSS SECTION
  ? 1
IS THERE SYMMETRY ABOUT THE Y-AXIS(1-YES,0-NO)
  ? 0
IS THERE SYMMETRY ABOUT THE Z-AXIS(1-YES,0-NO)
  ? 0
NUMBER OF NODAL POINT LINES TO BE INPUT
  ? 12
NUMBER OF ELEMENT DEFINITION LINES TO BE INPUT
  ? 5
NODAL POINT NUMBER, Y-COORD, Z-COORD
  ? 1,6,6.5
  ? 2,3.25,6.5
  ? 3,2.75,6.5
  ? 4,6,6
  ? 5,3.25,6
  ? 6,2.75,6
  ? 7,3.25,.5
  ? 8,2.75,.5
  ? 9,0,.5
  ? 10,3.25,0
  ? 11,2.75,0
  ? 12,0,0
ENTER NUMBER OF DIFFERENT KINDS OF MATERIALS OCCURRING
ON THE CROSS SECTION
  ? 1
MATERIAL PROPERTIES:
MODULUS OF ELASTICITY, POISSON'S RATIO
  ? 30.0E+06,.27
```

```
QUADRILATERAL DEFINITION
NODE1,NODE2,NODE3,NODE4,NUMBER OF ELEMENTS TO BE GENERATED
BY THE PROGRAM,MATERIAL CODE NUMBER
 ? 1,2,5,4,0,1
 ? 2,3,6,5,0,1
 ? 5,6,8,7,0,1
 ? 7,8,11,10,0,1
 ? 8,9,12,11,0,1

  ***************LOADING CONDITIONS***************

AXIAL FORCE
 ? -500
Z-COORD. OF AXIAL FORCE
 ? 4
Y-COORD. OF AXIAL FORCE
 ? 3
BENDING MOMENT ABOUT Y-AXIS
 ? 10000
BENDING MOMENT ABOUT Z-AXIS
 ? 2000
ENTER OPT3,WHERE:
     1-FOR PRINTOUT OF NORMAL STRESSES DUE TO BENDING MOMENTS ONLY
       (OPT1 MUST BE 2,3,OR 4)
     0-OTHERWISE
 ? 0
ENTER OPT4,WHERE:
     1-FOR PRINTOUT OF SHEAR STRESSES DUE TO SHEAR FORCES ONLY
       (OPT1 MUST BE 3 OR 4)
     0-OTHERWISE
 ? 0
ENTER OPT5,WHERE:
     1-FOR PRINTOUT OF SHEAR STRESSES DUE TO TWISTING MOMENT ONLY
       (OPT1 MUST BE 3 OR 4)
     0-OTHERWISE
 ? 0
ENTER OPT6,WHERE:
     1-FOR PRINTOUT OF NORMAL STRESSES DUE TO
       CONSTRAINED WARPING ONLY (OPT1 MUST BE 4)
     0-OTHERWISE
 ? 0
ENTER OPT7,WHERE:
     1-WARPING FUNCTION PRINTED (OPT1 MUST BE 3 OR 4)
     0-NOT PRINTED
 ? 0
ENTER OPT8,WHERE:
     1-GRAPH OF CROSS SECTION PRINTED
     0-NO GRAPH PRINTED
 ? 0

DO YOU WANT THE INPUT DATA FOR THE CROSS-SECTION PRINTED
(ANSWER:YES OR NO)
 ? NO

                 ***PROGRAM BEAMSTRESS - OUTPUT***


                 STRESSES ON THE CROSS SECTION


             COORDINATES OF
             ELEMENT CENTROID       NORMAL  STRESSES
                Y        Z              SIGMA

              4.625    6.250         14.944E+00
              3.000    6.250         22.160E+02
              3.000    3.250        -83.333E+00
              3.000     .250        -23.827E+02
              1.375     .250        -18.161E+01
```

CROSS-SECTIONAL PROPERTIES:

AREA OF SECTION...   60.00000E-01

Y-COORDINATE OF CENTROID...   30.00000E-01

Z-COORDINATE OF CENTROID...   32.50000E-01

Y-MOMENT OF INERTIA...   36.25000E+00

Z-MOMENT OF INERTIA...   90.62500E-01

PRODUCT OF INERTIA....   13.40625E+00

ANGLE TO PRINCIPAL AXES...   67.70

Y-RADIUS OF GYRATION   2.45798E+00

Z-RADIUS OF GYRATION   1.22899E+00

POLAR MOMENT OF INERTIA   4.53125E+01

Y-PRINCIPAL MOMENT OF INERTIA...   3.56391E+00

Z-PRINCIPAL MOMENT OF INERTIA...   4.17486E+01

IYZ-PRINCIPAL   0.

I MAX...   4.17486E+01

I MIN...   3.56391E+00

PARTIAL SUMMARY OF FORCES ON THE CROSS SECTION

TOTAL BENDING MOMENT MY...   96.25000E+02

TOTAL BENDING MOMENT MZ...   20.00000E+02

Example 2: Normal and Shear Stresses Analysis

Find all of the stresses, taking no constrained warping effects into account, and cross-sectional properties of the cross section in Fig. 13 subjected to the loadings: bending moment about y axis = 15,000 in-lb, bending moment about z axis = 5,000 in-lb, shear forces applied at y = 4 in., z = 4 in. with z component = 5,000 lb and y component = 500 lb, twisting moment about x axis = 2,000 in-lb.

The modulus of elasticity is 29 (10^6) psi and Poisson's ratio is 0.27. The selection of elements and nodal numbering is shown in Fig. 13. This example illustrates the prompting form of input; partial stress results are given.

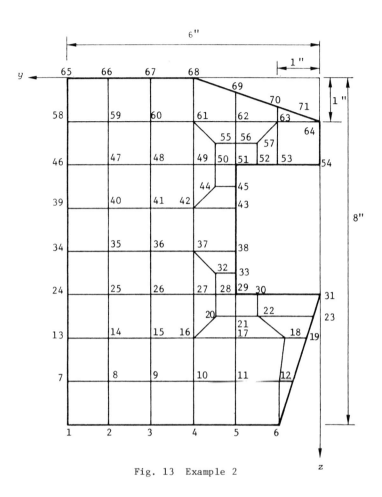

Fig. 13   Example 2

WILL INPUT BE FROM THE TERMINAL (ENTER 1)
OR FROM A PREVIOUSLY CREATED DATA FILE (ENTER 2)
? 1

DO YOU WANT TO SAVE A COPY OF YOUR INPUT DATA?
(TYPE 'YES' OR 'NO')
? YES

UNDER WHAT NAME?
? EXAM 2

```
************** PROGRAM BEAMSTRESS - DATA INPUT ***************
WHAT TYPE OF INPUT FORMAT DO YOU DESIRE
     1-PROMPTED
     2-NON-PROMPTED
     3-INPUT FROM DA FROM DATA FILE
  ? 1
INPUT PROBLEM TITLE
  ? EXAMPLE 2 NORMAL AND SHEAR STRESS ANALYSIS
ENTER OPT1,WHERE:
     1-ONLY CROSS-SECTIONAL PROPERTIES
     2-ONLY NORMAL STRESSES(WARPING EFFECTS NOT INCLUDED)
      AND CROSS-SECTIONAL PROPERTIES
     3-NORMAL AND SHEAR STRESSES(WARPING EFFECTS NOT INCLUDED)
      AND CROSS-SECTIONAL PROPERTIES
     4-NORMAL AND SHEAR STRESSES,INCLUDED CONSTRAINED WARPING
      EFFECTS,AND CROSS-SECTIONAL PROPERTIES
      WARPING SHEAR STRESSES ARE ACCURATE ONLY FOR THIN-WALLED
      OPEN SECTIONS AND REQUIRE A SUBSTANTIAL INCREASE
      IN THE AMOUNT OF INPUT
  ? 3
ENTER OPT2,WHERE:
     1-HOMOGENEOUS CROSS SECTION
     2-COMPOSITE CROSS SECTION
  ? 1
IS THERE SYMMETRY ABOUT THE Y-AXIS(1-YES,0-NO)
  ? 0
IS THERE SYMMETRY ABOUT THE Z-AXIS(1-YES,0-NO)
  ? 0
NUMBER OF NODAL POINT LINES TO BE INPUT
  ? 39
NUMBER OF ELEMENT DEFINITION LINES TO BE INPUT
  ? 23
NODAL POINT NUMBER, Y-COORD, Z-COORD
  ? 1,6,8
  ? 6,1,8
  ? 7,6,7
  ? 12,1,7
  ? 13,6,6
  ? 17,2,6
  ? 18,.9,6
  ? 19,.333,6
  ? 20,2.5,5.5
  ? 22,1.5,5.5
  ? 23,.167,5.5
  ? 24,6,5
  ? 27,3,5
  ? 29,2,5
  ? 30,1.5,5
  ? 31,0,5
  ? 32,2.5,4.5
  ? 33,2,4.5
  ? 34,6,4
  ? 37,3,4
  ? 38,2,4
  ? 39,6,3
  ? 42,3,3
  ? 43,2,3
  ? 44,2.5,2.5
  ? 45,2,2.5
  ? 46,6,2
  ? 49,3,2
  ? 53,1,2
  ? 54,0,2
  ? 55,2.5,1.5
```

```
? 57,1.5,1.5
? 58,6,1
? 64,0,1
? 65,6,0
? 68,3,0
? 69,2,.333
? 70,1,.666
? 71,.5,.833
```
ENTER NUMBER OF DIFFERENT KINDS OF MATERIALS OCCURRING
ON THE CROSS SECTION
```
? 1
```
MATERIAL PROPERTIES:
MODULUS OF ELASTICITY, POISSON'S RATIO
```
? 29.0E+06,.27
```
QUADRILATERAL DEFINITION
NODE1,NODE2,NODE3,NODE4,NUMBER OF ELEMENTS TO BE GENERATED
BY THE PROGRAM,MATERIAL CODE NUMBER
```
? 1,2,8,7,4,1
? 7,8,14,13,4,1
? 6,19,18,12,0,1
? 13,14,25,24,2,1
? 16,17,21,20,2,1
? 16,20,28,27,0,1
? 20,21,29,28,2,1
? 24,25,35,34,2,1
? 27,28,32,37,0,1
? 28,29,33,32,0,1
? 32,33,38,37,0,1
? 34,35,40,39,3,1
? 39,40,47,46,2,1
? 42,43,45,44,0,1
? 42,44,50,49,0,1
? 44,45,51,50,0,1
? 46,47,59,58,2,1
? 49,50,55,61,0,1
? 50,51,56,55,1,1
? 52,53,63,57,0,1
? 53,54,64,63,0,1
? 55,56,62,61,1,1
? 58,59,66,65,5,1
```

    ***************LOADING CONDITIONS***************

AXIAL FORCE
```
? 0
```
Z-COORD. OF AXIAL FORCE
```
? 0
```
Y-COORD. OF AXIAL FORCE
```
? 0
```
BENDING MOMENT ABOUT Y-AXIS
```
? 15000
```
BENDING MOMENT ABOUT Z-AXIS
```
? 5000
```
SHEAR FORCE IN Y-DIRECTION
```
? 500
```
SHEAR FORCE IN Z-DIRECTION
```
? 5000
```
Y-COORD. OF THE Z-COMPONENT OF THE SHEAR FORCE
```
? 4
```
Z-COORD. OF THE Y-COMPONENT OF THE SHEAR FORCE
```
? 4
```
APPLIED TWISTING MOMENT
```
? 2000
```
ENTER OPT3,WHERE:
     1-FOR PRINTOUT OF NORMAL STRESSES DUE TO BENDING MOMENTS ONLY
        (OPT1 MUST BE 2,3,OR 4)
     0-OTHERWISE
```
? 0
```
ENTER OPT4,WHERE:
     1-FOR PRINTOUT OF SHEAR STRESSES DUE TO SHEAR FORCES ONLY
        (OPT1 MUST BE 3 OR 4)
     0-OTHERWISE

```
    ? 0
ENTER OPT5,WHERE:
       1-FOR PRINTOUT OF SHEAR STRESSES DUE TO TWISTING MOMENT ONLY
         (OPT1 MUST BE 3 OR 4)
       0-OTHERWISE
    ? 0
ENTER OPT6,WHERE:
       1-FOR PRINTOUT OF NORMAL STRESSES DUE TO
         CONSTRAINED WARPING ONLY (OPT1 MUST BE 4)
       0-OTHERWISE
    ? 0
ENTER OPT7,WHERE:
       1-WARPING FUNCTION PRINTED (OPT1 MUST BE 3 OR 4)
       0-NOT PRINTED
    ? 0
ENTER OPT8,WHERE:
       1-GRAPH OF CROSS SECTION PRINTED
       0-NO GRAP-NO GRAPH PRINTED
    ? 0

DO YOU WANT THE INPUT DATA FOR THE CROSS-SECTION PRINTED
(ANSWER:YES OR NO)
.? NO

               ***PROGRAM BEAMSTRESS - OUTPUT***

    STRESSES ON THE CROSS SECTION


    COORDINATES OF
    ELEMENT CENTROID     NORMAL   STRESSES        SHEAR  STRESSES
       Y        Z            SIGMA           TXY             TXZ


     5.500    7.500      13.162E+01      -45.056E-01     53.461E+00
     4.500    7.500      18.123E+01      -83.105E-01     46.241E+00
     3.500    7.500      23.084E+01      -98.775E-01     41.198E+00
     2.500    7.500      28.045E+01      -80.437E-01     35.153E+00
     1.500    7.500      33.006E+01       38.263E-03     33.470E+00
     5.500    6.500      63.488E+00      -50.159E-02     13.948E+01
     4.500    6.500      11.310E+01      -42.159E-01     12.593E+01


              CROSS-SECTIONAL PROPERTIES:


         AREA OF SECTION...    39.00125E+00

         Y-COORDINATE OF CENTROID...    34.87107E-01

         Z-COORDINATE OF CENTROID...    41.02493E-01
         Z-MOMENT OF INERTIA...    91.25051E+00

         PRODUCT OF INERTIA....    -69.43380E-01

         ANGLE TO PRINCIPAL AXES...    -86.80

         Y-RADIUS OF GYRATION     2.34847E+00

         Z-RADIUS OF GYRATION     1.52960E+00

         POLAR MOMENT OF INERTIA    3.06355E+02

         Y-PRINCIPAL MOMENT OF INERTIA...    9.08625E+01

         Z-PRINCIPAL MOMENT OF INERTIA...    2.15493E+02

         IYZ-PRINCIPAL         0.

         I MAX...    2.15493E+02

         I MIN...    9.08625E+01
```

Y-COORDINATE OF SHEAR CENTER...   42.41476E-01

Z-COORDINATE OF SHEAR CENTER...   41.25179E-01

SHEAR COEFFICIENT AYY...   11.76942E-01

SHEAR COEFFICIENT AZZ...   14.66280E-01

SHEAR COEFFICIENT AYZ...   -57.74032E-04

WARPING CONSTANT...   28.49524E+01

TORSIONAL CONSTANT...   15.05642E+01

PARTIAL SUMMARY OF FORCES ON THE CROSS SECTION

TOTAL BENDING MOMENT MY...   15.00000E+03

TOTAL BENDING MOMENT MZ...   50.00000E+02

TOTAL TWISTING MOMENT...   85.52076E+01

Example 3:   Torsional Stress Analysis of Double Channel

This example illustrates the use of the nonprompting mode of input.
Input definitions for this input mode are given later in this chapter.
This input mode is sometimes best utilized once the user has mastered
the use of the prompting mode.

We wish to determine the shear stresses in the double channel
section shown in Fig. 14a due to a 1,000 in-lb twisting moment which
is applied at the centroid. Also, find the cross-sectional properties. Use a modulus of elasticity of $30(10^6)$ psi and Poisson's ratio
of 0.27. Do not take constrained warping effects into account.

As indicated in Fig. 14b, use is made of the symmetry options of
the program. The nodes are numbered as shown in Fig. 14b.

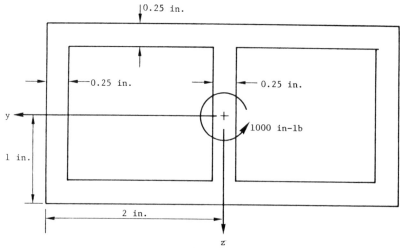

Fig. 14a   Example 3

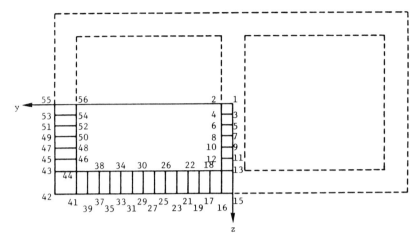

Fig. 14b   Example 3

```
WILL INPUT BE FROM THE TERMINAL (ENTER 1)
OR FROM A PREVIOUSLY CREATED DATA FILE (ENTER 2)
? 1
DO YOU WANT TO SAVE A COPY OF YOUR INPUT DATA?
(TYPE 'YES' OR 'NO')
? YES
UNDER WHAT NAME?
? EXAM 3


:::::::::::::: PROGRAM BEAMSTRESS - DATA INPUT ::::::::::::::

WHAT TYPE OF INPUT FORMAT DO YOU DESIRE
        1-PROMPTED
        2-NON-PROMPTED
        3-INPUT FROM DATA FILE
? 2
? EXAMPLE 3 TORSIONAL ANALYSIS OF TWO-CHANNEL SECTION
? 3
? 1
? 1
? 1
? 56
? 27
? 1,0,0
? 2,.125,0
? 3,0,.125
? 4,.125,.125
? 5,0,.25
? 6,.125,.25
? 7,0,.375
? 8,.125,.375
? 9,0,.5
? 10,.125,.5
? 11,0,.625
? 12,.125,.625
? 13,0,.75
? 14,.125,.75
? 15,0,1
? 16,.125,1
? 17,.25,1
```

```
?  18,.25,.75
?  19,.375,1
?  20,.375,.75
?  21,.5,1
?  22,.5,.75
?  23,.625,1
?  24,.625,.75
?  25,.75,1
?  26,.75,.75
?  27,.875,1
?  28,.875,.75
?  29,1,1
?  30,1,.75
?  31,1.125,1
?  32,1.125,.75
?  33,1.25,1
?  34,1.25,.75
?  35,1.375,1
?  36,1.375,.75
?  37,1.5,1
?  38,1.5,.75
?  39,1.625,1
?  40,1.625,.75
?  41,1.75,1
?  42,2,1
?  43,2,.75
?  44,1.75,.75
?  45,2,.625
?  46,1.75,.625
?  47,2,.5
?  48,1.75,.5
?  49,2,.375
?  50,1.75,.375
?  51,2,.25
?  52,1.75,.25
?  53,2,.125
?  54,1.75,.125
?  55,2,0
?  56,1.75,0
?  1
?  30.0E+06,0.27
?  1,2,4,3,0,1
?  3,4,6,5,0,1
?  5,6,8,7,0,1
?  7,8,10,9,0,1
?  9,10,12,11,0,1
?  11,12,14,13,0,1
?  13,14,16,15,0,1
?  14,18,17,16,0,1
?  18,20,19,17,0,1
?  20,22,21,19,0,1
?  22,24,23,21,0,1
?  24,26,25,23,0,1
?  26,28,27,25,0,1
?  28,30,29,27,0,1
?  30,32,31,29,0,1
?  32,34,33,31,0,1
?  34,36,35,33,0,1
?  36,38,37,35,0,1
?  38,40,39,37,0,1
?  40,44,41,39,0,1
?  44,43,42,41,0,1
?  46,45,43,44,0,1
?  48,47,45,46,0,1
?  50,49,47,48,0,1
?  52,51,49,50,0,1
?  54,53,51,52,0,1
?  56,55,53,54,0,1
?  0
?  0
```

```
? 0
? 0
? 0
? 0
? 0
? 0
? 0
? 1000
? 0
? 0
? 0
? 0
? 0
? 0
```

DO YOU WANT THE INPUT DATA FOR THE CROSS-SECTION PRINTED
(ANSWER:YES OR NO)
? NO

*************** PROGRAM BEAMSTRESS - OUTPUT ***************

EXAMPLE 3 TORSIONAL ANALYSIS OF TWO CHANNEL SECTION

      STRESSES ON THE CROSS SECTION

COORDINATES OF ELEMENT CENTROID		NORMAL STRESSES	SHEAR STRESSES	
Y	Z	SIGMA	TXY	TXZ
.063	.063	0.	-11.983E-03	29.687E+00
.063	.188	0.	-83.883E-03	29.639E+00
.063	.313	0.	-49.131E-02	29.352E+00
.063	.438	0.	-28.640E-01	27.674E+00
.063	.563	0.	-16.693E+00	17.896E+00
.063	.688	0.	-97.292E+00	-39.097E+00
.063	.875	0.	-25.405E+01	-14.285E+00
.188	.875	0.	-30.164E+01	-17.501E+00
.313	.875	0.	-30.164E+01	-39.402E-01
.438	.875	0.	-30.164E+01	-88.712E-02
.563	.875	0.	-30.164E+01	-19.965E-02
.688	.875	0.	-30.164E+01	-44.582E-03
.813	.875	0.	-30.164E+01	-83.982E-04
.938	.875	0.	-30.164E+01	53.901E-04
1.063	.875	0.	-30.164E+01	33.552E-03
1.188	.875	0.	-30.164E+01	15.119E-02
1.313	.875	0.	-30.164E+01	67.198E-02
1.438	.975	0.	-30.164E+01	29.847E-01
1.563	.875	0.	-30.164E+01	13.257E+00
1.688	.875	0.	-30.164E+01	58.880E+00
1.875	.875	0.	-12.582E+01	12.582E+01
1.875	.688	0.	-58.880E+00	30.164E+01
1.875	.563	0.	-13.257E+00	30.164E+01
1.875	.438	0.	-29.846E-01	30.164E+01
1.875	.313	0.	-67.162E-02	30.164E+01
1.875	.188	0.	-14.957E-02	30.164E+01
1.875	.063	0.	-26.395E-03	30.164E+01

          CROSS-SECTIONAL PROPERTIES:

        AREA OF SECTION...   31.25000E-01

        Y-COORDINATE OF CENTROID...   0.

        Z-COORDINATE OF CENTROID...   0.

```
Y-MOMENT OF INERTIA...     17.52604E-01

Z-MOMENT OF INERTIA...     53.09245E-01

PRODUCT OF INERTIA....          0.

ANGLE TO PRINCIPAL AXES...      0.

Y-RADIUS OF GYRATION       7.48888E-01

Z-RADIUS OF GYRATION       1.30344E+00

POLAR MOMENT OF INERTIA    7.06185E+00

Y-PRINCIPAL MOMENT OF INERTIA...     1.75260E+00

Z-PRINCIPAL MOMENT OF INERTIA...     5.30924E+00

IYZ-PRINCIPAL          0.

I MAX...     5.30924E+00

I MIN...     1.75260E+00

Y-COORDINATE OF SHEAR CENTER...          0.

Z-COORDINATE OF SHEAR CENTER...          0.

SHEAR COEFFICIENT AYY...     16.76364E-01

SHEAR COEFFICIENT AZZ...     24.32092E-01

SHEAR COEFFICIENT AYZ...          0.

WARPING CONSTANT...     40.92448E-02

TORSIONAL CONSTANT...     42.08872E-01

     PARTIAL SUMMARY OF FORCES ON THE CROSS SECTION

TOTAL BENDING MOMENT MY...          0.

TOTAL BENDING MOMENT MZ...          0.

TOTAL TWISTING MOMENT...     10.00000E+02
```

Example 4: Torsional Stress Analysis of Square Section

This example shows how to modify the data file which was generated
during the nonprompting input. The purpose of data modification is
either to correct the error(s) made during the nonprompting input or
to account for different loadings.
     The problem is to find the shear stresses, taking no constrained
warping effects into account, in the square section shown in Fig. 15
due to two loading conditions. These loading conditions are 100
in-lb and 150 in-lb twisting moments. The data file generated during
the nonprompting input of the first loading condition was saved under
the name of EXAM4. After completing the first run, the data file
EXAM4 is recalled and the modification is made by changing line number 275 from "100" to "150" and line number 305 from "0" to "1" (no gra
of the cross section printed). Then the first data set is replaced by
the modified set. The analysis for the second loading condition was
run by using the input from the modified data file EXAM4.

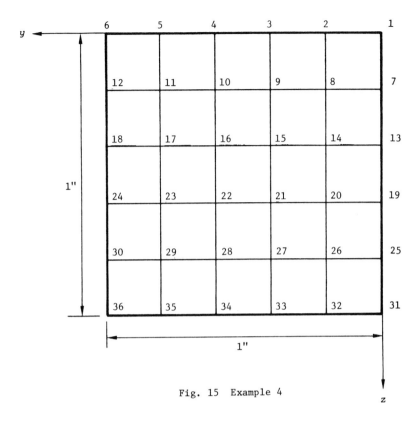

Fig. 15 Example 4

```
WILL INPUT BE FROM THE TERMINAL (ENTER 1)
OR FROM A PREVIOUSLY CREATED DATA FILE (ENTER 2)
? 1

DO YOU WANT TO SAVE A COPY OF YOUR INPUT DATA?
(TYPE 'YES' OR 'NO')
? YES

UNDER WHAT NAME?
? EXAM4

*************** PROGRAM BEAMSTRESS - DATA INPUT ***************

WHAT TYPE OF INPUT FORMAT DO YOU DESIRE
     1-PROMPTED
     2-NON-PROMPTED
     3-INPUT FROM DATA FILE
 ? 2
 ? EXAMPLE 4 TORSIONAL STRESS ANALYSIS OF SQUARE SECTION
 ? 3
 ? 1
 ? 0
 ? 0
```

```
? 12
? 5
? 1,0,0
? 6,1,0
? 7,0,.2
? 12,1,.2
? 13,0,.4
? 18,1,.4
? 19,0,.6
? 24,1,.6
? 25,0,.8
? 30,1,.8
? 31,0,1
? 36,1,1
? 1
? 29.0E+06,.27
? 1,2,8,7,4,1
? 7,8,14,13,4,1
? 13,14,20,19,4,1
? 19,20,26,25,4,1
? 25,26,32,31,4,1
? 0
? 0
? 0
? 0
? 0
? 0
? 0
? 0
? 0
? 100
? 0
? 0
? 0
? 0
? 0
? 0
```

DO YOU WANT THE INPUT DATA FOR THE CROSS-SECTION PRINTED
(ANSWER:YES OR NO)
? NO

PROGRAM BEAMSTRESS - OUTPUT

STRESSES ON THE CROSS SECTION

COORDINATES OF ELEMENT CENTROID		NORMAL STRESSES	SHEAR STRESSES	
Y	Z	SIGMA	TXY	TXZ
.100	.100	0.	14.631E+01	-14.631E+01
.300	.100	0.	30.197E+01	-49.809E+00
.500	.100	0.	34.555E+01	-91.244E-14
.700	.100	0.	30.197E+01	49.809E+00
.900	.100	0.	14.631E+01	14.631E+01
.100	.300	0.	49.809E+00	-30.197E+01
.300	.300	0.	12.452E+01	-12.452E+01
.500	.300	0.	14.943E+01	-18.249E-13
.700	.300	0.	12.452E+01	12.452E+01
.900	.300	0.	49.809E+00	30.197E+01
.100	.500	0.	-13.687E-13	-34.555E+01
.300	.500	0.	-21.290E-13	-14.943E+01
.500	.500	0.	-24.332E-13	-60.829E-14
.700	.500	0.	-22.811E-13	14.943E+01
.900	.500	0.	-13.687E-13	34.555E+01
.100	.700	0.	-49.809E+00	-30.197E+01
.300	.700	0.	-12.452E+01	-12.452E+01
.500	.700	0.	-14.943E+01	-45.622E-14
.700	.700	0.	-12.452E+01	12.452E+01

```
.900     .700      0.      -49.809E+00    30.197E+01
.100     .900      0.      -14.631E+01    14.631E+01
.300     .900      0.      -30.197E+01   -49.809E+00
.500     .900      0.      -34.555E+01   -15.207E-14
.700     .900      0.      -30.197E+01    49.809E+00
.900     .900      0.      -14.631E+01    14.631E+01
```

CROSS-SECTIONAL PROPERTIES:

AREA OF SECTION...   10.00000E-01

Y-COORDINATE OF CENTROID...   50.00000E-02

Z-COORDINATE OF CENTROID...   50.00000E-02

Y-MOMENT OF INERTIA...   83.33333E-03

Z-MOMENT OF INERTIA...   83.33333E-03

PRODUCT OF INERTIA....   35.52714E-16

ANGLE TO PRINCIPAL AXES...   0.

Y-RADIUS OF GYRATION   2.88675E-01

Z-RADIUS OF GYRATION   2.88675E-01
POLAR MOMENT OF INERTIA   1.66667E-01

Y-PRINCIPAL MOMENT OF INERTIA...   8.33333E-02

Z-PRINCIPAL MOMENT OF INERTIA...   8.33333E-02

IYZ-PRINCIPAL   0.

I MAX...   8.33333E-02

I MIN...   8.33333E-02

Y-COORDINATE OF SHEAR CENTER...   50.00000E-02

Z-COORDINATE OF SHEAR CENTER...   50.00000E-02

SHEAR COEFFICIENT AYY...   11.54215E-01

SHEAR COEFFICIENT AZZ...   11.54215E-01

SHEAR COEFFICIENT AYZ...   49.17326E-18

WARPING CONSTANT...   13.33609E-05

TORSIONAL CONSTANT...   14.60121E-02

PARTIAL SUMMARY OF FORCES ON THE CROSS SECTION

TOTAL BENDING MOMENT MY...   0.

TOTAL BENDING MOMENT MZ...   0.

TOTAL TWISTING MOMENT...   10.00000E+01

After the first run is completed, the second run is made by calling the program and using the data file created during the first run.

WILL INPUT BE FROM THE TERMINAL (ENTER 1)
OR FROM A PREVIOUSLY CREATED DATA FILE (ENTER 2)
? 2

WILL YOU WISH TO MODIFY YOUR DATA FILE?
(TYPE 'YES' OR 'NO')
? YES

```
WILL YOU WISH TO SAVE THE MODIFIED COPY?
('YES' OR 'NO')
? YES

UNDER WHAT NAME?
? EXAM4

::::::::::::: PROGRAM BEAMSTRESS - DATA INPUT :::::::::::::

WHAT TYPE OF INPUT FORMAT DO YOU DESIRE
          1-PROMPTED
          2-NON-PROMPTED
          3-INPUT FROM DATA FILE

DO YOU WISH TO MODIFY YOUR DATA FILE
? YES

BEGIN EDITING, TYPE 'L' TO LIST, 'Q' TO STOP

? L

100 EXAMPLE 4 TORSIONAL STRESS ANALYSIS OF SQUARE SECTION
105 3
110 1
115 0
120 0
125 12
130 5
135 1,0,0
140 6,1,0
145 7,0,.2
150 12,1,.2
155 13,0,.4
160 18,1,.4
165 19,0,.6
170 24,1,.6
175 25,0,.8
180 30,1,.8
185 31,0,1
190 36,1,1
195 1
200 29.0E+06,,.27
205 1,2,8,7,4,1
210 7,8,14,13,4,1
215 13,14,20,19,4,1
220 19,20,26,25,4,1
225 25,26,32,31,4,1
230 0
235 0
240 0
245 0
250 0
255 0
260 0
265 0
270 0
275 100
280 0
285 0
290 0
295 0
300 0
305 1
??275 150
?Q

DO YOU WANT THE INPUT DATA FOR THE CROSS-SECTION PRINTED
(ANSWER:YES OR NO)
 ? NO
```

PROGRAM BEAMSTRESS - OUTPUT

STRESSES ON THE CROSS SECTION

COORDINATES OF ELEMENT CENTROID		NORMAL STRESSES	SHEAR STRESSES	
Y	Z	SIGMA	TXY	TXZ
.100	.100	0.	21.947E+01	-21.947E+01
.300	.100	0.	45.295E+01	-74.714E+00
.500	.100	0.	51.833E+01	-13.687E-13
.700	.100	0.	45.295E+01	74.714E+00
.900	.100	0.	21.947E+01	21.947E+01
.100	.300	0.	74.714E+00	-45.295E+01
.300	.300	0.	18.678E+01	-18.678E+01

CROSS-SECTIONAL PROPERTIES:

AREA OF SECTION...   10.00000E-01

Y-COORDINATE OF CENTROID...   50.00000E-02

Z-COORDINATE OF CENTROID...   50.00000E-02

Y-MOMENT OF INERTIA...   83.33333E-03

Z-MOMENT OF INERTIA...   83.33333E-03

PRODUCT OF INERTIA....   35.52714E-16

ANGLE TO PRINCIPAL AXES...   0.

Y-RADIUS OF GYRATION   2.88675E-01

Z-RADIUS OF GYRATION   2.88675E-01

POLAR MOMENT_OF INERTIA   1.66667E-01

Y-PRINCIPAL MOMENT OF INERTIA...   8.33333E-02

Z-PRINCIPAL MOMENT OF INERTIA...   8.33333E-02

IYZ-PRINCIPAL   0.

I MAX...   8.33333E-02

I MIN...   8.33333E-02

Y-COORDINATE OF SHEAR CENTER...   50.00000E-02

Z-COORDINATE OF SHEAR CENTER...   50.00000E-02

SHEAR COEFFICIENT AYY...   11.54215E-01

SHEAR COEFFICIENT AZZ...   11.54215E-01

SHEAR COEFFICIENT AYZ...   49.17326E-18

WARPING CONSTANT...   13.33609E-05

TORSIONAL CONSTANT...   14.60121E-02

PARTIAL SUMMARY OF FORCES ON THE CROSS SECTION

TOTAL BENDING MOMENT MY...   0.

TOTAL BENDING MOMENT MZ...   0.

TOTAL TWISTING MOMENT...   15.00000E+01

Example 5:   Non-Shear-Related Cross-Sectional Properties of
Wing Section

This example shows how to create a data file. This can be done off-
line on paper tape and then fed into the teletype and saved as a
permanent file. Then the DATA FILE mode of input can be utilized.
    The problem is to determine the non-shear-related cross-section-
al properties for the wing section model shown in Fig. 16. Each
stringer is modeled by a single quadrilateral. For stringers of
other shapes, any convenient quadrilaterals with equivalent cross-
sectional areas can be used. The skins are ignored. Also, do not
consider constrained warping effects. The data file for this example
was created off line and then fed in and saved as a permanent file
under the name EXAM5.

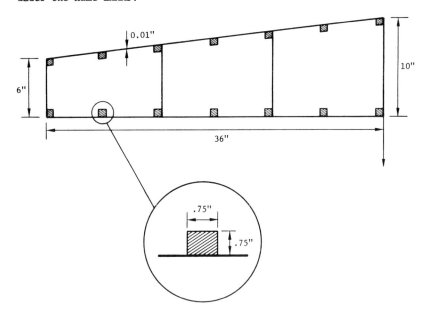

Fig. 16   Example 5

Create the data file off-line and save it. (See the instructions for
your computer system for the proper commands).

```
100 EXAMPLE 5 NON-SHEAR RELATED CROSS-SECTIONAL PROPERTIES
105 2
110 1
115 0
120 0
125 56
130 14
135 1,0,0
```

```
140  2,.75,0
145  3,.75,.75
150  4,0,.75
155  5,5.875,.6528
160  6,6.625,.6528
165  7,6.625,1.4028
170  8,5.875,1.4028
175  9,11.75,1.3056
180  10,12.5,1.3056
185  11,12.5,2.0556
190  12,11.75,2.0556
195  13,17.625,1.9583
200  14,18.375,1.9583
205  15,18.375,2.7083
210  16,17.625,2.7083
215  17,23.5,2.6111
220  18,24.25,2.6111
225  19,24.25,3.3611
230  20,23.5,3.3611
235  21,29.375,3.2639
240  22,30.125,3.2639
245  23,30.125,4.0139
250  24,29.375,4.0139
255  25,35.25,3.9167
260  26,36,3.9167
265  27,36,4.6667
270  28,35.25,4.6667
275  29,35.25,9.25
280  30,36,9.25
285  31,36,10
290  32,35.25,10
295  33,29.375,9.25
300  34,30.125,9.25
305  35,30.125,10
310  36,29.375,10
315  37,23.5,9.25
320  38,24.25,9.25
325  39,24.25,10
330  40,23.5,10
335  41,17.625,9.25
340  42,18.375,9.25
345  43,18.375,10
350  44,17.625,10
355  45,11.75,9.25
360  46,12.5,9.25
365  47,12.5,10
370  48,11.75,10
375  49,5.875,9.25
380  50,6.625,9.25
385  51,6.625,10
390  52,5.875,10
395  53,0,9.25
400  54,.75,9.25
405  55,.75,10
410  56,0,10
415  1
420  30.0E+06,.27
425  1,2,3,4,0,1
430  5,6,7,8,0,1
435  9,10,11,12,0,1
440  13,14,15,16,0,1
445  17,18,19,20,0,1
450  21,22,23,24,0,1
455  25,26,27,28,0,1
460  29,30,31,32,0,1
465  33,34,35,36,0,1
470  37,38,39,40,0,1
475  41,42,43,44,0,1
480  45,46,47,48,0,1
485  49,50,51,52,0,1
490  53,54,55,56,0,1
495  0
```

```
500 0
510 0
515 0
520 0
525 0
530 0
535 0
540 0
545 0
```

```
WILL INPUT BE FROM THE TERMINAL (ENTER 1)
OR FROM A PREVIOUSLY CREATED DATA FILE (ENTER 2)
? 2
ENTER FILE NAME
? EXAM5
WILL YOU WISH TO MODIFY YOUR DATA FILE (YES OR NO)
? NO

:::::::::::::: PROGRAM BEAMSTRESS - DATA INPUT ::::::::::::::

WHAT TYPE OF INPUT FORMAT DO YOU DESIRE
        1-PROMPTED
        2-NON-PROMPTED
        3-INPUT FROM DATA FILE
? 3
DO YOU WISH TO MODIFY YOUR DATA FILE
? NO

DO YOU WANT THE INPUT DATA FOR THE CROSS-SECTION PRINTED
(ANSWER:YES OR NO)
? NO

****************** PROGRAM BEAMSTRESS - OUTPUT ******************

EXAMPLE 5 NON-SHEAR RELATED CROSS-SECTIONAL PROPERTIES

             STRESSES ON THE CROSS SECTION
         COORDINATES OF
      ELEMENT CENTROID      NORMAL  STRESSES
          Y        Z              SIGMA

         .375     .375            0.
        6.250    1.028            0.
       12.125    1.681            0.
       18.000    2.333            0.
       23.875    2.986            0.
       29.750    3.639            0.
       35.625    4.292            0.
       35.625    9.625            0.
       29.750    9.625            0.
       23.875    9.625            0.
       18.000    9.625            0.
       12.125    9.625            0.
        6.250    9.625            0.
         .375    9.625            0.

              CROSS-SECTIONAL PROPERTIES:

          AREA OF SECTION...    78.75000E-01

          Y-COORDINATE OF CENTROID...    18.00000E+00

          Z-COORDINATE OF CENTROID...    59.79171E-01

          Y-MOMENT OF INERTIA...    11.17555E+01

          Z-MOMENT OF INERTIA...    10.87611E+02

          PRODUCT OF INERTIA....    60.40242E+00

          ANGLE TO PRINCIPAL AXES...    3.53

          Y-RADIUS OF GYRATION    3.76712E+00
```

```
Z-RADIUS OF GYRATION      1.17520E+01

POLAR MOMENT OF INERTIA     1.19937E+03

Y-PRINCIPAL MOMENT OF INERTIA...     1.08031E+02

Z-PRINCIPAL MOMENT OF INERTIA...     1.09134E+03
IYZ-PRINCIPAL          0.

I MAX...     1.09134E+03

I MIN...     1.08031E+02

     PARTIAL SUMMARY OF FORCES ON THE CROSS SECTION

TOTAL BENDING MOMENT MY...          0.

TOTAL BENDING MOMENT MZ...          0.
```

Example 6:   Restrained Torsional Warping Stresses on Zee Section

This and the following examples illustrate the use of the prompting mode of input. The problem is to find all of the restrained warping stresses and cross-sectional properties of the Zee section in Fig. 17 subjected to the loadings: bimoment = 239,055 lb-in^2, warping torque = 10,000 lb-in. The beam cross section is homogeneous,with the modulus of elasticity and Poisson's ratio being 29(10^6) psi and 0.27, respectively.

```
WILL INPUT BE FROM THE TERMINAL (ENTER 1)
OR FROM A PREVIOUSLY CREATED DATA FILE (ENTER 2)
? 1
DO YOU WANT TO SAVE A COPY OF YOUR INPUT DATA?
(TYPE 'YES' OR 'NO')
? YES
UNDER WHAT NAME?
? EXAM6
:::::::::::::: PROGRAM BEAMSTRESS - DATA INPUT ::::::::::::::

WHAT TYPE OF INPUT FORMAT DO YOU DESIRE
          1-PROMPTED
          2-NON-PROMPTED
          3-INPUT FROM DATA FILE
    ? 1
INPUT PROBLEM TITLE
    ? EXAMPLE 6 RESTRAINED WARPING STRESSES IN ZEE SECTION
ENTER OPT1,WHERE:
      1-ONLY CROSS-SECTIONAL PROPERTIES
      2-ONLY NORMAL STRESSES(WARPING EFFECTS NOT INCLUDED)
        AND CROSS-SECTIONAL PROPERTIES
      3-NORMAL AND SHEAR STRESSES(WARPING EFFECTS NOT INCLUDED)
        AND CROSS-SECTIONAL PROPERTIES
      4-NORMAL AND SHEAR STRESSES,INCLUDED CONSTRAINED WARPING
        EFFECTS,AND CROSS-SECTIONAL PROPERTIES
        WARPING SHEAR STRESSES ARE ACCURATE ONLY FOR THIN-WALLED
        OPEN SECTIONS AND REQUIRE A SUBSTANTIAL INCREASE
        IN THE AMOUNT OF INPUT
    ? 4
ENTER OPT2,WHERE:
      1-HOMOGENEOUS CROSS SECTION
      2-COMPOSITE CROSS SECTION
    ? 1
IS THERE SYMMETRY ABOUT THE Y-AXIS(1-YES,0-NO)
    ? 0
IS THERE SYMMETRY ABOUT THE Z-AXIS(1-YES,0-NO)
    ? 0
NUMBER OF NODAL POINT LINES TO BE INPUT
    ? 16
```

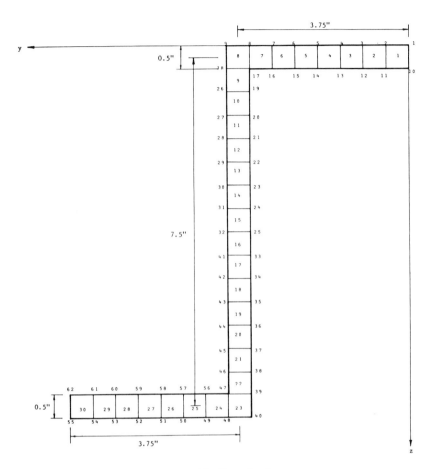

Fig. 17   Example 6

```
NODAL POINT NUMBER, Y-COORD, Z-COORD
 ?  1,0,0
 ?  9,4,0
 ?  10,0,.5
 ?  18,4,.5
 ?  19,3.5,1
 ?  25,3.5,4
 ?  26,4,1
 ?  32,4,4
 ?  33,3.5,4.5
 ?  40,3.5,8
 ?  41,4,4.5
 ?  48,4,8
 ?  49,4.5,8
 ?  55,7.5,8
 ?  56,4.5,7.5
 ?  62,7.5,7.5
```

```
ENTER NUMBER OF DIFFERENT KINDS OF MATERIALS OCCURRING
ON THE CROSS SECTION
 ? 1
MATERIAL PROPERTIES:
MODULUS OF ELASTICITY, POISSON'S RATIO
 ? 30.0E+06,.27
NUMBER OF THIN SEGMENTS
 ? 4
ENTER FOR EACH THIN SEGMENT <NROW1,NFREE> WHERE:
    NROW1=NUMBER OF ROWS OF QUADRILATERALS IN EACH THIN SEGMENT
    NFREE=INITIAL CONDITION OF EACH THIN SEGMENT
                 1=FREE EDGE
                 0=OTHERWISE
 ? 1,1
 ? 1,0
 ? 1,0
 ? 1,0
NUMBER OF ELEMENT DEFINITION LINES FOR EACH THIN SEGMENT
THESE SHOULD BE INPUT ACCORDING TO THE INPUT ORDER OF THIN SEGMENTS
 ? 1
 ? 2
 ? 2
 ? 2
QUADRILATERAL DEFINITION:
NODE1,NODE2,NODE3,NODE4,NUMBER OF ELEMENTS TO BE GENERATED,
MATERIAL CODE NUMBER
 ? 1,2,11,10,7,1
 ? 17,18,26,19,0,1
 ? 19,26,27,20,5,1
 ? 25,32,41,33,0,1
 ? 33,41,42,34,6,1
 ? 47,56,49,48,0,1
 ? 56,57,50,49,5,1


    ***************LOADING CONDITIONS***************

AXIAL FORCE
 ? 0
Z-COORD. OF AXIAL FORCE
 ? 0
Y-COORD. OF AXIAL FORCE
 ? 0
BENDING MOMENT ABOUT Y-AXIS
 ? 0
BENDING MOMENT ABOUT Z-AXIS
 ? 0
SHEAR FORCE IN Y-DIRECTION
 ? 0
SHEAR FORCE IN Z-DIRECTION
 ? 0
Y-COORD. OF THE Z-COMPONENT OF THE SHEAR FORCE
 ? 0
Z-COORD. OF THE Y-COMPONENT OF THE SHEAR FORCE
 ? 0
APPLIED TWISTING MOMENT
 ? 1000
BIMOMENT
 ? 239055
WARPING TORQUE
 ? 10000
ENTER OPT3,WHERE:
    1-FOR PRINTOUT OF NORMAL STRESSES DUE TO BENDING MOMENTS ONLY
      (OPT1 MUST BE 2,3,OR 4)
    0-OTHERWISE
 ? 0
ENTER OPT4,WHERE:
    1-FOR PRINTOUT OF SHEAR STRESSES DUE TO SHEAR FORCES ONLY
      (OPT1 MUST BE 3 OR 4)
    0-OTHERWISE
 ? 0
ENTER OPT5,WHERE:
    1-FOR PRINTOUT OF SHEAR STRESSES DUE TO TWISTING MOMENT ONLY
      (OPT1 MUST BE 3 OR 4)
```

```
       0-OTHERWISE
   ? 0
ENTER OPT6,WHERE:
       1-FOR PRINTOUT OF NORMAL STRESSES DUE TO
         CONSTRAINED WARPING ONLY (OPT1 MUST BE 4)
       0-OTHERWISE
   ? 1
ENTER OPT7,WHERE:
       1-WARPING FUNCTION PRINTED (OPT1 MUST BE 3 OR 4)
       0-NOT PRINTED
   ? 0
ENTER OPT8,WHERE:
       1-GRAPH OF CROSS SECTION PRINTED
       0-NO GRAPH PRINTED
   ? 0

DO YOU WANT THE INPUT DATA FOR THE CROSS-SECTION PRINTED
(ANSWER:YES OR NO)
   ? NO
```

PROGRAM BEAMSTRESS - OUTPUT

STRESSES ON THE CROSS SECTION

COORDINATES OF ELEMENT CENTROID		NORMAL STRESSES	SHEAR STRESSES	
Y	Z	SIGMA	TXY	TXZ
.250	.250	-14.890E+03	39.753E-11	-15.894E+01
.750	.250	-11.976E+03	61.436E-11	18.069E-11
1.250	.250	-90.633E+02	39.753E-11	18.069E-11
1.750	.250	-61.501E+02	48.787E-11	25.297E-11
2.250	.250	-32.369E+02	19.876E-11	19.876E-11
2.750	.250	-32.369E+01	25.297E-11	36.139E-12
3.250	.250	25.895E+02	27.104E-11	-52.980E+00

SHEAR FLOWS DUE TO CONSTRAINED WARPING

ELEMENT NUMBER	WARPING SHEAR FLOWS
1	0.
1	15.571E+01
2	28.096E+01
3	37.574E+01
4	44.006E+01
5	47.391E+01
6	47.730E+01
7	45.022E+01
8	39.335E+01

NORMAL STRESSES DUE TO CONSTRAINED WARPING

COORDINATES OF ELEMENT CENTROID		NORMAL STRESSES
Y	Z	SIGMA
.250	.250	-14.890E+03
.750	.250	-11.976E+03
1.250	.250	-90.633E+02

```
1.750       .250      -61.501E+02
2.250       .250      -32.369E+02
2.750       .250      -32.369E+01
3.250       .250       25.895E+02
```

CROSS-SECTIONAL PROPERTIES:

AREA OF SECTION...   75.00000E-01

Y-COORDINATE OF CENTROID...   37.50000E-01

Z-COORDINATE OF CENTROID...   40.00000E-01

Y-MOMENT OF INERTIA...   70.62500E+00

Z-MOMENT OF INERTIA...   17.65625E+00

PRODUCT OF INERTIA....   26.25000E+00

ANGLE TO PRINCIPAL AXES...   67.63

Y-RADIUS OF GYRATION   3.06866E+00

Z-RADIUS OF GYRATION   1.53433E+00

POLAR MOMENT OF INERTIA   8.82813E+01

Y-PRINCIPAL MOMENT OF INERTIA...   6.85142E+00

Z-PRINCIPAL MOMENT OF INERTIA...   8.14298E+01

IYZ-PRINCIPAL   0.

I MAX...   8.14298E+01

I MIN...   6.85142E+00

Y-COORDINATE OF SHEAR CENTER...   37.50000E-01

Z-COORDINATE OF SHEAR CENTER...   40.00000E-01

SHEAR COEFFICIENT AYY...   20.29275E-01

SHEAR COEFFICIENT AZZ...   21.94592E-01

SHEAR COEFFICIENT AYZ...   22.07667E-02

WARPING CONSTANT...   15.38617E+01

TORSIONAL CONSTANT...   78.64583E-02

PARTIAL SUMMARY OF FORCES ON THE CROSS SECTION

TOTAL BENDING MOMENT MY...   0.

TOTAL BENDING MOMENT MZ...   0.

TOTAL TWISTING MOMENT...   10.00000E+02

Example 7:   Restrained Torsional Warping Stresses in WF Section

Find all of the restrained warping stresses and cross-sectional
properties of the WF section in Fig. 18 subjected to a bimoment =
10,000 lb-in^2 and warping torque = 20,000 lb-in.   The beam cross section is homogeneous,with the modulus of elasticity and Poisson's
ratio being 29(10^6) psi and 0.27,respectively.

```
WILL INPUT BE FROM THE TERMINAL (ENTER 1)
OR FROM A PREVIOUSLY CREATED DATA FILE (ENTER 2)
 ? 1
DO YOU WANT TO SAVE A COPY OF YOUR INPUT DATA (YES OR NO)
 ? YES
UNDER WHAT NAME?
 ? EXAM7


*************** PROGRAM BEAMSTRESS - DATA INPUT ***************

WHAT TYPE OF INPUT FORMAT DO YOU DESIRE
        1-PROMPTED
        2-NON-PROMPTED
        3-INPUT FROM DATA FILE
 ? 1
INPUT PROBLEM TITLE
 ? EXAMPLE 7 RESTRAINED WARPING STRESSES IN WF SECTION
ENTER OPT1,WHERE:
        1-ONLY CROSS-SECTIONAL PROPERTIES
        2-ONLY NORMAL STRESSES(WARPING EFFECTS NOT INCLUDED)
         AND CROSS-SECTIONAL PROPERTIES
        3-NORMAL AND SHEAR STRESSES(WARPING EFFECTS NOT INCLUDED)
         AND CROSS-SECTIONAL PROPERTIES
        4-NORMAL AND SHEAR STRESSES,INCLUDED CONSTRAINED WARPING
         EFFECTS,AND CROSS-SECTIONAL PROPERTIES
         WARPING SHEAR STRESSES ARE ACCURATE ONLY FOR THIN-WALLED
         OPEN SECTIONS AND REQUIRE A SUBSTANTIAL INCREASE
         IN THE AMOUNT OF INPUT
 ? 4
ENTER OPT2,WHERE:
        1-HOMOGENEOUS CROSS SECTION
        2-COMPOSITE CROSS SECTION
 ? 1
IS THERE SYMMETRY ABOUT THE Y-AXIS(1-YES,0-NO)
 ? 0
IS THERE SYMMETRY ABOUT THE Z-AXIS(1-YES,0-NO)
 ? 0
NUMBER OF NODAL POINT LINES TO BE INPUT
 ? 24
NODAL POINT NUMBER, Y-COORD, Z-COORD
 ? 1,.75,0
 ? 9,3.75,0
 ? 10,.75,.5
 ? 18,3.75,.5
 ? 19,6.375,0
 ? 25,4.125,0
 ? 26,6.375,.5
 ? 32,4.125,.5
 ? 33,3.375,.875
 ? 41,3.375,3.875
 ? 42,3.75,.875
 ? 50,3.75,3.875
 ? 51,3.375,4.25
 ? 58,3.375,6.875
 ? 59,3.75,4.25
 ? 66,3.75,6.875
 ? 67,0,6.875
 ? 75,3,6.875
 ? 76,0,7.375
```

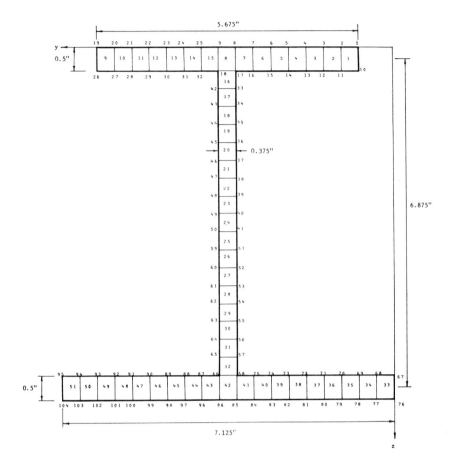

Fig. 18 Example 7

```
? 86,3.75,7.375
? 87,4.125,6.875
? 95,7.125,6.875
? 96,4.125,7.375
? 104,7.125,7.375
ENTER NUMBER OF DIFFERENT KINDS OF MATERIALS OCCURRING
ON THE CROSS SECTION
 ? 1
MATERIAL PROPERTIES:
MODULUS OF ELASTICITY, POISSON'S RATIO
 ? 30.0E+06,.27
NUMBER OF THIN SEGMENTS
 ? 6
ENTER FOR EACH THIN SEGMENT <NROW1,NFREE> WHERE:
     NROW1=NUMBER OF ROWS OF QUADRILATERALS IN EACH THIN SEGMENT
     NFREE=INITIAL CONDITION OF EACH THIN SEGMENT
                1=FREE EDGE
                0=OTHERWISE
```

```
?  1,1
?  1,1
?  1,0
?  1,0
?  1,1
?  1,0
```
NUMBER OF ELEMENT DEFINITION LINES FOR EACH THIN SEGMENT
THESE SHOULD BE INPUT ACCORDING TO THE INPUT ORDER OF THIN SEGMENTS
```
?  1
?  2
?  2
?  2
?  3
?  2
```
QUADRILATERAL DEFINITION:
NODE1,NODE2,NODE3,NODE4,NUMBER OF ELEMENTS TO BE GENERATED,
MATERIAL CODE NUMBER
```
?  1,2,11,10,7,1
?  20,19,26,27,5,1
?  9,25,32,18,0,1
?  17,18,42,33,0,1
?  33,42,43,34,7,1
?  41,50,59,51,0,1
?  51,59,60,52,6,1
?  67,68,77,76,7,1
?  75,58,85,84,0,1
?  58,66,86,85,0,1
?  66,87,96,86,0,1
?  87,88,97,96,7,1
```

*****************LOADING CONDITIONS***************

AXIAL FORCE
? 0
Z-COORD. OF AXIAL FORCE
? 0
Y-COORD. OF AXIAL FORCE
? 0
BENDING MOMENT ABOUT Y-AXIS
? 0
BENDING MOMENT ABOUT Z-AXIS
? 0
SHEAR FORCE IN Y-DIRECTION
? 0
SHEAR FORCE IN Z-DIRECTION
? 0
Y-COORD. OF THE Z-COMPONENT OF THE SHEAR FORCE
? 0
Z-COORD. OF THE Y-COMPONENT OF THE SHEAR FORCE
? 0
APPLIED TWISTING MOMENT
? 0
BIMOMENT
? 10000
WARPING TORQUE
? 20000
ENTER OPT3,WHERE:
    1-FOR PRINTOUT OF NORMAL STRESSES DUE TO BENDING MOMENTS ONLY
      (OPT1 MUST BE 2,3,OR 4)
    0-OTHERWISE
? 0
ENTER OPT4,WHERE:
    1-FOR PRINTOUT OF SHEAR STRESSES DUE TO SHEAR FORCES ONLY
      (OPT1 MUST BE 3 OR 4)
    0-OTHERWISE
? 0
ENTER OPT5,WHERE:
    1-FOR PRINTOUT OF SHEAR STRESSES DUE TO TWISTING MOMENT ONLY
      (OPT1 MUST BE 3 OR 4)
    0-OTHERWISE

```
? 0
ENTER OPT6,WHERE:
    1-FOR PRINTOUT OF NORMAL STRESSES DUE TO
    CONSTRAINED WARPING ONLY (OPT1 MUST BE 4)
    0-OTHERWISE
? 1
ENTER OPT7,WHERE:
    1-WARPING FUNCTION PRINTED (OPT1 MUST BE 3 OR 4)
    0-NOT PRINTED
? 0
ENTER OPT8,WHERE:
    1-GRAPH OF CROSS SECTION PRINTED
    0-NO GRAPH PRINTED
? 0

DO YOU WANT THE INPUT DATA FOR THE CROSS-SECTION PRINTED
(ANSWER:YES OR NO)
? NO

            ***PROGRAM BEAMSTRESS - OUTPUT***

    STRESSES ON THE CROSS SECTION
```

COORDINATES OF ELEMENT CENTROID		NORMAL STRESSES	SHEAR STRESSES	
Y	Z	SIGMA	TXY	TXZ
.938	.250	-51.602E+01	0.	0.
1.313	.250	-44.213E+01	0.	0.
1.688	.250	-36.823E+01	0.	0.
2.063	.250	-29.433E+01	0.	0.
2.438	.250	-22.043E+01	0.	0.
2.813	.250	-14.653E+01	0.	0.
3.188	.250	-72.633E+00	0.	0.
3.563	.250	-14.552E-10	0.	0.

```
    SHEAR FLOWS DUE TOS DUE TO CONSTRAINED WARPING
```

ELEMENT NUMBER	WARPING SHEAR FLOWS
1	0.
1	19.351E+01
2	35.931E+01
3	49.739E+01
4	60.777E+01
5	69.043E+01
6	74.538E+01
7	77.261E+01
8	77.261E+01

```
    NORMAL STRESSES DUE TO CONSTRAINED WARPING
```

COORDINATES OF ELEMENT CENTROID		NORMAL STRESSES
Y	Z	SIGMA
.938	.250	-51.602E+01
1.313	.250	-44.213E+01

```
1.688     .250     -36.823E+01
2.063     .250     -29.433E+01
2.438     .250     -22.043E+01
2.813     .250     -14.653E+01
3.188     .250     -72.633E+00
3.563     .250     -14.552E-10
6.188     .250      51.602E+01
```

CROSS-SECTIONAL PROPERTIES:

AREA OF SECTION...   87.65625E-01

Y-COORDINATE OF CENTROID...   35.62500E-01

Z-COORDINATE OF CENTROID...   39.81618E-01

Y-MOMENT OF INERTIA...   82.80050E+00

Z-MOMENT OF INERTIA...   22.51483E+00

PRODUCT OF INERTIA....   66.39311E-12

ANGLE TO PRINCIPAL AXES...   90.00

Y-RADIUS OF GYRATION   3.07344E+00

Z-RADIUS OF GYRATION   1.60267E+00

POLAR MOMENT OF INERTIA   1.05315E+02

Y-PRINCIPAL MOMENT OF INERTIA...   2.25148E+01

Z-PRINCIPAL MOMENT OF INERTIA...   8.28005E+01

IYZ-PRINCIPAL   0.

I MAX...   8.28005E+01

I MIN...   2.25148E+01

Y-COORDINATE OF SHEAR CENTER...   35.62500E-01

Z-COORDINATE OF SHEAR CENTER...   48.53192E-01

SHEAR COEFFICIENT AYY...   16.42660E-01

SHEAR COEFFICIENT AZZ...   35.13953E-01

SHEAR COEFFICIENT AYZ...   11.51182E-14

WARPING CONSTANT...   23.35873E+01

TORSIONAL CONSTANT...   78.04153E-02

PARTIAL SUMMARY OF FORCES ON THE CROSS SECTION

TOTAL BENDING MOMENT MY...   0.

TOTAL BENDING MOMENT MZ...   0.

TOTAL TWISTING MOMENT...   0.

Example 8:   Shear Stress Analysis of a Composite Beam

Find the shear stresses in the square section shown in Fig. 19.   Do
not include the effects of constrained warping.   The cross section is
composed of two materials as indicated in Fig. 19.   The modulii of
elasticity and Poisson's ratio for these materials are

Material number 1, $E = 30(10^6)$ psi $\nu = 0.27$

Material number 2, $E = 10(10^6)$ psi $\nu = 0.27$

The applied forces on the cross section are

Shear forces applied at y = 5 in, z = 5 in with
  z component = 5000 lb
  y component =   0 lb
Twisting moment about x axis = 2000 in-lb

Also calculate cross-sectional properties.

```
WILL INPUT BE FROM THE TERMINAL (ENTER 1)
OR FROM A PREVIOUSLY CREATED DATA FILE (ENTER 2)
? 1
DO YOU WANT TO SAVE A COPY OF YOUR INPUT DATA?
(TYPE 'YES' OR 'NO')
? YES

UNDER WHAT NAME?
? EXAM8

*************** PROGRAM BEAMSTRESS - DATA INPUT ***************

WHAT TYPE OF INPUT FORMAT DO YOU DESIRE
       1-PROMPTED
       2-NON-PROMPTED
       3-INPUT FROM DATA FILE
    ? 1
INPUT PROBLEM TITLE
    ? EXAMPLE 8 SHEAR STRESS ANALYSIS OF A COMPOSITE BEAM
ENTER OPT1,WHERE:
       1-ONLY CROSS-SECTIONAL PROPERTIES
       2-ONLY NORMAL STRESSES(WARPING EFFECTS NOT INCLUDED)
         AND CROSS-SECTIONAL PROPERTIES
       3-NORMAL AND SHEAR STRESSES(WARPING EFFECTS NOT INCLUDED)
         AND CROSS-SECTIONAL PROPERTIES
       4-NORMAL AND SHEAR STRESSES,INCLUDED CONSTRAINED WARPING
         EFFECTS,AND CROSS-SECTIONAL PROPERTIES
         WARPING SHEAR STRESSES ARE ACCURATE ONLY FOR THIN-WALLED
         OPEN SECTIONS AND REQUIRE A SUBSTANTIAL INCREASE
         IN THE AMOUNT OF INPUT
    ? 3
ENTER OPT2,WHERE:
       1-HOMOGENEOUS CROSS SECTION
       2-COMPOSITE CROSS SECTION
    ? 2
IS THERE SYMMETRY ABOUT THE Y-AXIS(1-YES,0-NO)
    ? 0
IS THERE SYMMETRY ABOUT THE Z-AXIS(1-YES,0-NO)
    ? 0
NUMBER OF NODAL POINT LINES TO BE INPUT
    ? 18
NUMBER OF ELEMENT DEFINITION LINES TO BE INPUT
    ? 8
NODAL POINT NUMBER, Y-COORD, Z-COORD
    ? 1,0,0
```

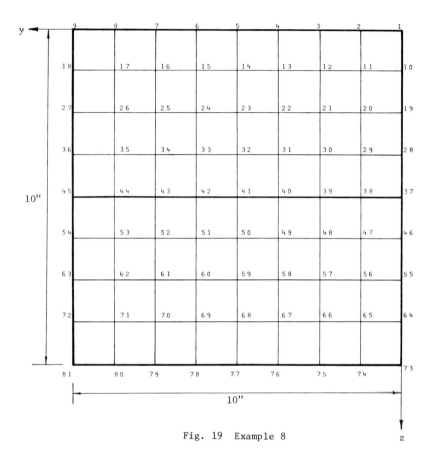

Fig. 19   Example 8

? 9,10,0
? 10,0,1.25
? 18,10,1.25
? 19,0,2.5
? 27,10,2.5
? 28,0,3.75
? 36,10,3.75
? 37,0,5
? 45,10,5
? 46,0,6.25
? 54,10,6.25
? 55,0,7.5
? 63,10,7.5
? 64,0,8.75
? 72,10,8.75
? 73,0,10
? 81,10,10
ENTER NUMBER OF DIFFERENT KINDS OF MATERIALS OCCURRING
ON THE CROSS SECTION
   ? 2

```
MATERIAL PROPERTIES:
MODULUS OF ELASTICITY, POISSON'S RATIO
 ? 30.0E+06,.27
 ? 10.0E+06,.27
QUADRILATERAL DEFINITION
NODE1,NODE2,NODE3,NODE4,NUMBER OF ELEMENTS TO BE GENERATED
BY THE PROGRAM,MATERIAL CODE NUMBER
 ? 1,2,11,10,7,1
 ? 10,11,20,19,7,1
 ? 19,20,29,28,7,1
 ? 28,29,38,37,7,1
 ? 37,38,47,46,7,2
 ? 46,47,56,55,7,2
 ? 55,56,65,64,7,2
 ? 64,65,74,73,7,2


  ****************LOADING CONDITIONS****************

AXIAL FORCE
 ? 0
Z-COORD. OF AXIAL FORCE
 ? 0
Y-COORD. OF AXIAL FORCE
 ? 0
BENDING MOMENT ABOUT Y-AXIS
 ? 0
BENDING MOMENT ABOUT Z-AXIS
 ? 0
SHEAR FORCE IN Y-DIRECTION
 ? 0
SHEAR FORCE IN Z-DIRECTION
 ? 10000
Y-COORD. OF THE Z-COMPONENT OF THE SHEAR FORCE
 ? 5
Z-COORD. OF THE Y-COMPONENT OF THE SHEAR FORCE
 ? 5
APPLIED TWISTING MOMENT
 ? 2000
ENTER OPT3,WHERE:
       1-FOR PRINTOUT OF NORMAL STRESSES DUE TO BENDING MOMENTS ONLY
         (OPT1 MUST BE 2,3,OR 4)
       0-OTHERWISE
 ? 0
ENTER OPT4,WHERE:
       1-FOR PRINTOUT OF SHEAR STRESSES DUE TO SHEAR FORCES ONLY
         (OPT1 MUST BE 3 OR 4)
       0-OTHERWISE
 ? 1
ENTER OPT5,WHERE:
       1-FOR PRINTOUT OF SHEAR STRESSES DUE TO TWISTING MOMENT ONLY
         (OPT1 MUST BE 3 OR 4)
       0-OTHERWISE
 ? 1
ENTER OPT6,WHERE:
       1-FOR PRINTOUT OF NORMAL STRESSES DUE TO
         CONSTRAINED WARPING ONLY (OPT1 MUST BE 4)
       0-OTHERWISE
 ? 0
ENTER OPT7,WHERE:
       1-WARPING FUNCTION PRINTED (OPT1 MUST BE 3 OR 4)
       0-NOT PRINTED
 ? 0
ENTER OPT8,WHERE:
       1-GRAPH OF CROSS SECTION PRINTED
       0-NO GRAPH PRINTED
 ? 0

DO YOU WANT THE INPUT DATA FOR THE CROSS-SECTION PRINTED
(ANSWER:YES OR NO)
 ? NO
```

PROGRAM BEAMSTRESS - OUTPUT

STRESSES ON THE CROSS SECTION

COORDINATES OF ELEMENT CENTROID		NORMAL STRESSES	SHEAR STRESSES	
Y	Z	SIGMA	TXY	TXZ
.625	.625	0.	-62.903E-01	51.685E+00
1.875	.625	0.	-78.727E-01	44.182E+00
3.125	.625	0.	-20.827E-01	41.617E+00
4.375	.625	0.	65.962E-01	40.826E+00
5.625	.625	0.	15.550E+00	41.281E+00
6.875	.625	0.	22.408E+00	43.147E+00
8.125	.625	0.	23.896E+00	47.431E+00
9.375	.625	0.	13.621E+00	59.062E+00
.625	1.875	0.	-11.706E-01	12.521E+01
1.875	1.875	0.	-18.592E-01	11.201E+01

SHEAR STRESSES DUE TO SHEAR FORCES

COORDINATES OF ELEMENT CENTROID		SHEAR STRESSES	
Y	Z	TXY	TXZ
.625	.625	-99.554E-01	55.373E+00
1.875	.625	-15.884E+00	45.806E+00
3.125	.625	-12.245E+00	42.382E+00
4.375	.625	-44.767E-01	41.053E+00
5.625	.625	44.767E-01	41.053E+00
6.875	.625	12.245E+00	42.382E+00
8.125	.625	15.884E+00	45.806E+00
9.375	.625	99.554E-01	55.373E+00
.625	1.875	-25.813E-01	13.311E+01
1.875	1.875	-55.948E-01	11.618E+01

SHEAR STRESSES DUE TO UNRESTRAINED TWISTING MOMENT

COORDINATES OF ELEMENT CENTROID		SHEAR STRESSES	
Y	Z	TXY	TXZ
.625	.625	36.651E-01	-36.886E-01
1.875	.625	80.116E-01	-16.244E-01
3.125	.625	10.163E+00	-76.534E-02
4.375	.625	11.073E+00	-22.758E-02
5.625	.625	11.073E+00	22.758E-02
6.875	.625	10.163E+00	76.534E-02
8.125	.625	80.116E-01	16.244E-01
9.375	.625	36.651E-01	36.886E-01
.625	1.875	14.108E-01	-78.944E-01
1.875	1.875	37.356E-01	-41.783E-01

MODULUS-WEIGHTED CROSS-SECTIONAL PROPERTIES

AREA OF SECTION...   66.66667E+00

Y-COORDINATE OF CENTROID...   50.00000E-01

Z-COORDINATE OF CENTROID...   37.50000E-01

Y-MOMENT OF INERTIA...   45.13889E+01

```
Z-MOMENT OF INERTIA...    55.55556E+01

PRODUCT OF INERTIA....    47.29372E-11
ANGLE TO PRINCIPAL AXES...         .00

Y-RADIUS OF GYRATION     2.60208E+00

Z-RADIUS OF GYRATION     2.88675E+00

POLAR MOMENT OF INERTIA     1.00694E+03

Y-PRINCIPAL MOMENT OF INERTIA...    4.51389E+02

Z-PRINCIPAL MOMENT OF INERTIA...    5.55556E+02

IYZ-PRINCIPAL          0.

I MAX...    5.55556E+02

I MIN...    4.51389E+02

Y-COORDINATE OF SHEAR CENTER...    50.00000E-01

Z-COORDINATE OF SHEAR CENTER...    38.50134E-01

SHEAR COEFFICIENT AYY...    17.83378E-01

SHEAR COEFFICIENT AZZ...    20.21310E-01

SHEAR COEFFICIENT AYZ...    68.59964E-15

WARPING CONSTANT...    24.36587E+01

TORSIONAL CONSTANT...    81.23105E+01


        PARTIAL SUMMARY OF FORCES ON THE CROSS SECTION

TOTAL BENDING MOMENT MY...         0.

TOTAL BENDING MOMENT MZ...         0.

TOTAL TWISTING MOMENT...    20.00000E+02
```

Example 9: Stress Analysis of Prestressed Concrete Bridge Girder

For the prestressed bridge girder illustrated in Figs. 20-21, compute
the stresses, taking no constrained warping effects into account, on
the cross section subjected to the following loadings:

Compressive axial force of 2 224 000 N (newtons) due to pre-
    stressing applied at

$$y = \quad 0 \text{ m (meter)}$$
$$z = 0.76 \text{ m (meter)}$$
Bending moment about y axis = 1 139 000 N·m
Bending moment about z axis = $\quad$ 0 N·m
Shear forces applied at y = 0 m, z = 0.5325 m with
            y component = $\quad$ 0 N
            z component = 143 400 N

Also, find the cross-sectional properties. The modulus of elasticity
is 27.79 (10^9) N/m^2 and Poisson's ratio is 0.15.
    As indicated in Fig. 20b, use is made of the symmetry option of
the program.
    The nonprompting mode of input is illustrated.

```
WILL INPUT BE FROM THE TERMINAL (ENTER 1)
OR FROM A PREVIOUSLY CREATED DATA FILE (ENTER 2)
? 1
DO YOU WANT TO SAVE A COPY OF YOUR INPUT DATA?
(TYPE 'YES' OR 'NO')
? YES
UNDER WHAT NAME?
? EXAM9

*************** PROGRAM BEAMSTRESS - DATA INPUT ****************

WHAT TYPE OF INPUT FORMAT DO YOU DESIRE
    1-PROMPTED
    2-NON-PROMPTED
    3-INPUT FROM DATA FILE
? 2
? EXAMPLE 9 STRESS ANALYSIS OF PRESTRESSED CONCRETE BRIDGE GIRDER
? 3
? 1
? 0
? 1
? 76
? 30
? 1,.3,0
? 5,.09,0
? 7,0,0
? 8,.3,.0375
? 12,.09,.0375
? 14,0,.0375
? 15,.3,.075
? 19,.09,.075
? 21,0,.075
? 22,.3,.1125
? 26,.09,.1125
? 28,0,.1125
? 29,.3,.15
? 33,.09,.15
? 35,0,.15
? 36,.27375,.159375
? 37,.2475,.16875
? 38,.195,.1875
? 40,.09,.1875
? 42,0,.1875
? 43,.16875,.196875
? 44,.1425,.20625
? 45,.09,.225
? 47,0,.225
? 48,.09,.27
? 50,0,.27
? 51,.09,.315
? 53,0,.315
? 54,.09,.36
? 56,0,.36
? 57,.09,.405
? 59,0,.405
? 60,.09,.45
? 62,0,.45
? 63,.09,.495
? 65,0,.495
? 66,.09,.54
? 68,0,.54
? 69,.09,.585
? 71,0,.585
```

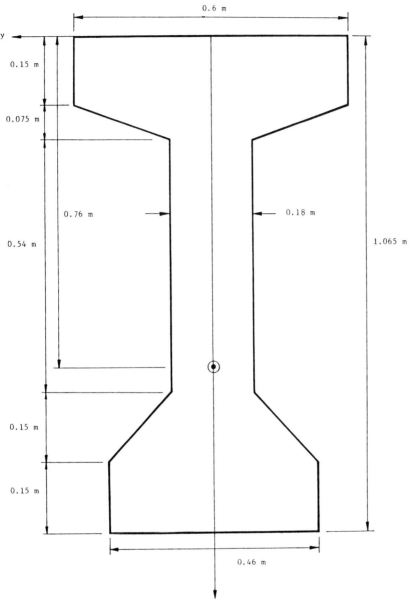

Fig. 20a   Example 9

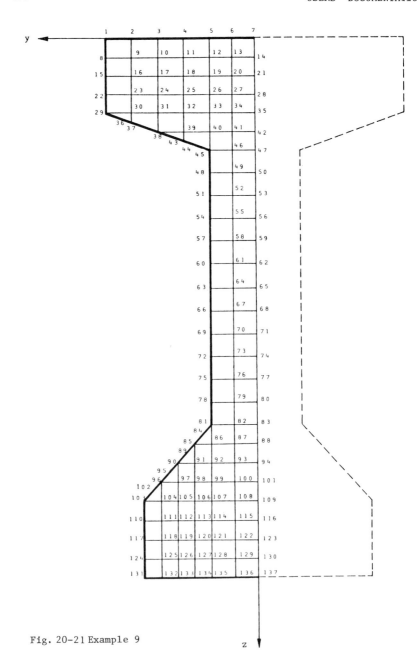

Fig. 20-21 Example 9

```
?  72,.09,.63
?  74,0,.63
?  75,.09,.675
?  77,0,.675
?  78,.09,.72
?  80,0,.72
?  81,.09,.765
?  83,0,.765
?  84,.1075,.78375
?  85,.125,.8025
?  86,.09,.8025
?  88,0,.8025
?  89,.1425,.82125
?  90,.16,.84
?  92,.09,.84
?  94,0,.84
?  95,.1775,.85875
?  96,.195,.8775
?  99,.09,.8775
?  101,0,.8775
?  102,.2125,.89625
?  103,.23,.915
?  107,.09,.915
?  109,0,.915
?  110,.23,.9525
?  114,.09,.9525
?  116,0,.9525
?  117,.23,.99
?  121,.09,.99
?  123,0,.99
?  124,.23,1.0275
?  128,.09,1.0275
?  130,0,1.0275
?  131,.23,1.065
?  135,.09,1.065
?  137,0,1.065
?  1
?  27790000000.,,.15
?  1,8,9,2,5,1
?  8,15,16,9,5,1
?  15,22,23,16,5,1
?  22,29,30,23,5,1
?  29,36,37,30,5,1
?  38,43,44,39,3,1
?  45,48,49,46,1,1
?  48,51,52,49,1,1
?  51,54,55,52,1,1
?  54,57,58,55,1,1
?  57,60,61,58,1,1
?  60,63,64,61,1,1
?  63,66,67,64,1,1
?  66,69,70,67,1,1
?  69,72,73,70,1,1
?  72,75,76,73,1,1
?  75,78,79,76,1,1
?  78,81,82,79,1,1
?  84,85,86,81,0,1
?  81,86,87,82,1,1
?  89,90,91,85,0,1
?  85,91,92,86,2,1
?  95,96,97,90,0,1
?  90,97,98,91,3,1
?  102,103,104,96,0,1
?  96,104,105,97,4,1
?  103,110,111,104,5,1
?  110,117,118,111,5,1
?  117,124,125,118,5,1
?  124,131,132,125,5,1
?  -2224000.
?  .76
?  0.
?  1139000.
```

```
? 0.
? 0.
? 143400.
? 0.
? 0.
? 0.
? 0
? 0
? 0
? 0
? 0
? 0
```

```
DO YOU WANT THE INPUT DATA FOR THE CROSS-SECTION PRINTED
(ANSWER:YES OR NO)
 ? NO
```

```
                ***PROGRAM BEAMSTRESS - OUTPUT***
```

EXAMPLE 9 STRESS ANALYSIS OF PRESTRESSED CONCRETE BRIDGE GIRDER

STRESSES ON THE CROSS SECTION

COORDINATES OF ELEMENT CENTROID		NORMAL STRESSES	SHEAR STRESSES	
Y	Z	SIGMA	TXY	TXZ
.274	.019	-13.027E+06	-21.388E+03	15.423E+03
.221	.019	-13.027E+06	-61.247E+03	18.147E+03
.169	.019	-13.027E+06	-85.341E+03	25.589E+03
.116	.019	-13.027E+06	-84.483E+03	34.955E+03
.067	.019	-13.027E+06	-59.731E+03	42.839E+03
.022	.019	-13.027E+06	-21.670E+03	46.986E+03
.274	.056	-12.540E+06	-26.575E+03	39.236E+03
.221	.056	-12.540E+06	-73.318E+03	49.739E+03
.169	.056	-12.540E+06	-10.145E+04	73.134E+03
.116	.056	-12.540E+06	-10.084E+04	10.293E+04

CROSS-SECTIONAL PROPERTIES:

AREA OF SECTION...   33.34500E-02

Y-COORDINATE OF CENTROID...   0.

Z-COORDINATE OF CENTROID...   50.77418E-02

Y-MOMENT OF INERTIA...   44.45468E-03

Z-MOMENT OF INERTIA...   51.45377E-04

PRODUCT OF INERTIA....   0.

ANGLE TO PRINCIPAL AXES...   0.

Y-RADIUS OF GYRATION   3.65127E-01

Z-RADIUS OF GYRATION   1.24220E-01

POLAR MOMENT OF INERTIA   4.96001E-02

Y-PRINCIPAL MOMENT OF INERTIA...   4.44547E-02

Z-PRINCIPAL MOMENT OF INERTIA...   5.14538E-03

IYZ-PRINCIPAL   0.

```
I MAX...    4.44547E-02

I MIN...    5.14538E-03

Y-COORDINATE OF SHEAR CENTER...          0.

Z-COORDINATE OF SHEAR CENTER...    40.98767E-02

SHEAR COEFFICIENT AYY...    15.05290E-01

SHEAR COEFFICIENT AZZ...    18.28797E-01

SHEAR COEFFICIENT AYZ...          0.

WARPING CONSTANT...    67.31917E-05

TORSIONAL CONSTANT...    51.25863E-04


     PARTIAL SUMMARY OF FORCES ON THE CROSS SECTION

TOTAL BENDING MOMENT MY...    57.79777E+04

TOTAL BENDING MOMENT MZ...          0.

TOTAL TWISTING MOMENT...          0.
```

INPUT DEFINITIONS

The definitions necessary to create an input data file or to use the nonprompting input option are presented in this section.

1. TITLE   Input problem title or other information

2. OPT1   Type of results desired
             1 = only cross-sectional properties
             2 = only normal stresses (warping effects not included)
                 and non-shear-related cross-sectional properties
             3 = normal and shear stresses (warping effects not in-
                 cluded) and cross-sectional properties
             4 = normal and shear stresses, included constrained
                 warping effects, and cross-sectional properties.
                 Warping shear stresses are accurate only for thin-
                 walled open sections and require a substantial in-
                 crease in the amount of input.

3. OPT2   Type of cross sections
             1 = homogeneous
             2 = composite

4. IYSYM   Symmetry of cross section about the y axis
             $\emptyset$ = NO
             1 = YES

5. IZSYM   Symmetry of cross section about the z axis
             $\emptyset$ = NO
             1 = YES

6. NNPC   Number of nodal point lines of input (see item 8) (max.
            200). For non-shear-related properties (OPT1 = 2) any
            convenient size quadrilaterals can be selected. Other-
            wise (OPT1 = 1, 3, or 4) a fine mesh size is required,
            especially near irregularities, as the accuracy of re-
            sults depends upon the mesh size.

7. NELEMC   Number of lines of input defining the elements (see item
            11) (max. 130) (not needed if OPT1 = 4; i.e., the warp-
            ing stresses are to be calculated)

8. N, Y(N), Z(N)   Nodal point number, y coordinate, z coordinate
            (number of these lines of input specified by item 6).
            One line is needed for each nodal point, except when
            using the automatic node generation option. Nodal point
            lines must be organized in increasing numerical sequence.
            If lines of input are omitted for a series of nodes,
            their coordinates are automatically generated by dividing
            the line connecting the defining nodes into equal inter-
            vals. See the introduction for suggestions in numbering
            nodal points such that the bandwidth will be minimized.
            The maximum difference between any two nodal point num-
            bers for a quadrilateral must not exceed 50.

9. NUME   Number of different kinds of materials occurring on the
            cross section (max. 5)

10. E$\emptyset$(I), NU$\emptyset$(I)   Modulus of elasticity, Poisson's ratio. One line
            of input is needed for each kind of material occurring
            on the cross section. The material in the first line
            will be called material number 1, in the second line will
            be called material number 2, and so on. The material
            numbers (material code numbers) will be used to identify
            the material property in each quadrilateral (on item 11
            or 15). The number of lines on this item must be equal
            to the number of kinds of material (NUME) designated on
            item 9.

11. NOD(N,1), NOD(N,2), NOD(N,3), NOD(N,4), NMIS, ENUM(N)
            Quadrilateral definition (nodes 1, 2, 3, 4 in counter-
            clockwise sequence), number of elements to be generated,
            material code number (from item 10) to specify the
            material property for each element (number of these
            lines specified by item 7). This item is not needed if
            the warping stresses are to be calculated (OPT1 = 4).
            Otherwise, one line is needed for each quadrilateral,
            except for the automatic element and material property
            generation described below. If element and material code
            lines are omitted, the program automatically generates
            the omitted information by incrementing the preceding
            nodal point numbers by one and assigning the same materi-
            al property of the preceding element to the elements
            with omitted information. Skip to item 16 if con-
            strained warping effects are not considered. (OPT1 = 1,

2, or 3.)

12. NPLATE   Number of thin segments that form the thin-walled section
              (see the introduction for definition and suggestions on
              thin segments) (not needed if OPT1 = 1, 2, 3)

13. NROW1(I), NFREE(I)   Number of rows of quadrilaterals in each
              thin segment, initial condition of each thin segment in
              which 1 = free edge, $\emptyset$ = if the initial end of the thin
              segment is connected to another thin segment(s). One
              line of input is needed for each thin segment. The num-
              ber of lines on this item must be equal to the number of
              thin segments (NPLATE) in item 12. This item is not
              needed if OPT1 = 1, 2, 3.

14. NELEC(I,J)   Number of quadrilateral lines of input, i.e. the
              number of input lines in item 15, for each row of each
              thin segment. These should be entered according to the
              input order of thin segments and rows. This item is not
              needed if OPT1 = 1, 2, 3.

15. NOD(N1,1) NOD(N1,2), NOD(N1,3), NOD(N1,4), NMIS, ENUM(N1)
              Quadrilateral definition (nodes 1, 2, 3, 4 in counter-
              clockwise sequence), number of elements to be generated,
              material code number (from item 10) to specify the
              material property for each element (number of these lines
              specified by item 14). This item is not needed if
              OPT1 = 1, 2, 3. Otherwise, one line is needed for each
              quadrilateral, except for the automatic element and
              material property generation described below. If ele-
              ment and material code lines are omitted, the program
              automatically generates the omitted information by incre-
              menting the preceding nodal point numbers by one and
              assigning the same material property of the preceding
              element to the elements with omitted information.

16. PX   Tensile axial force (not needed if OPT1 = 1). Use nega-
              tive sign if force is compressive.

17. ZP$\emptyset$ z coordinate of axial force (not needed if OPT1 = 1)
              $\emptyset$ if no axial force is applied

18. YP$\emptyset$ y coordinate of axial force (not needed if OPT1 = 1)
              $\emptyset$ if no axial force is applied

19. MY   Bending moment about y axis (not needed if OPT1 = 1) in
              addition to that due to P, the axial force. Positive if
              sense of vector is along the positive y axis.

20. MZ   Bending moment about z axis (not needed if OPT1 = 1) in
              addition to that due to P, the axial force. Positive if
              sense of vector is along the positive z axis.

21. VY   Shear force component in y direction (not needed if

OPT1 = 1 or 2). Positive if sense of vector is along
positive y axis.

22. VZ   Shear force component in z direction (not needed if
             OPT1 = 1 or 2). Positive if sense of vector is along
             positive z axis.

23. YØ   y coordinate of z component of shear force (not needed if
             OPTI = 1 or 2)
             Ø if no shear force is applied

24. ZØ   z coordinate of y component of shear force (not needed
             if OPT1 = 1 or 2)
             Ø if no shear force is applied

25. TMOMNT   Applied twisting moment (not needed if OPT1 = 1 or 2)
             in addition to that due to the Vy, Vz shear forces.
             Positive counterclockwise or, stated otherwise, positive
             if the sense of the vector is along the positive x axis.

26. BIMOM   Bimoment (not needed if OPT1 = 1, 2, or 3). Use the
             sign convention of the technical manual [4] or the Thin-
             walled Beam Response Program of the Structural Members
             Users Group.

27. VPSI   Warping torque (not needed if OPT1 = 1, 2 or 3). Use
             the sign convention of the technical manual [4] or the
             Thin-walled Beam Response Program.

28. OPT3   Printout of normal stresses due to bending moments only
             Ø = not printed
             1 = printed (OPT1 must be 2, 3, or 4)

29. OPT4   Printout of shear stresses due to shear forces only
             Ø = not printed
             1 = printed (OPT1 must be 3 or 4)

30. OPT5   Printout of shear stresses due to twisting moment only
             Ø = not printed
             1 = printed (OPT1 must be 3 or 4)

31. OPT6   Printout of normal stresses due to constrained warping
             only
             Ø = not printed
             1 = printed (OPT1 must be 4)

32. OPT7   Printout of warping function
             Ø = not printed
             1 = printed (OPT1 must be 3 or 4)

33. OPT8   Graph of the cross section printed
             Ø = no graph printed
             1 = graph printed

REFERENCES

1 Herrmann, L. R., "Elastic Torsional Analysis of Irregular Shapes," Journal of the Engineering Mechanics Division, ASCE, Vol. 91, 1965, pp. 11-19.

2 Mason, W. E., and Herrmann, L. R., "Elastic Shear Analysis of General Prismatic Beams," Journal of the Engineering Mechanics Division, ASCE, Vol. 94, 1968, pp. 965-83.

3 Chang, P. Y., Thasanatorn, C., and Pilkey, W. D., "Restrained Warping Stresses in Thin-Walled Open Sections," Journal of the Structural Division, ASCE, Vol. 101, 1975, pp. 2467-72.

4 Pilkey, W. D., and Chang, P. Y., Modern Formulas for Statics, Dynamics, and Stability: Shafts, Beams, Plates, and Shells, McGraw Hill, New York, 1977.

SHAFT: A PROGRAM FOR THE UNBALANCED RESPONSE AND CRITICAL
SPEEDS OF ROTATING SHAFTS

Walter D. Pilkey

University of Virginia

Pin Yu Chang

Hydronautics, Inc.

INTRODUCTION

The program SHAFT is for the flexural unbalanced response and critical speed of a rotating shaft with no cross-coupling coefficients in
the bearings. For unbalance problems, it calculates the component and
resultant deflection, slope, bending moment, shear force, and their
corresponding phase angles along the shaft. The critical speeds are
found for a rotor with no damping in the bearings. The corresponding
mode shapes are also printed out. The shaft can be formed of lumped
or continuous mass segments with foundations, any boundary conditions,
and any distribution of unbalanced masses. The user can include
any or all of bending, shear deformation, and rotary inertia effects.
The bearing systems can include springs, dampers, and a pedestal
mass. The computation for isotropic bearing systems is fully automated. For nonisotropic bearing systems, with no cross-coupling coefficients, the responses in the z and y directions are obtained by
using the program twice with different bearing system constants. The
results are combined as functions of time. Note that the orbit will
be elliptical rather than circular.
SHAFT is one of a family of computer programs for structural members and mechanical elements, e.g., rods, thin-walled beams, plates,
gridworks, torsional systems, shells, maintained by The Structural
Members Users Group.

GENERAL INFORMATION

Sign Convention

The shaft is considered to be in a horizontal position. The sign convention for the deflections, slopes, moments, and shear forces that
are calculated is shown in Fig. 1.

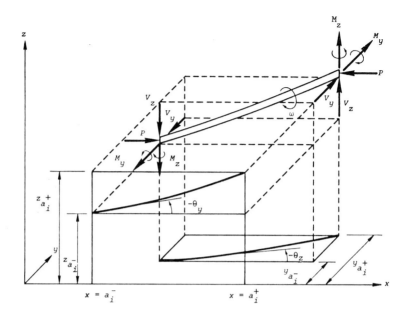

Fig. 1 Positive forces, moments, and slopes

Solution Method

The transfer matrix method is employed. The analysis starts at the
left end of the shaft and moves progressively to the right end.
Based on the data furnished by the user, the program will determine
the needed transfer matrices. However, if the user wishes, he may
choose to supply his own matrices for the entire shaft or any portion
of the shaft.

Technical Background

The underlying theory for the program, including derivations and a
tabulation of a wide array of transfer matrices, is provided in
Ref. [1].

Calculation of Critical Speeds

Critical speeds of the shaft are found by searching a characteristic

equation for its roots. That is, the critical speeds are those critical values that make the characteristic equation equal to zero. The
user inputs an estimated value for the lowest desired critical speed.
This estimated value should be somewhat less than what is thought to
be the actual value. The user also inputs a search increment. The
program then searches for the critical speeds by computing the value
of the characteristic equation using the estimated value, and then
the estimated value $+n\Delta$, $n = 1,2,3,\ldots$, where Δ is the search increment (Fig. 2). When the characteristic equation changes sign, the
computer program employs a root-finding scheme to converge to the
desired critical speed.

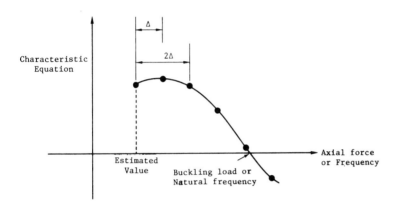

Fig. 2   Search for critical speeds

Since the program is set to search through an upper limit 50 incre--
ments, it is important to choose an estimated value-search increment
combination that will encompass the desired critical speed within 50
search increments.

The estimates for critical speeds higher than the first calculated speed are selected automatically by the computer program.

Accessing and Executing the Program

Three options of data input are provided for this shaft program: the
prompting mode, the nonprompting mode, and the use of input from a
previously created data file.

In the prompting mode of input, the user responds to questions
put forth by the program, thereby furnishing the relevant data for
his problem. In the nonprompting mode, the supportive questions are
suppressed and the user enters his data according to the sequence and
format given in the description of each program. In both modes of
input a file with data in the same sequence as the nonprompting input

is automatically generated. This file may be saved at the end of
each run. The third input capability of the program, i.e., input from
a data file, enables the user to call out his previously created
data file, modify his data, and then run the same problem. And of
course, he may simply run the problem using a data file without any
modification at all.

The program is FORTRAN coded. However, to use it, a minimal
knowledge of computer language, or even none at all, is assumed on
the user's part. All that is required is minimal familiarity with
the use of a terminal such as a teletype. All questions asked by the
programs are self-explanatory. The program will lead the user
through the input. Numerical data input is free-formatted. This
means that the user simply treats numbers the way he is most accustomed to without concern as to whether the numbers lie in particular
columns. Commas or blanks are inserted between numbers being input.
Of course, if one line is not long enough for the data, the user can
go to the next lines until his data list is satisfied.

The following pages, in combination with the system manuals for
the computer in question, should provide the necessary information to
access and begin using the program. The example problems provided
later in this documentation should appear similar on all systems as
far as content is concerned; system differences may cause output to
differ in appearance by including spurious line feeds, question
marks, etc.

Outline of Procedure to Access and Use the Program

1. Dial the nearest phone number for the computer system.
When the system responds with a high-pitched tone, place the phone
in the acoustic coupler and wait for the system to print something.

2. Log in according to the instructions given in the system's
reference manual. The system will give some message indicating it
is ready to accept your commands.

3. You are now ready to execute the program. A brief outline
of the user response and execution sequence for the program follows.
It should be noted that after each line of instruction to the computer is completed, the user signifies that he has finished a line of
instruction by hitting the carriage return key (CR). To invoke the
procedure files prepared on your system, type the name of the desired
program, SHAFT, followed by a return. In some case a variation to
the name is required. Consult your system manual.

4. The computer will print "WILL INPUT BE FROM THE TERMINAL
(ENTER 1) OR FROM A PREVIOUSLY CREATED DATA FILE (ENTER 2)?" These
are the two distinct modes in which the SHAFT program operates. If
input is to come from a data file, skip to step 8.

5. The computer will print "DO YOU WANT TO SAVE A COPY OF YOUR
INPUT DATA? (TYPE 'YES' OR 'NO')". This refers to the file which is
automatically generated containing a copy of the input data. If you
do not wish to save this file, skip to step 7.

6. The computer will reply "UNDER WHAT NAME?". Reply with the
name of the file you wish this data to be written on. The created
file will be accessible after the current run by this name. Note
that if a file with this name already exists it will be destroyed. In
some cases more than one name is required; consult your system manual.

7. The computer will print a message indicating the program has begun executing.

8. If the input is to be from a data file already in existence, the computer will print "ENTER FILE NAME". Enter the name of the data file previously created. The format is the same as in step 6.

9. The computer will print "WILL YOU WISH TO MODIFY YOUR DATA FILE? (TYPE 'YES' OR 'NO')". If you desire to modify the data on your file before running the program, type "YES", otherwise type "NO" and proceed to step 12. Note that the original copy of the data will not be altered.

10. The computer will respond with "WILL YOU WISH TO SAVE THE MODIFIED COPY? (TYPE 'YES' OR 'NO')". If you want the new version of your data to be saved, answer "YES". If not, the program will run once with the modified copy of the data and then discard it. If this is desired, answer "NO" and proceed to step 12.

11. The computer will print "UNDER WHAT NAME?". Respond as in step 6. The name of the original data file may be given here. In this case the modified copy will replace the original file, which will be destroyed.

12. The computer will print a message indicating the program has begun executing.

Input from a Data File and Modification

To execute a program with input from a data file either previously created or generated internally by the prompting or nonprompting mode of input, the user simply indicates this wish in executing the programs and specifies the file name. The user may also modify the data file before using it with the system editor. A simple editor is provided with this program and modifications may be made to data files after the program begins execution.

Each line in a data file always begins with a 3-digit line number followed by a blank. This number serves the dual purpose of identifying as well as sequencing a data line. Thus when a line of data is to be deleted, the user simply retypes its line number with nothing following. Also, new lines of data can be inserted between any two lines by using appropriate line numbers. While the program will automatically attach line numbers (with an increment of 10) for the data file generated in a prompting or a nonprompting input, the user must enter them for his data file created otherwise (see the examples in the following sections).

Modifications can be made by retyping the whole line (including the line number) which contains the item(s) to be changed, or if necessary, by adding a new line of data. It is important that the user makes all necessary associated changes, e.g., input parameter such as NSUP (number of in-span supports) as well as SIP(I), MTYP(I) (positions and type of supports). The user is allowed to enter as many data as space allows on a line so long as they are separated by a comma (or at least one blank). Furthermore, the new entries do not have to be in the same format as the replaced ones; e.g., the user may want to re-enter a number, say, 120.5, simply as

"120.5" instead of "1.205E+02" as it would appear on the data file.
The commands L and Q are available to list the current state of the
data file or quit (exit from editor). For more sophisticated manipulation of the data file, the user should refer to the appropriate
system reference manual.

Terminology

Field: The span of length over which a material property, e.g. mass
  density, or a loading remains unchanged.

Number of changes in . . .: One change is counted whenever a material
  property or a loading changes its magnitude at some point; 0
  (zero) should be entered if a material property or loading remains
  unchanged over the entire member.

Occurrence: An abrupt change in the magnitude of a geometrical, physical, or material property, e.g. a change in cross-sectional
  area or in distributed loading, or the application of a concentrate parameter.

Availability and Assistance

The program is available from and is maintained by The Structural
Members Users Group, P.O. Box 3958, University Station, Charlottesville, Va. 22903, phone 804-296-4906. Questions on using the program should be addressed to this organization.

EXAMPLE PROBLEMS

An array of example problems, illustrating all input options, are
presented in this section.

Example 1: Critical Speeds of a Uniform Rotating Shaft

Find the first three critical speeds of an undamped uniform shaft.
The ends are free. The shaft is 70 in. long. The elastic modulus
is 10^7 psi and Poisson's ratio is 0.3. The mass per unit length is
0.000813 lb-sec^2/in.   The shaft is solid, of radius 1 in. Consider
shear deformation and rotary inertia effects.
  We estimate that the first critical speed is 70 cps. This estimated value should always be somewhat less than the actual critical

speed.   We choose 10 cps as the increment for the critical speed
search.   This example illustrates the prompting form of input.

```
WILL INPUT BE FROM THE TERMINAL (ENTER 1)
OR FROM A PREVIOUSLY CREATED DATA FILE (ENTER 2)
?1

DO YOU WANT TO SAVE A COPY OF YOUR INPUTDATA?
(TYPE 'YES' OR 'NO')
?NO

*********************** PROGRAM SHAFT- DATA INPUT ***********************

DO YOU WANT A PROMPTING (ENTER 1) OR A NON-PROMPTING (ENTER 2) INPUT,
OR DO YOU WISH TO ENTER DATA FROM YOUR DATA FILE (ENTER 3)
? 1

INDICATE THE TYPE OF ANALYSIS DESIRED BY ENTERING
         1 FOR UNBALANCED RESPONSE
         2 FOR CRITICAL SPEEDS
? 2

YOU HAVE A CRITICAL SPEED PROBLEM.  ENTER BELOW THE DATA SET
(SP,DEL,NF), WHERE SP=YOUR ESTIMATE OF THE FIRST CRITICAL SPEED (IN CPS)
                   DEL=INCREMENT FOR CRITICAL SPEED SEARCH
                   NF=NO. OF SPEEDS TO BE DETERMINED
(SP,DEL,NF)
? 70,10,3

IS A LUMPED PARAMETER MODEL TO BE USED (YES OR NO)
? NO

LENGTH OF SHAFT =
? 70

         ********** END AND INSPAN SUPPORTS **********
ARE THE ENDS SUPPORTED BY ELASTIC BEARINGS (YES OR NO)
? NO

USING 1=FIXED, 2=PINNED, 3=FREE, 4=GUIDED, SPECIFY THE END SUPPORTS:
(NL,NR), WHERE NL=TYPE OF LEFT END SUPPORT
               NR=TYPE OF RIGHT END SUPPORT
(NL,NR)
? 3,3

NUMBER OF ELASTIC BEARINGS (0 IF NONE)
? 0

NUMBER OF OTHER INSPAN SUPPORTS (SHEAR  RELEASE,MOMENT RELEASE, GUIDE,
AND RIGID; 0 IF NONE)
? 0

         ********** MATERIAL AND GEOMETRICAL PROPERTIES **********
ENTER THE FOLLOWING DATA SET (NEY,NCS)
WHERE   NEY = NO. OF CHANGES IN MODULUS OF ELASTICITY,
        NCS = NO. OF CHANGES IN CROSS SECTION (0 IF UNCHANGED).

(NEY,NCS)
? 0,0

ENTER, CONSECUTIVELY, THE DATA SET (INITIAL POSITION,MAGNITUDE)
FOR ALL E FIELDS:

? 0,1.0E+07

ENTER THE DATA SET (INITIAL POSITION, INNER RADIUS, OUTER RADIUS)
FOR EACH CROSS SECTION FIELD:

? 0,0,1

IS SHEAR DEFORMATION TO BE CONSIDERED (YES OR NO)
? YES

THEN ENTER THE NUMBER OF CHANGES IN POISSON'S RATIO (0 IF UNCHANGED)
? 0
```

```
ENTER, CONSECUTIVELY, THE DATA SET (INITIAL POSITION,MAGNITUDE)
FOR ALL POISSON'S FIELDS:

? 0,.3

IS ROTARY INERTIA TO BE CONSIDERED (YES OR NO)
? YES

NO. OF CHANGES IN MASS PER UNIT OF SHAFT LENGTH
? 0

ENTER, CONSECUTIVELY, THE DATA SET (INITIAL POSITION,MAGNITUDE)
FOR ALL MASS FIELDS:

? 0,.000813

NO. OF AXIAL LOADS (INCLUDING REACTION AT LEFT END; 0 IF NONE)
? 0

DO YOU WISH TO HAVE THE TRACE OF CRITICAL SPEED SEARCH PRINTED OUT
(YES OR NO)
? YES

DO YOU WISH TO HAVE THE MODE SHAPES PRINTED OUT (YES OR NO)
? NO

DO YOU WANT A SUMMARY OF YOUR INPUT DATA (YES OR NO)
? NO

*************************** PROGRAM SHAFT - OUTPUT ***************************


    TRACE
      FREQ IN CYCLES/SEC  DETERMINANT

             7.00001E+01    -1.44283E+09
             8.00001E+01     1.68599E+10
             7.53942E+01     6.27930E+09
             7.30913E+01     2.44103E+09
             7.19398E+01     8.35646E+08
             7.07884E+01    -5.78408E+08
             7.12594E+01    -2.22899E+07
             7.17304E+01     5.64553E+08
             7.15038E+01     2.78386E+08
             7.13905E+01     1.39014E+08
             7.13339E+01     6.85003E+07
             7.13056E+01     3.39110E+07
             7.12914E+01     1.66581E+07
             7.12773E+01    -5.66924E+05

      FREQUENCY OF MODE    1 =     7.1277E+01 CYCLES PER SECOND


    TRACE
      FREQ IN CYCLES/SEC  DETERMINANT

             8.00001E+01     1.68599E+10
             1.00000E+02     1.29979E+11
             1.20000E+02     4.07014E+11
             1.40000E+02     8.57173E+11
             1.60000E+02     1.29198E+12
             1.80000E+02     1.16270E+12
             2.00000E+02    -5.74112E+11
             1.93389E+02     2.64219E+11
             1.95473E+02     3.31148E+10
             1.97556E+02    -2.27706E+11
             1.96647E+02    -1.10074E+11
             1.96192E+02    -5.34699E+10
             1.95965E+02    -2.57118E+10
             1.95737E+02     1.68710E+09

      FREQUENCY OF MODE    2 =     1.9574E+02 CYCLES PER SECOND


    TRACE
      FREQ IN CYCLES/SEC  DETERMINANT

             2.00000E+02    -5.74112E+11
             2.30000E+02    -9.69077E+12
             2.60000E+02    -3.19489E+13
             2.90000E+02    -6.94381E+13
             3.20000E+02    -1.10659E+14
             3.50000E+02    -1.17244E+14
```

3.80000E+02	-1.16034E+13
4.10000E+02	3.25987E+14
3.95516E+02	1.25109E+14
3.88273E+02	5.23890E+13
3.84652E+02	2.20409E+13
3.82842E+02	8.25746E+12
3.81031E+02	-4.64107E+12
3.81683E+02	-9.99564E+10
3.82334E+02	4.55314E+12
3.82015E+02	2.26249E+12
3.81856E+02	1.12729E+12
3.81776E+02	5.62215E+11
3.81736E+02	2.80307E+11
3.81717E+02	1.39510E+11

FREQUENCY OF MODE   3 =   3.8172E+02 CYCLES PER SECOND

MODE	NUMBER OF ITERATIONS	FREQUENCIES IN CYCLES PER SECOND
1	15	71.2773
2	15	195.7371
3	21	381.7166

Example 2: Unbalanced Response of a Single Mass System

This example illustrates the use of the nonprompting option of input. Find the unbalanced response of the shaft of Fig. 3 which is
rotating at 100 cycles/sec. The rotor is modeled as a massless shaft
with a single mass at the center that is offset by 0.01 in. at a
phase angle of 45 degrees. This is a solid shaft with an outer radius of 5 in. The modulus of elasticity is $3(10^7)$ psi.
    The data will be input using the nonprompting mode, which is
the same as the prompting mode except that the questions are deleted.
Here the input is entered according to the instructions in the final
section of this chapter. The data file created in this mode of input
is saved under a name of your choice (see the instructions for your
computer system). Note that the ends of the shaft are treated as
being free. The springs of the ends of the shaft are entered as
bearing systems, not as end conditions.

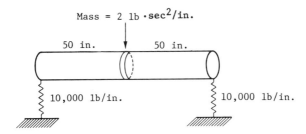

Fig. 3 Example 2

```
WILL INPUT BE FROM THE TERMINAL (ENTER 1)
OR FROM A PREVIOUSLY CREATED DATA FILE (ENTER 2)
 ? 1
DO YOU WANT TO SAVE A COPY OF YOUR INPUT DATA (YES OR NO)
 ? YES
UNDER WHAT NAME?
 ? DATA100


*********************** PROGRAM SHAFT- DATA INPUT ***********************

DO YOU WANT A PROMPTING (ENTER 1) OR A NON-PROMPTING (ENTER 2) INPUT,
OR DO YOU WISH TO ENTER DATA FROM YOUR DATA FILE (ENTER 3)
 ? 2
 ? 1
 ? 100
 ? YES
 ? 100,3,3
 ? 2
 ? 0,1,100,1
 ? 10000,0,0,0,0,10000,0,0,0,0
 ? 0
 ? 0,0
 ? 0,3.0E+07
 ? 0,0,5
 ? NO
 ? NO
 ? 0
 ? 0,0
 ? 1
 ? 50,2,45,.01
 ? 4

DO YOU WANT A SUMMARY OF YOUR INPUT DATA (YES OR NO)
 ? NO

************************** PROGRAM SHAFT - OUTPUT **************************
```

LOCATION	DEFLECTION	SLOPE	MOMENT	SHEAR	ANGLE
0.	9.9704E-03	-8.4632E-06	0.	9.9704E+01	4.4999E+01
10.00	1.0054E-02	-8.1247E-06	9.9704E+02	9.9704E+01	4.4999E+01
20.00	1.0131E-02	-7.1091E-06	1.9941E+03	9.9704E+01	4.4999E+01
30.00	1.0194E-02	-5.4164E-06	2.9911E103	9.9704E+01	4.4999E+01
40.00	1.0237E-02	-3.0467E-06	3.9882E+03	9.9704E+01	4.4999E+01
50.00	1.0253E-02	-5.2266E-17	4.9852E+03	-9.9704E+01	4.4999E+01
60.00	1.0237E-02	3.0467E-06	3.9882E+03	-9.9704E+01	4.4999E+01
70.00	1.0194E-02	5.4164E-06	2.9911E+03	-9.9704E+01	4.4999E+01
80.00	1.0131E-02	7.1091E-06	1.9941E+03	-9.9704E+01	4.4999E+01
90.00	1.0054E-02	8.1247E-06	9.9704E+02	-9.9704E+01	4.4999E+01
100.00	9.9704E-03	8.4632E-06	-6.0581E-08	-9.9704E+01	4.4999E+01

```
BEARING REACTIONS
```

LOCATION	FORCE	FORCE ANGLE	MOMENT	MOMENT ANGLE
0.	9.9704E+01	44.999	0.	0.
100.000	9.9704E+01	44.999	0.	0.

Example 3: Critical Speed of a Single Mass System

Find the first critical speed of the shaft of Fig. 3 using the data file, created in Example 2.

This change was made by changing lines 100, 110, 250, and 280, deleting lines 260 and 270, and adding the pertinent data in line 255. The mass entry was changed since, in a critical speed problem, eccentricity and phase are neglected.

```
WILL INPUT BE FROM THE TERMINAL (ENTER 1)
OR FROM A PREVIOUSLY CREATED DATA FILE (ENTER 2)
 ? 2
ENTER FILE NAME
 ? DATA100
WILL YOU WISH TO MODIFY YOUR DATA FILE (YES OR NO)
 ? YES
WILL YOU WISH TO SAVE THE MODIFIED COPY (YES OR NO)
 ? NO

******************** PROGRAM SHAFT- DATA INPUT ********************

DO YOU WANT A PROMPTING (ENTER 1) OR A NON-PROMPTING (ENTER 2) INPUT,
OR DO YOU WISH TO ENTER DATA FROM YOUR DATA FILE (ENTER 3)
? 3
DO YOU WISH TO MODIFY YOUR DATA FILE
? YES

BEGIN EDITING, ENTER Q TO STOP, L TO LIST.

? L

100   1
110   1.000E+02
120   YES
130   1.000E+02    3    3
140   2
150   0.         1  1.000E+02  1
160   1.000E+04    0.         0.         0.        0.
170   1.000E+04    0.         0.         0.        0.
180   0
190   0    0
200   0.         3.000E+07
210   0.         0.         5.000E+00
220   NO
230   NO
240   0
250   0    0
260   1
270   5.000E+01  2.000E+00  4.500E+01  1.000E-02
280   4

?100   2
?110   1    10    1
?250   1    0
?255   50    2
?260
?270
?280   0    1    0    0
?Q

************************ PROGRAM SHAFT - OUTPUT ************************
        TRACE
        FREQ IN CYCLES/SEC   DETERMINANT

            1.00000E+00    -9.95940E+11
            1.10000E+01    -5.08795E+11
            2.10000E+01     7.90258E+11
            1.79583E+01     3.09209E+11
            1.49167E+01    -9.67242E+10
            1.56414E+01    -6.81678E+09
            1.63662E+01     8.73554E+10
            1.60300E+01     4.31474E+10
            1.58620E+01     2.13874E+10
            1.57779E+01     1.05935E+10
            1.57359E+01     5.21797E+09
            1.56939E+01    -1.43181E+08

     FREQUENCY OF MODE   1 =      1.5694E+01 CYCLES PER SECOND

   MODE   NUMBER OF      FREQUENCIES IN
          ITERATIONS     CYCLES PER SECOND

     1        13              15.6939
```

Example 4: Unbalanced Response of a Lumped Mass Rotor

Find the unbalanced response of the shaft of Fig. 4 which is rotating at 50 cps. The elastic modulus is $3(10^7)$ psi. Each shaft
mass is 50 lb-sec^2/in. The bearing masses are 1 lb-sec^2/in. The
support spring and damping constants are 5000 lb/in and 50 lb-
sec/in, respectively. The third mass from the left is offset by a
distance of 0.01 in.

   The input used is a previously created data file. (See the instructions for your computer system for the proper commands.) The
data file can be developed on or off line. Follow the definitions of
the final section of this chapter in typing the data file.

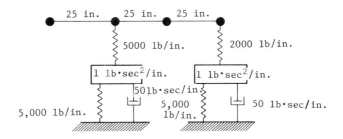

Fig. 4   Example 4

Create the data file off line and save it. (See the instructions for
your computer system for the proper commands.)

```
100   1
110   50
120   YES
130   75   3   3
140   2
150   25   1   75   1
160   5000   0   5000   50   1   5000   50   1
170   0
180   0   0
190   0   3.0E+07
200   0   0   2
210   NO
220   YES
230   0
240   3   0
250   0   50   25   50   75   50
260   1
270   50   50   0   .01
280   4


WILL INPUT BE FROM THE TERMINAL (ENTER 1)
OR FROM A PREVIOUSLY CREATED DATA FILE (ENTER 2)
?2

ENTER FILE NAME
?SHDATA

WILL YOU WISH TO MODIFY YOUR DATA FILE?
(TYPE 'YES' OR 'NO')
?NO
```

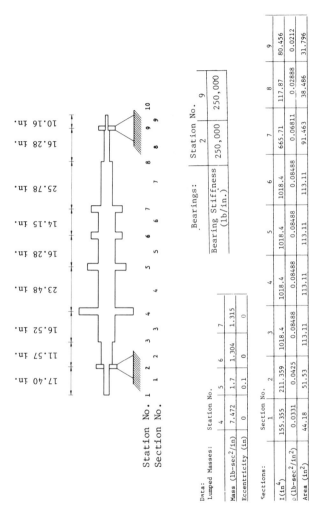

Fig. 5 Turbine, Example 5

```
********************** PROGRAM SHAFT- DATA INPUT ***********************

DO YOU WANT A PROMPTING (ENTER 1) OR A NON-PROMPTING (ENTER 2) INPUT,
OR DO YOU WISH TO ENTER DATA FROM YOUR DATA FILE (ENTER 3) ?3

WILL YOU WISH TO MODIFY YOUR DATA FILE ('YES' OR 'NO')
?NO

DO YOU WANT A SUMMARY OF YOUR INPUT DATA (YES OR NO)
? NO

************************** PROGRAM SHAFT - OUTPUT ************************
```

LOCATION	DEFLECTION	SLOPE	MOMENT	SHEAR	ANGLE
0.	-1.8143E-07	-2.0496E-04	0.	8.9533E-01	0.
5.00	1.0246E-03	-2.0493E-04	4.4767E+00	8.9533E-01	0.
10.00	2.0490E-03	-2.0484E-04	8.9533E+00	8.9533E-01	0.
15.00	3.0728E-03	-2.0469E-04	1.3430E+01	8.9533E-01	0.
20.00	4.0958E-03	-2.0448E-04	1.7907E+01	8.9533E-01	0.
25.00	5.1176E-03	-2.0422E-04	2.2383E+01	2.7926E+01	0.
30.00	6.1364E-03	-2.0299E-04	1.6201E+02	2.7926E+01	0.
35.00	7.1444E-03	-1.9992E-04	3.0164E+02	2.7926E+01	0.
40.00	8.1325E-03	-1.9499E-04	4.4127E+02	2.7926E+01	0.
45.00	9.0912E-03	-1.8821E-04	5.8090E+02	2.7926E+01	0.
50.00	1.0011E-02	-1.7958E-04	7.2452E+02	-2.8821E+01	0.
55.00	1.0887E-02	-1.7098E-04	5.7642E+02	-2.8821E+01	0.
60.00	1.1725E-02	-1.6429E-04	4.3231E+02	-2.8821E+01	0.
65.00	1.2533E-02	-1.5951E-04	2.8821E+02	-2.8821E+01	0.
70.00	1.3323E-02	-1.5665E-04	1.4410E+02	-2.8821E+01	0.
75.00	1.4103E-02	-1.5569E-04	8.6427E-07	-2.8821E+01	0.

```
BEARING REACTIONS
```

LOCATION	FORCE	FORCE ANGLE	MOMENT	MOMENT ANGLE
25.000	2.7030E+01	0.	0.	0.
75.000	2.8821E+01	0.	0.	0.

Example 5: Unbalanced Response of Turbine

Find the unbalanced response of the turbine of Fig. 5 which rotates at
60 cps. The bearing systems are modeled as simple springs with spring
constants of magnitude 250,000 lb/in. The elastic modulus is $3(10^7)$
psi. The second mass from the left end is offset with an eccentricity
of 0.1 in. The output is displayed.

```
WILL INPUT BE FROM THE TERMINAL (ENTER 1)
OR FROM A PREVIOUSLY CREATED DATA FILE (ENTER 2)
? 2
ENTER FILE NAME
? EXAM5
WILL YOU WISH TO MODIFY YOUR DATA FILE (YES OR NO)
? NO

************************** OUTPUT ******************************
```

LOC.	DEFLECTION	SLOPE	MOMENT	SHEAR	ANGLE
0.00	-9.7233E-04	-1.5412E-04	0.	0.	0.
17.40	1.7078E-03	-1.5385E-04	5.5905E+01	3.9680E+02	0.
28.97	3.4773E-03	-1.5009E-04	3.7165E+03	2.1535E+02	0.
45.49	5.9377EE03	-1.4833E-04	1.9439E+02	-7.0289E+03	0.
68.97	9.8373E-06	-2.1742E-04	-1.8851E+05	1.2558E+04	0.
85.25	1.4021E-02	-2.6648E-04	-1.9053E+03	7.6294E+03	0.
99.40	1.7743E-02	-2.4515E-04	8.7589E+04	1.5978E+03	0.
125.18	2.2550E-02	-1.3204E-04	6.5741E+04	-3.4914E+03	0.
141.46	2.2883E-02	2.0726E-05	-3.5411E+03	6.9789E+02	0.
151.62	2.2718E-02	1.5761E-05	0.	0.	0.

BEARING REACTIONS

LOCATION	FORCE	FORCE ANGLE	MOMENT	MOMENT ANGLE
17.400	4.2694E+02	0.000	0.	0.000
141.460	5.7208E+03	0.000	0.	0.000

INPUT DEFINITIONS

The definitions necessary to create an input data file or to use the nonprompting input system are presented in this section.

1. ID   Type of solution desired
   1 = Unbalanced response
   2 = Critical speeds

2. Choose one:
   SP   for unbalanced response speed of rotation of the shaft (cps)
   SP, DETE, NF   for critical speeds
        SP: Estimate of first critical speed. Choose a value lower than the actual critical speed.
      DETE: Increment for critical speed search
        NF: Number of critical speeds to be determined

3. ANSO   (YES or NO) Is a lumped parameter model to be used for the mass of the shaft (not including mass imbalances)?

4. BL, NB1, NB2
           BL: Total shaft length
   NB1, NB2: Left and right end conditions
               1 = fixed
               2 = simply supported
               3 = free
               4 = guided
               Ends with flexible (spring, mass, dashpot) bearing systems are treated as free boundaries since the bearing systems are entered as concentrated parameters and not as boundary conditions.

5. NLNB   Number of flexible bearing systems

   Skip to item 6 if no flexible bearing systems (NLNB = 0.)

5a. PB(1), LNT(1), PB(2), LNT(2), ... PB (NLNB), LNT(NLNB)
      PB(I):   Position of the Ith flexible bearing
     LNT(I):   Type of Ith bearing
                 1 = Linear bearing (extension) bearing only
                 2 = Linear and rotary bearing coefficients

5b. BS1(1), BD(1), SS(1), SD(1), BML(1), BS1(2), BD(2), SS(2), SD(2),
    BML(2) ... BS1(NLNB), BD(NLNL), SS(NLNB), SD(NLNB), (NLNB)

   BSL(I):   Linear bearing spring constant for the Ith bearing
           (k_{z3} of Fig. 6)

    BD(I):   Linear bearing damping coefficient (c_{z3} of Fig. 6)

    SS(I):   Linear support spring constant (k_{z4} of Fig. 6).
           0 for bearing with rigid pedestal.

    SD(I):   Linear support damping coefficient (c_{z4} of Fig. 6).
           0 for bearing with rigid pedestal.

   BML(I):   Bearing mass (M_{zi} of Fig. 6). 0 for bearing with
           rigid pedestal.

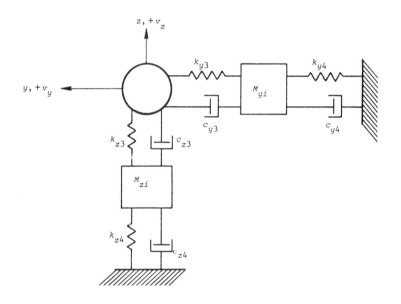

x-section view, x axis increases into the page

Fig. 6

5c. RBS(1), RBD(1), RSS(1), RSD(1), BMI(1), RBS(2), RBD(2), RSS(2),
    RSD(2), BMI(2) - - RBS(NLNB), RBD(NLNB), RSS(NLNB), RSD(NLNB),
    BMI(NLNB)

           These entries are made only if LNT(I) = 2 (Rotary
           (tilt) bearings). If for some bearing, LNT(I) = 1,
           skip these entries for that bearing. Note that
           each bearing is entered separately.

RBS(I):   Rotary bearing spring constant for the Ith bearing
RBD(I):   Rotary bearing damping coefficient for the Ith
          bearing
RSS(I):   Rotary support spring constant for the Ith bearing.
          0 for bearing with rigid pedestal.
RSD(I):   Rotary support damping coefficient for the Ith
          bearing. 0 for bearing with rigid pedestal.
BMI(I):   Bearing mass moment of inertia for the Ith bearing.
          0 for bearing with rigid pedestal.

6. NSUP   Number of other in-span supports

   Skip to item 7 if no other in-span supports.

6a. SUP(1), MTYP(1), SUP(2), MTYP(2), ... SUP(NSUP), MTYP(NSUP)
    SUP(I):   Position of the Ith in-span support
    MTYP(I): Type of support
              1 = shear release
              2 = moment release
              3 = guide
              4 = rigid support

7. NEY, NCS
      NEY: Number of changes in modulus of elasticity
      NCS: Number of changes in cross section

7a. ELAS(1), EY(1), ELAS(2), EY(2), ... ELAS(NEY + 1), EY(NEY + 1)
          Initial positions and magnitudes for all E fields
          (force/length^2)

7b. XINS(1), RAD1(1), RAD2(1), XINS(2), RAD1(2), RAD2(2), ... XINS
    (NCS + 1) RAD1(NCS + 1), RAD2(NCS + 1)
          Initial positions, inner and outer radii for all
          cross section fields

8. ANS3   (YES or NO) Is shear deformation to be considered?

   If NO, skip to item 9.

8a. NPO   Number of changes in Poisson's ratio

8b. POI(1), PI(1), POI(2), PI(2), ... POl(NPO + 1), PI(NPO + 1)

             Initial positions and magnitudes for all Poisson's
             fields

9. ANS4   (YES or NO) Is rotary inertia to be considered?
   Skip to item 11 if this is a lumped mas model (ANSO = YES).

10. NDM   Number of changes in mass per unit shaft length

10a. DEN(1), DM(1), DEN(2), DM(2), ... DEN(NDM + 1), DM(NDM + 1)
                Initial positions and magnitudes for all mass den-
                sity (mass/length) fields

11. NAXF   Number of axial forces, including reaction at left
                end. If no axial forces, skip to item 12.

11a. AXF(1), FA(1), AXF(2), FA(2), ... AXF(NAXF), FA(NAXF)
                Applied positions and magnitudes for all axial loads,
                compressive forces are positive

12. Skip to item 13 if this is not a lumped mass model (ANSO=
    NO).

    NCMA, NCR
        NCMA: Number of concentrated masses other than moment
                imbalances (eccentric mass)
        NCR: Number of concentrated rotary inertia

    Skip either of the following entries if the number of the concen-
    trated parameter associated with that entry is zero.

12a. CMA(1), CM(1), CMA(2), CM(2), ... CMA(NCMA), CM(NCMA)
                Positions and magnitudes of the concentrated masses

12b. CRI(1), CR(1), CRI(2), CR(2), ... CRI(NCR), CR(NCR)
                Positions and magnitudes of the concentrated rotary
                inertia

13. Skip to item 14 if critical speeds problem.

    NCMAL   Number of moment imbalances (eccentric masses)

    Skip to item 14 if no moment imbalamces.

13a. CMI(1), CM(1), CFF(1), ECC(1), CMI(2), CM(2), CFF(2), ECC(2), ...
     CMI(NCMAl), CM(NCMAl), CFF(NCMAl), ECC(NCMAl)
        CMI(I): Position of Ith moment imbalance
        CM(I):   Mass of Ith moment imbalance
        CFF(I): Phase angle of Ith mass (degrees)
        ECC(I): Eccentricity of Ith mass (length)

14. Choose one:
    NA   for unbalanced response problem
    NP, NM, NA for critical speed problem
        NP: 1 for printing trace of critical speed search
             0 otherwise
        NM: 1 for printing mode shape
             0 otherwise
        NA: Number of points for printing results between
             occurrences

REFERENCE

1 Pilkey, W. D., and Chang, P. Y., <u>Modern Formulas for Statics,
Dynamics, and Stability: Shafts, Beams, Plates and Shells</u>, McGraw
Hill, New York, 1977.

PART II

REVIEWS AND SUMMARIES

OF AVAILABLE PROGRAMS

COMPUTER-AIDED BUILDING DESIGN

Surenda K. Goel
Robert K. Waddick
Charles F. Beck

Sargent & Lundy Engineers

INTRODUCTION

Computers have become an accepted tool in today's engineering design offices. Engineering News Record in its annual survey of the top 500 design engineering firms in 1970 reported 78 percent of those firms were using computers [1]. This survey was indicative of trends in 1969. Indeed, in the years since then the percentage of computer users has increased substantially.

As with the number of users, the range of applications of computers has also been rapidly increasing. The earlier computer applications were aimed at providing an extra computational capability to the engineer. One level higher in complexity are the structural analysis programs. The level of competence reached in these programs is such that they are now routinely applied in most of the structural design offices.

Design programs are the most recent addition to structural engineering computer program libraries. One main reason that engineering design programs took so long in surfacing is that whereas there always exists a unique solution to the structural analysis problem depending upon the laws of structural mechanics, it is not necessarily so with the design problems. There can be more than one solution to a design problem with no explicit way to establish the superiority of one design over the other. It is like cakes baked with the same recipe but by different bakers; the cakes could taste quite different. This is true of design programs also.

This chapter discusses the various computer programs available to the writers in the area of building design. Capabilities of the programs, their merits, and their shortcomings are discussed. It is anticipated that this will help the reader make an enlightened judgment in choosing the best program available to suit his needs.

One of the fundamental requirements of a design program is a high degree of user-computer interaction capability. This attribute is desirable in any program but is absolutely necessary in a design program because of the essential nature of the design process. Because there is no unique solution to a design problem, an innovative designer can produce a solution to a design problem far more

imaginatively than a self-contained computer program. The design
programs should, therefore, aim at providing help to the designer
rather than at replacing him. In the computer programs discussed
in this chapter, this attribute has been one of the important considerations.

BUILDING SYSTEMS DESIGN

Building Components

In the traditional hand design procedure, the structure is visualized
as being composed of components, for example, beams, columns, slabs,
shear walls, etc. The forces acting on the structure give rise to
stresses, strains, and distortions in these building components.
Each component is then sized for a limiting value of these parameters.

A number of computer programs are available for the design of
building components based on this approach. These programs have been
serving a very useful purpose by relieving the designer of the repetitive calculations and allowing him more time for creative thinking.
However, the forces on various components of the system are computed
on the basis of some assumed stiffness of the components which may be
quite different from their actual stiffnesses.

Whole Building Design

An efficient and optimum design of each building component does not
necessarily ensure an optimized design for the whole building unless
it accounts for the interaction of the building components. In a
statically indeterminate structure, forces in a member depend not
only on its own stiffness but also on the stiffness of the adjoining
members [2]. There is also a redistribution of member forces when
any member buckles. Consequently, there have to be a number of
iterations between analysis and design, and the efficiency of convergence to the final design is an important attribute of any whole
building design program. Figure 1 shows a conceptual flow diagram of
such a design procedure.

Optimization

Attempts at designing buildings by writing an optimization function
and maximizing (or minimizing) that function have been made. It has
been noted that any optimization function becomes extremely large
and complicated even for a small structure. Consequently, these
rigorously formulated optimization programs either incorporate a
number of simplifying assumptions, solve a very small structure, or
both. This chapter will discuss only two optimization programs.

Iterations

In the iterative analysis and design procedure shown in Fig. 1, the convergence criteria must be selected judiciously to achieve rapid convergence to the final result. For a large structure, each extra iteration in the analysis-design procedure could mean a substantial investment in computer time and cost which must be balanced against the economy achieved in that extra iteration. The writers' experience is that it is best to have the convergence criteria incorporated as variables in the program. The user should have the option to control these variables to achieve the rate of convergence or the degree of convergence of his choice.

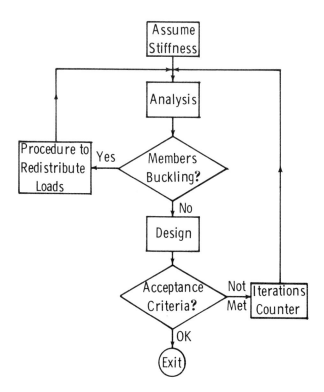

Fig. 1 Flow diagram of a design procedure

STATE OF THE ART

There has been a considerable investment of effort in design programs in recent years. The development of design programs has
reached a point at which there are several programs available which
perform the same function. The following pages contain a discussion
of a number of such programs. The discussion has been divided into
three parts.

1. Building Components Design Programs. These are generally
small programs performing design of one type of component. These
programs mostly require forces on the members as input data. The
members could be designed in steel, reinforced concrete, or prestressed concrete. Tables 1, 2, 3, and 4 give descriptions of the
design programs for beams, columns, flat plates, and footings. The
program owners and special features of these programs are noted with
the descriptions.

2. Whole Building Design Programs. These programs generally
include analysis, design, and checking of a number of members at the
same time. This frequently involves iterations between analysis and
design. Descriptions of a number of such programs are included.
Any special features which make a program outstanding are discussed.

3. Optimization Programs. These programs are generally based
on a minimum weight design. Examples of a rigorous formulation and
exhaustive search are discussed.

Building Component Design Programs

STAND System

The STAND system [3] is an integrated system of computer programs
performing design of steel structures especially suited for a design
office environment. The capabilities of the STAND system are:

1. Rolled beam analysis and design
2. Composite beam analysis and design
3. Plate girder design
4. Column with uniaxial or biaxial loading design
5. Column base plate design

The control over these various programs is exercised by an Executive
Program as the means of communication between the user and the program. The user has the flexibility of performing a multiple number
of tasks in a single run. For example, one run may consist of designing rolled beams for a whole floor plan with different materials.
The user can then choose the ones best suited to his requirements.
Similarly, it is possible to obtain alternate designs in rolled beams
and composite beams with cost comparisons between the two. It is
possible to transfer reactions from the tributary beams as loads on

the main beams. All beam designs include Type 2 connection designs
at both ends.
The plate girder program designs the girder by optimizing on
the weight. The design procedure includes such details as availability of plate sizes for the steel grade used in the flange and
web elements of the girders.
The program input consists of program control cards which control the flow of information within the program and input data. For
data, the fixed format has been found to be more convenient than
free format for design office use. The output consists of all the
pertinent design information, for example, size of members and
actual and allowable stresses at critical sections. Also, the input
data are printed in neatly tabulated form for filing and record maintenance. Special features include modular structure of the program
and dynamic linkage of program modules.
STAND system is a proprietary program of Sargent & Lundy, 55 E.
Monroe Street, Chicago, Illinois 60603. Sargent & Lundy uses the
STAND system for design of floor systems, plate girders, and columns
in its power plant designs. The program is, however, general enough
to be used on any kind of structure.
More building component design programs are described in Tables
1, 2, 3, and 4.

Whole Building Design Programs

STRUDL-II

STRUDL-II [4] is probably the most publicized and, therefore, the
most well known computer program available to the structural engineering profession. Its availability and that of its predecessor
program STRESS has made the greatest single impact of any computer
program on the practice of structural engineering.
The STRUDL system is a modular system of computer programs
capable of performing the analysis of the structure and the design
of members in steel or concrete. The analysis procedure is based
on a stiffness matrix formulation, an approach most widely used in
structural analysis programs. Elsewhere in this chapter a comparison is made with the relaxation technique used in AMECO-17.
The design of members in steel is based on a table look-up procedure from the standard shapes stored on the secondary storage of
the computer. The original MIT version of STRUDL was implemented
with the 1963 AISC Specification. Recent updates have included the
1969 AISC Specification and new member tables. New implementations
by Sperry Univac on 1100 series equipment and by McDonnell-Douglas
Automation Co. have increased the user base and expanded the program
in graphics, dynamics, and finite element analysis.
STRUDL's design of reinforced concrete member capabilities consists of rectangular or T-beams, rectangular or circular columns with
ties or spirals, flat slabs with or without capitals and drop panels,
and one-way solid or joist floor slabs. To proportion these elements, the user can specify one or more cross-sectional parameters
or specify identities between members. The output consists of

Table 1 Beam Design Programs

Program Name	Type	Program Owners	Remarks
OBEAM	Concrete Prestressed	Concrete Masonry Corporation Huron & Lowell St. Elyria, Ohio 45400	ACI 318-1971 Static, Simple supports prismatic
AISC	Steel	American Inst. of Steel Construction 1221 Avenue of the Americas New York, N.Y. 10020	Floor framing system. 1969 AISC Specification. Design and Investigation. 8K capacity
S107	Steel	Smith Hinchman Grylls Assoc., Inc. 455 W. Fort St. Detroit, Mich. 48226	Composite or Rolled WF Sections
S126	Concrete	"	Single Span R.C. Beam Design
S105	Concrete	"	R.C. Beams & One Way Slabs
Beam Elements	Concrete	KKBNA Engineers, Inc. 7456 W. 5th Ave. Denver, Colo. 80226	Web Openings Considered
Cont. Beams	Concrete	"	WSD or USD Prismatic or Non-prismatic
Prestressed Beams	Prestressed	KKBNA Denver, Colo.	Post-tensioned analysis, design & investigation
Comp. Beams	Composite	"	Design & analysis
Continuous Beam	Steel	KKBNA Denver, Colo.	
Plate Girder	Steel	"	Tapered or Non-tapered
SBCDN	Steel	Environmental Services, Inc. 140 Grand Ave. Englewood, N.J. 07432	Steel Beam-Column design

Table 1 (Continued)

Program Name	Type	Program Owners	Remarks
REBDN	Concrete	Environmental Services, Inc.	Ultimate Strength or Working Stress design of Concrete
REBDN	Concrete	"	Beams based on 1963 ACI Code
Beam$$	Concrete	Leap Associates P. O. Box 1053 Lakeland, Fla. 33802	For Rectangular or T-Beams; computes the reinforcement for given values of design moment and shear force
PRIEST$	Prestressed Concrete	Leap Associates Lakeland, Florida	Basically a trial program where the designer inputs at the terminal the section and the trial strand pattern. The computer gives the final prestress force required.
CONBM1	Concrete	Modular Computer System 188 Industrial Dr. Elmhurst, Ill. 60126	Continuous beams up to 20 spans + 2 cantilevers. Concentrated, uniform or triangular loading.
Conc. Beam	Concrete	Dalton-Dalton-Little-Newport 3605 Warrensville Center Rd. Cleveland, Ohio 44122	
Conc. Beam	Concrete	R.S. Fling & Partners 999 Crupper Ave. Columbus, Ohio 43229	
Conc. Beam	Concrete	Systems Professionals 3055 Overland Ave. Los Angeles, Calif. 90034	

Table 2 Column Design Programs

Program Name	Type	Program Owners	Remarks
INDIA	Concrete	Sargent & Lundy Chicago, Ill.	Interaction diagram
AISC	Steel	American Inst. of Steel Construction New York	Biaxial bending Calculates K-factors.
CISC	Steel	Canadian Inst. of Steel Construction 201 Consumers Rd. Street 300 Willowdale, Ontario M2J 4G8	Accounts for Column Drift
PCAUC	Concrete	Portland Cement Association 5420 Old Orchard Rd. Skokie, Ill. 60076 (Modified by Sargent & Lundy)	Ultimate Strength Design, ACI 318-71 Code
S104	Steel	Smith, Hinchman & Grylls Assocs. Detroit, Mich.	Axial load & biaxial moments. Accumulates moments from each story.
S114	Concrete	"	Rectangular or Round Columns. Ultimate Strength Design
Concrete Columns	Concrete	KKBNA Denver, Colo.	Ultimate Strength Design. Plotting of interaction dgm.
Steel Columns	Steel	"	Axial load & moment design & investigation
COLUMN$	Concrete	Leap Assocs. Lakeland, Florida	Computes column section and reinforcement for the given axial and flexural loading
STCOL1	Steel	Modular Computer System Wheaton, Ill.	Designs steel column section. Loading conditions. Axial load and moments.

9

Table 3 Flat Plate Design Programs

Program Name	Type	Program Owners	Remarks
S117	Concrete	Smith, Hinchman & Grylls Assocs. Detroit, Mich.	Ultimate Strength Design with or without drop panel
S120	Concrete	"	Working Stress Design
Flat Plates	Concrete	KKBNA Denver, Colo.	Working Stress or Ultimate Strength Design
FLAT PLATES	Concrete	PCA Skokie, Ill.	Analysis and design of Flat Slabs, Waffle Slabs and Continuous Frames according to ACI 318-71

Table 4 Footing Design Programs

Program Name	Type	Program Owners	Remarks
S112	Concrete	Smith, Hinchman & Grylls Assocs. Detroit, Mich.	Square or Rectangular for axial load or moment in both directions
STAND-BP	Concrete	Sargent & Lundy Chicago, Ill.	Base Plate design for given loading and column dimensions
Base Plate		KKBNA Denver, Colo.	Axial and/or moment design
SPRED1	Concrete	Modular Computer Systems Elmhurst, Ill.	Spread pedestal design. Optimum mat thickness and reinforcing.

cross-sectional dimensions complete with reinforcement information, including location and length of all bars.

The design procedures are in accordance with ACI 318-63, though it is understood that individual owners of the program may have modified their programs to conform to the ACI 318-71 Code.

The STRUDL analysis and design capabilities, even though broad based in their coverage, are, nevertheless, simple-minded in the sense that no attempt is made to automatically iterate between analysis and design. Thus, the member forces computed on the basis of trial member sizes may not be the correct member forces. Iteration, if desired by the user, has to be forced externally by judicious use of the STRUDL command language.

STRUDL's widespread use has led to the formation of ICES User's Group, Inc. The group holds semiannual conferences to discuss problems of common interest to the users. The deliberations of this group are indicative of the relative use of the different parts of the STRUDL system. The writers have noticed more discussions relative to the analysis part than to the design part of the program, indicating that perhaps the design features of the program have not caught the imaginations of the users as much as the analysis parts.

One of the problems with STRUDL is its large core storage requirement for execution. This makes it impossible for a significant number of in-house computer users with small machines to use the program. The program has been implemented only on the larger models of IBM System 360 and System 370 and UNIVAC models 1106, 1108, and 1110. Implementation is being initiated on CDC Cyber Systems.

The program is available through the ICES User's Group, Inc., P. O. Box 8243, Cranston, R. I., 02920. A large number of software centers have implemented STRUDL on their systems. McDonnell Douglas Automation Company's version of STRUDL has been modified extensively over the original MIT version of the program and therefore rates higher among users' reactions.

FRAME 90-D

This program was developed by the Computer Applications Group of the American Bridge Division of the U.S. Steel Corporation and is operational on that company's CDC 6500 computer in Pittsburgh. It is available for use by arrangement.

The program capabilities consist of analysis of plane frames composed of linear members with fixed or pinned ends and design of members in structural steel using the 1969 AISC Specification. Strength, deflection, and size constraints can be applied to the design. The analysis is performed according to the stiffness matrix formulation and draws upon a finite element technique developed for NASA.

The program can use either the U.S. Customary or S.I. metric units. For a 168-member frame, it took eight man-hours to prepare the input data, and the design time was 5.8 seconds per member for each load combination. The corresponding computer time for investigation of each member is of the order of 2.5 seconds.

AMECO-17

AMECO-17 [5] is a program incorporating the entire process of anal-
ysis/design, from geometry generation to material take off. Iteration between analysis and design is performed. As member sizes are
changed, the program recycles back to new load calculations, frame
analysis, and member proportioning until convergence is encountered.
    The unique feature of the program is its frame analysis proce-
dure which is based on relaxation methods. The developers of the
program claim that the accuracy attained is comparable to a stiffness
analysis program but the execution time is drastically reduced.
Figure 2 shows their comparison of execution times for programs based
on stiffness matrix formulations and relaxation methods. It is noted
that whereas the execution time for the stiffness matrix programs
increases exponentially with the size of the structure, it increases
only linearly for the relaxation method programs. As a comparison,
an 1128-joint frame took 3660 seconds for analysis by a stiffness

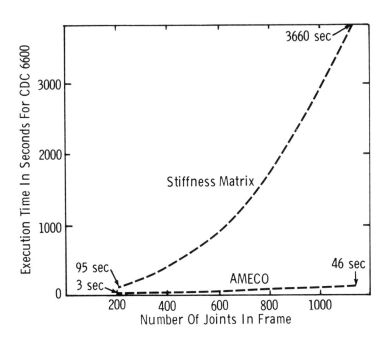

Fig. 2 Comparison of execution time for stiffness matrix and relaxation method programs

matrix program, whereas AMECO-17 took only 46 seconds. This start-
ling comparison should enhance the status of relaxation methods in
computer applications considerably. In fairness to the stiffness
matrix programs, however, it should be pointed out that this comparison holds only for one loading condition. For multiple loading conditions, the stiffness matrix program time increases only marginally,
whereas the relaxation program time will multiply by the number of
loading conditions.

The design capabilities of the AMECO-17 cover both concrete and
steel members. A choice of ten design codes including ACI and CSA
standards for concrete design and two design codes, AISC and CSA-516
for steel, are available to the AMECO-17 users. The program can
accept only two loading conditions, dead and live, which could be a
great handicap to a number of program users. The program iterates
between analysis and design until convergence is achieved.

The AMECO-17 is operational on CDC 6600 and CYBER-74 computers.
Some of the computer cost estimates provided by the program developers are 0.5 to 5 cents per joint for frame analysis, 10 to 40 cents
per member for concrete design, and 6 to 20 cents per member for
steel design. Further information is available from the Multiple
Access Computer Group, 800 Dorchester Blvd. West, Montreal, Canada
H3B1X9.

GENESYS

GENESYS is a computer system developed in the United Kingdom [6]. It
consists of a master program and a library of programs called subsystems. The subsystems operate under the control of the master
program and range in application over the whole construction field
from structures through highways to hydraulics. The GENESYS developers have encouraged the users of GENESYS to contribute to the
library of subsystems. The GENESYS Centre handles exchanges of subsystems between users for a brokerage fee.

One of the GENESYS subsystems is entitled RC-BUILDING/1. This
subsystem analyzes the components of a three-dimensional structure by
the techniques normally used by the engineers in their design
offices. A beam is analyzed by considering the substructure which
consists of beams and the columns supporting it but taken only to the
floor above and below. Thus, GENESYS does not use a global struc-
ural analysis procedure.

The program performs detailed design of beams, columns, and
slabs, calculating the size of reinforcement bars including such
details as their lengths and disposition. The slabs may be designed
one way or two way, with a variety of edge conditions.

The program output is in a form directly usable by the construction crews. The program developers estimate that detailing accounts
for 30 to 40 percent of design costs. Also, there is an acute short-
age of skilled detailers. The GENESYS approach, which replaces drawings from the site with well-conceived computer output makes good
sense and could radically transform the character of engineering
design offices. In most other respects, GENESYS remains a British
version of the ICES system. GENESYS started out with wide hopes of

a computer system independent of the computer hardware and transfer
of data from one subsystem to another. To the writers' knowledge,
this has not been as successful as originally intended.

The GENESYS system has been marketed internationally, although
its penetration into the United States market has been limited.
Nonetheless, its contribution to the applications of computers to
building design is recognized as significant. Inquiries about the
GENESYS system should be directed to GENESYS Limited, 2 Lemyngton
St., Loughborough, Leicestershire, LE111XA, U.K.

TRANTOWER

This is a special purpose program for the analysis and design of
steel transmission towers or space truss structures [8]. Iterations
between analysis and design, with the tolerance controlled by the
designer, are performed to achieve convergence to the final solution.
One important feature of the program is accounting for the buckling
of members, thus using a bilinear force-displacement relationship.

The program has the capability of generating symmetric portions
of the tower geometry, plotting isometric views of the tower, searching and stabilizing planar nodes, handling "tension only" members,
and optimizing on tower geometry by varying key node locations. For
analysis of the tower, a frontal equation solver with automatic renumbering has been employed, making the program extremely efficient.
Details of the program, its applications, and examples of its use are
given in Ref. [8]. It is a proprietary program of Sargent & Lundy,
55 E. Monroe St., Chicago, Ill. 60603.

Optimization Programs

Optimal structural design has been tried using least weight as the
basis employing rigorous mathematical programming techniques. However, these rigorous optimization procedures are still in their
infancy. Consequently, they have not reached the design office application stage because they get rather involved even for a reasonable
size structure. Moreover, the concept of optimized cost on the basis
of least weight can be deceptive because fabrication, erection, and
construction costs, which constitute a major component of the overall
cost, are not factors in the objective function. Some attempts to
include the fabrication costs have been made in recent years.

The alternative technique of making an exhaustive search has
been used in a number of applications. PLGIRD program described here
is an example of exhaustive search techniques. Again, the exhaustive
search is limited to problems with a small number of design variables.

DAPS

DAPS [9] is a computer program for the design and analysis of plastic
structures. Linear programming formulations are made for analysis

under proportional and shakedown loading by static and kinematic approaches. The program gives the plastic moment capacities at the
critical sections. However, the number of critical sections and
elementary mechanisms, together with the maximum number of sections
in any elementary mechanism, have to be identified external to the
program and are required input. This may be difficult for large
frames, but an experienced designer can generate the required information within a reasonable time. The procedure has great promise,
but its general application awaits further demonstration of its
capability for handling large frames.

The program was developed in the Solid Mechanics Division of the
University of Waterloo, Ontario, Canada. Report No. 26, obtainable
from the University, gives a complete description and listing of the
program.

PLGIRD

PLGIRD is a program for the design of fabricated steel girders on the
basis of 1969 AISC Specification. A least-weight girder design is
attained by the exhaustive search technique [10] under which a number
of girders are designed and the one with least weight is adopted as
the final design.

The variables considered in the optimization of the girder
weight are the depth of the girder and the web thickness. Figure 3

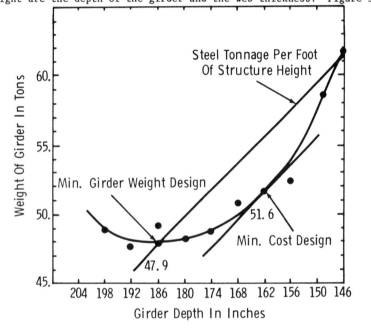

Fig. 3 Minimum weight design of plate girders

shows the variation of girder weight according to the depth of the
girder. The program can be implemented with any girder depth limitation and flange width limitation. Flange cut-off capability has been
provided in the program. The girder can be designed with or without
stiffeners.

The program takes about 3 seconds/girder on a UNIVAC 1106 computer. PLGIRD is a proprietary program of Sargent & Lundy, 55 E.
Monroe St., Chicago.

GRAPHICS

Graphical output has long been a highly desirable feature of computer
programs. Results for complex analysis and design programs can be
pictorially conveyed to the user in the most concise manner and the
shortest time. The user can thus pass judgment on the acceptability
of the results without a detailed study of a large array of numerical
data. Complicated analysis output may be reduced to graphical form
resulting in a considerable economy of man-time in its comprehension
and use. Programs with graphical output may be divided into two
major areas of interest based upon their emphasis on graphics: those
programs which are principally for analysis or design with graphic
output as an incidental aid and those with graphic output as the
primary output. The medium of graphics output may vary but is
primarily directed toward three classes of devices: printer graphics,
plotter output, CRT, and/or interactive CRT terminals.

The choice of graphic medium and format depends on the output to
be displayed and the cost justification. Very simple graphics can be
generated via the printer which may be useful in extracting design
requirements and diagnosing input data problems. More sophisticated
output to the extent of complete drawings may be produced on the
digital incremental plotter. CRT graphics is most helpful in input
stages and for the display of data to be used in an interactive mode.
The so-called soft image of interactive graphics is temporary and is
most effective when used in connection with sophisticated analysis
programs. An interesting offshoot of CRT graphics is the use of computer output on microfilm to produce microfilm or microfiche images
of plotter output for still viewing or for generating successive
views, a motion picture of structural response. The dynamic behavior
of complex structures can often be displayed and examined through
this technique.

Printer Graphics

Prior to the advent of low-cost digital plotting systems, the use of
the line printer to generate elementary graphical output was the only
graphical media available. Even today, the use of the line printer
has distinct advantages for simple presentations where graphical resolution accuracy is not demanded. The line printer can be used to
provide a satisfactory presentation and is generally returned to the
user with other primary output. No separate on-line or off-line
delay is required for such graphics. Low-cost, small-scale computer

installations rarely have any other graphical output available.
Thus, printer output is economically justifiable. Illustrated in
Fig. 4 are typical printer outputs from a PLOT PLANE and PLOT
DIAGRAM of MIT STRUDL-II. The moment diagram is plotted to scale.
This form of printer output is probably as accurate as most manually
drawn moment diagrams. Although the plane structure plot is not
aesthetically of high quality, it is schematically correct and satisfactory for input data debugging. Other ICES subsystem programs such
as BRIDGE and PROJECT have printer output which pictorially presents
the results of the numerical analysis. ICES subsystem ROADS makes
use of the printer to present scaled roadway cross sections.
Although these data are not acceptable as final project documents,
they are of great assistance in diagnosing the validity of input
data and evaluating program output.

Output using line printer overprinting capabilities can be utilized to display stress intensities as illustrated in Fig. 4c. Here,
the print density indicates the stress level. The output for this
figure was generated by the program SYMAP using numerical output from
a finite element stress analysis.

SYMAP is one of a series of graphics applications available from
Harvard University, Graduate School of Design, 114 Memorial Hall,
Cambridge, Mass. 02138.

A number of other programs which are of value to civil engineers
in the field of planning use printer graphics as the primary output.
It is apparent that printer graphics do not display the most satisfactory resolution nor the most desirable aesthetics. However, the
information is qualitatively accurate and timely. These facts, plus
the relatively low cost of printer graphics added to existing programs, serve to increase its effective use.

Plotter Graphics

Digital incremental plotters have been available to medium and large-
scale computer users since the mid-1950s. In recent years the cost
of plotters has decreased, making them available for smaller systems
also. Electrostatic printer/plotters have provided a bridge to the
incremental plotter. Printed output and reasonable plotter graphics
may be obtained with equal facility. Plotter applications, as
applied to building systems design, may be divided into two major
groups; overall structural graphics, and member detail and working
drawings. Plotter output is common for sophisticated stress analysis
programs, for example, finite element mesh plots, deformation plots,
isothermal, isostress contour plots, and vector field plots. In the
analysis of building systems programs, the plotter has most frequently been used in the area of input data diagnostics. The structures
illustrated in Fig. 5 would be typical examples for a plane or space
structure. Figure 5c illustrates the isometric view of a portion of
the piping system of a nuclear power plant. The ultimate responsi-
bility for appropriate use of computer output must be placed upon the
engineer [11]. Graphics output can greatly assist him in detecting
and correcting data and modeling errors. Wise use of printer and
graphical output can maximize the credibility of computer-aided
design.

a. Structure display from STRUDL

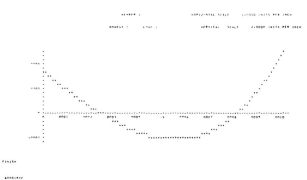

b. Moment diagram display from STRUDL

c. Stress intensities from finite element analysis

Fig. 4 Typical printer graphics output

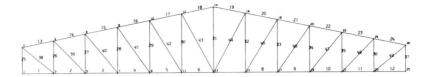

a. Plane structure display

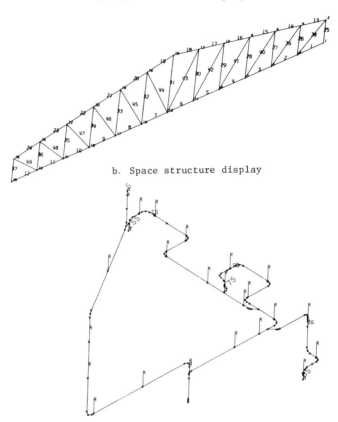

b. Space structure display

c. A portion of a complex piping system

Fig. 5 Typical plotter graphics output

Plotter output is used in the presentation of response spectrum
for selected points; time history analysis plots of accelerations,
displacements, and velocities; and for the display of mode shapes.
For static analysis, plotter output is used for the display of member
moment diagrams and structure displacements. Moment diagrams,
shapes, displacement time histories, etc., are used in the further
design process and in the compilation of various reports to clients
and regulatory agencies.

One of the more exciting applications of computer output following member design is the creation of an entire floor plan as shown
in Fig. 6. Members are identified and the plan is drawn to scale.
This specific drawing was extracted from a full 30x42-inch drawing
completely computer prepared by Taskmaster Computing Systems 609,
10240-124 St., Edmonton, Alberta, Canada, T5N 3W6, and is a fine
example of computer drafting of an engineering structure.

In addition to overall structure drawings, programs are available to prepare complete detailed drawings of members and connections. Illustrated in Fig. 7 is a member detail drawing produced
on the plotter. The plot is output from the UNISTRUCT-UNIPLOT system available for use through the CDC CYBERNET network. Note that
all linework is computer produced, but some lettering is varityped.
This mixture presents an excellent drawing which is well composed and
clearly understandable to the engineer and fabricator. Similar programs have been written to proceed with detailing of concrete structures, bar-bending diagrams, and foundation design in addition to
steel detailing.

Interactive Graphics

Member and joint data for the iterative analysis and design procedure
of the program TRANTOWER, discussed previously, are generated from the
coordinates and connectivity of a one-quarter structure by rotation
and reflection. Joint and member operation is permissible with the
one-quarter structure to further simplify the data-gathering task.
At present, primary program output consists of printed design and
analysis results. Plotter output of the structure, as shown in
Fig. 8, is limited to a geometry diagnostic aid. Potential expansions of output in the area of graphics are to include assembly drawings, member details, and connections as illustrated in Fig. 7.
Complete structure analysis and design, as shown by some of these
examples, can be made more effective through well-planned use of an
interactive terminal system with graphic display. A large computer
system, such as that currently in use at Sargent & Lundy, Chicago,
could be configured with suitable remote terminals as shown in
Fig. 9.

By its very nature, interactive graphics implies display to the
user for the purpose of modification of input or other action. Thus,
there is no final product of interactive graphics, and therefore the
image is considered a soft copy. The hard copy of the image may be
produced on a plotter, microfilm, or an electrostatic copier. Because of resolution difficulties, the soft image must be restricted
to simpler forms. When complex diagrams are involved, software must

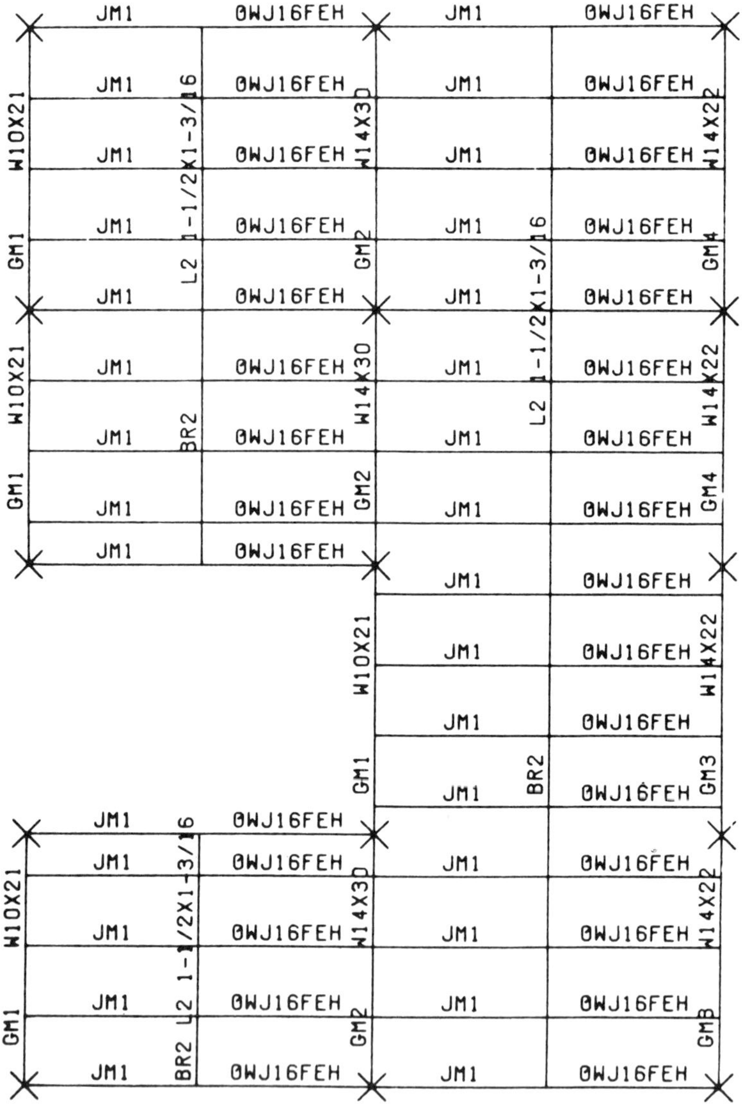

Fig. 6 Framing plan

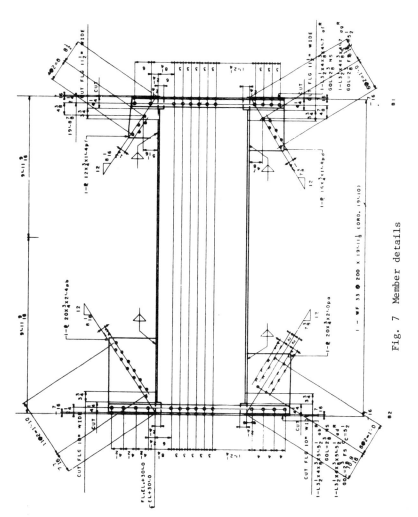

Fig. 7 Member details

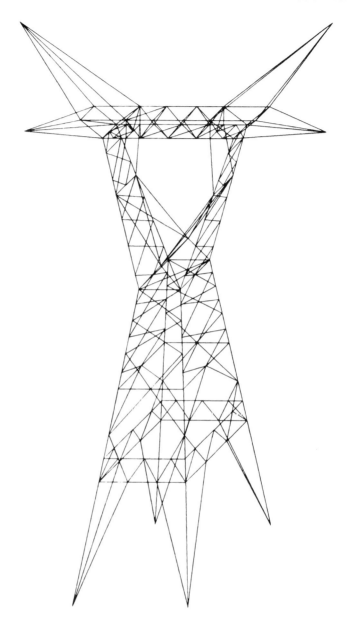

Fig. 8   TRANTOWER plotter output

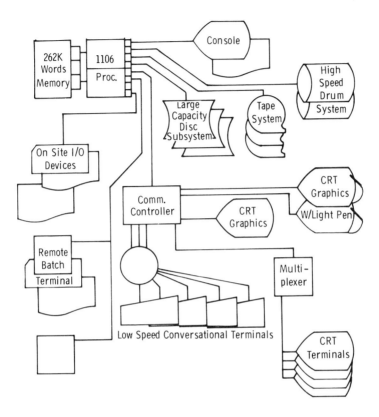

Fig. 9 Large-scale computer system with interactive display terminals

be so written as to provide for enlargement or blowup of specific areas for further detailed examination. A number of interactive finite element packages have been written to provide the user with mesh generation and output facilities comparable to those with plotter results but with the quick turnaround typical of interactive terminals. Interactive input of finite element data is unsurpassed for its efficiency and effective use of man-machine communications. Input of data for building design can be highly effective through interactive graphics. Although much data is of nongraphical nature, e.g., member properties, loading conditions, etc., through a combination of keyboard and manual selection techniques, these values can be generated with ease. Output of framing plans or fabrication details is not practical via interactive graphics. However, display of the deformed shape of structures, vibration modes, etc., can be extremely helpful in understanding the behavior of the structure. More recent raster scan devices have introduced color as another means of displaying data such as temperature, surface pressure, and overstressed or inelastic regions.

The principle of pictures replacing words is nowhere more valuable than in engineering language. Printer graphics, plotter output,
and interactive graphics have brought the pictures back to sophisticated engineering analysis and design. Future development along
these lines will bring to light concepts and ideas unthought of at
present. The engineering profession may find new forms of graphical
expression using the computer as the primary interpretive tool.

STANDARDIZATION AND PROGRAM EXCHANGE

The discussions in the previous sections indicate that there may be
several programs available to perform a certain task. Concern has
been raised about waste of effort due to unnecessary duplication [12].
On the other hand, the availability of a choice would be welcome because it may make feasible alternative design approaches.
To help exchange information about programs, groups such as CEPA,
APEC, and ICES User's Group have been formed and have been providing
useful service to the program users. Government, university, and
professional society sponsored conferences have brought together
persons and agencies of common interest and familiarity with similar
programs to discuss mutual applications problems.
     One of the problems encountered by users faced with a number of
programs is deciding which program to use under what conditions.
These users may not always have the facilities and means of testing
and comparing various programs. With this end in view, the ACI Committee 118 on Use of Computers has initiated a plan for evaluating
available programs on building design according to a standard format
and publishing the results in the ACI Journals.
     Also, CEPA, originally an organization of IBM 1130 hardware
users which has now been expanded in scope, has completed a study
entitled "Definition of a National Effort to Promote Effective Application of Computer Software in the Practice of Civil Engineering and
Building Construction." This study was funded by the National
Science Foundation and completed in the fall of 1975. The major
result of the CEPA-NSF study is a proposal for a National Institute
for Computers in Engineering to distribute, modify, and design computer programs and provide for user information exchange.
     The Conferences of the Office of Naval Research have also been
highly effective in spreading awareness of the current state of the
computer software in structural engineering.

CONCLUSIONS

There is a widespread awareness in the engineering profession that
computers have unlimited scope of application in the engineering
design process. Although there have been tremendous strides in this
direction, the net effect is only a scratch on the surface. Most of
the design programs available so far can perform only a few well-
defined tasks. Conspicuous by their absence are general purpose
design programs which may handle a variety of member types, materials, and codes and specifications. Engineer interaction should be

provided at every meaningful opportunity in the design of a computer-aided design system. Emphasis must be placed on the computer-"aided" aspect of complex systems.

Codes and specifications apply external constraints to design programs which greatly restrict their versatility. Programs written on the basis of one code cannot be used for any other code. Incorporating even the revised version of the original code often becomes a major undertaking. Typical of this situation is the STRUDL steel design program, which until recently was based on the 1963 AISC specification, and the STRUDL concrete design program, which is still based on the ACI 318-63.

Efforts have been made to redefine the design process so as to separate the constraint-checking process from the body of the design program. Decision Table formulations of codes and specifications have been suggested to accomplish this purpose [13]. This holds great promise.

Format-free problem-oriented languages, as used in the ICES system, are absolutely essential for operations from remote terminals but are not very efficient in a design office environment. There are two reasons for this: (1) A good engineer may not necessarily be a good typist and even if he is, it will be inefficient utilization of his time, and (2) the engineer must be encouraged to have all the required data on the very first trial in a problem. This can best be accomplished by use of some standardized forms.

There is a great deal of interest in the development of computer graphics. Computer graphics can be effectively used to supplement and extend current drafting personnel and make them available for more creative tasks. Output from the computer should be arranged so that it is directly usable by detailers or by the construction crews in the field. The use of graphics output and particularly interactive graphics must be carefully planned for. Waddick and Beck [14] have outlined general considerations for the formulation of system specifications. A well-designed system can be highly effective in building design. Efforts in Europe have apparently gone further in this respect than efforts in the North American continent and deserve immediate attention.

ACKNOWLEDGMENT

Considerable amounts of information in this chapter have been derived from program brochures and publications too numerous to mention individually. The writers' experience in the area of computer-aided analysis and design gained at Sargent & Lundy is gratefully acknowledged.

REFERENCES

1 "Top 500 Design Firms," Engineering News Record, Vol. 184, No. 21, May 21, 1970, pp. 62-86.

2 Cross, Hardy, "The Relation of Analysis to Structural Design," Transactions, ASCE, Vol. 101, 1936, pp. 1363-1408.

3 Chu, S. L., "STAND – An Integrated Computer System for Structural Analysis and Design," Illinois Institute of Technology, Summer Institute in Structural Design, Chicago, Illinois, 1972.

4 ICES STRUDL-II, Engineering User's Manuals, Vol. 1, Report 68-91, "Frame Analysis," Vol. 2, Report 68-92, "Additional Analysis Capabilities," and Vol. 3, Report 70-35, "Reinforced Concrete Structures," Massachusetts Institute of Technology, Department of Civil Engineering, Cambridge, Massachusetts.

5 Palejs, Andre A., and Freibergs, I. F., "Computerized Automatic Design of Concrete Buildings," Computers and Structures, Vol. 3, 1973, pp. 937-953.

6 Allwood, R. J., "Problem Oriented Language for the Design of Reinforced Concrete Structures," Impact of Computers on the Practice of Structural Engineering in Concrete, SP-33, pp. 47-62, American Concrete Institute, Detroit, Michigan, 1972.

7 Miller, C. L., "Man-Machine Communication in Civil Engineering," Journal of the Structural Division, ASCE, Vol. 89, No. ST4, 1963, pp. 5-29.

8 Lo. D. L. C., Morcos, A., and Goel, S. K., "Use of Computers in Transmission Tower Design," Journal of the Structural Division, ASCE, Vol. 101, No. ST7, 1973, pp. 1443-1453.

9 Parimi, S. R., Gosh, S. K., and Cohn, M. Z., "The Computer Programme DAPS for the Design and Analysis of Plastic Structures," Report No. 26, Solid Mechanics Division, University of Waterloo, Waterloo, Ontario, Canada, June 1973.

10 Beck, C. F., and Chu, S. L., "Minimum Weight Design of a Plate Girder," ASCE Joint Specialty Conference on Optimization and Nonlinear Problems, Chicago, Ill., April 18-20, 1968.

11 Beck, C. F., "Responsibilities of Computer-Aided Design," Civil Engineering, Vol. 42, No. 6, June 1972, pp. 58-60.

12 Fenves, S. J., "Scenario for a Third Computer Revolution in Structural Engineering," Journal of the Structural Division, ASCE, Vol. 97, No. ST1, 1971, pp. 3-11.

13 Goel, S. K., and Fenves, S. J., "Computer-Aided Processing of Design Specifications," Journal of the Structural Division, ASCE, Vol. 97, No. ST1, 1971, pp. 463-479.

14 Waddick, R. K., and Beck, C. F., "Specifications for Computer Software," Guidelines for Acquisition of Computer Software for Stress Analysis, ASCE National Structural Engineering Meeting, San Francisco, Calif., April 1973.

CURVED GIRDER BRIDGE SYSTEMS

David R. Schelling and Conrad P. Heins

University of Maryland

Glen H. Sikes

Georgia Department of Transportation

INTRODUCTION

The use of horizontally curved girder bridges and ramps has become increasingly popular. The requirements of highway alignment
along with aesthetic considerations often dictate the use of curved
members. Also, it has been shown [1, 2] that there exists an eco-
nomic incentive for using curved members in that the net costs for
curved beams are generally lower than those given for straight
chords. Thus, a survey [3] conducted by the Subcommittee on Curved
Girders (under the joint AASHTO-ASCE Committee on Flexural Members)
indicates a clear trend toward the increased use of curved girders
due to these factors. In fact, slightly over one half of the 507
curved member bridges surveyed in the report were constructed in
the 1968 to 1969 period, showing that the rate of use is increasing.
    Also indicated by the subcommittee report [3] and in a paper
surveying the state-of-the-art [2] is that much attention is currently being given to research in the development of analytical
techniques relating to the mechanics of curved members. This research is extensive and often entails the development or use of
various computer programs. The topic of curved girder bridge
analysis and design is, in fact, made tractable only through use
of the computer. This is due both to the large number of unknowns
that are involved in the determination of moments, shears,and deflections for an entire girder-diaphragm-cross-beam system and the
complex mechanics necessary for an analysis.
    This chapter presents information on the numerous computer pro-
grams that have been developed which may be used to analyze or design curved girder bridges. The material is limited to programs
applicable to curved bridges loaded normal to the plane of curvature
and does not consider rings or arches. Specifically discussed are
the capabilities which exist within 27 software systems (the total
number of separate programs is actually 31 if variants are counted).
These capabilities will be presented both in table form (see Tables
1, 2, 5,and 6) and in abstract form so as to be of maximum use to the
reader. Finally, a survey of usage is given along with current and

future requirements with respect to specific software needs within the curved girder area.

. The information and data given within this chapter were obtained through a review of the various software manuals and research reports, from the writers' experience in using the programs, and via direct contact with users and the authors of the various software packages. It represents the best interpretation as viewed by the writers of the most current information available.

CURRENT CAPABILITIES

The current interest in horizontally curved girder structures has stimulated a considerable amount of software development. The 27 systems which have been identified (see Table 1) fall into three general categories:

1. Production Programs - Software which has been used successfully by engineers in the design of curved girder bridges
2. Potential Production Programs - Software which, because of certain minor limitations, must undergo modification and verification in order to be used for design
3. Restrictive Programs - Software which, due to severe limitations or narrow scope, cannot easily be converted to production use

Summarized in Table 1 is information which, in very general terms, describes the capabilities of each of the systems which are available. Specifically given are: the program name (acronym), the program source, a brief description of the program, the date the program became available, the computer for which the program was designed, and the language used.

Indicated in Table 1 under Description is a brief statement as to the general category (defined above) in which the program falls. As can be noted a wide range of capability exists including 15 (or 54%), 4 (or 14%), and 9 (or 32%), programs which qualify as Production Programs, Potential Production Programs, and Restrictive Programs, respectively. Such a diversity probably indicates the degree of attention the topic is receiving and the difficulties encountered in extracting design information. In fact, it is generally acknowledged that the AASHTO code requires a computer solution beyond the current capabilities of existing software. This, coupled with research needs, indicates that the rate of software development should continue--hopefully culminating in improved production-oriented programs.

In order to accurately ascertain the level of current capabilities, it is necessary to quantitatively express the state-of-the-art limit for curved-girder software technology and to compare the various programs with this limit. Here numerous factors relating to the analysis, automation, and design of curved-girder bridges are given. These were chosen on the basis of the following criteria: (i) current need expressed by engineers, (ii) current AASHTO code requirements, and (iii) the features which exist in existing software. This resulted in the 57 items given within Tables

2, 5, and 6 which were used as a basis of comparison between the
various computer programs. To provide the descriptive detail, the
programs are abstracted in a standard 17-point format which can be
found in this chapter.

Analysis Capabilities

The difficulty that tends to deter engineers from recommending
curved girders has been the complex mathematical formulations that
are required in performing an analysis. Since horizontally curved
beams can be classified as linear elastic structures, many of the
standard analysis techniques have been employed regardless of their
suitability. Consequently, the 27 software packages identified
herein are based upon a wide variety of methodologies. Indeed, of
the 8 basic methods summarized by McManus, Ghulan, and Culver [2],
all but one have been identified as the basis for a computer program.

Although many analytical methods and variations of methods have
been used, 10 appear to be the most popular and probably the most
suitable for use by design engineers (see Table 3). Notably, of the
15 programs examined which have been classified as Production Programs, it can be seen from Table 2 that 7 (or 47%) utilize the
stiffness method (generally as a grid, finite element, or space frame),
5 (or 33%) employ various numerical methods (generally Fourier series or finite difference formulated to solve a set of governing
differential equations), and 3 (or 20%) use traditional beam analysis
techniques (such as conjugate beam [4], virtual work [5, 6], etc.).

Thus, it appears that the stiffness method is utilized more
within curved-girder production programs than any other technique.
Indeed, a further categorization discloses that the predominant
stiffness model of the gridwork accounts for 5 (or 33%) of the systems now in use (with 2 accounting for Finite Element). This is not
surprising when one considers:

1. that the finite element and space frame solutions currently
require large amounts of core, processing time, and input, making
analysis very costly;
2. that the problem of obtaining stresses due to lateral
flange bending is felt to be tractable via a gridwork model
[7] (although it is acknowledged that comparisons between test
data and the production programs identified are not satisfactory
for warping effects);
3. that the gridwork approach is the next level of complexity
above the traditional straight-beam solution and, therefore, is
more easily understood by practicing engineers (indeed, some
engineers are currently using the grid analysis in lieu of the
traditional continuous beam methods).

Also, the authors' experience and the data contained in Table 3 indicate that the overall most popular analysis vehicles are the
U.S. Steel method, as embodied in HCGA1 [8], and the stiffness
matrix grid method, as embodied in CUGAR [9, 10, 11, 12], CURVBRG
[7], and STRUDL [13]. A brief analysis of Tables 1, 2, 5, and 6

leads to the conclusion that although these methods are not as general as the finite element or the space frame formulations, they
have been enhanced in their design capabilities beyond other techniques.
        Another criterion which may be used to judge the practicality
and effectiveness of the various methods and programs is to identify
what engineers are using. In the "Survey of Curved Girder Bridges"
[3], it was found that 76% were designed by the approximate (U.S.
Steel) method and 22% were analyzed as a gridwork. Although the majority of the bridges were designed using the approximate method, it
must be pointed out that 58% of the spans were placed on radial supports, 53% were less than 100 ft. in length, and 52% had radii of
750 ft. or more, the condition for which the U.S. method is valid.
In the bridges where the configurations negated the use of the
approximate method, the grid model was used in all but 0.6% of the
cases.
        Another study was conducted in the latter part of 1975 by the
Tennessee Department of Transportation. Here, an inventory of information and usage of curved-girder analysis computer programs was
compiled for all 50 State Departments of Highways and Transportation.
Table 3 contains a summary of those states which have experience
with curved-girder analysis computer programs in a production mode
and/or have evaluated such programs. Evaluations vary from an extensive review of the program manuals to actually implementing and
testing the programs. The information was assembled by Tom
Cayce of the Tennessee DOT as part of its effort to provide a
Curved-Girder Analysis Computer Program, which is its responsi-
bility in the "Cooperative Effort to Upgrade Design Software" to
the southeastern states.
        Note here that only 30% of the states use computerized methods
for analyzing curved girders,and the 50% have made extensive evaluations; also, that a majority (52%) of the user states utilize the
stiffness matrix grid method as embodied in CUGAR, CURVBRG ,or
STRUDL. Also, of all the programs evaluated, approximately 25% have
been used in actual production, possibly indicating that the numerous other methods and software are not being utilized for design.
        If the response of all the states could be summarized, it would
be as follows:

        1.   The stiffness matrix grid method is the most popular, with
52% of the states using CUGAR, CURVBRG or STRUDL.
        2.   The State Departments of Highways and Transportation need
an effective curved-girder analysis/design computer program.
        3.   The various individual agencies cannot afford to develop
such a program and are expecting the software to be developed by
other sources.
        4.   The software which had been developed and which is avail-
able thus far has been a great disappointment from the users'
viewpoint.

Although the grid is becoming an important analysis technique, it
does present some problems in implementation. Consider Table 4, in
which the approximate requirements for grid size and computer

capacity based upon an analysis of data for over 418 curved girder
bridges presented in reference [3] are shown. Given are the percentage of bridges that could be analyzed for various geometrical
parameters and the resulting program sizes. For example, if a grid
program were able to analyze an 8-girder 4-span bridge with a diaphragm spacing of 10 ft. and span lengths under 200 ft. (median
limits), it would require approximately 258 k bytes of core and have
a 648-joint and 675-member capacity. Such a program could perform
the analysis for 88% of the bridges indicated. It must be emphasized here that the data given in Table 3 are approximate and intended only to show the rather large storage requirements necessary
to process a curved-girder bridge design. The basic data presented
in reference [3] are coarse and make it necessary to maximize parameters. However, the grid requirements are felt to be of the correct magnitudes in that although maximums do not occur simultaneously, the skewness of any bridge and the resulting increase in
the upper bandwidth could more than compensate for any savings in
core.

In conclusion, the grid model is proving to be the most popular
analysis technique as a general method. This is based upon the
software capability which currently exists in the form of production
programs, upon an increasing history of usage, and upon the huge input data and core requirements necessary for the implementation of
finite element or space frame models.

Degree of Automation

A further obstacle that tends to deter engineers from specifying
curved-girder bridges is the sheer amount of detail necessary to
extract a design. Specifically required are: the continual re-
definition of bridge properties throughout the design processes;
the full definition of all DL and construction conditions; the
determination of all LL envelopes for truck, interstate, and lane
loads with consideration given to the various loading options as
allowed by AASHTO; and finally, the determination of all girder and
diaphragm stress combinations including those for lateral flange
bending. It is felt that any effective computer program must automate these basic but formidable tasks or the analysis function will
always be an impediment to curved girder technology.

It should be noted that the types of stresses developed in a
curved girder are varied. The primary warping normal stress, also
known as lateral flange bending or bimoment, is considered by most
analytical computer techniques. An additional stress, called
secondary warping, is induced by the normal warping stress and con-
stitutes a lateral shear. Most computer techniques do not investigate this phenomenon. The other stress, normal warping distortional stress, is a self-equilibrating stress created by the cross
section's not retaining its shape. Again most analysis techniques do
not consider this stress state. These are noted in Table 5 under
STRESSES as: Primary (Normal) Warping, Secondary (Shear) Warping,
and Warping (Normal) Distortion, respectively.

In order to quantify the current level of automation that the
various computer programs have achieved, a summary table was constructed where the basic design functions are indicated. In Table 5
it can be seen that although 20 (71%) and 19 (68%) of the programs
automate the DL and bridge properties respectively, almost none
of the systems automate the LL totally or the stress computations
to any level of effectiveness. In fact, it can be determined by
comparing the completed activities indicated in Tables 2 and 5 that
the available software has progressed little beyond analysis. Since
the automation of basic tasks, such as the DL and LL functions, must
necessarily be accomplished before automated design can occur, it
can be concluded that the automation of basic analysis tasks is the
current obstacle not only to the use of curved girders but also
to the goal of automated design.

Design Capabilities

The last function which is generally implemented in the evolution
of any program application area is the design function. This is
verified in the sparse activities which are presented in Table 6,
on design capabilities. If a similar table on the design of straight
beams were prepared, almost all design features would be covered. A
great deal of time will elapse before the status of curved-girder
software will reach the capabilities represented by the continuous beam
bridge. The reasons that this probably will be the case are:

     1. Greater requirements exist for computer storage and pro-
cessing costs for curved-girder bridges (see Table 4) .
     2. More complex analysis techniques are required for the de-
sign of curved-girder bridges over those of straight girders.
     3. The ready availability of the approximate U.S. Steel method
(i.e., HCGA1) provides an inertia which could tend to inhibit new
development.
     4. The development costs for comprehensive curved-girder soft-
ware are high.

The realities are such that an almost fully automated design is required when one considers the complex code environment that exists
today. Also, if AASHTO incorporates load factor into curved-girder
design, it is felt that automated design would be a necessity.

PROJECTED REQUIREMENTS

The requirements for curved-girder oriented software are well
known in that specific needs have been established over the years
since curved-girder bridges have become popular. Specifically, the
features which are enumerated in Tables 1, 2, 5, and 6 are those
which are badly needed and would, saving drastic and unforeseen

changes in the design code, serve well in the future. In order to give an estimate on the scope and size of such a package, a hypothetical program, DESCUS (DESign of CUrved Systems)[1] is configured (see Table 4) as follows:

1. The system would utilize the stiffness matrix formulation of the grid model and would have the capacity to handle 500 joints, 800 members, have an upper band width of 48 (for skewed bridges) and would require approximately 340 kilobytes for the storage of variables. As can be noted from Table 4, this program would not be able to handle all maximums simultaneously but, since this rarely occurs, it would handle virtually all actual design cases.

2. Such a system would be written in FORTRAN IV, level G and be modular in its construction so as to achieve the maximum portability between computers. It should incorporate both a fixed input and a problem oriented language (POL) and have direct file access as options.

3. The system should incorporate all features as given in Tables 1, 2, 5 and 6 as specified under DESCUS in Table 4.

4. The system should have the capability of handling curved bridges of any geometrical configurations including spirals, simple curves, tangents, bifuractions, etc.

Although DESCUS would be intended primarily as a design tool for the engineer, it is foreseen that such a program could also serve the researcher as well. Specific areas of interest might include: the implementation of load factor design for curved girders; the effect of diaphragm spacing on the design with all DL and LL effects considered; the determination of more refined distribution factors for curved and straight girder systems; the definition of a more comprehensive specification for diaphragm design and connections.

Thus, not only would such an effective generalized curved girder design program serve to remove the current difficulties that tend to deter engineers from placing bridges on curves, it would also enhance the state-of-the-art as well in that it could provide much needed research data. It is felt that the cost of making such a system available for general use would be more than offset in better and more efficient structures, fewer erection problems, and lower design costs.

---

[1]It should be pointed out that such a system has been developed which incorporates all of the items listed except for the POL option. This program has operated on the IBM 370/155, the IBM 1130, and the Digital Scientific META 4 computer systems. The program requires about 1.5 megabytes of core on the IBM 370/155 and has handled extremely large curved girder bridges with 13 girders and up to 4 spans [49].

494

Table 1   Program Data

NAME	SOURCE	DESCRIPTION	DATE AVAIL.	COMPUTER	LANGUAGE
CUGAR 1,2,3	Univ. of Rhode Island	Production programs with a high degree of machine independence. Although limited due to a lack of automatic LL generation and design features, these have seen much use. Production program [9]	9/71	IBM 360	FORTRAN IV G-Level
CURVBRG	Univ. of California (Berkeley)	Performs a stress and deflection analysis of curved open girder bridges idealized as a grid. Production program [7].	5/73	CDC 6400/6600, IBM 360/370	FORTRAN IV
STACRB	Univ. of Pennsylvania	Performs a static analysis of open or box sections, straight or curved girder bridges using the finite element method. Potential production program [14].	6/73	IBM 370/165	FORTRAN IV
PACGRB	Univ. of Rhode Island	A basic grid analysis with straight or curved members using the stiffness matrix method. Restrictive program [15].	12/65	IBM 1410	FORTRAN IV
DYNCRB/BG	Univ. of Pennsylvania	Performs the dynamic analysis of curved box girder bridges using the finite element and the mass condensation methods. Restrictive program [16].	6/75	IBM 370/165	FORTRAN IV Level G

Table 1 Program Data (Cont.)

NAME	SOURCE	DESCRIPTION	DATE AVAIL.	COMPUTER	LANGUAGE
DYNCRB/IG	Univ. of Pennsylvania	Perform the dynamic analysis of curved I-girder bridges using the finite element and mass condensation methods. Restrictive program [17].	6/74	IBM 370/165	FORTRAN IV
HCGA1	Richardson, Gordon and Associates	Performs analysis of horizontally curved girders using the "Approximate Method" specified in the "Highway Structures Design Handbook," Vol.I. Production Program [18, 19].	4/68	IBM 1130	FORTRAN IV
BR200	Ministry of Transportation and Communications, Canada	Performs analysis of monolithic posttensioned curved bridges of arbitrary configuration and section. Production program [20]	10/75	IBM 370/168	FORTRAN IV
Unknown[21]	Univ. of Missouri (Columbia)	Static analysis of continuous curved radially supported girder or slab bridges. Method included to obtain influence surfaces. Restrictive program [21].	11/70	IBM 360/50	Unknown
PROG 1,2	Syracuse University	Static analysis of continuous composite or noncomposite straight or curved girder bridges via a space frame. Potential production [22].	4/72	IBM 360	FORTRAN

Table 1 Program Data (Cont.)

NAME	SOURCE	DESCRIPTION	DATE AVAIL.	COMPUTER	LANGUAGE
COBRA 1,2,3	Univ. of Maryland	Continuous orthotropic plate on flexible supports including diaphragms--Fourier Series Solution with Slope Deflection. Production [23, 24, 25, 26, 27].	6/68	UNIVAC 1108	FORTRAN IV
CURSYS	Univ. of Maryland	System of continuous Curved Girders with Diaphragms--Finite Difference Method. Production [28, 29].	9/73	UNIVAC 1108	FORTRAN IV
CURSGL	Univ. of Maryland	Analysis of multispan single continuous curved girders. Variable sections allowed with warping effects directly incorporated. Production [28, 29].		UNIVAC 1108	FORTRAN IV
BOX GIRD.	Univ. of Maryland	Single Span Curved Box. Production [30, 31, 32].	8/74	UNIVAC	FORTRAN IV
CUR. TUBE	Univ. of Maryland	Continuous Curved Tube/Box. Production [33].	11/75	UNIVAC	FORTRAN IV
PLS6DOF	Univ. of Texas at Austin	Performs the analysis of a curved bridge system by idealizing it as a shell-type structure using the finite element method of analysis (6 DOF). Restricted production [34].	8/73	CDC 6600 IBM 370/158	FORTRAN IV

Table 1 Program Data (Cont.)

NAME	SOURCE	DESCRIPTION	DATE AVAIL.	COMPUTER	LANGUAGE
SHELL 6	University of Texas at Austin	Performs the analysis of a curved bridge system by idealizing it as a shell-type structure using the finite element method of analysis (6 DOF). Restricted production [35].	1971	CDC 6600	FORTRAN IV
CPG 2,3	Michigan Dept. of Highways and Transportation	Performs the analysis of a single two- or three-span continuous curved girder using the approximate U.S. Steel method. Production [19].	6/70	Burroughs B5500	FORTRAN IV
E225	Connecticut Dept. of Transportation	Performs the analysis of a system of curved girders using the lateral flange bending method. Production.	1967	UNIVAC 1106	FORTRAN V
CUCBAN	Queen's Univ., Kingston, Ontario, Canada	Performs the analysis of a single continuous circular curved beam using the stiffness method. Restricted production [36].	8/75	Burroughs B6700 IBM 360/50	FORTRAN IV
CURSTR	Univ. of California, Berkeley	Performs the analysis of prismatic folded plate structures which are circular in plan and made up of orthotropic plate elements. Restricted production [37, 38, 39].	6/70	CDC 6400	FORTRAN IV

Table 1 Program Data (Cont.)

NAME	SOURCE	DESCRIPTION	DATE AVAIL.	COMPUTER	LANGUAGE
CELL	Univ. of California, Berkeley	Performs the analysis of cellular box girder structures using the finite element method with direct stiffness. Potential production [38, 39, 40].	9/70	CDC 6400	FORTRAN IV
FINPL 2	Univ. of California, Berkeley	Performs the analysis of general nonprismatic cellular box girder structures of varying width and direct stiffness method. Prcduction [38, 39, 41].	12/71	CDC 6400	FORTRAN IV
PCGR 2	Center for Highway Research, Univ. of Texas at Austin	Performs the analysis of a single line member (straight or curved) using finite element and direct stiffness method. Production[42]	6/71	IBM 370/158	FORTRAN IV
SHELL	Univ. of California, Berkeley and Univ. of Texas at Austin	Performs the analysis of a curved bridge system by idealizing it as a shell-type structure using the finite element method (6 DOF) Restricted production[34,43,44,45]	1969	CDC 6600 CDC 6400 IBM 370/158	FORTRAN IV
STRESS (IBM 1130 Version)	Various computer hardware	A general purpose system for performing linear analysis of 2- and 3-dimensional frame and truss structures and planar grids. The latter option has been used for the analysis of curved-(cont.)	1964	Virtually all major computer system. Version given here is for the IBM 1130.	FORTRAN IV

Table 1 Program Data (Cont.)

NAME	SOURCE	DESCRIPTION	DATE AVAIL.	COMPUTER	LANGUAGE
CBRIDG	Structures Laboratory, Department of Civil Engineering, McGill Univ., Montreal, Canada	girder bridges although no curved element has been implemented. Production program [46]. A three-dimensional finite element program for the static and vibration (free) analysis of prismatic curved box girder bridges with vertical elements. Potential production [47].	3/73	IBM 360/75	FORTRAN
STRUDL (Grid)	McDonnell—ECI ICES STRUDL DYNAL, McDonnell Douglas Automation Co., Box 516, St. Louis, MO.	A general 3-dimensional finite element program with curved member capabilities. System will handle statics, dynamics, plots, influence lines, automatic LL (not with curved elements). As in any general finite element system, it can handle virtually any bridge configuration and cross section. Other versions of STRUDL are available, but McAuto version considered to represent the state-of-the-art and most widely used version. Production [13].	1/74	IBM 360/370	CDL and FORTRAN

Table 2 Analysis Capability

NAME	METHOD	SIZE LIMITS — NUMBER SPANS	NUMBER GIRDERS	NUMBER JOINTS	NUMBER MEMBERS	ELEMENTS — STRAIGHT	CURVED	DIAPHRAGMS X or K	BEAM DIAPHRAGMS	LOAD TYPES — JOINT LOADS	CONCENTRATED MEM. LOADS	UNIFORM MEM. LOADS	GENERAL CAPABILITY — HINGES	OVERHANGS	WARPING DISTORTION	SKEWED SUPPORTS	CONTINUOUS SLAB
CUGAR	Gird via the Stiffness Method	—	—			X	X	X	X	X				X		X	
CURVBRG	Gird via the Stiffness Method	—	10			X	X	X	X	X	X	X	X	X	X	X	X
STACRB	Finite Element	—	—	400	300	X	X	X	X	X	X	X		X	X	X	X
PACGRB[15]	Stiffness Grid			65		X	X		X	X		X		X			
DYNCRB/BG	Finite Element			300	100	X	X		X	X	X			X			
DYNCRB/IG	Finite Element			400	300	X	X	X	X	X	X			X			
HCGA1	U.S. Steel Method [55]	5	6			X	X	X			X	X		X	X	X	X
BR 200	Virtual Work	14	Inf.			X	X				X	X		X			
Unknown[21]	Fourier Series	1				X					X	X					
PROG 1, 2	Space Frame via Stiffness Method			40	12	X		X		X							
COBRA 1,2,3	Slope-Deflection	3	10	—	—		X		X		X	X	X	X	X	X	X
CURSYS	Finite Difference	10	10	—	—		X	X	X	X		X			X		X

Table 2 Analysis Capability (Cont.)

NAME	SIZE LIMITS: NUMBER SPANS	NUMBER GIRDERS	NUMBER JOINTS	NUMBER MEMBERS	METHOD	ELEMENTS: STRAIGHT	CURVED	DIAPHRAGMS X or K	BEAM DIAPHRAGMS	LOAD TYPES: JOINT LOADS	CONCENTRATED MEM. LOADS	UNIFORM MEM. LOADS	GENERAL CAPABILITY: HINGES	OVERHANGS	WARPING DISTORTION	SKEWED SUPPORTS	CONTINUOUS SLAB
CURSGL	10	10	—	—	Finite Difference		X	X	X	X		X			X		X
BOX GIRD	1	1	—	—	Finite Difference		X		X	X		X			X		
CUR. TUBE	3	1	—	—	Finite Difference		X		X	X		X			X		
PLS6DOF		1	800	1200	Finite Element	X	X	X	X	X		X		X	X	X	
SHELL 6					Finite Element	X	X	X	X	X		X			X	X	
CPG 2,3	2/3	1			Approximate U.S. Steel Method	X	X				X	X		X			
E225					Grid via the Stiffness Method	X	X					X					
CUCBAN	1	1	51	50	Stiffness Matrix	X	X	X	X	X		X			X	X	
CURSTR	1				Finite Strip		X		X	X				X	X		
CELL					Finite Element		X		X	X					X		
FINPL 2					Finite Element	X	X		X	X					X	X	
PCGR		1			Finite Element	X				X		X			X		

Table 2 Analysis Capability (Cont.)

NAME	SIZE LIMITS				METHOD	ELEMENTS				LOAD TYPES			GENERAL CAPABILITY				
	NUMBER SPANS	NUMBER GIRDERS	NUMBER JOINTS	NUMBER MEMBERS		STRAIGHT	CURVED	X or K DIAPHRAGMS	BEAM DIAPHRAGMS	JOINT LOADS	CONCENTRATED MEM. LOADS	UNIFORM MEM. LOADS	HINGES	OVERHANGS	WARPING DISTORTION	SKEWED SUPPORTS	CONTINUOUS SLAB
SHELL	—	—	800	1200	Finite Element	X	X	X	X	X		X		X	X	X	
STRESS (IBM 1130 Vers.)	—	—	125	250	Stiffness Matrix Method (Grid)	X			X	X	X	X	X	X		X	X
CBRIDGE	—	—	NA	NA	Finite Element	X	X	X	X	X		X		X		X	
STRUDL	—	—	Inf.	30k	Generally Grid	X	X	X	X	X		X	X	X		X	

Table 3 Survey of Curved Girder Software Usage by State Highway
Departments

STATE	IN PRODUCTION	EVALUATED
Arizona	BR200	CURT Programs
Arkansas		TDAHCB, CUGAR2, CUGAR3, CIRGIR
California	CURVBRG	
Colorado		TDAHCB
Conn.	E225	CUGAR1, CUGAR2, CURVBRG, STACRB, STRUDL II (UNIVAC), NASTRAN
Delaware		CUGAR1
Georgia	CURVBRG	
Hawaii		TDAHCB, STACRB
Illinois	STRUDL II (McAUTO)	
Kansas	STRUDL II	
Mass.	CUGAR1	
Michigan	CPG2&3	
Montana		CUGAR1
Nebraska	Nebraska Program	TDAHCB
New Hamp.	New Hamp. Program	CURVGRG, COBRA, CURSEL, CURSYS, STACBR, TDAHCB
New York	CUGAR1, CPG2	CUGAR2, COBRA, CURVBRG, TDAHCB, STACBR
N.Carolina		CUGAR1, CUGAR2, STACBR, TDAHCB
Oklahoma		TDAHCB
Oregon	STRUDL	CUGAR
Penn.	CUGAR	CUGAR2, STACBR, TDAHCB, CURSYS, CURSEL, CPG2&3
Rhode Is.	CUGAR	
Tennessee		Evaluating all available programs

Table 3 Survey of Curved Girder Software Usage (Cont.)

STATE	IN PRODUCTION	EVALUATED
Texas	PCGR2, SHELL, PLS6DOF, SHELL6, CUGARI, TDAHCB	STACBR
Vermont		CUGAR II
Washington	STRUDL II	
Wisconsin		CUGAR, CURSYS, CURSEL

Table 4 Size Requirements for a General Purpose Curved-Girder Design Program

Item	Estimated Limits[1]			Envelope Limit (100%)	DESCUS[3] (Proposed)
	Lowest	Median	High		
A. ANALYSIS CAPABILITY					
Number of Girders	5	8	10	10	14
Diaphragm Spacing	12'	10'	10'	8'	Any
Number Spans	3	4	6	10	8
Span Length Range	100'-150'	150'-200'	200'-250'	200'-250'	Any
Percentage of Bridges Covered	53%	88%	96%	100%	100%
B. APPROXIMATE UPPER[2] REQUIREMENTS FOR A GRID					
Number of Joints	180	500	1000	3200	500
Number of Members	200	600	1200	3300	800
Upper Bandwidth	18	27	33	33	48
Variable Storage Requirements (kilobytes)	60	260	650	1500	340

1. Approximations based upon a two-dimensional grid utilizing the stiffness matrix method with 3 degrees-of-freedom at each joint.

2. The storage requirements were computed on the basis that all maximums (given above in A) occur simultaneously.

3. Values shown for DESCUS were arrived at through experience of the authors either in developing or using production software for the design of curved-girder bridges.

Table 5   Automatic Capabilities

NAME	DEAD LOAD: MOMENTS, SHEARS, AND REACTIONS	DEAD LOAD: DEFLECTIONS	LIVE LOAD: MOMENTS, SHEARS, AND REACTIONS	LIVE LOAD: DEFLECTIONS	LIVE LOAD: IMPACT	LIVE LOAD: MULTILANE REDUCTION	BRIDGE PROP: NONCOMPOSITE	BRIDGE PROP: COMPOSITE	BRIDGE PROP: WIDE FLANGE SECTION TABLES	BRIDGE PROP: PLATE GIRDERS	BRIDGE PROP: INDIVIDUAL BOXES	BRIDGE PROP: CONNECTED BOXES	BRIDGE PROP: TUBES	BRIDGE PROP: OTHER	STRESSES: ALLOWABLE WITH FATIGUE	STRESSES: ALLOWABLE	STRESSES: STRESS SUMMARY	STRESSES: PRIMARY (NORMAL) WARPING	STRESSES: SECONDARY (SHEAR) WARPING	STRESSES: WARPING (NORMAL) DISTORTION
CUGAR 1,2,3	X	X					X	X	X	X	X							X		
CURVBRG	X	X	X	X			X	X										X		
STACRB																				
PACGRB [15]																				
DYNCRB/BG					X		X	X			X	X								
DYNCRB/IG					X															
HCGA1	X	X	X	X	X	X	X	X										X		
BR 200	X	X	X	X	X						X	X		X						
Unknown[21]	X	X	X					X			X			X						
PROG 1,2																				
COBRA 1,2,3	X	X					X	X										X	X	

Table 5 Automatic Capabilities (Cont.)

NAME	DEAD LOAD		LIVE LOAD				BRIDGE PROPERTIES								STRESSES				
	MOMENTS, SHEARS, AND REACTIONS	DEFLECTIONS	MOMENTS, SHEARS, AND REACTIONS	DEFLECTIONS	IMPACT	MULTILANE REDUCTION	NONCOMPOSITE	COMPOSITE	WIDE FLANGE SECTION TABLES	PLATE GIRDERS	INDIVIDUAL BOXES	CONNECTED BOXES	TUBES	OTHER	ALLOWABLE WITH FATIGUE	ALLOWABLE STRESS SUMMARY	PRIMARY (NORMAL) WARPING	SECONDARY (SHEAR) WARPING	WARPING (NORMAL) DISTORTION
CURSYS	X	X					X	X									X	X	
CURSGL	X	X					X										X	X	
BOX GIRD	X	X					X	X			X						X	X	X
CUR. TUBE	X	X			X	X	X	X			X					X	X		
PLS6DOF	X	X	X	X			X												
SHELL 6	X	X	X	X			X							X					
CPG 2,3	X	X	X	X	X		X	X		X				X					
E225	X	X	X	X			X	X		X									
CUCBAN	X	X	X	X			X							X					
CURSTR	X	X	X	X			X				X	X		X					

Table 5   Automatic Capabilities (Cont.)

NAME	DEAD LOAD: MOMENTS, SHEARS, AND REACTIONS	DEAD LOAD: DEFLECTIONS	LIVE LOAD: MOMENTS, SHEARS, AND REACTIONS	LIVE LOAD: DEFLECTIONS	LIVE LOAD: IMPACT	LIVE LOAD: MULTILANE REDUCTION	BRIDGE PROPERTIES: NONCOMPOSITE	BRIDGE PROPERTIES: COMPOSITE	BRIDGE PROPERTIES: WIDE FLANGE SECTION TABLES	BRIDGE PROPERTIES: PLATE GIRDERS	BRIDGE PROPERTIES: INDIVIDUAL BOXES	BRIDGE PROPERTIES: CONNECTED BOXES	BRIDGE PROPERTIES: TUBES	BRIDGE PROPERTIES: OTHER	STRESSES: ALLOWABLE WITH FATIGUE	STRESSES: ALLOWABLE STRESS SUMMARY	STRESSES: WARPING PRIMARY (NORMAL)	STRESSES: WARPING SECONDARY (SHEAR)	STRESSES: WARPING (NORMAL) DISTORTION
CELL	X	X	X	X			X				X	X							
FINPL 2	X	X	X	X			X				X	X		X					
PCGR 2	X	X	X	X			X			X				X					
SHELL	X	X	X	X			X							X					
STRESS (IBM 1130 Vers.)																			
CBRIDG																	X		
STRUDL									X	X									

Table 6 Design Capabilities

NAME	AASHTO			OTHER CODE	FEATURES					GENERAL					OTHER
	YEAR	WORKING STRESS	LOAD FACTOR		COVER PLATE ENVELOPES	COVER PLATE CUT OFF	SHEAR CONNECTOR SPACINGS	STIFFENER SPACINGS	RECYCLED DESIGN	GEOMETRY PLOT	DESIGN ON STORED DATA	INTERACTIVE CAPABILITY	P O L	INFLUENCE LINE PLOTS	
CUGAR 1,2,3										X			X		Stores Envelopes
CURVBRG															
STACRB															
PACGRB [15]															
DYNCRB/BG															
DYNCRB/IG															
HCGA1															
BR 200	75	X													
Unknown[21]															
PROG 1, 2															
COBRA															

Table 6   Design Capabilities (Cont.)

NAME	AASHTO			OTHER CODE	FEATURES				GENERAL						OTHER
	YEAR	WORKING STRESS	LOAD FACTOR		COVER PLATE ENVELOPES	COVER PLATE CUT OFF	SHEAR CONNECTOR SPACINGS	STIFFENER SPACINGS	RECYCLED DESIGN	GEOMETRY PLOT	DESIGN ON STORED DATA	INTERACTIVE CAPABILITY	P O L	INFLUENCE LINE PLOTS	
CURSYS															
CURSGL															
BOX GIRD															
CUR. TUBE		X									X				
PLS6DOF															
SHELL 6															
CPG 2, 3	75	X				X	X	X							
E225															
CUCBAN															
CURSTR															
CELL															

Table 6 Design Capabilities (Cont.)

NAME	AASHTO YEAR	AASHTO WORKING STRESS	AASHTO LOAD FACTOR	OTHER CODE	FEATURES COVER PLATE ENVELOPES	FEATURES COVER PLATE CUT OFF	FEATURES SHEAR CONNECTOR SPACINGS	FEATURES STIFFENER SPACINGS	GENERAL RECYCLED DESIGN	GENERAL GEOMETRY PLOT	GENERAL DESIGN ON STORED DATA	GENERAL INTERACTIVE CAPABILITY	GENERAL PLOT	GENERAL INFLUENCE LINE PLOTS	OTHER
FINPL 2															
PCGR															
SHELL															
STRESS (IBM 1130 Version)										X			X		Various versions have design features.
CBRIDG															
STRUDL										X			X	X	

PROGRAM DETAILS

The Dynamic Response of Curved Bridges/I-Girder (DYNCRB/IG)

Categories: Curved girders; Bridges; Dynamics; Elasticity; Finite
    element; Structural engineering
Title: The Dynamic Response of Curved Girder Bridges/I-Girder
Author: S. Shore, S. K. Chaudhuri, Department of Civil and Urban
    Engineering, University of Pennsylvania, Philadelphia, Pa.,
    19104
Maintenance: Mr. James Cooper, Structural Research Engineer, Bridge
    Structures Group, FHWA, Office of Research (HRS-11), Washington,
    D.C., 20590
Date: June, 1974
Capability: Program was developed for obtaining dynamic and static
    responses of horizontally curved I-girder bridges under a
    moving vehicular loading. The load can be a 2-axle, 4-wheeled
    spring vehicle (which can be adjusted to simulate a single load)
    moving at constant speed along a circular path parallel to the
    centerline of the bridge. Centrifugal force exerted by the
    vehicle on the bridge is allowed in the analysis. The program
    utilizes many of the routines of the static program STACRB [14]
    and, therefore, incorporates much of its general and finite
    element capability.
Method: The finite element method is used where the bridge is
    modeled as follows:
        1. The concrete deck slab is discretized by annular sec-
            tor plate elements where the interaction between the
            vehicle and the deck is through these elements .
        2. The curved steel girders are represented by thin-
            walled curved-beam elements and the bridge supports
            are specified at appropriate nodes on these elements .
        3. The cross-diaphragms are discretized by beam or frame
            type elements.
    The mass condensation procedure coupled with the linear accel-
    eration method is utilized in obtaining dynamic effects.
Limitations: The assumptions and limitations for the structure and
    vehicle are as follows:
        1. The material is assumed to be homogeneous and to obey
            Hooke's law.
        2. All bridge deflections are assumed to be small .
        3. Inclined webs are not allowed .
        4. The torsional stiffness of the diaphragms are ne-
            glected .
        5. Only two-or three-axled vehicles are allowed .
        6. Unsprung vehicular mass is neglected .
        7. Only linear springs are allowed .
    Further, no automatic mesh generator or structural plot accom-
    panies the program, making the input voluminous and difficult
    to verify. The program also lacks an automatic AASHTO DL and
    LL generator.
Programming Language: FORTRAN IV, level G

Documentation: A user manual [17] and a research report for STACRB
   [14], which forms the basis of the static analysis, are available.
Input: Control information, coordinates of the nodes, element definition, connectivity, boundary conditions. Also required is
   the magnitude, configuration, location, and velocity of the
   moving loads along with those nodes for which the master de-
   gree-of-freedoms are to be selected.
Output: An echo check of all input along with detailed properties
   of the bridge and vehicle, displacements, static forces,
   natural frequencies, centrifugal forces, and impact factors
Software operation: Batch
Hardware: IBM 370/165 using 400K bytes of core and 18 (IBM 2311)
   disk files
Usage: Used as a research tool on the CURT Project at the Univer-
   sity of Pennsylvania
Typical running time: Unknown
Availability: Mr. James Cooper, Structural Research Engineer,
   Bridge Structures Group, FHWA, Office of Research (HRS-11),
   Washington, D.C. 20590

Curved Girder Analysis (CUGAR1, CUGAR2, CUGAR 3)

Categories: Curved girders; Bridges; Elasticity; Beams
Title: Curved Girder
Authors: F. H. Lavelle, R. A. Greg, H. R. Wimmer, University of
   Rhode Island, Kingston, Rhode Island, 02881
Maintenance: Mr. James Cooper, Structural Research Engineer, Bridge
   Structures Group, FHWA, Office of Research (HRS-11), Washington
   D.C. 20590
Dates: CUGAR1 (IBM 360), September 1971; CUGAR1 (IBM 1130), March
   1973; availability dates unknown for CUGAR2 and CUGAR 3
Capability: CUGAR1 [9, 10, 12], CUGAR2 and CUGAR3 [11, 12] are
   programs which analyze curved-girder bridges by stiffness
   matrix formulations of a linear elastic planar grid structure.
   The systems are oriented toward production and a maximum degree of machine independence. Numerous input/output options
   are available including geometry and section property generators.
      All CUGAR algorithms utilize curved and straight elements
   [16] as follows:
      1. CUGAR1 allows only I-sections and assumes the uniform
          torsion theory to provide torsional stiffness.
      2. CUGAR2 incorporates a lateral flange bending method to
          provide torsional stiffness.
      3. CUGAR3 analyzes box girder sections.
Method: The method of analysis was developed at the University of
   Rhode Island [16] and incorporates straight or curved elements
   in a stiffness formulation of planar gridworks.
Limitations: The curved-girder bridge is idealized as a linear
   elastic horizontal planar grid loaded normal to its plane. The
   specific limitations are as follows:

1. CUGAR1 requires an additional analysis to account for the axial stresses produced by twisting. Truss diaphragms must also be approximated as equivalent beams.
2. No automated LL feature is incorporated.
3. Allowables with respect to fatigue and nonfatigue stresses are not generated.
4. Loads are applied only at joints with equivalent concentrated loads substituted for distributed loads.

Programming language: FORTRAN IV, level G

Documentation: Complete documentation exists for CUGAR1 under Volume 1-Users Information [9] and Volume 2-System Information [10]. Status of documentation for CUGAR2 and CUGAR3 is unknown.

Input: The basic input consists of joint coordinates, support conditions, member (and diaphragm) properties, radii,and loading conditions. Various options that exist are as follows:

1. Coordinates and support conditions may be input either via a COGO option, various standard mesh generators, or individually.
2. Member properties may be calculated automatically for composite or noncomposite sections and by using AISC designations for rolled beams.
3. Maximums can be automatically calculated for Dead Load but must be positioned manually for Live Loading.

Output: Substantial output is generated from CUGAR including: an echo check of all input; reactions; displacements at each joint; moments; shear and torsion for each member at each joint. Also given are precision indicators, status checks, and error conditions along with a plot of the structure.

Software operation: Batch

Hardware: Program operates under 360/OS/HASP, requires less than 64,000 bytes of core storage, and uses four sequential access files (which can be on a single pack). Also required is a card reader, printer, and an optional card punch (or additional sequential access file).

The system has been converted to a Burroughs B-5500, an RCA Spectra 70 M35, Univac 1106,and the IBM 1130.

Usage: Program has been used extensively in the design of curved-girder bridges by various state agencies and numerous private consultants.

Availability: Mr. James Cooper, Structural Research Engineer, Bridge Structures Group, FHWA, Office of Research (HRS-11), Washington, D.C., 20590

The Dynamic Response of Horizontally Curved
Box Girder Bridges (DYNCRB/BG)

Category: Curved Girders; Bridges; Dynamics; Elasticity; Beams; Box girders

Title: The Dynamic Response of Horizontally Curved Box Girder Bridges

Authors: S. Shore, R. O. Rabizadeh, Department of Civil and Urban Engineering, University of Pennsylvania, Philadelphia, Pa., 19104

Maintenance: Mr. James Cooper, Structural Research Engineer,
    Bridge Structures Group, FHWA, Office of Research (HRS-11),
    Washington, D.C., 20590
Date: June, 1975
Capability: Program yields the dynamic deflections, stresses and
    reactions of box girder bridges caused by two moving loads
    traveling with constant velocity on circumferential paths. It
    also calculates the static responses of the same forces sta-
    tioned at different positions on the paths as well as centri-
    fugal force. Further, the program is capable of calculating
    the frequencies, related node shapes, and dynamic responses.
Method: The finite element method is used where the bridge is
    modeled as follows:
    1. An annular plate element is used for the top deck and
       bottom flanges .
    2. A cylindrical shell element is used for the web of the
       box·
    3. A rectangular plate element is used for the inter-
       mediate and end diaphragms·
    4. A pin-jointed bar element is used for diaphragms com-
       posed of struts.
Limitations: The assumptions and limitations for the structure and
    vehicle are as follows:
    1. The material is assumed to be homogeneous and obey
       Hooke's law .
    2. All bridge deflections are assumed to be small.
    3. Inclined webs are not allowed·
    4. Supports are located radially·
    5. The coupling of reactive forces is neglected.
    6. The moving vehicle is represented by 2 constant forces
       with no mass traveling with constant velocity·
    7. The damping of the structure is neglected.
    Further, no automatic mesh generator or structural plot accom-
    panies the program making the input voluminous and difficult to
    check. Program lacks an automatic AASHTO DL and LL generator.
Programming language: FORTRAN IV, level G
Documentation: Both a research report [16] and a user's manual [48]
    exist for the system.
Input: Control information, coordinates of the nodes, element de-
    finition, connectivity, boundary conditions, magnitude, loca-
    tion and velocity of the moving forces, and selection of the
    nodes from which the master freedoms are to be chosen
Output: Properties of the elements, boundary conditions, displace-
    ments, natural frequencies, impact factors
Software operation: Batch
Hardware: IBM 370/165 using 400 K bytes of core and 17 disk files
Usage: Used as a research tool on the CURT Project at the Univer-
    sity of Pennsylvania
Typical running time: Unknown
Availability: Mr. James Cooper, Structural Research Engineer,
    Bridge Structures Group, FHWA, Office of Research (HRS-11),
    Washington, D.C., 20590

Continuous Curved Bridge Program (BR200)

Category: Curved girders; Box girders; Voided slabs; Prestress;
    Concrete; Bridges; Beams
Title: Continuous Curved Bridge Program
Authors: N. J. Varmazis, D. C. Weeks, H. T. Chan, A. Urbanowicz,
    T. I. Campbell, T. J. Fritz, Engineering and Management Systems
    Branch, Ministry of Transportation and Communications, Ontario,
    Canada
Maintenance: Authors
Date: October 28, 1975
Capability: Performs the structural analysis of monolithic curved
    bridges. The bridge can be on a fully transitioned curved
    (tangent, spiral, circle) or any part thereof. The program
    calculates bending and torsional moments, shear forces,and
    deflections at tenth points for: DL, LL + I (AASHTO standard
    loads or special vehicle width up to 10 axles), prestress, and
    cantilevers. The system has been used to design many con-
    crete prestressed box and voided slab bridges in the U.S. and
    in Canada.
Method: Influence coefficients determined from the equations of
    virtual work cast in matrix form. The bridge section is re-
    duced to a line element with all the inertia concentrated at
    the center.
Limitations: Current versions have limits which can handle 1-14
    spans and 0-5 lanes of traffic. The analysis neglects the
    plate action of the bridge,making the analysis one-dimensional.
    Supports provide either full or no torsional restraint.
Programming language: Program is composed of about 8,000 source
    statements written in FORTRAN IV.
Documentation: Complete and current [20]
Input: The input data are entered on two input sheets for bridge
    data and section properties. Bridge data include : curve
    data, roadway width, LL definition, span lengths, constraints,
    and eccentricities. Section properties include: areas, mo-
    ments in inertia, and superimposed DL.
Output: Complete and well-formulated tables are output from the
    program including: an echo check of all input, geometry,
    section properties, various structural coefficients, influence
    lines for bending, torsion,and shear, as well as maximum
    bending, torsion,and shear resultants.
Software operation: Batch and RJE under OS with program being modi-
    fied to operate in interactive (TSO) mode
Hardware: Currently operating on an IBM 370/168. Has been modified
    throughout its history to run on IBM 7040, 7094, and 360/65
    computers. Program requires 150K of core and a card reader,
    printer,and one disc pack.
Usage: Program has or is currently being used for production by
    the states of Arizona and Maryland and the Ontario Ministry of
    Transportation and Communications.
Typical running time: The running times for two examples which were
    run on an IBM 370/168 are as follows: a 3-span, 2-lane bridge
    under an AASHTO Truck and Lane Loading required 17 seconds of
    CPU time and a cost of $3.90; a 12-span, 2-lane bridge under

a Special Truck Load required 264 seconds of CPU time and a
cost of $52.25.
Availability: Available to the various federal and state agencies
within the U.S. through the Ministry of Transportation and
Communications, Ontario, Canada (see Authors)

A Program to Analyze Curved-Girder Bridges (PACGRB)

Categories: Curved girders; Bridges; Beams; Stiffness method;
Elasticity
Title: A Program to Analyze Curved-Girder Bridges
Authors: F. H. Lavelle, J. S. Boick, University of Rhode Island,
Kingston, Rhode Island, 02881
Maintence: Unknown
Date: December 1965
Capability: Performs a basic analysis of planar grid structures
[15]. Joint or uniform member loads are allowed.
Method: The general stiffness matrix method is used with curved and
straight members.
Limitations: Program preceeds and forms the basis of analysis for
the CUGAR systems. It is not, however, meant to be a pro-
duction tool in that no geometry generation or design is
accomplished.
Programming language: FORTRAN IV
Documentation: In research report form [15]
Input: Joint coordinates, member properties and coincidences, and
loads
Output: Displacements, reactions, member moments, shears,and tor-
sion
Software operation: Batch
Hardware: IBM 1410 with 40,000 character core storage
Usage: Unknown
Typical running time: A 2-span, 3-girder bridge with 32 mem-
bers, 21 joints, and 4 loading conditions required 55 minutes.
Same problem required 1.7 minutes on the UNIVAC 1107.
Availability: Listing contained in Reference 15

Three-Dimensional Analysis of Horizontally Curved Bridges
(PROG1, PROG2)

Category: Curved girder; Box girders; Stiffness method; Bridges;
Space frame
Title: Three-Dimensional Analysis of Horizontally Curved Bridges
Authors: P. J. Brennan, J. A. Mandel, Department of Civil Engin-
eering, Syracuse University, Syracuse, New York, 13210
Maintenance: Mr. James Cooper, Structural Research Engineer,
Bridge Structures Group, FHWA, Office of Research (HRS-11),
Washington, D.C., 20590
Date: April, 1972 (Preliminary)
Capability: Performs a space frame analysis of composite or non-
composite curved or straight girder bridges via the stiffness

method. The system is composed of a two—program suite that
operates in series. Program 1 generates the geometry and
the physical properties of the bridge which are punched onto
cards and fed into Program 2. Program 2 solves for member
forces, moments and displacements.
Method: A three-dimensional space frame analysis utilizing the
stiffness method with a banding is incorporated into the
program.
Limitations: Severe limitations exist with respect to the number of
joints and members that can be accommodated. Also, intermediate diaphragms on curved bridges must be placed radially.
Section properties such as moments of inertia, areas,and torsional constants must be computed by the user. Only joint
loads are allowed and must be input manually to simulate DL
and LL conditions.
Programming language: FORTRAN
Documentation: Users manual is available [22] which includes user
instructions, examples,and source listings
Input: Program 1 requires punched cards containing physical data
which describe the bridge including material, section properties, geometry, splice information, and diaphragm locations.
Program 2 requires the specification of all joint coordinates,
member properties,and supports (which is output from Program 1).
Also required for Program 1 are the number of loading cases
along with the specific loads for each case.
Output: Program 1 outputs all geometric material and section pro-
perties for use in Program 2. Program 2 outputs reactions,
displacements (including rotations), moments,and forces in all
members for each load case along with various control data
(such as stiffness coefficients) for purposes of monitoring.
Software operations: Batch
Hardware: IBM 360
Usage: Used primarily as a research tool on the CURT project [12]
Availability: Mr. James Cooper, Structural Research Engineer,
Bridge Structures Group, FHWA, Office of Research (HRS-11),
Washington, D.C., 20590

Analysis of Horizontally Curved Multibeam Bridges

Categories: Beams; Bridges; Curved beams; Elasticity; Influence
surfaces; Plates; Structural engineering
Title: Analysis of Horizontally Curved Multibeam Bridges
Authors: Cenap Oran, S. C. Lin, Department of Civil Engineering,
University of Missouri, Columbia, Missouri, 65201
Maintenance: Unknown
Date: November, 1970
Capability: A static analysis of simple-span,curved,radially
supported girder or slab bridges is formulated utilizing
Fourier series. Poisson's ratio has been retained, and a
procedure has been included to accelerate the convergence
of bending moments in beams located directly under con-
centrated loads. A method also has been developed whereby

the influence surfaces for various effects may be obtained.
Program is not oriented toward practical application.
Method: Fourier series solutions are incorporated for an isotropic
curved plate over simple supports. The structure is idealized
as individual beams and slab panels assembled to satisfy continuity and equilibriums (unknowns are deflections and rotations making continuity automatically satisfied). The loading is expressed as a Fourier sine series in the circumferential direction so that superposition can be utilized to add
effects.
Limitations: Numerous limitations are inherent within the program:
       1. All supports must lie along a radial line.
       2. The beam and slab are simply supported .
       3. Each beam must have a constant cross section·
       4. All girders must be concentric·
       5. No circumferential overhang is allowed·
       6. The bridge slab is assumed isotropic.
       7. Diaphragms are neglected.
Programming language: Unknown
Documentation: No system documentation per se but an exposition
of the method exists in the form of a research report [21].
Input: Unknown
Output: Unknown
Software operation: Unknown
Hardware: IBM 350/50
Usage: Program has been declared a research vehicle by the authors
and is not oriented toward production.
Availability: Unknown

A Computer Program for the Analysis of
Curved Open Girder Bridges (CURVBRG)

Categories: Bridges; Curved girders; Stiffness method; Beams;
Elasticity; Structural analysis
Title: A Computer Program for the Analysis of Curved Open Girder
Bridges
Authors: G. H. Powell, D. P. Mondkar, University of California,
Berkeley, California, 94720
Maintenance: Mr. James Cooper, Structural Research Engineer,
Bridge Structures Group, FHWA, Office of Research (HRS-11),
Washington, D.C., 20590
Date: May, 1973
Capability: Performs a stress and deflection analysis of curved
open girder bridges using the stiffness method. The bridge
superstructure is idealized as a grid with an added degree of
freedom (in addition to the normal three degrees of freedom
for bending, shear,and torsion) to permit the consideration
of warping torsion effects. Five types of members are allowed:
prismatic or variable depth I-sections; composite decks where
the slab may be introduced by dividing it transversely between
joints on the girder; beam-type diaphragms which can be either
composite or noncomposite; diagonally braced cross frames; wind

bracing members. Support settlement and hinges may be specified.

Provision is included to specify construction stages as is a considerable LL capability. Truck loadings and load trains may be defined as standard patterns which may be positioned anywhere on a girder by command.

The program is considered to be excellent state-of-the-art work which could form the basis of an effective production program.

Method: The bridge is idealized as a two-dimensional grid which is analyzed by the direct stiffness method. The member stiffness matrix is determined by subdividing each member into eight straight submembers and assembling a substructure stiffness matrix. The degree of freedom which is returned to the subassemblage is then eliminated by static condensation to yield an equivalent grid member stiffness. Four degrees of freedom are formulated for each joint; namely, two rotations, one vertical displacement,and a warping displacement.

Limitations: Program is limited in that a fully automatic LL feature is not included. Also, it is indicated in the reference [7] that discrepancies exist between the program output and experimental data for stresses due to warping torsion (lateral flange bending). No design features are included within the system. Formating of output is also minimal.

Programming language: 6000 FORTRAN IV Statements

Documentation: Excellent user documentation exists with example problems [7]

Input: Control information (number of girders, etc.), material properties with variation for construction staging, joint and girder geometry, cross-sectional properties, supports and hinges, slab properties, diaphragms, construction type, wind bracing, cross section (for stress output), truck load patterns, load conditions,and load case combinations

Output: Vertical displacements at specified joints; support reactions; the stresses in the top and bottom fibers and web for sections specified; the moment at each end for each slab strip; stresses in the diaphragms and wind bracing for each load case combination; the specified sum of various envelopes; error messages

Software operation: Batch

Hardware: CDC 6400/6600. Also a double precision version for the IBM 360/370 is available. System requires 8 disc or tape files.

Usage: Used by the California and Georgia Departments of Transportation as well as various consultants (such as the Swindell-Dressler Co. where it is used for curved and straight girder bridges)

Typical running time: Unknown

Availability: Mr. James Cooper, Structural Research Engineer, Bridge Structures Group, FHWA, Office of Research (HRS-11), Washington, D.C., 20590

The Static Analysis of Curved Bridges (STACRB)

Category: Curved girders; Bridges; Finite element; Elasticity
Title: The Static Analysis of Curved Bridges
Author: S. Shore, Department of Civil and Urban Engineering,
University of Pennsylvania, Philadelphia, Pa., 19104
Maintenance: Mr. James Cooper, Structural Research Engineer,
Bridge Structures Group, FHWA, Office of Research (HRS-11),
Washington, D.C., 20590
Date: June, 1973
Capability: The program STACRB (Static Analysis of Horizontally
Curved Bridges) utilizes the finite element method to analyze
highway bridges of open (plate girder) and closed (box girder)
sections. The bridge structures are visualized as an assemblage of elements interconnected to a discrete number of nodal
points. Specifically, STACRB contains a library of 6 elements
(annular, cylindrical, rectangular diaphragm, single straight
beam, curved beam, and straight strut) in order that the bridge
can be modeled accurately and in detail [14].
Method: The finite element method is used wherein the bridge is
modeled from a library of 6 specialized elements (see Capability given above).
Limitations: The program is considered by the authors as a research
tool rather than a production program for the following reasons:
1. The input required to model an actual bridge is large.
2. The core requirements and running time for the analysis of even a small bridge (for all the required
cycled DL and LL calculations) could be very large.
3. No automatic AASHTO compatible DL and LL generator are
incorporated within the system.
4. No envelopes are stored for use by designers.
5. No design capability exists within the system.
6. No plot routine exists within the system where the
input could be visually verified.
However, since the analysis method has the inherent capability
of determining lateral flange bending, and since nonlinear
effects can be added, the program has a potential as a continuing research vehicle and perhaps a production tool for
special problems.
Programming language: FORTRAN IV
Documentation: User's manual [14] exists with an example problem.
Input: The input consists of 8 segments entered in free and fixed
format:
1. Primary Data - This includes basic bridge data such
as method of analysis, bridge type, number of spans,
loading type, etc., given in free format.
2. Control Data - This includes system control data such
as type of coordinate system, number of degrees of
freedom per joint, output options, etc., given in
free format.
3. Node Coordinates - The node coordinates along with
supports and skew angles given in fixed format.
4. Connectivity - The element types which connect the
various nodes given in fixed format.

5. Element Definition - The material and geometrical
    properties of each element given in fixed format.
6. Boundary Conditions - The 13 allowable possible
    degrees of freedom for each element given in fixed
    format.
7. Selecting Output - The various options whereby output
    can be selectively given.
8. Loads - The local or global definition of the static
    loading conditions given in free format.

Output: This is also given in segments. The first correspond to
    the output segments defined above (i.e., Primary Date, etc.).
    The last three are: Node Displacements, Stress Resultants,
    Stress Couples and Reactions.

Software operation: Batch

Hardware: IBM 370/165

Usage: Unknown

Availability: Mr. James Cooper, Structural Research Engineer,
    Bridge Structures Group, FHWA, Office of Research (HRS-11),
    Washington, D.C., 20590

Horizontal Curved Girder Analysis (HCGA1)

Categories: Curved girders; Bridges; Beams; Influence lines

Title: Horizontal Curved Girder Analysis Program

Authors: Harry J. Yoder, Richardson, Gordon and Associates,
    3 Gateway Center, Pittsburgh, Pennsylvania, 15230

Maintenance: Author

Date: May, 1968

Capability: This program performs the analysis for a horizontally
    curved girder system consisting of up to five continuous spans
    and six composite or noncomposite girders. The AASHTO Code is
    followed, and the program, along with the associated method, has
    been used in the design of innumerable curved-girder bridges.

Method: The "Approximate Method" described in the Highway Structure
    Design Handbook, Vol. 1 [19] has been used to obtain DL and LL
    moments, shear, reactions, and deflections in accordance with
    the AASHTO Specifications. The conjugate beam method and
    Maxwell's reciprocal theorem are used to determine results for
    straight continuous spans and then are modified to account for
    curvature.

Limitations: Numerous limitations are inherent within the method
    and are summarized as follows:

1. All girders must have the same relative stiffness.
2. All supports must be radial or the ratio of inside
    girders to outside girder span lengths must be
    consistent for all spans.
3. The torsion due to curvature is resisted by the inter-
    action of the girders and diaphragms and not by the
    stiffness of the individual members .
4. The curvature must be relatively small.
5. Each tenth panel within each span is idealized as be-
    ing prismatic.

Programming language: IBM 1130/1800 Basic FORTRAN IV

Documentation: Excellent combined user/system documentation is available [8]
Input: Span lengths, moments of inertia, location of changes in section, uniform initial and superimposed DL for each span, LL distribution factors, type of AASHTO live load, number of LL lanes on structure, radius of outside girder,and girder spacings
Output: Moments, shears, and deflections at the tenth points due to DL and LL, shear and moment envelopes are given. Also output are maximum reactions and uplift due to DL and LL for each girder along with maximum LL deflection in each span in the outside girder. Optional are: influence lines, loads,and load positions for maximum effects.
Software operation: Batch
Hardware: 8 Kiloword IBM 1130 with Card Read/Punch and an 1132 Printer
Usage: Program and method have been used extensively in the design of numerous curved-girder bridges.
Typical running time: From the author's experience, a 2-span, 5-girder noncomposite bridge on a 32 k IBM 1130 requires about 15 minutes.
Availability: Through the CEPA user group library and from Richardson, Gordon and Associates (see Authors)

Curved Orthotropic Bridge Analysis (COBRA)

Category: Curved girder; Orthotropic slab; Concrete; System; I-girder; Box girder; Diaphragms; Continuous analysis
Title: Curved Orthotropic Bridge Analysis
Authors: C. P. Heins, L. C. Bell, Civil Engineering Department, University of Maryland, College Park, Maryland, 20742
Maintenance: Authors
Date: September 1969
Capability: Analysis of single, two- or three-span continuous curved bridges, with radial supports. Considers continuous dead load and concentrated live loads. Interior diaphragms can be incorporated. Loads can be positioned at any location. The program had been used to design various curved bridges. Incorporates warping effects directly.
Method: Slope-Deflection Fourier series solution of continuous orthotropic plates on flexible supports
Limitations: 1, 2,or 3 span; 1-7 girders
Programming language: Program is composed of 1400 cards per system, i.e., 1, 2 or 3 span, and is written in FORTRAN IV
Documentation: Complete and current [23, 24, 25, 26, 27]
Input: The input data is entered on a series of cards, including load magnitude, radius and angle to load, girder and plate stiffness
Output: Gives deflection, slope, bending moment, shear force, St. Venant torsion moment, warping torsion moment, and bimoment at tenth points along each girder
Software operation: Batch

Hardware: Currently operating on IBM 7094 and UNIVAC 1108
    computers
Usage: Program has been used by various consultants, the Maryland
    State Highway Administration, the Federal Highway Adminis-
    tration, and the University of Maryland.
Typical running time: The running time on the IBM 7094 for a 4-gir-
    der bridge subjected to the AASHTO vehicle was .29 min. for a
    single span, .35 min. for two spans,and .34 min. for three
    spans.
Availability: Available to anyone through the Maryland State High-
    way Administration and C. P. Heins, University of Maryland
    (see Authors)

Curved System (CURSYS)

Category: Curved system; I-girder; Box girder; Diaphragms, Con-
    tinuous beam analysis
Title: Curved System
Authors: C. P. Heins, C. H. Yoo, Civil Engineering Department,
    University of Maryland, College Park, Maryland, 20742
Maintenance: Authors
Date: September 1974
Capability: Analysis of continuous span curved multigirder bridges.
    Variable section properties. Uniform patch or continuous loads
    and concentrated loads at specified node points. Diaphragms
    may be beams or trusses. Composite or noncomposite sections
    allowed.
Method: Finite difference solution of Vlasov equations
Limitation: Present version can have 1-15 spans, 1-10 girders.
Programming language: Program is composed of 1300 source statements
    written in FORTRAN IV
Documentation: Complete and current [28, 29]
Input: Girder stiffnesses and loads at specified nodes
Output: Deflection, rotations, bending moment, shear, bimoment,
    St. Venant torsion moment, warping torsion moment
Software operation: Batch
Hardware: Currently operating on UNIVAC 1108
Availability: Available to anyone through the Maryland State High-
    way Administration and C. P. Heins, University of Maryland
    (see Authors)

Curved Single Girder (CURSGL)

Category: Curved; Single girder; I-Girder; Box girder; Analysis
Title: Curved Single Girder
Authors: C. P. Heins, C. H. Yoo, Civil Engineering Department,
    University of Maryland, College Park, Maryland, 20742
Maintenance: Authors
Date: September, 1974
Capability: Analysis of multispan continuous single curved girder.
    Variable section properties, concentrated loads, patch uniform
    loads can be considered. Incorporates warping effects directly.

Method: Finite difference solution of Vlasov equations
Limitations: Present version is limited to 1-15 spans.
Programming language: Program is composed of 800 source statements written in FORTRAN IV.
Documentation: Complete and current [28, 29]
Input: Girder stiffness at various node points, loads at specified nodes.
Output: Deflection, rotations, bending moment, shear, bimoment, St. Venant torsion moment, and warping torsion moment
Software operation: Batch
Hardware: Currently operating on UNIVAC 1108
Usage: Civil Engineering Department of the University of Maryland and the Maryland State Highway Administration
Availability: Available to anyone through the Maryland State Highway Administration and C. P. Heins, University of Maryland (see Authors)

Curved Box (Box Girder)

Category: Curved girder; Box; Single-span; Composite; Noncomposite
Title: Curved Box
Authors: C. P. Heins, J. C. Oleinik, Civil Engineering Department, University of Maryland, College Park, Maryland, 20742
Maintenance: Authors
Date: August, 1974
Capability: Analysis of a single span curved box girder, composite and noncomposite. Includes effects of warping and distortion of cross section. Variable location of interior diaphragms included. Variable stiffness properties can be accommodated.
Method: Finite difference solution of Vlasov equations and BRF analogy using Dabrowski expressions
Limitation: One span, one box, infinite number of diaphragms
Programming language: Program is composed of 200 cards and is written in FORTRAN IV.
Documentation: Complete and current [30, 31, 32]
Input: Girder stiffnesses, location of interior diaphragms, and load locations at specific nodes
Output: Deflection, rotations, bending moment, shear, St. Venant torsion, bimoment, warping torsion, angular distortion, normal bending stress, normal warping stress, normal distortional stress
Software operation: Batch
Hardware: Currently operating on UNIVAC 1108
Availability: Available to anyone through C. P. Heins (see Authors)

Curved Tubular Girder (Cur. Tube)

Category: Curved girder; Boxes; Tubes; Analysis; Design continuous spans
Title: Continuous Curved Tube Girder Design
Authors: C. P. Heins, J. P. Stroczkowski, Civil Engineering Depart-

ment, University of Maryland, College Park, Maryland, 20742
Maintenance: Authors
Date: December 1975
Capability: Automatic design of continuous 2- to 3-span curved tubular
    or box girders. Develops force envelopes (moment, shear, tor-
    sion, bimoment) due to AASHTO loadings at tenth points along
    girder. Incorporates warping effects directly.
Method: Finite difference solution of Vlasov equations
Limitations: 2- or 3-span continuous single girder
Program language: Program is composed of 2800 cards, and is written
    in FORTRAN IV.
Documentation: Complete and current [33]
Input: Girder stiffness and loads at various node points
Output: Bending moment, shear, bimoment, and torsion moment enve-
    lopes. Maximum live and dead load deformations.
Software operation: Batch
Hardware: Currently operating on UNIVAC 1108
Running time: Two-span continuous requires approximately one minute
Availability: C. P. Heins (see Authors)

Analysis of Curved Folded Plate Structures (CURSTR)

Category: Curved folded plates; Curved bridges; Curved box girders
Title: Analysis of Folded Plate Structures
Authors: C. Meyer, A. C. Scordelis, University of California,
    Berkeley, California, 94720
Maintenance: Unknown
Date: June 1970
Capability: Performs the analysis of prismatic folded plate struc-
    tures which are circular in plan and made up of orthotropic
    plate elements. A curved open frame or box girder bridge can
    be idealized as a folded plate structure. The program solves
    for the internal forces and displacements.
Method: Each plate element is idealized by a number of circum-
    ferential finite strips. The finite strip method is used to
    determine the strip stiffness. The displacement patterns are
    assumed to vary as harmonics in a circumferential direction.
    In the tranverse direction, a linear variation of the in-plane
    displacements and a cubic variation of the normal displacements
    are chosen. A direct stiffness harmonic analysis is used to
    analyze the assembled structure.
Limitations: The structure must be simply supported by radial
    diaphragms at two ends.
Programming language: The program is written in FORTRAN IV.
Documentation: Complete [37, 38, 39]
Input: The input consists of the geometrics, properties of members
    and materials, and load data.
Output: Output consists of axial forces, moments, shears, and
    deflections due to applied loads.
Software operation: Batch or RJE to CDC 6400
Hardware: Program can be operated on most computers with Fortran
    capability. Program developed and run on CDC 6400.

Usage: The program has been used in a continuing program of research on curved box girders at the University of California
at Berkeley. Small-scale model tests were made at the University to verify the analytical solution and computer program.
Typical running time: The running time for a single-span, two-cell
box girder for one AASHTO truck loading position was 27 seconds.
Availability: Contact the Department of Civil Engineering, University of California, Berkeley (see Authors).

Cellular Structures of Arbitrary Plan Geometry (CELL)

Category: Curved bridges; Box girders
Title: Cellular Structures of Arbitrary Plan Geometry
Authors: K. J. William and A. C. Scordelis, University of Cal-
ifornia, Berkeley, California, 94720
Maintenance: Unknown
Date: September, 1970
Capability: Performs the analysis of cellular structures (box
girders) and determines the nodal point displacements and the
internal stresses in the member elements. Orthotropic plate
properties and arbitrary loadings and boundary conditions can
be treated.
Method: The solution is based on the method of finite elements.
For a general box bridge system, two-dimensional shell or plate
elements and one-dimensional transverse or longitudinal frame
type elements may be used.
Limitations: The program analyzes structures with constant depth.
The structure must be made up of top and bottom horizontal deck
slabs and vertical webs.
Programming language: FORTRAN IV
Documentation: Complete [38, 39, 40]
Input: The input consists of the geometrics, properties of members,
materials, and load data. Automatic element and coordinate
generation options minimize the required input data.
Output: Output consists of axial forces, moments, shear, and de-
flections due to the applied loads.
Software operations: Batch or RJE to CDC 6400
Hardware: Program can be operated on most computers with Fortran
capability. Program developed to run on CDC 6400.
Usage: The program has been used in a continuing program of research on curved box girders at the University of California
at Berkeley. Small-scale model tests were made at the Univer-
sity to verify the analytical solution and computer program.
Typical running time: The running time for a single-span, two-cell
box girder for one loading condition was 193 seconds.
Availability: Contact the authors at the University of California,
Berkeley (see Authors).

Nonprismatic Folded Plates with Plate and Beam Elements (FINPL2)

Category: Curved bridges; Box girders
Title: Nonprismatic Folded Plates with Plate and Beam Elements
Authors: C. Meyer and A. C. Scordelis, University of California,
    Berkeley, California, 94720
Maintenance: Unknown
Date: December, 1971
Capability: The program can analyze general nonprismatic cellular
    structures of varying width and depth. The program determines
    the nodal point displacements and the internal stresses in the
    member elements. Orthotropic plate properties and arbitrary
    loadings and boundary conditions can be treated.
Method: The solution is based on the method of finite elements.
    The structure is discretized by dividing it longitudinally into
    a certain number of vertical sections. Stiffness matrices
    which approximate the behavior in the continuum are developed
    for the finite elements based on assumed displacement patterns.
    Finally, an analysis based on the direct stiffness method is
    performed.
Limitations: The structure must be made up of top and bottom hori-
    zontal deck slabs and vertical webs.
Programming language: FORTRAN IV
Documentation: Complete [38, 39, 41]
Input: The input consists of the geometrics, properties of mem-
    bers, materials, and load data. Automatic element and coor-
    dinate generation options minimize the required input data.
Output: Output consists of axial forces, moments, shears, and de-
    flections due to the applied loads.
Software Operation: Batch or RJE to CDC 6400
Hardware: Program can be operated on most computers with FORTRAN
    capability. Program developed and run on CDC 6400.
Usage: The program has been used in a continuing program of re-
    search on curved box girders at the University of California
    at Berkeley. Small-scale model tests were made at the Univer-
    sity to verify the analytical solution and computer program.
Typical running time: The running time for a single-span, two-cell
    box girder for one AASHTO truck loading position was 300
    seconds.
Availability: Contact the authors at the University of California,
    Berkeley (see Authors).

Finite Element Method of Analysis for Plane Curved Girders (PCGR2)

Category: Curved girders; Bridges; Beams
Title: Finite Element Method of Analysis for Plane Curved Girders
Author: William P. Dawkins while with the Center for Highway Re-
    search, The University of Texas at Austin, 200-300 W. 21st,
    Austin, Texas, 78712
Maintenance: Unknown
Date: June, 1971
Capability: The program analyzes a single line member which may be
    composed of any variation of curved or straight segments. The

supports may be composed of linearly elastic spring restraints, both rotational and translational, which allow for simulation when analyzing a single member which is restrained by other members (such as diaphragms).

Method: The method of solution combines the ease of visualization of discrete element techniques and the efficiency of direct matrix structural analysis solution methods.

Limitations: Curved members must be divided into a series of straight chords. Systems with supports skewed to the radial direction cannot be satisfactorily handled by the program; that is, when a bridge system is simulated as a single member, the torsional stiffnesses of the members are not considered.

Programming language: FORTRAN IV

Documentation: Complete [42]

Input: Input data consist of the geometry, bending stiffness, twisting stiffness, support characteristics, and the loading system.

Output: The output data consist of a list of the input data, twisting moments, shear forces, joint displacements, and bending moments.

Software operation: The program operates in a batch or TSO environment.

Hardware: Currently operating on an IBM 370/158 at the Texas Department of Highways and Public Transportation

Usage: The program is currently being used by the Bridge Division of the Texas Department of Highways and Public Transportation.

Typical running time: A typical highway bridge girder analysis requires approximately 10 seconds of CPU time.

Availability: Contact the Center for Highway Research, University of Texas at Austin (see Authors).

The Analysis of Thin Shells (SHELL)

Category: Shell structures; Curved bridges; Finite elements

Title: The Analysis of Thin Shells

Author: C. P. Johnson while at the University of California, Berkeley, California, 94720

Maintenance: Center for Highway Research, University of Texas at Austin, 200-300 W. 21st, Austin, Texas, 78712

Date: 1969

Capability: The program can analyze a curved bridge system by idealizing it as a shell-type structure with one- and two-dimensional elements. Individual elements can vary in thickness. The analysis determines the displacements, reactions, element moment and stress resultants due to arbitrary loading and support conditions. Temperature effects and truss elements can be handled.

Method: The program uses finite elements employing a five degree-of-freedom nodal system of displacements. These consist of three translations but only two rotations.

Limitations: The capacity of the program is 800 nodes and 1200 elements. The significant limitations are the fact that the program is general purpose in nature and not specifically oriented to curved bridge analysis.

Programming language: The program is composed of approximately 2700
    source statements written in FORTRAN IV.

Documentation: Complete [34, 43, 44, 45]

Input: The input data are entered on general purpose forms (batch
    operation) in fixed format and consist of the geometry, nodal
    point coordinates, temperature differences, and surface direc-
    tion cosines and displacements, nodal forces, element stress
    resultants, averaged nodal stress resultants, element stresses,
    and principal stresses for the loading system.

Software Operation: Batch, RJE, or time sharing

Hardware: Currently operating on an IBM 370/158 at the Texas De-
    partment of Highways and Public Transportation

Usage: The program was demonstrated by the authors in the solution
    of a curved, through-type, continuous railroad bridge. The
    program is operational at the Texas Department of Highways and
    Public Transportation.

Typical running time: Unknown

Availability: Contact the Center for Highway Research, University
    of Texas at Austin (see Maintenance)

The Analysis of Thin Shells (PLS6DOF)

Category: Shell structures; Curved bridges; Finite Elements

Title: The Analysis of Thin Shells

Authors: C. P. Johnson, T. Thepchatri, K. M. Will while at the
    University of Texas at Austin, 200-300 W. 21st, Austin, Texas,
    78712

Maintenance: Center for Highway Research, University of Texas at
    Austin, 200-300 W. 21st, Austin, Texas, 78712

Date: August 1973

Capability: The program is a revised version of program SHELL and
    has the same general capabilities except that six degrees of
    freedom (DOF) are considered instead of five. In addition, a
    set of rather cumbersome inputs (required to define rotations)
    has been eliminated.

Method: The program uses finite elements employing a six DOF nodal
    system of displacements. The six DOF consist of three transla-
    tions and three rotations.

Limitations: The capacity of the program is 800 nodes and 1200
    elements. The significant limitations are the fact that the
    program is general purpose in nature and not specifically
    oriented to curved bridge analysis.

Programming language: FORTRAN IV

Documentation: General description [34]

Input: The input data are entered on general purpose forms (batch
    processing) in fixed format and consist of the geometry, nodal
    point coordinate generation features, nodal point numbering,
    boundary conditions, material properties, and loading condi-
    tions.

Output: The output consists of a duplicate list of the input data,
    nodal point coordinates, temperature differences, and surface
    direction cosines and displacement, nodal forces, element

stress resultants, averaged nodal stress resultants, element
stresses, and principal stresses for the loading system.
Software operation: Batch, RJE, or time sharing
Hardware: The program was developed on a CDC 6600 at the University
of Texas at Austin, and has been implemented on the Texas Department of Highways and Public Transportation's IBM 370/158.
Usage: The program is in use by the Texas Department of Highways
and Public Transportation.
Typical running time: Unknown
Availability: Contact the Center for Highway Research, University
of Texas at Austin (see Maintenance).

Finite Element Analysis of Shell-Type Structures (SHELL 6)

Category: Shell structures; Curved bridges; Finite elements
Title: Finite Element Analysis of Shell-Type Structures
Author: M. R. S. Abdelraouf while at the University of Texas at
Austin, 200-300 W. 21st, Austin, Texas, 78712
Maintenance: Unknown
Date: 1971
Capability: The program can analyze a curved bridge system by
idealizing it as a shell-type structure with one- and two-
dimensional elements. The analysis determines the displacements, reactions, element moment, and stress resultants due to
the loading system and support conditions.
Method: The program uses finite elements employing a six degree-of-
freedom (DOF) nodal system of displacements. It has an option
which enables the use of a refined membrane and bending element
in the analysis. The program is based on isotropic material
properties and constant element thickness.
Limitations: The significant limitation is the fact that the program is general purpose in nature and not specifically designed
for the analysis of curved highway bridge systems.
Programming language: FORTRAN IV
Documentation: Complete [35]
Input: The input consists basically of the geometry, material
properties, and loading systems.
Output: The output consists of a list of the input data, nodal
point coordinates, and effects (displacements, etc.) of the
load system.
Software operation: Batch or RJE mode
Hardware: The program was developed and run on a CDC 6600.
Usage: The program was used in a demonstration by the Center for
Highway Research at the University of Texas at Austin to assess
the values of program SHELL (5 DOF) in the analysis of a curved,
through-type, continuous railroad bridge.
Typical running time: Unknown
Availability: Contact the University of Texas at Austin (see
Author).

Continuous Plate Girder (CPG 2,3)

Category: Curved girders; Plate girder; Steel; Bridges
Title: Continuous Plate Girder
Author: Maurice Van Auken, Michigan Department of Highways and
    Transportation, State Highways Building, Lansing, Michigan,
    48904
Maintenance: Unknown
Date: June, 1970 (latest revision)
Capability: There are two programs - one for analyzing a two-span
    curved plate girder and the other for analyzing a three-span
    curved plate girder. Composite girders can be handled.
    Standard AASHTO live loads are automatically moved for maximum
    effects. Program considers fatigue, shear connectors, and
    transverse stiffeners. The girders may have cantilevers.
Method: The method of solution is for a straight continuous girder
    and the effects of curvature are added according to the U.S.
    Steel Handbook [19].
Limitations: Current versions analyze only two- and three-span
    curved continuous units. The programs handle only one girder
    and not a girder bridge system. Other limitations are noted
    in the approximate method used in the U.S. Steel Handbook.
Programming language: FORTRAN IV
Documentation: Input instructions and input data form
Input: The input data consist of girder and slab dimensions, span
    lengths, depth variations, live load type and distribution,
    noncomposite and composite loads, cantilever data, radii, num-
    ber of girders and diaphragm spacings.
Output: The output data consist of girder section properties, dead
    load and live load moments, tensile and compressive stresses
    in the top and bottom flanges with live load stress range, dead
    load and live load shears, deflections due to the beam weight
    and each deck pour, final plate thickness and length, live load
    deflections, stiffener spacing, shear connector spacings, re-
    actions, girder weight, and an echo print of the input. Mo-
    ments, stresses, etc., are given at the span tenth points.
Software operation: Batch processing on a Burroughs B5500
Hardware: The programs are currently operating on a Burroughs B5500.
Usage: The programs are being used by the states of Michigan and
    New York.
Typical running time: Approximately one minute of computer time for
    an average girder analysis
Availability: Contact the author at the Michigan Department of
    Highways and Transportation (see Author).

Analysis of I-Type Curved Girder Bridges (E225)

Category: Curved bridges; Curved I-beams; Steel; Bridges; Beams
Title: Analysis of I-Type Curved Girder Bridges
Author: Barry Miller, Bridge Design Section, Connecticut Department
    of Transportation, 24 Wolcott Hill Road, Wethersfield, Ct., 06109
Maintenance: Unknown
Date: 1967 (with later modification)

Capability: The program analyzes a system of curved girders, com-
    putes, and outputs displacements and dead and live load effects
    including stresses. Diaphragms can be beam- or truss-type mem-
    bers. Members may be composite or noncomposite.
Method: The program uses a stiffness matrix grid analysis developed
    by Lavelle as part of the CURT project and is referred to as
    the lateral flange bending method. The curved bridge is
    idealized as a planar grid. Warping torsion is included.
Limitations: The program is limited to open-framed girders. Loads
    are uniform along member or concentrated at joints. There is
    no automatic live load movement.
Programming language: FORTRAN V
Documentation: Input forms only
Input: For radially framed bridges, the program computes all mem-
    ber and joint numbering and joint coordinates. Otherwise,
    this data must be input. Input data are entered on special
    forms in fixed format and consist of girder properties, di-
    mensions, loads, etc.
Output: The output consists of an echo print of the input data,
    coordinates, section properties for members between joints,
    joint loads and displacements, dead load and live load
    effects (shear, torque, and moment) at each member end, and
    the flange stresses due to dead load and live load conditions
    at each end of each member. There are no summations.
Software operation: Batch or time sharing to a UNIVAC 1106
Hardware: The program is currently operating on a UNIVAC 1106 com-
    puter.
Usage: The program is used by the Connecticut DOT in a production
    environment.
Typical running time: 15 seconds for average two-span bridge
Availability: Contact the author in the Bridge Design Section of
    the Connecticut Department of Transportation (see Author).

Curved Continuous Beam Analysis (CUCBAN)

Category: Continuous curved beams; Curved prestressed girders
Title: Curved Continuous Beam Analysis
Authors: T. I. Campbell, B. Neil, M. Lacasse, D. Turcke, Queen's
    University, Department of Civil Engineering, Kingston, Ontario,
    Canada
Maintenance: Author
Date: August 1975
Capability: The program performs the analysis of a single contin-
    uous circular curved or straight beam, which may be prestressed,
    for general applied loads. Uniform loads can be handled as
    well as concentrated loads at the joints. Straight or para-
    bolic prestress profiles in any or all members are allowed.
Method: The stiffness method of analysis is used in the program to
    determine the effect of general loading conditions, including
    prestressing, on continuous circular curved beams. The beams
    to be analyzed are assumed to consist of members which are
    rigidly connected to each other and supported at various points
    along their length.

Limitations: The program is limited to single girders which must
    be prismatic. The analysis is limited to small deflections and
    homogeneous isotropic materials that obey Hooke's Law. Uniform
    distributed torque induced by eccentricity of the beam weight
    is not taken into account.
Programming language: FORTRAN IV
Documentation: User's Manual [36]
Input: Input data consist of structure parameters, elastic modulus,
    member designations and properties, joint restraint list, cum-
    ulative restraint list, number of loaded joint and members, and
    loads applied at joints.
Output: Output data consist of joint displacements, support re-
    actions, member end actions (moment, shear and torsion), an
    echo printout of the input data, and the stiffness matrix.
Software operation: Batch or RJE
Hardware: The program has been operated on an IBM 360/50 and the
    Burroughs B6700 computers. It can be operated on most computers
    with FORTRAN IV capability.
Usage: The program has been used in research studies at the Queen's
    University.
Availability: Contact authors at the Department of Civil Engin-
    eering, Queen's University, Kingston, Ontario, Canada (see
    Authors).

                Structural Engineering System Solver (STRESS)

Category: Grid; Stiffness method; Continuous beams
Title: Structural Engineering System Solver
Authors: S. J. Fenves, R. D. Logcher, S. I. Mauch, K. F. Rein-
    schmidt
Maintenance: Maintenance is provided by the various hardware ven-
    dors that support STRESS on their computer systems.
Date: 1964
Capability: STRESS is a system for performing the linear analysis
    on two- or three-dimensional frame and truss structures and
    planar grids. The latter option has been used for the analysis
    of curved girder bridges although no curved element has been
    known to have been incorporated. (The curvature being approxi-
    mated by straight chords.) The system incorporates a problem-
    oriented language (POL) which is used by the engineer to
    specify and solve general structural problems. Numerous
    versions are available including those for the IBM 1620,
    7090, 1130, 360, and 370 computer systems.
Method: The stiffness matrix method
Limitations: Numerous limitations exist in that the system was de-
    signed for solving a wide variety of structural problems.
    Specifically, no DL or LL capabilities exist for bridge
    structures, no curved element is available, and warping is
    not considered.
Programming language: FORTRAN IV
Documentation: Complete user's manual [46]

Input: Structure type, joint coordinates, member properties, re-
    leases and connectivity, support conditions, loadings
Output: Deflections, moments, shears at joints and all reactions
Software operation: Batch
Hardware: Currently operating on virtually all major computer sys-
    tems and even some programmable calculators
Usage: Program has been used to analyze numerous curved girder
    bridges by means of the grid formulation with straight chords.
    Diaphragms that are K or X trusses can be handled by using the
    "Alter Stiffness Matrix Statement", but it is not known if this
    is used extensively.
Typical running time: A plane grid consisting of 117 joints, 212
    members and one loading condition requires 2 hours, 48
    minutes on a minimal IBM 1130 configuration.
Availability: Through the various hardware vendors

Static and Free Vibration Analysis of Curved
Box Bridges (CBRIDG)

Category: Curved girder; Box girders; Static analysis; Vibration
Title: Static and Free Vibration Analysis of Curved Box Bridges
Author: A. R. M. Ram, McGill University, Montreal, Canada
Maintenance: Unknown
Date: March, 1973
Capability: A three-dimensional finite element model is adopted as
    as idealization for prismatic cellular bridges having straight
    or a curved alignment. Solutions of static or dynamic re-
    sponses are possible. The boxes may be formed by a single cell,
    contiguous cells,or separate cells. The cell shape can be
    rectangular or trapezoidal and be constructed of steel or
    concrete. A mesh generator is incorporated within the program.
Method: The finite element method is used where elements are con-
    figured to simulate the bridge in three dimension. The first
    lowest free vibration frequencies and the corresponding modes
    are calculated by using the simultaneous iteration method.
Limitation: No degree of automation for DL and LL is incorporated
    for the program. Also, the program is limited to curved box
    bridges with vertical web elements. No design is performed
    within the system.
Programming language: FORTRAN
Documentation: Complete [47]
Input: General nodal coordinates, element information (from which
    the specific elements are generated via the mesh generator),
    material properties, and loads.
Output: Nodal displacements, stresses, strains, and resultant
    forces and moments at the corners and at the center of
    each element. Also, the first lowest free vibration
    frequencies and modes are output.
Software operation: Batch
Hardware: IBM 360/75
Usage: Research at McGill University
Typical running time: 1000 equations with an upper bandwidth of

100 require 715 CPU seconds for one loading condition.
Availability: Unknown

McDonnell-ECI ICES STRUDL (STRUDL)

Categories: Curved girders; Finite elements; Elasticity; Structural engineering; Bridges
Title: McDonnell-ECI ICES STRUDL
Author: A system originally developed at MIT by R. Logcher and S. Fenves. Version discussed involved the enhancement by McDonnell Douglas Automation Co. and Multisystems (originally ECI). Many other systems, however, exist and are too numerous to include here.
Maintenance: McDonnell-ECI ICES STRUDL DYNAL, McDonnell Douglas Automation Co., Box 516, St. Louis, Mo
Date: January 1974
Capability: A general 3-dimensional finite element program with curved member or element capabilities. Curved girder analysis assumes a grid analysis with members curved horizontally, but a 3-dimensional model is possible by using a space frame or numerous elements. The system features include: statics, dynamics, plot, influence lines, automatic LL (not with curved elements). As in any general finite element system, it can also handle any bridge configuration and cross section.
Method: The bridge is idealized most often as a 2-dimensional grid using the direct stiffness finite element method.
Limitations: Program has few automatic or design features specialized to curved girder bridges. Also, no nonlinear warping effects are analyzed.
Programming language: CDL and ICETRAN
Documentation: Excellent system and users[13] documentation is available.
Input: Joint (or node) coordinates, member and element incidences, material properties joint and uniform member loads, member properties. Specialized "K" or "X" diaphragm must be input via a modification of the stiffness matrix.
Output: Echo check of all input, member moments, shears and axial forces, joint displacements, reactions, general dynamic effects.
Software operation: Batch and time share (for data checking only)
Hardware: IBM 360/370 (McDonnell Douglas version). System to be known to exist on UNIVAC 1108, and CDC 6600 series (pending Georgia Institute of Technology GT-ICES development).
Usage: A highly successful production system used by numerous consultants and some states (see Table 3)
Availability: Via McDonnell Douglas, and various other sources (contact ICES User Group for specific information).

REFERENCES

1 Schmitt, W., "Interchange Utilizes Arc Welded Horizontally Curved Girder Spans," unpublished paper submitted to Lincoln Arc Welding Foundation, 1966.

2 McManus, P. F., Nasir, G. A., Culver C. G., "Horizontally Curved Girders-State of the Art," ASCE Structural Journal, Vol. 95, No. ST 5, May 1969.

3 Subcommittee on Curved Girders, Joint AASHTO-ASCE Committee on Flexural Members, "Survey of Curved Girder Bridges", Civil Engineering-ASCE, pp. 54-56.

4 Bazant, Z. P., "Conjugate Analogy of Space Structures," J. Struct. Div., ASCE, Vol, 92, No. ST 3, Proc. Paper 4850, June 1966.

5 Schulz, M., and Chedraui, M., "Tables for Circularly Curved Horizontal Beams with Symmetric Uniform Load," Journal of American Concrete Institute, Vol. 53, Title No. 53-58, May 1957.

6 Engel, S., "Structural Analysis of Circular Curved Beams," J. Struct. Div., ASCE, Vol. 93, No. ST 1, Proc. paper 5099, Feb. 1967.

7 Powell, G. H., "CURVBRG: A Computer Program for Analysis of Curved Open Girder Bridges," University of California, Berkeley, California, June 1973.

8 Yoder, L. J., "Horizontal Curved Girder Analysis," Richardson, Gordon and Associates, Pittsburgh, Pennsylvania, April 1968.

9 Lavelle, F. H., Grieg, R. A., and Wemmer, H. R., "CUGAR 1 (Curved Girder Analysis Revision), A Program to Analyze Curved Girder Bridges, Volume 1 - Users Information," University of Rhode Island, Kingston, Rhode Island, 1971.

10 Lavelle, F. H., "1130 CUGAR, A Program to Analyze Curved Girder Bridges as Modified from CUGAR 1, Volume II, 1130 System Manual," University of Rhode Island, Kingston, Rhode Island, March 1973.

11 Powell, G. H., et al., "Fact Sheets for Computer Programs: CURVBRG, COBRA, CURSEL, SURSYS, Horizontal Curved Girder Analysis," (Richardson, Gordon and Associates), CUGAR 1, CUGAR 2, CUGAR 3, June 1973.

12 Lavelle, F. H., "The CUGAR Programs," University of Rhode Island, Kingston, Rhode Island, June 1973.

13 McDonnell - ECI ICES STRUDL, User Manual, McDonnell Douglas Automation Co., St. Louis, Mo., and Engineering Computer International, Cambridge, Mass., 1974.

14 Shore, S., "Users Manual for the Static Analysis of Curved Bridges (STACRB)," CURT Report No. TO 173, University of Pennsylvania, Philadelphia, Pennsylvania, June 1973.

15 Lavelle, Francis H., Boick, John S., "A Program to Analyze Curved Girder Bridges," University of Rhode Island, Division of Engineering Research and Development, Engineering Bulletin No. 8, December 1965.

16 Shore, S., Rabizadeh, R. O., "The Dynamic Response of Horizontally Curved Box Girder Bridges," CURT Resport No. TO 175, University of Pennsylvania, Philadelphia, Pennsylvania, June 1975.

17   Shore, S., Chaudhuri, S. K., "Users Manual for the Dynamic Response of Curved Bridges/I-Girder (DYNCRB/IG)," CURT Report No. TO 274, University of Pennsylvania, Philadelphia, Pennsylvania, June 1974.

18   Richardson, Gordon and Associates, Consulting Engineers, "Analysis and Design of Horizontally Curved Girder Steel Bridge Girders," United States Steel Corporation Structural Report, 1963.

19   United States Steel Corporation, Highway Structures Design Handbook, Volume I, Pittsburgh, Pennsylvania 1965.

20   Varmazis, H. J., et al., "Continuous Curved Bridge Analysis Program BR 200," Engineering and Management Systems Branch, Ministry of Transportation and Communications, Ontario, Canada, January 1976.

21   Oran, C., Lin, S. C., "Analysis of Horizontally Curved Multi-Beam Bridges," The College of Engineering, The University of Missouri-Columbia, November 1970.

22   Brennan, P. J., Mandel, J. A., "Preliminary Users Manual, Program for Three Dimensional Analysis of Horizontally Curved Bridges," Department of Civil Engineering, Syracuse University, April 1972.

23   Bell, L. C., Heins, C. P., "Curved Girder Computer Manual," Report No. 30, Department of Civil Engineering, University of Maryland, College Park, Maryland, September 1969.

24   Bell, L. C., Heins, C. P., "Analysis of Curved Girder Bridges," ASCE Structural Division Journal, Vol. 96, No ST 8, August 1970.

25   Heins, C. P., and Bell, L. C., "Curved Girder Bridge Analysis," Journal of Computers and Structures, Vol. 2, Pergamon Press, England, 1972, pp. 785-797.

26   Heins, C. P., The Presentation of the Slope-Deflection Method for the Analysis of Curved Orthotropic Highway Bridges," Civil Engineering Report, No. 15, June 1967.

27   Bell, L. C., and Heins, C. P., "The Solution of Curved Bridge Systems Using the Slope-Deflection Fourier Series Method," Civil Engineering Report, No. 19, June 1968.

28   Yoo, C., Heins, C. P., "Users Manual for the State Analysis of Curved Bridge Girder," Report No. 55, Department of Civil Engineering, University of Maryland, College Park, Maryland, September 1973.

29   Yoo, C. H., Evick, D. R., and Heins, C. P., "Non-Prismatic Curved Girder Analysis," Journal of Computers and Structures, Vol. 3, 1973.

30   Oleinik, and Heins, C. P., "Diaphragms for Curved Box Beam Bridges," ASCE Structural Division Journal, Vol. 101, No. ST 10, October 1975.

31   Heins, C. P., Oleinik, J. C., "Curved Box Beam Bridge Analysis," Journal of Computers and Structures, 1976.

32   Oleinik, J. C., Heins, C. P., "Diaphragm Requirements for Curved Box Girders," Civil Engineering Report, No. 58, September 1974.

33   Heins, C. P., Stroczkowski, J. P., "Computerized Design of Continuous Curved Tubular Girders," Journal of Computers and Structures, 1976.

34 Johnson, C. P., Thepchatri, T., Will, K. M., "Static and Buckling Analysis of Highway Bridges by Finite-Element Procedures," Research Report 155-1F, Center for Highway Research, University of Texas at Austin, August 1973.

35 Abdelraouf, M. R. S., "Finite Element Analysis of Shell-Type Structures," Thesis presented to the University of Texas at Austin in partial fulfillment of the requirements for the degree of Doctor of Philosophy, 1971.

36 Campbell, T. I., Neil, B., Lacasse, M., Turcke, D., "User's Manual for Curved Continuous Beam Analysis Programme," Department of Civil Engineering, Queen's University, Kingston, Ontario, Canada, August 1975.

37 Meyer, C., Scordelis, A. C., "Analysis of Curved Folded Plate Structures," UC-SESM, No. 70-8, University of California, Berkeley, June 1970.

38 Scordelis, A. C., "Analytical Solutions for Box Girder Bridges," Proceedings of the International Conference on Development in Bridge Design and Construction, Crosby Lockwood & Son, Ltd., England, 1971.

39 Scordelis, A. C., "Analytical and Experimental Studies of Multi-Cell Concrete Box Girder Bridges," Bulletin of the International Association for Shell and Spatial Structures, No. 58, Secretarial: Alfonso XII, 3, Madrid, Spain, 1975.

40 Willam, K. J., Scordelis, A. C., "Computer Program for Cellular Structures of Arbitrary Plan Geometry," UC-SESM, No. 70-10, University of California, Berkeley, September 1970.

41 Meyer, C., Scordelis, A. C., "Computer Program for Non-Prismatic Folded Plates with Plate and Beam Properties," UC-SESM, No. 71-23, University of California, Berkeley, December 1971.

42 Dawkins, W. P., "Finite Element Method of Analysis for Plane Curved Girders," Research Report 56-20, Center for Highway Research, University of Texas at Austin, June 1971.

43 Johnson, C. P., "The Analysis of Thin Shells by a Finite-Element Procedure," SEL Report No. 67-22, University of California, Berkeley 1967.

44 Johnson, C. P., Smith, P. G., "A Computer Program for the Analysis of Thin Shells," Structural Engineering Laboratory Report No. 69-5, University of California, Berkeley 1969.

45 Johnson, C. P., "Analysis of Thin Shells," A User's Manual, Department of Civil Engineering, University of Texas at Austin, October 1970.

46 "Structural Engineering Systems Solver (STRESS) for the IBM 1130 (1130-EC-03X), Version 2, Users Manual", IBM Application Program H20-0340-2, International Business Machines Corporation, White Plains, N.Y., 1967.

47 Fam, A. R. M., "Static and Free Vibration Analysis of Curved Box Bridges", Structural Dynamics Series No. 73-2, Department of Civil Engineering and Applied Mechanics, McGill University, Montreal, Canada, March 1973.

48 Shore, S., Rabizadeh, R. O., "Users Manual for the Dynamic Response of Curved Bridges/Box Girders (DYNCRB/BG)," CURT Report No. TO 273, University of Pennsylvania, Philadelphia, Pennsylvania, December 1973.

49 Schelling, D. R., "Automated Curved Girder Analysis and Design" U.S. DOT-CURT Symposium on Curved Girders, Boston, Massachusetts, June 1973.

SYMBOLIC AND ALGEBRAIC MANIPULATION LANGUAGES AND THEIR
APPLICATIONS IN MECHANICS

Jarl Jensen
Frithiof Niordson

The Technical University of Denmark

INTRODUCTION

In mechanics, as in all exact sciences, computers have served for
numerical calculations as long as they have been available. However,
their capacity for processing data has only recently been applied to
symbolic manipulation of formulae in mechanics. The meaning of
"symbolic manipulation" is, perhaps, most easily explained with the
help of a simple example.

Thus, to establish the identity

$$\left(x + \frac{4}{3}x^2 - \frac{6}{5}x^3\right)^4 = x^4 + \frac{16}{3}x^5 + \frac{88}{15}x^6 - \frac{1312}{135}x^7 - \frac{27944}{2025}x^8$$

$$+ \frac{2624}{225}x^9 + \frac{1056}{125}x^{10} - \frac{1152}{125}x^{11} + \frac{1296}{625}x^{12}$$

we have only to apply a few simple rules of arithmetic. Since
neither inventiveness nor imagination is necessary during the
process, the expansion of the left-hand side may well be (and was in
fact) performed by a suitably programmed computer.

Of course, this being possible, there is virtually no limit to
the complexity of problems of this kind that can be solved by automated algebraic manipulators other than that set by the capability
of the computer.

It seems that the first documented use of computers for
symbolic manipulation was made in 1953 [1,2]. About ten years later
the first general purpose systems appeared for algebraic calculations, i.e., ALPAK (a forerunner of ALTRAN) [3] and FORMAC [4]. Since
then, the development of systems and algorithms for processing
formulae on computers has been rapid. Today, there are a number of
general as well as more particular languages and algorithms that
may be implemented on a broad variety of computers. The purpose of
this chapter is to discuss some of these languages, namely

                              ALTRAN
                              REDUCE
                              SCHOONSCHIP
                              SAC-1
                              SYMBAL
                              MACSYMA
                              SCRATCHPAD
                              FORMAC

     The last language on the list, FORMAC, will be the subject of
a more detailed discussion, and with its help we shall demonstrate
the application of symbolic manipulation to some particular
problems in mechanics.
     With all the progress that has taken place in the last decade
or so in this field of computer applications, a large and rapidly
growing number of scientists might be expected to be making use of
this facility. But this does not seem to be the case. In fact, sur-
prisingly few are doing so, and one gets the impression that there
are more people designing systems than using them. This seems to be
the case in all fields of science, not only in mechanics, where the
number of documented applications known to the authors is below ten.
     Thus, many scientists familiar with the capacity of modern
computers for numerical work seem to be unaware of the fact that
they have facilities at hand that may be useful when the need arises
for large and complex manipulations of formulae.

USE OF SYMBOLIC AND ALGEBRAIC MANIPULATION LANGUAGES

The use of computers for symbolic and algebraic manipulation of
formulae is documented in the following areas: mathematics, group
theory, numerical analysis, general relativity, celestial mechanics,
theoretical seismology, quantum electrodynamics, and solid
mechanics. In addition, several authors have emphasized and applied
some special facilities of different systems. A study of these
cases indicates that the symbolic manipulation languages have a wide
range of applications.
     At one end, there is the need for an "algebraic desk calcula-
tor" with versatility and fast turnaround time. Interactive use of
the computer becomes necessary for such applications, which for instance, occur at certain stages of deductive work for deriving or
checking tedious algebraic derivations.
     At the other end, systems are derived for special purposes;
for instance, analytic series expansions with thousands of terms.
Such systems use large resources of core, cpu-time, and I/O operations, and often all of them.
     In between are the general purpose systems for algebraic
computations, corresponding to languages like ALGOL or FORTRAN in
numerical computations. The language discussed later, FORMAC, may be
considered as such a general tool.
     Computers are thus currently used for numerical computations
as well as for algebraic manipulations. It is, however, important to
realize that for scientific work the computer is probably best

utilized when both modes are applied simultaneously or in sequence.
Some problems require a numerical and some an analytical answer. In
either case, the road to the final answer may involve both numerical
and algebraic calculations.

There are, for instance, problems in mechanics for which
standard numerical procedures are available but which could be
solved more elegantly and accurately using analytical methods if
the formula work could be overcome. Automated formula manipulation
might afford the most effective solution to such problems. An
example of this (an eigenvalue problem) is given below.

SEVEN SYMBOLIC AND ALGEBRAIC MANIPULATION SYSTEMS

Considering the limited use of automated symbolic and algebraic
manipulations within structural mechanics until now, it seems to be
more important to describe common facilities and possibilities in
the field of symbolic and algebraic manipulation than to give a
complete description of all these systems. Hence, in the following,
we shall confine ourself to a short description of seven of the more
commonly used systems. Later, we shall concentrate on a more detailed description of FORMAC.

Our description of these seven systems will perhaps not en-
able the reader to decide which system is best suited to his
purpose. It will only be a guide. However, more often than not, we
are bound to use the systems that are installed on the computer
to which we have access, and the choice today is often very
limited.

The authors have, in fact, only had access to FORMAC. Hence,
our description of other systems is based solely on available
documentation.

ALTRAN

ALTRAN [5-7]: developed and maintained by Bell Telephone Laboratories. An early version of ALTRAN, ALPAK, was designed by M. D. McIlroy
and W. S. Brown in 1963. ALTRAN is a programming language for the
formal manipulation of rational functions in several variables with
integer coefficients. As in most scientific programming languages,
the elementary arithmetic operations $(+, -, *, /, **)$ are provided.
In addition, ALTRAN also provides a facility for substitution. More
complicated operations such as differentation and greatest common
devisor are available through procedure calls to library routines.

The ALTRAN system, composed of a translator, interpreter, and
run-time library, has been written almost entirely in FORTRAN IV.
Considerable effort has been spent to achieve a portable system
without undue sacrifice of efficiency.

The syntax of the language is FORTRAN-like (main program and
subroutines, no block structure, but recursivity). The semantics
are PL/1-like. Every dependent variable must be declared with type
and attributes. The system contains about 100 library routines for
matrix operations, truncation of power series, etc.

Table 1 Program Availability

PROGRAM NAME	SOURCE OF THE PROGRAM	HARDWARE	LANGUAGE	HOW SOLD	COST	MAINTAINED BY SOURCE
ALTRAN	Computing Information Services Bell Laboratories 600 Mountain Ave. Murray Hill, New Jersey 07974	any	FORTRAN	tape	license and patent fees for industrial users; $35 fee for educational use	no
REDUCE 2	REDUCE Secretary Department of Physics University of Utah Salt Lake City, Utah 84112 Digital Equipment Corp. Users Society Maynard, Mass. 01754	IBM 360/370 DEC PDP-10	LISP	user supplied tape tape	$35 $61	yes
SCHOONSHIP	M. Veltman CERN	CDC 6000/7000	COMPASS			
SAC 1	G. E. Collins University of Wisconsin Computer Sciences Dept. 1210 West Dayton St. Madison, Wisc. 53706	any	99% FORTRAN 1% Assembly Language	tape	$40	yes

Table 1 Program Availability (cont.)

PROGRAM NAME	SOURCE OF THE PROGRAM	HARDWARE	LANGUAGE	HOW SOLD	COST	MAINTAINED BY SOURCE
SYMBAL	M. E. Engeli Fides Trust Company Zurich, Switzerland	IBM 360/370 CDC 6000/CYBER ICL IV				
MACSYMA	Susan Poh MITRE Corp National Systems Design Dept. W185 1820 Dolly Madison Blvd. Westgate Research Park McLean, Va. 22101	ITS SYSTEM, M.I.T.	LISP	not sold; accessible on M.I.T. system		yes
FORMAC	IBM – Program Information Dept. 40 Sawmill River Rd. Hawthorne, N.Y. 10532 Order Program No. 360D-03.3.004 on the IBM Program Order Form		PL/1		$0	no

REDUCE

REDUCE [8,9]: written in LISP by A. C. Hearn and maintained at
the University of Utah. It originated as a system for solving some
particular problems arising in high-energy physics, but in 1967
REDUCE was announced to be a system for general purpose algebraic
simplification and released for distribution.

The latest version of REDUCE (REDUCE 2) offers the following
facilities:

Expansion and ordering of rational functions
Symbolic differentiation of rational functions
Substitution and pattern matching in a wide variety of forms
Automatic and user-controlled simplification of expressions
Calculations with symbolic matrices
Procedural facilities for defining functions and extending the
    system
Calculations of interest to high-energy physicists including
    spin $\frac{1}{2}$ and spin 1 algebra
Tensor operations

In general terms, REDUCE may be said to be command-oriented rather
than program-oriented. This is a consequence of the fact that REDUCE
is primarily intended for interactive calculations in a time-sharing
environment.

The syntax of individual commands in REDUCE bears more
resemblance to ALGOL 60 than to any of the other algebraic languages.
In fact, REDUCE can be regarded as an extension of a certain part
of ALGOL 60.

REDUCE 2 is available for use on most IBM 360 or 370 series
computers, the DEC PDP-10 and the CDC 6400, 6500, 6600 and 7600
machines.

SCHOONSCHIP

SCHOONSCHIP [10,11]: designed more than ten years ago by
M. Veltman at CERN. It is intended for doing long - but in
principle straightforward - analytic calculations. Its major applications are in the field of high-energy physics, but it is sufficiently general to have a broader field of applications.

Its syntax is quite different from that of the other
languages. Thus, it is designed to evaluate expressions of the form:

(A1 + B1 + ...)*(A2 + B2 + ...)*... + (AA1 + BB1 + ...)*...

where * denotes multiplication and where A1, B1, etc., may be
products of numbers, algebraic symbols, vectors, functions, etc.,
or further expressions enclosed in brackets. Moreover, an elaborate
set of substitutions and commands is provided, which allows us to
perform most of the commonly required algebraic manipulations.

SCHOONSCHIP is written almost entirely in CDC 6000/7000
machine code.

SAC-1

SAC-1 [12,13]: developed by G. E. Collins and his students at the
University of Wisconsin since 1967. SAC-1 is a program system for
performing operations on multivariable polynomials and rational
functions with infinite-precision coefficients.

It is, with the exception of a few simple primitives, a
hierarchial collection of subprograms written in ASA FORTRAN. One
uses the system by writing a FORTRAN subprogram which calls the appropriate SAC-1 subprograms, including utility subprograms for input, output, and memory management.

The following is a list of all the subsystems in the system:

List-processing system
Infinite-precision integer arithmetic system
Polynomial system
Rational function system
Modular arithmetic system
Rational function integration system
Polynomial real zero system
Polynomial greatest common divisor and resultant system
Polynomial factorization system
Polynomial linear algebra system
Rational polynomial system

SYMBAL

SYMBAL [14]: developed by M. E. Engeli, FIDES Trust Company, in
Zurich. It has been operable on the CDC 1604 since 1965 and on the
CDC 6000 computers since 1968.

Today the system is the result of a complete redesign in which
the experience gained has been utilized.

The syntax of SYMBAL is rather simple and is based on ALGOL.

A full set of instruments, including conditional statements,
recursively callable procedures, dynamically alterable go to, and
switching operations, is present. Since new values can only be formed in expressions, their power has been given particular consideration. The possibilities include:

Σ , Π operators.
Differentiation and substitution operators. The FOR clause
    may be used to generate substitution pairs.
Assignments within parentheses.
Logical expressions and relations.

A number of mode lists serve to control internal processes, namely:

smod: simplification, common denominator, truncation, non-
    commutativity
fmod: functional transformations
nmod: numerical computations
pmod: printing options
dmod: debugging levels

The system is presently available in versions for the IBM 360/370, the CDC 6000/CYBER, and the ICL IV computers.

MACSYMA

MACSYMA [15-17]: a large symbolic and algebraic manipulation system under development at Project MAC, M.I.T., since 1969. The original design decisions for MACSYMA were made in 1968 by C. Engelman, W. Martin, and J. Moses. The goal was to combine the results of the research made by Martin and Moses with the ideas in Engelman's MATHLAB.

MACSYMA is an interactive system written in LISP with an ALGOL-like syntax, with blocks, various FOR statements, and the like.
It contains capabilities in several areas, including:

Limit calculations
Symbolic integration
Solution of equations
Canonical simplification
User-level pattern matching
User-specified expression manipulation
Programming and bookkeeping assistance

The system utilizes four major internal representations: general, rational, power series, and Poisson series.

MACSYMA currently resides on a PDP-10 which has 512K memory and on a Honeywell 6180.

SCRATCHPAD

SCRATCHPAD [18,19]: an experimental interactive system for on-line symbolic mathematics under development at the IBM Thomas J. Watson Research Center, Yorktown Heights, New York 01598. The current version has been implemented in LISP primarily by J. H. Griesmer and R. D. Jenks. The SCRATCHPAD language has been described as a two-dimensional language designed for interactive symbolic computation, and for eventual use in on-line exploratory research with graphical input/output. But it may also be used as a language for the formal description of algorithms as well as a source language for their efficient implementation. The language unifies five language concepts within a single language:

1. A declarative language suitable for the interactive definition and manipulation of symbolic formulas and expressions
2. A pattern-matching language with evaluation described by a Markov algorithm
3. An extensible language
4. A formal description language allowing data representation free programming

5. A high-level implementation language

SCRATCHPAD includes significant portions of other systems such as REDUCE 2, MATHLAB, and SIN. Among the symbolic facilities currently available to the user are:

Manipulation of rational functions
Polynomial greatest common divisor
User-controlled simplification
Differentiation
Polynomial factorization
Symbolic integration
Manipulation of sequences and sets
Solution of linear differential equations
Solution of systems of linear equations
Unlimited precision rational arithmetic
Truncated power series
Symbolic matrix and APL array operations

The system runs on the VM/370 and TSS time-sharing systems. Communication to the system goes via IBM 2741 or 3277 terminals.

A COMPARISON

A comparison based on installation and use of six of the systems mentioned here has been carried out by Yngve Sundblad [20]. The results of his comparison of the systems from different aspects are collected in the following table, where the systems are given a subjective rating from 5 (best) to 1. A zero means that the system does not offer the corresponding possibility.

Property	ALTRAN	FORMAC	REDUCE	SAC-1	SCHOONSCHIP	SYMBAL
Smallness	3	4	2	5	4	4
Portability	5	1	3	4	2	1
Distribution	5	1	5	3	5	0
Maintenance	5	0	4	2	4	0
Interactivity	0	3	5	0	0	0
Syntax	3	2	4	1	1	5
Security	5	1	3	1	3	3
Debugging	5	4	2	1	2	3
Extensibility	2	2	5	2	1	2
Output	4	3	5	1	2	2
User's documentation	5	4	3	4	2	4
System documentation	5	0	5	5	3	0
Exact arithmetic	2	4	5	5	1	5
Floating point arithmetic	3	4	2	4	5	0
Unevaluated functions	2	5	4	2	4	2
Elementary functions	2	5	4	2	2	2

Pattern matching	3	3	5	1	5	2
Modern algorithms	3	0	4	5	0	0
Truncated power series	5	1	3	1	3	2
Rational functions	5	2	4	5	0	2
Vectors and matrices	3	2	5	1	5	3
Gamma matrix algebra	0	0	5	0	5	0
Noncommutative algebra	0	0	2	0	5	0
Secondary storage	2	3	3	2	5	1
Run-time-efficiency:						
Small problems	1	4	3	2	3	5
Moderate problems	2	1	3	4	5	5
Large problems	4	1	3	3	5	2

It must be noted that this comparison is from 1973 and that the development of all the systems has continued since then. This is especially true of FORMAC and SYMBAL, which, in 1973, were considered "dead" [20].

FORMAC

History

The first version of FORMAC, an extension of IBM 7090/94 FORTRAN IV, was an experimental programming system to assist in the symbolic manipulation of mathematical expressions [4,21]. The project originated in August 1962, and the system was released as a type III program in November 1964. It provided such capabilities as symbolic differentiation, expansion, substitution, comparison, and evaluation of expressions, in addition to the full arithmetic, testing loop-control, and I/O of the FORTRAN system. Comments of users [22] initiated the design and implementation of PL/1-FORMAC, a more powerful and more flexible system, based on the same principles [23]. The first version of PL/1-FORMAC was released in 1967, the second in September 1969, both again as a type III program, [24].

In 1970 IBM stopped support of FORMAC and released the source code. It was felt by some users that, in addition to some errors, the IBM preprocessor had a number of shortcomings. In April 1970 a new preprocessor became available. It was developed at KFA-Jülich, [25]. The errors were corrected and most of the proposed extensions were implemented.

A new version of FORMAC, called FORMAC73, is now available. A number of extensions and improvements have been incorporated into it and make FORMAC73 a more powerful and more modern system [26,27].

General System

PL/1-FORMAC can be considered to be an extension of PL/1. In addi-

tion to the PL/1 language elements, PL/1-FORMAC contains a package
of macro-statements for performing symbolic mathematical computations. These FORMAC macros may be considered to constitute a
separate language from PL/1. The fact that PL/1-FORMAC contains two
different entities has important consequences concerning the compilation and execution of a program. While the PL/1 statements are
translated into machine code by the PL/1 compiler in the usual manner, the FORMAC statements are not affected by the compiler. They
remain unchanged as character strings and are processed interpreta-
tively at execution time.

This concept is realized by means of the PL/1-FORMAC interpreter, an extension of the PL/1(F) compiler and originally designed to run under OS/360 on a model 40 or higher with at least 256K
bytes of core storage available. The interpreter consists of two
modules of assembled routines - the preprocessor and the object-time
library - in addition to a systems library. The preprocessor is used
to translate the PL/1-FORMAC program into a pure PL/1 program
containing a series of calls of external subroutines, the above
mentioned macros. The object-time library routines are then used
for the interpretation during execution time.

Conversational Systems

The object-time library routines that interpret the FORMAC macro-
statements deliver the base for an interactive system with all the
FORMAC facilities but without PL/1. Quite a large number of interactive systems are designed in this manner: FORDECAL, TUTOR, NETFORM,
and SYMBAS [28-30]. In addition to the FORMAC statements they all
have extended capabilities, either some of the PL/1 statements,
usual mathematical syntax, mathematical expressions on both sides
of the equality sign, analytic solution of a system of linear equations, or BASIC numerical capabilities.

Later we shall give an example from an interactive FORMAC
system extended with capabilities for symbolic manipulation of
general tensors.

The Language

The basic capabilities: expressions and assignments. The most basic
and important capability of FORMAC is its accommodation of mathematical expressions as symbolic entities at execution time. This
feature can best be illustrated by contrasting the nonnumerical
capability of FORMAC with the numerical capability of PL/1.
Execution of the PL/1 program segment

$$A = 4.2; \quad B = 3; \quad C = A/B + 0.8$$

results in the assignment of the value 2.2 to the PL/1 variable
C .

Execution, however, of the FORMAC program segment

```
LET( A = X+Y**2;   B = 2;   C = A/B + 0.8 )
```

results in the assignment of the expression $\frac{1}{2}(x + y^2) + 0.8$ to
the FORMAC variable C . This value of C is internally represented
as a list of coded symbols.

PL/1 and FORMAC assignment statements are distinguished by the
appearance of the word "LET". This distinction allows for the mixing
of FORMAC and PL/1 statements in any PL/1-FORMAC program. Although
only a minimum knowledge of PL/1 is necessary, the user has full access to all PL/1 facilities. Thus PL/1-FORMAC, containing PL/1 as a
subset, offers the combination of numerical and analytical techniques.

The execution of a FORMAC assignment or "LET" statement
results in the assignment of a FORMAC expression to a FORMAC variable.

FORMAC expressions are written in precisely the same way as
PL/1 or FORTRAN expressions, i.e., by combining variables and
constants by means of rational operators (+ , - , * , /), exponentia-
tion (**), and functions.

Variables. FORMAC variables can be of atomic or assigned type. An
atomic variable is one which has not been assigned an expression,
i.e., has not appeared on the left-hand side of an executed LET
statement. An assigned variable is one which has been assigned and
hence represents or names an expression. In the above example (taken
alone) X and Y are atomic variables, while A, B, and C are
assigned variables.

FORMAC variables do not have an associated base, scale or
precision and are not declared. They may be subscripted with up to
4 subscripts.

Constants. There are four kinds of FORMAC constants.

Floating point constants are internally maintained in double
precision, and all arithmetic operations on them are carried out in
double precision.

Integer constants are represented by up to 2295 digits.

Rational numbers are represented externally in FORMAC expressions in the form a/b , where a and b are integers. Rational
and integer numbers combine with floating point numbers to produce
floating point numbers. Arithmetic operations on rational numbers
are carried out using rational mode arithmetic with rational results
always reduced to lowest terms.

There are three reserved names used as system constants; #E
represents e = 2.7812... , #P represents π, and #I represents
i = $\sqrt{-1}$. These symbols are recognized by the system and certain
transformations involving them are carried out automatically. For
example, #I**2 will be simplified to -1 .

Built-in functions. Just as in PL/1, certain built-in functions can
be used in FORMAC in writing expressions, e.g., SIN, COS, LOG, ERF,

FAC, COMB, etc. The arguments of these functions may be any FORMAC expression, which itself may involve functions. For example, the execution of

$$\text{LET(A = X**2 + 7/3;}$$
$$\text{B = 3*SIN(A+1) + LOG(COS(Y)))}$$

results in $b = 3 \sin(x^2 + 10/3) + \ln(\cos(y))$.

User-defined functions. The user may define his own functions in FNC statements; for example

$$\text{LET(FNC(F) = 3*COS(\$(1)**2 + \$(2)) + 1);}$$
$$\text{LET(X = B + C);}$$
$$. \quad . \quad . \quad . \quad . \quad . \quad . \quad . \quad . \quad . \quad . \quad . \quad . \quad . \quad . \quad . \quad . \quad . \quad . \quad . $$
$$\text{LET(Y = F(X+4,3) + 2)}$$

results in $y = 3 \cos((b+c+4)^2 + 3) + 3$. The FNC statement defines F as a function of two variables: F($(1),$(2)) . The dollar-variables serve as dummy variables or parameters of the function F .

Unspecified functions. FORMAC provides for the use of unspecified functions by means of function variables. These may appear in FORMAC expressions with arbitrary expressions as arguments. For example

$$\text{LET(Y = G.(A+B,B+C) + SIN(H.(X+3)))}$$

Note the dot following the names of the function variables G and H . Function variables may be subscripted, e.g., MOM(I,J).(X1,X2) . For the TENSOR FORMAC system discussed later this is an important facility.

Chains. FORMAC variables may be assigned a list or chain of FORMAC expressions by means of the CHAIN function. For example

$$\text{LET(X = CHAIN(X1,X2,X3,X4))}$$

will cause X to be assigned the actual list consisting of X1,X2,X3,X4 . The CHAIN operation provides the capacity of building lists of arguments for FORMAC functions. For example, after the statement above has been executed, the statement

$$\text{LET(Y = F.(T,X))}$$

will cause Y to be assigned the expression F.(T,X1,X2,X3,X4) .

Automatic simplification. FORMAC provides facilities for two kinds

of simplification, automatic and user-controlled. Automatic simplification is carried out without any intervention of the user. Thus,
certain transformations such as $1x \to x$, $x^1 \to x$, $0 + x \to x$,
$e^{\log x} \to x$, $3x^2 + 5xyx - x^2 \to 2x^2 + 5x^2 y$ are performed automatically.

User-controlled simplification. There are many cases where the notion of "simpler" is not clear. Whereas we would all agree that
$3y^3/x$ is simpler than $18x^2 y^5/6x^3 y^2$, the choice between $a(b+c)$
and $ab + ac$ or between $\sin 2v$ and $2 \sin v \cos v$ might depend
upon the circumstances. Thus, the form selected will depend on the
use one wishes to make of the expression. In some cases, it is just
a matter of personal preference. FORMAC provides certain user-controlled simplification routines, EXPAND, MULT, DIST, CODEM, FRACTN,
GCF, and GCFOUT.
      EXPAND applies the distributive and multinomial laws to its
argument; for example

          LET(Z = EXPAND((X+4)**2 + 3*(2*X+Y)*(X-3)))

results in $z = 7x^2 - 10x + 3xy - 9y + 16$.
      GCFOUT factors out the greatest common factor of the terms of
a sum; for example

          LET(Z = GCFOUT(A*B**(3*C)*D**(A+X) + A*B**C*D**(E+X)))

results in $z = ab^c d^x (b^{2c} d^a + d^e)$.
      CODEM returns the argument expression in the general form
a/b , i.e., with a common denominator. For example

          LET(Z = CODEM(B/(A*X+A*Y) + C/(A*U + A*V)))

results in $z = (b(u+v) + c(x+y))/(a(x+y)(u+v))$.

Substitution. This is possible with the routines EVAL and REPLACE.
EVAL carries out parallel substitution to replace atomic variables
by expressions, and REPLACE carries out serial substitution to
replace subexpressions by expressions. For example

          LET(Z = EVAL(A + B*C,B,X + Y))

results in $z = a + (x+y)c$.

          LET(Z = REPLACE(A + B**2 + C,A + B**2,X + Y))

results in $z = x + y + c$.
      The routine REPLACE may also be demonstrated by integration of
a polynomium z with respect to x . Thus ZINT defined by

where $N   means "for any name," will be the integral of z .

Analytical differentiation.   This is possible with the routines
DERIVE, DIFF, and DRV.   For example

```
        LET( Z = DERIV(F.(4*X**3,V.(X)) + LOG(X),X,2) );
        PRINT_OUT( Z )
```

gives the result

```
            (1)        3               2   (1 2)        3
 Z = 24 X F     .( 4 X  , V.( X ) ) + ( 12 X   F       .( 4 X  , V.( X )
            2
        (2 )        3               (1)         (1)            2
  ) + F     .( 4 X  , V.( X ) ) V     .( X ) ; V    .( X ) + 12 X  (
        2
    2  (1 )        3                  (1 2)        3                (1)
 12 X  F     .( 4 X  , V.( X ) ) + F        .( 4 X  , V.( X ) ) V      .
        (2)        3               (2)              2
 ( X ) ) + F    .( 4 X  , V.( X ) ) V    .( X ) - 1 / X
```

which, in more common notation, may be written

$$z = 24x \frac{\partial F(u,v)}{\partial u} + \left[12x^2 \frac{\partial^2 F(u,v)}{\partial u \partial v} + \frac{\partial^2 F(u,v)}{\partial u^2} \frac{\partial v}{\partial x}\right]\frac{\partial v}{\partial x}$$

$$+ 12x^2\left[12x^2 \frac{\partial^2 F(u,v)}{\partial u^2} + \frac{\partial^2 F(u,v)}{\partial u \partial v} \frac{\partial v}{\partial x}\right] + \frac{\partial F(u,v)}{\partial v} \cdot \frac{\partial^2 v}{\partial x^2} - \frac{1}{x^2}$$

where $u(x) = 4x^3$.
        The use of EVAL and DERIV may be further demonstrated by the
following program segment. The result of an execution of the segment
is shown immediately after the segment.

```
    /*  THIS PROGRAM SEGMENT COMPUTES THE 13'TH DEGREE TAYLOR SERI-
        ES POLYNOMIAL  TAYL  AROUND THE POINT  X = A = 0  FOR THE
        FUNCTION  FX = SIN(X)*LOG(X+1) .                        */

        LET( FX = SIN(X)*LOG(X+1) );    LET( A = 0 );

        LET( TAYL = EVAL(FX,X,A) );
LOOP:       DO I = 1 TO 13;    LET( I = "I" );
            LET( FX = DERIV(FX,X) );
            LET( TAYL = TAYL + (X-A)**I*EVAL(FX,X,A)/FAC(I) );
            END LOOP;
        PRINT_OUT( TAYL );
```

$$
\begin{aligned}
TAYL = 2\ X^2\ /\ 2!\ -\ 3\ X^3\ /\ 3!\ +\ 4\ X^4\ /\ 4!\ -\ 20\ X^5\ /\ 5!\ +\ 110\ X^6 \\
/\ 6!\ -\ 651\ X^7\ /\ 7!\ +\ 4520\ X^8\ /\ 8!\ -\ 36000\ X^9\ /\ 9!\ +\ 322618\ X^{10} \\
/\ 10!\ -\ 3213595\ X^{11}\ /\ 11!\ +\ 35226860\ X^{12}\ /\ 12!\ -\ 421419492\ X^{13} \\
/\ 13!
\end{aligned}
$$

Comparison. A comparison of FORMAC expressions for identity is possible by means of the IDENT function, which returns a PL/1 bit-string of value '1'B if the two expressions are identical and '0'B otherwise. For example

```
LET( Y = A*A + 2*A*B + B**2 );
LET( Z = (A+B)**2 );
IF IDENT(Y;EXPAND(Z)) THEN GO TO ID
```

results in a transfer to ID.

Expression analysis routines. FORMAC provides a number of expression analysis facilities.

Polynomial analysis facilities allow the user to extract the coefficient of a subexpression by means of the routine COEFF and appraises him of the highest or lowest power of a subexpression using the routines HIGHPOW or LOWPOW, respectively. For example

```
LET( Y  = A + B + 2*C*(A+B)**2 + D*(A+B)**4 );
LET( Z1 = COEFF(Y,(A+B)**2) );
LET( Z2 = HIGHPOW(EXPAND(Y),B) );
LET( Z3 = LOWPOW(Y,A) )
```

results in $z_1 = 2c$, $z_2 = 4$, $z_3 = 1$.

The routines NUM and DENOM allow the user to obtain the numerator and denominator, respectively, in an expression with the general form a/b . For example

```
LET( Z = NUM((2*X*SIN(V) + X**2)/(A+B)) )
```

results in $z = 2x\ sinv + x^2$.

The routines LOP, NARGS, and ARG offer the user the opportunity of performing a general analysis of an expression. LOP returns the number of the leading operator of an expression (every operator has a number, for instance + is number 24 , - number 25, etc.). NARGS returns the number of arguments of the leading operator of an expression, and ARG returns the ith argument of the leading operator. For example

```
LET( Y = X + X**2*SIN(V) - X**3*(A-B)*COSH(U.(X)) );
I1 = LOP(Y);      LET( Z1 = ARG(3,Y) );      I2 = NARGS(Y);
I3 = LOP(Z1);     LET( Z2 = ARG(1,Z1) );
I4 = LOP(Z2);     LET( Z3 = ARG(3,Z2) );
I5 = LOP(Z3);     LET( Z4 = ARG(1,Z3) );
I6 = LOP(Z4);     LET( Z5 = ARG(2,Z4) );
I7 = LOP(Z5)
```

results in $z_1 = -x^3(a-b)\cosh(u(x))$, $z_2 = x^3(a-b)\cosh(u(x))$, $z_3 = \cosh(u(x))$, $z_4 = u(x)$, $z_5 = x$ and $i_1 = 24$, $i_2 = 3$, $i_3 = 25$, $i_4 = 26$, $i_5 = 9$, $i_6 = 21$, $i_7 = 44$.

FORMAC-PL/1 interface considerations. The fact that PL/1-FORMAC contains two different entities gives rise to the need for special facilities to allow the use of PL/1 values in FORMAC statements and vice versa.

PL/1 variables enclosed within double quotes may appear on both sides of the equality sign in LET statements. For example

```
DCL (A,B,Z) CHARACTER(25) VARYING;
Z = 'Z';     A = '(A*X**2 + DERIV(Y,X))';     B = '23/7';
LET( Y = SIN(X) );     C = 0.5;
LET( "Z" = "A"*A*"C" + "B" + 1/7 )
```

results in $z = 0.5a(ax^2 + \cos x) + \frac{24}{7}$.

The CHAREX statement is used to pass the value of a non-constant FORMAC expression to a PL/1 varying character-string variable. For example

```
LET( Y = A - C + B**2 );
CHAREX( Z = Y )
```

results in $z = $ 'Y = A-C + B**2' .

The functions INTEGER and ARITH convert FORMAC constants into PL/1 constants. INTEGER returns a fixed point binary number ARITH as a double precision floating point number.

A sample program. We shall demonstrate the compilation of a small program and, especially, the use of PL/1 variables in FORMAC statements and vice versa by the following example:

The system of differential equations

$$\frac{dy_1}{dx} = f_1(x,y_1,\ldots,y_n) \; ; \; y_1(0) = y_{10}$$

$$. \quad . \quad . \quad . \quad .$$

$$\frac{dy_n}{dx} = f_n(x, y_1, \ldots, y_n) \; ; \; y_n(0) = y_{n0}$$

where $f_1, \ldots, f_n$ are polynomials, may be solved by the following successive approximation scheme

$$y_1^{(m+1)} = y_{10} + \int_0^x f_1(x, y_1^{(m)}, \ldots, y_n^{(m)}) dx$$

$$\cdot \quad \cdot \quad \cdot \quad \cdot \quad \cdot$$

$$y_n^{(m+1)} = y_{n0} + \int_0^x f_n(x, y_1^{(m)}, \ldots, y_n^{(m)}) dx$$

where, in $y_k^{(m+1)}$, only the new term with the lowest power in x is retained when $y_k^{(m+1)}$ is compared with $y_k^{(m)}$.

The program is demonstrated with the set of equations

$$\frac{dy_1}{dx} = y_2 \, w/b \; ; \; y_1(0) = 0$$

$$\frac{dy_2}{dx} = -y_1 \, wb \; ; \; y_2(0) = ab$$

where a, b, and w are parameters.

```
//FORMAC.SYSIN DD *
  DIFE: PROC OPTIONS(MAIN);
          /*  ACTIVATE THE PREPROCESSOR.                              */
          FORMAC_OPTIONS;
          /*  SPECIFY LINELENGTH OF OUTPUT.                           */
          OPTSET(LINELENGTH = 70);

          /*  ALLOW THE CONSTRUCTION LET( "J" =  WHERE  J  IS A PL/1
              FIXED BINARY VARIABLE.                                  */
          CONVERT FIXED(J;L);

          /*  SET UP THE SPECIFIC PROBLEM, N  IS THE NUMBER OF EQUATIONS
              M  THE NUMBER OF ITERATIONS REQUESTED.                  */
          N = 2;    M = 10;
          LET( F(1) =   YP(2)*W/B;    Y0(1) = 0 );
          LET( F(2) = - YP(1)*W*B;    Y0(2) = A*B );

          /*  INITIALIZE THE APPROXIMATIONS  Y(K) .                   */
```

```
      DO I = 1 TO N;    LET( I = "I" );
      LET( Y(I) = Y0(I) );
      END;
      DO KK = 1 TO M;
         DO K = 1 TO N;    LET( K = "K" );

  /*  SUBSTITUTE THE CURRENT APPROXIMATION  Y(K)  INTO  F(K)
      IN PLACE OF THE   YP(K) .                              */
      LET( Y = F(K) );
         DO I = 1 TO N;    LET( I = "I" );
         LET( Y = EVAL(Y,YP(I),Y(I)) );
         END;

  /*  FIND AND INTEGRATE THE FIRST TERM OF ORDER GREATER THAN
      THE CURRENT APPROXIMATION  Y(K) .                      */
      LET(Y = EXPAND(X*Y) );
      LET( "J" = HIGHPOW(Y(K),X) );
      LET( "L" = HIGHPOW(Y,X) );
         DO I = J + 1 TO L;    LET( I = "I" );
         LET( YY = COEFF(Y,X**I)*X**I/I );
         IF LOP(YY) ⌐= 36 THEN GO TO FIFO; /* TRUE FOR YY ≠ 0  */
         END;

  /*  INTEGRATE THE LOW ORDER TERMS OF  Y  AND ADD THE INITIAL
      VALUE  Y0(K) .                                         */
  FIFO:        DO I = 1 TO J;    LET( I = "I" );
      LET( YY = YY + COEFF(Y,X**I)*X**I/I );
      END;
      LET( Y(K) = YY + Y0(K) );
  /*  Y(K)  IS NOW THE NEW APPROXIMATION.                    */
      END;
   END;

  /*  PRINT OUT THE RESULTING APPROXIMATIONS.                */
   DO I = 1 TO N;    PRINT_OUT( Y("I") );    END;
   END DIFE;
```

```
                        3   3            5   5              7   7
Y(1) = A X W - 1/6 A X   W   + 1/120 A X   W   - 1/5040 A X   W   + 1/
            9   9              11   11                  13   13
362880 A X   W   - 1/39916800 A X    W   + 1/6227020800 A X    W
          15   15                          17   17
 - 1/1307674368000 A X   W   + 1/355687428096000 A X   W    - 1/
                   19   19
1216451004088832000 A X   W
                        2   2            4   4              6   6
Y(2) = A B - 1/2 A X   W   B + 1/24 A X   W   B - 1/720 A X   W   B +
```

$1/40320 \ A \ X^8 \ W^8 \ B \ - \ 1/3628800 \ A \ X^{10} \ W^{10} \ B \ + \ 1/479001600 \ A \ X^{12} \ W^{12}$

$B \ - \ 1/87178291200 \ A \ X^{14} \ W^{14} \ B \ + \ 1/20922789888000 \ A \ X^{16} \ W^{16} \ B \ - \ 1/$

$6402373705728000 \ A \ X^{18} \ W^{18} \ B \ + \ 1/2432902008176640000 \ A \ X^{20} \ W^{20} \ B$

An Eigenvalue Problem

The natural frequencies and modes of an elastic beam of uniform mass
and stiffness exposed to a homogeneous gravitational field parallel
to the undeformed beam axis are governed by the differential equation

$$y'''' + q(xy')' = \lambda y \tag{1}$$

where q is a parameter taking the mass, the stiffness, and the
gravitation into account, and where λ is the eigenvalue.

Let us consider a beam free at the one end $x = 0$ and clamped
at the other end $x = 1$. Then the boundary conditions are

$$y(1) = y'(1) = y''(0) = y'''(0) = 0 \tag{2}$$

This eigenvalue problem is self-adjoint and, for not too big values
of q , fully definite.

If we write the differential equation for an eigenvalue
problem of this kind in the following way

$$M[y] = \lambda N[y] \tag{3}$$

we have, according to [31],

$$\lambda \leq RQ(F_n) \leq RQ(F_{n-1}) \tag{4}$$

where the Rayleigh Quotient $RQ(F_n)$ is given by

$$RQ(F_n) = \frac{\int_a^b F_n M[F_n] dx}{\int_a^b F_n N[F_n] dx} \tag{5}$$

and

$$\text{Min}\left\{\frac{F_{n-1}(x)}{F_n(x)}\right\} \le \lambda \le \text{Max}\left\{\frac{F_{n-1}(x)}{F_n(x)}\right\} \; ; \; a \le x \le b \qquad (6)$$

where

$$M[F_n] = N[F_{n-1}] \qquad (7)$$

and where $F_n(x)$ are "comparison functions," i.e., functions which satisfy all the boundary conditions and possess continuous derivatives, including the order of the differential operator $M[\ ]$.

In the solution of an eigenvalue problem, given by Eq. 3, by means of the method of successive interations, as given by Eq. 7, it is usual to apply Eq. 7, from right to left, such that F_n is determined from F_{n-1} by integration. In this case, the differential operator in Eq. 1, is such that it is not possible in general to reach F_n by analytical integration. Instead, we may choose to apply Eq. 7 from left to right, so that F_{n-1} is determined from F_n by differentiation.

Let us take F_3 to be a polynomial of order 12 in x with 12 unknown coefficients $A_1, A_2, \ldots A_{12}$. By using the iteration scheme Eq. 7 twice and the boundary conditions of Eq. 2 three times, we get 12 linear equations for the determination of the unknown A_i. The solution of the equation system gives three comparison functions, of which two are subsequently used in Eq. 5, 4 and 6.

```
EIGE:   PROC OPTIONS(MAIN);

        /*  SOLUTION OF AN EIGENVALUE PROBLEM BY MEANS OF A 12TH DE-
            GREE POLYNOMIUM AND BACKWARD SUCCESSIVE ITERATIONS.      */

        FORMAC_OPTIONS;    OPTSET(LINELENGTH = 70 );
        DCL N FIXED BINARY(31) INITIAL(12);

        /*  GENERATE A COMPARISON FUNCTION AS A N-TH DEGREE POLYNO-
            MIUM IN X                                               */
        LET( L = "N"/4 );   LET( K = L );   LET( PX(L) = 0 );
        DO I = 0 TO N;   LET( I = "I" );
        LET( PX(L) = PX(L) + A(I)*X**I );
        END;
        /*  FOR LATER USE THE CONSTANT  1  IN  PX(L)  IS NAMED  A(0)  */

        /*  BOUNDARY CONDITIONS                                     */
NEWA:LET( BC(1) = EVAL(PX(K),X,1) );
        LET( BC(2) = EVAL(DERIV(PX(K),X),X,1) );
```

```
LET( BC(3) = EVAL(DERIV(PX(K),X,2),X,0) );
LET( BC(4) = EVAL(DERIV(PX(K),X,3),X,0) );

/*  PLACE THE COEFFICIENTS OF  A(I)  IN A MATRIX.              */
DO J = 1 TO 4;   LET( J = "J" );
   DO I = 1 TO N;   LET( I = "I" );
   LET( CMAT((L-K)*4+J,I) = COEFF(BC(J),A(I)) );
   END;
END;

/*  THE SUCCESSIVE ITERATIONS WITH THE DIFFERENTIAL OPERATOR. */
IF INTEGER(K) = 1 THEN GO TO SOLV;
LET( PX(K-1) = EXPAND(DERIV(PX(K),X,4) + O*DERIV(X*DERIV(
               PX(K),X),X)) );
LET( K = K - 1 );
GO TO NEWA;

/*  SET UP THE RIGHT HAND SIDE OF THE LINEAR EQUATIONS.        */
SOLV:LET( RHS(1) = -1 );
DO I = 2 TO N;   LET( I = "I" );
LET( RHS(I) = 0 );
END;

/*  SOLVE THE LINEAR EQUATIONS.                                */
CALL LIEQ(N,'CMAT','RHS','B','B(0)');
/*  THE SUBROUTINE LIEQ SOLVES THE SYSTEM OF LINEAR EQUATIONS
    OF ORDER  N  WITH THE COEFFICIENT MATRIX  CMAT  AND THE
    RIGHT HAND SIDE  RHS . THE DETERMINANT OF THE COEFFICIENT
    MATRIX IS RETURNED UNDER THE NAME  B(0)  AND THE SOLUTION
    VECTOR MULTIPLIED BY THE DETERMINANT IS RETURNED UNDER THE
    NAME  B .                                                  */

/*             ************************************            */

/*  CALCULATE NOMINATOR AND DENOMINATOR IN THE RAYLEIGH QUO-
    TIENT (5).                                                 */
LET( RAYNOM = EXPAND(PX(L)*PX(L-1)) );
LET( RAYDEN = EXPAND(PX(L)*PX(L)) );
CALL INTGPO('RAYNOM','X','0','1','RAYNOM');
CALL INTGPO('RAYDEN','X','0','1','RAYDEN');
/*  THE SUBROUTINE INTGPO INTEGRATES A POLYNOMIUM  RAYNOM
    WITH RESPECT TO A VARIABLE  X  BETWEEN THE LIMITS  0  AND
    1  AND RETURNS THE RESULT UNDER THE NAME  RAYNOM .         */

/*  SUBSTITUTE  B(I)  FOR  A(I)  IN  RAYNOM  AND  RAYDEN .
    THE COMPARISON FUNCTIONS  PX  ARE HEREBY MULTIPLIED BY THE
```

```
          DETERMINANT  B(0) .                          */
  LET( CH = CHAIN(A(0),B(0)) );
  DO I = 1 TO N;    LET( I = "I" );
  LET( CH = CHAIN(CH,A(I),B(I)) );
  END;
  LET( RAYNOM = EVAL(RAYNOM,CH) );
  LET( RAYDEN = EVAL(RAYDEN,CH) );

  /*  CONVERT RATIONAL NUMBERS TO FLOATING POINT NUMBERS IN
      RAYNOM  AND  RAYDEN .                          */
  LET( RAYNOM = REPLACE(RAYNOM,Q,2.0*Q,Q,0.5*Q) + 1.0E-10 );
  LET( RAYDEN = REPLACE(RAYDEN,Q,2.0*Q,Q,0.5*Q) + 1.0E-10 );

  /*  THE NOMINATOR AND THE DENOMINATOR OF THE RAYLEIGH QUO-
      TIENT ARE FOR  N = 12  POLYNOMIALS IN  Q  UP TO THE POWER
      21 . THE COEFFICIENTS OF TERMS WITH INCREASING POWERS
      OF  Q  ARE STRONGLY DECREASING. TO DEMONSTRATE THE POWER
      SERIES TRUNCATION FACILITY WE MAY THEREFORE PRINT OUT THE
      NOMINATOR OF THE RAYLEIGH QUOTIENT UP TO THE SIXTH PO-
      WER.                                           */
  OPTSET(TRUNC = 6);
  LET( RAYNOM = RAYNOM );
  PRINT_OUT( RAYNOM );
  OPTSET(TRUNC = 100);

  /*        ************************************      */

  /*  CALCULATE THE QUOTIENT  PX(L-1)/PX(L)  USED IN (6).   */

  /*  SUBSTITUTE  B(I)  FOR  A(I)  IN  PX(L)  AND  PX(L-1) .

      PX(L)  AND  PX(L-1) ARE THEN POLYNOMIALS IN  X  AND  Q . */
  LET( PX(L) = EVAL(PX(L),CH) );
  LET( PX(L-1) = EVAL(PX(L-1),CH) );

  /*  REMOVE THE COMMON DOUBLE ROOT  X = 1  IN  PX(L)  AND
      PX(L-1) .                                      */
  LET( DOUBRO = EXPAND((X-1)**2) );
  CALL POLDIV('PX(L)','DOUBRO','X','PX(L)','REST');
  CALL POLDIV('PX(L-1)','DOUBRO','X','PX(L-1)','REST');
  /*  THE SUBROUTINE POLDIV DIVIDES THE POLYNOMIUM  PX(L)  WITH
      THE POLYNOMIUM  DOUBRO  WITH RESPECT TO  X  AND RETURNS
      THE QUOTIENT UNDER THE NAME  PX(L)  AND THE REST (HERE
      THE REST = 0) UNDER THE NAME  REST .             */

  /*        ************************************      */
```

```
/*  CALCULATE THE RAYLEIGH QUOTIENT AND THE MINIMUM AND MAXI-
    MUM OF THE QUOTIENT  PX(L-1)/PX(L)  FOR SOME VALUES OF  Q */

/*  FOR VALUES OF  Q  BETWEEN  0  AND  1  THE QUOTIENT
    PX(L-1)/PX(L)  HAS ITS MINIMUM FOR  X = 0  AND ITS MAXI-
    MUM FOR  X = 1 .                                           */
LET( PX3X0 = EVAL(PX(L),X,0.0) );
LET( PX3X1 = EVAL(PX(L),X,1.0) );
LET( PX2X0 = EVAL(PX(L-1),X,0.0) );
LET( PX2X1 = EVAL(PX(L-1),X,1.0) );
DO J = 0 TO 5;    LET( J = "J" );
LET( QQ = 0.20*J );
LET( RAYLEIGH = EVAL(RAYNOM/RAYDEN,Q,QQ) );
LET( MINFIX =    EVAL(PX2X0/PX3X0,Q,QQ) + 1.0E-10 );
LET( MAXFIX =    EVAL(PX2X1/PX3X1,Q,QQ) );
PRINT_OUT( MINFIX;RAYLEIGH;MAXFIX );
END;


END EIGE;
```

$$RAYNOM = 1.56130314E+41\ Q - 1.77979159E+40\ Q^2 - 2.68628605E+39\ Q^3 -$$
$$7.43229232E+37\ Q^4 + 1.54376852E+36\ Q^5 + 1.34113966E+42$$

MINFIX = 12.3580749	RAYLEIGH = 12.3623634	MAXFIX = 12.3903177
MINFIX = 12.0437112	RAYLEIGH = 12.0481575	MAXFIX = 12.0774422
MINFIX = 11.7299862	RAYLEIGH = 11.7338907	MAXFIX = 11.7597848
MINFIX = 11.4167284	RAYLEIGH = 11.4195627	MAXFIX = 11.4384101
MINFIX = 11.1037938	RAYLEIGH = 11.1051727	MAXFIX = 11.1142058
MINFIX = 10.7878964	RAYLEIGH = 10.7907107	MAXFIX = 10.7910632

TENSOR FORMAC

A Tensor-Oriented Symbolic Command Language

Introduction

General tensors are often used today to formulate fundamental relations in solid and fluid mechanics as well as in the theory of relativity. This is certainly due to the fact that the laws, when formulated correctly as tensor equations, remain valid regardless of
our arbitrary choice of coordinate systems.

However, the compactness, elegance, and clarity of tensor nota-

tion are to a certain extent balanced by the fact that tensor equations are not immediately suitable for analytical or numerical work.

Let us assume that we would like to apply the set of governing
relations given in tensor notation to a specific problem. When a
set of suitable coordinates for the problem has been selected, it
remains to write out the explicit form of the tensor equations for
this coordinate system. As well known to anybody that has tried it,
the transcription of tensor equations results as a rule in tedious
and cumbersome work in all but the simplest cases. In fact, the
formula-manipulating work involved in this often becomes too comprehensive to be done by hand and thus limits the use of exact
analytical formulations in favor of numerical approaches of, for
instance, the "finite element" type. However, this limitation in
the use of tensors may be removed by automated symbolic manipulation. Several [32-35] have in the past realized this.

In the following we shall discuss and demonstrate an extension
of PL/1-FORMAC: TENSOR FORMAC, a system which is capable of manipu-
lating tensors and tensor expressions.

General System

TENSOR FORMAC has been developed at the Department of Solid Mechanics,
the Technical University of Denmark [36]. It is based on the
object-time library routines of FORMAC and is designed to run as a
conversational system under TSO on an IBM 370/165. However, a TENSOR
FORMAC job may run in a batch under OS/MVT, too, and the output from
the batch job may later be applied at an interactive session.

The system is command-oriented and operates with four types of
commands: control commands and commands in MODE 1, 2, and 3.

Control commands offer the following possibilities:

    Definition of the dimension of the space
    Specification of different options
    Specification of the mode of the system
    Manipulation of secondary storage
    Information about the state of the system or of the tensors

MODE 1 commands involve solely tensors and offer the possibility
of combining tensors in expressions to define new tensors. The
system recognizes:

    Covariant and contravariant indices
    Tensors of the order zero to four
    Addition and subtraction
    Contraction
    Outer product and scalar product
    Covariant differentiation

The system automatically performs raising and lowering of indices
using the metric tensor.

MODE 2 commands offer possibilities for the definition of tensors by ordinary FORMAC expressions or by calls of standard procedures.

MODE 3 commands involve solely ordinary FORMAC variables and expressions. The full set of FORMAC statements from PL/1-FORMAC is available as commands.

A TENSOR FORMAC Example

We shall not give a detailed description of the TENSOR FORMAC system but restrict ourselves to a demonstration of a program handling a problem from the shell theory.

Free Vibrations of a Thick Cylindrical Shell

Consider a cylindrical shell with mean radius R, thickness h, and length L. The shell is assumed to be simply supported at both ends. Our problem is to consider free vibrations of the shell.

We choose coordinates such that a point (x^1, x^2) on the middle surface has Cartesian coordinates

$$(x, y, z) = (R\cos(x^1/R), \ R\sin(x^1/R), \ x^2) \tag{1}$$

where z is the axis of the shell. The strain tensor has the form

$$E_{\alpha\beta} = \frac{1}{2}(D_\alpha v_\beta + D_\beta v_\alpha) - d_{\alpha\beta}w \tag{2}$$

where v_α is the displacement vector in the tangential plane, w in the normal direction, D_α denotes covariant derivation, and $d_{\alpha\beta}$ is the curvature tensor [37]. Similarly, the bending tensor is given by

$$K_{\alpha\beta} = D_\alpha D_\beta w + d_{\alpha\gamma}D_\beta v^\gamma + d_{\beta\gamma}D_\alpha v^\gamma + v^\gamma D_\beta d_{\gamma\alpha} - d_{\beta\gamma}d^\gamma_\alpha w \tag{3}$$

The equations of equilibrium can be written in the form

$$D_\alpha N^{\alpha\beta} + 2d^\beta_\gamma D_\alpha M^{\alpha\gamma} + M^{\alpha\gamma}D_\alpha d^\beta_\gamma + F^\beta = 0 \tag{4}$$

$$D_\alpha D_\beta M^{\alpha\beta} - d_{\alpha\beta}d^\beta_\gamma M^{\alpha\gamma} - d_{\alpha\beta}N^{\alpha\beta} - p = 0 \tag{5}$$

where $N^{\alpha\beta}$ is the membrane stress tensor, $M^{\alpha\beta}$ the moment tensor, and F^α and p are the external loads per unit area of the middle surface acting in the tangential and in the normal directions, respectively.

We intend to derive equations that will also hold for moderately thick shells, i.e., for shells where the ratio h/R is of order unity. Therefore, we shall apply the constitutive equations from the refined shell theory given in Ref. [38].

$$
N^{\alpha\beta} = \tilde{E}h\left[E^{\alpha\beta} + \tilde{\nu}\, a^{\alpha\beta}\, E^{\gamma}_{\gamma}\right](1 + K\,h^2/12) + \tag{6}
$$

$$
+ \frac{1}{24}\,\tilde{E}h^3\left[- 3(d^{\alpha\gamma}\,K^{\beta}_{\gamma} + d^{\beta\gamma}\,K^{\alpha}_{\gamma}) + 2d\,K^{\alpha\beta} - \right.
$$

$$
- 4\tilde{\nu}\,a^{\alpha\beta}\,d^{\gamma\delta}\,K_{\gamma\delta} - 5\tilde{\nu}\,d^{\alpha\beta}\,K^{\gamma}_{\gamma} + \tilde{\nu}(2-3\tilde{\nu})d\,a^{\alpha\beta}\,K^{\gamma}_{\gamma} +
$$

$$
+ 4d^{\alpha\delta}\,d^{\gamma\beta}\,E_{\gamma\delta} + 2(1+5\tilde{\nu})d^{\alpha\beta}\,d^{\gamma\delta}\,E_{\gamma\delta} + \tilde{\nu}(6+5\tilde{\nu})d\,d^{\alpha\beta}\,E^{\gamma}_{\gamma} +
$$

$$
+ \tilde{\nu}(6+5\tilde{\nu})d\,a^{\alpha\beta}\,d^{\gamma\delta}\,E_{\gamma\delta} + 2d(d^{\alpha\gamma}\,E^{\beta}_{\gamma} + d^{\beta\gamma}\,E^{\alpha}_{\gamma}) +
$$

$$
+ 2\tilde{\nu}^2(2+\tilde{\nu})d^2\,a^{\alpha\beta}\,E^{\gamma}_{\gamma} - 12K\,E^{\alpha\beta} - 4\tilde{\nu}(5+3\tilde{\nu})K\,a^{\alpha\beta}\,E^{\gamma}_{\gamma}\Big] +
$$

$$
+ \frac{1}{12}\,\tilde{E}h^3(1-\tilde{\nu})(d^{\gamma\delta}\,E_{\gamma\delta} + \tilde{\nu}\,d\,E^{\gamma}_{\gamma})(d^{\alpha\beta} + \tilde{\nu}\,d\,a^{\alpha\beta})
$$

$$
M^{\alpha\beta} = \frac{1}{24}\,\tilde{E}h^3\left[2K^{\alpha\beta} + 2\tilde{\nu}\,a^{\alpha\beta}\,K^{\gamma}_{\gamma} - 3(d^{\alpha\gamma}\,E^{\beta}_{\gamma} + d^{\beta\gamma}\,E^{\alpha}_{\gamma}) + \right. \tag{7}
$$

$$
+ 2d\,E^{\alpha\beta} - 4\tilde{\nu}\,d^{\alpha\beta}\,E^{\gamma}_{\gamma} - 5\tilde{\nu}\,a^{\alpha\beta}\,d^{\gamma\delta}\,E_{\gamma\delta} +
$$

$$
+ \tilde{\nu}(2-3\tilde{\nu})d\,a^{\alpha\beta}\,E^{\gamma}_{\gamma}\Big]
$$

Here $a_{\alpha\beta}$ is the metric tensor, and $d = d^{\gamma}_{\gamma}$ and $K = d/a$ are the surface invariants. Furthermore

$$
\tilde{\nu} = \frac{\nu}{1-\nu} \quad ; \quad \tilde{E} = \frac{E}{1+\nu} \tag{8}
$$

where E is Young's modulus and ν is Poisson's ratio.

By using the accelerations of the middle surface and d'Alembert's principle and taking into account the differences in volume on each side of the middle surface, we find the external loads on the middle surface statically equivalent to the inertia forces

$$F^\alpha = \frac{\Omega}{R^2}\left[v^1\left(1 - \frac{h^2}{12R^2}\right)\ ,\ v^2\right]\ ;\ p = \frac{\Omega}{R^2}\,w \qquad (9)$$

where $\Omega = R^2\omega^2\rho h$, and where ω is the angular frequency of the harmonic motion and ρ the density of the material.

Substitution of Eqs. (2) and (3) in Eqs. (6) and (7) and Eqs. (6), (7), and (9) in Eqs. (4) and (5) yields the equations of motion in terms of the displacements and their derivatives.

The equations of motion and all the boundary conditions

$$v^1 = w = N^{22} = M^{22} = 0\ ;\ x^2 = 0, L \qquad (10)$$

are satisfied by the displacement functions

$$v^1 = A_{ij}\,\sin(i\ x^2/R)\sin(j\ x^1/R)$$

$$v^2 = B_{ij}\,\cos(i\ x^2/R)\cos(j\ x^1/R) \qquad (11)$$

$$w = C_{ij}\,\sin(i\ x^2/R)\cos(j\ x^1/R)$$

where $i = \frac{R}{L}\pi m$, $m = 0,1,2,\ldots$, and where $j = 0,1,2,\ldots$.

Substitution of Eq. 11 into the equations of motion yields three homogeneous linear equations for the constants A_{ij} , B_{ij}, and C_{ij} . A nonvanishing solution requires that the determinant of the coefficients must vanish.

The computations are straightforward, but of such complexity that automated formula manipulation is required. The TENSOR FORMAC session listed below successfully performs the formula manipulation described above.

TENSOR FORMAC session

```
/**  SPECIFY THE MULTINOMIAL AND THE DISTRIBUTIVE LAWS TO BE
     APPLIED DURING EVALUATION OF EXPRESSIONS.                    **/
OPTSET (EXPND);    OPTSET(LINELENGTH = 70);

/**  THE DEFAULT DIMENSION OF SPACE IS 2 , THUS NO DIMENSION
     COMMAND IS NECESSARY.                                        **/

/**  DEFINE THE PARAMETRIC RELATIONS FOR A CYLINDRICAL SURFACE.
     PF1, PF2 AND  PF3  ARE STANDARD NAMES IN THE SYSTEM FOR THE
```

```
        PARAMETRIC RELATIONS. THEY ARE TENSORS OF THE ORDER ZERO.    **/
   /**  X1  AND  X2  ARE THE STANDARD NAMES IN THE SYSTEM OF THE
        INDEPENDENT VARIABLES.                                       **/
   /**  SPECIFY THE SUCCEEDING COMMANDS TO BE INTERPRETED IN MODE 2 **/
  MODE 2;
  PF1 = R*COS(X1/R);
  PF2 = R*SIN(X1/R);
  PF3 = X2;


   /**  DEFINE A SUBSTITUTION PAIR FOR REPLACEMENT LATER IN THE SES-
        SION OF  COS(X1/R)  BY  ((1 - SIN(X1/R))**2)**(1/2) .        **/
  MODE 3;
  CHCOSI = CHAIN(COS(X1/R),(1 - SIN(X1/R)**2)**(1/2));
   /**  FOR CONVENIENCE  'LET(   )'  IS ALWAYS OMITTED IN MODE 3 IN
        TENSOR FORMAC.                                               **/


   /**  GENERATE THE COVARIANT METRIC TENSOR  MET(AB)  AND PRINT IT
        OUT.                                                         **/
  MODE 2;
  COV_MET;
  PRINT_OUT MET(AB);

MET(11) = SIN(X1*R**(-1 ))**2 + COS(X1*R**(-1 ))**2
MET(12) = 0
MET(21) = 0
MET(22) = 1


   /**  REDUCE THE METRIC TENSOR BY USING THE CHAIN  CHCOSI   AND
        PRINT IT OUT FOR CONTROL OF THE REDUCTION.                   **/
  REPLACE MET(AB),CHCOSI;
  PRINT_OUT MET(AB);

MET(11) = 1
MET(12) = 0
MET(21) = 0
MET(22) = 1


   /**  GENERATE THE DETERMINANT  MDE  OF THE COVARIANT METRIC TEN-
        SOR, THE CONTRAVARIANT METRIC TENSOR  MET(:AB), THE UNIT
        NORMAL TO THE SURFACE AND THE COVARIANT CURVATURE TENSOR
        CUR(AB) .                                                    **/
  MET_DET;
  CON_MET;
  NORMAL;
  CURVATURE;
  REPLACE CUR(AB),CHCOSI;
```

```
/** GENERATE THE DETERMINANT  CDE  OF THE COVARIANT CURVATURE
     TENSOR AND THE TRACE  CTR  OF THE MIXED CURVATURE TENSOR.  **/
MODE 1;
CDE = CUR(11)*CUR(22) - CUR(12)*CUR(12);
CTR = CUR(A:A);
   /** THE CHARACTER ':' INDICATES THAT IF THE PRECEEDING INDEX WAS
        A COVARIANT ONE THE NEXT ONE IS CONTRAVARIANT AND VICE VER-
        SA.                                                     **/

   /** DEFINE THE COVARIANT TANGENTIAL DISPLACEMENT VECTOR  VVV(A)
        AND THE NORMAL DISPLACEMENT  WWW  BY THE THREE FORMAC FUNC-
        TION VARIABLES  U.(X1,X2) , V.(X1,X2)  AND  W.(X1,X2) . ALL
        TENSOR NAMES CONSISTS OF THREE CHARACTERS, ALFABETIC OR NU-
        MERIC. THUS, THE PURPOSE OF THIS DEFINITION IS TO SHORTEN
        THE PRINT OUTS OF EXPRESSIONS INVOLVING THE DISPLACEMENTS. **/
MODE 2;
VVV(1) = U.(X);     VVV(2) = V.(X);     WWW = W.(X);
   /** X IS THE NAME OF THE CHAIN  X1,X2 .                       **/

   /** DEFINE THE EXTERNAL LOADS  FFF(:A)  AND  PPP  AS GIVEN BY
        (9).                                                    **/
FFF(:1) = OM*U.(X)*(1 - H**2/R**2/12)/R**2;
FFF(:2) = OM*V.(X)/R**2;     PPP = OM*W.(X)/R**2;

   /** DEFINE ALL THOSE CONSTANTS USED IN THE CONSTITUITIVE EQUA-
        TIONS (6), (7) AND IN (2) AND (4) AS TENSORS OF THE ORDER
        ZERO.                                                   **/
NNY = NY;     HP2 = H**2;
C01 = 1;     C02 = 2;     C03 = 3;     C04 = 4;     C05 = 5;     C12 = 1/12;
C24 = 1/24;     HAF = 1/2;     C23 = 2 - 3*NY;     C15 = 1 + 5*NY;
C65 = 6 + 5*NY;     C21 = 2 + NY;     C53 = 5 + 3*NY;     C11 = 1 - NY;

   /** GENERATE THE GAUSSIAN CURVATURE  CDE/MDE . CDE1(1,1,1,1)
        AND  MDE1(1,1,1,1)  ARE THE INTERNAL, I.E. FORMAC, NAMES
        FOR  CDE  AND  MDE .                                    **/
GAU = CDE1(1,1,1,1)/MDE1(1,1,1,1);

   /** CALCULATE THE COVARIANT STRAIN TENSOR  STR(AB)  AND THE CO-
        VARIANT BENDING TENSOR  BEN(AB)  AS GIVEN BY (2) AND (3).
        PRINT OUT THE BENDING TENSOR.                           **/
   /** THE CHARACTERS 'DA' IN FRONT OF  VVV(B)  DENOTES COVARIANT
        DIFFERENTIATION.                                        **/
MODE 1;
STR(AB)  = HAF*DAVVV(B) + HAF*DBVVV(A) - CUR(AB)*WWW;
BEN(AB)  = DADBWWW + CUR(AG)*DBVVV(:G) + CUR(BG)*DAVVV(:G) +
            VVV(:G)*DBCUR(GA) - CUR(BG)*CUR(A:G)*WWW;
PRINT_OUT BEN(AB);
```

```
BEN(11) = -R**(-2 )*W-R**(-1 )*U,1*2 + W,12
BEN(12) = -R**(-1 )*U,2 + W,1,2
BEN(21) = -R**(-1 )*U,2 + W,1,2
BEN(22) = W,22
   /** THE NOTATION  U,2  DENOTES THE PARTIAL DERIVATIVE OF  U
       WITH RESPECT TO  X2 , W,12  DENOTES THE PARTIAL DERIVATIVE
       OF SECOND ORDER OF  W  WITH RESPECT TO  X1  AND  W,1,2  DE-
       NOTES THE PARTIAL DERIVATIVE OF SECOND ORDER OF  W  WITH
       RESPECT TO  X1  AND  X2 .                            **/

   /** CALCULATE THE CONTRAVARIANT MEMBRANE STRESS TENSOR  MEM(:AB)
       GIVEN BY (6).                                        **/
   /** THE MEMBRANE STRESS TENSOR, THE MOMENT TENSOR, THE EQUA-
       TIONS OF EQUILIBRIUM AND HENCE THE EIGENVALUE ARE ALL FOR
       SHORTNESS DIVIDED BY  E*H .                           **/
ME0     = C01 + GAU*HP2*C12;
ME1(:AB) = ME0*STR(:AB) + ME0*NNY*MET(:AB)*STR(G:G);
ME2(:AB) = - C03*CUR(:AG)*BEN(G:B) - C03*CUR(:BG)*BEN(G:A)
           + C02*CTR*BEN(:AB) - C04*NNY*MET(:AB)*CUR(:GC)*BEN(GC)
           - C05*NNY*CUR(:AB)*BEN(G:G) + NNY*C23*CTR*MET(:AB)*BEN(G:G)
           + C04*CUR(:AC)*CUR(:GB)*STR(GC) + C02*C15*CUR(:AB)
           *CUR(:GC)*STR(GC) + NNY*C65*CTR*CUR(:AB)*STR(G:G)
           + NNY*C65*CTR*MET(:AB)*CUR(:GC)*STR(GC) + C02*CTR*CUR(:AG)
           *STR(G:B) + C02*CTR*CUR(:BG)*STR(G:A) + C02*NNY*NNY*C21
           *CTR*CTR*MET(:AB)*STR(G:G) - C03*C04*GAU*STR(:AB)
           - C04*NNY*C53*GAU*MET(:AB)*STR(G:G);
ME3     = CUR(:GC)*STR(GC) + NNY*CTR*STR(G:G);
ME4(:AB) = CUR(:AB) + NNY*CTR*MET(:AB);
MEM(:AB) = ME1(:AB) + C24*HP2*ME2(:AB) + C12*C11*HP2*ME3*ME4(:AB);

   /** CALCULATE THE CONTRAVARIANT MOMENT TENSOR  MOM(:AB)  GIVEN
       BY (7). PRINT OUT THE COMPONENT  MOM(:11)  OF THE MOMENT
       TENSOR.                                              **/
MO1(:AB) = C02*BEN(:AB) + C02*NNY*MET(:AB)*BEN(G:G) - C03*CUR(:AG)
           *STR(G:B) - C03*CUR(:BG)*STR(G:A) + C02*CTR*STR(:AB)
           - C04*NNY*CUR(:AB)*STR(G:G) - C05*NNY*MET(:AB)*CUR(:GC)
           *STR(GC) + NNY*C23*CTR*MET(:AB)*STR(G:G);
           + NNY*C23*CTR*MET(:AB)*STR(G:G);
MOM(:AB) = C24*HP2*MO1(:AB);
PRINT_OUT MOM(:11);


MOM(:11)  =  NY*H**2*R**(-2 )*W*(5/24 ) +  NY*H**2*R**(-1 )*U,1*(1/8)
   +  NY*H**2*R**(-1 )*V,2*(1/12 ) + NY*H**2*W,12*(1/12 ) + NY*H**2*W,2
2*(1/12 ) + NY**2*H**2*R**(-2 )*W*(1/8 ) + NY**2*H**2*R**(-1 )*U,1*(1/
8 ) + NY**2*H**2*R**(-1 )*V,2*(1/8 ) + H**2*R**(-2 )*W*(1/12 ) + H**2*
W,12*(1/12 )
```

```
/**   GENERATE THE EQUATIONS OF EQUILIBRIUM GIVEN BY (4) AND (5).
      THE LEFT HAND SIDE OF (4) AND (5) ARE NAMED  EQ1(:B)  AND
      EQ3 , RESPECTIVELY.                                       **/
EQ1(:B)  = DAMEM(:AB) + CO2*CUR(G:B)*DAMOM(:AG) + MOM(:AG)*DACUR(G:B)
           + FFF(:B);
EQ3      = DADBMOM(:AB) - CUR(AB)*CUR(G:B)*MMM(:AG) - CUR(AB)*MEM(:AB)
           - PPP;


   /**  PRINT OUT THE EQUATION OF EQUILIBRIUM NAMED  EQ3 .        **/
PRINT_OUT EQ3;


EQ3    =  - OM*R**(-2 )*W  +  NY*H**2*R**(-4 )*W*(1/2 )  +  NY*H**2*R**
(-3 )*U,1*(7/24 )  +  NY*H**2*R**(-3 )*V,2*(1/4 ) + NY*H**2*R**(-2 )*W
,12*(5/12 ) + NY*H**2*R**(-2 )*W,22*(1/12 )-NY*H**2*R**(-1 )*U,1,22*(1
/24 ) + NY*H**2*R**(-1 )*U,13*(1/8 ) + NY*H**2*R**(-1 )*V,12,2*(1/12 )
-NY*H**2*R**(-1 )*V,23*(1/12 ) + NY*H**2*W,12,22*(1/6 ) + NY*H**2*W,14
*(1/12 ) + NY*H**2*W,24*(1/12 ) + NY*R**(-2 )*W + NY*R**(-1 )*U,1 + NY
*R**(-1 )*V,2 + NY**2*H**2*R**(-4 )*W*(1/4 ) + NY**2*H**2*R**(-3 )*U,1
*(1/8 ) + NY**2*H**2*R**(-3 )*V,2*(1/4 ) + NY**2*H**2*R**(-2 )*W,12*(1
/4 ) + NY**2*H**2*R**(-2 )*W,22*(1/4 ) + NY**2*H**2*R**(-1 )*U,1,22*(1
/8 ) + NY**2*H**2*R**(-1 )*U,13*(1/8 ) + NY**2*H**2*R**(-1 )*V,12,2*(1
/8 ) + NY**2*H**2*R**(-1 )*V,23*(1/8 ) + H**2*R**(-4 )*W*(1/4 ) + H**2
*R**(-3 )*U,1*(1/6 ) + H**2*R**(-2 )*W,12*(1/6 )-H**2*R**(-1 )*U,1,22*
(1/8 ) + H**2*R**(-1 )*V,12,2*(1/24 )-H**2*R**(-1 )*V,23*(1/12 ) + H**
2*W,12,22*(1/6 ) + H**2*W,14*(1/12 ) + H**2*W,24*(1/12 ) + R**(-2 )*W
+ R**(-1 )*U,1


   /**  IN THE EQUATIONS OF EQUILIBRIUM REPLACE THE DISPLACEMENTS
        WITH THE ASSUMED VIBRATION MODES GIVEN BY (11).           **/
MODE 3;
VIBMOD = CHAIN(U.($),A*SIN(I*$(2)/R)*SIN(J*$(1)/R),
               V.($),B*COS(I*$(2)/R)*COS(J*$(1)/R),
               W.($),C*SIN(I*$(2)/R)*COS(J*$(1)/R));

MODE 1;
EVAL EQ1(:B),VIBMOD;
EVAL EQ3,VIBMOD;


   /**  REDUCE THE EQUATIONS OF EQUILIBRIUM BY ELIMINATING THE TRI-
        GONOMETRIC COEFFICIENTS, BY MULTIPLYING WITH R**2 AND BY
        SUBSTITUTING  K  FOR  H**2/R**2/12 .                     **/
MODE 3;
EQEQ1 = - R**2*EQ12(1,1,1,1)/(SIN(I*X2/R)*SIN(J*X1/R));
EQEQ2 = - R**2*EQ12(2,1,1,1)/(COS(I*X2/R)*COS(J*X1/R));
EQEQ3 =   R**2*EQ31(1,1,1,1)/(SIN(I*X2/R)*COS(J*X1/R));
EQEQ1 = REPLACE(EQEQ1,H**2,R**2*K*12);
EQEQ2 = REPLACE(EQEQ2,H**2,R**2*K*12);
EQEQ3 = REPLACE(EQEQ3,H**2,R**2*K*12);
```

```
/** PRINT OUT THE THIRD OF THE EQUILIBRIUM EQUATIONS.          **/
PRINT_OUT (EQEQ3);
```

$$EQEQ3 = C + 6\,NY\,K\,C - NY\,I^2\,K\,C + 2\,NY\,J^2\,I^2\,K\,C + 2\,J^2\,I^2\,K\,C - 3$$
$$NY^2\,I^2\,K\,C + I^4\,K\,C + NY\,I^4\,K\,C - 5\,NY\,J^2\,K\,C - 3\,NY^2\,J^2\,K\,C -$$
$$2\,J^2\,K\,C + J^4\,K\,C + NY\,J^4\,K\,C + 3\,NY^2\,K\,C + 3\,K\,C - OM\,C + NY\,C +$$
$$7/2\,NY\,J^2\,A\,K + 3/2\,NY^2\,J^2\,A\,K + 2\,J^2\,A\,K + 1/2\,NY\,J^2\,I^2\,A\,K - 3/2\,NY^2$$
$$J^2\,I^2\,A\,K + 3/2\,J^2\,I^2\,A\,K - 3/2\,NY\,J^3\,A\,K - 3/2\,NY^2\,J^3\,A\,K - 3\,NY\,B$$
$$I^2\,K - 3\,NY^2\,B\,I^2\,K + NY\,B\,J^2\,I^2\,K + 3/2\,NY^2\,B\,J^2\,I^2\,K + 1/2\,B\,J^2\,I^2$$
$$K - B\,I^3\,K - NY\,B\,I^3\,K + 3/2\,NY^2\,B^2\,I\,K + K + J\,A + NY\,J^3\,A - NY\,B\,I$$

```
/** FIND THE COEFFICIENTS OF A , B  AND  C  IN THE THREE EQUI-
    LIBRIUM EQUATIONS.                                    **/
EQ1A = COEFF(EQEO1,A);   EQ1B = COEFF(EQEO1,B);   EQ1C = COEFF(EQEO1,C);
EQ2A = COEFF(EQEO2,A);   EQ2B = COEFF(EOEO2,B);   EQ2C = COEFF(EOEQ2,C);
EQ3A = COEFF(EQEQ3,A);   EQ3B = COEFF(EQEQ3,B);   EQ3C = COEFF(EQEO3,C);

/** THIS TERMINATES THE ANALYTIC COMPUTATIONS. ALL NINE COEFFI-
    CIENTS ARE FOUND. AS AN EXAMPLE PRINT OUT THE COEFFICIENT OF
    C  IN THE THIRD EQUILIBRIUM EQUATION.                 **/
PRINT_OUT (EQ3C);
```

$$EQ3C = 3\,K - OM + NY + 6\,NY\,K - NY\,I^2\,K + 2\,NY\,J^2\,I^2\,K + 2\,J^2\,I^2\,K$$
$$- 3\,NY^2\,I^2\,K + I^4\,K + NY\,I^4\,K - 5\,NY\,J^2\,K - 3\,NY^2\,J^2\,K - 2\,J^2$$
$$K + J^4\,K + NY\,J^4\,K + 3\,NY^2\,K + 1$$

```
/** WITH THE NOEDIT OPTION WE MAY PRINT OR PUNCH THE NINE COEF-
    FICIENTS AS FORTRAN OR PL/1 COMPATIBLE EXPRESSIONS. FOR
    EXAMPLE                                               **/
OPTSET(NOEDIT);
PRINT_OUT (EQ3C);
EQ3C = K**3-OM + NY + K*NY*6-K*I**2*L**(-2)*NY*R**2 + K*I**2*L**(-2 )*J
**2*NY*R**2*2 + K*I**2*L**(-2 )*J**2*R**2*2-K*I**2*L**(-2 )*NY**2*R**2
*3 + K*I**4*L**(-4 )*NY*R**4 + K*I**4*L**(-4 )*R**4-K*J**2*NY*5-K*J**2
*NY**2*3-K*J**2*2 + K*J**4 + K*J**4*NY + K*NY**2*3 + 1

/** TERMINATE THE SESSION.                               **/
STOP;
```

The session is terminated when the coefficients of the constants A_{ij}, B_{ij}, and C_{ij} are obtained. The eigenvalues and the corresponding values of A_{ij}, B_{ij}, and C_{ij} may easily be obtained numerically. Hence, further treatment of the problem is of no interest here.

Of course, although this example is not trivial, it must be underlined that the capabilities of the TENSOR FORMAC system or the computer have by no means been exhausted.

REFERENCES

Symbolic and algebraic manipulation systems

1 Kahrimanian, H. G., "Analytic Differentiation by a Digital Computer," Master's Thesis, Temple University, Philadelphia, 1953, 43 p.

2 Nolan, J., "Analytic Differentiation on a Digital Computer," Master's Thesis, M.I.T., Cambridge Mass., 1953, 71 p.

3 Brown, W. S., "The ALPAK System for Nonnumerical Algebra on a Digital Computer - I: Polynomials in Several Variables and Truncated Power Series with Polynomial Coefficients," Bell Systems Technical Journal, Vol. 42, 1963, pp. 2081-2119.

4 Bond, E., et al., "FORMAC an Experimental Formula Manipulation Compiler," Proceedings of the 19th ACM Conference, 1964, pp. K2.1-1 - K2.1-18.

5 Hall, A. D., "The ALTRAN System for Rational Function Manipulation - A Survey," Proceedings of the Second Symposium on Symbolic and Algebraic Manipulation, March 1971, pp. 153-157.

6 Fedlman, S. I., "A Brief Description of ALTRAN," ACM SIGSAM Bulletin, November 1975, pp. 12-20.

7 Brown, W. S., "ALTRAN User's Manual," Third Edition, Bell Laboratories, 1973.

8 Hearn, A. C., "REDUCE 2: A System and Language for Algebraic Manipulation," Proceedings of the Second Symposium on Symbolic and Algebraic Manipulation, March 1971, pp. 128-133.

9 Hearn, A. C., "REDUCE 2 User's Manual," Second Ed., Tech. rep. UCP-19, Physics Department, University of Utah, 1973.

10 Strubbe, H., "Presentation of the SCHOONSCHIP System," ACM SIGSAM Bulletin, August 1974, pp. 55-60.

11 Strubbe, H., "Manual for SCHOONSCHIP, A CDC 6000/7000 Program for Symbolic Evolution of Algebraic Expressions," CERN-Data Handling Division, 1974, 48 p.

12 Collins, G. E., "The SAC-1 System: An Introduction and Survey," Proceedings of the Second Symposium on Symbolic and Algebraic Manipulation, March 1971, pp. 144-152.

13 Collins, G. E., "The SAC-1 Integer Arithmetic System - Version III," University of Wisconsin Computing Center, Technical Report No. 156, March 1973.

14 Engeli, M., "An Enhanced SYMBAL System," ACM SIGSAM Bulletin, November 1975, pp. 21-29.

15 Martin, W. A. and Fateman, R. J., "The MACSYMA system," Proceedings of the Second Symposium on Symbolic and Algebraic Manipulation, March 1971, pp. 59-75.

16 Moses, J., "MACSYMA - The Fifth Year," ACM SIGSAM Bulletin, August 1974, pp. 105-110.

17 Bogen, R. A., et al., "MACSYMA Reference Manual," Version 6, M.I.T., Cambridge, Mass., 1974.

18 Griesmer, J. H. and Jenks, R. D., "SCRATCHPAD/1 - An Interactive Facility for Symbolic Mathematics," Proceedings of the Second Symposium on Symbolic and Algebraic Manipulation, March 1971, pp. 42-58.

19 Jenks, R. D., "The SCRATCHPAD Language," ACM SIGSAM Bulletin, May 1974, pp. 20-30.

20 Sundblad, Y., "A User's Review of Algebraic System," Report TRITA-NA-73/3, Department of Computer Science, Royal Institute of Technology, Stockholm, 1973, 34 p.

FORMAC

21 Bond, E. R., et al., "Implementation of FORMAC," IBM Technical Report TR00.1260, March 1965.

22 Jensen, J., "Experience in Use of FORMAC," Proceedings of SEAS XII, 1967, pp. 050.1-050.13.

23 Xenakis, J., "The PL/1-FORMAC Interpreter," Second Symposium on Symbolic and Algebraic Manipulation, March 1971, pp. 105-114.

24 Tobey, R. G., et al., "PL/1-FORMAC Symbolic Mathematics Interpreter," SHARE Contributed Program Library, No. 360D-03.3.004, September 1969, 164 p.

25 Schwerdt, R., "The KFA FORMAC Preprocessor," KFA-Jülich Report Jul-676-MA, July 1970.

26 Bahr, K. A., "Toward a Revision of FORMAC," ACM SIGSAM Bulletin, February 1974, pp. 10-16.

27 Bahr, K. A., "Utilizing the FORMAC Novelties," Proceedings SEAS Anniversary Meeting, September 1974, pp. 236-245.

28 Laplace, A., "FORMAC Desk Calculator," Proceedings SEAS XVI, 1971.

29 Smit, J., "NETFORM, an Interactive FORMAC System with Special Facilities for Analysis of Electrical Networks," Technische Hogeschool Twente, June 1975, 112 p.

30 Smit, J., "Introduction to NETFORM," ACM SIGSAM Bulletin, May 1974, pp. 31-36.

31 Collatz, L., "Eigenwertaufgaben mit Technischen Anwendungen," Leipzig 1963, 500 p.

Symbolic Tensor Manipulation

32 Walton, J. J., "Tensor Calculations on the Computer," Comm. ACM, Vol. 9, No. 12, 1966, p. 864 and Comm. ACM, Vol. 10, No. 3, 1967, pp. 183-186.

33 Howard, J. C., "Computer Formulation of the Equations of Motion Using Tensor Notation," Comm. ACM, Vol. 10, No. 9, 1967, pp. 543-548.

34 Howard, J. C. and Tasjian, H., "An Algorithm for Deriving the Equations of Mathematical Physics by Symbolic Manipulations," Comm. ACM, Vol. 11, No. 12, 1968, pp. 814-818, 826.

35 Barton, D., "Some Applications of CAMAL 370," Proceedings SEAS Anniversary Meeting, September 1973, pp. 354-361.

36 Jensen, J., "Manual for the Symbolic Tensor Analysis Program, TENSOR FORMAC," Department of Solid Mechanics, Technical University of Denmark, 1975, 50 p.

37 Niordson, F. I., "Indledning til Skalteorien," Department of Solid Mechanics, Technical University of Denmark, 1974, 180 p.

38 Niordson, F. I., "A Consistent Refined Shell Theory," DCAMM Report No. 104, Technical University of Denmark, May 1976, 17 p.

Application of Symbolic and Algebraic Manipulation

39 Chepurniy, N., "Evaluation of High-Order Polynomial Triangular Finite Elements Using FORMAC," Proceedings of the Second Symposium on Symbolic and Algebraic Manipulation, March 1971, pp. 365-371.

40 Andersen, C. M. and Noor, A. K., "Use of Symbolic Manipulation in the Development of Two-Dimensional Finite Elements," SIAM 1973 National Meeting, Hampton, Virginia.

41 Pedersen, P., and Megahed, M. M., "Axisymmetric Element Analysis Using Analytic Computing," Computers & Structures, Vol. 5 pp. 241-247.

42 Cohen, J., "Symbolic and Numerical Computer Analysis of the Combined Local and Overall Buckling of Rectangular Thin-Walled Columns," Computer Methods in Applied Mechanics and Engineering, Vol. 7, 1976, pp. 17-38.

43 Pedersen, P., "On Computer-Aided Analytic Element Analysis and the Similarities of Tetrahedron Elements," to appear in International Jouranl for Numerical Methods in Engineering.

FLOOR ANALYSIS AND DESIGN

M. Daniel Vanderbilt

Colorado State University

INTRODUCTION

A floor is a structural subsystem which is planar, usually rectangular, may contain one or many panels, and supports a load applied normal to its plane. Each panel of a floor is a plate element, and many of the concepts of the classical theory of elastic plates are useful in analyzing floors. The input data required in floor analysis include a description of the geometry, material properties, and loadings. The basic output information consists of deflections, moments, and shears. Additional output data may include stresses, interlayer slips, fastener forces, prestressing forces, column reactions, reinforcing steel areas, and so forth, depending upon the type of construction material and program used.

Floors may be constructed of any of the major structural materials, e.g., wood, reinforced or prestressed concrete, steel, or combinations of these materials, e.g., wood joists with a concrete slab, or steel joists with metal deck and concrete slab. The analysis, or analysis and design of floors of each type of material presents problems not encountered with other materials. Thus this survey of types of available programs is categorized by materials. The following materials and programs are discussed.

1. Wood
       Program FEAFLO performs a finite element analysis of wood joist floors.
    2. Reinforced and Prestressed Concrete
       Program IRSLAB performs a finite difference analysis of irregular elastic slabs.
       Program CNCGRD performs analysis and design of continuous concrete beams and slabs.
       Program POSTEN performs analysis and design of continuous prestressed post-tensioned concrete beams and slabs.
       Program ADOSS(SR185) performs analysis and design of reinforced concrete floor slabs.

No special purpose programs for the analysis of steel floors are
available for review.

NOMENCLATURE

The symbols used in the chapter are listed below, except that symbols used only on a single page are not shown. Units for symbols
are given in parentheses.

A_i = cross-sectional area of ith layer (L^2)

CL, CS = widths of rectangular column in long and short directions, respectively (L)

E = modulus of elasticity (F/L^2)

E_i = modulus of elasticity of ith layer (F/L^2)

$EGI_{\|, \perp}$ = sheathing modulus of elasticity in bending, based on
gross section, in directions parallel and perpendicular
to face grain respectively (F/L^2)

$EGA_{\|, \perp}$ = sheathing modulus of elasticity for axial force, based
on gross section, in directions parallel and perpendic-
ular to face grain respectively (F/L^2)

f'_c = cylinder strength of concrete (F/L^2)

f_y = yield stress of reinforcing steel (F/L^2)

G = shear modulus of elasticity (F/L^2)

H = dimensionless ratio of EI of beam to EI of plate

I_i = moment of inertia of ith layer (L^4)

I = moment of inertia (L^4)

k_i = slip modulus of connector between ith and $(i+1)$th layers
(F/L)

ℓ = length of beam (L)

L = long span of rectangular plate (L)

n_i = number of rows of connectors between ith and $(i+1)$th
layers

n_L = number of layers

R = ratio of short to long spans of rectangular panel

S_i = spacing of connectors between ith and $(i+1)$th layers (L)

S = short span of rectangular plate (L)

u_i = axial deformation of ith layer at its midheight (L)

w = loading on beam (F/L)

x = coordinate along length of beam (L)

y = deflection of node point (L)

WOOD FLOORS

Theory

A wood joist floor typically consists of parallel wood joists, usually of equal size and spacing, covered with one or two layers of
sheathing. Sheathing materials include plywood, particle board,
wood boards, and concrete. The layers (the joists are treated as a
layer which is usually, but not necessarily, the bottom layer) are
fastened together with nails and/or elastomeric glues.

Although wood joist and sheathing systems are simple in concept and simply constructed, they are extremely complicated to
analyze. A wood floor is an orthotropic multilayered plate with
each layer made of orthotropic materials, and because of the fastener behavior there exists an interlayer slip of sufficient
magnitude to have a major effect on the deflections and stresses of
the system. In addition, gaps at joints in the sheathing layers
produce discontinuities which have a significant effect on the composite action. These factors, coupled with material variability in
each component, require a complex analysis technique to predict
system performance.

Theoretical bases for studies of layered wood systems and details of several analysis procedures including closed-form and
finite difference procedures have been described in numerous previous publications. Studies reported by Goodman [1,2,3],
Polensek [4], and others provide a background of experimental and
theoretical knowledge.

Finite Element Formulation

The finite element formulation on which program FEAFLO is based is
discussed in detail by Thompson, Vanderbilt, and Goodman [5]. This
program was developed as a part of a continuing research program
aimed at completing rational analysis and design procedures for layered wood systems as described in a report by Vanderbilt et al. [6].

A typical rectangular floor system is shown in Fig. 1a. For
purposes of the finite element analysis, the floor is idealized as a
set of crossing beams as shown. Each of the T-beams, in the direction of the joists, consists of a joist plus a composite flange of
one or more layers of sheathing, equal in width to the joist spacing, as shown in Fig. 1b. Each of the sheathing strips (Fig. 1c)
is either a simple beam (one layer of sheathing) or a layered beam
(multiple sheathing layers) of arbitrary width. At each node
(crossing) point the floor stiffness is obtained by summing the
contributions of the T-beam and sheathing strip which intersect at
that node. The assumption that the floor can be represented by
this idealization ignores the contribution of the torsional
stiffness of sheathing and T-beams. For wood-based materials, the
G/E ratio is usually small (typically 1/20 to 1/10), and thus this
assumption is felt to be valid. Deflections computed with this

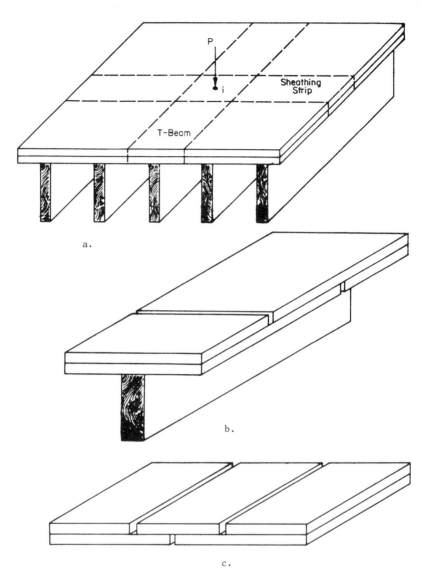

Fig. 1 Crossing beam model of wood joist floor:
         a.   division of floor into crossing beams
         b.   typical T-beam
         c.   typical sheathing strip

assumption may be expected to be slightly greater than those
measured,

The basic component in the program is that for the analysis of
a layered wood beam which includes the effects of interlayer slip,
orthotropy, gaps at joints, and variability of materials. The
finite element approximation for the layered beam component was developed considering the potential energy contributions of bending,
axial loads, external loading, and a special contribution due to interlayer slip effects. Axial and deflection displacements are
approximated by appropriate shape functions, and the usual methods
for formulating the stiffness matrix for each beam element are
applied. Gaps at joints and the resulting discontinuities are
modeled by using a soft element. Detailed descriptions of the development of the finite element method may be found in [5].

Capabilities of Program FEAFLO

General Description

The work described above culminated in the development of a computer
program for the finite element analysis of wood floor systems
(FEAFLO). This program can analyze rectangular wood joist floors
with one or two layers of sheathing subjected to any pattern of
force loading perpendicular to the plane of the sheathing. Joints
can be in both layers of sheathing independently as required. Input
data include a description of the floor geometry, number of layers
(two or three), material property information, gap data, slip
moduli, and load data. Output data at each node include the deflection, slip displacements, rotation in the T-beam direction,
extreme fiber stresses in each layer, and fastener forces.

Examples of Program Verification. Program FEAFLO has been used to
predict the measured deflections of full-scale floors for which the
material properties were measured using newly developed nondestruc-
tive testing techniques [7,8]. An example of the capability of
the program to properly predict the true behavior of a variety of
floor systems is shown in Fig. 2. The excellent agreement obtained
demonstrates the capability of the program to predict the performance of floor systems. This verification of the procedures used in
developing the mathematical model and the finite element analysis
allows the use of the program in a variety of applications. Complete details of the extensive studies made to verify the program
are given in [6].

Program Capabilities

Program FEAFLO is the only program currently available which properly incorporates all of the factors known to affect the response of

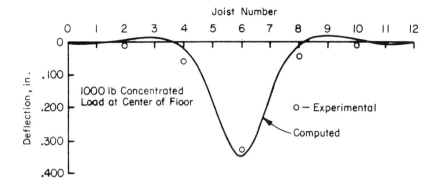

a. Deflection profile at centerline of joists

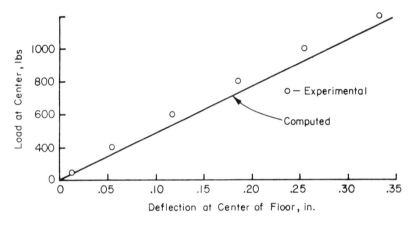

b. Load-deflection behavior

Fig. 2 Computed vs. measured results of floor specimen F6-8E16-2
(nails of top layer driven into joists)

wood floors to static loads. The program can be used as follows:

    1. Analysis of a given floor. Any rectangular wood joist floor with known material properties can be analyzed.

    2. Parameter studies. The effects of varying one parameter while holding all others constant can quickly be assessed. The results of one such study are shown in Fig. 3. The joist numbers of Fig. 3 are identified in Fig. 5. The effect of the modulus of elasticity, E, of the joist is seen to be of major importance. For example, reducing the basic E of 2,000,000 psi to 1,000,000 psi, while holding all other parameters constant, increases midspan deflections of the center joist by 40%.

    3. Simulation studies. The wood and wood-based materials used in floors have highly variable material properties due to species and grading differences. Studies by Dawson [9] and Fezio [10] have shown that the program may be used to evaluate the influence of known statistical distributions of input material properties using a Monte Carlo approach. An example of the results of a particular simulation study is given in Fig. 4. The cumulative frequencies of the occurrence of a given deflection are plotted versus the variability of joist modulus, E. It should be noted that even with high variability (coefficient of variation of 0.41) that the span/360° deflection of 0.44 in. was exceeded by only a few floors. Other variations in joist E (coefficient of variation for low variability was 0.06 and for medium variability was 0.20) produced even better results. Implications of these studies for improvement in grading methods for wood and for development of more realistic specifications for design of wood joist systems are clearly evident.

    4. Nonlinear analysis. The fastener load-slip curve becomes increasingly nonlinear at higher loads [11]. The program can be used in performing nonlinear analyses using an incremental approach.

Program Particulars

The backbone of program FEAFLO is subroutine FEABEA, Finite Element Analysis of BEAms. This subroutine develops the stiffness matrix for each of the crossing beams. Because these stiffness matrices are coupled only through the nodal point values of y at the crossing points, an LDU decomposition can be performed down to the equations representing these points. It is only these last stiffness coefficients (those relating the vertical displacements at the crossing points of the beams) that are returned to the main program to be incorporated into a larger stiffness matrix. The remaining LDU decomposition is read onto disc storage for later analysis of beam stresses and connector forces.

    The program is written to handle only rectangular floors loaded by concentrated forces at the crossing points of the beams. It is further designed so that all the T-beams should have the same dimensions and spacing; the same is true for the sheathing strips. However, the material properties and connector spacings may vary

Constant Data:
1. 3/4" plywood, 1.5"x7.25" joists
2. Conc. load=1100 lbs at center
3. E of plywood ‖ to grain=
    2.0×10^6 psi
    E of plywood ⊥ to grain=
    1.0×10^6 psi
4. s=8", n=1, k=30,000 lbs/in.

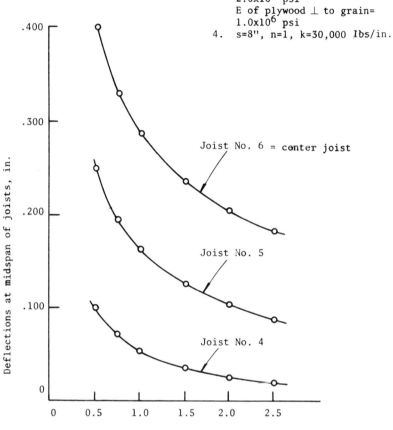

Fig. 3   Joist MOE vs joist deflections

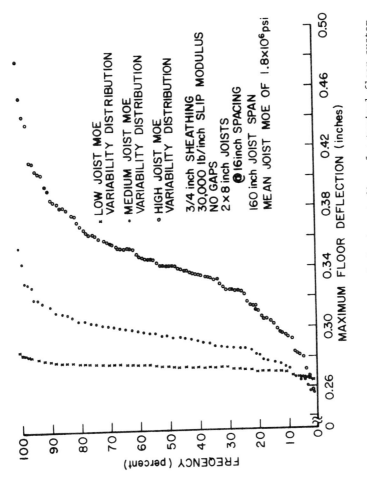

Fig. 4 Results of simulation studies of a typical floor system

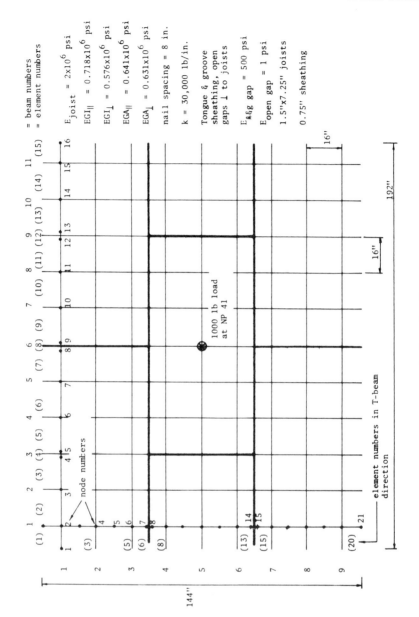

Fig. 5   Example floor

from beam to beam as well as along the beams. Although the program
has been written in this manner for ease of handling input data,
subroutine FEABEA does not depend on these restrictions. It would,
therefore, be an easy matter to alter the control program FEAFLO to
account for more geometrically complex layered wood systems if this
were desired.

Gaps are accounted for by placing short elements with low
moduli in the beams. In this manner, various stiffnesses can represent various degrees of gap behavior, from an open gap, to a glue-
filled gap, to a tightly butted gap. Work is in progress to more
adequately define gap stiffnesses. Openings can be simulated by
using several elements with a very low E throughout the region of
the opening.

Example Problem

Figure 5 is a schematic of the example floor analyzed to demonstrate input data requirements and output data obtained. Joist
and sheathing centerlines are shown as light lines and gaps as
heavy lines. Each sheathing strip is divided into 15 elements connected to 16 nodes. These nodes are spaced 16 in. apart except at
gaps when the element length is 1/16 in. The presence of a gap is
simulated by assigning a low modulus of elasticity to the short
element.

An echo of part of the input data is given in Figs. 6,7.
Layers are numbered from top to bottom of floor. Thus the joists
are layer two. The program also echoes load data and prints the
properties assigned to each element.

The output for T-beam No. 6 is given in Fig. 8. Since input
units were pounds and inches, the output units are pounds and inches
(slopes are dimensionless). Thus the stress in the joist directly
beneath the 1000 lb load (elements 10 and 11 at NP11) is 1139 psi,
which is only 41% of the stress computed using the only design procedure now available to engineers, i.e., the assumption that the
bare joist beneath the load supports the entire load.

Program FEAFLO Availability

Category: Analysis of wood floors
Title: Finite Element Analysis of Floors
Author: Dr. E. G. Thompson
         Professor of Civil Engineering
         Colorado State University
         Ft. Collins, Colorado 80523
Maintenance: same
Date: August, 1973
Capability: Analysis of rectangular wood joist floors for static
     load
Method: Finite element analysis as described above and in
     Ref. [5,12]. No technical manual is yet available.

INPUT DATA

    T-BEAM DATA

NBEAMS	NPNUM	LAYERS	SPAN
11	21	2	.144E+03

NODAL POINT COORDINATES, COORD

    COORD(J,I)
        J REFERS TO NPNUM ALONG T-BEAM(I)
        JCT CODES CROSSING OF A T-BEAM AND A S-STRIP BEAM AT A NP
            1=NP CROSSED BY BEAM SPANNING IN ORTHOGONAL DIRECTION
            0=NP NOT CROSSED BY BEAM SPANNING IN ORTHOGONAL DIRECTION
            AT GAPS NOT CROSSED EACH NP CODED 0
            AT GAPS CROSSED ONLY ONE NP CODED 1
            CODE GAPS AS MEMBERS WITH SMALL LENGTH AND LOW MOE

NP	COORD	JCT
1	0.00	0
2	8.00	1
3	16.00	0
4	24.00	1
5	32.00	0
6	40.00	1
7	47.97	0
8	48.03	0
9	56.00	1
10	64.00	0
11	72.00	1
12	80.00	0
13	88.00	1
14	95.97	0
15	96.03	0
16	104.00	1
17	112.00	0
18	120.00	1
19	128.00	0
20	136.00	1
21	144.00	0

LAYER DATA

LAYER	WIDTH	HEIGHT	EGI	EGA
1	.160E+02	.750E+00	.576E+06	.631E+06
2	.150E+01	.725E+01	.200E+07	.200E+07

INTERLAYER DATA

INTERFACE	RK1	S1	RN1
1	.300E+05	.800E+01	.100E+01

GAP-DATA

SHEATHING LAYER	GAP-MOE
1	.500E+03

Fig. 6 Echo of T-beam input data

INPUT DATA

   SHEATHING STRIP DATA

   NBEAMS   NPNUM   LAYERS   SPAN
      9   16   2   .192E+03

NODAL POINT COORDINATES, COORD

   COORD(J,I)
         J REFERS TO NPNUM ALONG SHEATHING STRIP BEAM(I)
      JCT CODES CROSSING OF A T-BEAM AND A S-STRIP BEAM AT A NP
         1=NP CROSSED BY BEAM SPANNING IN ORTHOGONAL DIRECTION
         0=NP NOT CROSSED BY BEAM SPANNING IN ORTHOGONAL DIRECTION
         AT GAPS NOT CROSSED EACH NP CODED 0
         AT GAPS CROSSED ONLY ONE NP CODED 1
         CODE GAPS AS MEMBERS WITH SMALL LENGTH AND LOW MOE

NP	COORD	JCT
1	0.00	0
2	16.00	1
3	32.00	1
4	47.97	0
5	48.03	1
6	64.00	1
7	80.00	1
8	95.97	0
9	96.03	1
10	112.00	1
11	128.00	1
12	143.97	0
13	144.03	1
14	160.00	1
15	176.00	1
16	192.00	0

LAYER DATA

LAYER	WIDTH	HEIGHT	EGI	EGA
1	.160E+02	.375E+00	.718E+06	.641E+06
2	.160E+02	.375E+00	.718E+06	.641E+06

INTERLAYER DATA

INTERFACE	RK1	S1	RN1
1	.100E+10	.160E+02	.100E+01

GAP-DATA

SHEATHING LAYER	GAP-MOE
1	.100E+01
2	.100E+01

Fig. 7 Echo of sheathing strip input data

OUTPUT DATA

T-BEAM NO.   6

NODE	DEFLECTION	SLOPE	ELONGATION LAYER1(U1)	ELONGATION LAYER2(U2)
1	.1121E-53	.4820E-02	-.1610E-01	-.1081E-63
2	.3842E-01	.4767E-02	-.1600E-01	-.3522E-04
3	.7600E-01	.4609E-02	-.1570E-01	-.1392E-03
4	.1119	.4341E-02	-.1522E-01	-.3068E-03
5	.1452	.3960E-02	-.1458E-01	-.5285E-03
6	.1749	.3454E-02	-.1383E-01	-.7834E-03
7	.2000	.2815E-02	-.1304E-01	-.1065E-02
8	.2001	.2809E-02	-.5251E-02	-.1068E-02
9	.2196	.2056E-02	-.4360E-02	-.1378E-02
10	.2325	.1147E-02	-.3301E-02	-.1746E-02
11	.2373	-.3325E-08	-.2148E-02	-.2148E-02
12	.2325	-.1147E-02	-.9945E-03	-.2549E-02
13	.2196	-.2056E-02	.6469E-04	-.2918E-02
14	.2001	-.2809E-02	.9551E-03	-.3228E-02
15	.2000	-.2815E-02	.8742E-02	-.3230E-02
16	.1749	-.3454E-02	.9535E-02	-.3506E-02
17	.1452	-.3960E-02	.1028E-01	-.3767E-02
18	.1119	-.4341E-02	.1092E-01	-.3989E-02
19	.7600E-01	-.4609E-02	.1140E-01	-.4157E-02
20	.3842E-01	-.4767E-02	.1170E-01	-.4261E-02
21	.1121E-53	-.4820E-02	.1180E-01	-.4296E-02

ELEMENT NUMBER	SLIP MODULUS	NAIL FORCE	STRESS TOP LAYER 1	STRESS BOT LAYER 1.	STRESS TOP LAYER 2	STRESS BOT LAYER 2
1	.3000E+05	94.34	9.403	6.558	38.93	-56.55
2	.3000E+05	89.76	27.84	19.29	117.5	-169.5
3	.3000E+05	79.98	45.20	30.75	200.6	-284.4
4	.3000E+05	63.64	60.54	39.93	290.4	-401.2
5	.3000E+05	38.46	72.73	45.45	392.7	-523.1
6	.3000E+05	.9513	80.14	45.46	512.6	-651.2
7	.3000E+05	95.12	62.41	62.38	582.5	-720.2
8	.3000E+05	184.4	90.93	50.08	607.6	-763.2
9	.3000E+05	124.1	108.1	58.99	732.0	-916.4
10	.3000E+05	45.47	121.9	60.02	938.6	-1139.
11	.3000E+05	45.47	121.9	60.02	938.6	-1139.
12	.3000E+05	124.1	108.1	58.99	732.0	-916.4
13	.3000E+05	184.4	90.92	50.08	607.6	-763.2
14	.3000E+05	95.12	62.41	62.38	582.5	-720.2
15	.3000E+05	.9521	80.14	45.46	512.6	-651.2
16	.3000E+05	38.46	72.73	45.45	392.7	-523.1
17	.3000E+05	63.64	60.54	39.93	290.4	-401.2
18	.3000E+05	79.98	45.20	30.75	200.6	-284.4
19	.3000E+05	89.76	27.84	19.29	117.5	-169.5
20	.3000E+05	94.34	9.403	6.558	38.93	-56.55

Fig. 8   Output for T-beam no. 6

Programming Language: FORTRAN IV
Documentation: See Ref. [5,12].
Input: See the example given above. In addition, numerous comment
cards in the program deck describe all required input.
Output: An echo of all input data and displacements, stresses, and
fastener forces at each node. See the example given above.
Software Operation: Batch only, no pre- or postprocessors
Hardware: CDC 6400 with 96K core
Usage: Used at CSU for research and consulting only
Typical Running Time: Using the SCOPE 3.3 operating system the pro-
gram compiles in 14 seconds. Execution time for the example
problem of Fig. 5 is 17 seconds.
Availability: A listing of the basic version of FEAFLO is given in
Ref. [12]. The basic version does not include the Monte Carlo
simulation capability. Costs of performing analyses on a con-
sulting basis are individually negotiated. Contact M. D.
Vanderbilt for further details.

CONCRETE FLOORS

Theory

Numerous methods are available for analyzing reinforced concrete
and prestressed concrete floor slab systems. These methods can be
classified as "continuum" or "analogy" methods. Continuum methods
treat a floor as an elastic continuum and utilize either the finite
difference or finite element method to predict the three-dimensional
deflected shape of the floor. After solving for the deflections,
normal and twisting moments and shears may then be computed. Analogy methods resort to the use of an analogy between the behavior of
the three-dimensional floor and some simpler (usually two-dimensional) structural system which can be analyzed using conventional
procedures, (i.e., moment distribution, stiffness analysis). Each
classification is discussed in more detail below.

Continuum Methods

Finite differences. The finite difference method gives excellent
results when used in analyzing certain classes of problems including
plate-bending problems. The finite difference method of solving the
governing differential equations for medium-thick elastic plates has
been described in detail by Timoshenko [13], Szilard [14], and numerous others. The procedure for analyzing a plate is as follows:

1. Node points are defined by constructing a rectangular,
triangular, or other shaped mesh which covers the plate.
2. A finite difference equation is written for each node. The
collection of finite difference equations for the complete plate is
assembled to give

$$[C]_{n \times n} \{y\}_n = \{A\}_n \tag{1}$$

where $[C]$ = coefficient matrix of finite difference equations
(usually unsymmetric), $\{y\}$ = vector of nodal deflections, and
$\{A\}$ = vector of nodal loads.

3. Equation (1) is solved for the n values of nodal deflections.

4. Using the nodal deflections the moments and shears throughout the plate are computed.

While conceptually simple, the labor involved in solving the
simplest structure is immense. The description of a study made by
Vanderbilt [15] serves to illustrate this point. Fig. 9 shows
one fourth of one panel of a continuous elastic plate. The panel
is assumed to be surrounded by a large number of identical panels
so that the quarter panel shown is bounded by lines of symmetry.
Thus the boundaries can deflect but not rotate. The finite difference operator to be applied at points not on beams is shown in
Fig. 10. Assume this operator is "applied" to node point 25.
Applying an operator means that the finite difference equation is
written for the node point in question. The equation for node 25 for
R = 1 is

$$(1)y_3 + (2)y_{13} + (-8)y_{14} + (2)y_{15} + (1)y_{23} + (-8)y_{24} + (20)y_{25}$$

$$+ (-8)y_{26} + (1)y_{27} + (2)y_{35} + (-8)y_{36} + (2)y_{37} + (1)y_{47} = Q_{25} \tag{2}$$

where Q_{25} is the load applied at node 25. A characteristic of the
finite difference method is that each equation is corrected for
boundary conditions as it is written. Equation (2) requires no
correction,but, for example, the equation for node 24 does require
correction as do all the points on or within one mesh spacing of a
boundary. Also the operator for nodes on beams must be modified to
account for the beams.

To analyze the plate of Fig. 9 program EPLATE (for Elastic
PLATE) was written. This program defines the quarter plate with up
to 120 nodes, writes the finite difference equation for each node,
solves for the nodal deflections, and uses these deflections to
compute the beam and plate moments at each node in both the x and
y directions. Results of analyses of a large number of cases have
been reported elsewhere [15]. An example of the results is given in
Fig. 11. A listing of program EPLATE may be obtained from M. D.
Vanderbilt. Execution time for one case on the CSU CDC 6400 computer is about 20 seconds.

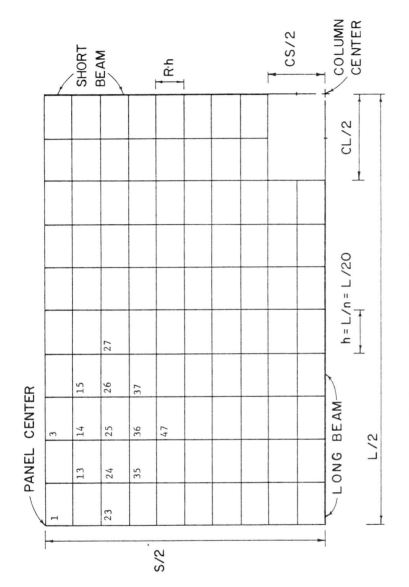

Fig. 9 One-fourth of a typical interior panel

PLATE OPERATOR

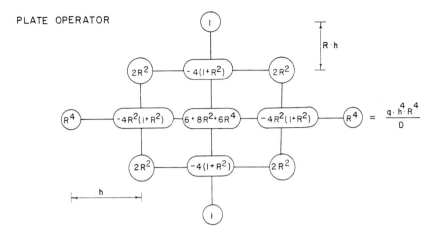

Fig. 10 Plate operator

The study described above involved the simplest type of geometry and boundary conditions. For more complex geometry, and
boundaries which both rotate and deflect, the classical finite difference method quickly becomes unwieldy. A physical analog of the
continuous elastic plate, developed by Newmark and discussed by Ang
and Newmark [16], may be used to develop operators for these more
complex cases. These operators are identical to those developed
using classical theory where such operators exist. However, for
many situations where an operator cannot be derived using classical
theory, use of the Newmark plate analog gives the needed operator.

Finite elements. Discussions of plate-bending elements suitable for
the analysis of floor slabs are given by Bathe and Wilson [17], Cook
[18], and numerous others. The procedure for analyzing a plate is
as follows:

     1. Nodes are defined by selecting a pattern of triangular or
rectangular finite elements. In contrast to the finite difference

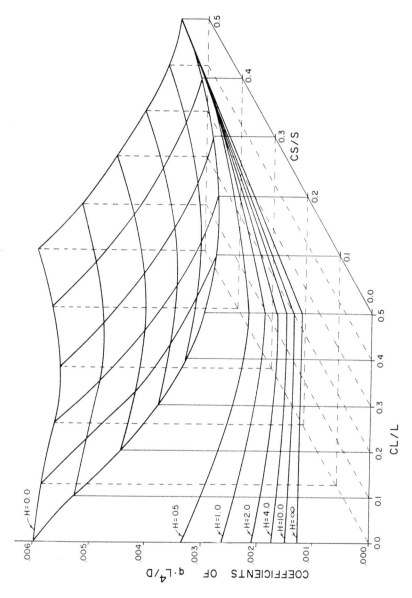

Fig. 11 Midpanel deflection coefficients, R = 1.0, IS = IL

method, which requires that all nodes be equally spaced, the analyst
can use small elements in regions of high curvature (e.g., around
columns) and larger elements elsewhere.

2. The stiffness matrix for each element is written and added
to the structure stiffness matrix to give

$$[S] \{D\} = \{A\} \tag{3}$$

where $[S]$ = stiffness matrix and $\{A\}$ and $\{D\}$ = vectors of actions
and displacements, respectively. Beams and columns are included by
using appropriate elements.

3. Equation (3) is corrected for boundary conditions, and
solved for the nodal displacements $\{D\}$.

4. Nodal actions are computed using standard procedures.

Many programs such as ANSYS, NASTRAN, SAP4, STRUDL,and others
are available. However, to analyze one panel of a continuous floor
requires a large amount of input data preparation, and the analysis
of several adjacent panels requires so much input data and execution
time as to be economically unfeasible except in rare cases. Hence
finite element analysis of concrete floors is not discussed further.

Analogs

The equivalent frame. The basic assumption on which the equivalent
frame analog is based is that the three-dimensional reinforced
concrete structure being analyzed can be replaced by a series of
two-dimensional plane frames. Each of these frames is analyzed
separately for one or more patterns of gravity loads. Analysis for
lateral loads may be made using the same frames as for the gravity
loads (i.e., the full width of floor in each frame is assumed effective), or a reduced effective width may be used. Results of the
analyses are then used in sizing the reinforcing steel.

. An example floor illustrating the basic assumption is shown in
Fig. 12. The floor is first divided into eight frames by cutting
the floor on the assumed locations of zero shear which are located
midway between column lines as shown by broken lines. The load
assigned to each frame is the total load between frame boundaries.
Thus each load is carried by two frames, one in the east-west and
one in the north-south direction. While the bending moments obtained from analyzing the eight frames are usually satisfactory for
sizing the flexural steel in both slab and columns, the sum of the
column axial forces will equal twice the total floor load. Hence
both the column axial forces and the punching shears must be corrected.

One of the major problems encountered in using the equivalent
frame method is in defining the stiffness properties of the frame
members. A portion of frame No. 1 at column al of Fig. 12 is shown
in Fig. 13. The beam member spanning between columns al and a2 has

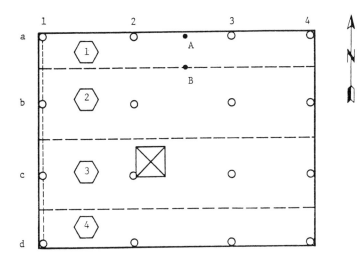

a.   East-west frames

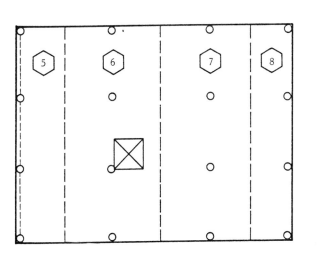

b.   North-south frames

Fig. 12   Selection of equivalent frames

width ℓ_2 as shown in Fig. 13. A portion of the moment transfer from
slab to column occurs directly over the column width c_2 as shown.
The remaining moment is transferred first from slab to beam and then
from beam to column in torsion. The column and its attached torsional member act as springs in series and are replaced by an equivalent column when making the analysis. The procedure for defining
the equivalent column stiffness was first developed by Corley [19]
and later modified by Corley and Jirsa [20]. The procedure for computing the equivalent column stiffness and for performing the equivalent frame analysis is contained in ACI 318-71 [21].

The equivalent frame analysis procedure was verified by Corley
for test structures subjected to uniformly distributed gravity
loads. Its validity when used in performing lateral load analysis
has never been demonstrated. In addition to uncertainty concerning
validity, other problems are encountered in attempting to use the
equivalent frame for lateral load analysis. These include the
following:

1. Assignment of stiffnesses of attached torsional members to
columns or beams
2. Definition of effective width of slab
3. Assigning lateral load to frames
4. Modifying member stiffness properties to account for
cracking

The procedure for performing an equivalent frame analysis contained in ACI 318-71 is intended for use in analyzing a single floor
with the far ends of all columns attached to the floor fixed against
displacement. Thus in computing the equivalent column stiffness for
the portion of the structure shown in Fig. 13 the torsional stiffness of the attached torsional member is assumed to act in series
with the sum of the flexural stiffnesses of columns A and B. For
lateral load analysis this procedure is invalid since each end of
each column, except at ground level, is free to displace. Studies
by Petrie and Vanderbilt [22] show that for this case the torsional
stiffness at a joint should be divided between the columns above and
below the joint in proportion to their relative flexural stiffnesses. It has recently been suggested by a number of investigators
that for lateral load analysis it may be more appropriate to assume
the torsional members act in series with the beams rather than the
the columns, thus giving effective beam rather than effective column
members. Pilot studies [22] show little difference between the
responses of a structure computed using the effective beam and
effective column formulations. However, ignoring the effects of the
torsional members (which is equivalent to assuming infinite torsional rigidity) leads to significant errors for both gravity and
lateral load analysis.

Studies by Khan and Sbarounis [23], Pecknold [24], and others
based on the behavior of elastic plates have indicated that for
lateral load analysis a reduced effective width ℓ_{2e} should be used

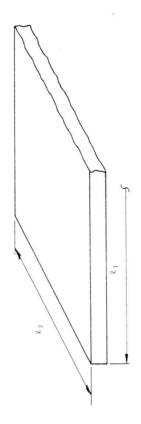

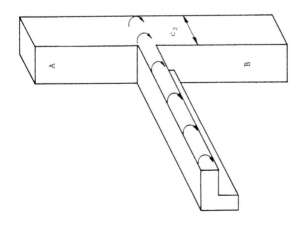

Fig. 13 Columns and attached torsional member

rather than the full transverse width ℓ_2. The primary factors identified as affecting the effective width ratio $\alpha = \ell_{2e}/\ell_2$ are the
aspect ratio ℓ_2/ℓ_1 and the ratio of column to panel size. The studies by Petrie and Vanderbilt [22] show that as α decreases, lateral
drift increases but the increases are not significant for $0.5 < \alpha \leq 1$.

Division of the lateral load acting on a three-dimensional
building among the equivalent frames assumed to represent the building should be made in proportion to the relative lateral stiffnesses
of the frames to ensure compatibility of drift deflections. However, to perform this type of distribution requires computing the
frame stiffnesses and is impractical. Hence use of a tributary
width equal to the frame transverse width is usually made.

Analysis of reinforced concrete structures is typically made
using the cross-sectional properties of the uncracked concrete
members and ignoring the presence of reinforcing. For gravity load
analysis of a single story this procedure is generally acceptable.
For lateral load analysis it may be advisable to reduce some of
the member properties to account for cracking. Except for the top
two or three stories the columns in a building usually carry sufficient axial load to warrant their being treated as uncracked.
However, the slabs are usually lightly reinforced and cracking
causes a marked reduction in their bending stiffness. Similarly
torsional cracking causes a severe decrease in torsional stiffness.
Insufficient data exist to give guidelines on what reductions should
be used.

The equivalent frame analysis method can be used to obtain deflections both at midspan and midpanel points. Conventional methods
such as numerical integration of the curvature diagrams can be used
to compute the deflections at midspan points such as point A in
Fig. 12a. Commerical programs which give deflections typically
give the midspan deflection or deflections at points along the span.
Procedures for obtaining the midpanel deflections have been developed by Nilson and Walters [25] and Vanderbilt [26]. To date, none
of the commercially available programs incorporate any technique for
predicting the midpanel deflections (point B in Fig. 12a.).

The equivalent grid. One floor of a reinforced concrete structure
can be modeled as a plane grid. The procedure, as suggested by
Ketchum [27], is to replace the continuous floor with a planar grid
of beams which simulate both the floor and its supporting columns.
An example floor containing a single panel and four supporting
columns is shown in Fig. 14a. The analogous grid is shown in
Fig. 14b. The flexural stiffnesses of one column about its two
principal axes are modeled by two orthogonal grid members. The
properties of the grid members simulating the slab are computed on
the basis of the portion of the slabs they represent. The advantage of the equivalent grid method is that it permits modeling a
space structure with a plane grid. Thus any available plane grid
program (STRUDL, etc.) can be used to analyze a floor. The disadvantages are the amount of time required to prepare the input

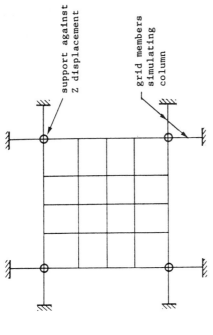

a. Single panel floor

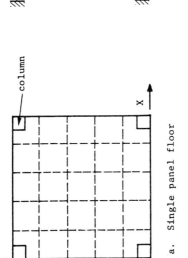

b. Plane grid analog

Fig. 14 Plane grid analog of floor

data and the lack of verification studies. The author has attempted
to use this procedure in analyzing one nine-panel test structure
with known properties and load-deflection behavior but obtained poor
results.

Program Availability

One program is available for performing finite difference analyses
of irregular floor slabs and is described below. Several programs
are available which use some type of plane frame analog for the
analysis of floor slabs. A representative sample of these is described below.

Finite Difference Analysis

Program IRSLAB

Category: Elastic analysis of IRregular SLABs and plates including
    raft foundations.
Author: D. Dorsey Moss
          2208 Indian Train Drive
          West Lafayette, Indiana 47907
Telephone: 317-494-8751
Date: 1966; revised 1976 to improve output
Capability: Static analysis of reactions, shears, moments, and de-
    flections in two-way floor and roof slabs and plates. Slabs
    may have a variety of special features, including: irregular
    boundaries, openings, beams, and thickened slabs. Slab sup-
    ports may be irregular in location, and columns may have finite
    dimensions and rigidity. Loads may be uniform, line, point, or
    may be proportional to the deflection. A load which is propor-
    tional to deflection represents the case of a slab on an elas-
    tic foundation, e.g., a raft foundation for a group of columns.
Method: Loads and slab details are defined for each point of a
    rectangular grid. Analysis is by finite difference equations
    using the Newmark plate analog.
Limitations: Maximum grid size is 4800 grid points.
Programming Language: FORTRAN IV
Documentation: Author's Ph.D. dissertation, available as Struc-
    tural Research Series No. 315, University of Illinois, Urbana,
    Illinois, includes theory and examples.
Input: Slab thickness, boundary locations, beam sizes and loca-
    tions, column sizes and locations, and loads
Output: Shears, moments, and deflections of slabs and beams; column
    reactions and moments
Software Operations: Batch processing. Preprocessor is used to
    verify input data.
Hardware: CDC 6500 150K (60 bit words)

Usage: The program has been used by the author on over 20 actual
jobs.
Typical Running Times: 1000 grid points - 2 minutes; 3000 grid
points - 10 minutes; 4800 grid points - 30 minutes
Availability: Data are submitted to the author for processing. Fee
for data preparation and job processing: $30 per hour. Com-
puter cost (CPU time): $10 per minute.

An example problem is shown in Fig. 15. The figure shows the
program printout describing one-fourth of a raft foundation mat for
a circular silo with the soil loading proportional to the mat deflection. The program generated 851 equations using 31 different
operators. The output includes an echo of input data, statics
checks, and the output described above. CPU time was 1.3 minutes.

Equivalent Frame Analysis

Program CNCGRD

Category: Elastic analysis and design of reinforced concrete slabs,
including waffle slabs and raft foundations and continuous
beams
Author: Hugh M. O'Neil, President
Hugh M. O'Neil Company
610 16th Street
Oakland, California 94612
Maintenance: by POSTEN PROGRAMS, a division of Hugh M. O'Neil
Company
Date: 1971, updated in July 1976 to include SI units
Capability: Performs equivalent frame analysis and design of reinforced concrete structures for gravity loads. Design features
are based on ACI 318-71. The program will accept one floor with
up to nine bays plus cantilever overhangs and with columns above
and below the floor having their far ends fixed. The program
automatically considers various live load patterns and sizes
both flexural and shear reinforcement. Numerous options are
available including the ability to use nonprismatic members
and a variety of loading patterns. The effective column stiffness in the equivalent frame can be suppressed. Since this
leads to unrealistically high moments at exterior columns and
at interior columns where unbalanced loads or spans are present, this option would normally be used for beam analysis but
not floor analysis.
Method: Moments are computed using moment distribution assuming
that moments of inertia are infinite over the widths of supports.
Limitations and Restrictions: Member stiffnesses are computed using
the gross section ignoring steel. Cantilevers must be prismatic. Column capitals are assumed square. Changes in cross
section can only occur at the tenth points of the clear span.

PLATE PATTERN

F = FREE EDGE
H = HINGED EDGE
X = FIXED EDGE

C = COLUMN
B = BEAM
T = THICKENED SLAB

• = TYPICAL INTERIOR POINT
= NO PLATE
C = SPECIFIED DEFLECTION

S = SYMMETRY EDGE
+ = POSITIVE SYMMETRY POINT
- = NEGATIVE SYMMETRY POINT

Compression steel is ignored in computing deflections.   Certain
assumptions are built into the steel sizing routine.
Documentation: A user's manual is available which contains specimen
data forms, a complete description of input and output data,
options available, and suggestions for efficient use of the
program.
Input: Description of the geometry of the structure including member sizes, load description, and material properties including
f'_c and weight of concrete and f_y of reinforcement
Output: Echo print of input data, maximum moments and shears at
tenth points of clear spans, worst reversal of moments at
tenth points, required flexural steel at tenth points, stirrup
sizes and spacings, short and long time deflections at tenth
points, punching shear stresses for flat plates and flat slabs
with drop panels, flexural steel area required near columns in
flat plates and slabs for moment transfer to columns
Software Operation: Batch or RJE time-sharing
Hardware: 1108 Univac with 65K core, CDC 6600 with 237K core
Usage: Approximately 100 users have designed over 5000 spans using
the program.
Typical Running Time: Execution time is approximately one to two
seconds per span.
Availability: A detailed price schedule is available from the author. Costs range from approximately $3.00 to $7.00 per span
depending upon options selected and whether the user selects
RJE data entry or has POSTEN PROGRAMS personnel prepare the in-
put data cards from the user's data sheet. The program is not
available for purchase or lease. Program usage is available
through (1) POSTEN PROGRAMS, 610   16th Street, Oakland,
California 94612, Phone: 415-832-2505. (2) United Computing
Systems (UCS), 1032 Elwell Court, Suite 217, Palo Alto,
California, or (3) Information Systems Design (ISD), 3205
Coronado Drive, Santa Clara, California 95051.

Program POSTEN

Category: Elastic analysis and design of post-tensioned concrete
slabs, including waffle slabs and raft foundations, and con-
tinuous beams
Author: Hugh M. O'Neil, President
        Hugh M. O'Neil Company
        610 16th Street
        Oakland, California 94612
Maintenance: by POSTEN PROGRAMS, a division of Hugh M. O'Neil
Company
Date: 1971, updated in July 1976 to include SI units
Capability: Analyzes and designs continous span bents with or with-
out cantilevers subjected to a wide variety of vertical loads.
Allows inputting separately determined lateral load moments.
Designs prismatic and nonprismatic members of a wide variety of
shapes including T, inverted T, and I sections. Has four main

options permitting design for maximum tensile stress, load
balancing, specified average effective prestress, or specified
drape and prestress for all spans. Permits inputting top or
bottom steps. Has approximately 30 auxiliary design options
for special cases including design for torsion, design for the
effects of shortening due to shrinkage, creep, etc., automatic
slab thickness determination, adding axial compressive force,
use of abbreviated input, automatic design to eliminate reinforcing, etc.

Method: See description of program CNCGRD.

Limitations and Restrictions: See description of program CNCGRD.

Program Language: FORTRAN IV

Documentation: A 68 page user's manual which contains extensive
discussions of data input preparation, options available, etc.,
is available from the author.

Input: f_c' and weight of concrete, f_y of reinforcement, strength of
tendons, pattern-loading data, span lengths, member dimensions,
loads, etc.

Output: Echo print of input data, effective prestress, drapes,
tendon ordinates, tendon stress loss, maximum top and bottom
tensile and compressive stresses, maximum bending moments,
balancing load moments, secondary moments, maximum shears,
shears due to balancing loads, allowable shear stresses, worst
reversal moments, stresses and moments for initial conditions,
flexural reinforcing areas for ultimate strength, flexural reinforcing based on formulas 18.5 and 18.6 of ACI 318-71, reinforcing for initial conditions, moment of inertia, section
modulus, area, distance to c. g., ordinates at tendon deflection points, balancing loads, stirrup diameters and spacings,
short and long term deflections, column moments, secondary
column moments, compressive shortening strain, punching shear
stress at columns, allowable punching shear stress, and reinforcing areas near columns for column moment transfer

Software Operation: Batch or RJE time sharing

Hardware: 1108 Univac with 65K core, CDC 6600 with 237K core
(octal)

Usage: Approximately 150 users have designed over 10,000 spans
using the program.

Typical Running Time: Execution time is approximately one to four
seconds per span.

Availability: A detailed price schedule is available from the
author. Costs range from approximately $6.00 to $11.00 per
span depending upon options and method of data input selected.
See description of program CNCGRD above.

Program ADOSS (SR185)

Category: Elastic analysis and design of reinforced concrete slabs
using the equivalent frame method

Descriptive Program Title: Analysis and Design of Slab Systems

Author: K. M. Kripanarayanan
Senior Structural Engineer
Portland Cement Association
Maintenance: Engineering Services Department
Portland Cement Association
Skokie, Ill. 60076
Date: October 1976
Capability: Analyzes and designs flat plates, flat slabs, waffle
slabs, two-way slabs, and continuous concrete frames, in accor-
dance with ACI 318-71, Building Code Requirements for
Reinforced Concrete. Analysis and design are for four com-
binations of vertical loads and four combinations of wind
moments combined with vertical loads.
Method: The equivalent frame method of ACI 318-71 is used. A frame
contains one floor with attached columns assumed fixed at their
far ends. A user's manual is available.
Limitations and Restrictions: Maximum of 12 spans with or without
cantilevers. Loading to be uniformly distributed. Slab thickness to be constant between spans.
Programming Language: FORTRAN IV
Documentation: Program description and user's manuals are available. Programmer's manual is not available.
Input: Input information consists of structure geometry, frame location (interior or exterior), loading conditions, exterior
support conditions, material properties, design method specifications, and lateral load moments or lateral loads, if the
combination of vertical and lateral load is required (typical
input is less than 10 to 12 cards per data set).
Output: The output provides the findings of the analysis (moments
and shears) and the resulting shear stresses. It also provides
a reinforcement schedule (bar size, number, and length), quantity estimates, and deflections. Typical output is less than 12
sheets of printout. Extent of output can be controlled by the
user.
Software Operation: Program available in source deck form. May be
used either on batch or time sharing systems.
Hardware: Source deck available for IBM 1130 (16K). A machine-
independent version of the program is also available for large
systems such as the IBM 360.
Usage: The program has been tested under both in-house and service
bureau operations. This is a new program. Previous versions
have been widely used.
Typical Running Time: 1 to 3 minutes per span on an IBM 1130 (16K)
system
Availability: Program source deck available from Engineering
Services Department, Portland Cement Association, Skokie, Ill.,
60076, upon signing nondisclosure licensing agreement at fee of
$750. Also available through many national computer service
bureaus.

REFERENCES

1 Goodman, J. R., and Popov, E. P., "Layered Beam Systems with Interlayer Slip," Journal of the Structural Division, ASCE, Vol. 94, No. ST11, Proc. Paper 6214, November 1968, pp. 2535-2547.

2 Goodman, J. R., "Layered Wood Systems with Interlayer Slip," Wood Science, Vol. 1, No. 3, 1969, pp. 148-158.

3 Goodman, J. R., et al., "Composite and Two-Way Action in Wood Joist Floor Systems," Wood Science, Vol. 7, No. 2, 1974, pp. 25-33.

4 Polensek, et al., "Response of Nailed Wood-Joist Floors to Static Loads," Forest Products Journal, Vol. 22, No. 9, Sept. 1972.

5 Thompson, E. G., Goodman, J. R., and Vanderbilt, M. D., "Finite Element Analysis of Layered Wood Systems," Journal of the Structural Division, ASCE., Vol. 101, No. ST12, December 1975, pp. 2659-2672.

6 Vanderbilt, M. D., et al., "A Rational Analysis and Design Procedure for Wood Joist Floors," Final Report on Grant No. GK-30853, Colorado State University, Fort Collins, Colorado, November 1974 (available through National Technical Information Service).

7 McLain, T. E., and Bodig, J., "Determination of Elastic Parameters of Full Size Wood Composite Boards," presented at Annual Meeting of Forest Products Research Society, Anaheim, California, June 1973.

8 Patterson, D. W., "Nailed Wood Joints Under Lateral Loads," M.S. Thesis, Colorado State University, 1973.

9 Dawson, P. R., "Variability Simulation of Joist Floor Systems," M.S. Thesis, Colorado State University, September 1974.

10 Fezio, R. V., "Material Variability and Wood Joist Floor Response," M.S. Thesis, Colorado State University, February 1976.

11 Tremblay, G. A., "Nonlinear Analysis of Layered T-Beams with Interlayer Slip," M.S. Thesis, Colorado State University, 1974.

12 Thompson, E. G., Vanderbilt, M. D., and Goodman, J. R., "FEAFLO: A Program for the Analysis of Layered Wood Systems," Journal of Computers and Structures, publication pending.

13 Timoshenko, S. P. and Woinowsky-Krieger, S., Theory of Plates and Shells, McGraw Hill Book Company, Inc., New York, N. Y., 1959.

14 Szilard, Rudolph, Theory and Analysis of Plates, Prentice Hall, Inc., Englewood Cliffs, New Jersey, 1974.

15 Vanderbilt, M. Daniel, "Deflection Calculations: Two-way Slabs," Proceedings of Symposium on Deflections of Structural Concrete, Montreal, Quebec, 22 October 1971.

16 Ang, A. H. S., and Newmark, N. M., "A Numerical Procedure for the Analysis of Continuous Plates," Proceedings of the 2nd ASCE Conference on Electronic Computation, 8-9 September 1960, Pittsburgh, Pennyslvania.

17 Bathe, K. J., and Wilson, E. L., Numerical Methods in Finite Element Analysis, Prentice Hall, Inc., Englewood Cliffs, N. J., 1976.

18 Cook, R. D., Concepts and Applications of Finite Element Analysis, John Wiley and Sons, Inc., New York, N. Y., 1973.

19 Corley, W. G., Sozen, M. A., and Siess, C. P., "The
Equivalent Frame Analysis for Reinforced Concrete Slabs," Structural
Research Series No. 218, Civil Engineering Department, University of
Illinois, Urbana, Illinois, June 1961.

20 Corley, W. G. and Jirsa, J. O., "Equivalent Frame Analysis
for Slab Design," Journal of the American Concrete Institute,
No. 11, November 1970.

21 "Building Code Requirements for Reinforced Concrete (ACI
318-71," American Concrete Institute, Detroit, Michigan, 1973.

22 Petrie, D. H. and Vanderbilt, M. D., "Equivalent Frame
Analysis for Lateral Loads," M.S. thesis, Colorado State University, in progress.

23 Khan, F. R. and Sbarounis, J. A., "Interaction of Shear
Walls and Frames," Journal of the Structural Division, No. ST3,
June 1964, pp. 285-325.

24 Pecknold, D. A., "Slab Effective Width for Equivalent Frame
Analysis," Journal of the American Concrete Institute, No. 4,
April 1975.

25 Nilson, A. H., and Walters, D. B., Jr.,"Deflection of Two-Way
Floor Systems by the Equivalent Frame Method," Journal of the
American Concrete Institute, No. 5, May 1975.

26 Vanderbilt, M. D., Sozen, M. A., and Siess, C. P., "Deflections of Reinforced Concrete Floor Slabs," Journal of the
Structural Division, ASCE, Vol. 91, No. ST4, August, 1965.

27 Ketchum, Milo S., "The Grid Method for Two-Way Concrete
Slabs," unpublished study.

THREE-DIMENSIONAL GROSS-MOTION CRASH VICTIM SIMULATORS

Ronald L. Huston

University of Cincinnati

INTRODUCTION

The past two decades have produced significant advances in hardware, software, and numerical methods. These advances have led to corresponding advances in finite element and finite segment modeling of mechanical systems. One of the most interesting and potentially useful areas of finite segment modeling is the gross motion simulation of the human body -- particularly the simulation of responses to crashes and high acceleration/impact environments. And, although advances in this area are directly related to advances in digital computer hardware and software, significant progress can also be attributed to new modeling approaches and more sophisticated computer coding of the models. Indeed, the technology has reached the point of being on the threshold of having several reliable, verified, well-documented, user oriented models which can be used to accurately and efficiently predict the human response, and hence potential injury, for a variety of crash and high acceleration/impact configurations.

Currently there are as many as ten distinct gross-motion simulators available including at least five three-dimensional models. Perhaps the first gross-motion simulator to be developed was a two-dimensional model advanced by McHenry [1] in 1963. This code was further developed and refined in subsequent years [2-5]. Other more recent two-dimensional simulators include those developed by Segal and McHenry [5,6,7], Danforth and Randall [8], Glancy and Larsen [9], Twigg, Karnes, Collins, et al. [10-13], and Robbins, Bowman, Bennett, et al. [14-17]. These simulators differ primarily in the variety of input-output opitons available. The three-dimensional simulators include those developed by Robbins, King, Patrick, et al. (HSRI) [18-23], Young (TTI) [24,25,26], Laananen (SOM-LA) [27-30], Bartz, Fleck, Karnes, et al. (CALSPAN) [31-36], and Huston et al. [37-41]. There is, of course, more diversity among these simulators because of their inherent complexity. It is the

objective of this paper to provide a summary of the relative
advantages, disadvantages, and ranges of application of these
three-dimensional simulators.

The balance of the paper is divided into four parts with
the first part containing a general discussion of the funda-
mentals of the modeling and the formulation of the codes. The
second part provides a summary of the vital features of the
simulators themselves. The third part provides a set of
conclusions about the state-of-the-art together with recommendations regarding applications and uses of the codes, and the
final part contains a condensed summary of the codes.

DEVELOPMENT OF A SIMULATOR

There are several major problem areas which need to be
resolved before a crash victim simulator is developed. First,
a modeling of the human body and its surroundings (or cockpit)
needs to be obtained. Even with the simplest codes, this
involves thought, judgment, and approximation. With the
more elaborate codes such as CALSPAN and UCIN, this can even
involve soft tissue modeling and the inclusion of airbags and
other occupants.

The modeling of the human body leads in turn to the major
problem of describing and accounting for the complex geometry
of the model itself and its many possible configurations. Also,
the problem of singularities and mathematically possible but
physically impossible configurations needs to be resolved.

Next, and perhaps most fundamental, governing dynamical
equations of motion need to be formulated and written. There
is still no apparent agreement among researchers about this.
Some simulators, such as TTI, HSRI, and SOM-LA, use Lagrange's
equations; CALSPAN uses a Newtonian approach; and UCIN uses a
combination virtual-work type approach called Lagrange's form
of d'Alembert's principle [42-45].

Following this, efficient algorithms need to be developed
to program the governing equations into a computer code. This,
in turn, involves finding a numerical integrator for the equations
of motion. After this, documentation and user manuals need to
be written so the code can be used by others. Indeed, this
latter area is perhaps the major current area of interest of
simulator researchers. It is probably the area which most needs
to be developed.

Finally, a simulation code needs to be verified experimentally.
It is extremely difficult to obtain reliable experimental data
to check the codes. It has only been recently with the work of
Begeman, King, Ewing, [46,50] that even the simplest kinds of
experimental verification have been obtained. This area also
still needs to receive attention by the researchers.

FIVE SPECIFIC SIMULATORS

In this part a summary of the major features of five of the
most widely used and accepted gross-motion crash victim
simulators (HSRI, TTI, SOM-LA, CALSPAN, and UCIN) is presented.
These five were selected on the basis of their documentation in
the literature, and their adoption by others, their continued
development, and their experimental verification. This is not
intended to imply that there are not other very useful and
suitable three-dimensional human body models and codes
available and under development. Indeed, the models of
Furusho, et al. [51,52,53], Smith, Kane , et al. [54,55], Huston,
Gallenstein, Abdelnour, et al. [57-60], and Ghosh and Boykin [61]
immediately come to mind. These are not specifically included
because of either their limited degrees of freedom or because
their development and application is not directed toward crash
victim simulation.

The HSRI Model

This code was developed by Robbins, King, Patrick, et al.
[18-23] at the Highway Safety Research Institute of the University
of Michigan (Ann Arbor, Mich. 48105). The model contains 6
mass segments providing 17 degrees of freedom. It contains both
hinge and ball-and-socket type joints simulating the human joints.
It has bilinear, unsymmetrical torsional springs at the joints with
coupling between the pitch roll and yaw stops. There is provision
for 4 seat-belt attachments to the torso of the model, and forces are
generated when the model strikes a cockpit intrusion surface. The
motion input is via the cockpit with provision for piecewise-linear
functions for as many as 6 (3 linear, 3 angular) cockpit accelerations. The governing equations are derived by using Lagrange's
equations, and they are numerically integrated using a Runge-Kutta,
predictor-corrector method. The computer code is written in FORTRAN,
and it requires approximately 400K bytes of core memory.
The developers of this code had the objective of formulating
an efficient, user-oriented, yet comprehensive model. This
necessitated a trade-off between the complexity (e.g., degrees of
freedom) of the model (and hence, its capability to accurately
predict physical phenomena) and the economy of user and run time.
The developers have apparently achieved a good balance between
the two. The code (like most of the other codes) probably needs
additional experimental verification.

The TTI Model

This code was developed by Young et al. [24,25,26] at
the Texas Transportation Institute of Texas A & M University
(College Station, Texas 77849). The model contains 12 mass segments providing 31 degrees of freedom. It has both hinge and
ball-and-socket joints, simulating the human joints. It employs

bilinear viscous damping at the joints to simulate muscle and
ligament forces. It has provision for lap and shoulder belt
restraints, and forces are generated when the model strikes a
cockpit surface. The motion input is via the cockpit by specifing
its linear and angular displacement as a function of time.
Lagrange's equations are used to develop the governing equations
and they are integrated numerically using a Runge-Kutta technique.
   This code is perhaps more specialized than the other codes.
That is, it is designed primarily for automobile crashes where
the automobile displacement is known as a function of time. Hence,
it does not provide as much flexibility on input as some of the
others. However, this allows the code to run more efficiently.
Also, the viscous joint stops eliminate unwanted resonance
characteristics which sometimes occur with spring stops. Finally,
further experimental verification would be desirable.

The SOM-LA Model

This code was developed by Laananen [27-30]   at the
Dynamic Sciences Division of Ultrasystems, Inc. (1850 W. Pinnacle
Peak Rd., Phoenix, Arizona 85027). The model contains 11 mass
segments connected by hinge and ball-and-socket joints, simulating the human joints. It has 28 degrees of freedom. It employs
nonlinear torsional springs and viscous dampers at the joints.
It contains a finite element seat model and sliding lap and
shoulder belts. The motion input is via the seat with provision
for 6 (3 linear, 3 angular) piecewise-linear acceleration
functions. The governing equations are derived using Lagrange's
equations, and they are numerically integrated using a Runge-
Kutta Adams-Moulton predictor-corrector method. The computer
code is written in FORTRAN, and it requires approximately 225K
bytes of core memory.
   The objective in the development of this model was to
provide an aid in seat and restraint design as opposed to
biodynamic research. Thus the model has the most elaborate
seat and restraint modeling of all the codes. Some experimental
verification with dummies has been obtained [30], but more is
needed.

The CALSPAN Model

This code was developed by Bartz, Fleck, Karnes, et al. [31,36]
at the Transportation Research Department of the Calspan Corp.
(Buffalo, N.Y. 14221). The model contains a variable number
of mass segments (up to 20) with the standard version using 15.
There may be either a null (locked), hinged, or ball-and-socket
connection at each joint providing as many as 63 degrees of
freedom. It has torsional and flexural spring and viscous joint
moments to simulate muscle and ligament action. It employs
extensible and sliding lap and shoulder restraint belts. It

has provision for contact forces generated when the model strikes
an intrusion surface of the cockpit or when segments of the
model strike each other. Air-bag force generation is also an
option. The motion input is via the cockpit with provision for 6
(3 linear, 3 angular) piecewise-linear acceleration functions.
It is also possible to accelerate the model by moving the cockpit surfaces onto the model. The governing equations are
derived using Newton's laws, and they are numerically integrated
using a Runge-Kutta, predictor-corrector method. The computer
code is written in FORTRAN, and it requires approximately 500K
bytes of core memory.

  This model and its code are the most elaborate and complex
of all the available codes. Indeed, probably far more effort
and research has been expended in the development of this code
than in any of the other codes. But, because of its complexity
and its various options, it is probably the most difficult and
expensive code to use. More user-oriented documentation is
needed. There is probably more experimental verification of this
code than the others, but more verification is still needed.

The UCIN Model

This code was developed by Huston et al. [37-41] at the University
of Cincinnati (Cincinnati, Ohio 45221). The model contains 12 mass
segments with a total of 34 degrees of freedom. It contains hinge
and ball-and-socket joints simulating the human joints and a translation connection at the neck to simulate neck stretch. It has
bilinear torsional and flexural viscous damping at the joints. It
has provision for up to 10 restraint belts (modeled as linear springs)
arbitrarily applied to the model. The motion input is via the cockpit with provision for 6 (3 linear, 3 angular) piecewise-linear
acceleration functions. The computer code is written in FORTRAN,
and it requires approximately 120K bytes of core memory.

  The principal feature of the UCIN code is its efficient
development of the governing equations and its efficient computer
algorithms. The governing equations are developed using a
virtual-work type principle called Lagrange's form of d'Alembert's
principle which is claimed to have the advantages of both the
Lagrangian and Newtonian approaches but without the corresponding
disadvantages [42-45]. The governing equations are numerically
integrated using a Runge-Kutta technique. This code is probably
the simplest, most efficient, and easiest to use of all the codes,
but it is also probably less specialized than most of the others.
And although the code has some good experimental verification,
more is still needed.

CONCLUSIONS AND RECOMMENDATIONS

There are currently available a number of three-dimensional
gross-motion simulators which can provide a reasonable analytical
computer simulation of human response to crash or high acceleration environments. Of the specific codes discussed here, none
is probably in its final finished (or "ideal") form. Each of
the codes needs more experimental verification. Each needs more
user-oriented documentation and better user's manuals. Better
numerical integration routines and better soft tissue modeling
is also needed.

  It seems to be clear that one or more advanced versions of
these codes should eventually take the place of dummies,
cadavers, and much of the current experimental work. The general
acceptance of the codes for such purposes by the researchers is,
of course, dependent upon further experimental verification of
the codes and the development of user-oriented documentation.

  Although a comparison of the various codes has been made
(see also the review papers King and Chou [62] and Robbins [63]),
it is probably unfair to select a "best" code or "most useful"
code since they have been developed with different end objectives.
However, data which would be useful (in addition to more
experimental verification) would be a comparison of the various
codes using the same input data for a variety of crash
configurations. It is hoped that such results will soon be
forthcoming.

SUMMARY

The HSRI Model

Name: HSRI 3D
Developers: D. H. Robbins, R. O. Bennett, and B. M. Bowman
             Highway Safety Research Institute
             University of Michigan
             Ann Arbor, Michigan 48105
Date: 1973
Objective: Efficient, comprehensive, user-oriented code
Degrees of Freedom: 17
Number of Mass Segments: 6
Language: Fortran IV
Hardware: IBM 360/370, Amdahl 470
Documentation and Verification: See References [18-23]
Availability: Contact D. H. Robbins at the above address.

The TTI Model

Name: TTI
Developer: R. D. Young
        Texas Transportation Institute
        Texas A & M University
        College Station, Texas   77849
Date: 1970
Objective: Auto crash simulation
Degrees of Freedom: 31
Number of Mass Segments: 12
Language: Fortran IV
Hardware: IBM 360/370
Documentation and Verification: See References [24,25,26]
Availability: Contact R. D. Young at the above address.

The SOM-LA Model

Name: SOM-LA
Developer: D. H. Laananen
        Dynamic Science Division
        Ultrasystems, Inc.
        1850 W. Pinnacle Peak Rd.
        Phoenix, Ariz.   85027
Date: 1975
Objective: Seat and restraint simulation
Degrees of Freedom: Occupant-28, Seat-16
Number of Mass Segments: 11
Language: Fortran IV
Hardware: Univac 1108, CDC 6600
Documentation and Verification: See References [27-30]
Availability: Contact Ultrasystems at the above address.

The CALSPAN Model

Name: CAL3D
Developers: J. A. Bartz, J. T. Fleck, et al.
        Transportation Research Department
        CALSPAN Corp.
        Buffalo, N.Y.   14221
Date: 1972
Objective: Comprehensive crash-victim simulation
Degrees of Freedom: Variable (Up to 63)
Number of Mass Segments: Variable (Up to 20)
Language: Fortran IV
Hardware: IBM 360/370, CDC 6600
Documentation and Verification: See References [31-36]
Availability: Contact J. T. Fleck at the above address

The UCIN Model

Name: UCIN
Developers: R. L. Huston, C. E. Passerello, M. W. Harlow
             Department of Engineering Science
             University of Cincinnati
             Cincinnati, Ohio 45221
Date: 1974
Objective: Comprehensive crash-victim simulation
Degrees of Freedom: 34
Number of Mass Segments: 12
Language: Fortran IV
Hardware: IBM 360/370, Amdahl 470
Documentation and Verification: See References [37-41]
Availability: Contact R. L. Huston at the above address

ACKNOWLEDGMENT

Support for the preparation of this paper was provided by the
Office of Naval Research under contract N00014-76C-0139.

REFERENCES

    1 McHenry, R. R., "Analysis of the Dynamics of Automobile
Passenger Restraint Systems," Proceedings of the 7th Stapp Car
Crash Conference, 1963, pp. 207-249.
    2 McHenry, R. R., and Naab, K. N., "Computer Simulation of
the Automobile Crash Victim - A Validation Study," Cornell
Aeronautical Laboratories, Inc., Report No. YB-2126-V-1R,
July, 1966.
    3 McHenry, R. R., and Naab, K. N., "Computer Simulation of
the Crash Victim - A Validation Study," Proceedings of the 10th
Stapp Car Crash Conference, Holloman AFB, N.M., 1966.
    4 McHenry, R. R., Naab, K. N., et al, "Cal Computer
Simulation Predicts Occupant Responses During Vehicle Head-On
Collision," SAE Journal, Vol. 75, No. 7, July, 1967, pp. 36-45.
    5 Segal, D. J., and McHenry, R. R., "Computer Simulation of
Automobile Crash Victim - Revision No. 1," Cornell Aeronautical
Laboratories, Inc., Report No. VJ-2492-V-1, March, 1968.
    6 Segal, D. J., "Revised Computer Simulation of the
Automobile Crash Victim," Cornell Aeronautical Laboratories, Inc.,
Report No. VJ-2759-V-2, Jan. 1971.
    7 Segal, D. J., "Computer Simulation of Pedestrial Accidents,"
Third Triennial Congress of the International Association for
Accident and Traffic Medicine, New York, N.Y., 1969.
    8 Danforth, J. P., and Randall, C. D., "Modified ROS
Occupant Dynamics Simulation User Manual," General Motors Corp.
Research Labs., Publication No. GMR-1254, Oct. 1972.

9 Glancy, J. J., and Larsen, S. E., "User Guide for Program SIMULA," Dynamic Science, Report TDR No. 72-23, 1972.

10 Karnes, R. N., Sebastian, J. D., Tocher, J. L., and Twigg, D. W., "A User-Oriented Program for Crash Dynamics," Proceedings of the International Conference on Vehicle Structural Mechanics, Detroit, Mich., March, 1974, pp. 154-163.

11 Twigg, D. W., and Karnes, R. N., "PROMETHEUS - A User-Oriented Program for Human Crash Dynamics (User Manual)," ONR Contract N00014-72-C-0223, Report No. BCS-40038, Nov. 1974.

12 Karnes, R. N., Tocher, J. L., and Twigg, D. W., "PROMETHEUS - A Crash Victim Simulator," Aircraft Crashworthiness, University Press of Virginia, 1975, pp. 327-345.

13 Collins, J. A., and Turnbow, J. W., "Response of a Seat-Passenger System," Symposium on Dynamic Response of Structures, Stanford, Ca., June, 1971.

14 Robbins, D. H., Bennett, R. O., and Roberts, V. L., "HSRI Two-Dimensional Crash Victim Simulator: Analysis, Verification, and Users' Manual," NTIS No. PB202 537, Dec. 1970.

15 Bowman, B. M., Bennett, R. O., and Robbins, D. H., "MVMA Two-Dimensional Crash Victim Simulation, Version 3," 3 volume report, NTIS Nos. 235 753/1, 236 907/2, 236 908/0, June, 1974.

16 Bennett, R. O., Bowman, B. M., and Robbins, D. N., "MVMA Two-Dimensional Crash Victim Simulation, Version 3 (3-75)," NSRI, University of Michigan, Ann Arbor, Mich., March 1975.

17 Robbins, D. H., Bowman, B. M., and Bennett, R. O., "The MVMA Two-Dimensional Crash Victim Simulation," Proceedings of the 18th Stapp Car Crash Conference, Warrendale, Pa., 1974, pp. 657-678.

18 Robbins, D. H., Bennett, R. O., and Bowman, B. M., "User-Oriented Mathematical Crash Victim Simulator," Proceedings of the 16th Stapp Car Crash Conference, Warrendale, Pa., 1972, pp. 128-148.

19 Robbins, D. H., Bennett, R. O., and Roberts, V. L., "HSRI Three-Dimensional Crash Victim Simulator: Analysis Verification, Users' Manual, and Pictorial Section," NTIS No. PB 208 242, June 1971.

20 Robbins, D. H., "Three-Dimensional Simulation of Advanced Automotive Restraint Systems," Paper No. 700421, 1970 International Automobile Safety Conference Compendium, P-30 SAE, Warrendale, Pa., May, 1970, pp. 1008-1023.

21 King, A. I., Chou, C. C., and Mackinder, J. A., "Mathematical Model of an Airbag for a Three-Dimensional Occupant Simulation," SAE Paper No. 720036, Warrendale, Pa., Jan. 1971.

22 Patrick, L. M., "Airbag Restraint for Automobile Drivers, Vol. II, Occupant Simulation Model," Final Report on DOT Contract FH-11-7607 for NHTSA, Wayne State University, Detroit, Mich., 1972.

23 Robbins, D. H., Bennett, R. O., and Bowman, B. M., "HSRI Six-Mass, Three-Dimensional Crash Victim Simulator," NTIS No. PB 239 476, Feb. 1973.

24 Young, R. D., "A Three-Dimensional Mathematical Model of an Automobile Passenger," Research Report 140-2, Texas Transportation Institute, Texas A and M University, College Station, Tex. NTIS NO. PB 197 159, Aug. 1970.

25 Young, R. D., Ross, H. E., and Lammert, W. F., "Simulation of the Pedestrian During Vehicle Impact," Proceedings of the 3rd International Congress on Automotive Safety, Paper No. 27, Vol. II, 1974.

26 Young, R. D., "Vehicle Exteriors and Pedestrian Injury Prevention, Vol. V, A Three-Dimensional Mathematical Simulation-Extension and Validation," Final NHTSA Contract Report, Texas Transportation Institute, College Station, Tex., 1975.

27 Laamanen, D. H., "A Digital Simulation Technique for Crashworthy Analysis of Aircraft Seats," SAE Paper No. 740371, Warrendale, Pa., April, 1974.

28 Laananen, D. H., "Development of a Scientific Basis for Analysis of Aircraft Seating Systems," Report No. FAA-NA-74-175, Ultrasystems, Inc., Dynamics Science Div., Phoenix, Az., Jan., 1975.

29 Laananen, D. H., "Implementation of a Digital Simulation Technique for Crashworthy Analysis of Aircraft Seats," Presentation 750541 at the SAE Business Aircraft Meeting, Wichita, Ka., April, 1975.

30 Laananen, D. H., "Simulation of an Aircraft Seat and Occupant in a Crash Environment," Aircraft Crashworthiness, University Press of Virginia, 1975, pp. 347-363.

31 Bartz, J. A., "Development and Validation of a Computer Simulation of a Crash Victim in Three Dimensions," Proceedings of the 16th Stapp Car Crash Conference, Warrendale, Pa. 1972, pp. 105-127.

32 Bartz, J. A., "A Three-Dimensional Computer Simulation of a Motor Vehicle Crash Victim, Phase I, Development of the Computer Program," Report CAL No. VJ-2978-V-1, Calspan Corp., Buffalo, N.Y., July, 1971.

33 Bartz, J. A., "A Three-Dimensional Computer Simulation of a Motor Vehicle Crash Victim, Phase II, Validation Study of the Model," Report Cal. No. VJ-2978-V-2, Calspan Corp., Buffalo, N.Y., Dec. 1972.

34 Fleck, J. T., Butler, F. E., and Vogel, S. L., "An Improved Three-Dimensional Computer Simulation of Motor Vehicle Crash Victims," Report CAL No. ZQ-5180-L-1, Calspan Corp., Buffalo, N.Y., 1974.

35 Karnes, R. N., "CAL 3D Crash Victim Simulation Computer Program User Manual," Document No. BCS-G0651, Boeing Computer Services, Inc., Seattle, Wash., March 1971.

36 Fleck, J. T., "Calspan Three-Dimensional Crash Victim Simulation Program," Aircraft Crashworthiness, University Press of Virginia, 1975, pp. 299-310.

37 Huston, R. L., Hessel, R. E., and Passerello, C. E., "A Three-Dimensional Vehicle-Man Model for Collision and High Acceleration Studies," SAE Paper No. 740275 Warrendale, Pa., Feb. 1974.

38 Huston, R. L., Passerello, C. E., Harlow, M. W., and
Winget, J. M., "The UCIN 3-Dimensional Aircraft Occupant,"
Aircraft Crashworthiness, University Press of Virginia, 1975,
pp. 311-324.
39 Huston, R. L., Hessel, R. E., and Winget, J. M.,
"Dynamics of a Crash Victim--A Finite Segment Model," AIAA
Journal, Vol. 14, No. 2, Feb. 1976, pp. 173-178.
40 Huston, R. L., Passerello, C. E., and Harlow, M. W.,
"UCIN Vehicle-Occupant/Crash Victim Simulation Model," Structural
Mechanics Software Series, University Press of Virginia, 1977.
41 Huston, R. L., Passerello, C. E., and Harlow, M. W.,
"User's Manual for UCIN Vehicle-Occupant Crash Study Model-
Version II," ONR Contract Report No. ONR-UC-EA-120/74-3, 1974.
42 Kane, T. R., "Dynamics of Nonholonomic Systems,"
Journal of Applied Mechanics, Vol. 28, 1961, pp. 574-578.
43 Kane, T. R., and Wang, C. F., "On the Derivation
of Equations of Motion," Journal of the Society for Industrial
and Applied Mathematics, Vol. 13, 1965, pp. 487-492.
44 Kane, T. R., Dynamics, Holt, Rinehart, and Winston,
New York, 1968.
45 Huston, R. L., and Passerello, C. E., "On Lagranges
Form of d'Alembert's Principle," The Matrix and Tensor Quarterly,
Vol. 23, 1973, pp. 109-112.
46 Begeman, P. C., King, A. I., and Prasad, P., "Spinal
Loads Resulting from - G_x Acceleration," Proceedings of the 17th
Stapp Car Crash Conference," Warrendale, Pa., 1973, pp. 343-360.
47 King, A. I., "Survey of the State of the Art of Human
Biodynamic Response," Aircraft Crashworthiness, University Press
of Virginia, 1975, pp. 83-120.
48 Ewing, C. L., and Thomas, D. J., "Response of Human Head
to Impact," Proceedings of the 17th Stapp Car Crash Conference,
Warrendale, Pa., 1973, pp. 309-342.
49 Ewing, C. L., Thomas, D. J., Patrick, L. M., Beeler, G. W.,
and Smith, M. J., "Living Human Dynamic Response to - G_x Impact
Acceleration II - Accelerations Measured on the Head and Neck,"
Proceedings of the 13th Stapp Car Crash Conference, Warrendale, Pa.,
1969, pp. 400-415.
50 Ewing, C. L., and Thomas, D. J., "Human Head and Neck
Response to Impact Acceleration," Army-Navy Joint Report, Naval
Aerospace Medical Research Laboratory, J.S., Army Aeromedical
Research Laboratory, Monograph 21, Aug. 1972.
51 Furusho, H., Yokoya, K., and Fujiki, S., "Dynamics of
Occupants in Collision: Vol. 1, Simulation of 3-D Man Model with
Five Masses," Society of Mechanical Engineers of Japan, Western
Division Meeting Reprint, No. 1970.
52 Furusho, H., and Yokoya, K., "Analysis of Occupants'
Movement in Head-On Collision," Transactions of the Society of
Automotive Engineers of Japan, No. 1, 1970, pp. 145-155.
53 Furusho, H., Yokoya, K., and Fujiki, S., "Analysis of
Occupant Movements in Rear-End Collision," Paper No. 13 of Safety
Research Tour in the U.S.A. from the Viewpoint of Vehicle
Dynamics, 1969.

54 Smith, P. G., and Kane, T. R., "On the Dynamics of the
Human Body in Free Fall," Journal of Applied Mechanics, Vol. 35,
1968, p. 167.
55 Kane, T. R., and Scher, M. P., "Human Self-Rotation by
Means of Limb Movements," Journal of Biomechanics, Vol. 3, 1970,
p. 39.
56 Passerello, C. E., and Huston, R. L., "Human Attitude
Control," Journal of Biomechanics, Vol. 4, 1971, pp. 95-102.
57 Huston, R. L., and Passerello, C. E., "On the Dynamics
of a Human Body," Journal of Biomechanics, Vol. 4, 1971,
pp. 369-378.
58 Gallenstein, J., and Huston, R. L., "Analysis of
Swimming Motions," Human Factors, Vol. 15, 1973, pp. 91-98.
59 Huston, R. L., Passerello, C. E., Hessel, R. E., and
Harlow, M. W., "On Human Body Dynamics," Annals of Biomedical
Engineering, Vol.4, 1976, pp. 25-43.
60 Abdelnour, T. A., Passerello, C. E., and Huston, R. L.,
"An Analytical Analysis of Walking," ASME Paper No. 75-WA/Bio-4,
ASME Winter Annual Meeting, Houston, Tex., 1975.
61 Ghosh, T. K., and Boykin, W. H., Jr., "Analytic Determina-
tion of an Optimal Human Motion," Journal of Optimization Theory
and Applications, Vol. 19, June, 1976, pp. 327-346.
62 King, A. I., and Chou, C. C., "Mathematical Modelling,
Simulation and Experimental Testing of Biomechanical System
Crash Response," AIAA Paper 75-272, AIAA 11th Annual Meeting
and Technical Display, Washington, D.C., Feb. 1975.
63 Robbins, D. H., "Simulation of Human Body Response to
Crash Loads," Shock and Vibration Computer Programs - Reviews and
Summaries, The Shock and Vibration Information Center, Naval
Research Laboratory, Washington, D.C., 1975, pp. 365-380.

INDEXES

SUBJECT INDEX OF PROGRAMS

See Alphabetical Index for page numbers of these listings